THE
CAMBRIDGE
ILLUMINATIONS

TEN CENTURIES OF BOOK PRODUCTION

IN THE MEDIEVAL WEST

This catalogue is published
to accompany the exhibition
The Cambridge Illuminations at the Fitzwilliam
Museum and the Cambridge University Library,
from 26 July to 11 December 2005

━━━━━

The exhibition has been generously sponsored by
The Arts and Humanities Research Council,
The Samuel H. Kress Foundation,
The Gladys Krieble Delmas Foundation,
International Partners on behalf of Melvin Seiden,
and Cambridge University Press

The catalogue has been sponsored by
International Partners on behalf of Melvin Seiden,
the executors of Mrs Mary Willis Parry's bequest,
and EEMLAC

THE CAMBRIDGE ILLUMINATIONS

TEN CENTURIES OF BOOK PRODUCTION
IN THE MEDIEVAL WEST

Edited by

PAUL BINSKI & STELLA PANAYOTOVA

HARVEY MILLER PUBLISHERS

*This catalogue
is published in honour of
James and Emily Marrow
and in memory of
Mary and Brian Parry*

HARVEY MILLER PUBLISHERS
An Imprint of Brepols Publishers
London / Turnhout

British Library Cataloguing in Publication Data
A catalogue record for this book is available
from the British Library

ISBN 1-872501-59-1 *(hardback)*
ISBN 1-872501-63-X *(paperback)*

Design and production: BLACKER DESIGN, East Grinstead, Sussex
Photography of Fitzwilliam Museum manuscripts:
ANDREW MORRIS and ANDREW NORMAN
Photography of Cambridge University Library and College manuscripts:
MARK SCUDDER and LES GOODEY
Printed and bound in China by 1010 Printing International Ltd on behalf of COMPASS PRESS

CONTENTS

ACKNOWLEDGEMENTS

LIKE MANY OF THE MEDIEVAL MANUSCRIPTS presented here, this catalogue and the exhibition it accompanies are truly collaborative ventures. Both became possible thanks to the colleges of Cambridge who agreed to lend their manuscripts to the University Library and the Fitzwilliam Museum on an unprecedented scale. We are greatly indebted to the guardians of all these treasures for their patience and enthusiasm, and especially to Gill Cannell, Christopher de Hamel, Jonathan Harris, David McKitterick, Jayne Ringrose, and Godfrey Waller, whose support went well beyond the call of duty.

The scope of the material included in this exhibition required a wide range of expertise and brought together a large number of scholars. Their contribution is significantly greater than this publication may convey. Long before they became contributors to the catalogue, they were already acting as the advisory committee on the exhibition. One of the most exciting aspects during the early stages of our work was the free and generous flow of ideas. It is delightful to see how many of them have come to fruition. The exhibition and catalogue brought together many more scholars who offered invaluable advice and criticism. We owe special thanks to Lillian Armstrong, François Avril, Chris Coppens, Patricia Easterling, Mirjam Foot, David Ganz, Richard Linenthal, Margaret Manion, Paul Needham, Laura Nuvoloni, Ann Payne, Nicolas Pickwoad, Nicholas Poole-Wilson, Robert Proctor, Michael Reeve, Suzanne Reynolds, Katrien Smeyers and many others whose names would easily fill up a book larger than this.

It takes inspired vision and tremendous generosity to transform ideas into reality. We were fortunate to find both in a number of individuals and institutions, while Kim McCann and Sharon Maurice steered the course with energy, precision, and elegance. The executors of the late Mary Parry offered the much-needed initial stimulus. International Partners on behalf of Melvin Seiden provided the indispensable funding for both catalogue and exhibition. The Samuel H. Kress Foundation, the Gladys Krieble Delmas Foundation, Sam Fogg and Mr Gifford Combs were extraordinarily generous with many other aspects of *The Cambridge Illuminations*. A major grant from the East of England Museums, Libraries, and Archives Council provided the photography for the catalogue. The future of the exhibition itself was secured by the Arts and Humanities Research Council who funded the technical assistant, John Lancaster. To him and his team of devoted and experienced volunteers we owe this splendid display. A complex exhibition like this one involves work on various fronts and benefits from the expert advice and moral support of colleagues and friends. We are hugely indebted to Sally-Ann Ashton, Fiona Brown, Lucilla Burn, Julie Dawson, Margaret Greeves, Dave Gunn, the late Nicholas Hadgraft, Craig Hartley, Robert Lloyd-Parry, Angela Metcalfe, Jane Munro, Elizabeth New, Lea Olsen, Shaun Osborne, Penny Price, Thyrza Smith, Anna Stopes, Frances Sword, Svetlana Taylor, Hanna Vorholt, John Wells, Mark Wingfield, and Patrick Zutshi. Special thanks go to the Museum's photographers, Andrew Morris and Andrew Norman, who turned trials into triumphs, and to Elly Miller and Elwyn Blacker who guided us through the editorial stages kindly and wisely.

Finally, this book is a tribute to Anne for her unfailing support and to John, Julie, and Patrick for their patience, understanding, and love.

THE EDITORS

IT HAS BEEN SAID that Cambridge contains the greatest concentration of illuminated manuscripts anywhere in the world, the Vatican excepted. But whereas the Vatican's collections are vested in the Holy See, those in Cambridge are to be found in both the University and many of the Colleges. This exhibition brings 'Cambridge Illuminations' together for the first time from no less than seventeen discrete sources. We are particularly grateful to the Governing Bodies of fifteen of our Colleges for agreeing to lend some of their greatest treasures to this exhibition which takes place simultaneously at the University Library and the Fitzwilliam Museum.

In recent years there have been a number of important exhibitions of illuminated manuscripts – that of Flemish manuscripts held at the J. Paul Getty Museum and the Royal Academy in 2003-2004 comes to mind – but these have tended to concentrate upon particular periods or schools. Our exhibition spans ten centuries of European art, from the sixth to the sixteenth of the Christian era. With two hundred and fifteen separate items on display it is one of the largest exhibitions of illuminated manuscripts ever mounted in this country; we are aware of only one larger, organised by Sydney Cockerell for the Burlington Fine Arts Club in 1908, co-incidentally or not the year in which he was appointed to the directorship of the Fitzwilliam Museum. One further and equally happy co-incidence is the acquisition by the Museum earlier this year of the Macclesfield Psalter, following a public appeal by the National Art Collections Fund to match a 50% grant from the Heritage Memorial Fund. Cockerell was unaware of its existence when, in 1907, he made the association between its two closest relatives, the Gorleston and Douai Psalters. The second of these had already been described by his predecessor at the Fitzwilliam, M R James, as 'absolutely faultless' and it was James who, in his Descriptive Catalogue of the Manuscripts in the Fitzwilliam Museum of 1895 encouraged collectors 'to think of the Fitzwilliam Museum as a place where (their) manuscripts would be choicely valued, religiously preserved, and minutely investigated'. It is this quintessentially Cambridge tradition of equal tenacity in terms of acquisition and erudition that our exhibition celebrates. For while certain of the manuscripts on display, notably those from the Parker Library at Corpus Christi College, have been in Cambridge since the Reformation of the sixteenth century, others are far more recent arrivals.

It remains for us to thank all of those who have helped to realise this ground-breaking exhibition which has been in preparation for several years. Professors James Marrow and Jonathan Alexander have served as its honorary curators. Stella Panayotova, Keeper of Manuscripts and Printed Books at the Fitzwilliam Museum, has masterminded the project, assisted in innumerable ways by an exhibition committee which included Paul Binski, Christopher de Hamel, Peter Jones, Rosamond McKitterick, Elly Miller, Nigel Morgan, Teresa Webber and Patrick Zutshi. We are grateful to them, to the other contributors to the catalogue and to the sponsors of the exhibition without whose financial support it could not have taken such splendid shape. We acknowledge in particular the generosity of the Arts and Humanities Research Council, the Samuel H. Kress Foundation, the Gladys Krieble Delmas Foundation, the East of England Museums, Libraries and Archives Council, the executors of the late Mary Parry, International Partners on behalf of Melvin Seiden, Sam Fogg and Mr Gifford Combs.

Finally, we are conscious that 'The Cambridge Illuminations' takes place at a time when our collegiate university is looking forward to celebrating its octocentenary. It would be hard to imagine a more appropriate overture to that anniversary than this exhibition which was conceived and executed as a collaboration between the University and the Colleges, in order to shed light on our collections as instruments of illumination and enrichment for all.

PETER FOX   DUNCAN ROBINSON
University Librarian   *Director, The Fitzwilliam Museum*

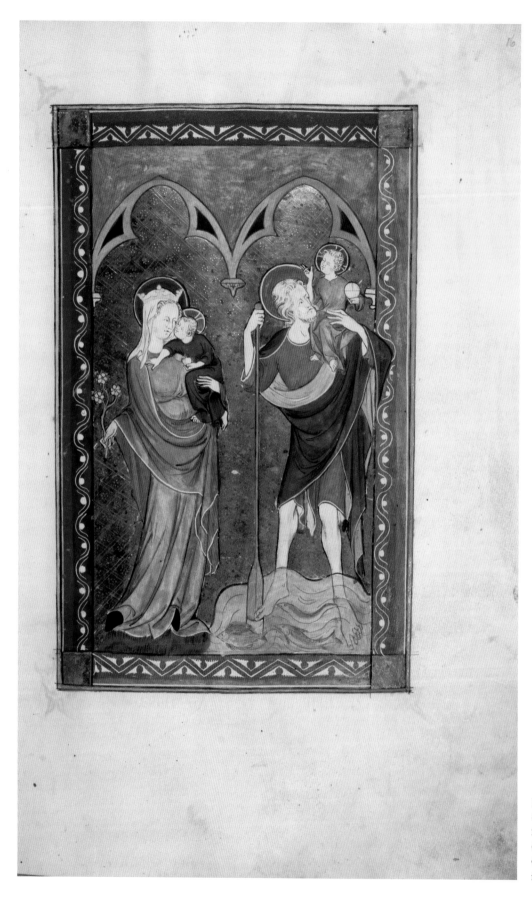

Fig 1. Virgin and
Child, and
St Christopher.
Corpus Christi
College, MS 53,
fol. 16

INTRODUCTION

Paul Binski

T HE PRESENT EXHIBITION puts before the general public a selection of the most important western medieval and Renaissance illuminated manuscripts held in collections in Cambridge. The University is blessed with such manuscripts in prodigious numbers: books of all types, hand-written or printed, decorated or plain, are a fundamental part of the University's intellectual capital as well as its daily life; but the illuminated ones, representing a thousand years of book art, add a special dimension. As the University approaches the celebration of its eight hundredth anniversary, a moment for general reflection on this remarkable heritage seems especially appropriate. Aside from being extremely beautiful, some of these books are landmarks in themselves of the religious, literary and cultural life of England and Western Europe – and it is right that these should be seen by an appreciative wide audience as part of the continuing mission of the University. This catalogue is intended for that audience while also, it is hoped, offering new ideas by a group of scholars, most of whom work within Cambridge University and who aspire to continue its traditions of study.

Well over three thousand manuscripts with significant illumination are dispersed throughout the collections of the University and, since only a minority of medieval books were ever illuminated, that figure represents a small proportion of the total holdings. Cambridge's individual collections have remarkable depth and character: consider the scope of English Romanesque and Gothic manuscripts at Trinity College or Corpus Christi College, or the Books of Hours at the Fitzwilliam, arguably the greatest smaller collection of its type. The Cambridge colleges, more than its University Library, were the beneficiaries of much older medieval library collections obtained from elsewhere, some of whose special character they preserve. Many centuries of accumulation have made it possible to put on show the largest exhibition of illuminated manuscripts to be held in the United Kingdom since that held almost a century ago, in 1908, at the Burlington Fine Arts Club, which included 269 items (London 1908). On display in Cambridge are 215 manuscripts and single miniatures which represent four or five per cent of the total in the University at large. Their selection has not been easy, and some may protest that their favourite manuscript, or one that is unjustly neglected, is not on show. In mitigation, it can be replied that this exhibition is part of a larger continuing project to catalogue all the Cambridge illuminations, which will be a friend to all such books.

Quantity aside, quality has been a major consideration in selecting what to show, for an opportunity such as this leaves no scope for false modesty. A decision to focus on illuminated books entails, *ipso facto*, a value judgement, even if the levels of quality of such books can be very variable. This exhibition includes some of the greatest books ever made, and displays them in the company of other manuscripts which are themselves amongst the best representatives of almost all types of book production and decoration. Of course, the value and importance of a book does not always lie solely in its beauty. For example, the first manuscript, the St Augustine Gospels at Corpus Christi College *(no. 1)*, is a sixth-century Italian copy of the Vulgate which may not be the most glamorous book known to us, but which, because of its great age and standing as a book associated with the foundation of the Christian identity of England, is quite simply unmatched. Since it is now used at the enthronement of the Archbishops of Canterbury it is the only manuscript in the selection which still retains something like its original liturgical function. We should reflect that many of the books in this exhibition form a significant part of the history of the English people and its literature. The roll-call begins with the great monastic historians Bede and Matthew Paris, whose unique copy of the *Chronica majora* or great chronicle, drawn up by himself, is preserved largely in two volumes at Corpus Christi College: on the basis of this text alone much of the subsequent history of medieval England in the time of the formation of its parliamentary system was based, for better or worse. It continues with the early religious writings of Ælfric and with the poetic literature of John Gower, John Lydgate and Geoffrey Chaucer, himself portrayed in a thoroughly courtly context in his *Troilus and Creseyde (no.129)*. European and wider literature is represented by, among others, Cicero, Pliny, Suetonius, Valerius Maximus, Josephus, Boethius, Prudentius, Gregory the Great, Guillaume de Lorris and Jean de Meun, Guillaume de Machaut and Christine de Pizan. No better start for an illuminated book may be imagined than a really great text. Yet artists about whom we know something, or whose portrait figures in their work, play their part too, such as the scribe (indeed 'Prince of Scribes') Eadwine, and the illuminators William de Brailes, Matthew Paris, Honoré and Jean Pucelle, as well as art-historical 'personalities' such as the Boucicaut Master, for all these are represented by their own work or by that of close associates. Finally we have the supreme masterpieces: from England and France alone before 1300, the Bury Bible, the Trinity College Apocalypse, the Isabella Psalter and the leaves from the workshop of Honoré *(nos. 19, 40, 72, 116)*. It can fairly be claimed that a near-complete history of the best in Western European illumination can easily and thoroughly be taught from within even a few of Cambridge's collections.

It is not surprising that just over half of a fairly representative selection such as this should consist of English or Insular manuscripts, and that books of such origin should be less apparent in the sections given over to the liturgy of the Church and to Christian devotion, since that merely reflects the major losses such types of book sustained at the Reformation and later. Other patterns are worth looking out for. We note for example how very few illuminated manuscripts of Continental origin (even including culturally closely-related spheres such as northern France) had arrived for certain in Cambridge collections before the seventeenth century, notably the Hrabanus manuscripts *(nos. 5, 6)*, the Peter Lombard *(no. 26)* and the Psalter of Count Achadeus *(no. 15)*. Granted that losses will have occurred, this still underlines the extent to which international currents of medieval book illumination were only known and appreciated in Cambridge after the Reformation and Renaissance. Such books will always have been of less importance to the day-to-day life of the University than those answering to the student curriculum. Then, as now, the wealth of individuals was often critical in determining book ownership and readership, except that illuminated books were almost fabulously expensive by the standards of the modern printed text. Very few young men in Cambridge will have been in the position of the thirteenth-century youth sent by his father to study at Bologna and Paris armed with a huge allowance, who to his father's manifest distress then squandered the lot on illuminated books 'enbabooned with gold letters' or as it were 'monkeyed-up' by the local booksellers (de Hamel 1986, 107).

There will always have been tempting Aristotles and law books for the connoisseur who could stretch to them.

Few will have been painted in Cambridge, however. In comparison with Oxford, where illuminated Bibles were certainly made and copies of curriculum texts were produced for copying in turn by students, Cambridge was relatively unimportant. Unlike older university cities, such as Paris or Bologna, Cambridge was for much of the Middle Ages distinctly provincial despite the fact that it was a city with rather over a dozen parish churches and chapels, a house of Augustinians at Barnwell, a Benedictine nunnery dedicated to St Radegund, and the usual houses of Franciscans, Dominicans, Carmelites and Austin Friars. Admittedly, all these will in theory have needed texts for worship and study which will in principle have created the occasion for decoration of some sort, even before consideration of the needs of the university curriculum. Reference survives to one Cambridge illuminator in the early fourteenth century, Robert le luminor (Michael 1988, 108 n. 10). Queen Eleanor of Castile's illuminator Godfrey purchased Psalters and Books of Hours in Cambridge, and there has in recent years been a tendency to stress the increasing importance of Cambridge as a centre towards the middle of the fourteenth century (Michael 1988, 109; Dennison 1986b, 54–6, 62). Yet very few surviving illuminated books or documents were demonstrably made in Cambridge, and those which almost certainly were (and they are included in the final section of the exhibition) are often done in somewhat run-of-the-mill contemporary styles. The best of them artistically is the refined Raymond of Peñafort's *Summa de casibus* made around 1250 *(no. 177)* which is sufficiently close to illuminated books made for monks in the Fenland area *(e.g. no. 68)* to illustrate how close was the overlap between early monastic and university books. The same point may be made about the rather robust fourteenth-century Psalter of the Bishop of Ely Simon de Montacute and one of the University's charters *(nos. 77, 179)*. But books such as the Peñafort or the Aristotle *(no. 175)* were post-medieval acquisitions. It is easy to forget how very modest were the University collections in the earliest years. They certainly existed by the second half of the fourteenth century and were large enough to warrant cataloguing in the period 1424–1440, when they numbered 122 volumes. This tally was probably more modest than some of the college collections, which themselves were assembled by institutions which were essentially mendicant in character, and thus subject to the vagaries of benefaction (Oates 1986). Substantial parts survive of the medieval collections of Peterhouse, Pembroke and Gonville Hall. Each has a different story to tell, but the fact is that most early university books are not picturesque. The library of Gonville Hall, of which some 350 books survive at Caius with clear indications of origin, comprised at least 64 works of theology, 20 books for the arts curriculum, 27 canon and civil law texts and 16 for medicine, of which only a minority are in any way decorated (Brooke 34–6). The liturgical books once found in every college chapel will not have passed into the academic library collections at the Reformation when they became useless, or downright suspect. Even in the fifteenth century the evidence for illumination in Cambridge is slim in comparison with other cities (Scott 1996, I, 28, 66–7 n. 27).

These various remarks are intended only to make a simple point: the 'Cambridge Illuminations' are the product above all of the tremendous surges of post-medieval acquisition that have built up the collections we know today. The most important of these was the product of socio-religious upheaval. As Christopher de Hamel shows in his essay, Cambridge University was a massive beneficiary of the English Reformation and Dissolution of the Monasteries which led to the wholesale transfer of batches of manuscripts, many of them illuminated and some of them of great antiquity, indirectly or directly from great monastic libraries. The gathering of Canterbury manuscripts at Trinity and Corpus Christi, helped to prevent the total loss of two of the most venerable, scholarly (and Catholic) libraries of England, of Christ Church and St Augustine's. As it is, the losses which were incurred are almost unimaginable, and the partial reconstitution, a sort of mental salvage, of these great lost libraries has itself been a significant preoccupation of such great modern scholars as M.R. James and N.R. Ker. Within a few generations, and as the result of donations by Matthew Parker, Richard Holdsworth, John Moore and many others, the modest scholarly libraries of Cambridge began to be transformed into the treasure-troves of today. Modern Renaissance tastes favoured the fairly early acquisition of many of the books with Humanist script and related Italianate styles of illustration to which a section of this exhibition is devoted. The actual use of what were always essentially practical, if beautiful, things was becoming secondary to their nature as art. By the modern era this produced colossal benefits, while also incurring serious costs. The collections of the Fitzwilliam Museum are testimony to the gradual but formidable rehabilitation of the art of the medieval as well as the Renaissance illuminated book, particularly devotional books of the later Middle Ages such as Books of Hours. Yet, just as such works became things of beauty, so they acquired value as art commodities; and this led in turn to abuse, namely the cutting out and dispersal of illuminations or illuminated pages as if they were framed paintings. In 1854 an unselfconscious entry was made in the diary of one of the greatest proponents of medieval art, John Ruskin: 'Cut up missal in evening – hard work' (Munby 1972, 160). Each one of us who has bought a Christmas card with some quaint scene from a Book of Hours is to an extent heir to this unfortunate outlook, represented by many examples in the Fitzwilliam Museum.

The very real efforts made in this catalogue precisely to take into account the relationship between text and image within a total concept of book art show how the understanding of these manuscripts has been a matter of constant development and change. The origins of Cambridge catalogues in the fifteenth century have already been noted. Early printed listings of books at Oxford and Cambridge include Thomas James's *Ecloga Oxonio-Cantabrigiensis* (1600) and Edward Bernard's and Humfrey Wanley's *Catalogus librorum manuscriptorum Angliae et Hiberniae* (1697). The first concerted catalogue of one of Cambridge's collections, that in the University Library, is also generally recognized as one of the weakest. It was published in 1856–1867 by C. Hardwick, J.E.B. Mayor (University Librarian, 1864–1867) and H. R. Luard (Registrary, 1864–1891) and is principally useful nowadays for some of its remarks on texts: the assertions it makes about illuminations and their dates are often wildly inaccurate and the product of obvious guesswork. The gulf between their work and that of M.R. James (1862–1936), the founding father of comprehensive manuscript cataloguing in Cambridge, is so great as to need no emphasis. For all their eccentricities and signs of haste, James's catalogues of the Fitzwilliam and college manuscripts, begun in earnest in the 1890s, mark a huge advance in the accuracy of even their most broad dating and localizations. Though not an art historian so much as an expert in all aspects of 'Christian archaeology'and textual history, James was a significant figure in the development of the printed manuscript facsimile with scholarly introduction which did so much to inform art-historical interest in, and knowledge of, illuminated manuscripts, so soundly continued by S.C. Cockerell and, nearer our own times, Francis Wormald and Phyllis Giles. James's sound Latinity, phenomenal grasp of published and unpublished texts, capacious memory for tiny but potentially important connections between manuscripts, ceaseless and truly Victorian energy and fearlessness in passing judgements (often hilarious) on manuscripts easily compensated for his dreadful handwriting and rather harsh comments on some of the Cambridge collections, 'Caius' (for example) 'being so dull that I must have some variety' (Pfaff 1980, 198). The one lacuna in Cambridge's cataloguing is the near-complete catalogue James drew up between 1925 and 1933 of the manuscripts in the University Library, for which he was paid £500, yet which was never published. Without the comparative wealth of the Fitzwilliam and the colleges, and their willingness to subvent the costs of such catalogues, the history of manuscript scholarship here would have been limited; without the amiable genius of the great Provost of King's, it might never have developed at all, and certainly not so quickly.

As noted earlier, the present exhibition is but part of a series of current projects to update radically the existing catalogues of illuminated manuscripts in Cambridge, including the University Library itself. The inspiration of the extraordinary general catalogues of illuminations at the Bodleian compiled by Otto Pächt and one of our own honorary curators, Jonathan Alexander, should be acknowledged here. But formal academic catalogues are not quite the same as those for exhibitions, and some words should be said here about the ways in which the present catalogue has been set out and presented. A century or more ago, a catalogue such as W.G. Searle's *The Illuminated Manuscripts in the Library of the Fitzwilliam Museum, Cambridge* of 1876 was arranged by national 'schools' of decoration – Italian, French, Flemish, Dutch, English – in keeping with contemporary ideas about the display of fine art. Later, an alternative was to arrange the books chronologically, as in Francis Wormald and Phyllis M. Giles's *Illuminated Manuscripts in the Fitzwilliam Museum* of 1966. In the present catalogue the arrangement is first by book type and function, and only secondly by date, style and origin. This shift in priority reflects the wide-ranging development in the study of illuminated manuscripts characteristic of the last two generations. Central to this understanding is a much more 'holistic' view of what a manuscript book is, as an object whose manufacture entailed the use of materials and skills, whose writing was governed by conventions regarding the layout and appearance of script, whose decoration very commonly reflected the nature and use of the text in question, and whose intended patronage and use were what medieval notions of causality would have identified as the 'efficient cause' of the manuscript in the first place. The book now stands at an interdisciplinary crossroads. All of these aspects of study require special interpretative skills, whether they be codicological (i.e. concerning the physical nature and make-up of books, or their 'archaeology'), palaeographical (concerning the history of script), scientific (concerning the analysis of the physical constituents of pigments and other materials) or literary and art-historical. As the essays by Christopher de Hamel, Stella Panayotova and Teresa Webber show, the history of collecting and the study of illuminating techniques are now special subjects in themselves; and as Rosamond McKitterick indicates, questions of literacy and the textual framework for illumination are now far more central than they would have been in Ruskin's day. All these things imply an outlook that is much more influenced by science, social theory and anthropology than would have been imaginable even half a century ago.

For every category selected in this catalogue – whether of religious manuscripts associated with the era of the Christian conversion of Europe, or medieval theology, liturgy and devotion, or history and literature, or science – a number of other, as it were 'virtual', categories will suggest themselves to viewers of the manuscripts, which allow quite different links and associations to those selected here to be built up. Consider for example the notion of tradition. The Cambridge Illuminations cover about one millennium's worth of Western European manuscript production that demonstrates the astonishing stability and continuity of book culture within certain places and institutions. Monasticism at Canterbury is one example. Of its contribution to the formation of libraries and the making of books we have several signal instances. As Rosamond McKitterick shows, the sixth-century St Augustine Gospels mentioned earlier *(no. 1)* belongs to an early phase of the history of Christianity as a religion of The Book. The Gospels were an important relic of St Augustine's Abbey in Canterbury. They enjoyed a tremendous pedigree. In another part of the exhibition is found the much later, fifteenth-century, chronicle of St Augustine's Abbey compiled by Thomas of Elmham, one of its monks *(no. 115)*. Thomas included in this manuscript a remarkable map of the Isle of Thanet, important to St Augustine's because Bede tells us in the first book of his Ecclesiastical History that St Augustine and his companions had landed there in the year 597 and had been greeted by King Ethelbert. Another map in Thomas's manuscript is a schematic view of the east end of his abbey's church showing the high altar and shrines. The books shown as relics over the main altar are labelled *libri missi a Gregorio ad Augustinum*, 'the books sent from Pope Gregory (the Great) to Augustine', and may include the St Augustine Gospels (Henderson 1999, 65–73). One of our manuscripts appears to 'document' the history of another. But the tradition is more developed still. Among the few surviving illustrations in the Gospels is a page of tiny framed miniatures showing the events from the Passion of Christ (p.46): the doctrine set out in one of Pope Gregory's most famous letters, that images allow the reader to learn something additional *(addiscere)* to the Gospel text, is here beautifully exemplified. That it remained relevant in the era of the Romanesque book half a millennium later is proved by the survival of a series of similar Bible pictures which originally adorned the very front of the great Eadwine Psalter *(no.25)* made at twelfth-century Christ Church, Canterbury, as a copy of the famous ninth-century Utrecht Psalter (Gibson, Heslop and Pfaff 1992, 25–42). In various ways, three of our books displayed in separate sections are related not just circumstantially, but in substantial ways proper to a tradition, the handing-down of, and participation in, a distinct body of ideas and things. Were it not for Matthew Parker, none of this might be known today.

Rosamond McKitterick and Teresa Webber show how the medieval book flourished at the heart of Western Europe from the period of its Christianization through to the formation of the sophisticated courtly and scholarly cultures of the Holy Roman Empire and twelfth-century northern France and southern England. Books such as the Eadwine Psalter were complex tools of scholarship which provide ample evidence of the concurrence in post-Conquest England and the twelfth century of more than one literary and linguistic culture, while reflecting back on the manuscript production of ninth-century Reims and the holdings of seventh-century Canterbury libraries. After 1200 or so, the grip of the ancient centres is not always so apparent. The small, beautifully written and increasingly standardized form of the single-volume Vulgate Bibles developed in thirteenth-century Paris points to the rise of new methods and places of production, as well as new needs; these will have included compact accessible books for university study, portable books for use by the new preaching Orders and, finally, commercial and more specialized books of various sorts for laypeople. Consider such Parisian books as the Isabella Psalter *(no. 72)* made for the sister of Louis IX of France, the leaves from the *Somme le Roi* attributed to Master Honoré *(no. 116)*, the Franciscan Breviary made for Marie de St Pol, Countess of Pembroke and founder of Pembroke College, Cambridge *(no. 49)* and the *Roman de la Rose* made by a husband-and-wife team *(no. 123)*. Royal courts, which produced such masterpieces as the Isabella Psalter (whose Calendar is that of the Sainte-Chapelle in Paris) or the Life of St Edward (made for the Plantagenet court of Henry III) *(no. 113)*, were also a significant factor in influencing the nature of urban book production precisely because such courts were now located in major urban centres.

Books such as Psalters, Breviaries and Lives of the Saints belonged to substantial and weighty traditions owing much to the continuing daily life of the Church and its liturgy, as well as providing historians with some indication of the ways in which 'private' forms of book and book use emerged from within such essentially public activities as church worship. The survival of significant illuminated manuscripts pertaining to the public liturgy of the Church is considered by Nigel Morgan. It was within this domain that many of the routines of ordinary Christian practice, as well as grand ceremonial, were shaped and perpetuated, with the assistance of the powerful language of the Mass and the daily Offices. It was within this sphere too that the rituals of the continuation and legitimization of power were conducted, as in the orders for the consecration, or coronation, of kings. But, as is indicated in the essay on devotional manuscripts, such highly conventional and public forms did not stand in opposition to private devotional life. On the contrary, the medieval 'best seller', the Book of Hours, a prayerbook which emerges first in the thirteenth century and which was produced in prodigious numbers by the fifteenth century and into the era of printing, was founded on the public offices of the Church collected in the Breviary. Daily life was steeped in the language and imagery of the liturgy; devotions, like liturgy, entailed discipline and generally-recognized orthodox procedures. To the modern eye they seem to have produced remarkable individual images, such as the Man of Sorrows, the Veronica, the *Pietà*, or other images seen with individual patrons at prayer. But it is worth recalling that in some cases (such as the Veronica) these images owed their standing to the indulgenced prayers which accompanied them, and hence much to the gradual formal establishment of the doctrine of Purgatory and of the efficacy of suffrages for the dead.

Of all the sections in the exhibition, that concerning history and literature is necessarily the most diverse, and here the need for 'virtual' connections of one sort or another is especially apparent. For one thing, within a predominantly Christian culture there were no harshly-drawn boundaries between notions of history governed by the idea of the Divine plan and other types of educative, improving or entertaining literature which might ordinarily be thought of as 'secular'. To both, clear and universal views of human conduct and the workings of justice in human affairs had applied since at least the time of Eusebius and Jerome. We certainly find them at work in the chronicle writing and hagiography of Matthew Paris *(nos. 113, 114)*; indeed works of hagiography could almost as easily have been classed with devotional manuscripts, for the saints were objects of devotion as well as models. There was also a constant interplay between ethical notions developed in the pre-Christian world and in Christianity itself. Roman writers such as Cicero and Valerius Maximus were widely read throughout the Middle Ages and Renaissance, and Aristotle's *Ethics* proved increasingly influential from the thirteenth century. The pastoral mission of the Church in the era following Gregorian reform had at its disposal methods of persuasion that were both pagan and Christian in character, including the visual image itself. These methods are equally apparent in the literature of the Church which aimed to lead men to the good, and in the literature concerning personal conduct, political governance and human frailty which fills so many of the distinguished later-medieval books in this section.

The holistic view of man as an ethical and spiritual entity within a larger order was not unrelated to a medieval cosmology founded on a belief in the ultimate harmony of creation, discussed in Peter Jones's essay on the medieval encyclopedia and science. As Peter Jones explains, the urge to arrive at a coherent and total understanding of the universe lay behind what he calls 'do-it-yourself encyclopedism' and the (to us) strange juxtaposition of texts about the observable world of plants, animals and the heavens which served the important purposes of moral estimation and prognostication. There could be no question here of the modern division of art and science discussed in C.P. Snow's famous *Two Cultures* (1959). 'Science' books could be works of art, and necessarily varied hugely in form and content, from the extraordinary gathering of Anglo-Norman texts made in the English Midlands around 1330 which forms one of the oddest-shaped books in Cambridge *(no. 151)*, to the courtly elegance of the text on the Properties of Things illuminated by the Boucicaut Master for a grandson of Jean, Duc de Berry, one of the greatest of medieval connoisseurs *(no. 152)*.

Our penultimate section is devoted to the Humanist manuscript. In one of the most famous (and controversial) put-downs in the history of art, Erwin Panofsky once remarked that from the middle of the fifteenth century book illumination (in northern Europe at least) had become a decadent and finally 'residual' art form secondary by far to 'real' painting: 'It has been said that book illumination was killed by the invention of printing; but it had already begun to commit suicide by converting itself into painting. Even without Gutenberg it would have died of an overdose of perspective' (Panofsky 1953b, 28). Whether or not this characteristically bold and eloquent estimation of the accomplishments of some of the latest 'Gothic' illuminations in our exhibition is fair – and many would now argue firmly that it is not – it is extremely hard to square with the new, fastidious and strange beauty of the Italian Renaissance page, which, as both Teresa Webber and Jonathan Alexander remark, was transformed in appearance by means not only of effects drawn from 'true' painting, but also by the new script, which led to a 'whiter' page than that afforded by the dense regular 'black letter' of Gothic script and early printing. This is an excellent instance of the importance of seeing the page as a whole, as was undoubtedly done by the greatest medieval and Renaissance book designers, whatever the specific language of design and colour they were working with. It will surely be agreed that these manuscripts form a fitting climax to this most comprehensive display of Cambridge treasures.

COLLECTORS AND COLLECTING IN CAMBRIDGE

Christopher de Hamel

ANYONE WOULD AGREE that books are at the core of university learning. There is appropriately a book in the centre of the coat of arms of Cambridge University. From the beginning the collegiate libraries of the medieval university included illuminated manuscripts, not for any antiquarian benefit but simply because they were necessary tools for daily study and Christian worship. Individual manuscripts may from time to time have already been of some antiquity, if only because many were acquired by the colleges as gifts from benefactors who would have obtained them on the second-hand market. There was no perceived interest in antiquarianism for its own sake. Any late medieval scholar intent on pursuing ancient or obsolete texts would doubtless have had access to the infinitely vaster libraries of the great English monasteries, which were still the repositories of nearly a thousand years of learning in the British Isles.

The Renaissance hit England at a bad time for manuscript studies. Towards the middle of the sixteenth century English academics began to catch the excitement of universal knowledge and the pursuit of classical and modern scholarship. They wanted books as never before, both personally and for their University. Printing had largely rendered manuscripts obsolete as reliable texts, and new advances in law and teaching looked back in despair on the archaic manuscript textbooks of the late Middle Ages. The closure of the monasteries in the 1530s and 1540s must then have thrown tens of thousands of medieval manuscripts on to the market. If such an event had happened today, one would expect some deal would be struck at governmental level between the royal commissioners and the University, and the monastic libraries would doubtless be transferred wholesale into the care of the University Library; but in the sixteenth century the universities were not ready for old books and were wisely cautious of aligning themselves too vigorously with suspected papist and Catholic scholarship. Cambridge embraced the Reformation, and may owe its survival to having done so. At the moment when books were more fashionable than they had ever been, bonfires of manuscripts in England were dedicated to eliminating utterly all evidence of an apparently erroneous and blasphemous past. It was heart-rending for the early antiquaries. Even in Cambridge (although not as much as in Oxford), medieval parchment manuscripts were cut up in their hundreds to provide strengthening for book-bindings or for domestic and commercial uses for pieces of waste paper and parchment.

The first great Reformation collectors for Cambridge were men of unquestionable orthodoxy, including several Archbishops of Canterbury, no less. Matthew Parker (1504–1575) is perhaps the most interesting for he provided a model for archiepiscopal accumulation and donation, which largely furnished the college libraries for centuries. Parker had been Master of Corpus (1544) and Vice-Chancellor of the University. He was exiled under Queen Mary and recalled in 1559 by Queen Elizabeth, who made him her first archbishop, with a mandate to make the English Reformation absolute and irrevocable. Parker edited and promulgated the Thirty-Nine Articles, the defining document of the Anglican Church.

Many of its clauses seemed at the time to be utterly revolutionary – the Bible and church services in the English language, for example, or married priests, and the Monarch (not the Pope) at the head of the Church. Parker, who was already a book collector and a historian by inclination, convinced himself that Anglo-Saxon England had represented a golden age of the English Church and language. He argued that the reformed Anglican Church was simply a reversion to precedent, and he selected books to prove the point. He obtained licence from the Queen to take into his own custody any former monastic manuscripts which would provide evidence that early England had had a special place in the destiny of the Christian faith. Many manuscripts were salvaged by him from sources close at hand: more than thirty-five came from the former Cathedral Priory of Christ Church in Canterbury, for instance, and about thirty from St Augustine's Abbey nearby, including the so-called 'Gospels of Saint Augustine' of the late sixth century *(no. 1)*. Others came especially from cathedral collections, such as Worcester, Winchester, Exeter and Norwich. In allowing an archbishop to acquire their manuscripts, many deans and chapters must have felt reassured that their ancient books were at least safe.

Parker's decision to locate his collections in Cambridge, rather than at Lambeth, Westminster or Canterbury, established the precedent which came to supply the college libraries of Cambridge with such remarkable and often quite unexpected collections of medieval manuscripts. Parker's indenture of 1574 entrusted his vast library into the care of Corpus Christi College but with conditions attached, including a clause that if Corpus should fail to preserve them appropriately, the collection should revert instead to Gonville and Caius College or in turn to Trinity Hall. It marks an important moment in library history, for the Cambridge colleges became the repositories of choice for those with the moral dilemma of what to do with sequestered monastic books. Learning that had been enshrined in religious houses now seemed more appropriate in collegiate hands. William Smart, portreeve of Ipswich, was persuaded in 1599 to lodge more than a hundred manuscripts at Pembroke College, including well over a third of the entire surviving library of Bury St Edmunds Abbey. A further clutch of manuscripts at Pembroke came *en bloc* from the former Abbey of Reading. The antiquary Robert Hare (*c*.1530–1611) gave manuscripts to several libraries in Cambridge, including Trinity Hall and the University Library. Other archbishops continued Parker's raids on the remaining collections in Canterbury, with less focus on the selection of texts and more now on acquisition for Cambridge. John Whitgift (*c*.1530–1604) followed Parker in being Master of his college (Trinity, 1567), Vice-Chancellor, and Archbishop of Canterbury from 1583. He too gathered into his possession runs of manuscripts from former religious houses, notably Buildwas Abbey in Shropshire, perhaps acquired when he was Bishop of Worcester (1577–1583). On his death most of Whitgift's library remained at Lambeth Palace but all his best medieval manuscripts, about one hundred and fifty volumes altogether, were bequeathed to Trinity College in Cambridge, including more than fifty formerly at Christ Church Cathedral Priory. By now most of the medieval books from Canterbury seemed to have been relocated in Cambridge. It must have appeared sensible for Thomas Nevile (*c*.1548–1615) to complete the job. Nevile's elder brother had been Matthew Parker's secretary. Probably on Whitgift's recommendation, Nevile had become Master of Trinity in 1593 and Dean of Canterbury in 1597. In about 1611 he sent one hundred and twenty six manuscripts from Canterbury and elsewhere to Cambridge, including the magnificent twelfth-century Canterbury or Eadwine Psalter *(no. 25)*.

In the seventeenth century illuminated manuscripts were acquiring an antiquarian value in their own right. Even between Parker and Nevile one can watch a shift of taste from rigorously textual and evidential to the bibliophilic, or at least towards a desire for books which a college might expect to display as symbols of luxury and patriotic adherence to English antiquity. St John's College acquired marvellous illuminated manuscripts from the collection of Shakespeare's patron, Henry Wriothesley (1573–1624), third Earl of Southampton. Wriothesley himself had probably acquired many of them from the poet and theologian, William Crashaw (1572–1626), Canon of York. The books finally reached the college in 1635 from Wriothesley's widow and son, the fourth Earl. The bequest included books from both the medieval monastic libraries of Canterbury, and from those of Rochester, Dover, Syon, Guisborough, Durham and elsewhere. Manuscripts once at Durham and other northern monasteries came to Jesus College too from Thomas Man (d.1690), priest and medical doctor, the son of the vicar of Northallerton, in northern Yorkshire. Emmanuel College acquired manuscripts from Thomas Leigh (d.1686), master of the grammar school at Bishop's Stortford, and from the classicist, Joshua Barnes (1654–1712), both fellows of the college. Others – though slight – reached Emmanuel from a third Archbishop of Canterbury, William Sancroft (1617–1693), former fellow and bursar. One of the greatest of all Gothic manuscripts in England, the breathtaking Trinity Apocalypse *(no. 40)*, was given to Trinity College in 1660 by Anne Sadleir, daughter of Sir Edward Coke. Trinity College was further enriched in 1738 with the combined collections of the antiquaries, father and son, Thomas Gale (1635/1636–1702), Dean of York, and Roger Gale (1672–1744). English monastic manuscripts were still available in their time. Thomas had married the cousin of the diarist Samuel Pepys (1633–1703), the greatest English bibliophile of the period. Pepys' own collection comprised relatively few manuscripts compared with his printed books, but they were a connoisseur's choice, chosen for delight as much as for instruction. His whole library is beautifully preserved even in his own bookcases in Magdalene College, but regrettably Pepys is not represented in this exhibition because the conditions of his bequest, partly modelled on those of Parker, added the refinement of prohibiting loans.

By the early eighteenth century the college libraries of Cambridge were extremely strong in their holdings of illuminated manuscripts, many of them salvaged and preserved from the dissolution of the English monasteries almost two centuries earlier. This is one great difference between the libraries of Oxford and Cambridge. In Oxford donations of manuscripts were almost all focused on the Bodleian Library, which was (and in many areas of medieval manuscripts still is) incomparably greater and more diverse than its opposite number in Cambridge University Library. The Oxford college libraries, however, with the possible exception of St John's, generally slumbered with the dwindling residues of their medieval collections. If there is a single reaction we expect from the current exhibition it is how extraordinarily rich in manuscripts the libraries of the individual colleges in Cambridge became in the fall-out of the Reformation. This imbalance between the colleges and the central library was first readdressed with the acquisition of the huge manuscript collection of John Moore (1646–1714). Moore came from a family with Oxford connections but was himself a fellow of Clare College in

Cambridge. He became successively Bishop of Norwich (1691–1707) and Ely (1707–1714). Thomas Tanner, the collector, was one of his chaplains. Moore's enormous library eventually filled eight great rooms in London, including almost two thousand manuscripts, among which the eighth-century Moore Bede *(no. 3)* was probably the most famous. Like the contemporary collection of Robert Harley, Earl of Oxford, Moore gathered books from the Continent as well as from England. In an extraordinary piece of strategic diplomacy, intended at least in part to endear the new Hanoverian monarchy to Cambridge, George I was persuaded by Lord Townshend, Secretary of State, to buy Moore's collection *en bloc* in 1714 and to present it to the University Library. Although a central library of the University had certainly existed since about 1420 (and Parker himself had given it a number of manuscripts), it was the acquisition of the library of Bishop Moore which launched it on its present path as one of the great national repositories of medieval books. It is now the only manuscript library in Cambridge still with a consistent programme of acquisition.

Medieval and illuminated manuscripts have always been valuable and collectible, but collectors have sought them for different reasons. If sixteenth-century owners gathered manuscripts for political and religious motives and seventeenth-century collectors for antiquity's sake and for the diversity of texts, the bibliophiles of the late eighteenth century began to enjoy illuminated manuscripts as works of art in their own right. This is exemplified in the collecting taste of Richard Fitzwilliam (1745–1816), seventh Viscount Fitzwilliam of Merrion, founder of the University Museum of Cambridge. Only one manuscript in his library had been inherited from his family (a Missal from York, made for an ancestor who died in 1479, now MS 34) but all others were bought by him towards the end of his life, many during his frequent trips to France. As the English Reformation had disgorged monastic texts on to the market in the sixteenth century, so the upheavals of the French Revolution scattered vast monastic and aristocratic libraries onto the market, to the delight of connoisseurs of book illumination, many of them English. The dispersals themselves affected collecting taste. Beginning in 1789, Lord Fitzwilliam began his cumulative acquisition of one hundred and thirty illuminated manuscripts, nearly a hundred of which were Books of Hours. These beautiful books had generally been ignored by the early collectors, for their textual value is often slight and their illustrations are overtly Catholic. In fact, the religiosity of late medieval illumination caught the imagination of collectors of the romantic era, and they enjoyed the discovery that the manuscripts' delicate artwork was often of the highest order. Lord Fitzwilliam bequeathed his entire collections to Cambridge University, paintings and works of art of all kinds as well as illuminated manuscripts, together with £100,000 for the creation of a suitable museum. It is notable that from that time onwards most manuscripts acquired by Cambridge were bought for the sake of their art, a criterion that would have puzzled or even shocked Matthew Parker. The Fitzwilliam now has one of the largest and finest collections of Books of Hours in the world, second in England only to the British Library.

Nineteenth-century collectors often expressed their connoisseurship of Gothic illumination by cutting out the miniatures to exhibit them as works of art in their own right. Choir Books and other illustrated manuscripts were dismembered in Italy especially and were brought to England for sale as individual medieval paintings. One of the largest such collections ever made, with two hundred and forty five cuttings, eventually reached the Fitzwilliam Museum with the bequest of Charles Brinsley Marlay (1831–1912). Others came individually, such as the first of the magnificent single miniatures by Honoré from the finest known copy of the *Somme le Roi (no. 116)*, acquired by the Fitzwilliam in 1892 from Samuel Sandars (1837–1894). Three successive directors of the Museum were specialists in manuscripts. They were J.H. Middleton, author of *Illuminated Manuscripts of Classical and Medieval Times* (1892), director 1889–1893; M.R. James, the pioneer cataloguer of Cambridge manuscripts and writer of antiquarian ghost stories, Director 1893–1908; and the irresistible and irrepressible magician of manuscripts, Sydney Cockerell, Director 1908–1937. Each in turn conjured gifts and bequests of manuscripts and illuminations, the most extensive of which came from Frank McClean (1837–1904). He was a railway engineer by profession but retired to Tunbridge Wells in his early thirties to devote his life to astronomy and collecting. He bequeathed just over two hundred illuminated manuscripts to the Fitzwilliam, gathered from the great sales of the turn of the century, including those of Sir Thomas Phillipps, Lord Ashburnham, Henry White, William Morris, and others. One of Cockerell's many innovations was the establishment of honorary keepers of the Fitzwilliam Museum as a device for maintaining the profile of the collections. Those for illuminated manuscripts have included Francis Wormald, Jonathan Alexander and James Marrow.

The dispersals of the English Reformation are still not quite over. Even as this catalogue was in press, news arrived of the acquisition by the Fitzwilliam Museum of an enchanting English fourteenth-century manuscript from Suffolk, the Macclesfield Psalter (now added to this Catalogue, *no. 78, fig. 2*), which has been unknown in private hands since the suppression of the monasteries. It is richly illuminated. It is not only appropriate that such a book should be gathered into the collections of Cambridge but its arrival is part of a long migration that began 500 years ago and will, with luck and the imagination of the University's benefactors, continue for centuries to come.

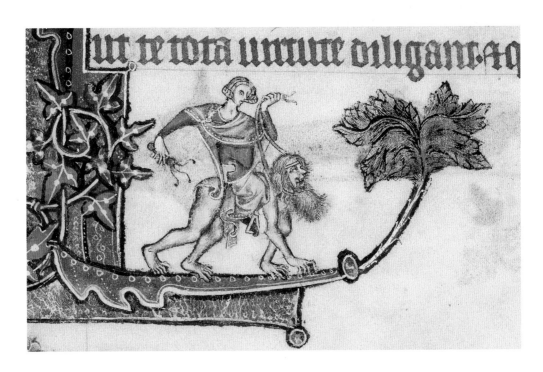

Fig. 2.
Man riding a wildman.
Fitzwilliam Museum,
MS1–2005,
fol. 110v, detail

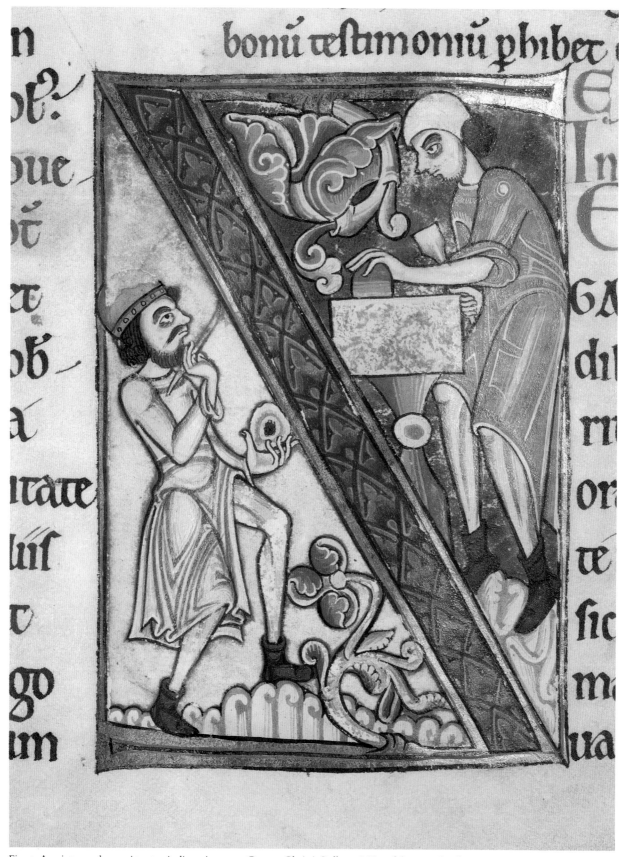

Fig. 3. A painter and an assistant grinding pigments. Corpus Christi College, MS 4, fol. 242v, detail

MAKING AN ILLUMINATED MANUSCRIPT

Stella Panayotova and Teresa Webber

To a modern audience, hand-written and painted books may appear as extravagant survivors of a bygone age. Our books are no longer copied, let alone decorated, by hand. In addition, our appreciation for contemporary art is often inseparable from the artists' identity, but we still marvel at the works of medieval masters who remain largely anonymous. Artists' signatures are rare before the fourteenth century; self-portraits, such as that of the Dover Bible master and his apprentice *(fig. 3, no. 21)* are unique. For some ten centuries, however, illuminated manuscripts were a dominant art medium, powerful symbols of wealth and status, and the main repository of learning and devotion. They preserved the texts of classical Antiquity, accommodated medieval history and literature as well as the quintessential text of Christianity – the Bible – and disseminated the works of the early Renaissance, of Dante, Petrarch, and Chaucer.

The Middle Ages gave us the book as we know it today. In the course of the fourth century AD the papyrus scroll of ancient texts was replaced by the codex, a volume written on a more durable material, animal skin, or parchment. Regardless of its size, a volume bound between two covers proved far easier to use than the scroll – whether for communal worship, private devotion, in-depth research, quick reference, or leisurely reading *(fig. 4)*. The texts in which the scroll endured throughout the medieval and Renaissance period were mainly chronicles, genealogies, and documents

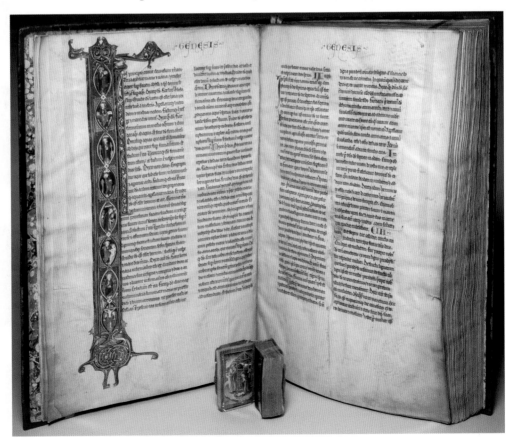

Fig. 4. A Book of Hours and a Bible. Fitzwilliam Museum, MS 149 and anonymous loan

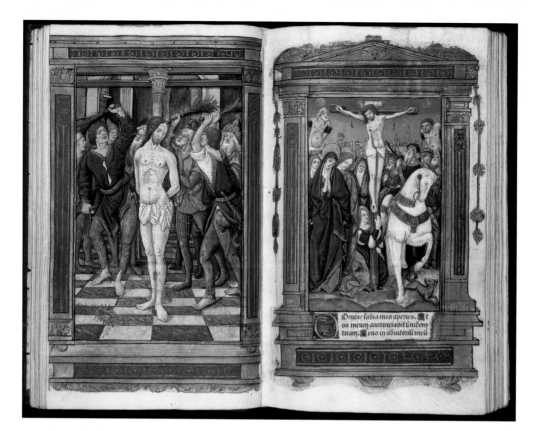

Fig. 5. Flagellation and Crucifixion. Fitzwilliam Museum, Book of Hours, Paris, 1512, fols. 24v–25

(nos. 110, 136). However, even there the old format gave way to the codex, as demonstrated by a genealogy that was written on a scroll, but subsequently folded and bound as a book (Cambridge, Queens' College, MS Horne 35). The introduction of the new book format and material transformed European civilization in a way equalled only by the invention of printing ten centuries later. In fact, they survived the advent of the new technology. The early printers ensured that their most presentable books were printed on parchment and did not differ in appearance from illuminated manuscripts. The rich pigments of the Flagellation and Crucifixion images in a de luxe Parisian Book of Hours printed on parchment by Gillet Hardouin in 1512 were applied over woodcuts designed at the Parisian workshop of Jean Pichore *(fig. 5)*.[1]

The centuries-long traditions of manuscript illumination were recorded and disseminated in artists' manuals, model books, and collections of pigment recipes.[2] Cambridge has numerous collections of recipes[3] and two famous model books, one from twelfth-century Tuscany and the other from fifteenth-century England (Magdalene College, Pepys MS 1916). The latter preserves not only stock motifs, but also signs of tracing. The finest tracing material available to medieval artists was made of tissue-thin kid parchment, which could be oiled to increase its transparency. Designs could also be transferred by pouncing. The contours of an image were pricked and the design 'dusted' through the holes on to the new surface, which could be parchment, paper, wood or fabric. The Clifford-Pabenham Hours *(no. 81)* preserves pouncing holes, although one can never be certain when exactly they were made or used. Artists were sometimes guided by marginal sketches such as those found in an alphabetical biblical dictionary (King's College, MS 40). Such designs may suggest that no pictorial exemplar was available, a challenge artists faced most frequently with texts that had no established iconographic programmes. For common subjects a verbal prompt would have been sufficient. Matteo Torelli and his assistants translated the marginal instruction *lastoria de magi* into a charming Epiphany scene in Cardinal Angelo Acciaiuoli's Missal (Fitzwilliam Museum, MS 30, fol. 16v). The artists of a fifteenth-

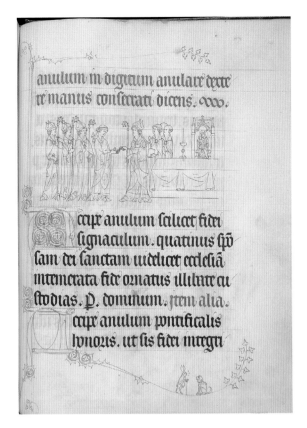

Fig. 6. Ink drawing. Fitzwilliam Museum, MS 298, fol. 129

century *Privity of the Passion* (Trinity College, MS B.10.12) had their instructions written either in the lower margin or within the space left blank for the miniature. Repeated use could transform instructions into image captions. A late thirteenth-century French Psalter with illustrations for each Psalm lists at its very beginning the subject-matter of every image.[4] What was originally a list of instructions circulating among the artists of contemporary fully-illustrated Psalters, had become an integral part of the book, a list of illustrations, as we would call it today.

Such peculiarities are among the most fascinating and revealing aspects of illuminated manuscripts. They demonstrate unusual, often unique approaches to book production and serve as correctives to generalizations. For instance, it is commonly believed – often justly – that until the twelfth century manuscripts were produced mainly by the members of religious communities, but subsequently the growing wealth and learning in the new urban and university centres demanded the services of secular professionals. Master Hugo who painted the great twelfth-century Bible for the Benedictine monastery of Bury St Edmunds, however, was, in all likelihood, a secular professional *(no. 19)*. The late fourteenth-century Psalter made for Mary de Bohun was illuminated by Augustinian friars 'seconded' from their house to work at Pleshey Castle, the residence of Mary's father *(no. 79)*. Alexander Antonii Simonis, who copied the sumptuous Hours of Lorenzo Strozzi *(no. 100)* in 1478, was an Augustinian hermit. His colophons contain verbose pleas for eternal salvation. The copying of a manuscript, like its illumination, was an act of piety in the small devotional book of a Renaissance businessman no less than it had been in the enormous lectern Bibles made for religious communities.

Nothing reveals how a medieval book was made better than an unfinished manuscript. A particularly instructive and refined example is the Metz Pontifical *(no. 52)*. Begun for Renaut de Bar, Bishop of Metz (1303–1316), it remained incomplete, presumably because of the patron's death in 1316. If one leafs through the manuscript starting from the end, one may reconstruct the order and procedures followed by scribes and artists in the majority of the medieval and Renaissance manuscripts *(figs. 6, 7)*.

Fig. 7. Unfinished miniature. Fitzwilliam Museum, MS 298, fol. 106, detail

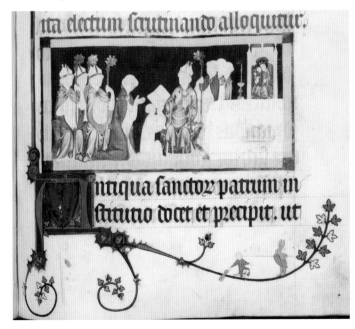

Parchment

For a luxury manuscript like the Metz Pontifical the scribe would first obtain parchment of the highest quality. The choice of animal skins and their treatment was determined by local economy and by the type of book for which they were intended.[5] Goatskins were most commonly used in Italy. Sheepskins were favoured for documents, since they showed erasures more noticeably than other materials and discouraged alteration. Large and thick calfskins were most suitable for giant lectern Bibles and Choir Books. Thirteenth-century pocket size Bibles used skins that had been split up or pared down to tissue-thin sheets, sometimes called 'uterine vellum' after their unlikely source, aborted calves. Calfskins of medium thickness would have provided the durable and yet supple material for manuscripts of the size and quality of the Metz Pontifical.

Quire structure

The clean and dry parchment was cut to the required size. Very large sheets could be folded several times and their edges cut open to form the basic unit of a book, the so-called quire, gathering, or, in the language of printers, signature. Smaller sheets were folded only once to create a bifolium, that is two leaves or four pages. Bifolia were inserted inside one another to form a quire. The quires of the Metz Pontifical are made up of four bifolia each, that is of eight leaves or sixteen pages, while those of the fifteenth-century Florentine Book of Hours *(no.104)*, shown here while it was disbound for conservation *(fig. 8)*, contain five bifolia each, that is ten leaves and twenty pages. In both manuscripts, the arrangement of the leaves follows a pattern common throughout the medieval period – hair side faces hair side and flesh side faces flesh side. The aesthetics of a medieval manuscript were determined well before work on the page layout, let alone the decoration, could

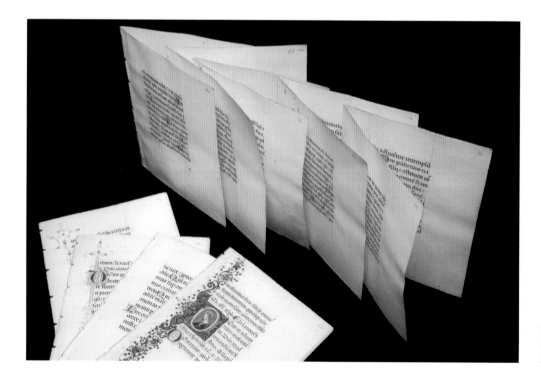

Fig. 8. Manuscript quires. Fitzwilliam Museum, MS 154

begin. The quires were often distributed among scribes and artists to speed up the work. The division of labour in such manuscripts corresponds to the division of quires. This is obvious in the Psalter and Hours of Isabelle of France *(no. 72)*. The different stages of completion in the Metz Pontifical coincide with the beginning of gatherings. Scribes used various devices to signal the order of quires: quire marks (consecutive numbers written on the last verso of a gathering), quire and leaf signatures (combinations of letters and numbers on the leaves in the first half of a gathering), or catchwords (the first words of the next gathering written at the end of the previous one).

Binding

The binder would use these clues to put the quires in order. Once re-assembled, they were sewn to a number of supports made of hemp cord or animal skin and held vertically under tension in a frame *(fig. 9)*. The number of supports and the pattern of sewing could vary considerably depending on the region, period, size and quality of the book. Released from the sewing frame, the supports were attached to the book covers, usually made of oak or beech. Finally, the boards were covered with tanned or tawed skin, vellum or velvet. Metal bosses were sometimes attached to protect the surface. Leather or fabric straps kept the volume closed. When examined together with the structure, the decoration of a binding may offer a fairly reliable guide to the book's origin and provenance, as well as to the specific context in which it was used. While the two enormous volumes of a twelfth-century monastic copy of Gilbert of Poitiers' gloss on the Psalms were well protected within their thick and prickly seal fur (Queens' College, MSS Horne 18 and 18★), soft red velvet was favoured in aristocratic books *(nos. 48, 142)*. The covers of liturgical manuscripts were embellished with gold, silver, precious stones and

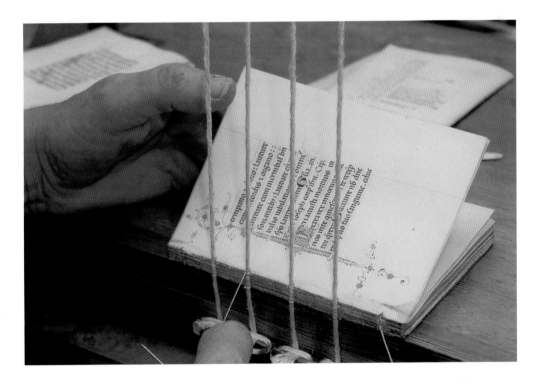

Fig. 9. Quires sewn on the binder's frame. Fitzwilliam Museum, MS 154

27

relics. The exceptionally thick upper cover of a twelfth-century Gospel Lectionary preserves the traces of a solid metal plate and gems that were secured deep into the board (Fitzwilliam Museum, MS McClean 22). Tanned or tawed skins received tooled or stamped decoration in blind or gold *(nos. 57 and 92)*. Ornamental motifs could be developed into complex overall designs, for example, the rope-work interlace characteristic of Italian humanistic books *(no. 165)*.[6] Tanned skins could also receive elaborate figural compositions, such as the Sacrifice of Isaac stamped from an engraved plate through gold leaf onto the cover of Fitzwilliam Museum, MS McClean 93.[7]

The decoration often declared the ownership of a book: the flint-and-steel badge relates the binding of the Statutes of the Golden Fleece to one of the Order's Chancellors *(no. 138)* and a thirteenth-century copy of Peter of Poitiers' *Genealogy of Christ* was later covered with the devices of Henry VIII and Catherine of Aragon, while integrating the *fenestra* from a previous binding (Cambridge University Library, MS Add. 4081). The *fenestra*, the horn window which protected the author and title label inscribed on one of the covers, was often transferred to a new binding *(nos. 121 and 168)*, and so were bosses and clasps *(no. 127)*. The *chemise*, or shirt, which was made of velvet or leather and wrapped over the covers gave manuscripts extra protection *(no. 34)* and glamour (Cambridge University Library, MS Add. 4082). From animal skin to animal skin, the process of making a manuscript was complete.

Writing materials

Before writing, scribes rubbed the parchment with pumice, cuttle fish or ground chalk to remove impurities and make the surface smooth and absorbent *(fig. 10)*.[8] They pricked the margins, often through several stacked sheets, and linked the pricks across the page or double opening to rule the lines and frame the text space. The ruling instrument varied in different areas and periods. A hard point, stylus or awl, was favoured in the early Middle Ages and again during the Renaissance;

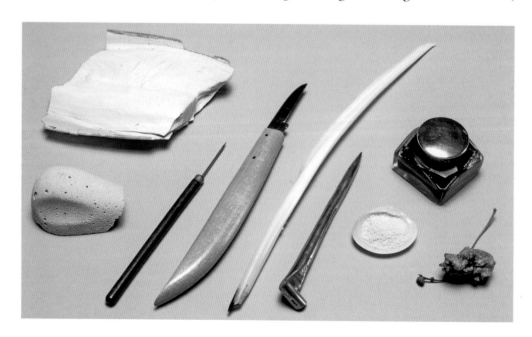

Fig. 10. Writing tools and materials: cuttle fish, pumice, stylus, pen-knife, quill, plummet, oak galls, iron sulphate, and ink pot

it produced a furrow and edge effect on the page. A plummet, or metal point made of lead or silver, was common from the eleventh or twelfth century onwards; it left a trace resembling a pencil mark, as in the Metz Pontifical *(no. 52)*. A fuzzy brown-grey line not unlike a modern crayon was also popular between the twelfth and fifteenth centuries. A pen dipped in black, red or purple ink added to the appeal of late medieval manuscripts. The choices of ruling materials show not only aesthetic concerns, but also economy of effort. Several pens could be attached to an instrument that resembled a gardener's rake and was run across the page to produce parallel lines. One can detect the use of the scribe's rake in manuscripts whose lines quiver 'in time'.

Black ink had several sources. Sepia, the natural ink from the glands of cuttle fish, was known since Antiquity. Just as common was the carbon black ink made of crushed charcoal or lamp black dissolved in water. But the material medieval and Renaissance scribes favoured above all was the iron-gall ink. Its tendency to bond with, or 'bite into', the parchment guaranteed durability and its lustre was irresistible. Its source was the tumour-like growth around the gall wasp eggs laid in the buds or soft twigs of oak trees. The crushed or powdered galls were boiled in water and the black liquid was thickened with gum Arabic, that is the water-soluble sap of acacia or, more commonly, cherry, plum or almond trees. The red lead, or minium, used for titles, headings, and important parts of the text, as in the Metz Pontifical, is responsible for our wider use of 'rubric' today; it derives from the Latin word for 'red', *ruber*.

Scribes made their quills by cutting a goose, swan, or crow feather with a pen-knife, which was also used to steady the parchment and to erase mistakes *(no. 43)*. The width of the nib determined the degree of contrast between pen strokes, thick or thin according to the direction in which they were traced, and also had a bearing upon the scale of the writing. Smaller handwriting generally required a narrower nib. With the parchment, quill and ink ready, the scribe could start work on the text.

Scripts

Medieval books display a bewildering array of scripts, but all derive ultimately from the handwriting of the late Roman world.[9] The earliest formal book scripts were majuscule scripts, in which few of the letter-forms contain strokes that project beneath the ruled line or above the headline. Although there was originally no correlation between script-types and categories of text, by the sixth century Uncial *(no. 1)* and Half-uncial, rather than Capitals, were the scripts in which the author-itative texts of Christianity were disseminated. These were formal majuscule scripts which had evolved from cursive handwriting during the later Roman period. Imported books in Uncial provided models for scribes in Anglo-Saxon England, but the most formal grade of script in the Insular tradition of handwriting was a distinctive variety of Half-uncial, characterized by wedge-shaped serifs at the top of the vertical strokes of letters such as 'i', 'm', 'n', 'u', 'h' and 'l' *(no. 2)*. These were impressive scripts, as befitted the status of the texts for which they were used. During the eighth century, however, a growing demand for books among religious communities prompted the adoption of more economical types of handwriting ('minuscule' scripts), derived from the smaller and more informal handwriting that had evolved variously in the different parts of Latin Europe from the administrative and everyday cursive handwriting of the late Roman period. In minuscule handwriting, the bodies of letters are smaller than those of majuscule script, and several of the letters are distinguished from each other by elements that project below the base-line and above the height of letters such as 'm' and 'n', as in our modern lower-case script. In the mid-eighth century, for example, scribes at the Northumbrian twin monasteries of Monkwearmouth-Jarrow refined the informal Insular minuscule to make it suitable as a book script, in response to the heavy demand for copies of the works of their house-author, Bede *(no. 3)*. Similar initiatives took place in a number of centres across Western Europe, resulting in a plethora of local and regional minuscules, which retained to a greater or lesser extent features of the cursive scripts from which they had evolved, such as variant forms of the same letter and elaborate ligatures which often distorted the shape of the linked letters.

In the 770s and 780s, scribes active at the northern Frankish monastery of Corbie and elsewhere (perhaps connected with the court of Charlemagne) sought to simplify their minuscule script in order to reduce the possibility for confusion and error, by reducing the number of variant forms and ligatures, and modifying certain letters. These reforms resulted in the emergence of a script known as Caroline minuscule, which became diffused throughout the Carolingian Empire during the first half of the ninth century *(nos. 5, 7, 8)*. It would ultimately become the basis for Roman type, and hence most of its forms are easily recognizable to us. Elsewhere, the local minuscules were only slowly supplanted. Until the later tenth century, Anglo-Saxon scribes, for example, continued to use varieties of Insular minuscule *(nos. 111 and 112)*, but by the early eleventh century Caroline minuscule had come to be regarded as the usual script for Latin texts in England *(nos. 11 and 12)*.

Caroline minuscule is characterized by the essential simplicity of its forms, each letter being comprised of the minimum basic elements required to distinguish it from similar letters (for example: 'i', 'n', 'm' and 'u'; 'b', 'd', 'p' and 'q'; 'c', 'e' and 'o'). From the later eleventh century, however, scribes began to explore ways in which to apply features of style to these forms: for example, replacing curved elements with broken strokes; increasing the contrast between thick and thin strokes, and emphasizing the headline and the baseline of the script with serifs added to the tops and bottoms of minim strokes *(no. 23)*. The proportions of the script changed: ascenders of letters such as 'b', 'h' and 'l' became shorter, and in northern Europe the essentially rounded forms of Caroline minuscule became more compressed and rectangular, reinforcing a tendency for the arches of letters such as 'm' and 'n' to be replaced with broken strokes *(no. 25)*. By the late twelfth century, these new stylistic features were being accompanied by other developments, such as the fusion of consecutive letters formed with facing curved elements, for example, 'o' or 'e' following 'b'. From the thirteenth century, these features of style came to dominate the script to such an extent that it can no longer be called Caroline minuscule. The term 'Gothic' has generally been applied to such handwriting, but a more precise term is *Textualis*.[10] When writing in the largest and most formal grade (*Textualis formata*), scribes refined every detail of the script: note, for example, in the Metz Pontifical *(no. 52)* the stylized treatment of the top and base of each vertical stroke, and the extreme contrast between thick and thin strokes, further emphasized by decorative hairline extensions curling from the final letter of most words.

From the fourteenth century, however, the elaborate *Textualis* began to give way to scripts which had their origin in the more rapid and informal varieties of Caroline minuscule that increasingly came to be used as business hands during the twelfth and early thirteenth century. Scribes who employed these cursive scripts in the course of their work as royal, ecclesiastical, and lay administrators, began also to be involved in copying literary texts, writing to a slightly larger scale, and with greater deliberation, lifting the pen more frequently when tracing the component elements of each letter. Some varieties of cursive bookhand achieved a considerable elegance, suitable even for luxury books. One of the most notable of these is the variety known as *Bastarda* (or *Bâtarde*), with its distinctive tapering strokes of letters such as 'f' and long 's', best known from the magnificent illuminated books associated with the Duchy of Burgundy and the Burgundian Netherlands *(see also no. 127)*.

The highly stylized, dense and heavily abbreviated writing characteristic of books of the thirteenth and fourteenth centuries, was not to everyone's taste. In the years on either side of 1400, scribes within the circle of Coluccio Salutati (d.1406), a Humanist and Chancellor of Florence, developed a consciously archaizing hand *(see also Introduction to Section 7)*. The most distinguished among them were Niccolò Niccoli (d.1437) and Poggio Bracciolini (d.1459). They took as their models the Caroline minuscule of late eleventh- and early twelfth-century copies of classical and patristic texts, which they perceived as *antiqua* and hence more appropriate for the authoritative texts of Antiquity.[11] In this new humanistic script letters are more clearly separated, there are fewer abbreviations, ascenders are taller, and there is a preference for more 'open' forms: for example, 'd' with a straight rather than a bent-over shaft, and long rather than round 's'. The generally 'whiter' appearance of the page thus created was further enhanced by the use of a narrower nib that produced less contrast between the thickness of the strokes, and by a reversion to ruling with a hard point *(fig. 11)*. Within a few decades the script had spread first to Venice, and then throughout Italy.[12] By the mid-fifteenth century, scribes associated with Humanist scholars in Northern Europe had begun to adopt the script. A humanistic cursive was also devised, a more flowing script in which, for example, 'f' and tall 's' curl elegantly below the ruled line, and which permitted the scribe to indulge in a greater degree of personal calligraphic expression *(no. 167)*.[13]

Fig. 11. Humanistic minuscule by Antonio Sinibaldi. Fitzwilliam Museum, MS McClean 160, fol. 139

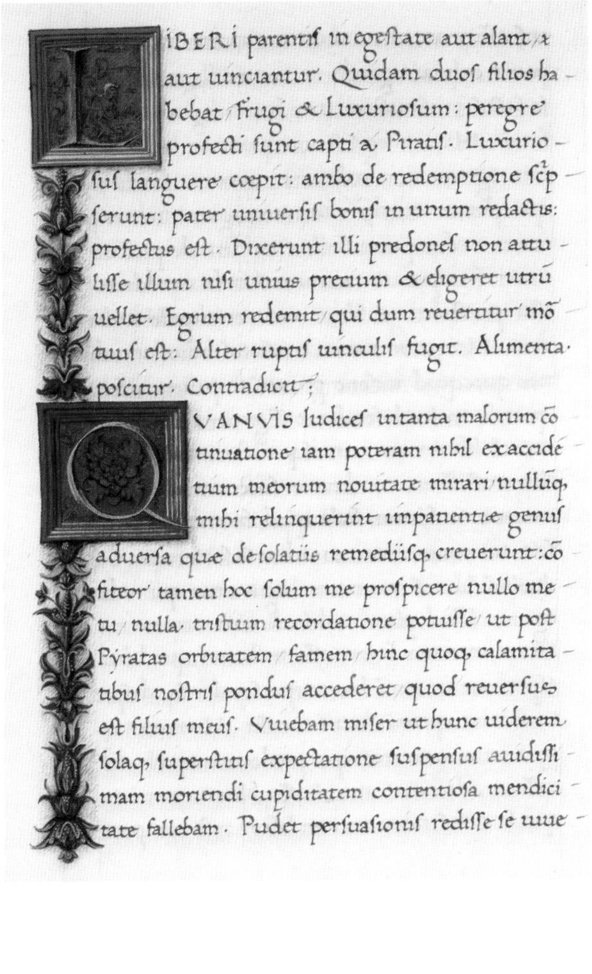

Design and decoration

Since most manuscripts were written before they were decorated, scribes often doubled as page designers.[14] Planning the hierarchy of decoration in line with the articulation of the text, they left room for the illumination, prompted artists by inserting faint letters in the spaces where initials

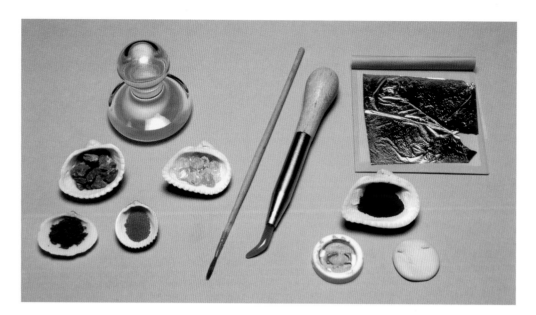

Fig. 12.
Illumination tools
and materials:
pestle, lapis lazuli,
malachite,
vermillion, gum
arabic, miniver
brush, agate
burnisher, liquid
gold, gesso pellet,
Armenian bole,
and gold leaf

were to be painted, and sometimes ruled right across the areas left blank for minia-tures. The lines proved useful for the definition of settings and for the transfer of designs, especially when they differed in scale from the model. The Metz Pontifical documents these practices. The artist almost always painted the initials suggested by the scribe and made good use of the lines ruled across the miniature spaces when transferring compositions that recur throughout the volume. He first sketched out the design with plummet and then firmed it up into an ink drawing *(fig. 6)*. The plummet is just barely visible and must have provided only a very basic suggestion of the subject-matter. Without following a detailed under-drawing, the inked compositions develop the miniatures to a remarkable level of detail, show-ing the confidence and fluidity of a truly accomplished artist.

The next stage was the application of gold. Beaten into sheets thinner than tissue, loose gold leaf crinkles at the faintest current of air, dissolves into dust when handled roughly, and clings to painted surfaces *(fig. 12)*. It was carefully laid over areas brushed with gum arabic, fish glue, or beaten and strained egg-white known as glair. Flat gold leaf was often left unburnished, as the staffs and details in the Metz Pontifical reveal *(fig. 7)*. For a raised effect, gold leaf was laid over gesso, a compound of plaster, white lead, sugar, and glue, which was often coloured with salmon-pink or orange-brown clay, known as Armenian bole, to enhance the glowing warmth of the gold. This 'cushion' made the thinnest gold leaf look solid and provided support for patterns incised with metal tools *(nos. 68, 80)*. Burnished with a 'dog's tooth', a smooth, hard stone, such as agate, the gold leaf glows and shimmers with the light, revealing the dazzling beauty and true essence of an illuminated manuscript.

Pigments

Once the gold leaf was burnished and any residue brushed away, the artist was ready to apply the colours. In the Metz Pontifical, the spaces to be painted were first coated with white transparent ground, leaving the facial features and details fully visible. The artist worked from lighter to darker tones, creating volume and texture *(fig. 7)*. Finally, he outlined all painted surfaces, and re-asserted the details of faces and drapery with a very fine brush or pen *(see no. 52)*. The tangible immediacy of materials and fabrics is created through the exquisite modelling and multi-layered application of colours of varying composition and saturation.

Individual pigments required different treatment, while the optical qualities of the same pigment could change significantly if prepared and tempered in different ways. Malachite had to be ground very gently and never reduced to powder or it lost its brilliance, while vermillion only improved if repeatedly placed on the slab. Grinding was essential and masters entrusted it to their most skilful assistants. No wonder the illuminator of the Dover Bible included his assistant in what is one of the earliest self-portraits in English painting *(fig. 3, and see no. 21)*. The assistant is shown grinding the pigment with a muller on a red porphyry slab, the hard stone recommended in Cennini's manual *Il libro dell'arte*, but not readily available outside Italy.[15]

The ground pigments were tempered with a variety of binding media which transformed them into paints and made them adhere to the parchment. The most delicate medium was the beaten and strained egg-white, or glair, which preserved the individual appearance of pigments. Gum arabic was a more powerful medium. It enhanced both the transparency and the saturation of certain colours, blue in particular, and became the dominant tempera from the fourteenth century onwards. Egg-yolk, the common medium for panels before the Northern invention of oil painting was introduced in Italy during the fifteenth century, was too heavy and greasy for manuscript illumination. While it could be mixed with glair to increase the lustre of rubrics, its use in miniatures, particularly in combination with gesso, may suggest that the illuminator was also a panel painter. Many artists represented in this exhibition excelled in both types of painting and practised in other media as well. Master Hugo, who illuminated the twelfth-century Bury Bible, was one of the earliest *(no. 19)* and Noël Bellemare, who painted the mannerist Parisian Book of Hours in the 1520s *(no. 106)*, one of the latest. Pacino di Bonaguida *(no. 58)* and Sano di Pietro *(no. 47)* were equally prolific in painting and illumination, while Guido Mazzoni, who also practised as a sculptor *(no. 105)*, and Benedetto Bordone, who designed woodcuts *(nos. 139 and 172)*, were among the most versatile. The ease with which artists moved between different media is reflected in the wide range of materials and techniques covered by manuals, such as Theophilus' *De diversis artibus* and Cennini's *Il libro dell' arte*. 'It is true that you may use on parchment any of the colours which you use on panel; but they must be ground very fine', advised Cennini.

Medieval manuals and recipe books provide plentiful, but ambiguous information on the preparation and use of pigments. Present-day technology introduces some clarity, as it makes sample-free analysis increasingly reliable. A recent analysis of the Metz Pontifical[16] confirmed that the green is malachite, as expected for a de luxe manuscript of that period, and not verdigris, the corrosive copper acetate commonly found in early medieval books. The pigments in the red-orange spectrum are red lead and vermillion. The latter was produced by heating mercury and sulphur, thus creating a synthetic alternative to cinnabar, the naturally occurring and highly poisonous mercuric sulphide. The red lead, or minium, is responsible for the term 'miniature' commonly used to define a picture in an illuminated manuscript. To our medieval and Renaissance predecessors, *miniare* meant to write or paint in minium. It was not until the sixteenth century that illuminators began to produce portrait miniatures in significant numbers and their small sizes gradually became associated with painting on parchment. Many of the paintings, or miniatures, in the manuscripts displayed in this exhibition are not only significantly larger than later portrait miniatures, but they are comparable in size to many contemporary panel paintings.

In addition to the naturally occurring minerals, such as malachite, cinnabar or orpiment, the poisonous arsenic sulphide used for yellow hues, and the man-made alternatives, red or white lead, vermillion, and verdigris, medieval artists had access to a wide range of organic pigments. From the thirteenth century onwards, they tended to replace highly corrosive pigments such as orpiment and verdigris. Saffron provided yellow, indigo – blue, the madder plant – rose, brazilwood – brownish red, and the turnsole plants a large spectrum of purple hues, from blue through violet to crimson. Certain pigments still vex modern scientists, conservators, and art historians. One of them is the Tyrian purple whose alleged source, kermes, gave rise to our 'crimson'. Used for imperial books in Late Antiquity, it was combined with silver and gold in the most opulent manuscripts of the Carolingian and Ottonian periods (no. 7) and revived in the all'antica manuscripts of the Italian Humanists (no. 166).[17] While the pigment was almost certainly extracted from insects, it remains unclear whether kermes, grain, murex (or shellfish), and cochineal beetles were alternative sources for the same pigment in different parts of the medieval world. Even more bewildering is the pigment probably obtained from the sap of the East Asian rattan palm tree, but called by Pliny 'dragon's blood' and described in medieval sources as flowing from the mutual slaughter of elephants and dragons. Recipe books are replete with mysterious materials and procedures drawing on legend as much as on Aristotelian theory and alchemical practice.[18]

The king of all colours was ultramarine. As its name suggests, the source, lapis lazuli, and the recipe came from beyond the sea, all the way from ancient Persia or modern-day Afghanistan. Inevitably, cheaper substitutes were found, notably azurite. The analysis of the Metz Pontifical revealed the use of ultramarine and azurite both independently and in a multi-layered combination, although the naked eye cannot distinguish between the two. The ability to economize on materials without compromising the quality is the ultimate proof of the artist's exceptional skill.

Only one other pigment matched the prestige and cost of ultramarine. This was liquid gold, also known as shell gold or gold ink, because it was used for writing (no. 7). The mixture of powdered gold and gum arabic, glue, or glair was more expensive than gold leaf, with which it could be combined to create subtle contrasts of light and texture. Liquid gold dominated the borders of late medieval manuscripts and introduced resplendent highlights to draperies and ornamental details (nos. 88, 103, 106).

Imagery: form and meaning

The choice of pigments and techniques can only be fully appreciated when considered in the light of the image's subject-matter, and the book's content, patronage and intended use. Delicate hues imbue the Alexis Master's miniature of the bride and groom with lyrical mysticism, most appropriate in a monastic commentary on the Song of Songs (no. 24). A similarly restrained, understated colour scheme characterizes some of the most elegant thirteenth-century English aristocratic and royal books (no. 113). By contrast, a manuscript, which may have been produced for members of the gentry, rather than the high nobility, displays a lavish use of gold and heavy pigments as well as the patrons' overwhelming desire for self-representation *(no. 81)*. The choice of grisaille, a refined and yet subdued idiom, corresponds to the intro-spective mood of a most peculiar image: a roundel with scenes from Christ's Passion and the lives of Saints Mary of Egypt, Paul the Hermit, Alexis, and Jerome *(fig. 13)*. Its earlier association with Francesco Marmitta, though rejected more recently, deserves to be reconsidered in the light of other fragments from devotional and liturgical manuscripts illuminated by Marmitta in the 1490s.[19] While its original context is hard to determine, its content and format suggest a highly personalized use, perhaps by a friar-hermit, in a cycle of contemplative exercises. The initial with St John the Baptist pasted in the centre may have introduced his feast in a Choir Book or his suffrage in a Book of Hours, but the roundel itself need not have come from the same or from any other manuscript. Passion scenes painted in grisaille and conceived in a circular format appear, for instance, on the reverse of Hieronymus Bosch's panel of St John on Patmos (Berlin, Gemäldegalerie). The Fitzwilliam roundel may have functioned as an independent devotional image. Grisaille was highly appropriate for images intended to support intense prayer and meditation, but it was also fashionable in literary manuscripts produced for aristocratic bibliophiles.

While the aesthetic qualities of an image are inseparable from its meaning, certain

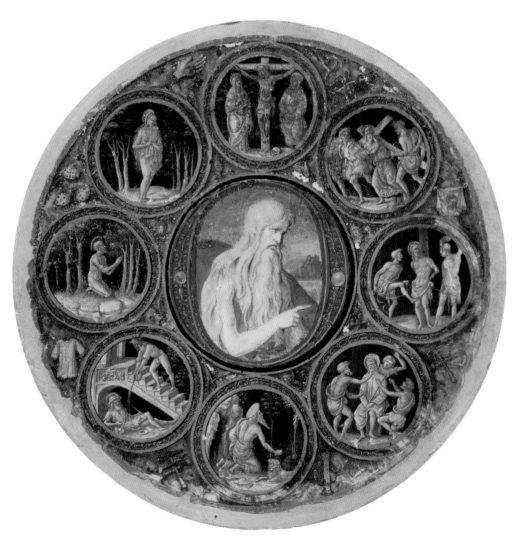

Fig. 13. St John the Baptist, Hermits and Passion Scenes. Fitzwilliam Museum, MS 269–1949

manuscripts extend the semantic role of their illuminations well beyond the usual boundaries and transform them into messengers more powerful and immediate than the text itself. The figural poems of Hrabanus Maurus are one example *(no. 6)*, the marginal images in the twelfth-century copy of Peter Lombard's *Magna Glossatura* made at Thomas Becket's request is another *(no. 26)*. The latter was a major editorial project carried out by Becket's secretary Herbert of Bosham. Herbert inserted profuse notes into the margins for the scribes and artists, instructing them to correct errors, and add cross-references. He used marginal figures to indicate his editorial contributions and to illustrate the specific themes of the Psalms.[20]

Herbert of Bosham's volumes exemplify one of the most engaging and rewarding aspects of manuscript studies. Unlike other works of art, whose context usually needs to be reconstructed outside their physical entity, manuscripts often carry their own context and offer rich internal evidence about their makers and users. In addition to their importance as sources on all aspects of contemporary life, they are the richest and best-preserved monuments of medieval art.

REFERENCES

1   See also Introduction to Section 7 and nos. 172–174.
2   Thompson 1956, Alexander 1992, Scheller 1995.
3   Clarke 2001, 63–66.
4   Cambridge University Library, MS Ee.4.24, fols. 4–5v; see Peterson 1994.
5   Federici, di Majo and Palma 1996. For an excellent summary on parchment making and other aspects of manuscript production see de Hamel 1992b.
6   It reached Northern Europe in bewildering combinations, such as the Italian-Northern hybrid with pseudo-Greek end-bands currently studied by Nicholas Pickwoad (Fitzwilliam Museum, MS 42–1950).
7   Mirjam Foot examined this binding recently and associated it with mid-sixteenth-century Germany.
8   For a practical approach to scribal materials and techniques, with a sound historical background, see Lovett 2000.
9   Bischoff 1990, 83–149.
10 Derolez 2003.
11 de la Mare 1977.
12 Ullmann 1960, de la Mare 1973.
13 Wardrop 1963.
14 For the design, materials and techniques of illumination, see Martin and Vezin 1990, Alexander 1992, de Hamel 2001b, and Watson 2003.
15 Thompson 1960, 21.
16 Dr Spike Bucklow from the Hamilton Kerr Institute and Dr Trevor Emmett from the Forensic Science Department at Anglia Polytechnic University carried out a preliminary examination of the Mezt Pontifical using a Video Spectral Comparator. The results will be presented at a Conference at the end of this exhibition (8–10 December 2005).
17 Longo 1998.
18 Bucklow 2000, Clarke 2001.
19 Wormald and Giles 1982, 411–12; Hindman et al. 1997, 189; Bacchi et al. 1995, 344.
20 Panayotova 2005a, Panayotova 2006.

CATALOGUE

CONTRIBUTORS

Jonathan Alexander

Paul Binski [PB] Richard Beadle [RB]

Christopher de Hamel [C DE H] Peter Jones [PJ] James Marrow [JHM]

Jean-Michel Massing [JMM] Nigel Morgan [NJM]

David McKitterick [DMCK] Rosamond McKitterick [RMCK]

Stella Panayotova [SP] Jayne Ringrose [JR]

Nicholas Rogers [NR] Teresa Webber [TW]

Patrick Zutshi [PNRZ]

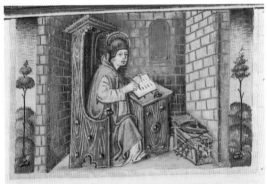

Detail of fol. 1, Cambridge University Library MS Gg.3.22

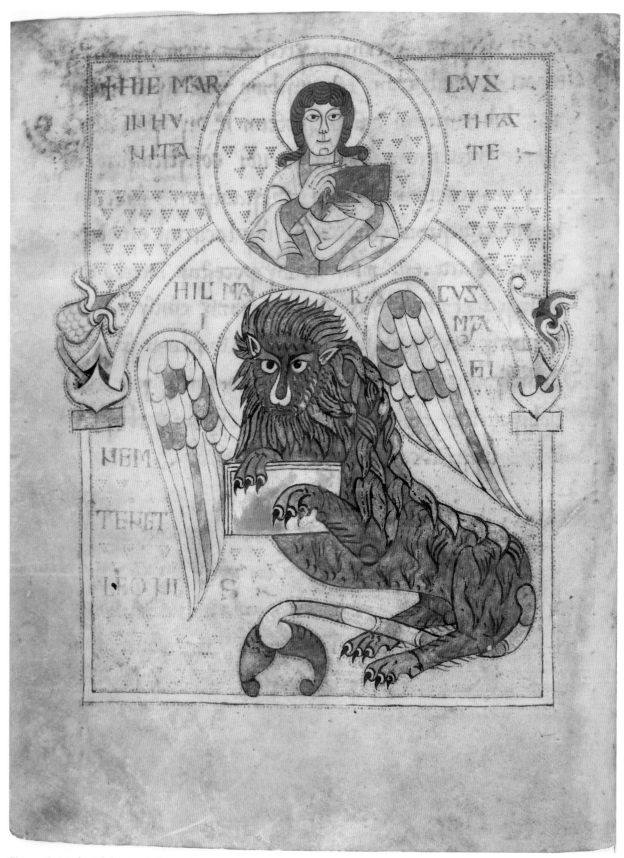

Fig. 14. St Mark with his Symbol. Cambridge University Library, MS Ll.1.10, fol. 12v

1

THE COMING OF CHRISTIANITY: PAGANS AND MISSIONARIES

Rosamond McKitterick

I N HIS *Ecclesiastical History of the English People*, the eighth-century Anglo-Saxon author Bede tells us that Pope Gregory I sent 'a servant of God named Augustine and other monks' from Rome 'to preach the word of God to the English people'. Augustine landed at Thanet in 597 and met Ethelbert, the King of Kent, who gave him permission to stay in Canterbury and teach the people about Christianity. From these small beginnings grew the English Church (Mayr-Harting 1991). The north-east of England, initially converted by the Roman missionary Paulinus was subsequently inspired by Aidan and other Irish missionaries in the middle of the seventh century. Ireland had been Christian since its conversion by Palladius and Patrick in the fifth century and the Irish missionaries brought to Northumbria far older Christian practices which had been conserved in Ireland. In due course the northern and the southern Christian communities made common cause but Ireland remained a source of great religious learning and inspiration for centuries to come. The Irish also played an important role in the expansion and consolidation of Christianity on the Continent.

The growth of the English Church charted by Bede over a hundred years after Augustine's arrival in Kent draws on the early records from Canterbury and Rome as well as on what contemporaries were able to tell him. One of Bede's purposes in writing his history was to insist on the close links between the new English Church and the Church of Rome, extolled by Bede as the See of St Peter, the rock on whom Christ had built his Church. Such links were not only expressed in the form of respect for the Pope and for orthodox Christian faith, but also in observance of what were understood to be the institutional structures and Christian devotional practices current in Rome. The latter included the liturgy, the law of the Church known as Canon Law, the forms of worship, and even the dates of the liturgical year. Indeed, one of the most dramatic disputes recorded by Bede is that between the clergy who wished to retain the Irish method of calculating the date of Easter and those advocating the newer and more accurate method according to the rules set out by Dionysius Exiguus in the sixth century and favoured in Rome. At the Synod of Whitby in 664, the Roman party, whose spokesman was Bishop Wilfrid of Hexham, won.

Because southern Britain had once been part of the Roman Empire, Christianity had also reached the Britons long before the English arrived. St Patrick had reached Ireland from western Britain in the fifth century and Bede himself records some instances of the Christian observance of the Roman-British people, not least the martyrdom of St Alban. Even when the English began to settle in greater numbers in Britain in the course of the fifth and sixth centuries, there remained Christian communities in Wales, in north-western Britain, Cornwall and Devon which subsequently had some contact with the English converts and the Roman missionaries and their successors who became bishops in the newly created dioceses of England. Influences from Gaul also were, and remained, of considerable importance in the development of both the Irish and the English Churches.

The success of Christianity in England was gradual. Just as the triumph of Christianity within the Roman Empire owed much to the conversion of the Roman Emperor Constantine in the early fourth century, so the adoption of Christianity in the various regions of England and the other barbarian states, successors of the western Roman Empire in Spain, Gaul and Italy, was initiated and supported by their rulers (Wallace-Hadrill 1983). Christianity played a significant role in enhancing the image of rulership. Bishops and the clergy in general were involved at many levels in the political life of their kingdoms. The organization of the Church in most parts of medieval Europe was itself an extension of the Roman administrative structures, with dioceses headed by bishops grouped into ecclesiastic provinces. Thus England, for example, was organized with the Province of Canterbury at first; subsequently a second Province, with the Archbishop of York at its centre, was created in 735. Apart from a short-lived elevation of Lichfield to the status of archbishopric by King Offa of Mercia in the eighth century, this is the structure of the English, and after the Reformation, Anglican Church that has been maintained to this day. The Christian Church throughout its history has depended on the lay population for its material support as well as for a continuous supply of new blood to become priests and deacons as well as bishops.

Monasticism added an extra dimension to the Christian life. Originally a movement starting in upper Egypt in the fourth century, the wish to fulfil an ascetic life, whether in solitude or as a member of a monastic community became a remarkable source of religious inspiration and expression all over Europe (Chadwick 2001). Many monasteries were founded in order to put the ideals into practice and the communities devoted themselves to a life of prayer, religious contemplation and devotion. Many of these were family affairs but gradually particular interpretations of the monastic life, of which the most influential in the early centuries was the sixth-century Rule of St Benedict of Nursia, were adopted by a number of houses. Monastic practice was extraordinarily diverse in the early Middle Ages. It was not until the tenth century that any semblance of uniformity, based upon the Rule of St Benedict, was achieved. In England this was the outcome of the reform movement of the later tenth century presided over by the reforming Bishops Ethelwold, Dunstan and Oswald, and zealously supported by King Edgar and his wife (Parsons 1975; Yorke 1988). Major monasteries had been established at Lindisfarne, Canterbury, Wearmouth-Jarrow, Malmesbury, Whitby, Wimborne and Winchester in the early years of the English Church. Furthermore, the monastic character of the cathedral clergy remained a very distinctive element of English ecclesiastical life for many centuries.

From the area once covered by the Roman Empire, Christianity expanded as a consequence of the activities of both missionaries and conquering armies into territories far beyond the former Roman frontiers (Wood 2001). Early conversions, such as those of the Copts, Syrians, Armenians and Goths, had often been an independent Christianization of whole communities. Others, like Augustine's mission to Canterbury or Boniface of Mainz's reconnaissance of Germany, had papal backing. Travelling monks, notably those from the British Isles, did much to inspire newly converted Christians to consolidate the faith with zeal. There was also considerable missionary activity in the German, Scandinavian and Slav regions of Europe between the eighth and the eleventh centuries. Many of these missionary enterprises were part of political expansion, especially on the Continent. With papal and royal backing new bishoprics were established in Denmark, Saxony, Poland, Bohemia, and Hungary in the tenth and early eleventh centuries. Prince Vladimir of Kiev adopted Byzantine Christianity and there was a mass baptism of the citizens of Kiev in the River Dnieper in 988. Iceland had accepted Christianity by *c.*1000, but it was not until 1387 that Lithuania formally began the process of abandoning paganism. Conversion in the Middle Ages can to a considerable degree be regarded as a form of cultural imperialism. It was not just the Christian religion that was introduced into these areas, but the entire cultural, moral and educational framework that it supported. In many instances, such as the production of texts in Gothic, Old High German, Old Church Slavonic or Old English, this involved the introduction of written forms of the vernacular and even the creation of new alphabets such as Gothic and Glagolitic.

From the beginning of its history, Christianity has been associated with books. Like Judaism and Islam it is a 'religion of the book'. Not only are there the four Gospel narratives by Matthew, Mark, Luke and John, but also the Acts of the Apostles, the Epistles of St Paul and other apostolic letters, and the Revelation or Apocalypse of St John the Divine. These were all written within the first one hundred and fifty years after the Crucifixion of Jesus Christ and disseminated rapidly throughout the expanding Christian communities of the Mediterranean region, the Middle East and Europe. The Old Testament was also regarded as essential for Christians, containing the account of God's creation of the world and of Man, the Fall, the history of the Jewish people and many prophesies interpreted by Christians as foretelling Christ's coming. Latin translations of many of the originally Greek, Hebrew and Aramaic texts were made as early as the second century AD, but the most successful Latin translation of the Bible and the form in which it was best known during the western Middle Ages was the so-called Vulgate Latin translation and compilation made by St Jerome (d.420). Many other kinds of texts were produced by scholars and holy men, including reflections on the faith, detailed theological discussions, guides to the Christian life, and biographies and histories of the Christian men and women who contributed to the growth of the Church.

Yet Christians in the early years had also been educated according to the pagan classical tradition known as *paideia*. Many elements of this were maintained in the Christian schools of the early Middle Ages in Britain and Ireland as well as on the Continent. Education and learning had formerly been concentrated in the secular school of the Roman cities but became increasingly the prerogative of the monastic and cathedral centres of the barbarian successor kingdoms. This monopoly of education was maintained until the establishment of the first universities in the late twelfth and early thirteenth centuries. There was an accompanying shift in emphasis in Late Antiquity from secular and classical to Christian learning with a curriculum that comprised the *trivium* (grammar, rhetoric and dialectic) and the *quadrivium* (arithmetic, geometry, music and astronomy), that is, the so-called seven liberal arts first defined by the Roman writer Martianus Capella in the fifth century. Throughout the Middle Ages these *artes* remained the basis of the curriculum whose goal was Christian knowledge and understanding. Classical texts were preserved in copies made in the scriptoria and writing centres of Europe, and many new works were added to the corpus of human learning over the centuries. Among the enormous variety of books and texts, many represented in this exhibition, were classical philosophy, rhetoric, poetry, grammar, history and science, Christian liturgical books, tracts on spiritual discipline, the works of the Early Christian Fathers and commentaries on books of the Bible. There were new works by medieval writers in all fields, theology, grammar, poetry, encyclopedias, geography, astronomy, philosophy, mathematics, law, saints' lives, practical manuals, biblical exegesis, history, and music. A core canon of knowledge was created with many additional and original contributions. Library catalogues surviving from as early as the ninth century give us a very clear understanding of what was to be found in these libraries. So too, of course, do the books themselves.

For the most part, conversion to Christianity in Western Europe also brought with it the Latin of the early Church, for the liturgy, law and scholarship of the Christian Church were all in Latin. In England, Latin became a major second language although the English Christians in due course began also to produce translations and new texts in their native Anglo-Saxon, just as in Ireland texts were translated into Irish, and somewhat later in Wales and Scotland into Welsh and Gaelic. Similarly, on the Continent Latin was the language of religion, government and education but gradually vernaculars, such as Germanic and Slavic or the Romance languages emerging from Latin, began to be written down. Inevitably the languages in use could enrich each other, but Latin's use in religion, education and scholarship also provided a means of communicating with Christians across Europe and beyond.

This first section of the exhibition includes a selection of Christian books from early medieval Britain and the Continent. Whether serving individuals or communities, they all reinforce the importance of Latin, of the Christian religion, and of an enduring educational tradition. In many instances these books provide the only evidence we have for the existence of a Christian community at all; in others they contribute to a rich understanding of major cultural centres. The oldest book in the exhibition *(no. 1)* is associated with St Augustine of Canterbury himself. Appropriately, it is a Gospel Book containing the texts most vital for the teaching of the Christian religion and for the daily liturgy. It was brought from Italy, but the English soon learnt how to produce books themselves. Scribes learnt how to write and developed distinctive forms of script known as Insular half-uncial and minuscule, as well as an English variety of uncial, the Roman formal book hand. Artists introduced decorative motifs and patterns from their native metalwork and sculpture, adopted and adapted designs and motifs they found in the books brought by the missionaries, notably the canon tables and Evangelist portraits in Gospel Books such as can be seen in the St Augustine Gospels.

The books themselves, therefore, are witness to a remarkable process of cultural migration and adaptation in a new context, with older Christian texts interpreted in visually new forms. Corpus Christi College MS 197B *(no. 2)* and the Book of Cerne *(no. 4)* are striking examples of a distinctly Insular presentation of the text and illumination. Yet the latter also contains newly composed texts, the product of the new Christians' efforts to instruct readers or their audience in devotion and learning. Further manifestations of the English contributions to religious instruction are to be seen in the two books of homilies by Ælfric and his contemporaries *(nos. 13, 14)*. These sermons show how much Christian learning their authors had imbibed and how familiar they were with the text of the Bible itself. The reception of Christian texts and the adaptation to new circumstances is also evident in books from the Continent, such as the St Gallen Epistolary *(no. 7)* and the McClean Gospels *(fig. 15, no. 8)*. Like the earlier English examples, these present the essential New Testament texts in a new medium of contemporary script and decoration, renewing the Christian message for another generation. Similarly, the Southampton Psalter *(no. 16)* demonstrates not only Irish decoration and script but also a special organization of the Psalm texts, prayers and Canticles for its audience and readers.

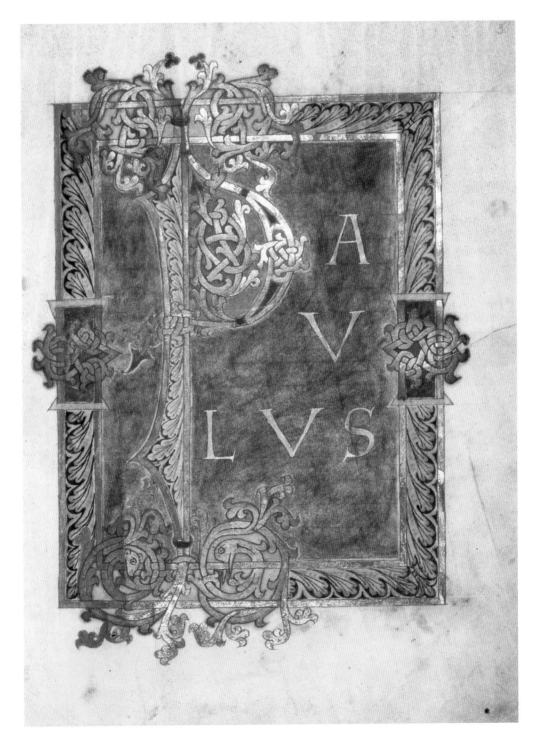

Fig. 15. Opening of St Paul's Epistles. Fitzwilliam Museum, MS McClean 30, fol. 3

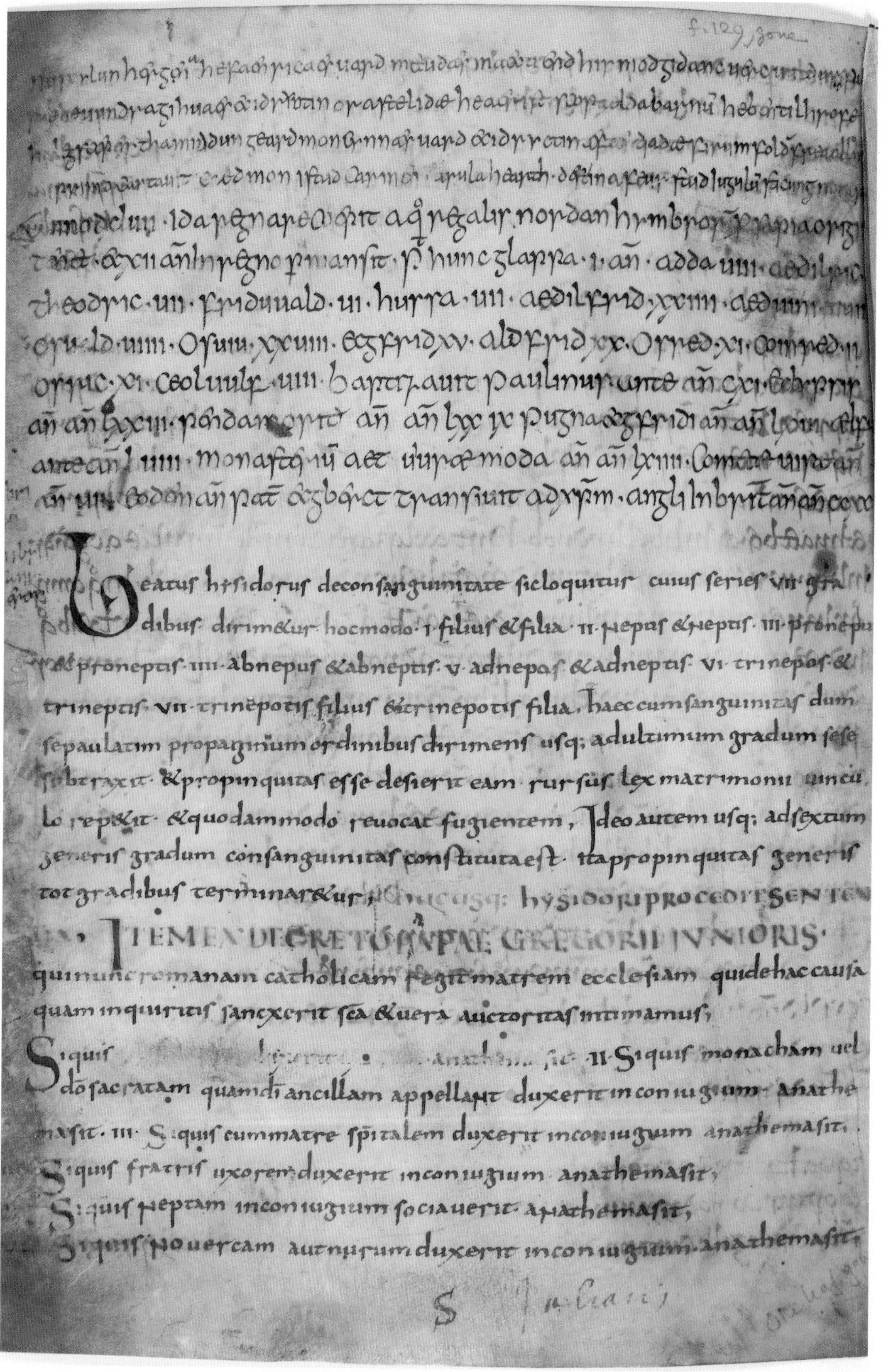

Fig. 16. Late eighth-century Continental additions to the Moore Bede. Cambridge University Library, MS Kk.5.16, fol. 128v

Yet Britain and the newly converted areas were also receptive to the importance of texts, both new ones written by missionaries to promote Christianity and older, patristic ones preserved and introduced into fresh pastures. They were probably discovered by people travelling abroad on pilgrimage or business. Some of the books in this exhibition have been in England for as far back as their provenance can be traced, and with a strong likelihood that they were acquired by people in England very soon after they were first produced. Others have only ended up in Cambridge as a result of the massive upheavals in institutional book ownership brought about by the Reformation, the French Wars of Religion, the Thirty Years War, the French Revolution, the Napoleonic Wars, and of course the two World Wars *(see Collectors and Collecting in Cambridge, pp.17–21 above)*. One extraordinary instance of a book travelling across time and place is the Moore Bede *(fig. 16, no. 3)*. First produced in Bede's own monastery of Jarrow about the time of his death, it appears to have been taken or sent to the Frankish kingdom within fifty years of its creation and was at the court of the Frankish ruler Charlemagne by the end of the eighth century. This manuscript became the parent of many more copies and played a very large role in the dissemination of Bede's account of the conversion of the English and the establishment of the Christian Church throughout the regions we now call France, Germany and Switzerland. Yet its history cannot be traced for most of the Middle Ages and it is not until its more recent history in the diocese of Le Mans and its purchase by Bishop John Moore that we pick up its tracks once more.

Other English texts undoubtedly were imported to Continental centres, especially the missionary centres of Germany founded by English missionaries, both men and women, in the course of the eighth century (Levison 1946). Equally, however, there are instances of books from the Continent being imported into England: ninth-century contacts of members of King Alfred's court with West Francia, tenth-century diplomatic links with Germany, and the tenth-century monastic reform provide the context in which copies of Arator's poetic version of the Acts of the Apostles *(no. 12)* and Prudentius's moral-didactic poem on the Virtues and Vices *(no. 11)* were introduced into England. These texts as well as the works of the great ninth-century abbot of Fulda in Germany, Hraban Maur, such as the *Liber de laudibus sanctae crucis* and the commentaries on St Paul's letters *(nos. 5, 6)*, are witness to the intellectual contacts and exchange between religious centres in Britain and on the Continent. Missionaries and travelling scholars, envoys, pilgrims, diplomats and messengers have all played a role in physically bringing together different aspects of Christian history and culture. Yet the manuscripts demonstrate not just the reproduction of the texts received but also an endlessly and richly creative process of adaptation and reinterpretation of these texts and their illumination in new contexts.

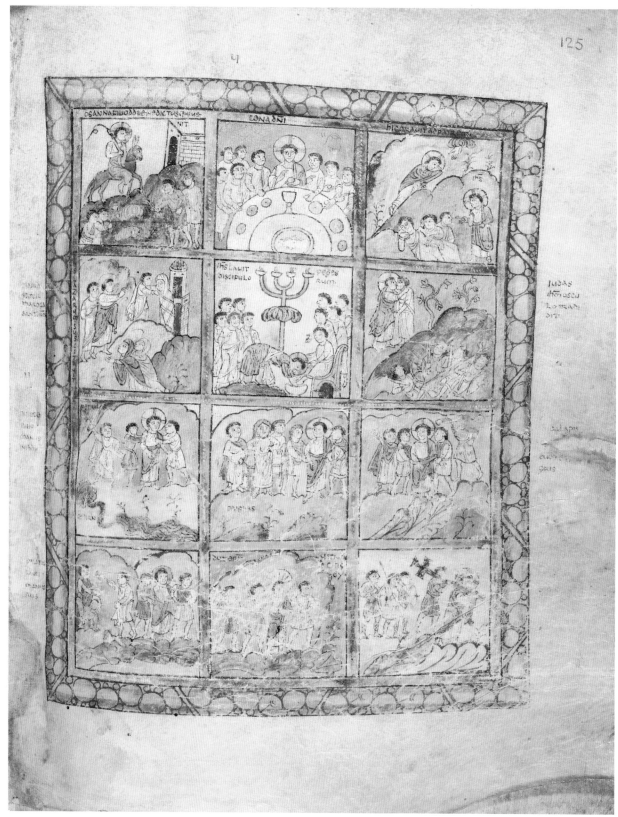

Passion narrative in pictures. Corpus Christi College, MS 286, fol. 125

1

The Gospels of St Augustine of Canterbury

In Latin
Italy or Gaul, sixth century

Parchment, iii + 1★ + 265 + v fols., 251 × 196 mm,
text 184 × 135 mm, 2 columns, 25 lines, ruled in hard point

SCRIPT: Uncial and Insular minuscule

BINDING: quarter-binding in goatskin and oak boards, 1949,
with one eighteenth-century endpaper from the 1748 binding

Corpus Christi College, MS 286

USED FOR THE ENTHRONEMENT of Archbishops of Canterbury since 1945, this manuscript was probably brought to England by St Augustine of Canterbury in 597, when he came to Kent to convert the English to Christianity, or by Archbishop Theodore of Canterbury (668–690) when he was appointed to the See. A long established tradition maintains that it was the former. It was certainly in England by the late seventh century. The Italian or Frankish uncial of the main text received running headings in Insular minuscule and captions in English uncial were added to the images.

The Vulgate text of the Gospels of Matthew, Mark, Luke and John was a revised version of the Old Latin Gospels made by Jerome (341–420) as part of his massive project initiated by Pope Damasus to provide a completely revised Latin version of the Old and New Testaments. In the case of the Old Testament books, Jerome went beyond the Greek and Old Latin translations available to the original Hebrew and made entirely new translations. Jerome wrote dedications and explanatory letters to Pope Damasus about his translation, as well as chapter lists and prefaces for each Gospel. Most early medieval Gospel Books also include the Eusebian canon tables, a series of synoptic tables compiled in order to show which sections of the Gospel story could be found in any of the four Gospels. Much of the prefatory material may have been lost along with other illustrated pages from this codex for only the *capitula* and prefaces, the Luke frontispiece and a repositioned endleaf with illustrations of the Passion narrative (fol. 125) survive in this book. Rough sketches were added between the ninth and eleventh centuries.

The text, written in a beautiful, regular and well-proportioned uncial, is laid out *per cola et commata*. This was a scheme for line-by-line layout according to phrases and sense units, rather than a division of sentences with punctuation marks favoured by Jerome himself. This

Vulgate version of the Gospels is close to the so-called *Codex Oxoniensis* (Oxford, Bodleian Library, MS Auct. D.2.14), a seventh-century manuscript, and is the Italian type. There are clear indications throughout the Corpus text of someone collating it against another copy of the Gospels and attempting to correct it. This witnesses to the interest in establishing the text of Scripture in early medieval England.

The presentation of the Passion narrative in comic-strip style with little frames is very unusual, especially for this early period. It illustrates twelve scenes from the final period of Christ's life and passion drawn from all four Gospel accounts. These are as follows: the Entry into Jerusalem on Palm Sunday; the Last Supper with the blessing of the bread (though only eight disciples are depicted); Christ's Agony in the Garden of Gethsemane and his reproach to the disciples; the Raising of Lazarus; Christ washing the feet of the Disciples (this is only recorded by St John); the Betrayal of Christ, with Judas kissing Christ and the crowd of Jewish guards; the Trial of Christ and the High Priest rending his garments; Christ before Pontius Pilate; Pilate washing his hands and Christ led away to be crucified; the Mocking of Christ; Christ carrying the Cross assisted by Simon of Cyrene. All these pictures are set in landscapes with delicate washes of colour. The book also contains a full-page author portrait of the Evangelist Luke seated on a throne under an arch and accompanied by his symbol, the calf. Both hold the Gospel Book. Little pictures in frames inserted between the columns to either side of Luke illustrate episodes from the Gospel of Luke. Markedly didactic in its scheme of illustration, the manuscript was clearly one of the highest quality. It might even have been intended as a gift to King Ethelbert of Kent.

PROVENANCE: St Augustine's Abbey, Canterbury; Matthew Parker (1504–1575); his bequest, 1575.

EXHIBITED: Cambridge 1975, no. 1; London 1991, no. 1; London 1997, no. 92.

LITERATURE: James 1912b, II, 52–56; Wormald 1954; McGurk 1961, 25–26; Henderson 1982; Henderson 1993–1994; Budny 1997, 1–50; Kauffmann 2003, 51, 77, 225.

RMCK

2

Gospels of St Luke and St John

In Latin
England, Northumbria, early eighth century

Parchment, ii + 36 + ii fols., 288 × 215 mm, text 235 × 175mm, 19 long lines, ruled in hard point

SCRIPT: Insular half-uncial

BINDING: pigskin over oak boards, by Nicholas Pickwood, 1987

Corpus Christi College, MS 197B

THIS MANUSCRIPT, a fragmentary version of the Gospels in the Latin Vulgate with Insular variants, is part of a larger codex, once comprising approximately 110 folios and now divided between Cambridge and London. The Corpus portion contains parts of the Gospels of John and Luke. Sixty-four charred fragments from the Gospels of Matthew and Mark survived the fire of 1731 (London, British Library, Cotton MS Otho C.v). London, British Library, Royal MS 7 C.xii, fols. 2–3 possibly preserves a fragment of the canon tables, which may have belonged to this book. The Corpus part of the volume has been associated with a group of

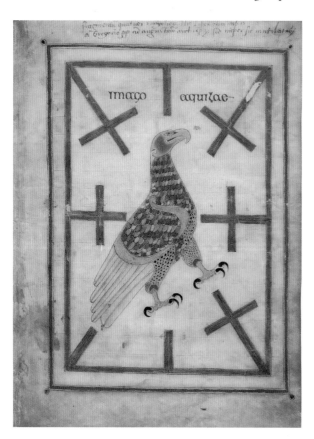

resplendent Gospel Books decorated in a very flamboyant and distinctive Insular style produced in Northumbria in the late seventh and eight centuries. The group includes the Lindisfarne Gospels (London, British Library, Cotton MS Nero D.iv) and the Durham Gospels (Durham Cathedral Library, MS A. II. 17) as well as the Book of Kells (Trinity College Dublin MS A. I. 6[58]).

Of the many illustrations which once adorned the whole Gospel Book, only the Evangelist symbol, the fine eagle on fol. 1, and the *incipit* page of St John's Gospel survive. The first four words of St John's Gospel (*In principio erat verbum*, 'In the beginning was the Word') are set out on fol. 2 with a very stylized *In* and the shaft of the *p* ornamented with two bows so that it looks like a *b*. These are filled in with elaborate interlaced foliage and geometric patterns, with spiral ornament on the finials and interlace birds in the bowls. The fancy capitals are written in stylized geometric shapes and form a pattern characteristic of these early Insular Gospel Books.

Despite the probable Northumbrian origin, the later additions suggest a scribe trained in southern England. Unlike the St Augustine Gospels *(no. 1)* with its *per cola et commata* layout, the text in this book was set out by its two scribes in long lines. Thus the initials divide up the text and there is some word division and a minimal use of punctuation with medial points and a triangular pattern of dots for main pauses. The ends of sections have sequences of dots and flourishes, often in red. Like many Gospel Books, the Eusebian Canon cross references, indicating which of the other Gospel accounts refer to the same incident, have been inserted in the margin. The script is very fine and regular, with firm wedged-shaped serifs on the letters. At the beginning of each section is a lovely initial with decorated finials, outlined in red dots, with *diminuendo* for the first few letters of the word.

PROVENANCE: probably at St Augustine's Abbey, Canterbury, by 8th or 9th c.; Matthew Parker (1504–1575); his bequest, 1575.

EXHIBITED: Cambridge 1975, no. 2; London 1991, no. 83b; London 2003, 47.

LITERATURE: James 1912b, I, 472–75; McGurk 1961, 24; Henderson 1987, 57–97; Pickwood 1994; Budny 1997, 55–73; Kendrick 1999, 164–66.

RMCK

LEFT AND OPPOSITE: Opening of St John's Gospel. Corpus Christi College, MS 197B, fols. 1 & 2

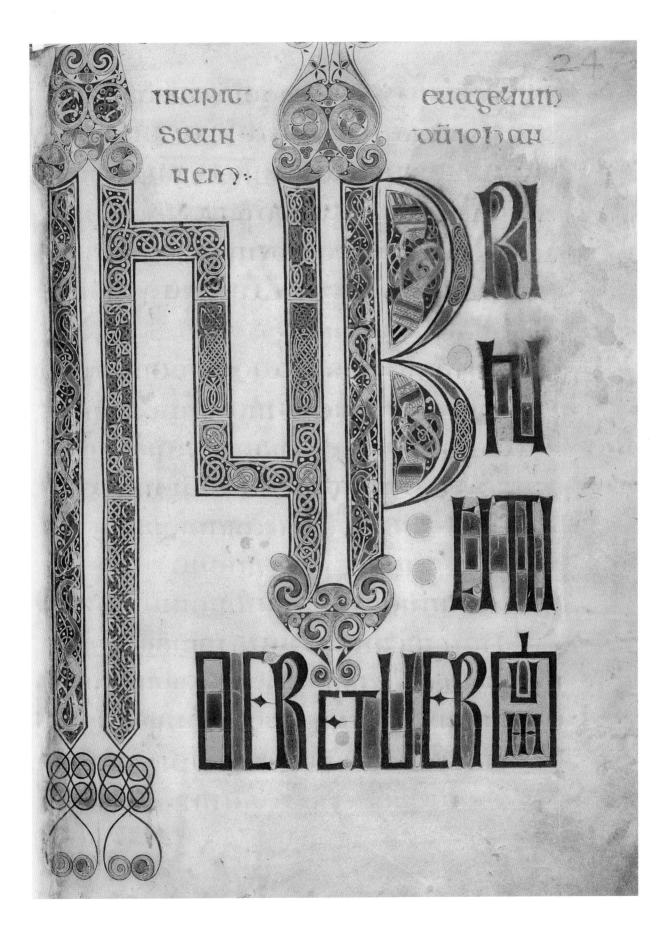

peortdon peada primo tdige multum noxapiep onturp portione
utdixtt iutir ruae In protonpore epop parchalip. Complecup In
trib. an p Intpactonon pondan regir rebellaruntaducepup re
zonorum ducep zodtoir mep cior Immin. & eapa & eadbep & leuato
Impzon uulph epe pilio dompondan adulep contequon occultum
prin augrant & lecup primcipib regirn prprirp nep puor portit
pimul & libertatem pecepup unt picq cumpuo rege liber xpo ucpop p
prompcip no In caelir pegno prp un re gaudebant. p punup p ciden
zota mep cior annip x & uii. habucq primum chrp trum hep de
quopupra diximup p dun lapuman. tch ceaddan. quap urmp p
omnep hip por dinen pibim & pucceden cep pub pegeuulph epe
zchtir mep cior chrir copatup t pimcu p chir copa ap ceqr or di
In ea aidano chir dehacurta publato pinan p illo gradum
natura cmip pup acceppepat qui In Inpula bin dip p par uch p
per cordam chir copali pedi d zruag. tn more pcotop n dela
pidep ep depob orepcto totam p por uncatq hap un di netcht
p ton por epequen ce peuep ertup pimur archi chir theodopip
In honope beati apoptp chir dedi caurt p ed & chir loci ip pur
eadbep ct ablata hap un de me plumbi lam minir eam tota hoc p
& cdecum &lp por qq parierp p coop chir re curaurt. hip tmpo
rib. q: p pcio pacta: prequen chir & magna deo byp uatione parche
d pirmancib. Sirq un de currt at de zalli p aducheparntq prtt
domm cum p arch e di on p trauiniu chr pa lir & cclie morem cele
braprent. Sira t In hir acceprimur uch p par chaed chir pr nomin
ponan. nacione quid dom p urttar ped In zalli ae t italiae partib.
pegulam & cclep cap uch rtarir edocurp. qui cum pinano pplichrir
multor quid dom co prprpcrt t adpolep tio pr uch rtatur Inquirtion
acchortt nequag. tn pinanum chir cida pepotuit. qui Impotiup p
& t homo peh ocir animm accer uno pecaptizando crantum uih p
rita tip aduchpurpurum pedidit. obprp uabatchr Iacob diac p
quondam ut pupra docuimur uchrchrabili par chren
paulin

3

Bede, *Historia ecclesiastica gentis anglorum*

In Latin
England, Northumbria, Wearmouth-Jarrow, 734–737

Parchment, 128 fols. (with a fragment of fol. 129), 290 × 215 mm, text 250 × 190 mm, 29–31 long lines, ruled in hard point

SCRIPT: Uncial and Insular minuscule

BINDING: quarter niger and marbled paper over boards, by S. Cockerell, 1959

Cambridge University Library, MS Kk.5.16

THIS REMARKABLE BOOK contains the most famous of Bede's works and was written around 735, the year of his death. Bede was the first important historian of the English people and of their religion, and the present book occupies a central place in the transmission of his *History*. The text focuses on the conversion of the English to Christianity, and on the development of the Church and Christian kingdoms of Anglo-Saxon England up to the early eighth century. His account drew on many sources then available to him, including an earlier, sixth-century narrative of the coming of the English to Britain, and the archives of Canterbury Cathedral. Bede's perspective, as one would expect, is markedly Northumbrian. But he was also a staunch advocate of the links between Anglo-Saxon England and Rome and the Papacy. This is most obvious in his account of the Synod of Whitby in 664, the beginning of which is illustrated here. This famous meeting settled the calculation of the date of Easter according to the method used in Rome. Bede prefaced his history with a wonderful description of the geography of the island of Britain for which he drew on the geographers of classical Antiquity.

The manuscript is associated with the St Petersburg Bede (St Petersburg, Saltykov-Schedrin Public Library, MS Q.v.I.18), a far more accurate text. No fewer than eight ninth- and tenth-century copies were made on the Continent directly from it. Many eleventh- and twelfth-century copies were derived from it, and it also formed the basis of most subsequent printed editions, from that of John and George Smith (Cambridge, 1722) onwards. At the end of the present manuscript two short texts have been added in a north French Caroline minuscule of the late eighth century. These comprise material by Isidore of Seville on consanguinity and part of the Roman synod of 721 presided over by Pope Gregory II. The same hand has expanded Insular contractions and abbreviations in the main text to make them intelligible for a Continental reader.

In addition to the very striking and accomplished Insular minuscule, the leaves within each quire are arranged in the manner common to the British Isles in the early Middle Ages, namely, with the flesh side out and with ruling drawn after the leaves had been folded and pricked in both margins. The gatherings are unusual in that they comprise both quinions and quaternions. Red, now much faded, was used for headings and *capitula*, and the simple capital letters at the beginning of each chapter are outlined with red dots, another characteristically Insular feature.

The manuscript has no illumination. Its text is written in *scriptio continua*, that is, with no space between the words. Originally, it had very little punctuation. Abbreviations were used extensively throughout and the text is full of errors: missing words, wrong tenses, and occasionally incorrect word order. These look like short cuts by an expert scribe, whose regularity of script is truly impressive. The book seems, therefore, to have been written at speed to meet some now unknown deadline. Indeed, the Insular minuscule in this and other early copies of Bede's works may have been specifically devised by the scribes of Wearmouth-Jarrow in the eighth century in order to meet the well-attested demand for these works from clerics in the Anglo-Saxon mission fields in Germany.

PROVENANCE: at Charlemagne's court by late 8th c.; at St Julien's Cathedral, Le Mans by 16th c.; purchased there by J.B. Hautin; purchased between 1697 and 1702 for John Moore, Bishop of Ely (1707–1714); presented to the Library by George I in 1715.

EXHIBITED: London 1991, no. 2.

LITERATURE: University Library 1856–1867, III, 688–89; Ker 1957, 38–39; Hunter Blair and Mynors 1959; Bischoff 1965; Parkes 1982; McKitterick 1986, 135–37; Robinson 1988, no. 68, pls. 1–2.

RMCK

Bede's account of the Synod of Whitby (664).
Cambridge University Library, MS Kk.5.16, fol. 63

4

The Book of Cerne

In Latin and Old English
England, Mercia, 820–840, fourteenth- to sixteenth-century additions

Parchment, 98 fols. (foliated 2–99, fols. 1–26 and the last 28 leaves are later additions), 285 × 225 mm, text 230 × 195 mm, 17–20 long lines, ruled in hard point

SCRIPT: Insular minuscule and half-uncial

BINDING: full niger morocco, by S. Cockerell, 1962

Cambridge University Library, MS Ll.1.10

THE MIDDLE PORTION of this manuscript dates from the ninth century and contains extracts from all four Gospels concerning the Passion and Resurrection, invocatory prayers and litany, including three prayers to the Trinity and the *Lorica of Laidcenn* (glossed in Old English), hymns and a Breviate Psalter ascribed to 'Bishop Oethilwald'. The final text about the Harrowing of Hell is incomplete. The content of some of the prayers can be compared to the Southampton Psalter *(no. 16)*. The name of Bishop Adeluald, to whom the Breviate Psalter on fol. 87v has been ascribed, appears in an acrostic poem on fol. 21. The volume seems to be a personal compilation for meditation and private devotion focusing on the communion of saints. It may have drawn on a set of older texts probably associated with Bishop Athilwald of Lindisfarne (714/724–740) or Bishop Athilwald of Lichfield (818–830). The later material at either end of the volume comprises fifty charters and seventy-six sequences probably added at Cerne in the later Middle Ages.

The manuscript's decoration was carefully planned and executed with great skill and exuberance. The major illustrations follow the conventions of the full texts from which the extracts are taken. There are miniatures of each of the Evangelists, including a meek Mark in a roundel, with his lion dominating the image illustrated here (fols. 12v–13). The Cerne Evangelist portraits have been described as composite designs. They seem to conflate a wide variety of Insular and Continental visual sources exploring the relationships between the Evangelists, Christ and the faithful Christian. The regular and stylish script, and the balanced page design demonstrate the mastery of the scribe and artists. Numerous text pages received similarly rich ornamentation. Initials with

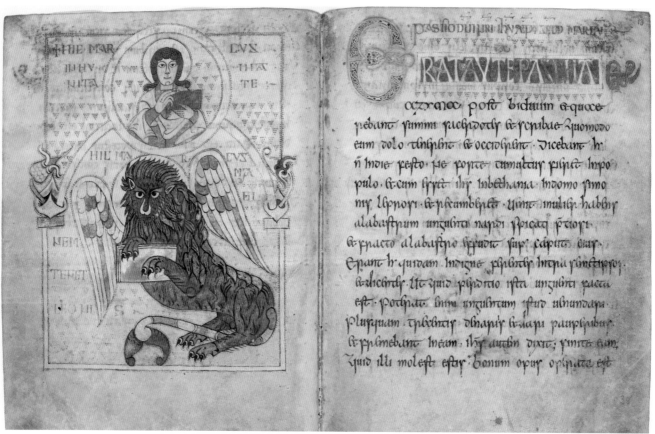

St Mark with his Symbol. Cambridge University Library, MS Ll.1.10, fols. 12v–13

colourful infill and display capitals with zoomorphic finials open the prayers. On fol. 71v a hole in the parchment has been transformed into a tortoise. On fol. 92v little creatures gambol among the lines of text.

This approach to the layout of text and decoration in the Book of Cerne is very close to manuscripts from the so-called 'Tiberius group', such as the Vespasian Psalter (London, British Library, Cotton MS Vespasian A.1). Two other books, Salisbury Cathedral Library, MS 117 and Oxford, Bodleian Library, MS Hatton 93 were produced in the same Mercian scriptorium as the Book of Cerne. The members of this scriptorium were used to writing both manuscripts and charters in Latin and in Old English in a very competent cursive Insular minuscule, and numbered skilled artists among them. The scriptorium was located in a broad area of Mercian cultural activity or 'Mercian script province' which included Kent. The late medieval Cerne sections of the manuscript probably became associated with the ninth-century portions after the Dissolution of the Monasteries and bear no relationship to its earlier provenance.

PROVENANCE: the early medieval section may have been connected with Worcester until the 13th c.; by 1697 it belonged to John Moore, Bishop of Ely (1707–1714); presented to the Library by George I in 1715.

EXHIBITED: London 1991, no. 165; London 1997, no. 124.

LITERATURE: University Library 1856–1867, IV, 5–6; Kuypers 1902; Cabrol 1904; Ker 1957, 39–40; Hughes 1970; Dumville 1972; Alexander 1978, no. 66; Robinson, 1988, no. 73, pl. 3; Brown 1996; Kauffmann 2003, 33.

RMCK

5

Hraban Maur, *Super Epistolas Pauli libri XIX*

In Latin
France, Reims, second half of the ninth century

Parchment, 256 + 1 fols., 300 × 210 mm, text 204 × 105 mm, 35 long lines, ruled in hard point

SCRIPT: Caroline minuscule

BINDING: full brown goat skin, 20th c.

Pembroke College, MS 308

HRABAN MAUR (d.856) was one of the most prolific and influential scholars in the Carolingian empire. His works were widely circulated. A pupil of the English scholar Alcuin at Tours, Hraban became Abbot of Fulda

in 822 and was later Archbishop of Mainz. His commentary on St Paul's Epistles was one of a long series of biblical commentaries. His method of exegesis was to offer the reader a commentary full of quotations and references to the interpretations of earlier authorities. A number of his biblical commentaries were dedicated to the Frankish rulers and it may well be that Fulda sent copies of his works to other communities to transcribe.

This manuscript was certainly made at Reims and may be an indication of connections between the major archbishoprics of Reims and Mainz, and of the way in which the works of an early medieval author were disseminated. It is quite clear from the structure and scribal annotations in this book that they were working from an exemplar, possibly sent from Fulda. The volume preserves the annotations of nine scribes, indicating the extent of the portions they had copied. It is one of the few early medieval manuscripts to offer specific evidence of the individual scribes responsible for the copying, for they all signed their names at the beginning of their stints. Each seems to have been allocated a particular number of gatherings. Iotmar copied the first 47 folios (i.e. the first six quires), Solvio wrote the next three gatherings (fols. 48–71v) and signed off with the words *et hic finit* ('and here finishes') and Hranigil, whose signature is illustrated here *(see overleaf)*, started his portion on fol. 72 with the words *hic inc. port. Hranigili* ('here begins the portion of Hranigil'). The opening display shows the writing of both Solvio and Hranigil. They distinguished the different levels of text they copied. They provide the *lemmata* of the Pauline text in rustic capitals and indicate the citations for the patristic authorities, Ambrose, Gregory, and Augustine, on whom Hraban drew for this portion of text. Bernard, Hrotald, Haimo, Adelrad, Ausold and Communis complete the book, though each only wrote one or two gatherings of eight leaves.

The book was originally given by Archbishop Hincmar of Reims to the abbey library of St Mary, Reims. His dedication note was written across a number of openings of the many manuscripts he gave, HINCMARUS ARCHIEP[ISCOPU]S DEDIT S[AN]C[T]AE MARIAE REMENSI. Gneuss suggests that the manuscript reached England by the late ninth century, presumably in association with Grimbald of St Bertin who was at the court of King Alfred in the 890s. Unfortunately there is no evidence to substantiate this hypothesis.

PROVENANCE: Abbey of St Mary, Reims; Cathedral Priory of Ely by 14th c.; acquired in the late sixteenth century by Lancelot Andrewes, Master of Pembroke College, and given by him to the College in 1589.

LITERATURE: James 1905a, 275–76; Vezin 1973; Robinson, 1988, no. 277, pl. 4a, 4b; Gneuss 2001, 41.

RMCK

Script of Solvio and Hranigil, with Hranigil's signature. Pembroke College, MS 308, fols. 71v – 72

6

Hraban Maur, *Opus in honorem sanctae crucis*

In Latin
Germany, probably Fulda, mid–ninth century or
England, tenth century

Parchment, iii (i–ii paper) + 45 fols., 415 × 335 mm, text
275–320 × 250–278 mm, 36–40 long lines for the poem, 35–54
long lines for the commentary, 35 long lines per page in Book II,
pricking in outer margin, ruled in hard point

SCRIPT: Rustic capitals and Insular minuscule

BINDING: gold-tooled calf over pasteboards, arms of John
Whitgift, 16th c., rebacked.

Trinity College, MS B.16.3

IN ADDITION to an encyclopedia, treatises about ecclesiastical organization, and a vast series of biblical commentaries, Hraban also composed early in his career this extraordinary poem in praise of the Holy Cross (Müller 1973; Ernst 1991; Spilling 1992; Ferrari 1999). It is accompanied by a prose commentary. Hraban devised the poem in a highly ingenious form known as *carmina figurata*. Every page is laid out in the form of a cross, either clearly outlined (as on the illustrated example with the cherubim and seraphim around the cross and praising Christ), or formed by the patterns made out of sections of the text. Phrases have also been highlighted in the outlines of many of the pictures and patterns to signal key concepts in the poems. The commentary explains how the poem is to be understood, and a second book essentially transposes into prose the poetry of the *carmina figurata*. The work is thus an *opus geminum*, that is a prose and verse version of the same text in one book.

This format presented a challenge to the scribe and artist of this copy, as well as to many of their colleagues

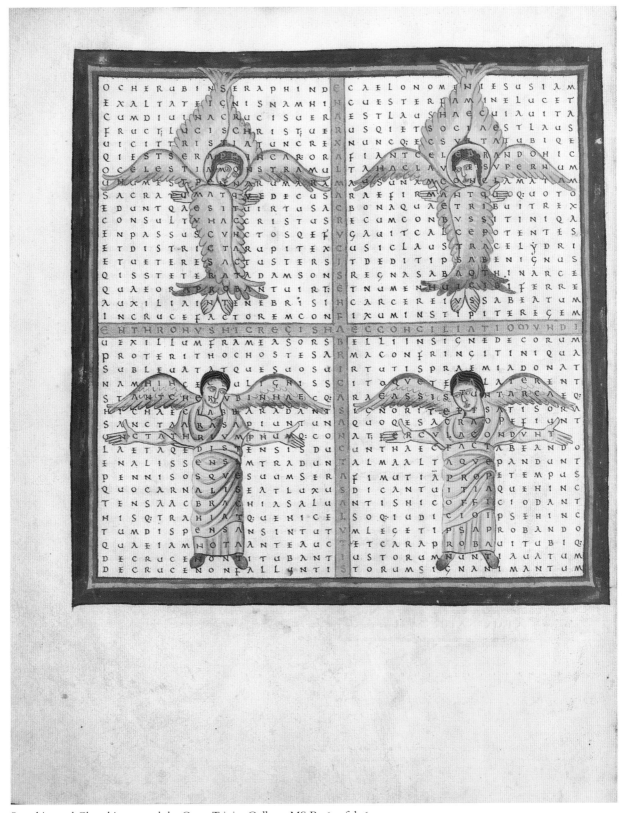

Seraphim and Cherubim around the Cross. Trinity College, MS B.16.3, fol. 6v

and even to the earliest printer who in 1503 responded to its technical difficulties. Nine copies (if the Trinity Hraban be included) were made in the ninth century alone, either at Fulda or directly from Fulda copies, and some were dedicated to Pope Gregory IV, to the Emperor Louis the Pious (814–840) and to Archbishop Otgar of Mainz (826–847). The grand format and luxurious colour scheme of the Trinity copy suggest a similarly distinguished original owner.

Both the rustic capitals and minuscule script of the book present considerable puzzles. Hitherto the minuscule has been regarded as an example of 'English square minuscule' and dated to the later tenth century, perhaps at Canterbury. But no comparisons have so far been made with the products of the Continental centre where the *Opus in honorem sanctae crucis* originated, namely Fulda in Germany. Yet Fulda manuscripts of the later eighth and ninth centuries are famous for their strong Insular characteristics. So are late eighth- and early ninth-century manuscripts associated with the Anglo-Saxon missionary centres of Würzburg, Fritzlar and Hersfeld. The Trinity Hraban has much closer similarities to the 'Continental Insular minuscule' produced there (e.g. Vienna, Österreichische Nationalbibliothek, MS 430★ or Würzburg, Universitätsbibliothek, MS M. p.th.f.144), than to English square minuscule. The figures in the dedication picture are also closely related to Fulda painting of the middle of the ninth century. A Continental attribution would also resolve other difficulties about positing an English origin for the manuscript, not least the character of the rustic capital sections. These too have their closest parallels with Fulda work of the ninth century. The abbreviations include both the typical Insular symbols for *autem* and (from one of the scribes) for *et*, but most of the others are standard Continental forms, such as the *et*-ligature, the *-tur* abbreviation and the form of the question mark. These aspects are not entirely covered by supposing a ninth-century exemplar. Even the method of the cryptogram *ast capiat uite premia perpetue* (fol. ★1, 'and may he receive the rewards of eternal life') is as common in Continental as in Anglo-Saxon manuscripts.

PROVENANCE: the inscription, *Eadwine*, on fol. ★1v suggests that the volume was in England by the late 10th c., if it was not in fact copied there; ownership inscription 'Willyam Porter' (16th c.); Gilbert Bourne, Bishop of Bath and Wells (d.1569); John Whitgift, Archbishop of Canterbury; his bequest, 1604.

EXHIBITED: Cambridge 1985, no. 3.

LITERATURE: James 1900–1904, I, 516–17; Spilling 1978; Spilling 1980; Vezin 1980; Dumville 1987; Perrin 1989; Spilling 1996; Keynes 1992, 11–14.

RMCK

7

Epistle Lectionary

In Latin
Alemannia, St Gallen, *c*.970

Parchment, 153 + iii fols., 268 × 193 mm, text 192 × 113 mm, 22 long lines, ruled in hard point

SCRIPT: Caroline minuscule

BINDING: gold–tooled morocco over wooden boards, 19th c.; the ivory carving of Christ Pantocrator once inset into the upper cover has been removed (Department of Applied Arts, M. 13–1904) and replaced with a photograph.

Fitzwilliam Museum, MS McClean 30

THE MANUSCRIPT is a sumptuous book of such expert and lavish decoration in the Reichenau style that it may originally have been intended for a very wealthy bishop or a royal chapel. The large and stately Caroline minuscule written in rich dark brown ink or pure gold is typical of tenth-century Ottonian manuscripts. Elaborate initials preface the readings for major feasts: Christmas, the Purification of the Virgin, Palm Sunday, Easter, Ascension, Pentecost, Trinity Sunday, the Assumption of the Virgin, St John the Baptist, St Peter, St Simon and St Jude, and All Saints. The latter was a feast day inaugurated in the ninth century. Some of these initials occupy a full page framed within gold borders, painted in resplendent turquoise or red, and filled with liquid gold ornament on luxurious purple background. Musical notation was added to the texts for the feast of St Stephen and St John the Evangelist in neumes of a St Gallen type (fols. 7, 8v). The readings, mostly from the Pauline Epistles, are set out with a range of complementary readings from the Old Testament. Like the list of Pericopes in Gospel Books *(see no. 8)*, they preserve in the headings not only the note of the feast day but also the stational church in Rome with which the reading was associated. Thus for the feasts of Quinquagesima, Sexagesima, Septuagesima, introduced in Rome in the early sixth century, late sixth and seventh centuries respectively, the stational churches mentioned are St Lawrence, San Paolo fuori le mura and St Peter's. The Common of Saints begins on fol. 139 and is succeeded by a number of votive Mass readings, such as that for the dedication of a church (fol. 150).

The manuscript reflects the 'Gallican' or Frankish system of three lessons in the Mass, one from the Old Testament, one from the Gospel and one from the 'Apostle' used in France and Germany in the ninth and tenth centuries. There are slight indications that the 'Galllican' system may have been based on a very early

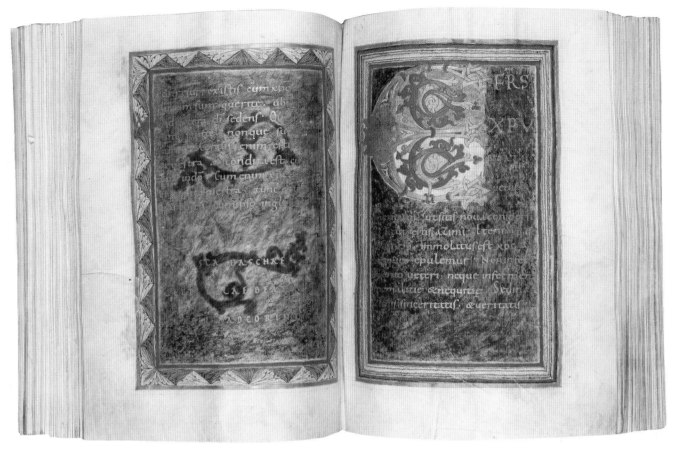

Easter readings. Fitzwilliam Museum, MS McClean 30, fols. 73v–74

Roman one (Vogel 1986). Including readings from both the Old Testament (mostly the Prophets) and the Epistles of St Paul, this manuscript is one of the very few extant Epistolaries from the eighth, ninth and tenth centuries. It includes the eighth-century letter to Constantius attributed to Jerome (fol. IV) in which the author gives the collection of scriptural passages the title of 'Comes'. He presents the list to his 'venerable and dearly beloved brother' who had urged him to make it, and describes how he has excerpted from the Bible passages suitable for particular feasts, arranging them in the order for reading starting with Christmas Eve. In the section for Lent he has also included some passages on moral edification. This suggests that the manuscript was intended for episcopal use, justifying its exceptional refinement and de luxe illumination.

PROVENANCE: Monsieur D. Petit, no. 353 in his catalogue (inscription on fol. 3); Jean-Baptiste-Joseph Barrois (1784–1855); acquired by Bertram, 4th Earl of Ashburnham in 1849 (Ashburnham 1853–1861, II, no. VI); his sale, Sotheby's, London, 10–14 June 1901, lot 189; purchased by Frank McClean (1837–1904); his bequest, 1904.

EXHIBITED: Cambridge 1966, no. 8.

LITERATURE: Frere 1894–1932, no. 1017; James 1912a, 53–55; Merton 1912, 83, pl. LXXXIX; Frere 1935, 68, 74–77; Gamber 1963, 435, no. 1022; Dodwell and Turner. 1965, 63; Hoffmann 1986, 378.

RMCK

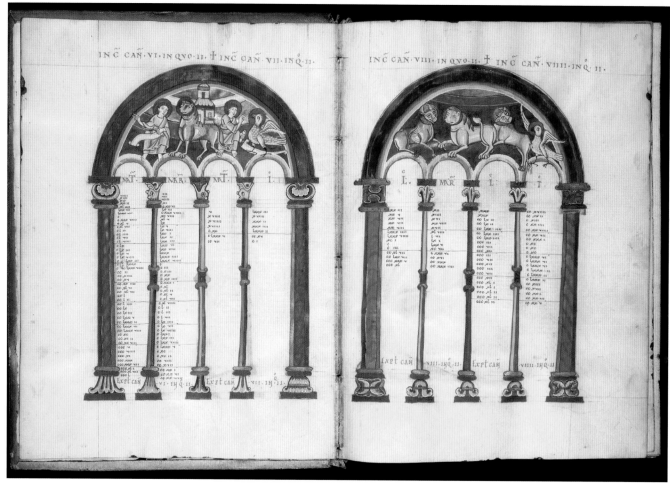

Canon Tables. Fitzwilliam Museum, MS McClean 20, fols. 7v–8

8

Gospels

In Latin
Bavaria, Freising, beginning of the eleventh century

Parchment, 144 fols., 278 × 200 mm, text 215 × 125 mm, 29–30
long lines, ruled in hard point

SCRIPT: Caroline minuscule

BINDING: blind-stamped pigskin over wooden boards, two metal
clasps, 16th c.; vellum label on spine 'MS pergament um 1000'.

Fitzwilliam Museum, MS McClean 20

T HIS MANUSCRIPT contains the complete text of the
four Gospels, equipped with a wide-ranging apparatus to guide readers through the Gospel narrative and
the liturgical year. The first two quires include Jerome's
letters to Pope Damasus, beginning *Novum opus* and
Sciendum etiam est, and discussing the canon tables and
Jerome's Vulgate edition of the Gospels adapted from
existing translations at the Pope's request around 384.
Next come Eusebius's letter to the Carpiani, beginning

Ammonius quidam alexandrino, the general prologue
beginning *Plures fuisse*, a *Breviarium* for each Gospel,
Jerome's *argumentum*, the *capitula*, and the short explanation on the Gospel narratives by Sedulius Scottus, an
Irish scholar working in Liège c.841–850 (fols. 15–17v).
The volume ends with a list of the Gospel Pericopes
providing the sequence of Gospel readings for the liturgical year. This started with Christmas Eve and was based
originally on a Roman list, for it includes notes of the
stational churches of Rome. The Sanctoral in this section
includes Saints Vitus, Sixtus, Sinicius and Willibald.
Although listed in November instead of July, possibly by
confusion with his compatriot Willibrord of Utrecht, St
Willibald was an Anglo-Saxon missionary and former
Bishop of Eichstätt. He was famous in the eighth century
for his journey to the Holy Land recorded in Hugeburc
of Heidenheim's *Hodoeporicon*.

The manuscript opens with the canon tables set
within richly decorated columns and arches. Devised by
Eusebius (260–340) and borrowed by Jerome, the tables
presented concordances between the narratives of the
four Evangelists, which also appear as marginal notes
throughout the Gospels. The text is laid out with great
care and clarity. The beginnings of verses are signalled

58

by red capitals; the headings are styled in rustic capitals; each section opens with large gold initials surrounded by foliage and terminating in biting animal heads. The *incipit* pages of each Gospel contain elaborate initials on purple ground, set within gold and red frames. Although the miniature of St Luke is missing, the other Evangelists are portrayed with consummate skill. They are distinguished through their symbols and individual activities. Matthew is shown writing, Mark thinking and John pausing to mend his pen. The style of painting is that of the renowned Regensburg school. Although it seems likely that this volume was produced for use in the diocese of Eichstätt, the illumination finds its closest parallels in manuscripts from Freising produced in the time of Bishop Ellenhart.

The skilled drawing, the rich palette, and the lavish use of gold and silver indicate an exceptionally wealthy commissioner. The use of purple, a prodigiously expensive pigment used as an imperial status symbol, may suggest royal patronage.

PROVENANCE: at Würzburg in 1273; Duke of Hamilton; purchased at the Hamilton Palace sale, Sotheby's, 23 May 1889, lot 34 by Quaritch; his catalogue no. 118, Dec. 1891; Frank McClean (1837–1904); his bequest, 1904.

EXHIBITED: Manchester 1959, no. 10; Cambridge 1966, no. 10.

LITERATURE: Frere 1894–1932, no. 1019; Swarzenski 1901, 131; James 1912a, 36–39, pl. X; Bange 1923, 92–97, figs. 88–90; Klauser 1935, XLII, no. 57; Garrison 1953, 114, fig. 22.

RMCK

9

Gospels

In Latin
England, first half of the eleventh century

Parchment, ii + 132 + ii fols., 292 × 220 mm, text 200 × 149 mm, 28 long lines, ruled in hard point

SCRIPT: Caroline minuscule

BINDING: tawed skin (originally pink) over boards, five bosses on the upper and four on the lower cover, 15th c.

Pembroke College, MS 301

THE GOSPEL BOOKS produced in England during the late tenth century and first half of the eleventh are among the finest as well as best surviving class of late Anglo-Saxon illuminated manuscripts. Much, however, remains obscure about the precise details of when, where and for whom these books were made.

Pembroke 301 is typical of late Anglo-Saxon Gospel Books in many respects: the text of the four Gospels is preceded by elaborately decorated Eusebian canon tables that provide tables of corresponding (or 'concordant') passages in the different Gospel accounts, whilst each Gospel is introduced with a full-page Evangelist portrait followed by elaborately decorated rubrics, opening initial and words of the Gospel text. Rubrics and ornamented initials throughout are in gold, indicating the high status of the book and the expense involved in its production. Yet, like a surprising number of late Anglo-Saxon illuminated books including other Gospel Books, it is unfinished. The accompanying textual apparatus is incomplete: the marginal concordance numbers that provide the reference to the relevant canon table were never supplied, nor were all the rubrics. The illustration and decoration were carried out in two phases, yet were still left unfinished. The canon tables on fols. 1v–6v, the portrait of Matthew and the decorated *incipit* to Matthew's Gospel were drawn and painted by an artist who employed pale shades of pink, orange, ochre and green, which did not obscure the elaborate pen-drawn ornament and draperies. The remainder of the canon tables (fols. 7–8v) and the other Evangelist portraits and *incipit* pages were partially painted a little later by at least one other, less skilled artist, in somewhat clumsily applied opaque and darker hues, in particular dark blue and brown.

Textual and scribal evidence has proved inconclusive in establishing where and for whom the book was produced. In general respects, Pembroke 301 is textually related to several early eleventh-century English illuminated Gospel Books, but with none is the relationship sufficiently close to indicate a common exemplar or place of origin. An oddity in the manuscript is the inclusion of the preface to Acts after the end of John's Gospel, which might suggest a Bible or New Testament as the exemplar, a possibility reinforced by a close textual relationship with the prefaces and text of the Gospels in a late tenth-century two-volume Bible (London, British Library, Royal MSS 1 E.vii and 1 E.viii) which was owned by Christ Church, Canterbury by at least the early twelfth century.

Pembroke 301 was written by a single scribe writing an English variety of Caroline minuscule, but in a rather mannered and idiosyncratic fashion. Bishop believed the hand to be that of the scribe he designated 'Scribe C' who contributed to one of the Gospel Books with which Pembroke 301 shares a general textual affinity, the Kederminster Gospels (London, British Library, Loan MS 11), and to another (London, British Library, Royal MS 1 D.ix), in both of which he worked in collaboration with the scribe of the Trinity Gospels *(no. 10)*. Scribe C also copied the original part of a copy of Bede's *Historia ecclesiastica* (Oxford, Bodleian Library, MS Bodley 163),

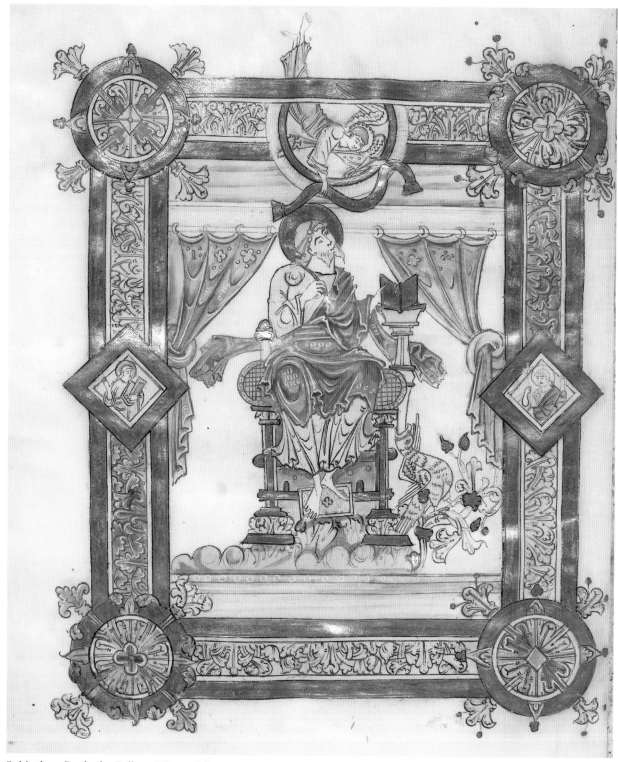

St Matthew. Pembroke College, MS 301, fol. 10v

which was at Peterborough by the early twelfth century. Dumville, however, has questioned the attribution of the hand of the scribe of Pembroke 301 to Scribe C, and there is thus doubt as to whether the manuscript was produced at Christ Church, Canterbury or at Peterborough.

PROVENANCE: 'Andrewe Jenour' (17th–c. inscription, fol. 1); source and date of College acquisition unknown.

EXHIBITED: London 1984a, no. 53.

LITERATURE: James 1905a, 163–66; Bishop 1971, 21; Temple 1976, no. 73; McGurk 1986, 43–63; Dumville 1991–1995, 41–42; Gneuss 2001, no. 138.

TW

10

Gospels

In Latin
England, first half of the eleventh century

Parchment, iii (modern parchment) + 174 + iii (modern parchment) fols., 320 × 232 mm, text 224 × 150 mm, 27 long lines, ruled in hard point

SCRIPT: Caroline minuscule

BINDING: dark brown leather over boards, 20th c.

Trinity College, MS B.10.4

THE TRINITY GOSPELS are a masterpiece of late Anglo-Saxon book production, and are the most sumptuous of all surviving late Anglo-Saxon Gospel Books. The manuscript was written by a single expert scribe on very fine parchment, rubricated throughout in gold, and accompanied by a full set of magnificently decorated canon tables, Evangelist portraits and *incipit* pages, as well as a miniature of Christ in Majesty (fol. 16v). It is the only extant late Anglo-Saxon Gospel Book in which all the *incipit* pages are complete. Together with the Grimbald Gospels (London, British Library, Add. MS 34890), it is also the most sophisticated in its layout. The Gospel text itself is set out in short paragraphs, each concordance beginning on a new line with a gold initial.

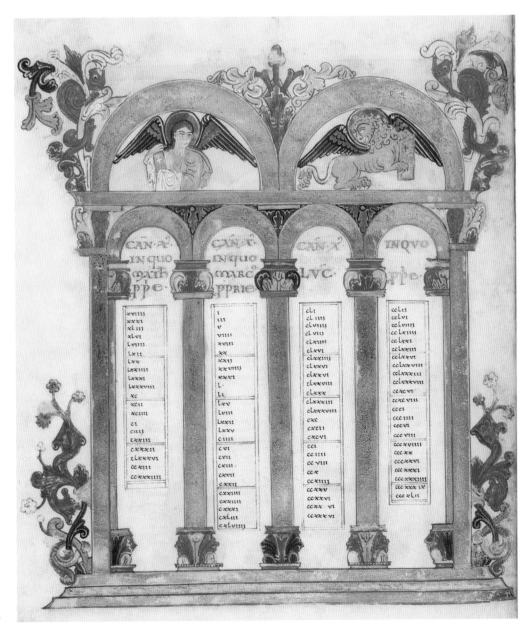

Canon Tables.
Trinity College,
MS B.10.4, fol. 15v

A hierarchy of script is used to provide visual articulation for rubrics, *incipits* and the texts themselves, including three sizes of minuscule for the Gospel text, the chapter lists and the list of Gospel lections respectively. In the account of the Passion in each of the Gospels, the passages that record the utterances of Christ are indicated with a cross, those of other characters with an 's' and the intervening words of the Evangelist with a 'c'.

Materials of the very highest quality were used. The colour of the parchment is unusually even throughout; some of the text leaves are remarkably thin, almost comparable with that of thirteenth-century single-volume Bibles, whilst a much stouter parchment was selected for the more heavily painted pages bearing the canon tables, Evangelist portraits and Gospel *incipits*. The quality of the parchment, the lavish use of gold, and the expert craftsmanship point to a very high-status patron. Such books were sometimes made for lay owners. Four Gospel Books, for example, were made for Judith, daughter of the Count of Flanders. By contrast with these, however, which lack (perhaps deliberately) the apparatus of *incipits* and *explicits*, general prefaces, canon tables, chapter lists, and marginal concordance references and chapter numbers, the Trinity Gospels are outstanding for the comprehensiveness and accuracy of the accompanying textual apparatus, which may indicate clerical or monastic use. Yet the book contains not the slightest indication of medieval ownership. Gospel Books were sometimes regarded as an appropriate location to copy records of property, rights or other information of special importance to their owner, whether an individual or community, as for example in Pembroke College, MS 302 *(no. 43)*, but the Trinity Gospels contain no medieval additions of any kind.

The scribe, however, has been identified in other books. Bishop, who designated him 'Scribe B', demonstrated that he wrote most of London, British Library, Royal MS 1 D.ix, perhaps before 1017/1020. Scribe B also wrote all but the general prefaces and capitulary of the Kederminster Gospels (London, British Library, Loan MS 11). Since the Trinity Gospels are the most developed in their contents and layout, it seems likely that they were the latest of the Gospel Books written wholly or in part by this scribe. Unfortunately too little is known about the circumstances of luxury book production during the first half of the eleventh century to permit us to assume an exclusively monastic context for Scribe B's activity, let alone identify a particular place of origin.

PROVENANCE: Matthew Parker (1504–1575), whose name is just visible on fol. 1; gift of Thomas Nevile (1548–1615), Master of Trinity College (1593–1615).

EXHIBITED: London 1984a, no. 49; Cambridge 1985, no. 20.

LITERATURE: James 1900–1904, I, 287–92; Bishop 1967; Temple 1976, no. 65; Brownrigg 1978, 264–66; McGurk 1986, 43–63; Heslop 1990, 154 n.10, 166, 172; Keynes 1992, 32–33; McGurk and Rosenthal 1995, 258–62; Ohlgren 1992, no. 7; Gneuss 2001, no. 172; Kauffmann 2003, 57.

TW

11

Prudentius, *Psychomachia*

In Latin with some Old English glosses and titles
England, probably Canterbury, late tenth or
early eleventh century

Parchment, ii + 104 fols., 365 × 287 mm, text 270 × 198 mm, 30 long lines in verse layout with provision of unlined spaces for the illustrations

SCRIPT: Caroline minuscule

BINDING: pigskin over oak boards, by Nicholas Pickwoad, 1988

Corpus Christi College, MS 23, part 1

THIS VERY LARGE COPY of the *Psychomachia* or 'the spiritual combat' occupies fols. 1–40v in the manuscript. It is bound together with a twelfth century copy from Dover of Orosius's *Seven books of history against the pagans*, which constitutes part 2 of the manuscript.

Prudentius (348–410), a native of Spain, wrote at a time when the Christian Church was still establishing itself within the Roman Empire and endeavouring both to provide alternatives to pagan institutions and ideals, and to deal with dissension among the Christians themselves. His elaborate, dramatic and highly rhetorical poem presents a battle between the Virtues and Vices for possession of the human soul (Cunningham 1966; Smith 1976; Haworth 1980). All the Virtues, personified as women, fight their opposite Vices either in single combat or in groups. Faith takes the field at the head of her army of Virtues against worship of the old Gods. Chastity combats Lust, Patience is pitted against Wrath and so on. The most insatiable and destructive vice of all, however, is *Avaritia*, Greed, who has a host of terrible children, including Fear, Anguish, Meanness, Corruption, Falsehood and Treachery. These are eventually overcome by Reason and Good Works. At the end of the poem, Faith, Concord and Wisdom triumph over Evil and Discord.

The pictures were added by a single artist after the text had been written. The marginal titles for the illustrations were written in Latin in rustic capitals and in English within the frame. Large titles in ornate monochrome capitals set out the text and are accompanied by ornamental initials with interlace, contorted birds and foliage.

Each line of the poem begins with a red capital letter and the first line is usually written in rustic capitals. The eighty-nine framed ink drawings outlined in blue, green and red in this book are characteristic of Canterbury illumination. The original drawings are claimed to be based on a hypothetical lost fifth- or sixth-century archetype, but the style was immediately inspired by the Utrecht Psalter produced at Reims around 820 and known at Canterbury (Noel 1995; Utrecht 1996). Those in the present book are clearly based on a Carolingian exemplar. This is especially evident in the drawing of the horses, swords and helmets of the warriors, though the text and illustrations do not always match. Yet, the pictures have been adapted to become distinctively English. The most magnificent example of this English style is the Harley Psalter in the British Library (Harley MS 603). Its most striking characteristics are the fluttering drapery and animation of the tall figures with their small heads and feet, as well as the coloured outlines. Occasionally stylized plant motifs are added. The page illustrated here is from the preface, where Prudentius draws a parallel and creates a scriptural allegory between the rescue of Lot by his uncle Abraham from the 'five kings' who had captured him, and the triumph of faith and the spirit's battle against monstrous vices.

There are twenty manuscripts of Prudentius' *Psychomachia* surviving from before the thirteenth century which indicate the popularity of this text in the earlier Middle Ages. Not only are there a number of Carolingian examples, but there are also three other surviving Anglo-Saxon copies of similar date. Some glosses indicate attentive reading. A further indication of this book's probable didactic purpose is the extensive series of marginal and interlinear glosses copied into the manuscript from the exemplar and the provision of the explanatory biography of Prudentius taken from Jerome-Gennadius, *De viris illustribus*. There are also many unillustrated copies, many of which also include detailed glosses explaining Prudentius's text.

PROVENANCE: presented to the Abbey of Malmesbury in the middle of the eleventh century by Aethelweard, conceivably the abbot of that name from 1040–1050; Matthew Parker (1504–1575); his bequest, 1575.

EXHIBITED: Cambridge 1975, no. 7.

LITERATURE: Stettiner 1895–1905, 17–22, pl. 31–34, 49–66; James 1912b, I, 44–46; Woodruff 1930, 8–9; Thomson 1949, I, 274–343; Ker 1957, 42–43; Temple 1976, no. 48; Thomson 1982; Wieland 1985; Budny 1997, 275–437; Kauffmann 2003, 39, 41.

RMCK

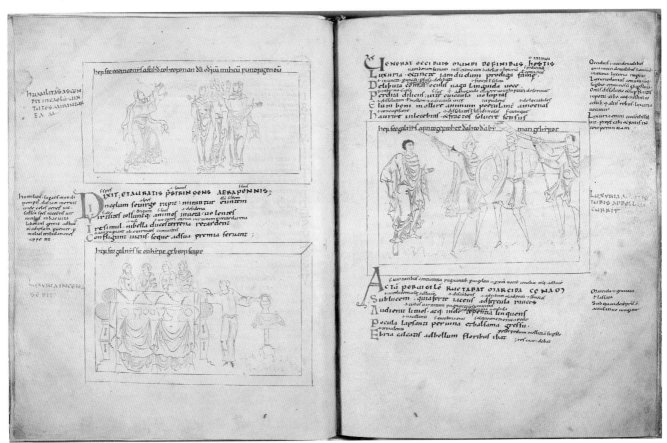

Humility and Luxury. Corpus Christi College, MS 23, fols. 17v–18

12

Arator, *De actibus apostolorum*

In Latin
England, Canterbury, Christ Church, late tenth or
early eleventh century

Parchment, 66 fols. (fols. 1–4 are flyleaves from a ninth-century
copy from Italy, Nonantola, of Ambrose on Psalm 118),
241 × 173 mm, text 177 × 91 mm, ruled in hard point
SCRIPT: Caroline minuscule
BINDING: full calf, arms of George Willmer, c.1610; rebacked.

Trinity College, MS B.14.3

A RATOR had been trained in the great schools of Milan,
Pavia and Ravenna in Theodoric the Ostrogoth's
Italy. He became a subdeacon in Rome and dedicated his
work to Pope Vigilius (537–555). His versified rendering of the Acts of the Apostles was composed soon after
he took up holy orders and is often grouped with other
Late Antique works written in response to the aversion
of Christians to pagan classical texts. Using the classical
form of hexameter verse, Arator described the history of
the expansion of the Apostolic Church and the conver-

sion of Macedonia, Greece and Asia, culminating in
St Paul's first visit to Rome. He uses a vocabulary associated by those of literary bent with heroes, soldiers and
athletes. The prominent Apostles in the story are Peter
and Paul and a major topic is the descent of the Holy
Spirit at Pentecost. To appreciate the poem, one needs a
good knowledge not just of Acts but also of the Bible as
a whole. Arator seizes many opportunities to expand on
the spiritual meaning of the events he describes and
points up the moral of various topics, such as Mary
making up for Eve's sin in the Garden of Eden. He also
added an opening of twenty lines on the Christian's
descent into Hell and the Resurrection. These are not in
Acts. Apparently he gave the poem a public reading in
April and May 544. With the encores, the epic reputedly
took four days to recite, which says much for the stam-
ina of his audience. Over one hundred codices extant of
this rather peculiar work attest to its popularity throughout Western Europe in the early Middle Ages, particularly from the ninth to the eleventh centuries.

The several hands in this manuscript have been found
in other Canterbury books and documents. One of the
scribes was also responsible for King Ethelred's charter for
Muchelney Abbey in 995 and the gloss in a Canterbury
copy of Boethius, *De consolatione philosophiae* (Oxford,
Bodleian Library, MS Auct. F.1.15 part i). These are
accomplished hands, capable also of writing slender rustic

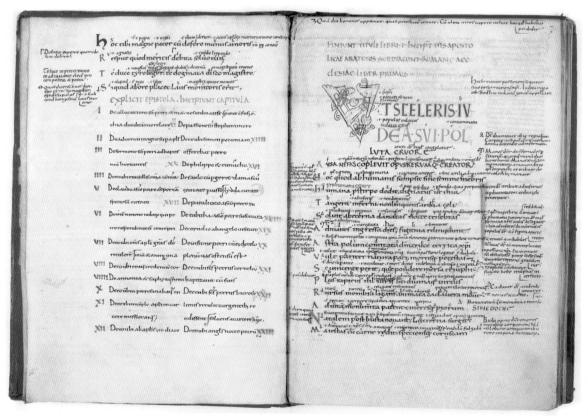

Ornamental
initial. Trinity
College, MS
B.14.3, fol. 2v–3

capitals in various colours (green, red, blue, black and dark red) for the first five lines of the text as well as the square capitals for the *incipit*. The V initial is formed by vegetative and zoomorphic motifs. While a number of hands added the interlinear and marginal glosses, there was one main glossator. It may have been he who added various letters and dots about the words in a system, more commonly found in grammatical texts, designed to construe the Latin word order, presumably for the benefit of English native speakers. These letters, 'a', 'b', 'c', 'd' etc. can clearly be seen in the illustration. In addition to the glosses, the same hand added an explanatory note about Arator himself in the top margin. This is in the style of the biographical entries in Jerome-Gennadius-Isidore, *De viris illustribus*, and was probably put together from the information supplied by Arator himself in his dedicatory letters. This and the frequent codicological context of Arator's poem alongside other school and didactic texts may be a further indication of the use of this manuscript in teaching.

PROVENANCE: Christ Church, Canterbury (listed in the *c.*1170 catalogue of the cathedral library, to which the mark FF above the later shelf mark on fol. 5 relates, and in Prior Eastry's catalogue of 1300); given to Trinity College by George Willmer, *c.*1610.

EXHIBITED: Cambridge 1985, no. 16.

LITERATURE: James 1900–1904, I, 404–406; MacKinlay 1942, 41–2; MacKinlay 1951; Ker 1957, 129–30; Bishop 1971, 7; Lapidge 1982, 116–20; Wieland 1985; Keynes 1992, 27–8; Schrader, Roberts and Makowski 1992.

RMCK

13

Ælfric, Homilies

In Old English
England, Canterbury, Christ Church,
mid-eleventh century

Parchment, iv + 216 + iv fols., 248 × 161 mm, text 200 × 95 mm, 21 long lines, ruled in hard point

SCRIPT: Insular minuscule

BINDING: gold-tooled calf over pasteboards, gauffered edges, arms of John Whitgift, 16th c.; rebacked.

Trinity College, MS B.15.34

THIS APPARENTLY INCOMPLETE BOOK contains the homilies by Ælfric, Abbot of Eynsham (*c.*950 – *c.*1010) for the nineteen weeks of Sundays and feast days after Easter to the eleventh Sunday after Pentecost. It once possibly continued to the beginning of Advent and may be the surviving part of a two-volume set of homilies, the first of which ran from Advent to Easter. Ælfric did not pull his punches in his sermons, and berates the afflictions of the people in the form of taxes and laws, his audience for their perversion of God's laws, and the cowardice of the English who submit to the Danes. Ælfric's sermons focus on biblical texts and his analyses are based on earlier medieval Latin writers such as Jerome, Gregory the Great, Bede, Haymo of Auxerre and Smaragdus of St Mihiel. Nevertheless, his own work was more a process of adaptation and new composition than of translation. He offered interpretations of the Bible which included allegorical explanations and he discussed a range of Christian theological topics and local devotional practices and beliefs, such as divination. His expected audience appears to have been the people outside as well as within the cloister, for one of his aims was to write for the 'edification of the simple'.

These sermons were written late in Ælfric's life. Educated at Winchester, Ælfric wrote works in both Latin and Old English, including a guide to Latin grammar written in English. His English prose is particularly elegant and stylish. Indeed, it is his Old English that is regarded as a model for modern analysis of the development of the English language.

Copied by a single scribe in a large and confident hand similar to that of the Winchcombe Psalter *(no. 17)* and the same as that of the Canterbury Benedictional (London, British Library, Harley MS 2892), the script has marked serifs on the ascenders of the tall letters, and shows in the forms of the 'n', 'm', 'a' and 's' in particular some influence from Caroline minuscule. The titles are written in red rustic capitals and each homily starts with a large green initial letter. There is only one illustration in the book. It is a full-page ink drawing, highlighted in green and red, of Christ the just Judge sitting in a mandorla. This drawing style is associated with early eleventh-century Canterbury manuscripts but the book itself may have been produced at Canterbury for use elsewhere. It is not possible to establish whether this manuscript was designed for a clerical or monastic community, or for use by a priest as guidance for the laity. The image of Christ as Judge may have been intended to pursue the line of thought in Ælfric's important eschatological sermon for the first Sunday after Pentecost, illustrated here, for it discusses death, the state of the human soul, Doomsday and the Last Judgement. The feast of the Trinity was not as yet securely established in the medieval liturgical Calendar, but Ælfric appears to have wanted this homily to cover topics he felt appropriate for the octave of Pentecost. It is based on the *Prognosticon futuri saeculi* of the Spanish bishop, Julian of Toledo (d.690) an epitome of which Ælfric had created earlier in his career.

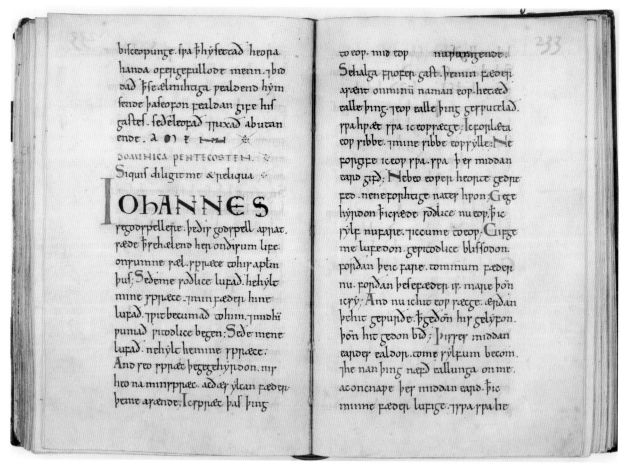

Sermon for the first Sunday after Pentecost. Trinity College, MS B.15.34, fols. 232–33

PROVENANCE: Matthew Parker (1504–1575); John Parker; given to Trinity College by John Whitgift in 1604.

EXHIBITED: Cambridge 1985, no. 22.

LITERATURE: James 1900–1904, I, 500–502; Ker 1957, 130–32; Gatch 1977, 95–101, 129–46; Strongman 1977; Gatch 1991; Bately 1991; Keynes 1992, 34–35.

RMCK

14

Anglo-Saxon Homilies

In Old English
England, first half of the eleventh century; additions made in Exeter, second half of the eleventh century

Parchment, ii + 366 + ii fols., 206 × 128 mm, text 172 × 95 mm, 19 long lines, ruled in hard point
SCRIPT: Insular minuscule
BINDING: full undyed goatskin over millboards, by J.P. Gray, 1954

Corpus Christi College, MS 421

THIS SERMON collection includes homilies by two of the most celebrated Anglo-Saxon sermon writers in English, Wulfstan 'the homilist' (d.1023), Bishop of London (996–1002), and then Bishop of Worcester (1002–1016) and Archbishop of York (1002–1023) simultaneously, and Ælfric, Abbot of Eynsham (c.950–c.1010). Like the English prose of Ælfric (see no. 13) Wulfstan's English is very distinctive though rather more idiosyncratic. Wulfstan used complex patterns of alliteration, two-stress phrases and sound play. There are other texts in the codex whose authors remain unidentified. One of them purports to be a letter by Christ from Heaven known as the 'Sunday Letter'. Another is an expanded translation of an apocalyptic treatise on the Antichrist in Latin, by Adso of Montier-en-Der (978–992). The Ælfric sermons can be linked textually to those in Trinity College MS B.15.34 (no. 13). The initial composition of the English texts in this manuscript attests to the wide distribution of talented and versatile writers within the eleventh-century Anglo-Saxon Church and the degree to which they were in contact with each other as well as receptive to Continental ecclesiastical texts and ideas. Their presence in a collection like this, created in two stages and probably made for a non-monastic church in south-eastern England, is also an indication of how widely English texts were circulated alongside Latin ones. There

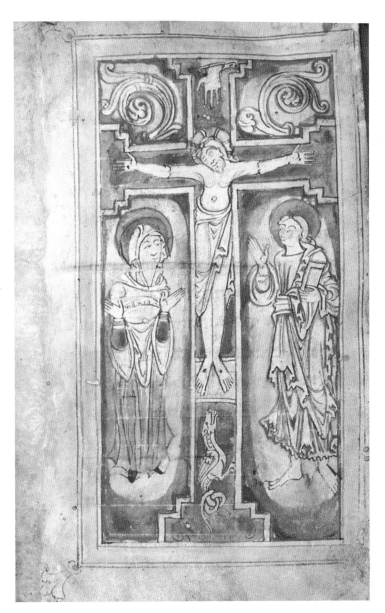

Crucifixion. Corpus Christi College, MS 421, fol. 1

is a strongly eschatological theme to the collection, further augmented by Ælfric's sermon to the people on the octave of Pentecost. This again seems to reflect a certain preoccupation with the Last Things among prominent English ecclesiastics in the eleventh century. The script is large and confident with little hammer-shaped serifs on the ascenders and lines of rustic capitals for the titles as well as ornamented display capitals for the beginning of each new sermon.

The Crucifixion drawing is a further indication of the cosmopolitanism of late Anglo-Saxon culture. The drawing itself originally belonged as a frontispiece to its companion volume, Cambridge, Corpus Christi College, MS 419, partly written by the same scribe. The drawing is in brown outline and washed in red. The style, with its fluttering draperies and elongated figures, is characteristic of southern English drawing and painting in this period. The image is a standard early medieval representation of Christ on the cross, with the hand of God above and Mary and John, neatly labelled *maria* and *johannes*,

to either side of Christ. A variant is offered, however, by the little dragon or serpent entwined around the foot of the cross. This may be an allusion to the serpent in the Garden of Eden which caused the Fall of Man redeemed by Christ. It is a motif uncommon in Anglo-Saxon illumination and is thought to be derived from a Carolingian model. The foliate scrolls in the upper left and right appear to be substitutes for the representations of the sun and the moon which appear in some Frankish portrayals of the Crucifixion. The limited range of colour, with only yellow and orangey red paint, the smallish format and the low quality parchment all indicate a relatively impoverished centre of production.

PROVENANCE: at Exeter by 11th c.; Matthew Parker (1504–1575); his bequest, 1575.

LITERATURE: James 1912b, II, 313–15; Betherum 1952; Ker 1957, 117–18; Pope 1967–1968; Napier 1967, no. XLII; Temple 1976, no. 82; Gatch 1977; Robinson, 1988, no. 164, pl. 27; Budny 1997, 525–34.   RMCK

15

Psalter of Count Achadeus

In Latin
West Frankish Kingdom, Reims, 883–884

Parchment, 183 fols., 264 × 204 mm, text 165 × 117 mm,
20 long lines, ruled in hard point

SCRIPT: Caroline minuscule and Rustic capitals

BINDING: full undyed goatskin over millboards, by J.P. Gray, 1954

Corpus Christi College, MS 272

THIS CODEX is one of a number of liturgical books that can be associated with devout laymen and lay women in the early Middle Ages. According to the note written in gold on fol. 150, *Achadeus misericordia dei comes. Hunc psalterium scribere iussit* ('Achadeus, by the grace of God Count, ordered this Psalter to be written'), this beautiful Psalter was commissioned by Count Achadeus between 883 and 884, possibly from the scriptorium of St Remi at Reims. Yet it is also possible that the book was intended as a gift to a monastery in the diocese of Reims. This is suggested first of all by the highlighting of

Columbanus, an Irish *peregrinus* monk famous for the rigour of his ascetic life and the inspiration he offered for the foundation of many monasteries in Frankish Gaul in the late sixth and seventh centuries. Secondly, prayers for St Benedict and *orationes* for the monastic hours as well as the full range of Canticles, the *Te deum*, Lord's Prayer, Apostle's Creed and *Quicunque vult* may point to a monastic church rather than a household chapel. The size of the main text script may indicate liturgical use, but the extensive glosses throughout the Psalter text, penned in a minute script, suggest private study.

Although there are no illustrations, the manuscript is beautifully written and decorated with glosses and titles in red rustic capitals as well as ornamented initials (though a number are now missing together with leaves that appear to have been removed from the book). These large decorated initials are painted in gold and colours, and that for the Collect on fol. 98 is particularly fine. Each Psalm verse begins with a gold capital letter. Each Psalm concludes with a Collect. The Litany is presented in fine double columns with decorated arches and pedimented columns, and coloured in yellow, red, purple and green. Plants and birds also ornament the columns and arches. Fol. 174v preserves French musical notation of the tenth century.

It may be supposed that Count Achadeus also asked for the additional material to be included, such as the

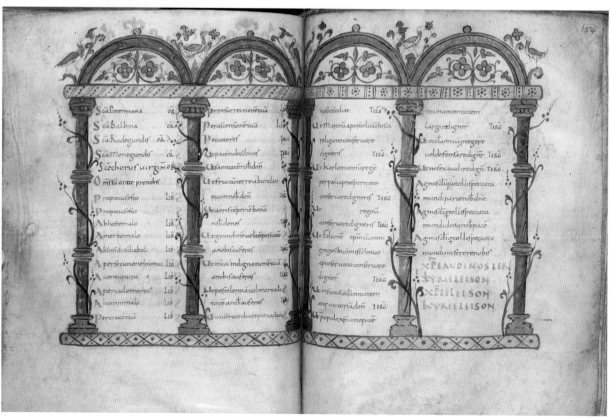

Litany. Corpus Christi College, MS 272, fols. 153v–154

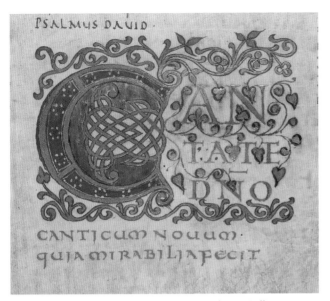

Ornamental initial to Psalm 97. Corpus Christi College, MS 272, fol. 98, detail

16

Psalter and Canticles (The Southampton Psalter)

In Latin, with Latin and Irish glosses
Ireland, end of the ninth century

Parchment, i + 98 fols. (3 leaves lost from the beginning and the foliation starts with fol. 4), 264 × 184 mm, text 167–174 × 90–110 mm, 30–31 long lines, ruled in hard point

SCRIPT: Insular half-uncial

BINDING: diced russia, probably 1818 (watermarks on flyleaves dated 1817 and 1818)

St John's College, MS C.9 (James no. 59)

elaborate Litany and the series of Canticles. The saints mentioned in the Litany, such as Sixtus, Sinicius, Remigius, Nivardus, Simdulfus, Theodulf and Cilinia suggest a Reims connection. Further, the manuscript can be dated precisely thanks to the inclusion of Pope Marinus (882–884), Fulco, Archbishop of Reims (883–900), and Carloman, King of the West Franks (882–884) in the Litany of those living to be prayed for. The highlighted invocation to Remigius in the Litany reinforces the book's association with the Diocese of Reims. Count Achadeus was also mentioned by Flodoard, the tenth-century historian of Reims.

The manuscript might have been brought to England as early as 887 by Grimbald of the monastery of St Bertin in the Diocese of Reims, who came to King Alfred's court. This seems rather soon after it was produced. There is no indication as to how the manuscript might have come into Grimbald's possession, or whether he subsequently presented it to Canterbury. The full-page initial B, added as a frontispiece in the early thirteenth century, has animals hiding among foliage and portrait busts of King David and his musicians.

PROVENANCE: Count Achadeus; fragments of fourteenth- and fifteenth-century Canterbury account rolls in the binding indicate that the book had reached Christ Church Canterbury by then; Matthew Parker (1504–1575); his bequest, 1575.

EXHIBITED: Cambridge 1975, no. 4.

LITERATURE: Flodoard 1886, 546; Frere 1894–1932, no. 886; James 1912b, II, 27–32; Boutemy 1954–1955; Robinson 1988, no. 149, pl. 7; Keynes and Lapidge 1983, 214 n. 26.

RMCK

THROUGHOUT THE MONASTERIES of medieval Europe the 150 Psalms were sung as part of the monastic office and the text was also used for private devotion and teaching. A number of commentaries on the Psalms were produced in order to explain and interpret the text, not least those sections of it thought to be prophetic statements about the Life and Passion of Christ. Many Psalters were illustrated with exegetical pictures in order to enhance the Christian interpretations, and many were richly ornamented. This particular example was clearly a book used in the liturgy. Its text is the Gallican version (Jerome's second revision of the Latin text of the Psalms). Not only is the text divided into the customary three parts of fifty Psalms each, but each Psalm has its verses divided neatly into sections, with two or three sections per Psalm. Each Psalm begins with a four- or five-line initial with animal head finials and red dot surrounds. The body of the letter is filled with fine interlace of either the 'ribbon animal' or 'knotted wire' type. The text is set out with *diminuendo* in the first line of the verse and each verse starts with an enlarged one and a half- or two-line initial filled with alternating colours of yellow and purple. A limited range of colours, red, yellow and two shades of purple, are used in the illuminations.

The book was also studied, judging from the explanatory marginal and interlinear glosses (perhaps taken from older books) and on-the-spot annotations both Latin and Old Irish, also written in Insular script. One of these, at the beginning of Psalm 51, provides a clue to the date of the manuscript for the annotator has noted 'Beltane today that is Wednesday'. Beltane (or 1st May) falling on a Wednesday in the late tenth century, as suggested by the characteristics of the half-uncial script of the manuscript, would date the manuscript to 989 or 995. A reader would also have been assisted in studying the text by the short *argumentum* or introduction put in

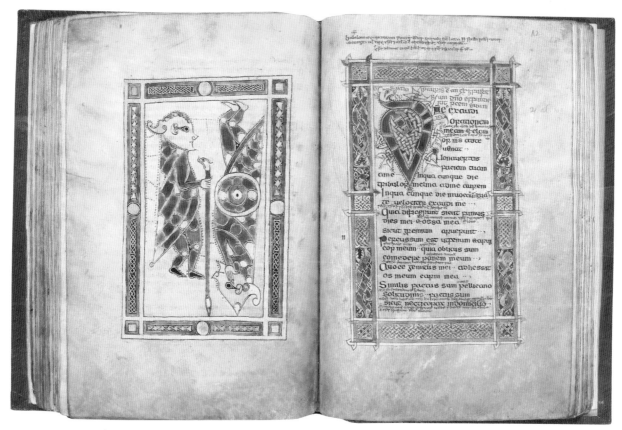

David fighting Goliath and Psalm 101 annotated in Irish. St John's College, MS C.9, fols. 68v–69

the margin beside each Psalm's opening initial. As is customary for Irish Psalters, each group of fifty Psalms is also followed by a special sequence of groups of prayers and Canticles, including the Canticles of Isaiah and Ezekiel, Anna, mother of Samuel, Mary, the sister of Moses, and Habbakuk.

A striking full-page image opens each group of fifty Psalms and decorated borders with interlace and serpent patterns embrace the initial letters *B*, *Q* and *D* respectively facing each picture. On fol. 4v David is represented as a shepherd and the *B* of *Beatus* at the beginning of Psalm 1 is rendered as a serpent. Fol. 38v depicts the Crucified Christ with three figures who most probably represent God the Father, Mary and John; flanking the Cross are Longinus with his spear and Stephaton with the reed and sponge. At the beginning of Psalm 101 is a picture of David fighting Goliath opposite the text page with the note about Beltane. The representations of human figures and animals are highly stylized and totally unlike anything produced in England during the tenth century. They resemble more closely contemporary Breton illuminations.

PROVENANCE: St Martin's Priory Dover; R. Benet (16th c.); William Crashaw; Henry Wriothesley; acquired by Thomas Wriothesley, 4th Earl of Southampton in 1635 and presented to the College.

EXHIBITED: London 1908, no. 3.

LITERATURE: James 1913, 76–78; Bannister 1910–1911; Henry 1960; Alexander 1978, 88; Kauffmann 2003, 106.   RMCK

17

Psalter (The Winchcombe Psalter)

In Latin and Old English
England, first half of the eleventh century

Parchment, iii (parchment, foliated 1–3) + 278 (foliated 4–281) + iii (parchment) fols., 273 × 160 mm, text 251 × 114 mm, 32 long lines, ruled in hard point.

SCRIPT: Anglo-Saxon minuscule

BINDING: gold-tooled calf over boards, 16th c.

Cambridge University Library, MS Ff.1.23

THIS IS THE MOST UNUSUAL of the nine surviving late Anglo-Saxon illuminated Psalters in which the Latin is accompanied by an Old English translation. The vernacular text, instead of being supplied in a smaller script as an interlinear gloss, is in the same scale of handwriting as the Latin (Latin and Old English being written on alternate lines), and is written in red. The general character of the handwriting and decoration is also without clear parallels in other manuscripts.

The *Romanum* found in this manuscript was the usual version of the Psalms in southern England until it was gradually supplanted by the *Gallicanum* during the later tenth and early eleventh centuries. In this copy, the

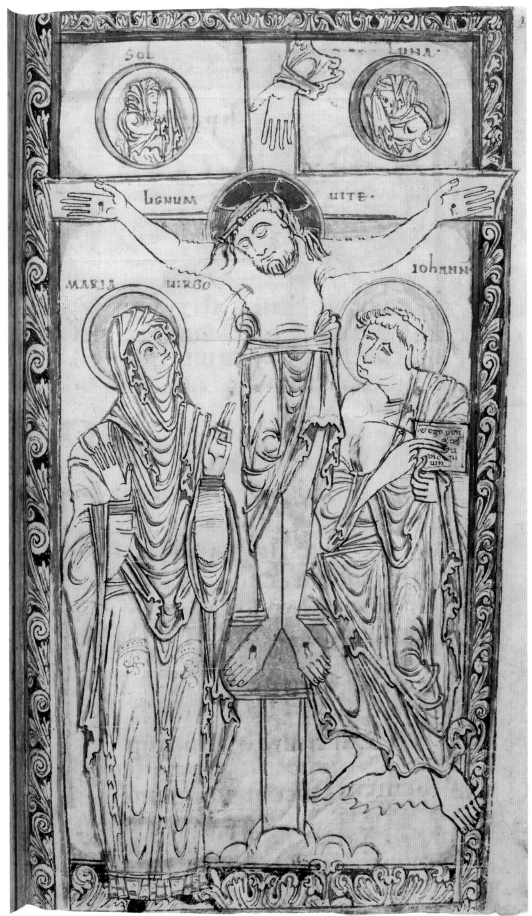

The Crucifixion.
Cambridge
University
Library, MS
Ff.1.23, fol. 88

Psalms are followed by the Canticles (all but the Apostles Creed in both Latin and Old English), a Litany and some twenty Latin prayers – typical accompaniments of the Psalms in late Anglo-Saxon Psalters. The 150 Psalms are presented as three groups of 50, each introduced with a full-page miniature (King David for Psalm 1, the Crucifixion for Psalm 51, and Christ in Majesty for Psalm 101), and a framed *incipit* page. A further division is likewise marked at Psalm 109, one of the eight-fold or 'liturgical' divisions of the Psalter, with a miniature depicting Christ triumphant over the dragon. Each of the remaining Psalms, Canticles and other texts begins with an ornamented initial.

The illustration and decoration, though copious, is not opulent, being drawn in a dark brownish outline, sometimes washed in brown and green with details supplied in green, orange and yellow. The iconography and much of the ornament is an eclectic mixture of Anglo-Saxon traditions, but some of the motifs display a similarity with Scandinavian ornament to a degree otherwise unprecedented in late Anglo-Saxon illumination. Scholars disagree, however, as to how such evidence should be interpreted.

The manuscript is written in one large and ungainly hand; the display script is especially clumsy. The scribe at first attempted to write the Latin text in Caroline minuscule, and the vernacular in Anglo-Saxon minuscule—a distinction that became the norm in the early eleventh century. However, by fol. 6v he had ceased to do so, and throughout the remainder of the book employed Insular forms even when writing the Latin. In a manuscript written in an established centre of book production, such as Christ Church or St Augustine's Canterbury, such inconsistency would indicate a date not much later than the beginning of the eleventh century, but the handwriting and other features of the book are so anomalous as perhaps to render it unwise to attempt to date and classify the script according to the norms of the known major centres of production.

Textual evidence for the place and date of origin is equally problematic. The Old English gloss is very closely related to that in the Vespasian Psalter (London, British Library, Cotton MS Vespasian A.1), at St Augustine's Canterbury by the eleventh century, but it is not yet clear whether it was copied directly or at one stage removed. The Litany (fols. 274–76) had appeared to offer more conclusive evidence. The prominence accorded St Kenelm in the Litany had been considered evidence that the book was made for Winchcombe Abbey (Gloucestershire), whilst the naming of St Martial as Apostle was believed to indicate a date after 1029. Doubt has been cast on both pieces of evidence. Lapidge uses the combined evidence of Kenelm and other saints commemorated in the Litany to argue that this text was compiled at Ramsey under the influence of Germanus, first Abbot of Winchcombe, who, after being driven into exile at Fleury, went to the Fenland abbey of Ramsey *c*.992. This, however, may only point to the source of the text of the Litany, not to the place of origin of the manuscript itself. Toswell, in her recent review of the manuscript and documentary evidence, suggests that a *terminus ante quem non* of 1029 cannot be assumed, since Martial was sometimes termed Apostle before the Bishop of Limoges officially proclaimed him as such in 1029.

PROVENANCE: given by Archbishop Matthew Parker to Sir Nicholas Bacon, who presented it to the Library in 1574.

EXHIBITED: London 1984a, no. 64.

LITERATURE: University Library 1856–1867, II, 312–13; Ker 1957, 11–12; Temple 1976, no. 80; Fuglesang 1980, 70–72; Robinson 1988, no. 29, pl. 17; Dumville 1991–1995, 40–41; Lapidge 1992; Toswell 1997; Gneuss 2001, no. 4.

TW

18

Psalter

In Latin
England, late tenth or early eleventh century

Parchment, i (paper) + iii (parchment) + 140 + vi (parchment) + i (paper) fols., 210 × 148 mm, text 152 × 88 mm, 23 long lines, ruled in hard point

SCRIPT: Caroline minuscule

BINDING: Parchment over pasteboards, 18th c.

Corpus Christi College, MS 411

Like UNIVERSITY LIBRARY MS Ff.1.23 *(no. 17)*, the Psalms in this book are accompanied by the Canticles, Prayers and a Litany, but in all other respects it represents a marked contrast to the Anglo-Saxon traditions of text, script and decoration reflected in Ff.1.23. It contains, instead, the *Gallicanum* version, widely used on the Continent from the Carolingian period, but only introduced to southern England during the later tenth century. It is written in Caroline rather than Anglo-Saxon minuscule. Indeed, both its script and decoration follow ninth- and early tenth-century Continental traditions so closely that it was once thought to have been produced on the Continent. It is now generally agreed to be the work of an English scribe, whose style of script was very closely modelled on a variety of Continental Caroline minuscule. Bishop, moreover,

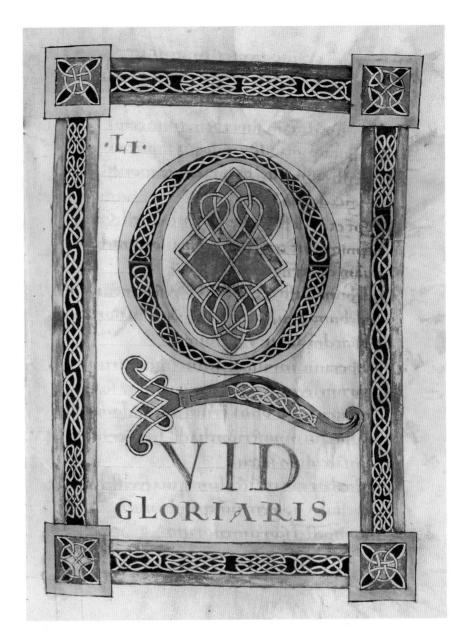

Ornamental initial to Psalm 51. Corpus Christi College, MS 411, fol. 40

identified his hand in a late tenth- or early eleventh-century glossed copy of Boethius's *Consolations of Philosophy* (Cambridge, Corpus Christi College, MS 214). The ornament of the framed display pages that introduce Psalms 1, 51 and 101, and the decorated initials of the *incipits* to Psalms 51 and 101 are likewise unusually close imitations of the Continental Franco-Saxon style, lacking any obvious English influence.

The contents offer few clues to the book's origin or first owners. A prayer to all confessors names Pope Gregory and Augustine (of Canterbury), but this, on its own, is insufficient evidence to prove a Canterbury origin. An added second Litany, written in a much more obviously English Caroline minuscule, gives prominence to Saints Benedict, Peter, Vincent, Eustacius and companions. The Benedictine abbey of Abingdon is known to have possessed relics of Vincent and Eustacius, but may not have been the only house to have commemorated these saints. A pen-drawn figure of a man standing holding a book was added on fol. 1v, but the hand of the artist has not been identified elsewhere. The book was certainly at Christ Church, Canterbury by the early twelfth century, but twelfth-century provenance is not always a reliable guide to earlier Anglo-Saxon origin.

PROVENANCE: Christ Church, Canterbury, early twelfth century (additions); Matthew Parker (1504–1575); a note in his hand records a tradition of ownership by Archbishops of Canterbury, including Thomas Becket, and a former binding with silver-gilt plaques and gems, but not listed as one of Becket's books in Prior Eastry's early fourteenth-century catalogue of Christ Church books (some of Parker's other attributions can be shown to be implausible); his bequest, 1575.

LITERATURE: James 1912b, II, 296–98; Bishop 1954–1958, 187; Temple 1976, no. 40; Dumville 1992, 151; Lapidge 1991, 65–66, 120–24; Budny 1997, no. 22; Gneuss 2001, no. 106.

TW

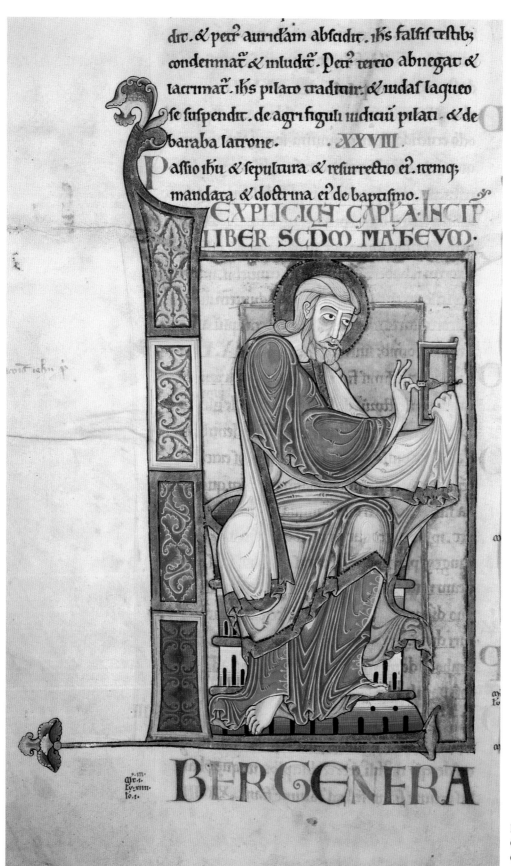

dir. & petr' auriclam abscidit. ihs falsis testib;
condempnat & mludit. Petr' tercio abnegat &
lacrimat. ihs pilato traditur. & iudas laqueo
se suspendit. de agri figuli iudicii pilati. & de
baraba latrone.   XXVIII
Passio ihu & sepultura & resurrectio ei. itemq;
mandata & doctrina ei de baptismo.
EXPLICIT CAP'LA. INCIP
LIBER SCDM MATHEVM.

BERGENERA

Fig. 17. St Matthew.
Corpus Christi
College, MS 4,
fol. 169v, detail

2

THE BIBLE AND ITS STUDY:
FROM THE CLOISTERS TO THE UNIVERSITY

Teresa Webber

'For what page or what utterance of the divinely-inspired books of the Old and the New Testament is not a most unerring rule of human life? Or what book of the holy Catholic Fathers is not manifestly devoted to teaching us the straight road to our Creator?'

THE CONCLUDING CHAPTER of the Rule of St Benedict takes as its main theme the centrality of the Bible to the monastic life, and the importance of the Fathers of the Church as its orthodox interpreters (McCann 1952, chapter 73). At the universities, especially Paris and Oxford, study of the sacred page (*sacra pagina*) marked the final stage of study; for those wishing to become masters of theology, lectures on Scripture were an essential requirement. The Bible was, without qualification, 'the most studied book of the middle ages' (Smalley 1983, xxvii). It was not surprisingly the most copied, though by no means always produced in its entirety. Until the thirteenth century, it was read and studied less from copies of the complete text than from volumes containing a single book or group of related books. This was true not only of the Gospels and the Psalms, the texts read most frequently as part of the cycle of readings of the Mass and the Office, but of the other books as well (McGurk 1994; Marsden 1994; de Hamel 2001). Biblical manuscripts display great diversity in their size and the visual presentation of the text, reflecting differences in use as well as the historical contexts within which they were produced (Martin and Vezin 1990, 57–111; Gameson 1994; de Hamel 2001).

All study of the Bible during the Middle Ages, whether by monks, clerics or friars, was underpinned by a familiarity with the Scriptures gained aurally from their regular repetition as part of the liturgy and also, within monastic communities, from public reading in the refectory. Within Benedictine houses, for example, the book of Psalms was recited each week, while readings from the rest of the Bible followed an annual cycle (Guarda 1986; Chadd 2002, 674–85; Grémont 1971). It is appropriate, therefore, to begin this brief survey of the Bible and its study with manuscripts intended in the first instance for communal use and public delivery rather than private study.

Gospel Books are by far the best surviving category of biblical manuscript from before the twelfth century. No doubt because of their role in the celebration of the Mass, they were accorded an especially high status by their owners, a status reflected in the unusual level of embellishment of the text compared with other types of book, sometimes further enhanced with a sumptuous binding made from precious metals and jewels. A mid-twelfth-century inventory from Ely, for example, lists some eighteen Gospel Books with precious bindings (Blake 1962, 290–91). In early medieval Insular Gospel Books, such as Corpus Christi College, MS 197B *(no. 2)* the beginning of each Gospel is typically marked with a full-page miniature depicting the Evangelist's symbol (for example, the eagle of St John), followed by an elaborated *incipit* page comprising large ornamental initials or monograms, accompanied by display lettering for the remainder of the first few words of the text. In eleventh-century Gospel Books *(e.g. nos. 8, 9, 10)*, the full-page miniature commonly takes the form of an Evangelist portrait, and the display script of the *incipit* page is often in gold. It was usual for the Gospel texts to be preceded by pages containing canon tables, listing the concordant passages found in two or more of the Gospels, arranged as columns set within arcades, which provided further opportunities for elaborate decoration. These features are also found in Gospel Lectionaries – manuscripts that contain only the Gospel readings for the Mass, arranged according to the liturgical cycle, or in their order of appearance in the full text, as in Pembroke College, MS 302 *(no. 43)*.

The other biblical text that enjoyed special prominence was the book of Psalms. It not only provided the bulk of the texts for the monastic offices but was also used for private devotion and study. In early medieval Psalters, decorative or pictorial embellishment was employed primarily to indicate the various major divisions into which the Psalms fell, most commonly the formal three-fold division at Psalms 1, 51 and 101. A more elaborate eight-fold, or 'liturgical' division (at Psalms 1, 26, 38, 52, 68, 80, 97, 109: seven for the days of the week, and an eighth forming a separate series for Vespers), became popular in England, for example, after the Norman Conquest. Each division might be introduced with a large ornamental initial and display script *(no. 18)* or, additionally, with a pictorial image. In a late Anglo-Saxon Psalter *(no. 17)*, full-page miniatures introduce each of the three-fold divisions, and depict King David (Psalm 1), the Crucifixion (Psalm 51), and Christ in Majesty (Psalm 101), with a further miniature of Christ trampling the beasts and spearing the dragon with his cross prefacing Psalm 109: 'The Lord said unto my Lord, sit thou at my right hand until I make thine enemies my footstool'. During the twelfth century, it became more common for the divisions other than Psalm 1 to be marked with historiated initials in place of *incipit* pages and full-page minia-tures, but a prefatory set of miniatures might precede the Psalms as a whole, such as those which probably once formed part of the Eadwine Psalter *(no. 25)*, and perhaps those now bound with a New Testament in Pembroke College *(no. 20)*. Throughout the twelfth and thirteenth centuries these typically depict scenes from the Old and New Testament *(e.g. nos. 69, 74)*, and, like the miniatures in the Winch-combe Psalter, were intended primarily to emphasize the Christological significance of the Psalms, interpreted typologically as prefiguring Christ and the Church.

Complete Bibles are a rarity during the early Middle Ages, with the exception of the Carolingian period, when they were copied in some profusion, most notably at the Abbey of Tours, whose scribes are estimated to have produced two single-volume Bibles a year over the course of the first half of the ninth century (Ganz 1994). The later eleventh century saw a revival in the production of complete Bibles, stimulated by new movements of monastic and clerical reform (Cahn 1982). The earliest of these Bibles are closely associated with bishops and cathedral communities. In England, for example, William of Saint-Calais (d.1096) gave a splendid two-volume Bible to his community at Durham (the second volume survives as Durham, Cathedral Library, MS A.II.4). Two-volume Bibles of about this date also survive from Lincoln Cathedral (Lincoln, Cathedral Library, MS 1 and Cambridge, Trinity College, MS B.5.2) and Rochester Cathedral Priory (San Marino, Huntington Library, MS HM 62), the latter associated with Bishop Gundulf (d.1108). By the middle decades of the twelfth century the major monastic communities had also acquired large-format Bibles. These stately volumes would appear to have supplanted Gospel Books as visually the most impressive category of illuminated manuscript during the twelfth century, and they provide us with some of the finest examples of Romanesque art. One of the most outstanding is the Bury Bible *(no. 19)*, commissioned according to the thirteenth-century *Gesta sacristarum* by the sacrist, Herveus, which is embellished not only with historiated initials and display scripts, but also with magnificent full-page miniatures acting as frontispieces to several of the books. Less opulent, but also a masterpiece of twelfth-century book production in its harmony of script and hierarchy of initials and display scripts, is the Dover Bible *(no. 21)*, produced at Christ Church, Canterbury in the mid-twelfth century. These massive volumes affirmed the centrality of biblical study to the monastic life, and were also impressive symbols of the prestige and wealth of the community to which they belonged.

The size of these volumes strongly suggests that they were made for public reading from a lectern in the church or refectory. Alcuin, who prepared the text disseminated in the ninth-century Tours Bibles, certainly intended them to be used liturgically (Ganz 1994, 55–6). Some of the later Tours Bibles employed the tiny 'capitular' minuscule of the chapter lists (*capitula*) for the texts of the Gospels and the Psalms as well, presumably because for these books a Gospel Book or Psalter would be used instead (Ganz 1994, 59). This is a feature also of the late-eleventh-century Gundulf Bible from Rochester (de Hamel 2001, 75). A liturgical function is also suggested by the Dover Bible, the first volume of which opens with a detailed list of the annual cycle of biblical readings. But we should not rule out the possibility that these books were also consulted for scholarly purposes. Other manuscripts designed for liturgical use can also be shown to have had a dual function as books for personal, scholarly scrutiny as well, such as the Southampton Psalter *(no. 16)*, produced in Ireland in the late ninth century, which contains an apparatus of marginal and interlinear glosses, and a short explanatory *argumentum* beside the opening initial to each gloss, and contains added notes indicative of private study. But it is perhaps inappropriate, especially within a monastic context, to draw too sharp a distinction between liturgy and study. One exceptional manuscript can be used to exemplify the fundamental unity of purpose that underlay the different ways in which the word of God was heard and read: the remarkable Eadwine Psalter *(no. 25)*, produced at Christ Church, Canterbury at about the same time as the Dover Bible. It contains within one volume all three Latin versions of the Psalms, accompanied by not only the texts normally found within a liturgical Psalter (Calendar, Collects, Canticles, Lord's Prayer and Creeds) but also the standard Latin scholarly apparatus of the mid-twelfth century (the *parva glossatura*) as well as interlinear vernacular translations in Old English and Anglo-Norman French.

As St Benedict emphasized in his Rule, the true meaning of the Word of God as recorded in the Scriptures could not be apprehended without assistance. An orthodox understanding of both its literal sense and its layers of spiritual meaning could only be gained safely with the help of the authoritative teaching of the Fathers of the Church. It is no coincidence that the revival of the production of complete Bibles during the later eleventh and twelfth centuries was accompanied by an increase in the production of works of the Fathers, and especially those works that supported the study of Scripture. At the Norman Abbey of Fécamp, for example, the annual cycle of biblical readings delivered in the refectory at mealtimes included relevant passages from the commentaries of Augustine on St John's Gospel, of Jerome on Matthew and Mark, and Ambrose on Luke, and other patristic texts (Chadd 2002, 674–85; Grémont 1971). These public readings supplemented the monks' individual devotional reading, in particular the book assigned to each at the annual Lenten distribution, in fulfilment of the requirement of chapter 48 of the Rule. Some, perhaps many of these texts, had not previously been widely available, especially outside the major Carolingian communities. The speed at which they were replicated during the decades on either side of 1100, in England and elsewhere, is striking, and involved the circulation of exemplars between religious houses. In some instances, an exemplar and its copy still survive. Trinity College, MS O.4.7 *(no. 23)*, produced before *c.*1123 at Rochester Cathedral Priory, was copied from a book made just a few years earlier at nearby Christ Church, Canterbury (Trinity College, MS B.2.34). Both manuscripts contain a collection of shorter works on the Old Testament by Jerome, who was the principal guide to the philological interpretation of the Old Testament, with its myriad of unfamiliar Hebrew names and terms. The principal mode of biblical exegesis during this period, however, was allegorical rather than literal, in particular concerning the Christological and ecclesiological significance of the books of the Old Testament. This interpretation was sometimes given pictorial form in the historiated initials found in some of the more heavily embellished manuscripts. An elaborate example is the superb historiated initial that opens the beginning of Bede's commentary on the Song of Songs *(no. 24)*, which depicts the bridegroom and bride, interpreted typologically by Bede as Christ and his Church. On the whole, however, these manuscripts are not lavishly decorated. Major initials are more usually ornamental, and form part of a hierarchy of display script to articulate the major divisions. Most of these initials comprise purely foliate forms, as for example, at the opening of Book 2 of Bede's commentary on the Song of Songs in the same manuscript *(fig. 18)*. Some initials incorporate human or animal figures, as in the terminals of the foliage spirals of the initial F at the beginning of the second book of Gregory the Great's *Dialogues (fig. 19)*, and, on an appropriately grander scale, in the initial at the very beginning of the same manuscript *(no. 22)*.

From the late eleventh century, scholars began to congregate at some of the cathedral schools of northern France to hear masters who had become renowned for lecturing on the Bible. These early centres of biblical study were ephemeral, lasting only as long as the master or masters who had made them famous. But during the second quarter of the twelfth century, the rapidly growing city of Paris emerged as a place where a concentration of such masters might be found, as well as other resources for study at the numerous religious houses within and on the outskirts of the city, such as the Augustinian Abbey of Saint-Victor. It was the schools at Paris that popularized a new reference tool for the study of the Bible, the *Glossa ordinaria*, in which the biblical text was written in a narrow column, with commentary drawn largely from the inherited wisdom of the Fathers and the early medieval commentators, written in smaller script as glosses in the margins and between the lines. Like the content, the presentation of the text in such a form was not new – there were Carolingian prototypes – but the existence of a standard

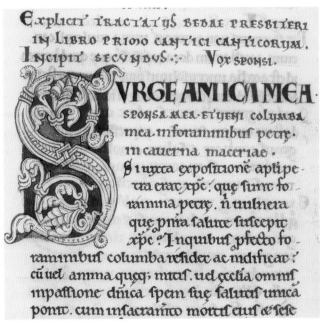

Fig. 18. Ornamental initial. Cambridge, King's College, MS 19, fol. 54v, detail

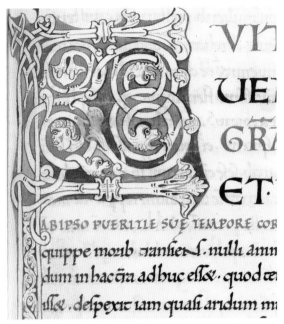

Fig. 19. Ornamental initial. Cambridge, Clare College, MS N1.1.8 (James no. 30), fol. 22, detail

reference tool of the entire Bible, in volumes of single books or groups of books, was unprecedented (de Hamel 1984; Gibson 1989; Gibson 1994). Some glossed books of the Bible are associated with the names of individual scholars, but large sets were only affordable under the patronage of religious communities and wealthy ecclesiastics. The presence within monastic libraries of glossed books of the Bible and other works emanating from the schools reminds us that the world of the cloister was not cut off from that of the emergent universities (see, for example, the magnificent glossed books acquired by St Albans, *nos. 24 and 27*). It became a requirement for larger religious houses to send monks to the universities, which formalized channels through which new tools for the study of the Bible came to supplement or supplant the volumes of glossed books upon the shelves of monastic book-cupboards. Chief among these were the *Postillae in totam Bibliam* of the Dominican Hugh of Saint-Cher (d.1263), a digest of patristic and early medieval teaching supplemented by that of twelfth- and thirteenth-century masters. In its turn, it was later supplemented by the *Postillae literalis in Vetus et Novum Testamentum* of the Franciscan, Nicholas of Lyra (d.1340), a superb copy of which was made for St Albans Abbey in the mid-fifteenth century *(no. 37)*.

The small-format, chunky, single-volume Bible that we are familiar with today, was a northern French creation of the late twelfth and early thirteenth centuries. Biblical scholars at Paris, like Peter the Chanter (d.1197) and Stephen Langton (d.1228), concerned themselves with various aspects of the biblical text, such as variant readings, and a more standardized system of chapter divisions and numbers (Smalley 1983, 214–224; Light 1984; Light 1994). It was, however, the new orders of mendicant friars who were responsible for the widespread production and diffusion of quantities of portable one-volume Bibles, written in a tiny script, with a more-or-less standard order of books, their divisions articulated with a hierarchy of historiated or ornamental initials, pen-flourished and plain one-line initials alternating in red and blue, and running titles (de Hamel 2001, 114–39). The itinerant character of the friars' practice of the religious life, and their role as preachers, teachers and confessors, required portable personal collections of the authoritative writings of the orthodox faith, and, above all, the Bible, together with new tools to aid rapid reference of these texts, such as concordances and *tabulae*. By the mid-thirteenth century, Bibles of very similar contents and design were being produced by specialist, professional craftsmen in Paris, Bologna (the locations of the two largest Dominican houses in Europe), and Oxford. Other religious and clergy also came to acquire these Bibles. The exhibited volumes *(nos. 29, 30, 31, 32, and 33)* are all rather larger than most thirteenth-century portable Bibles, and appear to have been made deliberately on a more lavish scale. Two of these *(nos. 29 and 31)* were made for Carthusian communities, and are marked up according to the annual cycle of monastic readings.

Lay princes and leading members of the aristocracy of the early Middle Ages had been owners and commissioners of Psalters and other liturgical and devotional volumes *(no. 15)*, a practice which increased during the later Middle Ages with the growing incidence of lay literacy *(nos. 71, 72, 74, 77, 79)*. In England, during the thirteenth century, the Apocalypse, with its strange visions of St John the Divine, came to rival the Psalms as a text suitable for treatment as luxury books. Illustrated Apocalypses, in Latin or French, often accompanied by a commentary, also either in Latin or French, are among the most splendid English illuminated manuscripts from the mid-thirteenth to the mid-fourteenth centuries *(nos. 40 and 41)*. The Trinity Apocalypse *(no. 40)*, dating from the 1250s is an outstanding example, made perhaps for a royal or aristocratic laywoman. Scribes and artists from the thirteenth century onwards also presented the substance of the Old and New Testaments in new ways with the needs of the laity in mind, such as the sumptuously illustrated *Bible moralisée*, the *Biblia pauperum*, and the *Speculum humanae salvationis (no. 36)*, a versified rendering of extracts from the Old Testament in one column with their New Testament parallels in an adjacent column, each pair of passages introduced with an illustration (de Hamel 2001, 140–65). These were luxury books, however, affordable only by the wealthy. For the most part, the Bible and its study remained the preserve of religious and scholars throughout the manuscript age.

19

The Bury Bible

In Latin

England, Bury St Edmunds, *c.*1130–*c.*1135

ARTIST: Master Hugo (act. *c.*1130–*c.*1160)

Parchment, divided since 1912 into 3 volumes, iii (modern paper) + 121 +iii (modern paper) fols.; iii (modern paper) + 120 (foliated 122–241) + iii (modern paper) fols.; iii (modern paper) + 116 (foliated 242–357) + iii (modern paper) fols.; 524 × 350 mm, text 382 × 235 mm, 2 columns, 42 lines, ruled vertically in hard point and horizontally in plummet

SCRIPT: Gothic bookhand (textualis)

BINDING: blind-tooled blue morocco, British Museum bindery, 1956

Corpus Christi College, MS 2, part I

THIS VAST BOOK is one of the noblest and most sublime of all English Romanesque manuscripts. It is also one of the best documented, for we know the name of the illuminator, Master Hugo, the earliest English professional artist whose work is extant and whose identity is independently documented. However, like the ruins of Bury Abbey itself, the manuscript is a fragment of what it once was. Only the first volume survives, doubtless of two, with text from Genesis to Job. Even in this portion six of the twelve illustrations once present are lost, peeled away or cut out before the manuscript was acquired by Matthew Parker.

The Benedictine abbey at Bury St Edmunds was a relatively minor late Anglo-Saxon foundation, which benefited enormously from the Norman Conquest. By the time of Domesday Book it was the fourth richest monastery in England. A series of able administrators culminated in Anselm, Abbot 1121–1148, a nephew of his namesake St Anselm of Canterbury (1033–1109) and

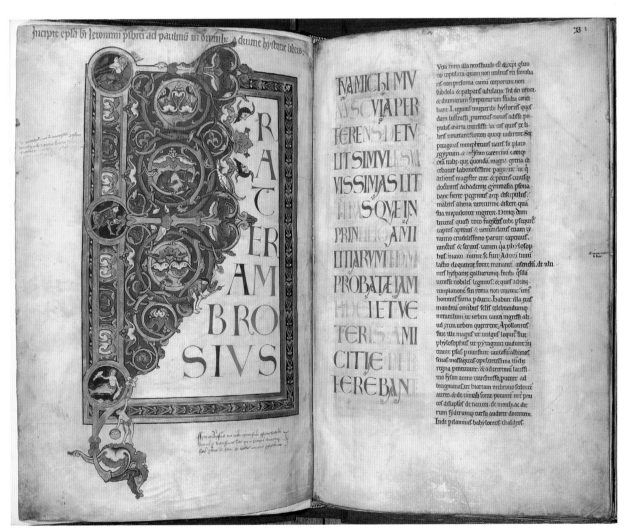

Jerome's Prologue. Corpus Christi College, MS 2, part I, fols. IV–2

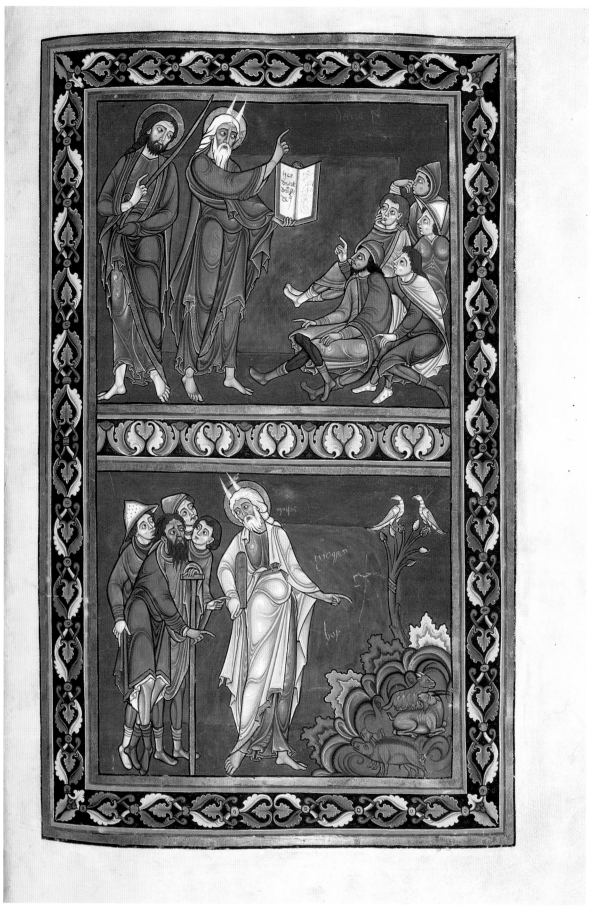

Moses. Corpus Christi College, MS 2, part 1, fol. 94

previously abbot at Saints Alexius and Sabas in Rome. In his time Bury St Edmunds set about acquiring fine copies of the great books of religion and scholarship. Giant monumental Bibles were a new Italian fashion, initiated in Italy by the reforms of Gregory VII (Pope 1073–1085). The full-page opening initial of the Bury Bible, unique in England, has parallels with Roman giant Bibles of the late eleventh century. Abbot Anselm might have brought an exemplar from Rome.

However, the Bible was not commissioned by the abbot but by the sacrist. The monastery's thirteenth-century *Gesta Sacristarum* records that Herveus, brother of Prior Talbot (in office *c.*1125–*c.*1136), found the money for a great Bible and had it incomparably painted by Master Hugo, and that as suitable calf skins were not to be found locally, they acquired parchment in Scotland. This unusual observation about the parchment is probably reflected in the fact that all six large paintings and sixteen of the illuminated initials are on separate pieces of parchment pasted into place. There must have been some difference in the quality which made it more suitable for decoration. Master Hugo was clearly a multi-talented craftsman, for he also appears in the records as having executed for the abbey a great bell in the crossing tower, a set of decorated metal church doors probably in bronze, which were still there in 1535, and, in the time of Abbot Ording, 1148–1156, a beautiful cross for the abbey choir. The word 'incomparable' is used several times. Clearly the monks thought a great deal of him and preserved his name for centuries.

To judge from his title 'Master', Hugo was not a monk. He may have been English, although 'Hugo' is not an Anglo-Saxon name, and he was clearly familiar with English book illumination of the early twelfth century. He was doubtless one of those fascinating, shadowy, Romanesque professional artists who moved from place to place seeking work. The magnificent colour patterns of his paintings and the startlingly new Byzantine draperies and deep staring eyes all suggest that he had travelled at least to southern Italy and probably to Cyprus, Byzantium or the Holy Land. Perhaps he had been involved with the English occupation of the Latin Kingdom of Jerusalem. His illustration of Moses and Aaron with the Jews, fol. 94, shows two dark-skinned North Africans painted with a realism which suggests direct experience.

The Bible is the only work securely attributed to Hugo. There are ingenious attempts, depending on a cumulation of coincidences (every one of which is individually possible but scarcely credible in total), to argue that the magnificent ivory cross in the Metropolitan Museum of Art in New York (Metropolitan Museum, Cloisters Collection, 63.12), might actually be the cross made by Hugo for the choir at Bury. Perhaps more likely

is Thomson's suggestion that Hugo later executed the fresco of Saint Paul and the viper in St Anselm's chapel in Canterbury Cathedral, *c.*1160.

The Bible was probably intended for the refectory at Bury, or was moved there when a new Bible was acquired under Abbot Hugh II (1215–1229). It has the Bury pressmark 'B.1' ('B' is for *Biblia*). It is unlikely to have been acquired by Matthew Parker directly from Bury, which was not one of his sources. A tiny fragment of the lost second volume recently emerged in a collection of mainly Oxford book-binders' waste, which suggests that the Bible was starting to be dismembered in the trade in the sixteenth century.

PROVENANCE: Bury St Edmunds Abbey; Matthew Parker (1504–1575); his bequest, 1575.

EXHIBITED: Cambridge 1975, nos. 10–11; London 1984b, no. 44.

LITERATURE: James 1912b, I, 3–8; Kauffmann 1975, no. 56; Cahn 1982, 160–64; Robinson, 1988, no. 199, pls. 45, 46; Parker and Little 1994; Kauffmann 1996; Thomson 2001; de Hamel 2001, 78–84; Kauffmann 2003, 89–104, figs. 64–66, 68, 71–73; Bloomfield-Smith 2004.

C DE H

20

Narrative picture cycle of the Ministry and Passion of Christ; New Testament

In Latin
England, probably Bury St Edmunds, *c.*1125–*c.*1150; England, mid-twelfth century

Parchment, (Part I) 6 + (Part II) 175 (foliated 7–182) fols., 410 × 270 mm, Part I framed area 330 × 213 mm, Part II text 302 × 185 mm, 2 columns, 35 lines, ruled in crayon
SCRIPT: late Caroline minuscule/early Gothic bookhand (textualis)
BINDING: light brown leather over boards, 20th c., medieval pastedowns

Pembroke College, MS 120

THIS VOLUME is a composite of elements drawn from two originally separate manuscripts, one perhaps made at Bury St Edmunds, the other given to Bury in the fourteenth century.

Part I comprises six leaves bearing a cycle of thirty-nine outline drawings of scenes from the New Testament, drawn by an artist whose style derives closely from that of the Alexis Master, the artist of the St Albans Psalter

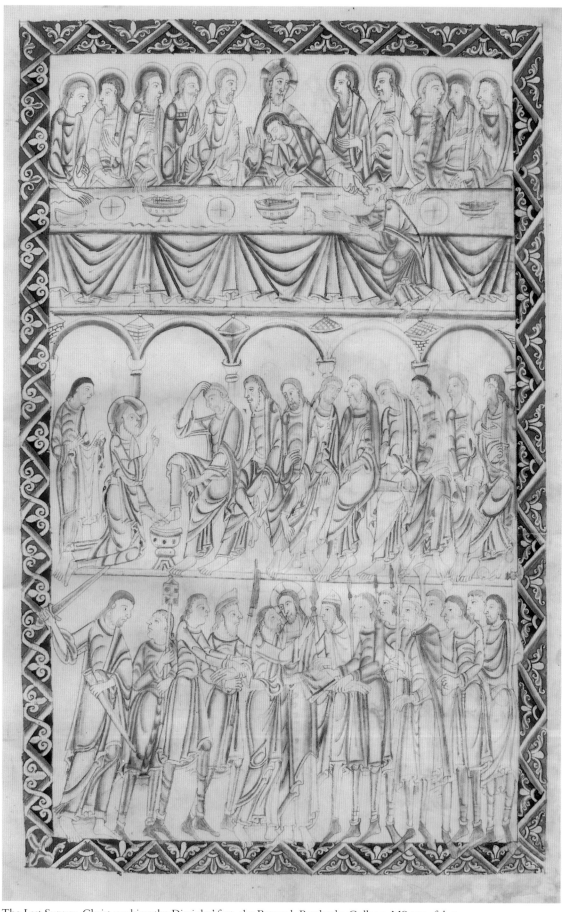

The Last Supper, Christ washing the Disciples' feet, the Betrayal. Pembroke College, MS 120, fol. 3

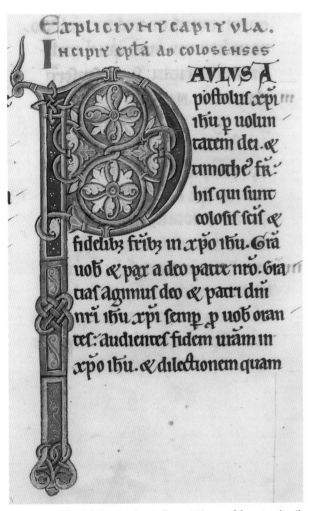

Ornamental initial. Pembroke College, MS 120, fol. 158v, detail

(Hildesheim, Pfarrbibliothek, St Godehard, MS 1) and other St Albans books (e.g. *no. 24*), whose work has been shown to have been of fundamental importance for the diffusion of a new style of Romanesque art in England. A Bury origin for the leaves has been suggested since the style of the Alexis Master was known at Bury: a very close follower illustrated a Life of St Edmund (New York, Pierpont Morgan Library, M. 736), presumably at Bury, since the text is in the hand of a Bury scribe. The under-drawings of the Life may have been the work of the Alexis Master himself. Furthermore, the first three leaves were subsequently tinted by another less competent artist, whose colouring in the borders may reflect the influence of the Bury Bible, certainly produced at and for the abbey *(no. 19)*.

The iconography corresponds in many respects to the cycle of pictures that prefaces the St Albans Psalter, and the more extensive cycle that once prefaced the Eadwine Psalter *(no. 25)*. Some of the iconography, however, is more unusual, and displays a close relationship with

Ottonian picture traditions, most especially those in eleventh-century manuscripts from Echternach, near Trier (an influence also detectable, though to a lesser extent, in the Eadwine picture cycle).

The leaves probably once formed, or were intended to form, part of a larger manuscript, but it is unclear what type of book this might have been. Surviving manuscripts suggest that biblical picture cycles normally accompanied Psalters, yet the proportions of the Bury leaves are much larger than those of twelfth-century Psalters (apart from the Eadwine Psalter which is exceptional), and are more typical of the large format Romanesque Bibles, such as the Bury and Dover Bibles *(no. 19 and 21)*. The absence of any Old Testament scenes is also anomalous.

The second element is a copy of the New Testament, produced in the mid-twelfth century by a single expert scribe who identifies himself as William in a colophon on fol. 182v. Major divisions of the text are marked with initials in rich body-colour and gold; five are historiated and the remainder ornamented with tight foliage spirals, monsters, birds and human figures. A second level of textual division is indicated with flat-colour 'arabesque' initials. The script is unlike that of the numerous surviving books produced at Bury St Edmunds during the mid-twelfth century, neither do the arabesque initials contain any of the motifs typical of Bury decoration of this date. It is especially notable for the iconography of its Evangelist portraits, in particular that of Mark, which E. Parker McLachlan believes to be unique in manuscript art of the twelfth century and earlier in depicting him as a tetramorph. His lion-symbol surmounts a seated human body with three further heads comprising the symbols of the other three Evangelists. The figure is shown turning to his left and cutting off his thumb, an act attributed to Mark in the prologue that accompanies the Gospel. Other aspects of the style and iconography of the major initials can be paralleled in English Romanesque manuscripts but without shedding light on a possible place of origin. It is assumed that this part of the manuscript only came to Bury in the four-teenth century, as the gift of the sacrist, Reginald of Denham.

PROVENANCE: Part II (fols. 7–182) given to Bury St Edmunds by Reginald of Denham, sacrist in the early fourteenth century (donation inscription, fol. 7); probably given to Pembroke College by Edmund Boldero, Master of Jesus College (1663–1679).

EXHIBITED: London 1984b, no. 21.

LITERATURE: James 1905a, 117–25; Parker 1969, 263–302; McLachlan 1975; Kauffmann 1975, no. 35; Kauffmann 2003, 122, 261.

TW

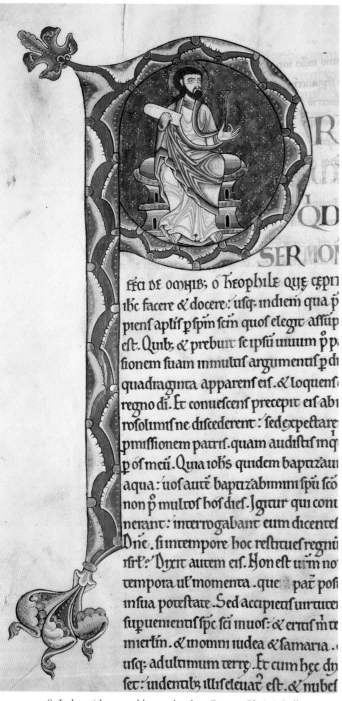

St Luke with wax tablets and stylus. Corpus Christi College,
MS 4, fol. 221v, detail

21

The Dover Bible

In Latin
England, Canterbury, Christ Church,
mid-twelfth century

Parchment, ii (paper) + 9 (parchment, 15th c.) + 274 (foliated
8–274) + ii (paper) fols., 534 × 355 mm, text 400 × 247 mm,
2 columns, 44 lines, ruled in crayon.
SCRIPT: late Caroline minuscule/early Gothic bookhand (textualis)
BINDING: brown leather over boards, 20th c.

Corpus Christi College, MS 4

ALTHOUGH LESS LAVISHLY ILLUSTRATED than some
of the large format Bibles produced in England and
elsewhere in Western Europe during the eleventh and
twelfth centuries (e.g. *no. 19*), the appearance of the two-
volume Dover Bible (Corpus Christi College, MSS 3–4)
– of which only Volume 1 is exhibited here – is truly
impressive. It is one of a small group of outstanding
manuscripts produced at Christ Church during the
middle decades of the twelfth century, of which the
most remarkable is the Eadwine Psalter *(no. 25)*.

The regularity and harmony of the handwriting of
these books is striking. During the mid-twelfth century,
scribes at Christ Church developed a style of handwriting very different from the rather angular variety of
Caroline minuscule cultivated in the late eleventh and
early twelfth centuries. It is upright, and generally large
(as befitted the status of the books for which it was used),
with a remarkable homogeneity even in minor details,
which makes identifying the hands of individual scribes
rather difficult. A smaller scale of the same script was
employed for the chapter lists. The features of handwriting in both volumes of the Dover Bible closely
correspond with those of the two main hands of the
Eadwine Psalter, and especially that of the scribe who
wrote the bulk of the volume. More detailed analysis,
however, is required to establish how many hands were
involved, and their possible identity with either of the
main scribes of the Eadwine Psalter.

The major textual divisions in both volumes are
marked with historiated or ornamented initials in full
body-colour, the only other major decoration being the
elaborately decorated Eusebian canon tables that precede
the Gospels. A different artist worked on each of the
volumes. The figure style of both reflects the influence
of contemporary Byzantine art, but certain aspects of the
facial features of the artist of this manuscript are highly
unusual, such as the staring eyes, heavy eyebrows, and

exaggerated curling moustaches. The iconography of some of his illustrations, such as the Judgement scene in the initial to Wisdom, is also unparalleled. His hand has also been identified in the Eadwine Psalter (the illustration to Psalm 4). The major initials form part of a well-developed hierarchy of initials and script, with secondary divisions indicated with flat-colour 'arabesque' initials, and a less elaborate scheme of display script being employed for their rubrics and opening words.

PROVENANCE: perhaps the 'Biblia Edwini', no. 322 in Prior Eastry's early fourteenth-century catalogue of the books of Christ Church, Canterbury, although not recorded as two volumes; by 1389 at Dover Priory, a cell of Christ Church: items 2 and 3 of section 'A:I' in John Whytefelde's catalogue; Matthew Parker (1504–1575); his bequest, 1575.

EXHIBITED: Cambridge 1975, nos. 12–13.

LITERATURE: James 1903, 51; James 1912b, I, 10–14; Dodwell 1954, 48, 57–59, 84–88, 92–94; Kauffmann 1975, no. 69; Stoneman 1999, 48; Kauffmann 2003. 77, 87; ills. 56, 63.

TW

22

Gregory the Great, *Dialogi*, etc.

In Latin
England, Worcester Cathedral Priory, last third of the eleventh century

Parchment, i (modern parchment) + 207 + i (modern parchment) fols., 327 × 220 mm, text 253–259 × 142–144 mm, 30 long lines, ruled in hard point

SCRIPT: Caroline minuscule

BINDING: white tawed skin over boards, 20th c.

Clare College, MS N1.1.8 (James no. 30)

Among the contents of this manuscript are two texts much read for spiritual and moral edification within early medieval monastic communities: the *Dialogues* of Gregory the Great, and the *Liber scintillarum* of the monk Defensor of Ligugé, an ascetic compilation of extracts mainly from the Bible and works of the Fathers. The book opens with the *Dialogues* which have been accorded a far more elaborate level of display than the other contents. Since the end of this text coincides with a quire boundary and also, perhaps, a change of scribe, it is possible that it may originally have formed an independent manuscript. Alternatively, the disparity in the level of decoration may reflect the especially high esteem in which the works of Gregory were held in Anglo-

Saxon England as the Pope who had sent Augustine as the apostle to the English. The *Dialogues* held particular significance for monastic communities since they provided the fullest account of the life of St Benedict. Their importance at Worcester, however, may have predated its reform as a monastic community in the late tenth century, since Asser, in his Life of King Alfred, attributes the Old English translation of the *Dialogues* to Werferth, Bishop of Worcester *c*.872 to 915. In general, eleventh- and early twelfth-century Worcester manuscripts are only modestly decorated; the impressive opening display page for the preface to the *Dialogues* is exceptional.

Worcester is one of the few English monastic houses for which fairly continuous manuscript production can be traced from the late tenth through to the twelfth

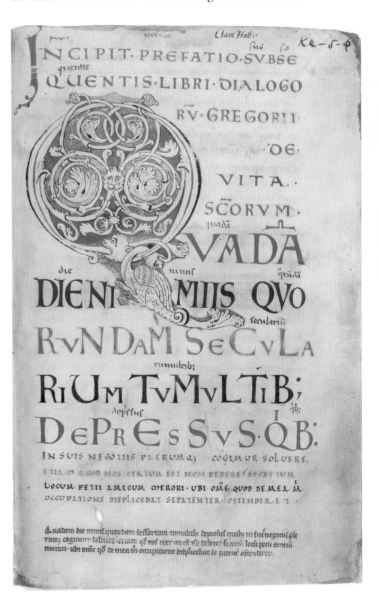

Ornamental initial. Clare College, MS N1.1.8, fol. 2

century. The books from the second half of the eleventh century are especially important for the evidence they provide of how traditions of handwriting and decoration evolved in a centre comparatively little affected by changes of personnel in the wake of the Norman Conquest. The scribe (or scribes) of this manuscript wrote a variety of English Caroline minuscule only slightly modified from that written at Worcester in the mid-eleventh century, but the major decorated initials to the preface and each book of the *Dialogues* display new motifs – dragons and spirals terminating in foliage or human and animal heads, motifs that are ubiquitous in Anglo-Norman and Norman books of the late eleventh and early twelfth centuries. Similar initials are found in other late-eleventh-century Worcester manuscripts. The minor initials are especially diagnostic of a Worcester origin, a number of them being decorated with the typically 'large and chunky' version of an otherwise widespread motif of a disc between two almost horizontal bars.

This manuscript may also bear witness to another work of art at Worcester in the twelfth century. On the originally blank first leaf of the first quire, a late-twelfth-century hand has added verses which M.R. James believed were intended to accompany an otherwise unattested set of pictures of the Book of Maccabees.

PROVENANCE: annotated at Worcester by the prolific early thirteenth-century annotator, 'the tremulous hand'; contemporary copies of thirteenth-century letters concerning the community at Worcester (fol. 1v); it is not known when the manuscript came to the College.

EXHIBITED: London 1984b, no. 10.

LITERATURE: James 1905b, 47–50; Kauffmann 1975, no. 4; Mason 1990, pls. 4–7; Gameson 1996, 223–26; Gullick 1996–1999, 89–91; Gameson 1999, nos. 50–51; Gneuss 2001, no. 34.

TW

23

Jerome, shorter works on the Old Testament

In Latin
England, Rochester Cathedral Priory, first quarter of the twelfth century

Parchment, i + 170 (fols 25, 169–170 replacement leaves, 13th c.) fols., 335 × 235 mm, text 230 × 150 mm, 2 columns, 32 lines, ruled in hard point.

SCRIPT: late Caroline minuscule

BINDING: alum tawed skin over wooden boards, 12th c.

Trinity College, MS O.4.7

ROCHESTER CATHEDRAL PRIORY, like several other religious houses in England, rapidly multiplied its holdings of patristic and other texts during the late eleventh and earlier twelfth century, in part by importing books but also by producing the books in-house. This endeavour required not only the relevant scribal and other skills but also the provision of exemplars. Exemplars of texts that had previously not been widely available, if at all, in England, were sometimes circulated between religious houses. The textual affiliations of the Rochester manuscripts indicate that they copied manuscripts from exemplars borrowed from various houses, but that Christ Church, Canterbury was a particularly important source.

Trinity MS O.4.7 is one such example, being a duplicate of a slightly earlier Christ Church manuscript, Cambridge, Trinity College, MS B.2.34. It contains a group of texts by (or attributed to) Jerome, which were regarded as an essential guide to the interpretation of the books of the Old Testament. It was written by one highly skilled scribe who played an important role within the Rochester scriptorium; his work includes the compilation of laws, charters and other texts, including a catalogue of the Rochester books, known as the *Textus Roffensis* (Rochester, Cathedral Library, MS A.3.5), probably datable to 1122–1123. A comparison of Trinity MS O.4.7 with its exemplar reveals how intelligent a copyist he was, improving the clarity and accuracy of the texts in various ways. For example, he introduced consistent conventions for word-division, orthography and use of *litterae notabiliores*, whilst a two- rather than single-column layout and numbered sections, with the first initial off-set in the margin, improved the legibility of the text and facilitated its use for reference purposes.

The major texts are introduced with pen-drawn initials incorporating foliate spirals, dragons, humans

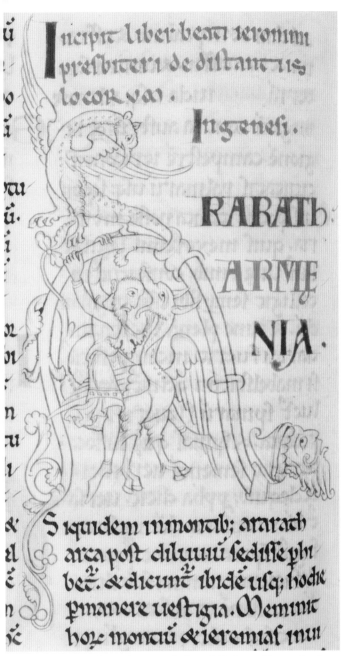

Ornamental initial. Trinity College, MS O.4.7, fol. 45v, detail

and animals in a manner typical of late eleventh and early twelfth-century Anglo-Norman books. Although only one of these (the initial to Jerome's *Quaestiones in librum regum*, fol. 112) is historiated, the images in at least one of the other initials may have been intended to be more than purely decorative. Camille argued that the illustration within the initial A at the beginning of Jerome's text on the interpretation of Hebrew names (fol. 75, depicting a man teaching a bear the ABC), may have had a didactic or at least mnemonic function for readers

grappling with Jerome's lengthy alphabetical list of names and their spiritual significance. T.A. Heslop has identified the artist in other books from both Rochester and Christ Church, Canterbury.

PROVENANCE: listed in two early twelfth-century Rochester catalogues (B77.29; B78.11) and in the catalogue of 1202 (B79. 46); 14th-century Rochester *ex libris* inscription (fol. 1); in the Royal Library in 1542 (H2.791); Dr Thomas Gale (1635/1636–1702); given to Trinity College by his son, Roger Gale in 1738.

EXHIBITED: London 1984b, no. 42.

LITERATURE: James 1900–1904, III, 254–56; Kauffmann 1975, no. 23; Waller 1981,161–66; Camille 1985a, 29–30; Heslop 1984, 200; Robinson, 1988, no. 376, pl.50; Sharpe 1996, 478, 494, 503; Gameson 1999, no. 167; Carley 2000, 150.

TW

24

Bede, *Super Cantica canticorum*

In Latin
England, St Albans, first quarter of the twelfth century
ARTIST: the Alexis Master (act. *c.*1100–*c.*1130)

Parchment, vii (fols. i–iii modern parchment, fols. iv–vii medieval parchment) + 203 (foliated 5–202, 204; fol. 203 missing) fols., 255 × 175 mm, text 164 × 101 mm, 26 lines, ruled mostly in hard point, some in plummet

SCRIPT: late Caroline minuscule

BINDING: alum tawed skin over boards, 20th c.

King's College, MS 19

THE MOST DETAILED EVIDENCE for the increasing involvement of specialist lay craftsmen in monastic book production during the late eleventh and twelfth centuries is provided by the *Gesta abbatum* of St Albans Abbey, first compiled during the thirteenth century by Matthew Paris, but drawing upon earlier records. The descriptions of arrangements made by various abbots for the provision of resources for book production, including the employment of laymen, are confirmed by the evidence of the surviving manuscripts, such as this one *(see also no. 27)*.

King's MS 19 is an exquisite small-format volume, smaller than most contemporary volumes containing biblical commentaries, in which the text has been carefully and elegantly articulated with decorated initials, rubrics and display script. It was copied by scribes whose hands are all closely similar, and indicate a common training. The hand of the corrector, which is found in other St Albans books, also reflects this training. One of the rubricators (who rubricated other St Albans books as well) has been identified in a manuscript of unknown provenance, written by a Norman scribe who also wrote books for Bishop William of St Calais, Bishop of Durham (d.1096) and Bishop Osbern of Exeter (d.1103). Since the decoration is typical of St Albans books of the earlier twelfth century, this Norman scribe must have travelled to St Albans to copy the book, and was probably a professional.

The seven major initials in King's MS 19 are in the 'St Albans' style. The historiated initial to the first book of Bede's commentary on the Song of Songs provides further evidence of professional craftsmen working at St Albans. It is notable for its very human depiction of the *Sponsus-Sponsa*, the mystical bridegroom and bride interpreted allegorically as Christ and the Church. By contrast with the formal enthroned figures in earlier representations, here they are embracing and about to kiss. These figures have been identified as the work of the so-called 'Alexis Master', the principal illuminator of the St Albans Psalter, who was almost certainly an itinerant specialist craftsman.

PROVENANCE: thirteenth-century St Albans *ex libris*; bequeathed to the College by John Holland in 1547.

LITERATURE: James 1895b, 35–36; Kauffmann 1975, 46; Thomson 1985, I, 23–24, 84; Gullick 1998, 7, 20; Gameson 1999, no. 108; Kauffmann 2003, 78, fig. 57.

TW

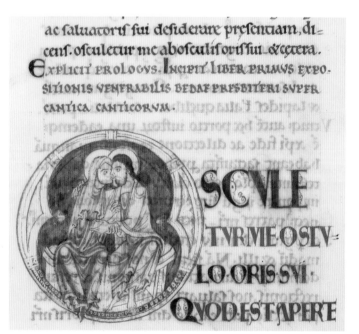

The Bride and the Groom. King's College, MS 19, fol. 21v, detail

25

Triple Psalter, with *Glossa ordinaria* (The Eadwine Psalter)

In Latin with Old English and Old French interlinear translations
England, Canterbury, Christ Church, mid-twelfth century
SCRIBES: Eadwine and others

Parchment, 286 fols., 460 × 330mm, text 305–325 × 287 mm, three columns, 36 lines, ruled in plummet
SCRIPT: late Caroline minuscule/early Gothic bookhand (textualis)
BINDING: gold-tooled brown leather over wooden boards, central boss on each cover, early 17th c.

Trinity College, MS R.17.1

OF ALL SURVIVING TWELFTH-CENTURY MANUSCRIPTS this is the most complex in design as well as the most heavily illuminated. It is the second of three Psalters made at Christ Church, Canterbury in the eleventh and twelfth centuries that derived their pictorial content from the ninth-century Utrecht Psalter (Utrecht, Universiteitsbibliotheek, MS 32). By contrast with its predecessors, the tinted outline drawings that preface each of the Psalms and the Canticles in the Eadwine Psalter have been integrated within a much more complex textual and decorative programme. Instead of a single version of the Psalms, all three Latin versions are present in parallel columns. The *Gallicanum* is given precedence, being written in a larger script, in a wider column on alternate ruled lines. It is presented as a typical mid-twelfth-century glossed Psalter, being accompanied by interlinear and marginal glosses comprising the standard Latin commentary, subsequently known as the *Parva glossatura*. The *Romanum* is glossed with an interlinear Old English translation, and the *Hebraicum* with an Anglo-Norman French translation. Each Psalm begins with a prologue and *titulus* and concludes with a collect. All three versions are embellished with major painted initials in solid body-colour, highlighted in gold (over five hundred in all), and each verse begins with a plain gold or silver initial. The manuscript now begins with a Calendar, but it is possible that four leaves, now in London and New York, containing a cycle of biblical scenes, also once prefaced the Psalms.

The Eadwine Psalter is an outstanding example of English Romanesque book production, in which a harmony of page-design is achieved without any loss of clarity of the individual constituent texts, despite the extraordinary complexity of the layout. Ten or more

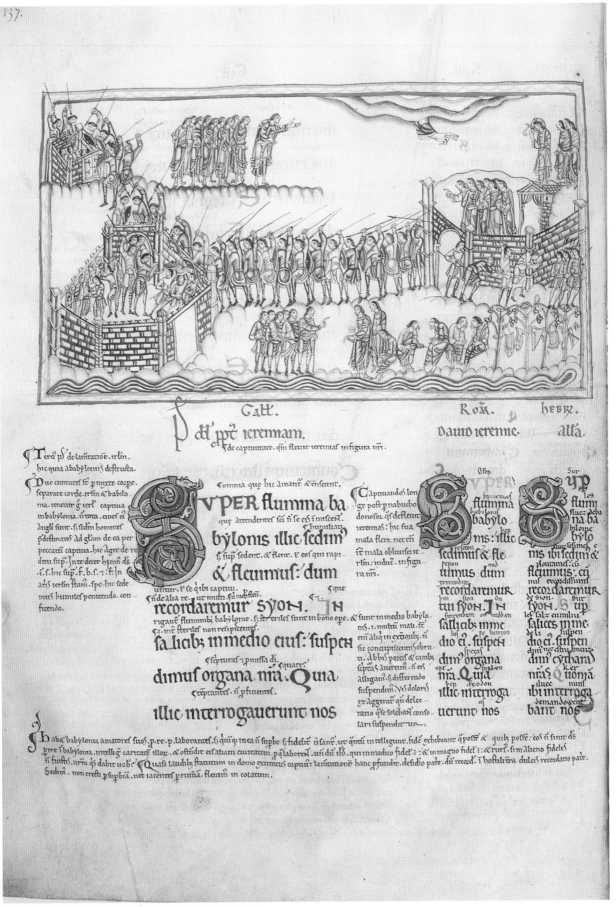

Psalm 136, 'By the Waters of Babylon'. Trinity College, MS R.17.1, fol. 243v

scribes and six artists were involved, but the bulk of the copying and illumination were executed by one scribe and one artist. The complex layout of the book, however, was the work of a different scribe. If the scribe Eadwine, named in a prayer at the end of the Psalms and whose portrait is found at the end of the book, was one of the scribes, then he may have been the designer rather than the main scribe. The hands of these two scribes bear close similarity to those of charters and other documents produced at Christ Church during the 1150s, and provide better dating evidence for the book than a marginal annotation once believed to refer to the 1147 appearance of Halley's comet. The hand of the main scribe has also been identified in other Christ Church-made books. It is possible that these scribes were members of the community. The artists are more likely to have been itinerant professionals. Only one of them has been identified elsewhere – the artist of the illustration to Psalm 4, who illuminated the second volume of the Dover Bible *(no. 36)*.

Given its combination of liturgical and scholarly elements, and its immense size and weight, it is difficult to envisage how the book may have been used. One explanation is that its function was primarily symbolic: a monument to the community's inherited textual and pictorial traditions of representing and understanding the biblical text most central to monastic life. A commemorative function might also best explain the presence of two further remarkable pictorial elements, one (or perhaps both) added shortly after the book had been completed: the full-page portrait of Eadwine 'prince of scribes' (unique as a scribal portrait in twelfth-century English manuscript art in its iconography and scale), and an elaborate plan of the waterworks at Christ Church, Canterbury installed by Prior Wibert (1153–1167), depicted within a tinted outline drawing of the Priory's buildings and grounds.

PROVENANCE: no. 323 in Prior Eastry's early-fourteenth-century catalogue of the books of Christ Church, Canterbury; a partially erased fifteenth-century inscription (fol. 4v) refers to Archbishop Thomas Arundel (1399–1414); given to Cambridge University by Richard Arkinstall perhaps in 1585 (fol. 1, inscription visible under ultra-violet light), but evidently returned to Canterbury; gift of Thomas Nevile (1548–1615), Master of Trinity College (1593–1615).

EXHIBITED: London 1984b, no. 62; Cambridge 1985, no. 26; Utrecht 1996, no. 29.

LITERATURE: James 1900–1904, II, 402–410; James 1903, 51; James 1935; Ker 1957, 135–36; Kauffmann 1975, no. 68; Robinson 1988, no. 358, pls. 63–64; Gibson, Heslop and Pfaff 1992; Kauffmann 2003, 77, 112, 114, 115, 133, 227, fig. 79.

TW

26

Peter Lombard, *Magna glossatura* on the Psalms

In Latin
Northern France, *c.*1164– *c.*1177

Parchment, ii + 184 + ii fols., 440 × 320 mm, text 300 × 170 mm, 2 columns, 52 lines, ruled for the gloss in plummet

SCRIPT: Gothic bookhand (textualis) and glossing hand

BINDING: calf over pasteboards, 16th c.; rebacked.

Trinity College, MS B.5.4

PART OF A FOUR-VOLUME SET, this manuscript is both representative of the twelfth-century best-seller, the glossed books of the Bible, and exceptional in being one of the most ambitious enterprises of its time. The set contains Peter Lombard's *Magna glossatura* on the Psalter (Cambridge, Trinity College, MS B.5.4; Oxford, Bodleian Library, MS Auct. E.inf.6) and the Pauline Epistles (Cambridge, Trinity College, MSS B.5.6 and B.5.7). Commissioned by Thomas Becket, the manuscripts were written and illuminated in Northern France between 1164 and 1177. The project was master-minded by Herbert of Bosham (*c.*1120 – *c.*1194), Becket's secretary and theological adviser. The corpus was begun during their exile at Pontigny (1164–1165), where the Archbishop studied the Bible daily under Herbert's supervision and asked him to prepare a special edition of Lombard's gloss. Since this was far from complete at Becket's death, Herbert added a re-dedication to his new patron, William of the White Hands, Archbishop of Sens, and probably had the martyr's portrait altered accordingly in the presentation image. The Pauline Epistles are prefaced by a letter from Herbert's friend William le Mire who became Abbot of St Denis in 1173. This was also the date of Becket's canonization and since Herbert refers to him as Saint Thomas in the preface, the main text and images must have been completed after 1173 and before 1177 when the new dedicatee, William, left the Archbishopric of Sens for Reims. He never received the volumes. Herbert never stopped working on them. Unreconciled with Henry II after Becket's death, striving to establish himself as an exiled academic in Paris, and seeking the patronage of powerful ecclesiastics, he pressed his erudition and association with Becket into service, as this volume demonstrates.

It shows the page layout designed for glossed biblical books in the 1160s. Lombard's commentary, incorporating the biblical text underlined in red, is written in a glossing hand in two columns. Inset within each column,

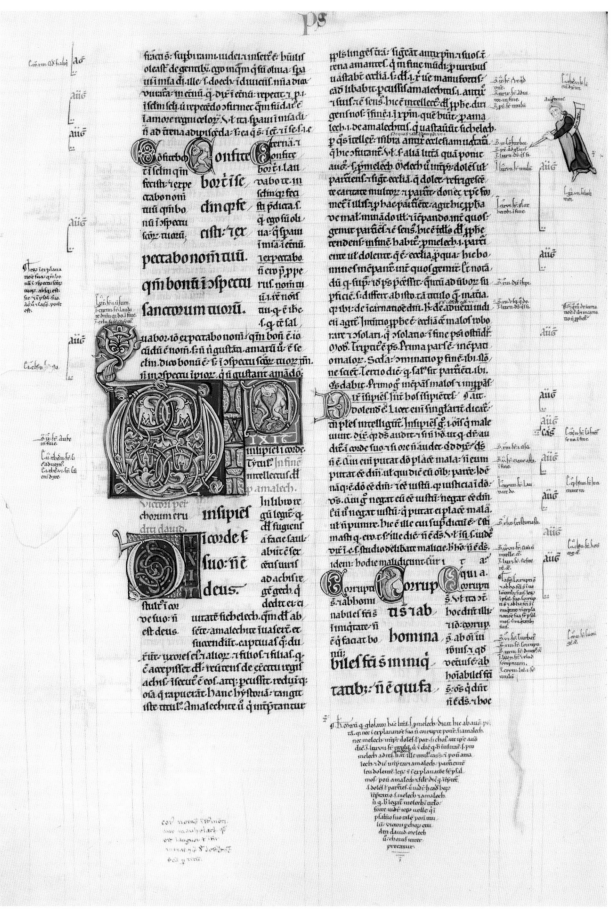

Psalm 52 and St Augustine correcting an attribution. Trinity College, MS B.5.4, fol. 135v

93

but written in a large Gothic script on alternate lines, is the Gallican text of the Psalms. In the margins, the names of the commentators on whose works the *Great gloss* was based, alternate in red and blue, with lines marking the quotes and dotted symbols signalling their beginning and end within the text. Herbert was not content with producing a copy of his master's work; he prepared a critical edition. An accomplished Hebraist, he supplemented the Gallican text of the Psalms with Jerome's translation from the Hebrew. The Hebraica appears on the left hand side of the text columns and is marked, like the Gallican version and Lombard's gloss, with ornamental initials. The marginal columns on either side show cross-references to Psalms and Epistles.

Herbert's main contribution was in identifying the passages wrongly attributed to the authorities responsible for the commentaries. Preserving the integrity of Lombard's text, he relegated his corrections to the margins, as one could see beneath the left-hand text column shown here. Yet, he drew attention to them with a cunning visual device. The figures protesting 'Not me', like Augustine with his 'Non ego' scroll shown here, point a long lance, not just a finger, at the wrong attributions. Herbert added another unique feature to this visual *apparatus criticus*. Numerous Psalms received marginal pictorial summaries of their main theme. As with the figures of the authorities, Herbert used images to stimulate a critical examination of the text, to facilitate the reader's search and memory, and, no doubt, to please the eye.

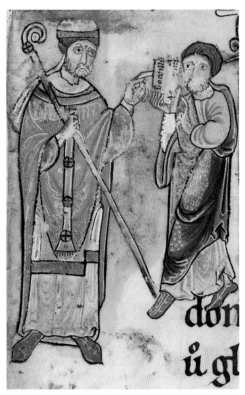

Herbert of Bosham presenting the manuscript to Thomas Becket. Trinity College, MS B.5.4, fol. 1, detail

Two illuminators were responsible for the presentation miniature and historiated initials at the beginning of the volume (fols. 1, 1v, 6v, 10). At least two more assisted them with the marginal images, authority figures, and ornamental initials. With varying degrees of success, they followed their masters' examples of the new type of foliage initials, tight-coiled and inhabited by white lions, that emerged around 1170 in Parisian glossed books of the Bible. Yet, the heavy modelling of the faces, the striking colour scheme, and the decorative treatment of fabrics place the artists outside the main stream of contemporary Parisian illumination. While it seems obvious that they and Herbert of Bosham worked in close proximity, their precise location awaits further research.

PROVENANCE: Herbert of Bosham; Christ Church, Canterbury; gift of Thomas Nevile (1548–1615), Master of Trinity College (1593–1615).

EXHIBITED: London 1908, no. 24; London 1984b, no. 69.

LITERATURE: James 1900–1904, I, 188–94; James 1903, 85, 154; Glunz 1933, 214, 218–21, 341–50; Smalley 1937, 374–75; Dodwell 1954, 105–06; Smalley 1973, 82; Kauffmann 1975, 27; de Hamel 1980, 38–41; de Hamel 1984, 42–43, 60; Robinson 1988, no. 329, pl. 84; de Hamel 1992, 179–84; Smith 2001, 45–48; Panayotova 2005a; Panayotova 2006.

SP

27

Peter Lombard, *Magna glossatura* on the Pauline Epistles

In Latin
England, St Albans, last third of the twelfth century
ARTIST: the Simon Master (act. *c.*1170–*c.*1190)

Parchment, iii (i modern parchment, ii parchment, iii paper) + 236 + ii (i paper, ii parchment) fols., 380 × 270 mm, text 245 × 168 mm, 50 lines, ruled for the gloss in plummet
SCRIPT: late Caroline minuscule/early Gothic bookhand (textualis)
BINDING: calf over wooden boards, remains of two clasps, 16th c.

Trinity College, MS O.5.8

THE DETAILED PROVISIONS for book production made by post-Conquest Abbots of St Albans were revived and reorganized by Abbot Simon (1167–1182) who, according to the *Gesta Abbatum*, 'repaired the scriptorium, at that time almost disused and in poor repair, and introduced into it certain praiseworthy customs; and he increased its revenues'. Abbot Simon was especially keen to acquire copies of glossed books of the Bible, which by

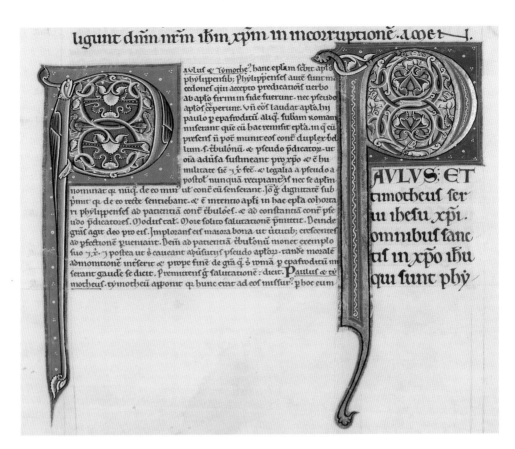

Ornamental initials.
Trinity College, MS
O.5.8, fol. 163v, detail

the middle of the twelfth century had become the standard reference tool for the study of the Bible: 'After he had been made abbot he continued to have written fine books and volumes of both the Old and New Testaments, glossed and corrected, faultlessly finished, which we have not seen bettered'. None of the surviving books that can be securely attributed to the period of Simon's abbacy is a glossed book, but Trinity MS O.5.8 is closely related to them in its script and decoration, and may have been written at this time, or shortly afterwards.

The manuscript contains the expanded gloss on the Pauline Epistles of Peter Lombard, who taught at Paris during the mid-twelfth century. Christpher de Hamel has argued that the greatly expanded nature of this gloss and Peter Lombard's other 'great gloss' on the Psalms, were contributory factors in prompting the more widespread use or development of various devices in the presentation of glossed books in Paris from the 1150s. These included an integrated system of ruling, in which the biblical text was written on alternate lines, a more sophisticated system of linking text and gloss as well as a heavier and more precise use of citations, red underlining of biblical quotations within the gloss, a more rectangular and stylized script for the main biblical text, and a smaller, slightly simpler variety of the same script for the gloss. Trinity MS O.5.8 displays all these devices, including the slightly later development of placing the biblical text at the left-hand side of the text-block, with the gloss surrounding it on three sides. Although it is possible that St Albans scribes travelled to Paris to use exemplars available there, knowledge of the new layout may already have been disseminated to England, either through exemplars or scribes. St Albans maintained close contacts with the Augustinian house of St Victor in Paris and is known to have sent scribes there to copy new texts, but such contacts could also have facilitated the importing of exemplars.

All but two of the major initials, like those of the books demonstrably made for Abbot Simon, are in the so-called 'Channel Style', which perhaps originated in Paris in the mid-twelfth century and quickly became widely diffused in England in the 1160s and 1170s. Characteristic of this style are controlled concentric foliage spirals, often inhabited with small white 'lions', the use of elongated 'blue giants' to form the descenders of letters such as P, and human features heavily influenced by Byzantine art. The first chief exponent of this style at St Albans was an itinerant craftsman known, from his involvement in Abbot Simon's books, as 'the Simon Master', who was active on both sides of the Channel. Thomson suggests that all of the Channel Style initials in Trinity MS O.5.8 may be in his hand.

PROVENANCE: St Albans *ex libris*, 13th c.; two similarly worded incomplete notes in the lower margins of fols. 153–153v refer to a former monk of the abbey, William Este, as 'archidiaconus . . . Sancti Albani', an office to which he was appointed after the Dissolution in 1544 (Emden 1974, 193); given to the College by Roger Gale (1672–1744) in 1738.

LITERATURE: James 1900–1904, III, 312–13; Thomson 1985, I, 54–56, 87–88; de Hamel 1984, 22–23, 56.

TW

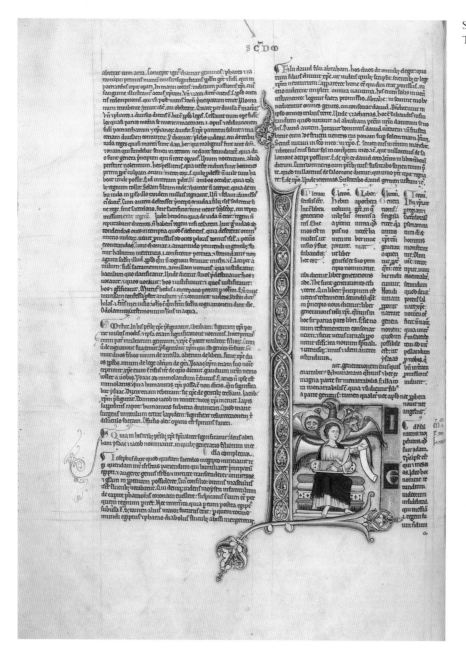

St Matthew's Gospel.
Trinity College, MS B.5.3, fol. 4v

28

Glossed Gospels

In Latin
England, St Albans, *c.*1200

Parchment, 236 fols., 410 × 310 mm, text 310 × 230 mm,
2 columns, 62 lines, ruled in plummet

SCRIPT: Gothic bookhand (textualis)

BINDING: blind-stamped calf over wooden boards, remains of
two clasps, old leather mounted on new spine, 16th c.

Trinity College, MS B.5.3

THESE GOSPELS are a magnificent illustration of the
high quality of book production for St Albans Abbey
around 1200 (Thomson 1982). Fol. 2v has an early inscription of ownership by the monastery. The volume
opens with a series of canon tables unusual in a glossed
Gospels. Each Gospel is preceded by a fine fully painted
and gilded initial incorporated into the complex page
design *(see nos. 26 and 27)*. The script is extremely handsome, but the bold initials are masterpieces of late Romanesque or early Gothic illumination. The book is open at
fol. 4v, the start of St Matthew's Gospel, *Liber Generationis
Iesu Christi filii David*, 'The book of the generation of Jesus
Christ, the son of David'. The large initial L is filled with
foliage medallions and extended with fleshy blossoms,

and in its base is the seated image of the symbol of Matthew, the angel writing and holding a scroll, with the other three Evangelist symbols connected to his head. The figure is ample and smoothly drawn, and the level of technical finish, in brilliant enamel-like colours and gilding, is admirable.

The artist's work is very similar to that of the author of the illuminations in the main part of a Psalter of *c.*1200 associated with another Benedictine establishment, Westminster Abbey (London, British Library, Royal MS 2 A. xxii; Morgan 1982–1988, no. 2). In general this style evolved from that of the last artists to have worked at Winchester Cathedral Priory on the Winchester Bible towards the end of the twelfth century. This was the heyday of quality book production at such monastic establishments in England, the products rivalling anything produced in a late Byzantine idiom anywhere in Western Europe. It is likely that such manuscripts provided a yardstick of quality for artists working as early as the thirteenth century. Matthew Paris of St Albans, ever on the lookout for good material *(see no. 114)* knew and used this book, since he copied a small figure on fol. 111v in one of his own drawings made a couple of generations later (Lewis 1987, 31, figs. 9–10).

PROVENANCE: St Albans Abbey; given by Thomas Nevile (1548–1615), Master of Trinity College (1593–1615).

EXHIBITED: London 1984b, no. 83.

LITERATURE: James 1900–1904, I, 186–88; Thomson 1982, 54, 61–62; Morgan 1982–1988, no.3.

PB

29

Bible

In Latin
England, probably Oxford, *c.*1230–*c.*1240

Parchment, i + 393 + i fols., 332 × 205 mm, text 188 × 121 mm, 2 columns, 59 lines, ruled in plummet

SCRIPT: Gothic bookhand (textualis)

BINDING: contemporary wooden boards, re-covered with later paper

Cambridge University Library, MS Ee.2.23

THE LATIN BIBLE arranged as a single volume with its various books in a standard order, from Genesis to the Book of Revelation, was principally an invention of late twelfth-century France. These new one-volume Bibles went through various processes of evolution and

refinement until about 1220–1230, by which time copies were clearly being produced in some quantities on a commercial basis, especially in the university cities of Paris, Bologna and Oxford. (Cambridge does not seem to have made Bibles until much later.) If one were

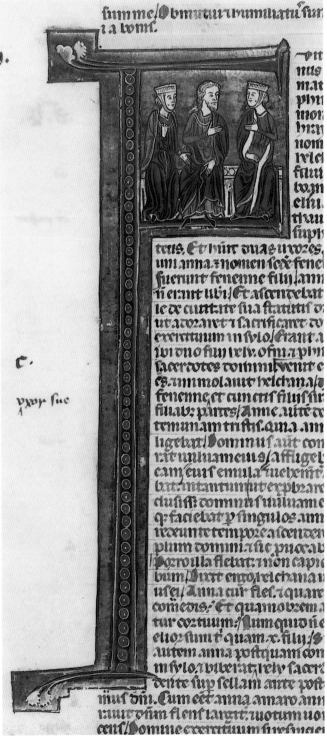

Elkanah with his Wives. Cambridge University Library, MS Ee.2.23, fol.79v

to judge from the text pages alone, one might well ascribe the present Bible to Oxford, for it is certainly English and it is written in a rather round hand, reminiscent of Oxford law books, and the smooth parchment darker on the hair side is common in thirteenth-century Oxford manuscripts. The very fine illumination too suggests a centre of some professionalism. Morgan describes it as 'one of the best preserved and most completely illustrated of all English Bibles of the first half of the thirteenth century'. He notes that the same artists worked on at least two other Bibles (Peterborough, Cathedral Library, MS 10, and Paris, Bibliothèque nationale de France, MS lat. 10431), and that the principal painter collaborated with W. de Brailes in a Psalter, now in Stockholm (Nationalmuseum, B. 2010). It is generally accepted that de Brailes, at least, was an Oxford illuminator, probably the same as the William de Brailes recorded there from about 1230 (see no. 30, 70).

The manuscript belonged to a Carthusian priory. It is marked up for reading throughout the year in the distinctively Carthusian system of dividing chapters into seven parts, lettered alphabetically from 'a' to 'g', and then by the letters 'P', 'S' and 'T', for *prima*, *secunda* and *tercia*. At least twice the markings refer to readings 'in refectorio', the annual cycle of monastic readings during meals (fols. 18 and 255). The text is extensively corrected. The Carthusians were preoccupied with biblical accuracy. This may be reflected in the thirteenth-century note in red on fol. 259, '*iste iiii* carte non sunt corr', 'these four pages are not corrected'.

The Carthusians were never widely established in England. Until the mid-fourteenth century there were only two Carthusian houses in the country, Witham (founded 1178–1179) and Hinton (founded 1227), both in Somerset. The Bible must have belonged to one or the other. Carthusian monks lived in separate cells, each with a small private garden. The script of the Bible is probably too small for easy public reading, unless with exceptionally good eyesight or bright light, and it is more likely that this was a monk's own copy, marked up by him for private re-reading back in his cell or garden before or after meals. It contains many annotations and marks of study. A piece of ancient grass is loosely enclosed as a bookmark between fols. 22 and 23.

PROVENANCE: a Carthusian priory (probably Witham or Hinton); Sir Thomas Knyvett (his MS. 11 in 1618); John Moore, Bishop of Ely (1707–1714); presented to the Library by George I in 1715.

LITERATURE: University Library 1856–1867, II, 40; McKitterick 1978, 158; Morgan 1982–1988, I, 112, no. 65; Avril and Stirnemann 1987, 74; Ker and Piper 1992, 168.

C DE H

30

Bible

In Latin
England, probably Oxford, *c.*1230– *c.*1240
ARTIST: workshop of William de Brailes
(doc. 1238–1252)

Parchment, 360 fols., 250 × 180 mm, text 165 × 105 mm, 2 columns, 59 lines, ruled in black ink

SCRIPT: Gothic bookhand (textualis)

BINDING: blind-tooled red leather over old oak boards, clasps and bosses gone, repaired by J.P. Gray and sons, 1914

Gonville and Caius College, MS 350/567

IN KEEPING with developments in single-volume Bible production in thirteenth-century Paris, this manuscript, though English, is of comparatively small size and is finely written, with a series of small illuminations at the head of each book of the Bible, as well as the preface shown here. The manuscript is in fact quite thoroughly illustrated, though the pattern of illumination differs somewhat from the Parisian Bibles of the period and illustrates the uneven English reaction to the Parisian Vulgate standard (Bennett 1973, 47–48, 312). This manuscript is of particular interest because, as Adelaide Bennett first noted (Bennett 1973, 48), it comes from the Oxford-based workshop of William de Brailes, whose output is well represented in Cambridge (*see no. 70*). This shop was producing Bibles in quantity since at least one other exists (Oxford, Bodleian Library, MS lat. bibl. e. 7; Morgan 1982–1988, no. 69). Some of the illumination in the Caius book looks as though it is the work of de Brailes' own hand, but there are discrepancies which suggest the cooperation of more than one hand, or which point to aspects of de Brailes' personal style which are still poorly understood. The striking thing is the extent to which the very slight deviations from his style (as represented by the undoubtedly autograph Fitzwilliam Museum leaves, *no. 70*) point to knowledge of, and a desire to emulate, Parisian Bible illumination of the type which developed in the sphere of the huge *Bibles moralisées* executed in Paris in the first half of the century. The immense prestige of the Latin Bible promulgated for use in the Paris schools, which were attended by many English students, must in part explain this. The general size of this book is however somewhat larger than most of the tiny and very finely written Parisian single-volume Bibles of the period, and the parchment is certainly less thin. It is exhibited at fol. 3, showing the Crucifixion and events from the

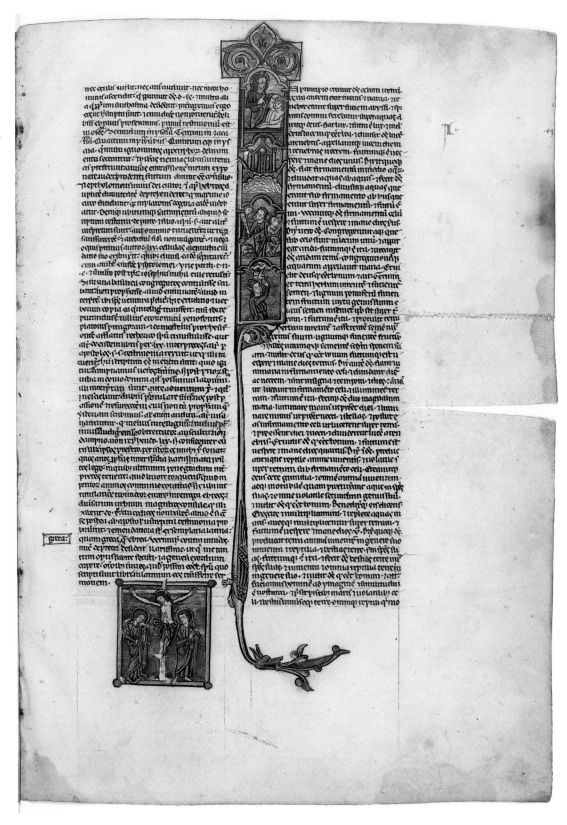

Opening of
the Book of
Genesis.
Gonville and
Caius College,
MS 350/567,
fol. 3

Book of Genesis. Note the decorative marginal extension
terminating in a dragon: de Brailes' shop was among the
first to develop this feature in English book decoration.

PROVENANCE: 'Master Rawson, gentilman and merser of
London' (16th c., endleaf); presented by John Gostlin, Master of
Gonville and Caius College, in 1627.

LITERATURE: James 1907–1914, I, 395–97; Bennett 1973, 48;
Morgan 1982–1988, no. 70; Noel 2004.

PB

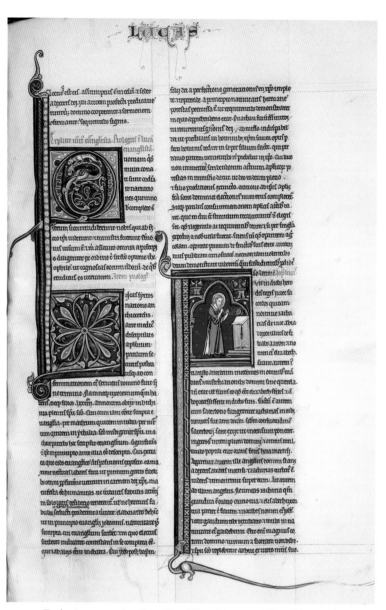

Zacharias censes the Altar. Fitzwilliam Museum, MS 1, fol. 372, detail

31

Bible

In Latin
France, Paris, *c.*1240–*c.*1260

Parchment, iii + 478 + i fols., 380 × 248 mm, text 255 × 146 mm, 2 columns, 48 lines, ruled in plummet

SCRIPT: Gothic bookhand (textualis)

BINDING: gold-tooled black morocco, 18th c., probably French.

Fitzwilliam Museum, MS 1

DESPITE BEING NUMBERED 'MS 1', this was a late purchase by Lord Fitzwilliam, for it was bought in 1814, perhaps in France, to judge from the large number of French books he acquired that year. It was a noble

choice, for it is a manuscript of great refinement and sophistication. The illuminated initials are attributable to the Parisian artists, active *c.*1240–1260, known collectively as the '*Vie de Saint Denis* atelier', named after a manuscript made for the royal Abbey of Saint-Denis near Paris (Paris, Bibliothèque nationale de France, MS nouv. acq. fr. 1098). At least three other manuscripts by the same illuminators are associated with Saint-Denis. Branner, who first ascribed the Fitzwilliam book to the workshop, called it 'perhaps the most beautiful and impressive single volume produced by this group'. It is a Bible on a large scale, for display rather than private study. The text concludes with a rhyming scribal colophon on fol. 478, alluding to the noise and the effort of copying with a quill: *Penna silens siste, laudes refero tibi christe, Cesset onus triste, labor et liber explicit iste* ('Rest silent, pen; I give praise to you, O Christ; may the melancholy duty be over; the work and this book are finished.')

There is an erased inscription on fol. 3v which James interpreted as referring to Groendaal Abbey in Belgium. In fact, it says '*Ista biblia est de domo vallis viridis prope parisius ordinis cartusiensis*', the Carthusian monastery of Vauvert in Paris. It was founded in 1257 by St Louis, King of France as Louis IX (1226–1270), and established in the former château de Vauvert the following year. The King endowed the foundation with lands and other benefactions and took it under his protection in 1259. There are no apparent records of the medieval library, but Louis customarily gave manuscripts to each of his monastic foundations. It is extremely possible that he would have presented a Bible of royal quality, and he may have commissioned the Vauvert Bible specially in 1257–1259.

The text has been marked up for public reading throughout the church year, using the distinctively Carthusian method of dividing each chapter by letters of the alphabet and by 'P', 'S' and 'T' *(see no. 29)*. These are now mostly erased but visible. Vauvert was suppressed in 1790 but the book had clearly already left the monastery by about 1700, for there is an untidy inscription, apparently 'Ex libris de Remond de Cours', perhaps Nicolas Rémond des Cours (d.1716), and rambling notes attributing the script to monks of the Order of Saint Basil, on no likely evidence. It may well be no. 6 in the catalogue of Auguste Chardin, *Catalogue de livres précieux, manuscrits et imprimés sur peau-vélin, du cabinet de M.★★*, Paris, 1811, from which Lord Fitzwilliam bought at least two other manuscripts *(see no. 161)*.

PROVENANCE: the Carthusian monastery of Vauvert, Paris; Rémond de Cours; probably Auguste Chardin (no. 6 in his catalogue of 1811); acquired by Viscount Fitzwilliam in 1814; his bequest, 1816.

EXHIBITED: Cambridge 1966, no. 44.

LITERATURE: James 1895a, 1–6; Branner 1977, 90, 192, 224, figs. 254, 256.

C DE H

32

Bible

In Latin
England, perhaps Oxford, *c.*1260–*c.*1270

Parchment, ii (i paper, ii parchment pasted to paper) + 349 + ii (paper) fols., 312 × 270 mm, text 272 × 152 mm, 2 columns, 54 lines, ruled in plummet

SCRIPT: Gothic bookhand (textualis)

BINDING: calf over boards, 18th c., rebacked

Emmanuel College, MS 116 (2.I.6)

O NE MIGHT HAVE THOUGHT, on seeing the great scale of the four thirteenth-century Bibles exhibited here, that such manuscripts were customarily in folio format. They are not at all. In fact, most Bibles of the thirteenth century (and they are not rare) are less than a quarter of this size, thick squat books which can be held on the palm of one hand. Thirteenth-century Bibles usually have microscopic illumination, tiny initials with perfect little pictures compressed with clarity into a space of a few millimetres high. If that was the familiar norm in the thirteenth century, we must consider these exceptional and luxurious copies as being conscious enlargements, inflated symbols of wealth, display or religious commitment. Pictures in most illuminated manuscripts are scaled-down versions of something commonly larger; these big thirteenth-century Bibles, however, in the experience of those who saw them new, are magnifications. This helps explain the use of historiated initials, when a picture would have fitted the design better, and the relatively simple compositions which sometimes seem to teeter uncomfortably and appear over-inflated in their unaccustomed space.

As early as 1697, the manuscript was described by Edward Bernard as being ornamented with *'literis pulcherrimis'*. It is almost a twin of Oxford, Bodleian Library, MS Auct. D.1.7, and it belongs among a wider group of loosely related manuscripts which include the well-known Bible signed by its scribe, William of Devon

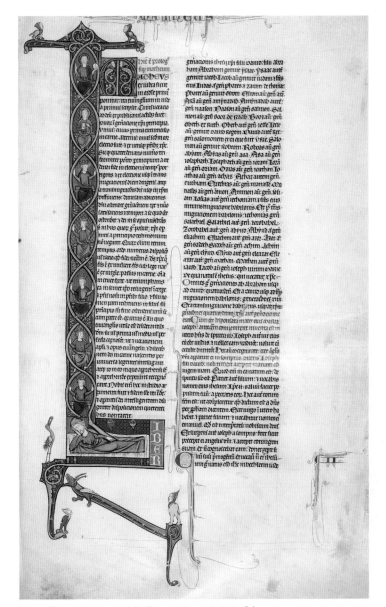

Tree of Jesse. Emmanuel College, MS 116 (2.I.6), fol. 250

(London, British Library, Royal MS 1.D.i; Morgan 1982, no. 159–64). They all show strong stylistic connections with contemporary Parisian illumination, and indeed the Bodleian manuscript was originally assumed to be French. However, there can be no doubt that the Emmanuel College Bible was made in England and its red and blue meandering penwork is entirely English. Its historiated initials support long bar borders embellished with little grotesques, birds, and hybrid half-human creatures balancing on or stepping off the decoration.

Very unusually in a Bible, the scribe himself has supplied little whimsical sketches of faces or other small pictures up against the edge of the text to indicate notable passages or to show different people speaking, as recounted in the narrative. One of these, illustrating Maccabees 12:43 on the pieces of silver sent to Jerusalem, is a recognizable drawing of a long-cross silver penny of Henry III. These coins were introduced in England in 1247 and must still have been a novelty.

PROVENANCE: at Emmanuel College by 1697.

LITERATURE: Bernard 1697, 91, no. 43; James 1904, 102–105; Morgan 1982–1988, no. 163; Lewis 1995, 349.

C DE H

33

Bible

In Latin
Italy, Bologna, *c.*1260–*c.*1270

Parchment, 583 fols., 295 × 210 mm, text 177 × 120 mm, 2 columns, 45 lines, ruled in plummet

SCRIPT: Gothic bookhand (textualis)

BINDING: reversed calf over wooden boards, engraved and pierced metal bosses and clasps, 15th c.

Fitzwilliam Museum, MS 1056–1975

THIS BIBLE has travelled widely around Europe. It was illuminated in Italy, doubtless in Bologna, in the so-called '*prima maniera*', or first Bolognese style (Conti 1981). It is one of a group of closely related Bibles, which include Vatican City, Biblioteca Apostolica Vaticana, MS Vat. Lat. 20, and Oxford, Bodleian Library, MS Canon. bibl. lat. 56 dated 1265. Every book of the Bible opens with an historiated initial. Their frames sprout like rapidly growing beanstalks into coloured tendrils in the manuscript's margins, wrapping around other decoration. Sometimes these include realistic animals and birds. Some borders include tonsured figures in black habits, apparently Benedictine monks rather than Dominican friars, as suggested by Wormald and Giles (fols. 1, 4v, 156v, 448); on other pages monks are brought into the initials themselves, even to accompany one of the ancestors of Christ in the lowest compartment of the Jesse Tree (fol. 434v). The book was probably commissioned by a Benedictine monastery. The text has been collated in the Middle Ages against a second copy, given the *siglum* 'k' ('k. non', etc.).

The manuscript was bought by Johann Weynrich for 12 Hungarian florins in 1468, according to the buyer's note on fol. 1. It was probably rebound for him in its present high Gothic covers. It soon afterwards belonged to a nun, perhaps his daughter, for it is inscribed inside the upper cover as being the book of Sister Katherina Zelchern, the gift of her father. It has the large bookplate of Ferdinand Hoffmann, Freiherr von Grünpühel und Strechau, whose library descended to the Princes of Dietrichstein at Schloss Nikolsburg in Moravia, until its eventual dispersal in Lucerne in 1933 when this manuscript realized 1500 Swiss francs. It was acquired by Pierre Hollier Larousse, of the French publishing family, and then by Henry Davis (d.1977), primarily a collector of book bindings, who gave it to the Fitzwilliam.

PROVENANCE: Johannes Weynrich, 1468; Katherina Zelchern; Ferdinand Hoffmann (1540–1607); the Dietrichstein library; sale of *Bibliothek Alexander Fürst Dietrichstein*, Lucerne, 21–22 November 1933, lot 424; Pierre Hollier Larousse; Henry Davis; his gift, 1975.

LITERATURE: Wormald and Giles 1982, 456–59.

C DE H

Creation and Passion scenes at the opening of Genesis. Fitzwilliam Museum, MS 1056–1975, fol. 4v

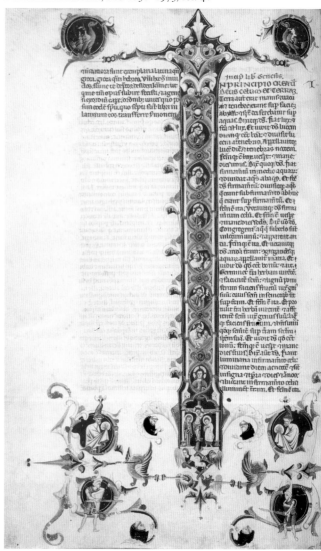

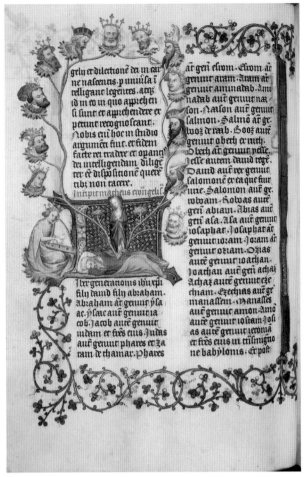

Tree of Jesse. Fitzwilliam Museum,
MS 289, vol. 3, fol. 67v

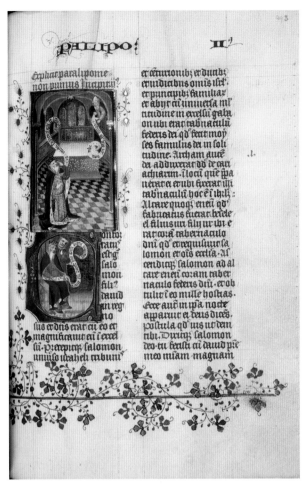

David kneeling before an altar. Fitzwilliam Museum,
MS 289, vol. 1, fol. 493

34

Bible

In Latin
The Netherlands, Utrecht, *c.*1420–*c.*1430
ARTISTS: Masters of Zweder van Culemborg
(act. *c.*1415–*c.*1445) and others

Parchment, 3 vols., i + 533 + ii; 574; 462 fols., 220 × 165 mm,
text in two columns, 132–134 × 94–96 mm, 29 lines, ruled in red
or purple ink.

SCRIPT: Gothic bookhand (textualis)

BINDING: modern red morocco (replacement, 1987, for old
brown calf, possibly original) over oak boards, with chemise
wrappings of doeskin secured to each cover with five metal
bosses (some modern replacements); two catches on the upper
covers and remains of leather bands for two clasps on lower
covers; paintings on all three edges of a shield held by an angel
with the arms of the Utrecht family of Lochorst.

Fitzwilliam Museum, MS 289, vol. 1

THERE WAS AN EFFLORESCENCE of Bible study and use
in the Northern Netherlands during the fifteenth
century, stimulated particularly by the religious reform
movement known as the *Devotio moderna*. Two types of
Bibles were predominant in Dutch illuminated manuscripts of the period: large Latin Bibles, made primarily
in and for use in monastic settings, which are illustrated
only sparely if at all; and vernacular History Bibles, some
of which were accompanied by extensive cycles of miniatures closely tied to the narrative of the text (Hindman
1977b). The Lochorst Bible belongs to neither of these
traditions. In its contents, the sequence of its books, the
choice of its biblical prologues, its dimensions, and its
layout and scheme of illustration, it recalls university
Bibles of the thirteenth and fourteenth centuries. It is the
only example known to us in Dutch illumination of a
Latin Bible in which each of the biblical books and major
divisions in the Psalter is introduced by a column miniature, a historiated initial, or both, and each of the biblical prologues and some subdivisions of the dictionary of
Hebrew names (a text commonly found in university

103

Bibles) by a historiated or a decorated initial. Most of the leaves with illustrations or large decorated initials are also accompanied by marginal decoration.

At least half a dozen painters belonging to two major stylistic groups contributed to the decoration of the manuscript. Miniatures from the more old-fashioned of the two groups feature small and limber figures. Some of the painters in this group favour figures executed largely in grisaille accented with pale and pastel tones modelled in a fine, almost pointillist technique. Male figures tend to have thin, angular faces, and females simple, puppet-like physiognomies. Settings range from prop-like architectural frameworks with abstract backgrounds, to simple, coloured ground planes and sky-like, stippled backgrounds, or landscape backgrounds rising almost to the top of the picture space and portrayed as if from birds' eye view. Many of these traits recall works of the so-called International Gothic style of the turn of the fifteenth century. Thus far we have encountered no other works by the painters belonging to this group elsewhere in Dutch manuscript illumination.

The second major miniature style found in the manuscript is that of the Masters of Zweder van Culemborg. Named after illustrations found in a Missal made *c.*1425 for Zweder van Culemborg, Bishop-elect of Utrecht (Bressanone, Seminario Maggiore, MS C. 20), the miniature style was among the most important practised in Utrecht *c.*1415–1445. Miniatures by these painters feature complex and spatially developed landscape and interior settings. Figures tend to be larger, their forms executed in paint, rather than in grisaille or delicate stippling, and the palette is richer and more variegated. The pictorial naturalism of these artists has analogies with works of early Netherlandish painting, and a few miniatures contain compositional or figural features reminiscent of illustrations in the Turin-Milan Hours (Turin, Museo Civico d'Arte Antica, Inv. no. 47).

This richly illustrated Bible was made for a member of the Lochorst family of Utrecht. The Lochorst arms are painted on shields held by angels on the edges of each of the three volumes and in a banner portrayed in one of the miniatures. Members of this family were deeply involved in civic and religious life in and around Utrecht. Possible patrons include Gijsbrecht van Lochorst (*c.*1380–1454), Canon of Oudmunster and of Utrecht Cathedral, and his brother Herman I van Lochorst (*c.*1365–1438), who was likewise a Canon of Oudmunster, possessor of prebends in all five chapters of Utrecht, and Dean of Utrecht Cathedral. Gijsbrecht or other family members may have commissioned two Dutch History Bibles of *c.*1440 decorated with arms of the Lochorst family (London, British Library, Add. MS 10043 and Add. MS 38122). The second of these books was illustrated in the style of the Master of Catherine of Cleves,

who succeeded the Masters of Zweder van Culemborg as the leading illuminator in Utrecht.

PROVENANCE: made for a member of the Lochorst family, whose arms appear on the edges of all three volumes and in the miniature in vol. 3, fol. 39v (partially erased); given by Sarah and Robert Wight to Maria Matthews in 1866, and by her to her sister Anne Byam Wight in 1871; Rev. E.S. Dewick; his bequest, 1917.

EXHIBITED: London 1908, no. 146; Cambridge 1966, no. 80.

LITERATURE: Byvanck and Hoogewerff 1922–1926, no. 25, pls. 106–108, 125–26, 143; Byvanck 1923b, 187; de Wit 1927, 71–72, 98–103, 113; de Wit 1929a, 266; de Wit 1929b, 276, fig. 3; Byvanck 1930, 130; Byvanck 1937, 47–51, 126, figs. 79–88; Hoogewerff 1936, 173, 421–27, 433, 434, figs. 215–218; Holter 1938, 56–59; Byvanck 1943, 25–27, figs. 13–16; Panofsky 1953a, 97–98, 101 n. 21; Hoogewerff 1961; Finke 1963; Marrow 1968, 55 n. 14; Gorissen 1973, 602, 658, 793, 801, 806–808, 824–25, 827–29, 963; Pächt and Jenni 1975, 13, 16–17, 19–22, 65, 75, figs. 13–14, 16–18, 20–21; Hindman 1977b, 41, 42 n. 24, 46–47, 48, 63, figs. 5, 9; Wormald and Giles 1982, 258–65, figs. 56–61; Hamburger 1988, 16, 18, fig. 12; Calkins 1991, 328, fig. 2; Hamburger 1991, 164–65; Lacaze 1991, 257; Marrow 1991, 58, fig. 15; van Buren 1996, 321 n. 30.

JHM

35

Gregory the Great, *Moralia in Job*

In Latin
England, probably Norwich, *c.*1320

Parchment, 223 fols., 470 × 310 mm, text 370 × 207 mm, 2 columns, 70 lines, ruled in ink

SCRIPT: Gothic bookhand (textualis)

BINDING: calf over pasteboards, 18th c., rebacked

Emmanuel College, MS 112 (2.I.1)

ST GREGORY THE GREAT (d.604) wrote a number of significant scholarly works in Constantinople at the request of Leander, Bishop of Seville, notably his famous *Moralia in Job* begun in the 590s as a series of lectures delivered to monks in the circle of Gregory. The text is a mystical and allegorical exposition of the many levels of signification of the Book of Job, and it was to be regarded as a storehouse of moral theology throughout the Middle Ages. This manuscript is one of the finest illuminated versions of the text in existence. Though some of its leaves and illuminations have been cut out, its remaining twenty-two historiated initials provide magnificent testimony to the technical quality of manuscript illumination in East Anglia in the first half of the fourteenth century. The book is open at fol. 92v, the start of Book 15, where the author, Gregory, is shown in his tiara standing on a stem in the left-hand border, bearing a scroll with the legend *Ducunt in bonis dies suos et in puncto ad inferna descendunt*, 'They spend their days in wealth, and in an instant go down to Hell' (Job 21:13). In the initial sit two men conversing, each holding a purse; below, they plunge into the inferno.

This manuscript is generally regarded as having been made for monastic use. On fol. 154 at the start of Book 26 Christ is shown holding a scroll with the legend *Discite a me quia mitis sum et humilis corde* 'Learn of me, for I am meek and lowly in heart' (Matthew 11:29). Benedictine monks, embodiments of the monastic virtue of humility, kneel in the border. These figures are the nearest we get to an indication of the patrons. The stylistic affiliation of the illumination is with the great Ormesby Psalter (Oxford, Bodleian Library, MS Douce 366) and books related to it, notably the Bromholm Psalter (Oxford, Bodleian Library, MS Ashmole 1523) and the Dublin Apocalypse (Dublin, Trinity College, MS 64; Sandler 1986, nos. 43, 44, 46). These manuscripts contain evidence of association with Norfolk, and the Cathedral Priory of Norwich especially in the case of the Ormesby Psalter. Though the Emmanuel College *Moralia in Job* has no Norwich Cathedral Priory press-mark, an association with Norwich Cathedral or with another Benedictine establishment in Norfolk seems likely. It was donated to the College by Ralph Cudworth who, as James noted, gave other books also from Norwich. The patronage was certainly splendid. The book's script is magnificent and its illuminations, conducted in pale and somewhat flat and dry colours, are sharply delineated and beautifully finished. These painters were connected to the workshop that produced the Thornham Parva Retable, in oil on oak, for one of East Anglia's Dominican houses, probably that at Thetford, *c*.1335.

PROVENANCE: possibly Norwich Benedictine Cathedral Priory; given to the College by Ralph Cudworth in 1600.

EXHIBITED: Norwich 1973, no. 24.

LITERATURE: James 1904, 97–100; Sandler 1986, no. 45.

PB

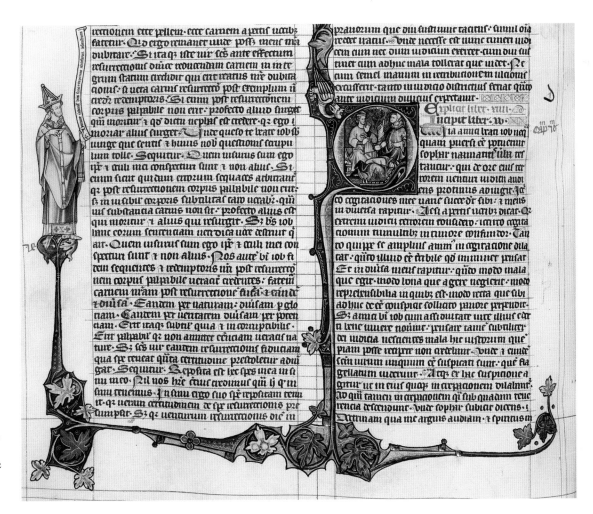

The Rewards of Earthly Treasure. Emmanuel College, MS 112 (2.I.1), fol. 92v, detail

36

Speculum Humanae Salvationis

In Latin
Italy, perhaps Tuscany, late fourteenth century

Parchment, 25 double-sided cuttings, each approximately
143 × 193 mm, text below almost entirely cut away, now inset
into thin card 490 × 335mm

SCRIPT: fragments of Gothic bookhand (textualis)

BINDING: gilt brown morocco, by Rivière, probably 1876

Fitzwilliam Museum, MS 43–1950

THIS GROUP OF CUTTINGS from a single manuscript is now divided between Cambridge and Paris (Bibliothèque nationale de France, MS lat. 9854, bought from the Parisian bookseller Creuzet in 1838). The portion exhibited here belonged by at least 1856 to the artist Sir William Boxhall who was later director of the National Gallery in London. Between them the two parts comprise one hundred and seventy-six illustrations out of a probable original total of one hundred and ninety-two, from a magnificent manuscript of the *Speculum Humanae Salvationis*, or 'Mirror of Human Salvation'. The *Speculum* was a popular verse text, which graphically presented events in the Old Testament as prophecies that were afterwards fulfilled or echoed in parallel incidents of the New Testament. The text is preserved in about four hundred copies, mostly German. Only ten are of Italian origin, of which two (including the Paris portion of the Fitzwilliam cuttings) record uniquely that the text was compiled in 1324. This date is generally accepted as credible. The author may have been Ludolph of Saxony (d.1377).

The manuscript originally consisted of two columns in Latin with a pair of illustrations at the top of each page showing scenes from the Old and New Testaments

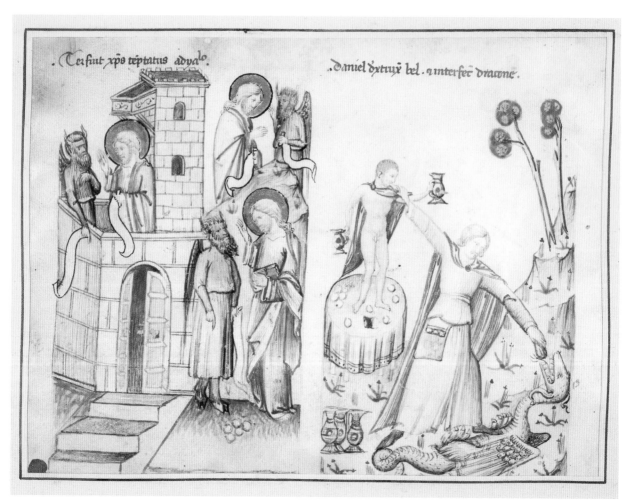

Christ's Temptation, Daniel destroying Bel. Fitzwilliam Museum, MS 43–1950, fol. 5v

side by side. They are gracefully drawn and filled with softly coloured washes, sometimes embellished with small areas of highly burnished gold lines, as thick as piped icing on a cake. The pictures were enormously admired in the nineteenth century, when this was known as the 'Boxhall Speculum'. They were described at length by Gustav Waagen (1857), when they were bound together as an oblong book. He ascribed them to Florence and praised their utmost 'beauty of purity of expression … rendered with so little labour as to merit admiration'. Samples were engraved in Anna Jameson and Elizabeth Eastlake, *The History of Our Lord as Exemplified in Works of Art*, London, 1864, and elsewhere. A full facsimile of both portions was published by James and Berenson in 1926. By then Berenson, uncharacteristically, was at a loss to attribute the drawing precisely, beyond the assumption that the artist was probably Florentine. In 1930 he returned to the problem of attribution and commented on general similarities with the work of the painters Spinello Aretino and

Lorenzo Nicolò. He observed influences from France, Spain, Byzantium, North Africa and even China. When the Paris portion of the manuscript was exhibited in 1984, Avril merely noted that the floral borders and initials were not, in fact, typical of Florence or Siena. It is a rare instance of manuscript scholarship becoming less precise with the passage of time.

PROVENANCE: Sir William Boxhall (1800–1879), acquired by 1857; given by him in 1876 to Sir John Duke (1820–1894), first Lord Coleridge, Lord Chief Justice; purchased from the Coleridge family by T.H. Riches in 1923; his bequest, 1935.

EXHIBITED: Cambridge 1966, no. 63.

LITERATURE: Waagen 1857, 196–98; James and Berenson 1926; Berenson 1930, 102–21; Wormald and Giles 1982, II, 456–59, pl. 36; Paris 1984a, 72; Wilson and Wilson 1984, 30–32 (as being in Oxford); Neisner 1995, 22.

C DE H

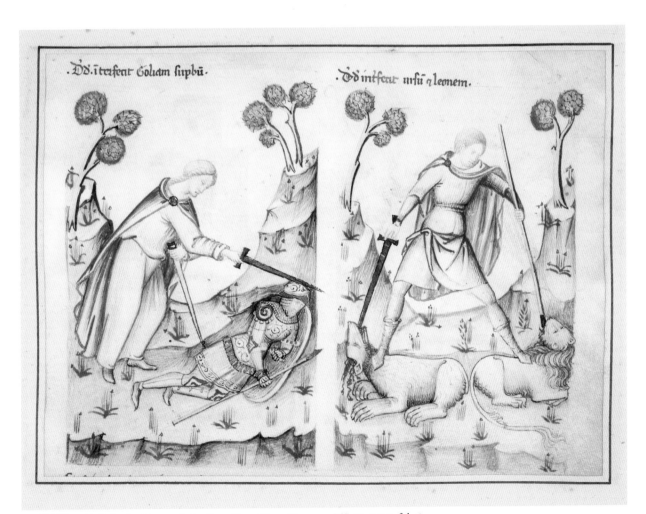

David killing Goliath, the Lion and the Bear. Fitzwilliam Museum, MS 43–1950, fol. 6

37

Nicholas of Lyra, *Postilla Litteralis in Vetus et Novum Testamentum*

In Latin
England, probably London, *c.*1425–*c.*1445, before 1457
SCRIBE: Stephen Dodesham (d.1481/1482)

Parchment, iv (i modern paper, ii–iii old paper, iv medieval parchment) + 319 (foliation begins on flyleaf but repeats 170) + ii (i medieval parchment, ii modern paper) fols., 472 × 330 mm, text 308 × 208 mm, 2 columns, 55 lines, ruled in purple ink

SCRIPT: Gothic bookhand (anglicana formata)

BINDING: modern brown goatskin preserving sides of early blind-tooled calf, probably 16th c.

Cambridge University Library, MS Dd.7.7

The Ark of the Covenant. Cambridge University Library, MS Dd.7.7, fol. 78v

THIS TRULY ENORMOUS BOOK is only the first in a set of four volumes, comprising the influential commentary on the literal meaning of the entire Latin Bible compiled by the Franciscan friar, Nicholas of Lyra (*c.*1270–1340). This volume deals with *Genesis* to *Esther*; the subsequent books in the set are MSS Dd.7.8, Dd.7.9, and Dd.7.10. They were copied by the well-known English scribe Stephen Dodesham, a Carthusian monk, and presented to the Abbey of St Albans in 1457. Two of the volumes, including this, preserve copies of a detailed indenture recording the formal donation of the manuscripts to the abbot and convent of St Albans on 17 May 1457 by Dame Eleanor Hull and Roger Huswyff, clerk, although they were to be reserved for the personal use of Huswyff during his lifetime. These are identifiable people. Eleanor Hull was the daughter of Sir John Malet, retainer of Henry Bolingbroke. She is first mentioned in 1413, already married to Sir John Hull (d. *c.*1420–21). She was in the service of Joan of Navarre, second wife of Henry V, and was a member of the confraternity of St Albans by 1417. Huswyff was her executor. He had been a scholar of both Winchester School (1400) and

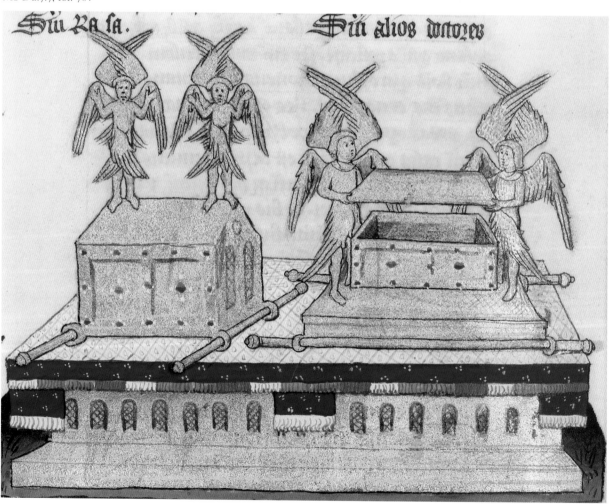

New College, Oxford (1402). He qualified as a lawyer and then changed careers to become a priest. He was still alive in 1465. In the fullness of time, the set evidently came into the Abbey's possession, as agreed.

What seems like a reference to the same set of books occurs in the Latin chronicle of St Albans Abbey preserved in the British Library (Cotton MS Nero D.vii, fol.32), recounting the merits of John Whethamstede, Abbot 1420–1440 and 1451–1465. 'In his time', the account records, 'the said abbot had the commentary of Nicholas of Lyra on the whole Bible begun, [written] in a hand of great distinction'. It seems very unlikely that two complete sets were made. Whethamstede was a notable patron of books and learning and a friend of Humfrey, Duke of Gloucester. He also knew Huswyff, whom he had appointed as his attorney during an absence in Italy in 1423. Whethamstede sponsored many manuscripts for his Abbey. Perhaps he originally commissioned these volumes, but they were finished at the expense of others, or perhaps the abbot was simply accorded credit for initiating Eleanor Hull's benefaction. According to Barratt (1995), the marginal notes are in Whethamstede's hand. Since Huswyff outlived him, the set was perhaps already in St Albans in Whethamstede's time, or it might have been made there.

It is commonly asserted (usually with some truth) that almost no manuscripts were made in English monasteries or by monks after the thirteenth century. St Albans was a notable exception, for books were certainly still being produced there throughout the fifteenth century (and a printing press was brought to the Abbey precincts around 1479). Stephen Dodesham was himself a monk, of the Carthusian Order. He was at Witham Priory in Somerset in 1469 when he was reprimanded for some unspecified misdemeanor against the prior. Later, whether by choice or expulsion, he had joined or returned to Sheen Abbey, to the west of London. He died there in 1481–1482. Dodesham may have been a professional scribe before joining a monastery, and he certainly continued to write books for outside clients throughout his life, including several for Syon Abbey, across the river from Sheen. Some twenty books are now ascribed to him, from the first quarter of the fifteenth century to about 1475, in Middle English as well as Latin. This is by far the most lengthy.

Certainly the utter professionalism of the manuscript does not suggest an amateur or home-made production. The pages are spaciously laid out, carefully corrected, and splendidly decorated. Unusually for a biblical commentary, de Lyra's text makes provision for explanatory illustrations. This volume alone has fifteen pages with magnificent pictures or diagrams, mostly brilliantly coloured and shimmering with gold. The artist is tentatively identified (by Scott 1996) as having worked in

several other books, including the Hours of Katherine of Valois, first wife of Henry V (London, British Library, Add. MS 65100), and a *Sanctilogium Salvatoris* made for Margaret, Duchess of Clarence and wife of the King's brother, who gave it to Syon (Karlsruhe, Badische Landesbibliothek, Skt. Georgen cod. 12). Given the royal connections of both Eleanor Hull and Whethamstede, it is likely that the St Albans book was illuminated in London or possibly at Sheen or Syon, both founded by Henry V. Dodesham, maverick among monks, was evidently familiar in such circles. The scale of the present enterprise makes it exceptional. All four volumes total more than 2400 pages of writing, over 250,000 lines of unwavering text. An owner of *c.*1600 comments on this on fol.1v in Latin ending, 'What diligence! What indolence of our own times!'

PROVENANCE: Dame Eleanor Hull and Roger Huswyff; St Albans Abbey; at the University Library by 1600 (James 1600, nos. 226–230)

LITERATURE: University Library 1856–1867, I, 327–28.; Ker 1964, 165, 335; Parkes 1979, 6; Ayto and Barratt 1984, xxxi–xxxii; Robinson 1988, no. 9, pl. 262; Doyle 1990, 14; Edwards 1991, 187; Barratt 1995, xxxi; Scott 1996, I, 71 n. 33 and II, 214; Doyle 1997, 97 n. 13, 99–101, 105, 115.

CDEH

38

Jerome, Letters and minor works

In Latin
England, Canterbury, Christ Church, 1478
SCRIBE: Theodoricus Werken (act. *c.*1444–*c.*1478)

Parchment, ii (i paper, ii parchment) + 308 + ii (i parchment, ii paper) fols., 540 × 370 mm, text 351 × 237 mm, 46 lines, ruled in hard point and crayon.

SCRIPT: Humanistic minuscule

BINDING: blind-stamped calf over wooden boards, 19th c., rebacked

Trinity College, MS R.17.5

THIS IS THE SECOND VOLUME of a massive two-volume copy of letters and other minor works by Jerome (or attributed to him), made for Christ Church, Canterbury in 1477–1478 by the Dutch scribe, Theodoricus Werken of Abbenbroek. These are luxury volumes, written in a large well-spaced script on over six hundred large sheets of parchment of a very high quality. In volume II, the fine two-sided border accompanying the

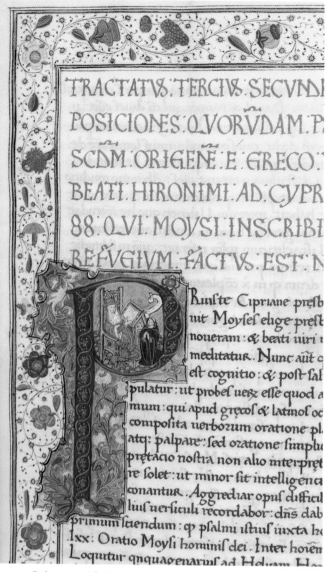

St Jerome with Lion and Benedictine monk. Trinity College, MS R.17.5, fol. 9, detail

prefatory letter to Pope Paul II, and the four-sided border of the opening page of the Letters themselves, with a historiated initial depicting Jerome and a kneeling Benedictine monk, are the work of an artist trained on the Continent. The decoration elsewhere in the volume is much less elaborate, comprising largely pen-drawn initials. Werken's exemplar was Giovanni Andrea Bussi's revised edition of Jerome's letters, printed in Rome by Sweynheym and Pannartz in 1468. He carefully reproduced aspects of the appearance of the printed exemplar, such as the layout of the text and rubrics, as well as imitating in a humanistic hand even minor details of the edition's roman type, and employing unobtrusive hard-point ruling.

Werken is one of a number of Dutch and German scribes who worked for English patrons during the mid-fifteenth century. During his earlier career he had been a close associate of the English Humanists, William Gray (later Bishop of Ely) and Richard Bole, Fellow of Balliol College, Oxford, and acted as a scribe for both. He accompanied Gray to Italy in 1444 or 1445 and probably learned there to write a humanistic hand. In the 1470s, however, he was based at or near Christ Church, Canterbury where he not only wrote supply leaves for two of the Cathedral Priory's twelfth-century Passionals (Canterbury, Cathedral Archives, MS Lit. E.42, fols. 69–74), but also produced a number of patristic texts (it is not known whether at the behest of the community or perhaps that of Prior Sellyng, a noted Humanist). These commissions are striking for their size and script, and for the use of recent printed editions. They reveal a Benedictine monastery supplementing or replacing its earlier copies of patristic texts with new copies reflecting humanistic influence in their script and, in two instances, their printed exemplars.

PROVENANCE: no. 112 in Ingram's list of books in the library of Christ Church, Canterbury in 1508; gift of Thomas Nevile (1548–1615), Master of Trinity College (1593–1615).

LITERATURE: James 1900–1904, II, 413; James 1903, 156; Mynors 1949–1953, 103–104; de la Mare 1972–1976; de la Mare and Hellinga 1977–1980, 191–92, 229; Robinson 1988, I, 100, II, pl. 316; Parkes 1997, 110–11, 134–35.

TW

39

Bede, Commentary on the Apocalypse, etc.

In Latin
England, probably Ramsey, second half of the twelfth century

Parchment, iv + 212 + i fols., 270 × 180 mm, text 172–81 × 95–103 mm, 21 lines, ruled in plummet and crayon.

SCRIPT: late Caroline minuscule/early Gothic bookhand (textualis)

BINDING: white tawed skin over boards, 12th c.

St John's College, MS H.6 (James no. 209)

THIS VOLUME contains copies of the commentaries on the Apocalypse by Bede and Caesarius (here attributed to Gennadius), Folcard's Life of St Botulph and Ambrose's *De Helia et ieiunio* (which now ends incomplete). The texts are preceded by a quire of four leaves, the first of which was originally blank, containing on fols. ii–iii verso a somewhat unusual and well-executed set of full-page framed pen drawings relating to the Apocalypse.

The quality of the drawings is in marked contrast to the script of the texts which was executed by a rather poor scribe who was, perhaps, the rubricator. The texts contain three mediocre decorated multi-coloured major initials, ornamented with zoomorphic and foliate elements. Both script and decoration look conservative for a manuscript, which, from the evidence of the drawings and inscriptions on the preliminary leaves must have been produced during the second half of the twelfth century. Another conservative feature is the absence of prickings in the inner margin to guide the horizontal ruling.

At first sight the drawings and the texts appear to have a common origin, since the hand of the inscriptions is clearly the same as that of the rubrics, apparently confirming the image on fol. ii verso of a man kneeling in humble supplication before the figure of St John as a portrait of the scribe of the following texts (*scriptor libri ueniam precatur*, 'the scribe of the book begs pardon'). However, Michael Gullick has drawn attention to the cramped and ill-spaced character of the inscriptions, and the difference in the quality of the parchment of these prefatory leaves and that of the main contents of the manuscript, which may suggest that the inscriptions were added. This would allow for the possibility that the drawings were produced elsewhere (conceivably even on the Continent, given the comparisons scholars have drawn between the treatment of the drapery folds and that of North German enamels of *c*.1170), and were only subsequently brought together with a manuscript that appropriately began with two commentaries on the Apocalypse. The rubricator of the manuscript may at that point have converted a purely devotional image into a scribal portrait.

The quality and conservatism of the script, decoration and codicology suggest that the texts at least were produced for local consumption in a 'provincial' centre. This may have been Ramsey Abbey, which certainly owned the

book in the late Middle Ages. A Fenland origin may also be indicated by the inclusion of Folcard's Life of St Botulf. Botulph was a seventh-century East Anglian saint, and his late eleventh-century hagiographer, Folcard, was, for a time, abbot at nearby Thorney. The text, however, is addressed to Bishop Walkelin of Winchester, and interest in it may have extended beyond the

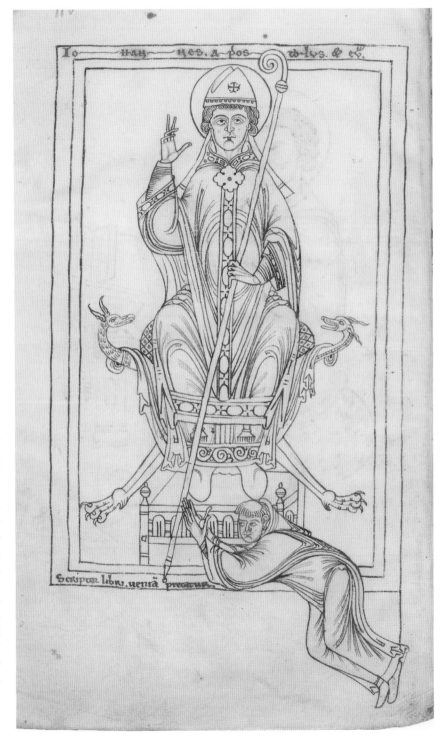

St John with kneeling supplicant. St John's College, MS H.6, fol. ii verso

Fens during the twelfth century. Although one of the other four surviving twelfth-century copies has a Peterborough provenance, the origin and ownership of the other three are unknown. Copies (now lost) are attested later at Reading and Saint-Évroult.

PROVENANCE: partially erased 15th-century *ex libris* inscription of Ramsey Abbey, fol. 1; William Crashaw (1572–1626); Henry Wriothesley, Earl of Southampton (*c*.1615); given to St John's College by his son Thomas in 1635.

EXHIBITED: London 1984b, no. 66.

LITERATURE: James 1913, 240–42; Kauffmann 1975, no. 86; Sharpe 1997, 117.

TW

40

Apocalypse

In Anglo-Norman French
England, *c*.1255–*c*.1260

Parchment, i + 32 fols., 430 × 304 mm, text 360 × 225 mm, 2 columns, 56 lines, ruled in plummet

SCRIPT: Gothic bookhand (textualis)

BINDING: gold-tooled white leather over wooden boards, royal arms and crown in the centre, 16th c.

Trinity College MS R.16.2

THIS IS THE LARGEST and most sumptuously illuminated of all thirteenth-century English Apocalypses. It has seventy-five framed pictures illustrating the Apocalypse text accompanied by extracts from the commentary of Berengaudus, both in French. Several of these contain more than one scene: there are ninety-seven scenes altogether, in addition to eleven pages of the scenes of the Life of St John the Evangelist, thought to be the author of the Apocalypse. These are divided into two sections, the first before he is exiled by the Emperor Domitian to the Isle of Patmos where he receives the apocalyptic visions; the second following the illustrations of the Apocalypse and telling of his preaching and miracles in Ephesus, and of his death. All these illustrations are in gold frames fully painted with the figures and animals set against counter-changed red and blue panelled grounds, in some cases gold grounds. The pictures closely follow the Apocalypse text with occasional influence from the commentary. The artists were evidently aware of the two basic iconographic models of English Apocalypse pictures already established by *c*.1255 when the Trinity Apocalypse was in the making (the Morgan-Bodleian and Metz-Lambeth cycles), but in most cases they reinter-

preted the material in their own way. In a few cases influence from a *c*.1225 Spanish Beatus Apocalypse is evident, similar to Paris, Bibliothèque nationale de France, MS nouv. acq. lat. 2290. The individual iconography has negligible influence on subsequent artists. Notable is the frequent inclusion of inscriptions and texts on scrolls and placards in the pictures. The Life of St John scenes mostly derive their imagery and some of their inscriptions from the text of his life in Anglo-Norman French (Paris, Bibliothèque nationale de France, MS fr. 19525).

Four artists worked on the book. The first painted fols. 1–16v, 25, 28–30v; the second fols. 17–24v, 27; the third the picture of the Heavenly Jerusalem on fol. 25v; and the fourth the final two pages of the life of St John on fols. 31–31v, separate from the final gathering and possibly done later. If this was the case, the life of St John was cut off on fol. 30v in the middle of the story of the robber youth. The third and fourth artists worked in the new French 'Court Style', which came to England in the mid-1250s. The first two show some stylistic similarities with the Rutland and Evesham Psalters (London, British Library, Add. MSS 62925 and 44874), but are not identical with their artists.

The ownership and patronage context is suggested by the inclusion in six scenes of a lady in company with men in brown-grey friars' habits (fols. 7v, 14, 14v, 17v, 20v, 24v), probably intended as Franciscans even though they lack their characteristic cord girdle. This group either fights against evil or is shown among the saved who escape the punishment of the wicked. Some have suggested that this woman was Henry III's queen, Eleanor of Provence, but she could be any of the high aristocratic women who are documented as patrons of illustrated manuscripts in England at this time.

There is no evidence from script or artistic style as to where in England this book was made. A city close to a major residence of the royal family, London, Salisbury or Winchester, is a possible place for its production.

PROVENANCE: Anne Sadleir, daughter of Edward Coke, and wife of Ralph Sadleir of Standon, Herts.; in a note on the front flyleaf, dated 20th August 1649, she commits the book to Ralph Brownrig, Bishop of Exeter (1592–1659), instructing him to give it to Trinity College where it arrived in 1660.

EXHIBITED: London 1987–1988, no. 349.

LITERATURE: James 1900–1904, II, 369–82, no. 950; James 1909b; Brieger 1967; Henderson 1967, 105, 117–35, pls. 9–11; Henderson 1968, 108–13; Otaka and Fukui 1977; Marks and Morgan 1981, 62–65, pls. 12–13; Emmerson and Lewis 1985, no. 50; Morgan 1982–1988, no. 110, frontispiece, ills. 60–66; Schiller 1990–1991, I, 261–62; II, *passim*, pls. 46, 113–15, 152, 168, 176, 204–05, 245, 280, 308–09, 334, 378, 384, 393, 427, 475–77, 496, 514, 538–39, 585–89, 644, 648, 659, 687, 730, 733, 737, 744, 772, 779; Lewis 1995, *passim*; Kauffmann 2003, 166; McKitterick et al. 2004; *Trinity Apokalypse* 2004.

NJM

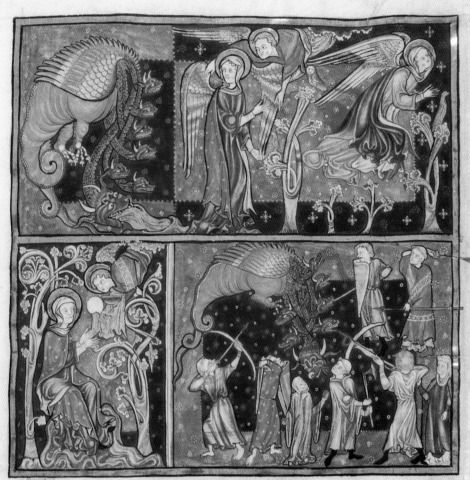

Epus ke li dragun uir ke il fu iete en tere: il pur
siwi la feme ke enfaunta le masle. e deul ele
de un graunt egle sunt dunes a la femme ke ole uo
last en deser lu. u ole est nurrie par un tens. e par
plusurs tens. e par demi tens. de la fate al serpent.
E la serpent mist hors de sa buche apres la femme
ewe ausi cum un fluue. ke il la frist estre tret del flu
ue. e la tere aida a la femme. e la tere oueŕa sa buche
e transglutra le fluue ke le dragun mist hors de sa
buche. E le dragun curire a cuntre la femme: a la fe
re bataile od les autres de sa semence. ki gardent les
comaundemenz deu. e uint le tesmoine iesu.

Epus ke li diable uir ke il auerr pdu graunt mul
titudine del esluz. e enclos de deus les destreises des
queors des reprouez. il pursiwi la femme co est seinte
eglise. Kar il enusa les empeŕurs de roume e tute la
multitudine des maues a pursiwere le poeple deu.
P le egle poum entendre est. Deul eles sunt deul testa
menz. Deul eles sunt donel a seinte eglise. co sut deul
testamenz. ke ole eschapet le diable. e ke ole munrre

al pais celestre p le apriſe de eus. Il apele cest pais deser
si cum nostre seignur dist en le ewangile. kaunt il dist
sai auert lasse nonaunte nof oŵailes en le desert e auert
ale querr une ke auert erre. Bapele le lu de seinte eglise
cest pais. si eul dura en le iugemer. Les bens eim munn
pere receueis. e receueis le regne ke est aparie auus de
la neſaunte del munde. P un tens. e plusur tens e
demi tens. le teus de la passiun ihu ist. treske a la fin
del munde est signifie. Le fluue de ewe sur charneus
desirs. Kaunt li diable uerr ke seinte eglise ne pot estre
abatue par pseruruns. mes destre e estre fermee. il
enuerr la multitudine de charn eus desirs. ke il la fa
ce estre tret par eus. Nus poum entendre les reprouez
p la tere. ki furent receiuurs des charneus desirs. Anus po
um entendre par meimes la tere ist. u p la buche de la tere n
poü entedre la poustre de est. La tere aida a la feme co est
ist. seinte eglise. Il ouerr le sen de sa misericorde. e sa poul
re esteint del tut enturr le fluue de uices. Les autres de la
semence de seinte eglise sunt les esluz ki sunt a nostre en la
fin del munde. od les queus aunrest le combarera.

41

Apocalypse

In Latin and English
England, probably Peterborough, *c*.1320–*c*.1335

Parchment, iii (paper) + i + 65 + iii (paper) fols., 305 × 203 mm,
text 225 × 135 mm, 2 columns of 18–19 lines (fols. 1–39v),
2 columns of 43–44 lines (fols. 40–65v), ruled in brown ink

SCRIPT: Gothic bookhand (textualis)

BINDING: brown leather, 1996, reusing old pastedowns on inner
covers

Magdalene College, Old Library, MS 5

THE BOOK is in two parts: an illustrated Apocalypse
in Latin with the commentary of Berengaudus
(fols. 1–39v), and an added fifteenth-century unillustrated Apocalypse commentary in English translated
from a thirteenth-century French prose Apocalypse
commentary. The Latin text is divided into two sections,
a passage from the Apocalypse illustrated in a rectangular picture above, followed by an excerpt from the late
eleventh-century commentary of Berengaudus explaining what is signified by the dramatic and often bizarre
events narrated in the Apocalypse text. There are seventy-
eight pictures portraying the visions of St John, who is
often shown standing outside the frame observing the
dreadful beasts, disasters of fire, earthquakes and thun-
ders, which are described in the text. This arrangement
and the selection of text passages derives from a group
of Apocalypses created in the middle years of the thirteenth century. These are named the Metz-Lambeth
group after the two earliest manuscripts, Metz, Bibliothèque municipale, MS Salis 38 of *c*.1250–1255 (destroyed by bombing in 1944), and London, Lambeth
Palace, MS 209 of *c*.1260–1267. The Tanner Apocalypse
of *c*.1255–1260 (Oxford, Bodleian Library, MS Tanner
184) made some modifications of the iconography of
the Apocalypse scenes, and has two fourteenth-century
followers, the Magdalene Apocalypse shown here and
the Canonici Apocalypse (Oxford, Bodleian Library,
MS Canon. bibl. lat. 62). The Canonici Apocalypse is
closely related in the figure style of its pictures to a
Psalter made for the Benedictine Abbey of Peterborough
(Oxford, Bodleian Library, MS Barlow 22), whereas the
Magdalene Apocalypse almost certainly was owned by
the nearby Benedictine Abbey of Croyland, referred to
in notes on fols. i, 65. This has led to the conclusion that
both Apocalypses were made in the Fenland region,
possibly in Peterborough.

The Magdalene and Canonici Apocalypses have almost
identical iconography for their seventy-eight scenes, and
both have the figures, painted with light colour washes
of blue, green, pink and grey, with gold only used for
haloes, crowns and a few other details, silhouetted against
the blank parchment ground. Characteristic of both is a
strong interest in shadowing in black and grey partly by
means of close parallel lines. The Canonici manuscript
is by two artists, and one of them may be the same as the
artist of the Magdalene College Apocalypse. The similarity of facial types, poses, and folds is particularly
evident in the opening pictures of the latter, although
later in the book the drawing line becomes sketchier. It
seems that during the decoration of the book the artist
took up a new style, that of the Queen Mary Psalter
workshop *(see nos. 80, 117, 149 and fig. 1)*. This influence
could have come from the Psalter *(no. 149)* which passed
to Peterborough Abbey before 1321 from an owner in
the Norwich diocese. The miniatures of the Prophets
and Apostles in tinted drawing in this Psalter, with their
mannered poses and small heads on tall thin bodies, are
just the sort of art which may have influenced the
Magdalene Apocalypse artist causing him to change his
style in the course of illustrating the book. Another link
with the Canonici Apocalypse is the delicate red penwork border extensions from the text initials, with leaves
and hybrid human or animal grotesques in the Magdalene College book. Work of the same sort, probably
by the same artist, is found in a supplementary text
section of the Meditations of St Bernard in the Canonici
Apocalypse. The dating of both manuscripts is likely to
be contemporary with the Barlow Psalter, which can be
dated after 1321 and before 1338.

PROVENANCE: Benedictine Abbey of Croyland (an almost erased
reference to ownership by a monk of Croyland on fol. i and a
reference to John London, monk of Croyland, on fol. 65); given
to the College by the antiquarian Simon Gunton (1609–1676).

EXHIBITED: Norwich 1973, no. 10.

LITERATURE: James 1909a, 5–10; Robbins 1952, 93–94, 259–60;
Sandler 1974, 110–17, 153–54; Emmerson and Lewis 1985, no.
46; Sandler 1986, no. 93, ill. 241.

NJM

The Fourth Rider. Magdalene College,
Old Library, MS 5, fol. 6

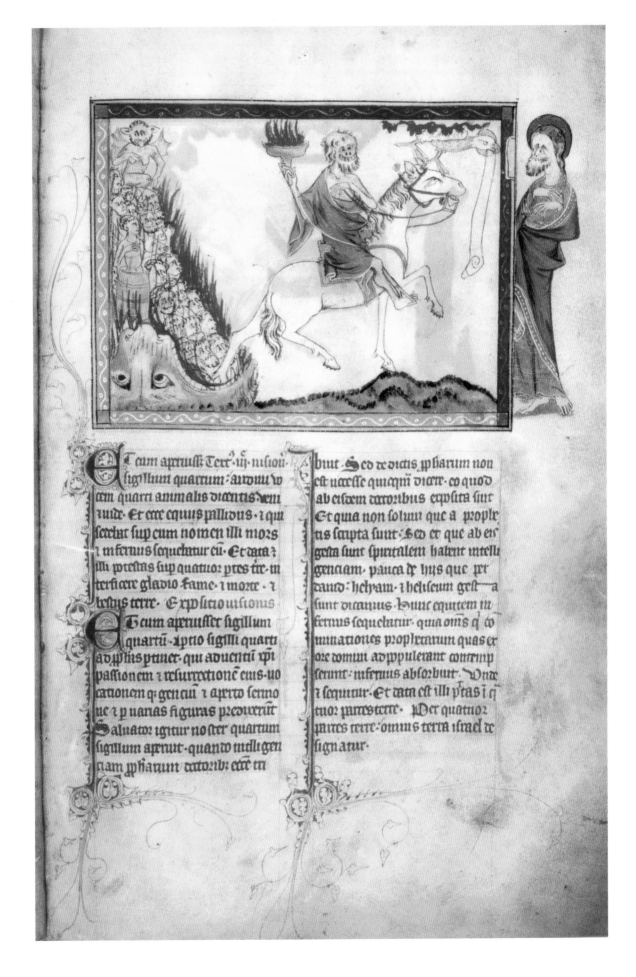

Et cum aprruifit Terr . iij . uisiou
sigrllum quartum: audiui uo
cem quarti animalis dicentis. veni
uidc. Et ecce equus pallidus . ⁊ qui
sedebat sup cum nomen illi mors
⁊ infernus sequebatur cu. Et data é
illi potestas sup quatuor ptes tir- in
tersicere gladio fame . ⁊ morte . ⁊
bestiis terre . Exposicio uisionis

Et cum aprruisset sigillum
quartu . aptio sigilli quarti
ad ipsis ptinet . qui aduenti xpi
passionem ⁊ resurrectione eius-uo
cationem qr gentiu ⁊ aprito sermo
ne ⁊ p uarias figuras preduxerit
Saluator igitur noster quartum
sigillum aprruit. quando intelligen
ciam ipharum certoribz ecce tri

buit . Sed de dictis ipharum non
est necesse quicqni dicere . eo quod
ab eisdem cterroribus exposita sunt
Et quia non solum que a prople
tis scripta sunt . Sed ⁊ que ab eis
gesta sunt spiritalem habent intelli
genciam . pauca de hijs que pr
dicando . hebram . thesiceum gest
sunt dicamus . Hunc equitem in
fernus sequebatur . quia omis q co
minaciones propletarum quas ex
ore domini adppulerant contrip
serunt infernus absorbuit . Unde
⁊ sequitur . Et data est illi ptas in q
tuor partes terre . Per quatuor
partes terre . omnis terra israel de
signatur .

42

Apocalypse with Commentary by Alexander of Bremen

In Latin
Germany, Cologne or Lower Saxony, *c.*1270–*c.*1275

Parchment, i (paper) + 205 + i (paper) fols., 250 × 180 mm, text 183 × 117 mm, 37 long lines, ruled in brown-black ink

SCRIPT: Gothic bookhand (textualis)

BINDING: marbled paper over wooden boards, by D. Cockerell, 1972

Cambridge University Library, MS Mm.5.31

THE COMMENTARY on the Apocalypse by Alexander (d.1271), a Franciscan who lived in the diocese of Bremen, is found in illustrated editions. Four copies, in addition to the Cambridge manuscript, have come down to us: Dresden, Sächsische Landesbibliothek, MS A. 117 (*c.*1300); Prague, Knihovna Metropolitni Kapituli, MS Cim. 5 (*c.*1336); Vatican City, Biblioteca Apostolica Vaticana, MS Vat. Lat. 3819); Wroclaw, Bibliotheka Uniwersytecka, MS I.Q.19 (*c.*1270–*c.*1275). The two earliest manuscripts in Cambridge and Wroclaw are closely related. Alexander's commentary presents the past and present history of the world as illustrative of the prophecies of the Apocalypse. This is done by other medieval Apocalypse commentators, but not, as here, by constructing the historical parallels in systematic order beginning with the Romans and the Early Church and ending with their own times. In chapter 20 Alexander takes his interpretation into near contemporary history at the time of the Second Crusade. His interpretation is clearly influenced by the apocalyptic writings by the late twelfth-century Calabrian abbot, Joachim of Fiore (d.1202), whose works were of interest to many Franciscans in the thirteenth century. Alexander quotes him in his commentary of the closing chapters of the Apocalypse. In the commentary to chapter 22 he refers to the coming of St Francis and the Franciscans. The illustrations in the Cambridge copy include Cistercians, which might suggest it was produced for a Cistercian Abbey.

Alexander first wrote his commentary around 1235 but revised it several times until its final version in 1249. Joachim had prophesied the coming end of the world in 1260, but for Alexander the Last Judgement would not take place until 1326. The Cambridge copy has seventy-one illustrations, having lost thirty-five folios, whereas in the Wroclaw text there are eighty-three, and

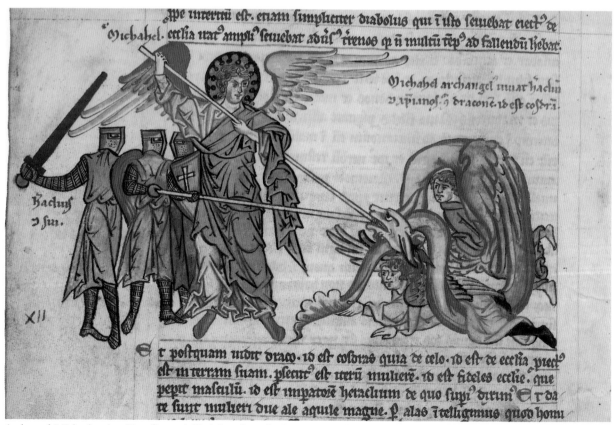

Archangel Michael saving Heraclius and Christians from the Dragon. Cambridge University Library, MS Mm.5.31, fol. 78v, detail

the maximum number in the other manuscripts is eighty-five (Prague copy). These are set as unframed illustrations at various positions on the text page. The figures and architectural settings, silhouetted against the blank vellum, are brightly coloured with thick painting and a sense for modelling and highlighting. Text inscriptions and speech scrolls are placed in the pictures to clarify their meaning, even though this is also explained in the text. Historical events and personages mentioned in the commentary are interpolated with the visions of the Apocalypse or are referred to by the interpolated inscriptions.

The iconography of some of the scenes suggests influence from the established cycles of Apocalypse illustration in mid-thirteenth century England (e.g. *no. 40*). This could be explained by one of these Apocalypses having been available in Cologne in the early 1270s, the time when the Cambridge and Wroclaw manuscripts were made. The English Franciscan, Peter of Tewkesbury, was lector for the Cologne Franciscans in the 1270s, and he could have brought with him the English Apocalypse that might have been used as a model. The location of the production of the two manuscripts in Cologne is made on stylistic grounds, namely because of their particular form of late *Zackenstil* (zig-zag style) of *c.*1250–*c.*1270 comparable to manuscripts such as the

Cartulary of the Brotherhood of the Three Kings (Hannover, Kestner Museum, Inv. 3986) of the 1250s, and the panel paintings of the Apostles in St Ursula. The style of Cologne wall painting of *c.*1250 in the Baptistery of St Gereon is also comparable, and albeit in a more mannered version, the *c.*1270 Crucifixion in the Baptistery of St Kunibert. Some have compared the style of these two manuscripts to painting of the Thuringian-Saxon school of the same period, but the parallels with Cologne painting seem closer.

PROVENANCE: Jo. Conyers, perhaps John Conyers, apothecary and antiquary (1633–1694); John Moore, Bishop of Ely (1707–1714); presented to the Library by George I in 1715.

EXHIBITED: London 1999– 2000, no. 14.

LITERATURE: University Library 1856–1867, IV, 359; Gilson 1922, 20–36; Huggler 1934, 113–16, 122–50; Wachtel 1955, XIV–XVI, XLIV–LIX, 1–510 (edition of the text); Leclercq 1956, 305–06; Mroczko 1966, 10–21, 27–31, 35, 44–45, figs. 1–4, 7–9; Emmerson and Lewis 1986, 443–44, no. 118; Schiller 1990–1991, I, 219–27; II, *passim*, pls. 98, 99, 138, 174–75, 199, 200, 238–40, 328, 372, 418, 456–59, 509, 532–34, 575–78, 637–38, 666, 686, 719–20; Schmolinsky 1991, *passim*; Lewis 2001; Derolez 2003, pl. 73.

NJM

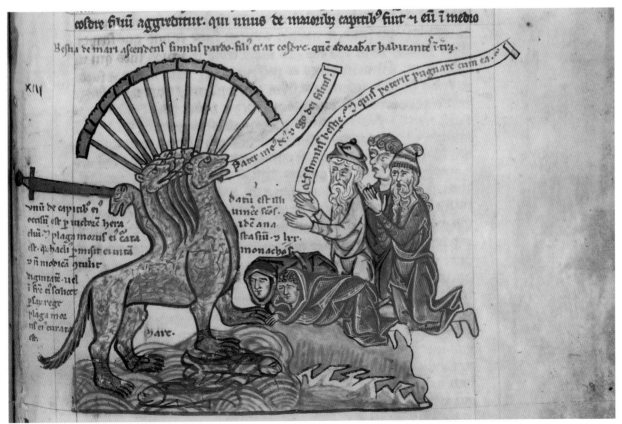

Worship of the Seven-Headed Beast rising from the Sea. Cambridge University Library, MS Mm.5.31, fol. 79, detail

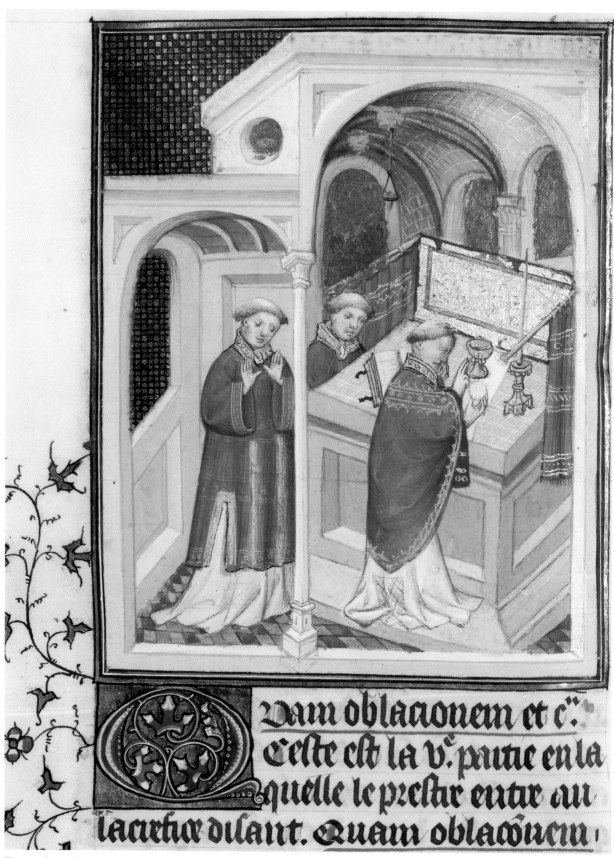

Fig. 20. Canon Prayer at Mass. Guillaume Durand, *Rational des Divins Offices*, Cambridge, St John's College, MS T. 8, fol. 121v, detail

THE LITURGY AND THE OFFICES

Nigel Morgan

Books used for the liturgical services in the Middle Ages in most cases were of high quality in their script and decoration, and quite often of exceptional luxury. These books can be divided into those used for the Mass and those for the Divine Office, and even the smallest parish church was expected to have a set of the basic texts required.[1]

There were many books for the Mass in the early Middle Ages. From the second half of the twelfth century many of these became amalgamated into a single book, the Missal (*nos. 45, 46, 47, 48*).[2] Before that time a book called a Sacramentary (*no. 44*, which includes some additional texts) contained only those parts of the Mass which were recited by the priest. The Collectar for the Collects, the Lectionaries for the Epistle (*no. 7*) and the Gospel (*no. 43*), and the Gradual for the musical parts of the Mass existed as separate volumes. The Gospel readings at Mass were often not arranged in a Gospel Lectionary but read directly from a text of the four Gospels, and in that sense the often richly decorated Gospel Book (*nos. 1, 8, 9, 10*) is an essential part of the set of liturgical books required in the earlier centuries of the Middle Ages. Gospel Books of this type cease to be produced after the twelfth century. Of these individual texts, only the Gradual survives extensively as a separate book from the thirteenth century onwards.[3] In Northern Europe Graduals very rarely had much illumination, but in Italy from the thirteenth to the sixteenth centuries these very large books had historiated initials and decorative borders. Many of them were mutilated, particularly in the nineteenth century, by cutting out pages or initials and these survive as cuttings (*nos. 59, 60, 62*). Very occasionally a church would possess separate Epistle and Gospel Lectionaries, and two such illuminated books from fifteenth-century England are Cambridge, Trinity College, MSS B.11.12 and B.11.13. Collectars of the later Middle Ages exist for some religious Orders, such as a *c.*1450–1470 illuminated copy for the Dominicans of Dunstable (Cambridge, University Library, MS Add. 2770).[4] Most churches would only possess a Missal and a Gradual, although larger churches would have several copies of each. Additional to these would be a Processional containing the texts and music for processions before the Mass.[5] Processionals hardly ever have much, if any, illumination: a Spanish copy of the early sixteenth century with decorative initials is Fitzwilliam Museum, MS McClean 53.

The Divine Office is the series of services for the hours of prayer: Matins, Lauds, Prime, Terce, Sext, None, Vespers and Compline.[6] All these would be services in choir for the religious Orders, collegiate churches and some would be held in a few large urban parish churches. For smaller parish churches, save on major feast days when some of the hours would be as services in choir, the priest or priests would be expected to read these hours of prayer privately in his Breviary. The hymns, collects, readings and prayers of the Divine Office are arranged around the weekly recitation of all hundred and fifty Psalms spread over the services of the hours.[7] The Psalter was absolutely essential for the Office. Many Psalters in the Middle Ages, however, were made for private devotional reading rather than use in the public liturgy *(nos. 72, 73, 79, 99, 101)*. In the early Middle Ages, other than the Psalter, an Office Lectionary would be required for the readings and an Antiphonal and Hymnal for the sung parts of the service.[8] In the twelfth century all these various texts were combined into one book, the Breviary *(nos. 49, 50)*, but the Antiphonal *(no. 61)* and Hymnal with full musical notation remained as separate books.[9] Hymnals were often attached to Psalters *(no. 101)*, often with the hymn texts only, without music. Occasionally a church had a separate Office Lectionary for the readings, but this is very rare after 1200 when the texts for the readings were included in the Breviary.

Missals, Breviaries and Psalters contain liturgical Calendars, usually placed at the beginning of the Missal and Psalter, but in the Breviary in the middle, preceding the Psalter. The Calendars are of the Use of a particular diocese or of a particular religious Order, or in the case of the Benedictines an individual house of their Order.[10] Analysis of the Calendar is the easiest way to determine the intended destination or origin of the text. In addition to their liturgical content most Calendars contain computistical material relating to the date of Easter and other moveable feasts.[11]

In addition to these essential books all churches needed two others, the Manual and the Ordinal.[12] The Manual contained all of the 'occasional Offices' required from the priest: e.g. Baptism, Marriage, Extreme Unction (the anointing of the seriously ill and dying), the Commendation of the Soul (the prayers and Psalms recited immediately following death), and the funeral and burial services, together with many other minor functions. The Ordinal is essentially a directory which outlines what services have to be done during the church year and how they should be done. These books rarely receive much illumination.

Bishops needed special books for the services only they could perform, and these usually had rich illumination appropriate to the status of their owners. These were contained in two books, the Benedictional *(e.g. no. 57)*; the *c.*900 Augsburg Benedictional, Fitzwilliam Museum, MS 27; the fifteenth-century Treviso Benedictional, Fitzwilliam Museum, MS McClean 52) and the Pontifical *(nos. 52, 54, 55* and the *c.*1500 French Pontifical, Fitzwilliam Museum, MS 29). The Benedictional contained the special blessings given to those present by the bishop after the consecration at Mass, and blessings for certain other occasions.[13] It occasionally exists as a separate book but usually constitutes one of the sections of the Pontifical. Pontificals are usually very large books and must have been inconvenient to use for the long and complex pontifical ceremonies.[14] This resulted in smaller books that included only certain sections of the full Pontifical text *(no. 57* containing the Benedictional and some other pontifical Offices; *no. 56* mainly containing pontifical Vespers and Mass, and the early fifteenth-century Spanish selection of pontifical Offices, Fitzwilliam Museum, MS McClean 54). One of the most important services at which bishops presided was the Coronation of a king and queen, emperor and empress.[15] It was either included in Pontificals or found separately *(no. 51)*.

Treatises on the liturgy were written to explain the ceremonies and texts, their symbolism and theological meaning. The most extensive of these was the *Rationale divinorum officiorum* by Guillaume Durand, Bishop of Mende. In the late fourteenth century the Latin text was translated into French and this edition exists in a series of illuminated copies.[16] One of the most extensively illustrated copies of the French version was made in Paris in the early fifteenth century *(fig. 20, no. 53)*.

The most numerous illuminated liturgical books in Cambridge libraries are of English provenance dating from the tenth century *(nos. 43, 44)* to the Reformation.[17] The liturgy in England had two periods of change. The first was in the fifty years after the Norman Conquest when older Anglo-Saxon liturgical practices were in part reformed according to the texts and rites of Normandy. The second, which began in the second half of the thirteenth century and ended in the early fifteenth century, was the adoption by almost all the English dioceses of the province of Canterbury of the liturgical texts of Salisbury Cathedral, the Use of Sarum.[18] The northern province of York retained its own Use of York, and for reasons yet to be explained, one diocese, Hereford, kept its own texts and ceremonies.[19] In the province of Canterbury, all secular Missals and Breviaries from the mid-fourteenth century until the Reformation were of Sarum Use, but sometimes contained feast days of saints and other special Uses of a particular diocese, diocesan supplements as the are called. Similarly, the popular devotional text, the Book of Hours, followed the Use of Sarum, and so did the Calendars, Litanies and Offices of the Dead in Psalters and Books of Hours.

Liturgical books from other European countries, mainly France and Italy, are fewer in Cambridge. They range from the tenth century *(no. 7* and the German Benedictional and Epistle Lectionary, Fitzwilliam Museum, MS 27) to the Reformation, but are mostly of the fourteenth and fifteenth centuries. They come from a great range of dioceses, but some are of the Use of Rome, which was adopted by some dioceses, particularly in Italy, in the fifteenth century.[20]

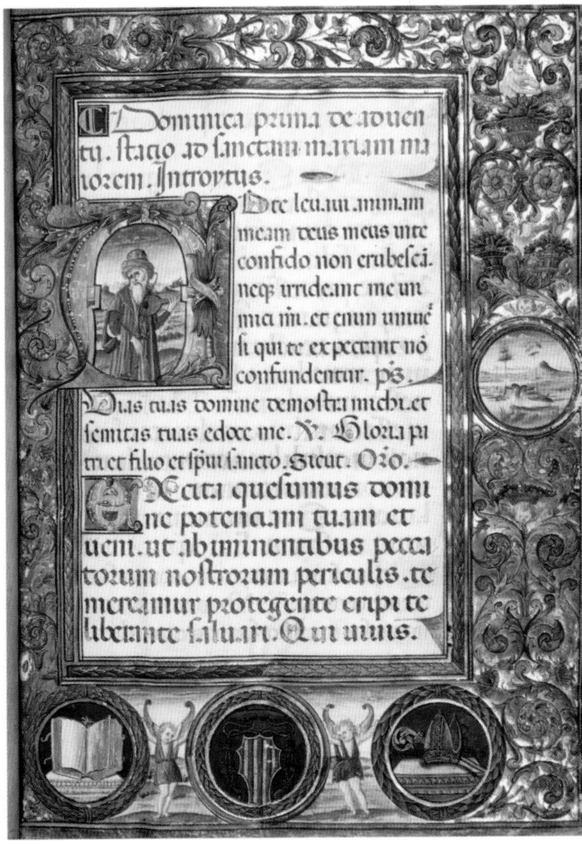

The illumination of liturgical books marks the services for the main feasts of the church year with historiated and ornamental initials or framed miniatures. The liturgical year in Missals and Breviaries is divided into two parts, the Temporal and the Sanctoral. The Temporal contains the feasts of the church year and all the Sunday Masses, whereas the Sanctoral contains the feasts of the saints, including those of the Virgin Mary. The Temporal usually ends with the feast of the Dedication of a Church whose date would of course vary from church to church, and this is often given an historiated initial. Another section of Missals and Breviaries is the Common, which contains the texts for the general categories of apostles, martyrs, confessors and virgins, and usually there is an historiated initial at the beginning of the Common. Finally there is a section of Votive Masses in the Missal and Votive Offices in the Breviary. These contain the Masses and Offices for the Holy Trinity, Holy Spirit, the Virgin Mary, the Dead and for many other specific occasions. Many Missals contain the marriage service with the accompanying nuptial Mass. In addition, in the centre of a Breviary, between the Temporal and the Sanctoral, is the Psalter, because the recitation of the Psalms forms the core of the

Fig. 21. David as a musician. Missal. Fitzwilliam Museum, MS Marlay 10, fol. 5

Divine Office. The Psalms of the liturgical divisions (the first Psalms for Matins of each day of the week, and the first Psalm for Sunday Vespers) are given large historiated or ornamental initials, and this results in the same system being used for Psalters for private use *(nos. 72, 73, 79)*.[21]

The position of the historiated initials for Missals is usually at the *Introit (fig. 21)*, the text sung at the entrance of the priest at the beginning of Mass.[22] Very occasionally it is found at the Collect which follows the singing of the *Kyrie* and the *Gloria* after the *Introit*. Missals also have large historiated or ornamental initials sometimes at the beginning of the Preface (*Vere dignum et iustum est*) and always at the beginning of the Canon Prayer (*Te igitur clementissime Pater*) *(nos. 45, 48)*. In Breviaries, the historiated initial is usually at Matins, either for the first Antiphon to the Psalms of the first Nocturn, at the beginning of the first lesson at Matins, or at its responsory, a text which was sung to an elaborate chant at choral Matins. Occasionally for great feasts there is Vespers on the vigil of the feast, and sometimes the historiated initial occurs at the first Antiphon to the Psalms for first Vespers *(fig. 22)*, or at the *Capitulum* reading *(fig. 23)*.

Other special formats of illustration are found in Gospel Lectionaries and Missals. These books often have full-page miniatures of the four Evangelists for Lectionaries and a full-page miniature of the Crucifixion at the beginning of the Canon Prayer (*Te igitur*) for Missals *(nos. 46, 47, 48)*. Gospel Lectionaries occasionally also have full-page miniatures for the main feasts of the liturgical year, as in the *c.*1170–1180 Eichstätt Lectionary, Fitzwilliam Museum, MS McClean 22.

The corresponding musical books to the Missal and the Breviary are the Gradual and the Antiphonal *(nos. 59, 60, 61, 62, 63, 66)*. In Italy, they were of exceptionally large size and elaborate illumination, but smaller and less ornate in other parts of Europe. The system of decoration is as for Missals and Breviaries in placing historiated or ornamental initials at the beginning of the main feasts of the Temporal, Sanctoral and at the beginning of the Common. In Graduals, as in Missals, the historiated initial usually occurs at the *Introit*, and in Antiphonals either at the responsory for the first lesson of Matins, or at the first Antiphon to the Psalms at first Vespers. In addition to music books used in the formal liturgy of the Church, the Italian religious confraternities, the *laudesi*, had an elaborately illuminated book, the *laudario*, containing the vernacular hymns (*laude*) sung at their extra-liturgical services. These, like many Italian Graduals and Antiphonals, have often been mutilated by cutting out pages or initials *(no. 58)*.

The bishop's books, the Benedictional and Pontifical, have images at the major divisions of the text *(fig. 24)*, or in

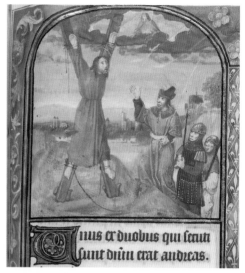

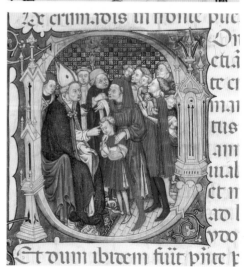

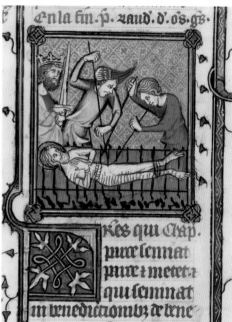

the case of a Benedictional for the main feast days on which the blessings are given *(nos. 52, 54, 55, 56, 57)*.[23] The arrangement of the texts of a Pontifical varied considerably until Guillaume Durand produced a standard text in the late thirteenth century *(no. 55)*. The text was used widely, but not exclusively, in the later centuries of the Middle Ages.[24] Other than the elaborate decoration at the beginning of the major divisions, many Pontificals have historiated initials *(no. 55)* or miniatures *(nos. 52, 54* and Fitzwilliam Museum, MS 29) illustrating the various ceremonies performed by the bishop *(e.g. fig. 24)*. These illustrations of ceremonies in Pontificals are necessarily rather simplified, and only give an approximate indication of the ways in which the rites were performed.

REFERENCES

1   For the different types of books see Harper 1991; Hughes 1982; Plummer 1964; specifically for England see the still useful Wordsworth and Littlehales 1904.

2   For the development of liturgical books up to the early thirteenth century see Palazzo 1998. For Missals and Sacramentaries the most extensive study is Leroquais 1924.

3   The Gradual is very well discussed in *The New Grove Dictionary of Music and Musicians*, 1980, VII, 598–609, and in Huglo 1988.

4   For the Dominican liturgy see Bonniwell 1944.

5   On this text see Bailey 1971 and Wormald 1972.

6   In addition to the books cited in nn. 1,2 see Fassler and Baltzer 2000 and for the English Benedictines, Roper 1993.

7   For tables showing the different way the Psalms were distributed over the hours of the Office in secular and monastic use see Gy 1984, 546–9.

8   The Antiphonal is very well discussed in *The New Grove Dictionary of Music and Musicians*, 1980, I, 482–90, in Hesbert 1963–1979, and in Huglo 1988. For the Hymnal see Mearns 1913 and Walpole and Mason 1922.

9   For the Breviary see Leroquais 1934 and Salmon 1962.

10 Calendars of the religious Orders and some Dioceses are printed in Grotefend 1891–1898; for Paris Calendars, see Perdrizet 1933, and for Oxford University (with a section on Cambridge) Wordsworth 1904. See Wormald 1939 and Wormald 1946 for English Benedictine Calendars.

11 On this aspect of Calendars see Pickering 1980.

12 For the Manual and Ordinal of the Use of Sarum see Collins 1960 and Wordsworth 1901–1902.

13 On Benedictionals see Brückmann 1973; Palazzo 1998, 200–1 and Rasmussen 1998, 492–95.

14 On Pontificals see Frere 1901–1908, Leroquais 1937, Andrieu 1938–1942, Brückmann 1973, Rasmussen 1998 and Palazzo 1999.

15 For the texts of Coronation rites see Legg 1900 and Legg 1901.

16 Rabel 1991.

17 The fundamental short entry catalogue of liturgical books in Cambridge collections is Frere 1894–1932, II, 76–169, nos. 759–1031. Their illumination is not described.

18 Morgan 2001 discusses the date of the introduction of Sarum Use into the dioceses of England. Texts of the Sarum Missals and Breviaries are published in Dickinson 1861–1883, Proctor and Wordsworth 1879–1886, Legg 1916, and Sandon 1984–.

19 Texts of the York and Hereford Missals and Breviaries are published in Henderson 1874, Lawley 1880–1883, Frere and Brown 1904–1915

20 There is an edition in Lippe 1899–1907 of the 1474 Missal of the Use of Rome before that Use was reformed in the sixteenth century following the Council of Trent. Regrettably, there is no modern edition of the pre-Trent Roman Breviary. For the origins of the Missal and Breviary of the Use of Rome see van Dijk and Walker 1960 and van Dijk 1963.

21 For the texts and illumination of Psalters see Haseloff 1938 and Leroquais 1940–1941.

22 See Leroquais, 1924 for the illustration of Missals.

23 For the decoration of Pontificals see Leroquais 1937 and Palazzo 1999.

24 For the text of the Durandus Pontifical see Andrieu 1940, 327–662.

Fig. 22. Martyrdom of St Andrew. Breviary. St John's College, MS H. 13, fol. 103, detail

Fig. 23. Martyrdom of St Laurence. Breviary. Cambridge, University Library, MS Dd.5.5, fol. 264, detail

Fig. 24. Confirmation of a child. Pontifical. Fitzwilliam Museum, MS 28, fol. 1, detail

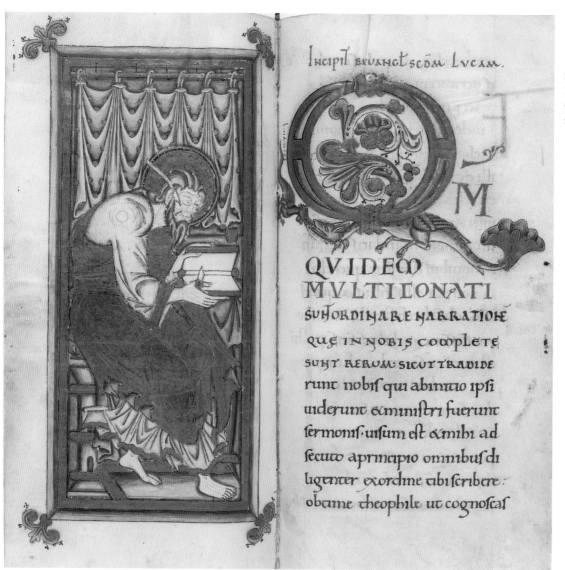

43

Gospel Lectionary

In Latin
England, middle or second half of the eleventh century

Parchment, ii (paper) + 117 + iii (paper) fols., 197 × 100 mm, text 157 × 67 mm, 20 long lines, ruled in hard point

SCRIPT: Caroline minuscule

BINDING: gold-tooled dark green morocco, 18th c.

Pembroke College, MS 302

A GOSPEL LECTIONARY is a collection of the Gospel readings arranged either according to the liturgical cycle or in order of their appearance in the Gospels. Pembroke 302 is of the latter type. As in copies of the complete text of the Gospels, the volume begins with a full set of elaborately decorated Eusebian canon tables,

and each Gospel is introduced with a full-page framed Evangelist portrait and *incipit* page in display script. The accounts of the Passion in Matthew and Mark have been annotated to indicate the utterances of Christ, his disciples and other characters, but otherwise the volume lacks further apparatus.

Soon after it was made, Pembroke 302 was probably owned by the bishop or community at Hereford Cathedral. An Old English description of the eastern boundaries of the diocese of Hereford, as established by Bishop Æthelstan (1012–1056), was added on the recto of an originally blank leaf between the canon tables and the Gospels, in an Anglo-Saxon minuscule datable to the middle or second half of the eleventh century. The origin of the book, however, remains unknown.

The book is very well made: the work of an excellent scribe and artist, the latter making plentiful use of gold and colours of great intensity. It is a small, portable volume, its tall and narrow proportions similar to those of a mid-eleventh-century Troper (London, British

Library, Cotton MS Caligula A.xiv, fols. 1–92). As in the Caligula Troper, the closest parallels to the intense colouring and the style of the draperies and figures are found not in late Anglo-Saxon illumination but in manuscripts from the Low Countries and the Rhineland. Teviotdale's detailed analyses of both books, however, conclude that they are not the work of the same artist or even the same centre, since a number of features typical of late Anglo-Saxon manuscripts, such as the treatment of gold, colour, and facial expressions, are more pronounced in the Gospel Lectionary than in the Caligula Troper.

The minuscule script of the Lectionary also conforms more fully to the distinctive letter-forms of English Caroline minuscule of the mid- and later eleventh century, although certain details, such as the form of 'r', are reminiscent of the hand of the Caligula Troper. Although not identical, their display scripts also share a number of features found in some other contemporary manuscripts, such as the hairline finials of the display capitals and elongated ascenders and descenders of the rustic capitals.

PROVENANCE: Hereford, second half of the eleventh century; given to Pembroke College by William Mundy, a Fellow, in 1730.

EXHIBITED: London 1984a, no. 70.

LITERATURE: James 1905a, 266–69; Ker 1957, 125–26; Temple 1976, no. 96; Ohlgren 1992, no. 14; Teviotdale 1992; Teviotdale 1995; Gneuss 2001, no. 139.

TW

44

Liturgical compendium

In Latin and Old English
England, c.1062

Parchment, i (modern paper) + 13 (Part I, paginated 1–26) + 280 (Part II, paginated 27–586) + i (modern paper) fols., Part II: 190 × 130 mm, text 158 × 80–83 mm, 20 long lines, ruled in hard point

SCRIPT: Caroline minuscule

BINDING: half-binding of tanned pigskin with blue paper sides over boards, 20th c.

Corpus Christi College, MS 422, Part II, pp. 27–586

CORPUS 422, PART II, although small in format, is a chunky compendium of liturgical texts, largely relating to the Mass. Since the twelfth century, they were bound with a fragmentary copy of the Old English

Dialogue of Solomon and Saturn. In addition to Masses (some including full texts of chants and lections), it contains a Calendar, Easter tables, benedictions, the liturgy for ordeals, exorcisms and other rituals, and various offices. A number of additions were made during the late eleventh and the first half of the twelfth centuries. It is, for the most part, undecorated, apart from rather plain minor initials in green, orange or red. The exception is the splendid opening of the Preface and Canon of the Mass on pp. 51–53, comprising an *incipit* page in display script and now somewhat faded historiated initials depicting Christ in Majesty and the Crucifixion.

The compendium is of immense liturgical interest, both for the unusual extent to which it has been rubricated with instructions in Old English and for a number of texts not found in other Anglo-Saxon liturgical manuscripts, including the earliest known text of the

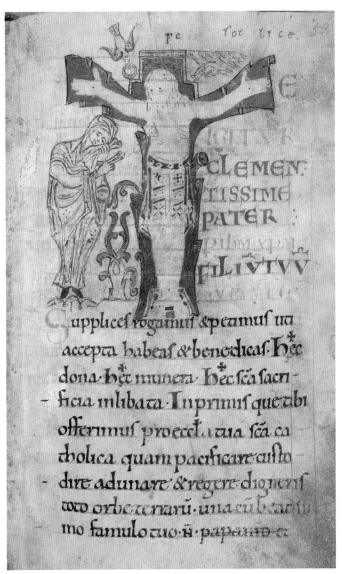

The Crucifixion. Corpus Christi College, MS 422, p. 53

Mass of St Olaf. Its generally plain appearance and the various additions made periodically to it, demonstrate that it was intended for practical purposes. In addition, although the original contents make plain that it was produced for the use of a priest within a monastic context, the text and rubrics of some of the offices, such as that for baptism, and for the visitation and unction of the sick, reveal that its owner was also involved in the pastoral care of women and children (both boys and girls). It is thus an important witness to the practical application of the pastoral reforms advocated by members of the monastic reform movement, notably Ælfric of Cerne.

The original compendium was copied by one or more very similar hands writing the distinctive variety of English Caroline minuscule that became widely diffused in southern England during the third quarter of the eleventh century. It is datable on the basis of the Easter tables covering the years 1061–1098. Since the year 1061 occurs towards the end of one Dionysiac cycle (1045–1063), it seems likely that the choice was deliberate and that the book was produced around 1061.

In the sixteenth century this volume was known as 'the rede boke of Dareley', referring to Darley Dale, near Matlock, Derbyshire, but it originated in southern England. Liturgical evidence points to Sherborne. The Calendar for January gives special prominence to the entry on 8 January for Wulfsige, Bishop of Sherborne (993–1002), who brought his community under the rule of St Benedict, and whose cult appears to have been confined to Sherborne and Westminster where he had been abbot. The inclusion of the otherwise unknown feast of the translation at Cerne of Eadwold the Anchorite clearly indicates Sherborne rather than Westminster. Scholars, however, have also noted the commemoration of several Winchester feasts as well as the prominence accorded in the Litany to Grimbald, first Abbot of the New Minster, Winchester. An explanation for these Winchester commemorations in a book otherwise apparently made for Sherborne has recently been provided by Keynes, in the person of Ælfwold, Bishop of Sherborne (1045–1062), who had previously been a monk at the Old Minster, Winchester.

PROVENANCE: probably at the Church of St Helen, Darley Dale, in the twelfth century, when a Mass for St Helen was added; Darley Dale, near Matlock, in the sixteenth century; Margaret Rollysley, widow (ownership inscriptions, 16th c., pp. 130–31); given by Richard Wendesley to Matthew Parker (1504–1575); his bequest, 1575.

LITERATURE: James 1912b, II, 315–22; Ker 1957, 119–20; Hohler 1972; Temple 1976, no. 104; Robinson 1988, no. 165, pl. 30; Pfaff 1995, 21–24, 56–57, 100–08; Budney 1997, no. 44; Gneuss 2001, no. 111; Rushforth 2002, no. 20; Keynes 2005.

TW

45

Missal

In Latin
England, London, *c*.1425–*c*.1430

Parchment, iii + 363 + i fols., 232 × 165 mm, text 152 × 96 mm, 2 columns, 33 lines, ruled in violet ink

SCRIPT: Gothic bookhand (textualis)

BINDING: blind-stamped calf, arms of Nevile embossed in colour, 17th c., rebacked

Trinity College, MS B.11.11

THIS MISSAL is of the Use of Sarum with no full set of diocesan supplements in the Calendar or Sanctoral to point to a specific diocese. Only the Translation of Edmund (29 April) and Mildred (13 July) are in the original hand of the Calendar, suggesting the Norwich and Canterbury dioceses respectively. The feasts of saints introduced into Sarum in the fifteenth century, David (1 March), Chad (2 March), John of Beverley (7 May), and Winifred (3 Nov.), were added to the Calendar, and so was the Translation of Etheldreda (17 Oct.). Although the first four were approved by the Convocation of Canterbury in 1415–1416, their absence from a Sarum Calendar does not indicate that it was written before that date. They are often absent from much later books, had to be added to the Calendar, and their Mass Propers were added on the flyleaves. The Translation of Etheldreda was not approved by the Convocation until 1480. The Sanctoral is a standard Sarum text with no diocesan supplements. In the late fifteenth century, the Masses for the feasts of the Visitation (2 July), the Transfiguration (6 Aug.), and the Name of Jesus (7 Aug.) were added on fols. 359–63. The first was officially introduced into Sarum in 1480 and the other two in 1487.

The Missal was probably not made for the use of a priest, but for Anne Plantagenet, wife of William Bourchier, probably after her husband died in 1420. The arms of Stafford (she had formerly been married to Edmund Stafford, d.1403), Thomas of Woodstock and Bourchier are on fol. 7 and in other borders. The second owner of the book was Anne's son, Thomas Bourchier, successively bishop, archbishop and cardinal. His name, T.B. Cantuariensis, was recorded on fol. ii after 1454 when he became Archbishop of Canterbury. The high-born first owner may account for the decoration of this Missal being more elaborate than most Sarum Missals (*see no. 46*). There are twenty historiated initials for the main feast days of the Temporal and Sanctoral, with full decorative borders with pink, green and blue acanthus

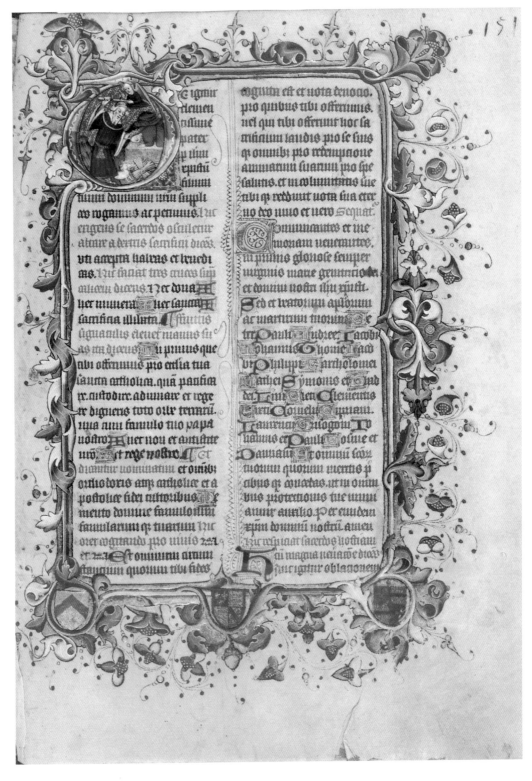

Sacrifice of Isaac.
Trinity College,
MS B.11.11,
fol. 151

leaves, occasional blossoms, and black sprays with green blobs: blessing of salt and water (fol. 7), a priest kneeling at an altar (Advent Sunday, fol. 8v), Nativity (fol. 24), Circumcision (fol. 30), Adoration of the Magi (fol. 31v), Sacrifice of Isaac (Canon Prayer, fol. 151), Resurrection (fol. 165), Ascension (fol. 182v), Pentecost (fol. 187), Trinity (fol. 195v), a host in a chalice held by two angels (Corpus Christi, fol. 197), dedication of a church (fol. 229v), St Andrew (fol. 233), Presentation in the Temple (fol. 244), John the Baptist (fol. 261), Assumption (fol. 277), Nativity of the Virgin (fol. 284), Christ with saints (All Saints, fol. 296), an Apostle (Common of Apostles, fols. 301v, 302v).

There are two main artists for the figural initials. The first was responsible for fols. 7, 8v, 24, 30, 151, 165, 195v, 197, 233, 244, 277, 301v, and 302v. He also worked on the Prayer Book made c.1417–1424 for Charles, Duke of Orléans, while he was in captivity after the battle of

Agincourt (Paris, Bibliothèque nationale de France, MS lat. 1196). He was an Englishman who collaborated with Herman Scheerre, the leading German illuminator working in London from c.1405–1425. The artist of the decorative borders in the Trinity Missal also worked on the Prayer Book. The second artist who painted the initials on fols. 31v, 182v, 187, 229v, 261, 284, and 296 was a follower of Johannes, the other leading London illuminator in the first quarter of the fifteenth century.

PROVENANCE: Anne Plantagenet (1382–1438), daughter of Thomas Woodstock, Duke of Gloucester (1355–97); her son, Thomas Bourchier (1404–1486), Bishop of Worcester (1433–1443), Bishop of Ely (1443–1454), Archbishop of Canterbury (1454–1486) and Cardinal from 1473; gift of Thomas Nevile (1548–1615), Master of Trinity College (1593–1615).

LITERATURE: James 1900–1904, I, 350–52; Dearmer 1922, 42–43, pl. VII; Frere 1894–1932, II, no. 965; Brussels 1973, 111; Scott 1996, I, 29, 40, 70 n. 5, figs. 244–47, II, no. 61, 72, 95, 179, 180, 236, 380–81.

NJM

46

Missal

In Latin
England, c.1475–c.1480

Parchment, iii + 233 + i fols., 328 × 228 mm, text 229 × 145 mm, 2 columns, 36–37 lines (33 lines on fols. 96–105), ruled in brown ink

SCRIPT: Gothic bookhand (textualis)

BINDING: brown morocco stamped binding by Rivière, inscribed 'Harold E. Young, Sandgate, Blundellsands', 20th c.

Newnham College, MS 3

THOUGH NOT of the same high artistic quality of other missals in Cambridge collections, this manuscript is a typical example of the Sarum Missal that would have been found in all parish churches of the Province of Canterbury. Its relatively large size allows the script to be sufficiently large for easy reading as an altar Missal. Its Calendar has no full set of diocesan

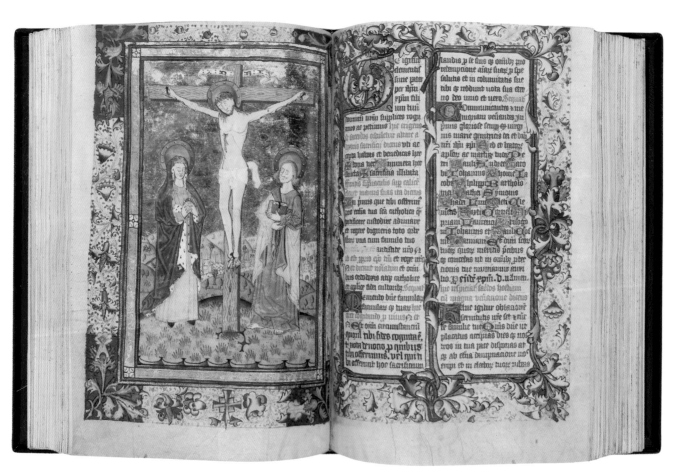

Crucifixion and the opening of the Canon Prayer. Newnham College, MS 3, fols. 100v–101

supplements. Only Oswald (28 Feb.), one of the supplements of the diocese of Worcester, appears in the original hand, with an added note *non-Sarum*. The feast is not in the Sanctoral and probably no particular significance is to be attached to its presence. The remaining feasts in the Calendar and Sanctoral are the new feasts added to Sarum in the fifteenth century, and some of them help in the dating of the book. The Calendar has in the original hand: Chad (2 March), John of Beverley (7 May), Translation of Osmund (16 July), Winifred (3 Nov.) and Osmund (4 Dec.). All of these feasts were introduced in 1415–1416, except that of Osmund, which came in after his canonization in 1457. His Translation, but not the December feast, is also in the Sanctoral. Winifred is also in the Sanctoral and so is John of Beverley's Translation (25 Oct.), though not his May feast. Winifred is mentioned in the Sanctoral but the full text of her Mass had to be added on fol. 235v at the end of the book. In the Sanctoral, although not in the Calendar, is the Mass for the Visitation (2 July), which is the key entry for dating as it was not officially introduced into England until 1475–1480. Some English Missals do have the feast before that date, because although only promulgated by Pope Sixtus IV in 1475, it had been decreed to be observed by the Council of Basel in 1441. A date around 1475–1480 is consistent with the style of the figural and ornamental decoration of the Newnham Missal.

Except for a few leaves excised at the beginning, the Missal is complete. It contains the ritual of the blessing of salt and water with which all Sarum Missal texts begin, and it includes the full-page Crucifixion which faces the opening of the Canon Prayer, *Te igitur clementissime Pater*. The Crucifixion with Mary and John, surrounded by a frame of acanthus leaves is set against a crudely painted green landscape. This is the only figure work in the book. The ornamental decoration is of higher quality. There are illuminated foliage initials with full or partial decorative borders of blue, pink and green acanthus leaves among black sprays with small green leaves and gold blobs for all the main feasts of the church year beginning with Advent: first Sunday of Advent (fol. 9), Christmas Day (fol. 18v), Epiphany (fol. 25), Easter Sunday (fol. 105v), Ascension Day (fol. 117v), Pentecost (fol. 121), Trinity Sunday (fol. 126v), Corpus Christi (fol. 127v), Dedication of the Church (fol. 150), Common for an Apostle (fols. 152v, 153), St Andrew (fol. 182v), Candlemas (fol. 189v), Assumption (fol. 214), Nativity of the Virgin (fol. 219), and All Saints (fol. 227v). The feast of St Andrew (30 Nov.) received elaborate decoration because it is the first feast of the Sanctoral at the beginning of the church year, the Advent season. The Ordinary of the Mass (fols. 94v–105) has large gold initials for many of its sections, and large illuminated initials and borders for *Per omnia secula seculorum* preceding the Preface *Vere dignum et iustum est*, and at the beginning of the Canon Prayer, *Te igitur clementissime Pater*. The Ordinary, as is common in English late medieval Missals, is placed between the liturgy of Holy Saturday and the Mass of Easter Sunday.

PROVENANCE: W.V. Campbell-Wyndham-Long; acquired in 1929 by Harold Edgar Young who donated it to Newnham College.

LITERATURE: Ker 1977, 238–39 (his foliation does not correspond with the present foliation).

NJM

47

Missal

In Latin
Italy, Siena, *c*.1455–*c*.1465
ARTIST: Sano di Pietro (1405–1481)

Parchment, i + 338 + I fols., 369 × 263 mm, text 233 × 163 mm, 2 columns, 28 lines, ruled in plummet and black ink

SCRIPT: Gothic bookhand (textualis)

BINDING: blind-tooled brown leather over wooden boards, two straps with gilt clasps; 15th c.

Fitzwilliam Museum, MS 6–1954

THIS RICHLY ILLUMINATED MISSAL was made for the Augustinian friars of Siena. The Calendar and Sanctoral make its provenance absolutely clear. The Calendar has: William of Malavalla (10 Feb.), Translation of Augustine (28 Feb.), Monica (4 May), Conversion of Augustine (5 May), Canonization of Nicholas of Tolentino (5 June), Octave of Augustine (4 Sept.), Nicholas of Tolentino (10 Sept.), Translation of Augustine (11 Oct.), Crescentius (12 Oct.), Ansanus (1 Dec.), and Galganus (3 Dec.). In the Sanctoral are Monica, a sequence provided for the feast of St Augustine (28 Aug.), and a note to the feast of Nicholas of Tolentino recording his canonization on 5 June 1446. He was an Augustinian friar, and the many feasts of Augustine and his mother, Monica, indicate that the Missal was made for the Augustinian Order, while William of Malavalla, Crescentius, Ansanus and Galganus point to Siena.

There are six historiated initials in the Temporal, and eleven in the Sanctoral. The Ordinary follows the liturgy of Holy Saturday with the Canon prayer, *Te igitur*, preceded by a three-quarter page miniature of the Crucifixion. The initials for the Temporal, which are for the

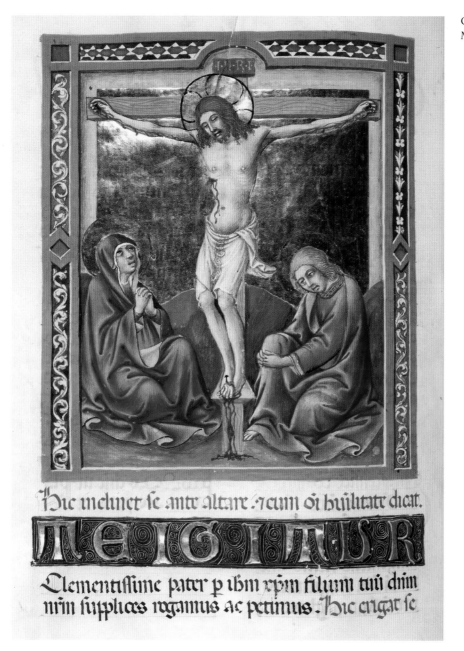

Crucifixion. Fitzwilliam Museum, MS 6–1954, fol. 160v, detail

Collects, are: Christ blessing (First Sunday of Advent, fol. 7), Nativity (Christmas, fol. 18), Adoration of the Magi (Epiphany, fol. 25v), Resurrection (Easter Sunday, fol. 166v), Pentecost (fol. 183v), and a priest elevating the Host (Corpus Christi, fol. 192v). Those for the Sanctoral, also for the Collects, are: St Andrew (fol. 220), St Agatha (fol. 229), Annunciation (fol. 232v), St Monica (fol. 236v), St John the Baptist (fol. 242), Saints Peter and Paul (fol. 245), St Mary Magdalene (fol. 250v), Assumption (fol. 258v), St Augustine (fol. 261), Nativity of the Virgin (fol. 264), St Nicholas of Tolentino (fol. 265), and All Saints (fol. 274v). The first page has a full border extending from the initial of green, blue and orange-red acanthus leaves,

gold blobs, daisy buds and a butterfly. The other initials have smaller partial borders of the same type.

The three-quarter page Crucifixion has a characteristic frame containing panels of leaf ornament with diamond shapes. The Crucifixion, set against a burnished gold ground, is of the 'humility' type in which both Mary and John the Evangelist sit on the ground by the cross in poses of grief. Mary, clasping her hands, looks up at her suffering son, while John looks despairingly down, clasping his knee in his hands. Mary and John have strongly modelled faces and draperies giving bulk to their figures. This relatively large picture is like a miniature panel painting. There has been dispute as to whether this, and most of the historiated initials, are by the Sienese painter, Sano Pietro, who worked both on panels and illuminated manuscripts (New York 1989). It seems beyond doubt that the Crucifixion miniature is by him. It is closely paralleled in figure style and frame type by his documented, large, framed miniatures of the Nativity, St John on Patmos and the Baptism of Christ in an Antiphonary made in 1459–1463 (Bologna, Museo Civico Medievale, MS 562; New York 1988–1989, pls. on 155–57). The figure style and ornament of the Fitzwilliam Missal can also been compared with three Graduals, an Antiphoner and a Psalter (Siena, Museo dell'Opera del Duomo MSS 95.1, 96.2, 97.3, 90.L, 107.13), a 1471–1472 Gradual for Siena Cathedral (Siena, Libreria Piccolomini, MS 27.11), and a Choir Book (Siena, Biblioteca dell'Osservanza, MS Corale 6). In the latter, the initial with the Crucifixion of 'humility' on fol. 264v is particularly close to the large miniature in the Fitzwilliam Missal.

PROVENANCE: Siena, Augustinian Friars Hermits; Bichi family, 16th century (arms, fol. 7); M. Didier-Petit of Lyons, c.1843; Mme. Etienne Mallet, sold in 1926 to H.A. Brölemann; sold by Bernard Quaritch (1926–1946) to Viscount Lee of Fareham (1868–1947); his bequest, 1947; presented to the Museum by his widow in 1954.

EXHIBITED: Cambridge 1966, no. 88.

LITERATURE: Diringer 1967, 334, pl. VI–20; Wormald and Giles 1982, 504–06, pl. 63; Ciardi Dupré dal Poggetto 1984, 141; Hindman et al. 1997, 142–46.

NJM

48

Missal

In Latin
Italy, Naples, 1488

Parchment, ii (paper) + 268 + ii (paper) fols., 390 × 274 mm, text 235 × 156 mm, 19 long lines, ruled in plummet

SCRIPT: Gothic bookhand (textualis)

BINDING: red velvet over wooden boards, embroidered with the arms of Cardinal Alessandro Crivelli (1511–1574), fore-edges painted with the arms of Antonio Scarampa, Bishop of Nola (1546–1569), 16th c.

Fitzwilliam Museum, MS Marlay 10

THE ARMS of the original owner of this Missal on fols. 5 and 163v have been overpainted, but are still legible as the arms of Carafa under a green bishop's hat

with four tassels on each side. The manuscript is dated 1488 within the marginal decoration on fols. 122 and 230. It has always been said to have been made for Cardinal Oliviero Carafa (1430–1511), who was Archbishop of Naples (1458–1484) and became cardinal in 1464. If this was so, one would expect to see the red cardinal's hat on fols. 5 and 163v. Unless the colour has been carefully changed to green, which seems unlikely, the first owner of the Missal was probably Oliviero's brother, Alessandro, who succeeded him as Archbishop of Naples after his resignation in 1484. The heraldry on fols. 5 and 163v was changed from that of Carafa to Scarampa when the book passed to Antonio Scarampa, Bishop of Nola in the mid-sixteenth century. His name was added in the border on fol. 163v.

The Missal contains the Temporal from Advent to Holy Saturday (fols. 5–143v), the Ordinary (fols. 143v–175v), the Temporal from Easter Sunday to Corpus Christi (fols. 175v–200v), the Sanctoral of select feasts (fols. 200v–228), Masses for the Dead (fols. 228–240v), Mass of the Dedication of a church (fols. 241–243), Votive Masses (fols. 243–257v), and Marriage service and Nuptial Mass (fols. 257v–266v). This is the normal content of a Missal save for the abbreviated Sanctoral which contains only the masses for the major feasts of the Virgin, Peter and Paul, All Saints and, significantly, Januarius, or San Gennaro, the patron saint of Naples. There are historiated initials and full ornamental borders for the beginning of the Temporal, the first Sunday of Advent, David playing a viol (fol. 5, *fig. 21*), and for the beginning of the Canon prayer, *Te igitur*, the Elevation of the Host (fol. 164). A full-page Crucifixion with a wide ornamental frame (fol. 163v) faces the Canon prayer. For the main feasts, nine in the Temporal and eight in the Sanctoral, there are historiated initials with partial borders varying in size.

The decoration is in one style. The Crucifixion, the initial with David, and a medallion on the same page have expansive landscapes in the background, which recede to distant mountains, and slender trees in the foreground. Such landscapes appear in contemporary panel painting in Naples, notably in the work of the Neapolitan Francesco Pagano. In 1487–1489 he was working with Antoniazzo Romano in Rome on the absidal frescoes of the Legend of the True Cross in Santa Croce in Gerusalemme which have very similar landscapes. The large ornamental borders for the beginning of the Temporal and the Crucifixion have symmetrical systems of coils of blue and pink feathery acanthus leaves and pairs of blue and pink flowers, and a repertoire of Early Renaissance ornament, busts and heads of putti, a herm and vases, all set against a gold ground. This border ornament is difficult to parallel exactly in Neapolitan manuscripts but may derive from that of two copies of Agathias, *De bello Gothorum*, made in Naples in 1483–1484

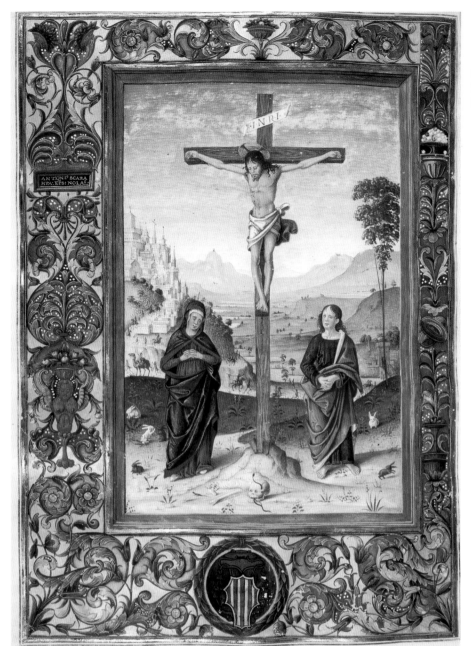

Crucifixion. Fitzwilliam Museum, MS Marlay 10, fol. 163v

for Beatrice of Aragon and Lorenzo de' Medici respectively (Budapest, National Széchényi Library, MS Clmae 413; Florence, Biblioteca Medicea Laurenziana, MS Plut. 68,23).

PROVENANCE: probably made for Alessandro Carafa, Archbishop of Naples (1484–1503); Antonio Scarampa, Bishop of Nola (1546–1569); Cardinal Alessandro Crivelli (1511–1574) acquired it perhaps through his wife, Margherita of the Scarampa family, becoming a priest after her death; Pierre Gélis-Didot (his bookplate on inner front cover); his sale, Paris, 12 April 1897, lot 22; Charles Brinsley Marlay (1831–1912); his bequest, 1912.

EXHIBITED: Cambridge 1966, no. 103.

LITERATURE: Wormald and Giles 1982, 70–73; Robinson 1988, no. 214, pl. 331; Baroffio 1999, 42; Derolez 2003, pl. 74.

NJM

49

Breviary

In Latin and French
France, Paris, *c.*1330–*c.*1342
ARTISTS: Mahiet (act. *c.*1320–*c.*1345) and another artist

Parchment, i (paper) + 438 (some represented by stubs only) + i (paper) fols., 195 × 130 mm, text 130 × 83 mm, 2 columns, 30 lines, ruled in brown ink

SCRIPT: Gothic bookhand (textualis)

BINDING: alum tawed skin, 1980; diamond pattern painted on fore-edge.

Cambridge University Library, MS Dd.5.5

THIS BREVIARY of Franciscan Use, containing the summer and autumn part from Pentecost until the week before Advent, was commissioned and owned by Mary de St Pol, Countess of Pembroke, the wife of Aymer de Valence (d.1324). Represented with the arms of Châtillon-St Pol impaled with Valence, which feature throughout the book, she kneels before Saints Mary Magdalene, Clare and Cecilia (fols. 236, 274, 388). During her long period of widowhood of over fifty years, she founded in 1347 the Hall of Valence Mary in the University of Cambridge, later to become Pembroke College. In 1342 she founded the Franciscan Abbey of nuns at Denney near Cambridge. She visited it frequently and was buried there. It is possible that the Breviary may have been commissioned for Denney or have passed there before her death as a gift from her to one of the nuns. As foundress of the Abbey it would be quite appropriate for her to be depicted in one of the nuns' books. By 1351, the nuns at Denney had incorporated all those from the nearby Abbey of Waterbeach founded in 1294. There were then only three houses of the Franciscan nuns in England, all following the special rule of the French royal foundation of Longchamp. Apart from Mary de St Pol being French herself, this connection of the English Franciscan nuns with Longchamp may explain why this Breviary was made in Paris rather than in England.

The manuscript is richly decorated by two artists with thirty-nine miniatures for the main feasts, all accompanied by decorative borders inhabited by animals, birds and grotesques. These decorative borders are also found on many other pages of the book.

The decoration, according to Richard Rouse, is all by an artist called Mahiet who was associated with the famous illuminator, Jean Pucelle. Mahiet was working in Paris c.1320–c.1340, and has been identified as the

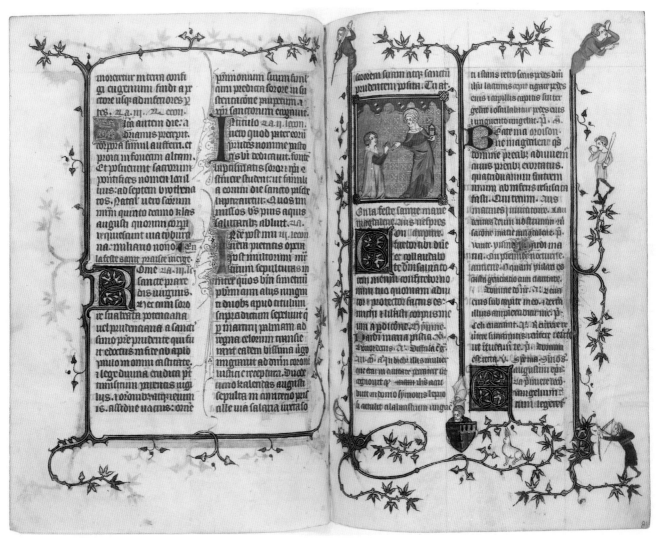

Mary de St Pol before St Mary Magdalen. Cambridge University Library, MS Dd.5.5, fols. 235v–236

artist of the *Vie de Saint Louis* (Paris, Bibliothèque nationale de France, MS fr. 5716). Pucelle himself had died in 1334 but his fellow artists continued to produce manuscripts decorated in the style and iconography initiated by him for at least twenty-five years after his death. The numerous artists involved are difficult to separate as individuals, save for two, Mahiet and Jean le Noir. François Avril (Paris 1981, 291–300) has defined many of these artists working in the tradition of Jean Pucelle, but unfortunately does not mention the Cambridge Breviary. It is particularly difficult to date the manuscripts of the period after Pucelle's death because these artists work in a very conservative tradition.

No less than six Franciscan Breviaries have come down to us from this group of artists; the earliest was illuminated around 1325 by Jean Pucelle himself for Queen Jeanne d'Evreux (Chantilly, Musée Condé, MS 51). The Breviary in the J. Paul Getty Museum (MS Ludwig IX 2) is very similar in appearance to the Cambridge Breviary. Of particular significance for Marie de St Pol's commission of a Breviary is that her sister Mahaut (d.1358), who married Charles of Valois (d.1325), father of Philip VI of France, also commissioned a Franciscan Breviary from one of the Pucelle-influenced artists in which she kneels clothed in the arms of Châtillon-St Pol (Cividale, Museo Archeologico Nazionale, MS CXL; Bergamini 1986). Marie de St Pol may have commissioned the Breviary in Paris through her sister. This seems preferable to identifying it with a Breviary mentioned in Marie's will as given to her by the Queen (of England, presumably) and left to her confessor. Certain features in Marie's Breviary, such as the frames with quatrefoils in the corners and the miniatures placed in inner frames of barbed quatrefoils, predominate in the work of these artists deriving from Pucelle in the period *c.*1330–*c.*1340, thus suggesting a date for this manuscript.

PROVENANCE: Marie de St Pol, Countess of Pembroke (d.1377); at the University Library by the mid-eighteenth century when it was entered in the 1754–1756 list (MS Oo.7.53).

LITERATURE: Meyer 1886, 350–51; Jenkinson 1915, 425–26; Frere 1894–1932, II, no. 772; Little 1937, 63–64, pls. 9, 13; Morand 1962, 49; Randall 1966, figs. 67, 394, 470, 595, 720; von Euw and Plotzek 1982, 72; Grimstone 1997, 1–7 with col. pl.

NJM

50

Breviary

In Latin
Flanders, Ghent, *c.*1475–*c.*1480
ARTIST: Vienna Master of Mary of Burgundy
(act. *c.*1470–*c.*1480)

Parchment, i (paper) + 263 + ii (paper) fols., 264 × 186 mm, text 175 × 124 mm, 2 columns, 30 lines, ruled in brown ink

SCRIPT: Gothic bookhand (textualis)

BINDING: gold-tooled brown leather over pasteboards, marbled edges, 17th c.

St John's College, MS H. 13 (James no. 215)

MARGARET OF YORK, wife of Charles the Bold, Duke of Burgundy (d.1477), was a major patroness of illuminators and scribes. She favoured devotional and didactic texts above all others and employed the best artists of the time. Many scholars, though not all, agree that this Breviary was painted in part by the Vienna Master of Mary of Burgundy. Margaret's ownership is indicated by her motto *Bien en aviegne* ('May good come of it') and the initials C and M, which appear in other books owned by her and her husband, and may suggest that the Breviary was made before Charles's death in 1477.

The Breviary is of Sarum use, as would be expected for an English woman, even though she was living in a country which followed a different liturgical use. It is only the part from Lent until the Old Testament readings for Sundays after Trinity, and the remaining part of the year has not survived. Regrettably, many leaves have been removed and some have been bound into Sir Robert Cotton's manuscripts now in the British Library (Brown 1998). The surviving decoration has square miniatures in the first column of the text and full decorative borders for the main feasts of the church year. In the Temporal are the Ascension (fol. 51v) and the Last Supper (Corpus Christi, fol. 57v), and in the Sanctoral the Crucifixion of St Andrew (fol. 103), the Presentation in the Temple (Candlemas, fol. 122), the Annunciation (fol. 134), and the Nativity of John the Baptist (fol. 151v). The miniatures show receding three-dimensional domestic interiors and spacious airy landscapes with complex grouping of figures. The Last Supper has the table stretching from the front to the back of the room, with the servants at the hatch, and the sideboard and fireplace at the walls of the room. The characteristic landscapes are in the Ascension and St Andrew miniatures. The artist used a painterly style with soft contours,

Last Supper. St John's
College, MS H. 13, fol. 57v

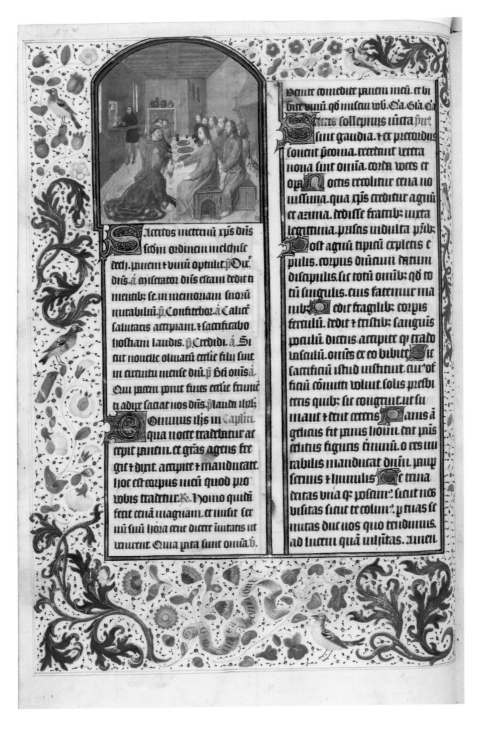

and a solemn serenity of poses and facial expressions. This phase of his style and iconography has been compared to that in the contemporary Voustre Demeure Hours (Madrid, Biblioteca Nacional, MS Vit. 25–5). The text pages are framed by wide decorative borders at the main divisions and by partial borders throughout the rest of the book. These borders may belong to two campaigns of decoration, separated by a few years. The first consists of the new *trompe-l'oeil* border type, showing gold and silver acanthus leaf coils interspersed with illusionistically depicted flowers and birds against a fully painted ground (fols. 51v, 103, 122, 151v). Such borders occur in other works by the Vienna Master of Mary of Burgundy, notably the Hours of Mary of Burgundy of *c.*1475 (Vienna, Österreichische Nationalbibliothek, MS 1857) and the Hours of Engelbert of Nassau of *c.*1475–1480 (Oxford, Bodleian Library, MS Douce 219). The other border type, used for the partial borders on the ordinary text pages, has blue and gold acanthus leaves, flowers, birds and fruit, and black tendrils with blobs of gold, set against the plain vellum background. It can be compared with earlier Flemish and North French works, for example the border surrounding Simon Marmion's miniature in *L'Instruction d'un jeune prince (no. 121)* and the copy of devotional treatises made for Margaret of York (Oxford, Bodleian Library, MS Douce 365). The borders with the fully painted grounds are particularly close to those in the 1477 Register of the Ghent Guild of St Anne (Windsor Castle, Royal Library). This strongly suggests that the Cambridge manuscript was made in Ghent where the Vienna Master of Mary of Burgundy was most probably based.

PROVENANCE: Margaret of York, Duchess of Burgundy (1446–1503); given to the College *c.*1618 by Sir Thomas Gardiner (1591–1652).

EXHIBITED: Brussels 1959, no. 198; Cambridge 1993, no. 49; Los Angeles and London 2003–2004, no. 22.

LITERATURE: James 1913, 244–45; Frere 1894–1932, II, no. 915; Pächt 1948, 42, 64, pl. 23a; Lieftinck 1969, 1–7, pls. I–II; Alexander 1970a; Hughes 1984, 58–59; Dogaer 1987, 149; Kren 1992, 14, 41, 58, 60, 65, 261; Brown 1998, 287–89, figs. 169, 170, pls. 8, 9.

NJM

51

Metrical Apocalypse, Descent into Hell and Visions of St Paul, and Coronation Order

In Latin and Anglo-Norman French
England, *c.*1335– *c.*1339

Parchment, 72 + v fols., 370 × 260 mm, text 260 × 190 mm, 2 columns, 32 lines, ruled in black ink
SCRIPT: Gothic bookhand (textualis)
BINDING: alum tawed skin over oak boards, 1990

Corpus Christi College, MS 20

THIS MANUSCRIPT is an unusual compilation illuminated in a uniform style within a single campaign. Folios 1–60 consist of a Latin Apocalypse which runs in parallel with an Anglo-Norman French metrical version and prose commentary (Meyer 1896; Delisle and Meyer 1901, no. 35; Justice 1993). The Apocalypse is richly illuminated with a hundred and six framed miniatures. They open with scenes of the Last Supper and St John's

exile to Patmos. The Last Supper was selected because it shows St John asleep on Christ's breast, the moment when, according to some commentaries, Christ imparted to John the final Revelation. Beneath kneels an armed man in heraldic surcoat, identifiable as Henry, 1st Lord of Cobham (d.1339). During his later years, when he commissioned the manuscript, he spent more time in Somerset than in Kent (Saul 2001, 19). The Apocalypse sits well with the material which follows on fols. 61–68, the Descent of St Paul into Hell and his Visions, with fourteen miniatures which are related to a manuscript in Toulouse (Bibliothèque municipale, MS 815; Meyer 1895; Morgan 2004, 252, 256–57).

Much more unusual is the combination of such visionary eschatology with a liturgical text, that of the English Coronation Order, with which the book ends. It too is in the French vernacular (Legg 1900, xxxi–xxxvii, 39–49). It opens with a large miniature of the Coronation (fol. 68). The form of the rite is essentially that of the fourth and final medieval recension of the Westminster Abbey ritual, drawn up for the coronation of Edward II in 1308. It can be shown that the version of the text upon which this copy was based was the Order for the coronation of Edward II, not Edward III, since it ends on fol. 72v with a prayer for Edward the new king's father, 'who has gone to heaven' (*la pleine benescon de dieux veigne sur la gendrure Eduix que a cil mounta*; Legg 1900, 49; Binski 1995, 131). This state of affairs could not have pertained at the coronation of Edward III in 1327, since his father Edward II was still alive at the time (cf. however Sandler 1986, 113). The prayer is thus for Edward I. The Order is that found in a later illustrated version, Westminster Abbey MS 38, the so-called *Liber Regalis* of the 1390s (Sandler 1986, no. 155; Binski 1997). Unlike the *Liber Regalis* and the even more spectacular step-by-step illustrations in the Coronation Book of Charles V of France (London, British Library, Cotton MS Tiberius B.viii; O'Meara 2001), the Corpus Christi manuscript has only the single illustration of the rite shown here. The crown is being positioned or secured on the enthroned king's head; the monarch holding an elaborate sceptre and orb is accompanied by a throng of mitred clerics and barons, two of whom extend to the king half-opened pyx-like gold containers.

It would be a mistake to see this monumental composition as an illustration of any specific moment of the rite; it acts instead as a vivid and compelling memento of the ritual as a whole. Its planned presence in this manuscript indicates direct personal connection with the coronation rite. According to the opening text of the Order (Legg 1900, 39; Binski 1995, 128) certain families or *grans seigneurs* had offices in the coronation ritual by hereditary right. The Lord Beauchamp was responsible for providing precious carpets, the Earl of

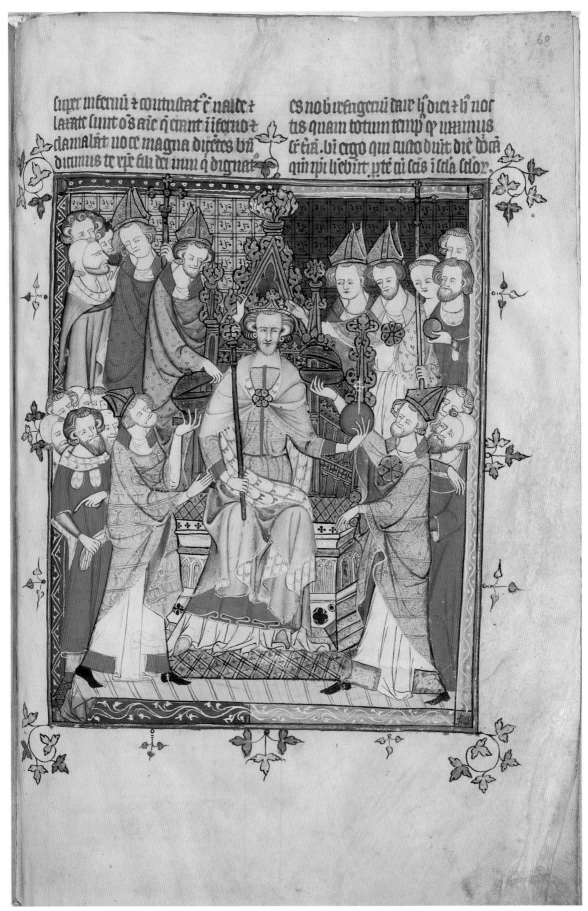

Coronation. Corpus Christi College, MS 20, fol. 68

Chester for processing the sword called *curtana*, and the Earl of Huntingdon another sword. Henry was a Warden of the Cinque Ports, the barons of which carried a canopy over the king in the procession (Legg 1900, 39). After 1339 the book appears to have passed from Henry to Juliana de Leybourn, Countess of Huntingdon (d. 1367). Juliana was buried at St Augustine's Abbey and bequeathed the book to the monastery *(see also no. 77)*.

Sandler correctly relates the style of the illuminations to the Taymouth Hours and the Smithfield Decretals (London, British Library, Yates Thompson MS 13 and Royal MS 10.E.iv; Sandler 1986, no. 98. no. 101). These connections place the production of the Corpus volume in the London area. The painting is of consistently good quality with strong, light oranges, pinks, greens and blues with gilding, and rather dry and hard drawing. The tight buttoned tunic of the bowman in the bas-de-page of fol. 1 is cut in a way fashionable only from the mid-1330s onwards, and a date nearing 1339 for the execution is thus probable.

PROVENANCE: Henry, 1st Lord Cobham (d. 1339); Juliana de Leybourn (d. 1367), inscription on top of fol. iii verso; St Augustine's Abbey, Canterbury; Matthew Parker (1504–1575); his bequest, 1575.

EXHIBITED: London 1987–1988, no. 11.

LITERATURE: James 1912b, I, 37–41; Sandler 1986, no. 103.

PB

52

Pontifical

In Latin
France, Metz or Verdun, 1303–1316

Parchment, 140 fols., 320 × 245 mm, text 225 × 150 mm, 14 long lines, ruled in plummet

SCRIPT: Gothic bookhand (textualis)

BINDING: red velvet over wooden boards, 18th c., rebacked and repaired

Fitzwilliam Museum, MS 298

THE PONTIFICAL is the book containing all the ceremonies and services only a bishop can perform. Many books are very richly decorated and this is one of the most luxurious examples. It was made for Renaut de Bar, Bishop of Metz (1303–1316; Balteau et al. 1929–, V, cols. 141–42). It has forty-two large rectangular miniatures and one hundred and thirty-seven historiated initials for the ceremonies of the dedication of a church

(fols. 1–62v), the blessing of abbots and abbesses (fols. 63–97v), the celebration of a synod (fols. 98–102v), and the consecration of a bishop (fols. 103–139v). In addition there are many decorative borders with grotesques of a humorous nature – a fashion of the time in the ornamentation of Psalters and Books of Hours, perhaps surprising to find in a Pontifical. The painting was left incomplete from fol. 98 onwards and from fol. 127 to the end the ink drawings reveal the confident hand of an accomplished artist *(see figs. 6, 7)*. This state of incompleteness is not uncommon in sumptuously illuminated medieval manuscripts and may have resulted from a firm deadline which the artists failed to meet.

The remaining part of this Pontifical, bound as a separate volume, is now in Prague (University Library, MS XXIII.c.120; Kvĕt 1931, 224–25, 229, figs. 79–81; Urbánková 1957, 25–26, pl. 46). It was recorded as still being in the possession of a Bishop of Metz late in the fourteenth century. Another book belonging to Renaut de Bar, a Ritual (Metz, Bibliothèque municipale, MS 43, destroyed in 1944), contained additional liturgical Offices for the use of the Bishop. There is much heraldry in the decoration of the Pontifical with the arms of Bar and Châtillon-Toucy (Renaut's mother's arms) leaving no doubt as to his ownership, partly overpainted in the Cambridge part when the book passed to another bishop, but unaltered in the Prague part. In the blessings for abbots and abbesses the Church of Metz is mentioned, confirming that it was made for a bishop of that diocese.

Renaut de Bar had a particular interest in elaborately illustrated books. His Breviary in two volumes was also profusely illuminated (London, British Library, Yates Thompson MS 8 and Verdun, Bibliothèque municipale, MS 107). It is of the Use of Verdun and was made around 1302–1305 while Renaut was a canon of Verdun, before becoming Bishop of Metz. As in the case of his Pontifical, the illuminators left the end of the summer part incomplete. The Cambridge Pontifical is by a single artist who illuminated a major part of the Breviary as well as Renaut's Missal (Verdun, Bibliothèque municipale, MS 98). The Prague part is by three artists. The figure style of the artist of the Cambridge part is characterized by elegant but restrained poses with ordered groupings of the figures balancing the elements of architecture or church furnishing. His style is well suited to portraying the solemn dignity of the pontifical ceremonies. The backgrounds are of delicate diaper patterns against which the figures are silhouetted. His restraint is also evident in the placing of just one or two grotesques on the elegantly curving tendrils of the bottom border, contrasting with contemporary manuscripts from Lorraine such as the Aspremont Psalter-Hours (Melbourne, National Gallery of Victoria, MS Felton 171/3; Oxford,

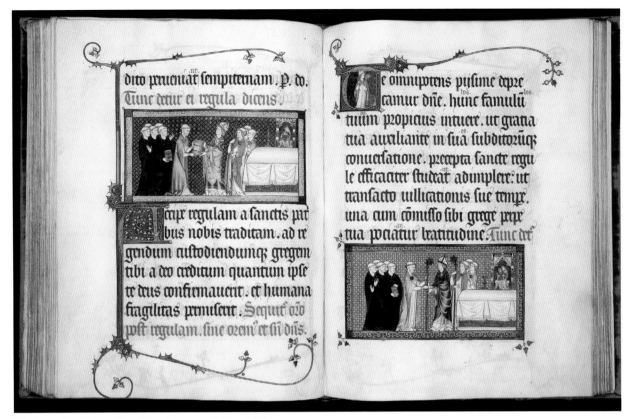

Blessing of an Abbot. Fitzwilliam Museum, MS 298, fols. 72v–73

Bodleian Library, MS Douce 118) whose borders over-flow with grotesques. François Avril has convincingly suggested that this artist may have come from Paris and was probably trained in the workshop of the 'Cholet Group' operating there c.1270–c.1285.

PROVENANCE: Renaut de Bar, bishop of Metz (1303–1316); Count MacCarthy; his sale, Paris, 1817, lot 231; purchased by F.S. Ellis from an antiquarian bookseller in Dijon; Sir Thomas Brooke (1830–1908); bequeathed by him to Henry Yates Thompson (1838–1928); his gift to the Museum, 1918.

EXHIBITED: London 1959, no. 478; Cambridge 1966, no. 50; Cambridge 1982, no. 20; Nancy 1984, no. 77; Paris 1998, no. 216.

LITERATURE: Dewick1895; Dewick 1902; Vitzthum 1907, 220–21; Kvĕt 1931, 224; Randall 1966, 32, figs. 169, 326, 354, 365, 566, 598, 635, 664, 665; de Winter 1980, 34, 38, 46, figs. 5, 12; Wormald and Giles 1982, 276–77, pls. 25, 28; Robinson 1988, no. 201, pl.131; Metz 1989, 52–53, fig. 2; Palazzo 1999, 172, 173, 243. 337, 352, 353; Derolez 2003, pl. 26.

NJM

53

Guillaume Durand, *Rational des Divins Offices*

In French and Latin
France, Paris, c.1410

Parchment, 359 + ii fols., 355 × 263 mm, text 226 × 168 mm, 2 columns, 40 lines, ruled in dark brown ink

SCRIPT: Gothic bookhand (textualis)

BINDING: brown leather over pasteboards, 18th c; unidentified arms painted on fore-edge.

St John's College, MS T.8 (James no. 260)

GUILLAUME DURAND, or Durandus, Bishop of Mende (1285–1296) and compiler of the standard edition of the Pontifical *(see no. 55)*, also wrote an extensive and widely-known treatise on all aspects of the liturgy, the *Rationale divinorum officiorum* (Davril and Thibodeau 1995–2000). In 1372, the Latin text was translated into French by the Carmelite Jean Golein for King Charles V of France (Barthelémy 1854; Jackson 1969). Richly

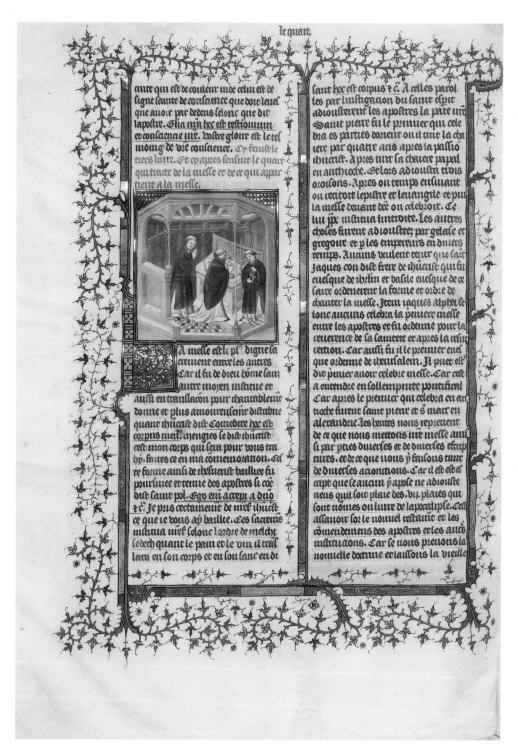

Offertory at Mass.
St John's College,
MS T. 8, fol. 77v

illuminated copies were made for distinguished patrons, including the King himself (Paris, Bibliothèque nationale de France, MS fr. 437). The St John's copy was made in Paris *c.*1410 and illustrated with thirty-nine miniatures. Together with a Burgundian manuscript of *c.*1450 (Beaune, Bibliothèque municipale, MS 21; Paris 1993, 193–95), the St John's volume is the most extensively illustrated of all extant copies of the text. This lengthy work is divided into eight books: I, the Church, the Altar, Church Ornaments, Dedication of Churches, the Sacraments (fols. 1–47v); II, the Orders of Ministers and Ordinations (fols. 48–60v); III, Vestments (fols. 61–77); IV, the Mass (fols. 77v–153v); V, the Divine Office (fols. 154–184v); VI, the Feasts of the Church Year (fols. 185–331); VII, the Feasts of the Saints (fols. 331v–358); VIII, Computistica, not included in the St John's manuscript, but mentioned on fol. 358 as 'the concern of the astronomers'. The translation into French, evidently to cater for lay readership, survives in nine manuscripts, six of them illustrated, and in a printed edition of 1503 published in Paris by Antoine Vérard (Durand 1503).

The framed miniatures are set in a single text column

at the beginning of books, most of them complete with decorative border bars with ivy leaf tendrils. The only exception is the elaborate opening miniature, which consists of four compartments spread over both text columns. It shows Christ blessing, the Sainte-Chapelle in Paris, Charles V receiving the book from Jean Golein, and Jean Golein instructing students. The smaller miniatures relating to the liturgy are: Book I, bells (fol. 17v), burial in a cemetery (fol. 19v), dedication of a church (fol. 22v), dedication of an altar (fol. 29), coronation of a king (fol. 37v); Book II, bishop blessing (fol. 48), bishop at altar (fol. 59); Book III, a priest vesting (fol. 61); Book IV, the Offertory (fol. 77v), the Canon prayer (fol. 116), parallel with Old Testament offerings (fol. 116v), reception of communion (fol. 119), *quam oblationem* (fol. 121v), sub-deacon bringing back the paten at *Pater noster* (fol. 144), giving of the peace (fol. 147), communion of the priest (fol. 148v); Book V, God on a mountain showing a mirror to a prophet, kings, a monk, and a friar (fol. 154). Those relating to the feasts of the year are: Book VI, St John the Baptist preaching (Advent, fol. 189v), bishop and clerics (Ember days, fol. 199), Presentation in the Temple (Candlemas, fol. 206v), Apostles bringing ass to Christ (Palm Sunday, fol. 244), Crucifixion (Good Friday, fol. 263), Resurrection (fol. 285v), Pentecost (fol. 308v), Trinity (fol. 314); Book VII, Saints (fol. 331v), Purification of the Virgin (fol. 337v), Peter enthroned (*Cathedra Petri*, fol. 338), Annunciation (fol. 338v), St Michael and the angels (fol. 339v), St John the Baptist (fol. 340), Saints Peter and Paul (fol. 341), St James the Great (fol. 342), St Stephen (fol. 342v), Presentation of the Virgin in the Temple (mistakenly included instead of her Nativity, fol. 343v), All Saints (fol. 344), Requiem Mass (All Souls, fol. 344v).

The scenes are often set within three-dimensional architectural structures, with the buildings painted in pastel colours of green, mauve, pink, blue and brown. Some of the faces are lightly modelled in grey-green and the figures are often set against chequered grounds of gold and colours. The two artists seem related to the workshops of the Master of the Cité de Dames and the Boucicaut Master, while the architecture is reminiscent of that of the Orosius Master.

PROVENANCE: Charles de Pradel, Bishop of Montpelier (1676–1696); Charles-Joachim Colbert de Croissy, Bishop of Montpelier (1697–1738); sale of the Pradel-Colbert de Croissy library, 1740; William Grove, Fellow of St John's, who gave it to the College in 1762.

LITERATURE: Meyer 1879, 306–08; James 1913, 296–99; Rabel 1992, 175–76, 181, fig. 5.

NJM

54

Pontifical

In Latin
England, probably London, *c.*1397–1407, 1407–1421, 1421–1435

Parchment, ii (paper) + 286 + ii (paper) fols., 400 × 255 mm, text 290 × 170 mm, 2 columns, 30 lines, ruled in brown ink and plummet

SCRIPT: Gothic bookhand (textualis)

BINDING: green board with leather spine, 1952

Corpus Christi College, MS 79

THIS PONTIFICAL belonged to three successive bishops. The first, Guy de Mohun, Bishop of St David's, whose arms are on fol. 151, seems to have been the commissioner of the book. The character of the figure style and border decoration on fols. 21–286 seems to be of the closing years of the fourteenth century or the earliest years of the fifteenth. Some have thought the book was only begun for Bishop Mohun, but that it passed to Bishop Clifford, whose arms are on fol. 25, under whom the decoration of fols. 21–286 may have been completed. It seems preferable to suggest that Bishop Clifford's arms, together with the royal arms and those of Eglesfield, which also occur on fol. 25, were painted over the carefully erased arms of the original owner, Bishop Mohun, and two other unknown families, and that the decoration was substantially complete when it came into Clifford's possession. The colours of the paint of these three arms do not match the rest of the page and suggest a different artist, whereas on fol. 151 the arms of Mohun appear to be by the painter of the whole page. The connection of the Eglesfield family with Bishop Clifford has yet to be explained. It might be argued that Bishop Clifford acquired the book as Bishop of Worcester, and that it remained at Worcester Cathedral when he transferred to London in 1407. The third owner was Philip Morgan, Bishop of Worcester (1419–1426), who added a section of text containing the Penitential Psalms and the blessing of a hermit on fols. 13–20v, with his arms on fol. 13. In 1489 the Pontifical was at St Paul's Cathedral; the text for the ceremony held there when Henry VII was presented with a papal sword and cap by Innocent VIII's nuncio was added on fols. 1v–2.

The book has forty-one small framed miniatures set in the columns of the text and illustrating the various pontifical Offices, and thirty-four historiated initials. Many pages are wholly or partially framed by illuminated

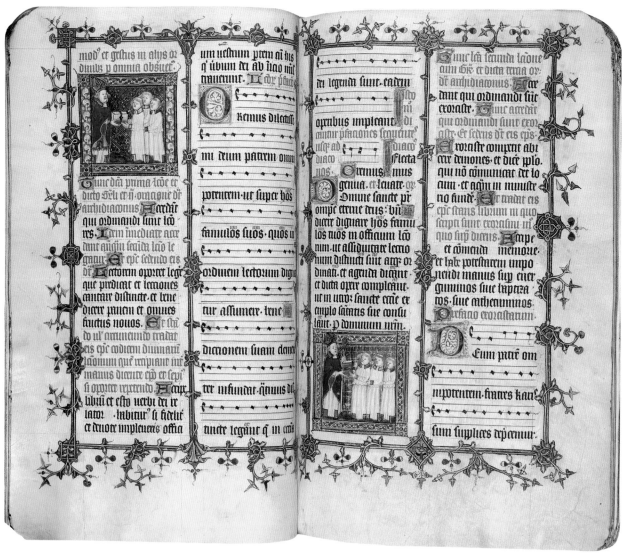

Ordinations. Corpus Christi College, MS 79, fols. 42v–43

decorative borders. The figures are squat and block-like in proportion, with prominent black dots for their eyes. This style is comparable with work produced in the period 1380–1400 in manuscripts such as the Litlyngton Missal (London, Westminster Abbey, MS 37) and a Psalter in Hatfield House (MS C.P. 292). Also the borders have kidney- and diamond-shaped leaves, and daisy buds, which are characteristic of the late fourteenth century, and do not include the acanthus type leaves which increasingly predominate in early fifteenth century borders. If the book was not completed for Bishop Mohun before his death in 1407, and was still being decorated for Bishop Clifford after 1407, the artists were working in a conservative style. Two artists worked on the main section, fols. 21–286. The master painted only the pages at the major divisions of the Pontifical (fols. 25, 151, 179, 182v). His assistant completed the

extensive decoration of the rest of the book. A third artist painted the section written for Bishop Morgan after 1419, which has two historiated initials.

PROVENANCE: Guy de Mohun, Bishop of St David's (1397–1407), arms on fol. 151; Richard Clifford, Bishop of Worcester (1401–1407) and Bishop of London (1407–1421), arms on fol. 25; Philip Morgan, Bishop of Worcester (1419–26) and Bishop of Ely (1426–1435), arms on fol. 13; Matthew Parker (1504–1575); his bequest, 1575.

LITERATURE: Frere 1901–1908, I, 87–9, II, pls. I–IX; James 1912b, I, 158–64; Frere 1894–1932, II, 133, no. 896; Brückmann 1973, 404–405; Robinson 1988, nos. 129–131, pls. 183, 205; Scott 1996, I, 28, 32, 51, 76 n. 17, figs. 73–79 and II, no. 18, 32, 37, 99, 213; Lowden 2003, 40–43, figs. 10–12.   NJM

55

Pontifical

In Latin
Italy, Milan or Pavia, *c*.1435–*c*.1440
ARTIST: Master of the Vitae Imperatorum
(act. *c*.1430–*c*.1450)

Parchment, i (paper) + viii (parchment) + 444 + ii (parchment) + i (paper) fols, 358 × 255 mm., text 218 × 154 mm., single column of 22 lines, ruled in faint grey plummet

SCRIPT: Gothic bookhand (textualis)

BINDING: alum tawed skin over oak boards, two straps and metal clasps, by Robert Proctor, 2001

Fitzwilliam Museum, MS 28

IN THE PERIOD *c*.1370–*c*.1440 Milan and Pavia were major centres of manuscript illumination. Both had castles of the Visconti family, under whose patronage Lombard artists such as Giovannino de'Grassi and Michelino da Besozzo absorbed Parisian influences and created a Milanese version of the International Gothic style. One of the last artists to work in this manner was the Master of the Vitae Imperatorum, named after a manuscript of Suetonius's lives of the Roman Emperors (Paris, Bibliothèque nationale de France, MS ital. 131), which he illuminated for Filippo Maria Visconti in 1431 *(see no. 160)*. Shortly afterwards he worked on this magnificent Pontifical for the Archbishop of Milan, Francesco Pizolpasso, whose arms occur in the borders of fols. 1, 135v, and 253. It has been argued that the book might have been made for him before 1435, when he was still Bishop of Pavia. This is because some of the manuscripts illuminated for him have a crosier beside his arms while others show a cross. The latter suggests the archbishop's processional cross he assumed when he became Archbishop of Milan. This Pontifical always shows the crosier and not the cross. However, what at first sight might seem to be the lappets of the mitre surmounting his arms on fol. 1 is in fact a strip of white cloth passing inside the mitre and marked with black crosses. This might be interpreted as the pallium, and may signify that the book was made after he became Archbishop in 1435. The significance of crosier or cross in his other manuscripts remains uncertain.

The text of this Pontifical is of the 'standard edition' compiled by the liturgist, Guillaume Durand, or Durandus, Bishop of Mende (1285–1296) in the south of France (Andrieu 1940, 327–662). While up to his time there was a diversity of Pontificals, in the course of the fourteenth century his edition was adopted throughout most of Europe, although there were exceptions, such as the English Pontifical of *c*.1400 discussed above *(no. 54)*. Durandus's Pontifical is divided into three books preceded by a prologue and a list of contents. Book 1 deals with confirmation, ordinations and special blessings of persons; Book 2 with the dedication of a church and the blessings of objects; Book 3 with pontifical ceremonies in Lent and Holy

Laying the Foundations of a Church.
Fitzwilliam Museum, MS 28, fol. 135v

143

Week, councils and synods, suspension, excommunication and reconciliation, visitations and finally the ceremonial of the pontifical Mass. Each of the three books (fols. 1, 135v, 253) and the Benedictional, the various blessings during the church year given by the bishop at the pontifical Mass (fol. 409), begin with an elaborately decorated page with a large historiated initial and decorative border. In addition, there are one hundred and eleven historiated initials with small border extensions illustrating the pontifical ceremonies. The historiated initials of the pages with full borders are: confirmation of a child (fol. 1), laying the foundation stone of a church (fol. 135v), expulsion of the penitents at the beginning of Lent (fol. 253), and the bishop giving the pontifical blessing at Mass (fol. 409). The four main decorated pages have full borders incorporating heraldry, naturalistic animals, birds and insects set beside leaves and flowers in gold, blue, pink and green. On fol. 1 two putti play pipe and mandolin. The interest in naturalistic portrayal of birds and animals (Treuherz 1972) is reflected in the drawing books of Lombard artists of the time, such as that of Giovannino dei Grassi (Bergamo, Biblioteca Civica MS Cassa. 1.21).

PROVENANCE: Francesco Pizolpasso, Bishop of Pavia (1427–1435), Archbishop of Milan (1435–1443); in the 1443 catalogue of Biblioteca Capitolare, Milan Cathedral; acquired by Viscount Fitzwilliam in 1807; his bequest, 1816.

EXHIBITED: Cambridge 1966, no. 85.

LITERATURE: James 1895a, 71–76, pl. IV; Frere 1894–1932, II, no. 1026; Pellegrin 1955–1969, 55, Supplément, 35; Paredi 1961, 77, 86, 163–68, pls. XII, XIII; Stones 1969, 11; Brückmann 1973, 408; Melograni 1992, 119, 137 n. 16, fig. 5; Turner 1996, XX, 783; Baroffio 1999, 42.

NJM

56

Pontifical Offices

In Latin
Italy, Florence, c.1485–c.1490
ARTISTS: Gherardo di Giovanni del Fora (1446–1497) and workshop

Parchment, i (parchment lined with yellow silk) + 63 + i (parchment lined with yellow silk) fols., 222 × 160 mm, text 143 × 90 mm, 25 long lines, ruled in plummet and faint-brown ink

SCRIPT: Gothic bookhand (textualis)

BINDING: blind- and gold-tooled yellow morocco, six *Agnus Dei* stamps on spine, gilt and gauffered edges, 19th c.

Cambridge University Library, MS Add. 4127

THE VERY LARGE SIZE AND WEIGHT of most complete Pontificals made them inconvenient to use, and sometimes smaller books were made, containing only a few sections of the Pontifical. This is such a book, consisting of sections excerpted partly from Book 3 of the Durandus Pontifical and partly from a Pontifical Ritual (the Office of Vespers). It contains the texts for Pontifical Mass and Vespers (fols. 1–23v), with those for Mass and Vespers when the bishop is present but not celebrant or officiant (fols. 24–27), the Maundy Thursday liturgy for the consecration of the holy oils (fols. 27–46v), the texts for celebrating a provincial council or synod (fols. 46v–56), for the commencement of a journey (fols. 56–57v), for the reception of a greater prelate or legate (fols. 57v–59v) and for a parochial visitation (fols. 59v–63v).

The manuscript opens with a small miniature showing the bishop in a cope, standing at the altar and celebrating Vespers with two assistants in copes holding his crosier and mitre (fol. 1). This represents the moment during the *Magnificat* when the bishop leaves his throne and goes to the altar for the incensation. The side chapels of the church can be seen partly shadowed in the background. The rubric text defining the ceremonial is surrounded by a heavy border. The wreath at the bottom contains a shield surmounted by a green bishop's hat with six tassels on either side. Unfortunately when the book passed to another owner the arms were erased but possibly had a cross on a *gules* ground. The heavy border has clumps of pink blue and green acanthus leaves, pairs of blue and pink flowers, nine whole figures of putti, brooches of gems surrounded by pearls, vases, and cornucopiae, all set against small tendrils with gold blobs. This border decoration is characteristic of Florence c.1475–c.1490, particularly of the workshop of Gherardo di Giovanni del Fora before he developed a heavier type of border in the late years of the century *(see no. 101)*. Similar borders decorate the Dialogues of St Gregory (Modena, Biblioteca Estense, MS lat. 449) and St Jerome's Commentary on Galatians (Budapest, National Széchényi Library, MS Clmae 347), both made for Matthias Corvinus c.1488–c.1490. Suggested by the stylistic parallels, a date in the late 1480s or early 1490s for the Cambridge manuscript is also supported by the indulgence on fol. 17v. It was granted by Benedictus de Paganostis of Florence, Bishop of Vaison (1485/1489–1523), and provides a *terminus post quem*.

Gherardo was strongly influenced by Netherlandish painting, which may have resulted in the dark, sombre *chiaroscuro* interior of the Vespers scene, with the back wall set in deep shadow. The second picture of the vesting of the bishop is a bas-de-page roundel on fol. 6. The text describes the vesting of the bishop in the sacristy before Pontifical Mass when the bishop has his buskins

Bishop celebrating
Vespers. Cambridge
University Library,
MS Add. 4127, fol. 1

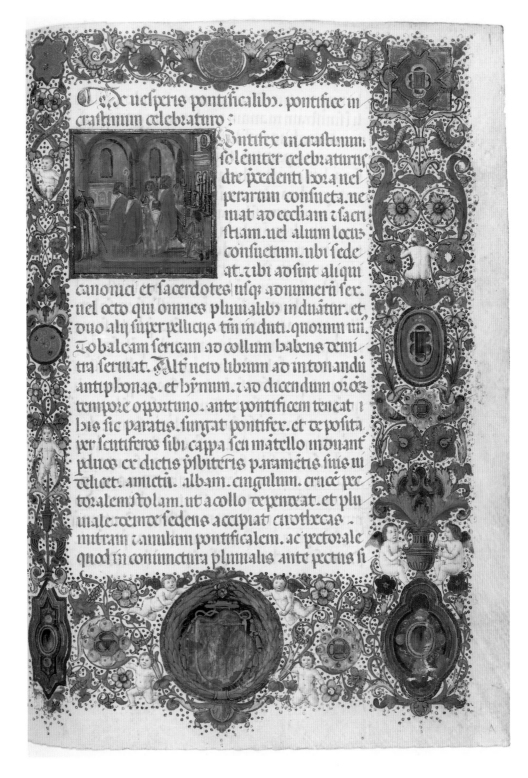

and sandals put on. This is what we see in the roundel, a scene of great rarity in art. The remaining decoration of the manuscript consists of ornamental initials at the main text divisions, surrounded by partial borders of the same character as the larger border on fol. 6 (fols. 4v, 24, 24v, 27, 46v, 56, 57v, 59v).

PROVENANCE: Alexander Boswell, Lord Auchinleck (1706–1782); Mrs Mounsey; her sale, Sotheby's, London, 23 June 1893, lot 712; purchased by Samuel Sandars (1837–1894); his bequest, 1894.

LITERATURE: Frere 1894–1932, II, no. 853.

NJM

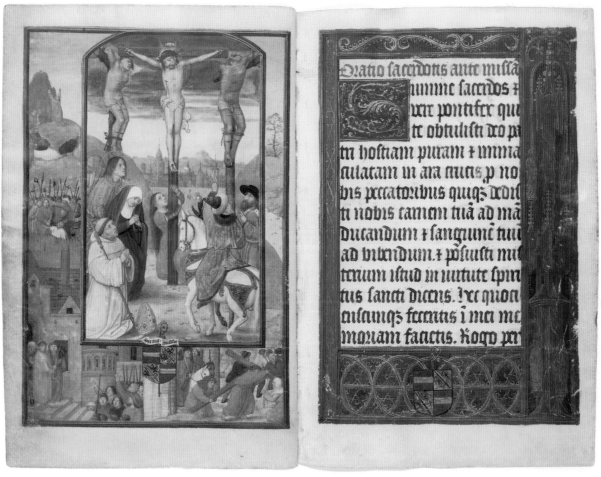

Crucifixion and Prayer before Mass. Cambridge University Library, MS Nn.4.1, fols. 4v–5

57

Benedictional of Robert de Clercq

In Latin, with short texts in French and Dutch
Flanders, Bruges, *c.*1520
ARTISTS: Simon Bening (1483–1561) and assistants

Parchment, 119 fols. (foliated 1–70a, 70b–118), 200 × 140 mm,
text 125 × 80 mm, 14 long lines ruled in red ink

SCRIPT: Gothic bookhand (textualis)

BINDING: original blind-stamped brown calf over boards, sewn
on six supports, traces of two clasps and catchplates, gauffered
and gilt edges, by Ludovicus Bloc of Bruges (d.1529).

Cambridge University Library, MS Nn.4.1

THE BENEDICTIONAL, a relatively rare type of book, contains the texts of blessings, prayers and rites destined for the personal use of an abbot. Among its contents are prayers and associated texts to be read before and after Mass, blessings, or benedictions, to be dispensed on major feast days of the liturgical year (commencing with the Vigil of the Nativity, extending to the Dedication of a Church, and encompassing twenty-nine feasts from the Temporal and the Sanctoral), blessings for church furnishings (patens, chalices, liturgical garments), holy water, and for brides and grooms (including the texts of their marital vows, given here in Dutch and French forms), and rites for the performance of baptisms and the profession of nuns and monks.

Included among the decorated and illustrated pages of the manuscript are the coats of arms, the motto *Sperans gaudebo* ('In hope I will rejoice'), and the initials of its patron, Robert de Clercq, who served from 1519 to 1557 as the thirty-third abbot of the Cistercian monastery of Ter Duinen ('Les Dunes') at Kokside near Bruges. He is portrayed kneeling in prayer in his white Cistercian habit, accompanied by his abbatial crosier and mitre, in the first illustrated page of the manuscript, the full-page miniature of the Crucifixion shown here. The Cambridge Benedictional was one of several manuscripts commissioned or owned by Robert de Clercq, who followed a succession of other abbots of Ter Duinen (Jan Crabbe, Petrus Vaillant, and Christian de Hondt) in commissioning illuminated manuscripts and other works of art for use in the Abbey (Smeyers 1999, 456–59).

Six of the eight miniatures in the manuscript (two

full-page, three half-page, and one column miniature), including the opening Crucifixion and its illustrated border of scenes from the Passion, are by Simon Bening, one of the foremost Flemish miniaturists of his time *(see no. 97)*. Active in Bruges for much of the first half of the sixteenth century, Bening received or participated in some of the most prestigious commissions of the period, including those from leading aristocratic and ecclesiastical patrons in Germany, Spain, Portugal and Italy. The Benedictional of Robert de Clercq is one of the more modest commissions undertaken by Bening and one of the few that he is known to have received from an ecclesiastical patron in Flanders. Bening was employed, above all, to illustrate Books of Hours and Prayer Books treating the life and Passion of Christ, which called for depictions ranging from hieratically conceived devotional images and sweetly idealized figures to works of vivid narrative and dramatic expressive intensity. He was prized for his pictorial qualities, evident in his highly developed and atmospheric landscapes and his ability to vary the focus of his depictions from distant views to extreme close-ups (an example of which can be seen in the small, half-length depiction of the Madonna and Child, fol. 33r). The Benedictional is comparable in size to Flemish Books of Hours of the period and its programme of illustration is consonant with the type of pictures typically found in such books, which may account for Robert de Clercq having entrusted the commission to Bening. The decoration of simulated architectural forms, jewellery, foliage, flowers, insects, birds, animals, grotesques and garlands portrayed in *trompe-l'oeil* on gold or coloured panels in the margins of the text and miniature pages, as well as the pictorial border of the text page on fol. 45v, appear to have been contributed by one or more collaborators, presumably border specialists. Two of the full-page miniatures must also be assigned to different, unidentified painters, the Blessing Saviour in half-length (fol. 69v) and the Baptism of Christ (fol. 79v), which derives from an engraving of the same subject by Martin Schongauer (Lehrs 8).

The binding is by Ludovicus Bloc, a well-known binder from Bruges, who also bound another manuscript illuminated by Simon Bening for a Flemish monastic patron, the Prayer Book of Joanna of Ghistelles, Abbess of Messines (London, British Library, Egerton MS 2125; Los Angeles and London 2003–2004, no. 141). Since Robert de Clercq was chosen as Abbot of Ter Duinen in 1519 and Bloc died in 1529, the Benedictional must have been produced between those years. On stylistic grounds, the manuscript is usually assigned to *c.*1520, shortly after Robert de Clercq assumed the abbacy.

PROVENANCE: Robert de Clercq, Abbot of Ter Duinen (1519–1557); subsequently the property of the abbey (*Liber Beate*

Marie de Dunis inscribed inside the upper cover); at the University Library by 1796, when it was recorded in James Nasmyth's handwritten catalogue (MS Nn. 6. 42–4).

EXHIBITED: London 1953–1954, no. 621; Cambridge 1993, no. 42.

LITERATURE: University Library 1856–1867, IV, 490–92; McKitterick 1986, 550; Testa 1986, 44–45; Hindman 1989, 17; Saint Petersburg and Florence 1996, 44; Hindman et al. 1997, 98; Smeyers 1999, 459.

JHM

58

Two Miniatures from a *Laudario*

Italy, Florence, *c.*1340
ARTIST: Pacino di Bonaguida (doc. 1303–1330)
In Italian

(a) The Resurrection and the Three Marys at the Tomb

Parchment, 456 × 330 mm

Fitzwilliam Museum, MS 194

(b) The Martyrdom of Saints Peter and Paul

Parchment, 195 × 230 mm

SCRIPT: Gothic bookhand (textualis) on reverse

Fitzwilliam Museum, Marlay cutting It. 83

THESE MINIATURES once belonged to a celebrated *Laudario*, which was arguably the most richly illuminated Florentine manuscript known from the first half of the fourteenth century. A *Laudario* is a Choir Book for the laity, consisting of hymns of praise (laudes) to the Virgin and Saints arranged roughly in the order of feasts throughout the liturgical year. Written in Italian in the thirteenth century and sung by the members of a religious society, or a confraternity, the hymns were often gathered in sumptuously illustrated volumes. They signalled the growing wealth of Florentine society and the increasing desire of the laity to emulate the communal devotions of those in holy orders (Wilson 1992; Henderson 1994; Betka 2002).

The *Laudario* from which these and some twenty other miniatures were excised was made for the Compagnia di Sant' Agnese in Santa Maria del Carmine in Florence. The identification is based on the combined evidence of images of Carmelite saints in a Washington fragment (National Gallery of Art, Inv. no. 1950.1.8), a depiction of St Agnes on a leaf in London (British

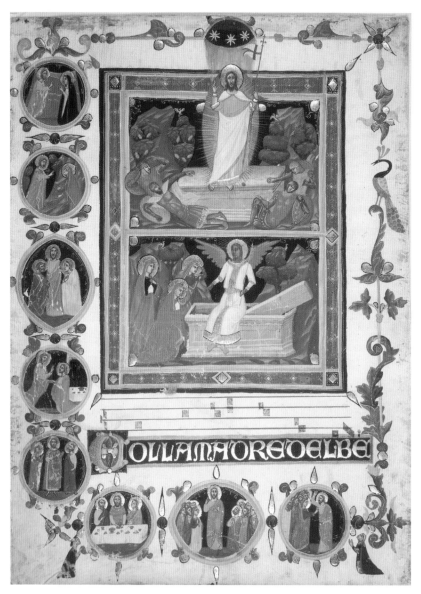

Resurrection scenes.
Fitzwilliam Museum, MS 194

Library, Add. MS 18196), and the inventory of the Compagnia made in 1466 (New York 1994, 58–80; Ziino and Zamei 1999). Two of its members are depicted in the bas-de-page of the Resurrection leaf shown here. The Easter hymn *Colla madre del beato* opens with an extended narrative frontispiece drawing on the Gospels and the *Golden Legend (see no. 128).* In the border medallions, the risen Christ appears to the Virgin, to Mary Magdalene, to Saints Peter and John, and to James the Less, before joining his disciples for the Supper at Emmaus and revealing himself to the Apostles and to the doubting Thomas.

The second miniature introduces the feast of Saints Peter and Paul (29 June). On the left, St Peter is crucified head down at his own request, lest his death be equalled with Christ's sacrifice. The monuments represent the goal markers thought to identify the site of St Peter's martyrdom. On the right, St Paul appears after his death to the devout Plautilla and returns her veil used, according to the *Golden Legend,* to blindfold him

during the decollation. While the iconographic details tell the story, the main protagonists remain detached from it. Their solemn expressions and hieratic postures imbue the narrative with the timeless aura of an icon. This combination may explain the enormous success of Pacino di Bonaguida who was a prolific painter and illuminator and head of a workshop that virtually monopolized Florentine book illustration in the first half of the fourteenth century. This *Laudario* was a late work and among his most prestigious commissions.

(a) PROVENANCE: Compagnia di Sant'Agnese, Florence, *c.*1340; William Young Ottley (1771–1836); his sale, Sotheby's, London, 11 May 1838, lot 178; N.P. Simes of Strood Park, Horsham; his sale, Sotheby's, London, 9 July 1886, part of lot 1095; purchased by the Museum in 1891.

EXHIBITED: New York 1994, no. 4e.

LITERATURE: James 1895a, 401–402; Offner 1930, 26, pl. X; Ziino 1978, 44–45, pl. 4; Partsch 1981, no. 5, pl. 19, fig. 61; Boskovits 1984, 52 n. 179; Offner and Boskovits 1987, 200–203, pl. LXXIII–IV; Henderson 1994, pl. 3.4.

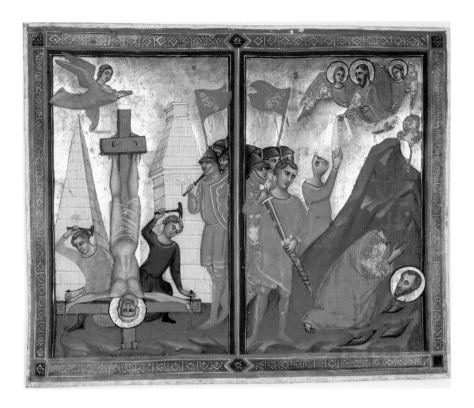

The Martyrdom of Saints Peter and Paul. Fitzwilliam Museum, Marlay cutting It. 83

(b) PROVENANCE: Compagnia di Sant'Agnese, Florence, *c.*1340; Thomas Miller Whitehead, acquired in 1855; acquired before 1886 by Charles Brinsley Marlay (1831–1912); his bequest, 1912.

EXHIBITED: London 1886, no. 7; New York 1994, no. 4j.

LITERATURE: Wormald and Giles 1982, 142–43; Betka 2002, 391–92.   SP

59

The Presentation in the Temple

Historiated initial from a Gradual
In Latin
Italy, Florence, 1371–1375
ARTIST: Don Silvestro dei Gherarducci (1339–1399)

Parchment, 300 × 270 mm

Fitzwilliam Museum, Marlay cutting It. 13A

THE PRESENTATION IN THE TEMPLE within the initial *S* once introduced the *Introit* for the Mass for the feast of the Purification of the Virgin: *Suscepimus, Deus, misericordiam tuam in medio templi tui* ('We have received your kindness, O Lord, within your temple'). As fol. 42 of a splendid Gradual for the Sanctorale made for the Camaldolese monastery of Santa Maria degli Angeli in Florence, it was among the twenty most richly illuminated leaves which were removed from the volume dur-

ing the Napoleonic campaigns in Italy. While the mutilated Gradual entered the Biblioteca Laurenziana in 1809 as Corale 2, by 1800 the cuttings were in the collection of William Young Ottley *(see no. 64).* Though subsequently dispersed, all but one have now been identified in public and private collections (D'Ancona 1994; New York 1994, 131–38, no. 16; Freuler 1997). Three more historiated initials from the Choir Books of Santa Maria degli Angeli are in the Fitzwilliam Museum (MS 5– 1979, Marlay cuttings It. 13.i and ii).

The Presentation in the Temple (*illustration overleaf*) is among the finest works of Don Silvestro dei Gherarducci, the leading Florentine illuminator of the last quarter of the fourteenth century. Vasari praised him as Lorenzo Monaco's most distinguished precursor. Don Silvestro worked exclusively for the Camaldolese order and mainly for Santa Maria degli Angeli where he arrived as a novice in 1348 and died as a prior in 1399. Of the numerous Choir Books that he illuminated for his monastery, Corale 2 is the most sumptuous. Conceived on a grand scale and imbued with solemn introspection, Don Silvestro's scenes and figures have the impact of monumental paintings. Indeed, the Presentation in the Temple is based on Ambrogio Lorenzetti's eponymous altarpiece completed in 1342 for the Crescentius Chapel in Siena Cathedral (now in the Uffizi). Further comparisons of Don Silvestro's compositions with panels and frescoes reveal the artist's exceptional skill in blending the refined nuances and exquisite delicacy of manuscript illumination with the sweeping freedom and powerful immediacy of a monumental painting. He adapted a large panel, conceived within an architectural setting, to the scale and context of manuscript painting. Don

Silvestro simplified the architectural complexity of Lorenzetti's panel and re-arranged the figures so as to convey the sense of depth while offering the viewer a closer observation of details and emotions. In a medieval tradition, he conflated Christ's Circumcision with the Purification of the Virgin. By placing the doves required by the Jewish rite in Joseph's hands, Don Silvestro linked the image to the feast it illustrates in the manuscript and to the liturgical text which he heard and probably sang together with his fellow monks from this Gradual.

PROVENANCE: Santa Maria degli Angeli, Florence; Francis Douce (1757–1834); Sir Samuel Rush Meyrick (1783–1848); acquired before 1886 by Charles Brinsley Marlay (1831–1912); his bequest, 1912.

EXHIBITED: London 1886, no. 6; London 1983, no. 45; New York 1994, no. 16b.

LITERATURE: D'Ancona 1957, 18–19, fig. 6; Boskovits 1975, 114, 216 n. 86, 421; D'Ancona 1978, 221; Wormald and Giles 1982, 110; D'Ancona 1994, 14–20, 90; Freuler 1997, 352 n. 5, 362, 365, 378–79, 380 n. 1, 437, pl. XLI.29.

SP

The Presentation in the Temple. Fitzwilliam Museum, Marlay cutting It. 13A

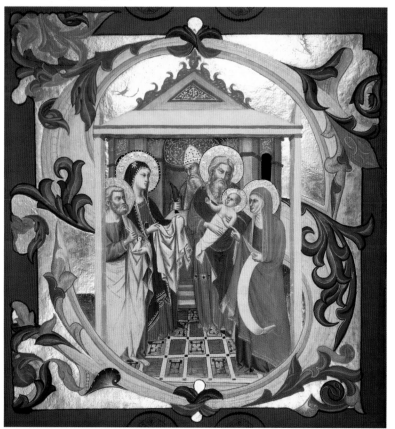

60

Two Historiated Initials from a Gradual

In Latin
Italy, Venice, c.1420
ARTIST: The Master of the Murano Gradual
(act. c.1420 – c.1440)

(a) The Dormition of the Virgin

Parchment, 305 × 320 mm

SCRIPT: Gothic bookhand (textualis) on reverse

Fitzwilliam Museum, Marlay cutting It. 18

(b) Female Saint

Parchment, 143 × 96 mm

SCRIPT: Gothic bookhand (textualis) on reverse

Cambridge University Library, MS Add. 4165(10)

THE G-INITIAL with the Dormition of the Virgin once opened the *Introit* for the Mass for the Assumption of the Virgin in a magnificent Gradual: *Gaudeamus omnes in Domino, diem festum celebrantes* ('Let us all rejoice in the Lord as we celebrate the feast'). The continuation of the text is partially preserved on the verso:…*honore Marie virginis de cuius [assumptio]ne gaudent angeli et…* ('…in honour of the Virgin Mary at whose assumption the angels rejoice and…'). Saints Peter and Paul read the Vigil of the Dead over the Virgin's bier and St John holds the Palm of Paradise while God receives Mary's soul in heaven. The crippled people in the foreground refer to the lame and blind who, according to the Apocryphal New Testament, were healed by touching the house where the Virgin lay dying. By bringing them in as witnesses of a divine revelation, positioning them in direct contact with Mary's body, and offering them the viewer's perspective on the unfolding events, the artist has created a unified, monumental composition and has heightened the sense of immediate participation in the drama and mystery of the Assumption.

The identification of the female saint in the second initial is uncertain, due to the trimmed letter shape, which may have been an O, D, C or G, and to the fragmentary text on the verso (…*um ver…*). It is possible that

The Dormition of the Virgin. Fitzwilliam Museum, Marlay cutting It. 18

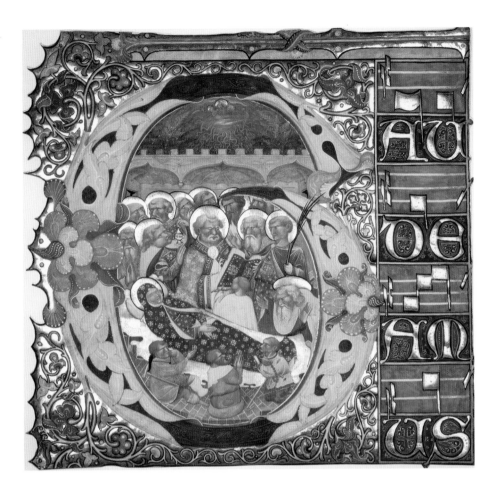

she represented St Clare at the *Introit* for the Mass for her feast, *O virginale lilium* ('O purest lily').

These two fragments and many more scattered in public and private collections across the world came from a Gradual for the Sanctorale made for the Venetian Camaldolese monastery of San Mattia in Murano. They are closely related in style to a Murano Gradual for the Temporale (Berlin, Kupferstichkabinett, MS 78 F.1). Pietro Toesca was the first to identify the artist of some of these cuttings with the artist of the Berlin Gradual and to suggest that he was a Venetian follower of Belbello da Pavia (Toesca 1930, 93–94). Some scholars have identified the Murano Master with Belbello da Pavia, either in his early years around 1420 or during his last sojourn in Venice after 1461, while others have seen him as a Venetian master who collaborated with, and even influenced, Belbello (Salmi 1951, 325; D'Ancona 1970, 35–59; Nordenfalk 1975, 70–74; Padovani 1978; Cadei 1984, 210–11; Milan 1988, 14–15; Hindman et al. 1997, 176–77; Cleveland/San Francisco/New York 2003, no. 60).

A close examination of the Cambridge fragments confirms the distinct style and personality of the Murano Master. Among his salient features are the monumental, voluminous, tubular fabrics whose complex hatching pattern is most obvious in the white robes of the female

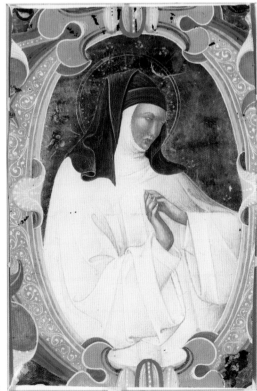

Female Saint. Cambridge University Library, MS Add. 4165(10)

saint and finds close parallels in the Wildenstein miniature of the Apostle's Mission and the initial with a seated Evangelist (Paris, Musée Marmottan, Inv. M 6030, Inv. M 6039); the haloes with floral patterns or pseudo-kufic lettering; the long white nails on delicately drawn hands; and the plasticity of the faces, whose bone-structure appears as if sculpted above the parchment surface, and whose eyes, with their strong white highlights, sparkle against their dark, sun-blushed complexion. It is the expression of the faces, calm and dreamy for the women, but tense, questioning, grave, sometimes even fierce for the men, that constitutes the Murano Master's hallmark. It may have evolved, together with the decorative vocabulary and the monumental compositions, from the Florentine models to which the artist aspired. In their work on the Choir Books for San Mattia in Murano (Berlin, Kupferstichkabinett, MS 78 F.1 and Milan, Biblioteca Nazionale Braidense, MS AB–XVII.28), the Murano Master and Cristoforo Cortese drew on two Graduals illuminated for the sister house of San Michele in Murano by Don Silvestro dei Gherarducci in the 1390s (Milan 1988, 232–35; New York 1994, 155–76, no. 17; Freuler 1997, 453–64). Yet, Don Silvestro's faces share the calm, introspective, somewhat melancholic grandeur of his figures, while the animosity of the Murano Master's protagonists seems closer to the intense, grave expressions found in the work of Don Silvestro's great successor at Santa Maria degli Angeli, Lorenzo Monaco (d.1423/1424). The plasticity with which Don Lorenzo renders human flesh, his dynamic compositions and daring juxtaposition of bright colours provide further parallels to the Murano Master's work. Unlike Don Silvestro, Don Lorenzo is not known to have worked for the Camaldolese houses in Venice. Yet, the connections between Santa Maria degli Angeli and San Michele in Murano were particularly close during the first two decades of the fifteenth century while Lorenzo Monaco dominated Florentine illumination. This was also the formative period of the Murano Master. Our understanding of his importance will be greatly advanced by a reconstruction of the Murano Choir Books.

(a) PROVENANCE: William Young Ottley (1771–1836); his sale, Sotheby's, London, 11 May 1838, lot 191; Rev. John Fuller; Thomas Miller Whitehead, 1853; note on original mount: '1887. No. 2396'; Charles Brinsley Marlay (1831–1912); his bequest, 1912.

EXHIBITED: Cambridge 1966, no. 89.

LITERATURE: D'Ancona 1970, 54; Nordenfalk 1975, no. 21, n. 2; Padovani 1978, fig. 22; Russell 1980, n. 14; Wormald and Giles 1982, 112–13.

(b) PROVENANCE: Edward Hailstone; his sale, Sotheby's, London, 4 Feb. 1891, part of lot 1465 or 1466; purchased by Samuel Sandars (1837–1894); his bequest, 1894.

LITERATURE: unpublished   SP

61

Antiphonal

In Latin
Flanders or Brabant, c.1510

Parchment, i + 153 + i fols., 485–488 × 342 mm, text 412 × 242 mm, 10 long lines each of music (4-line red staves) and text ruled in light brown or grey ink

SCRIPT: Gothic bookhand (textualis)

BINDING: blind-tooled brown calf over wooden boards, brass corners and shoes at tail, four domed circular brass bosses and a cast brass boss at the centre of each board, two brass clasps and catchplates, late 16th or early 17th c., restored and re-backed by the Cockerell Bindery, 1982.

Fitzwilliam Museum, MS 41

Because of their large size and the complexity of the Divine Office, which called for the recitation and singing of different prayers, lessons and chants throughout the liturgical year by the members of religious communities, Antiphonals frequently came in multi-volume sets comprising the variable chants for different parts of the year. The present volume, containing only the Antiphons and related chants for the winter portion of the liturgical year (Temporal feasts from Advent to the Eve of Easter) was presumably originally complemented by at least one other volume containing the antiphonal chants for other parts of the liturgical year as well as for the Sanctoral and the Common of Saints. Thus far, however, no other volume from the same set has been identified, and the present volume lacks clear-cut evidence of its destination or place of production.

Fitzwilliam MS 41 has five decorated and illustrated leaves for the feasts of Advent (an unusual depiction apparently of Daniel in the Lion's Den), Christmas Day (Nativity and Annunciation to the Shepherds), the First Sunday after the Octave of Epiphany (King David in Penitence), Septuagesima (God creating the Animals) and the First Sunday in Lent (the Temptation of Christ). Although the scope of the painted decoration is modest, its quality is high. The decoration and illustration are in the style of the so-called Ghent-Bruges school of illumination: miniatures are conceived as veritable pictures set in expansive and atmospheric landscapes or interior settings, and they are accompanied by gilt or coloured panel borders decorated with foliage, flowers, insects, birds, and animals in *trompe-l'oeil*, and, on fol. 31, also incorporating an illustrated corner piece.

The miniaturist has not yet been identified, but some of the illustrations are rooted in known traditions of Flemish painting. The depiction of the Nativity (fol. 31),

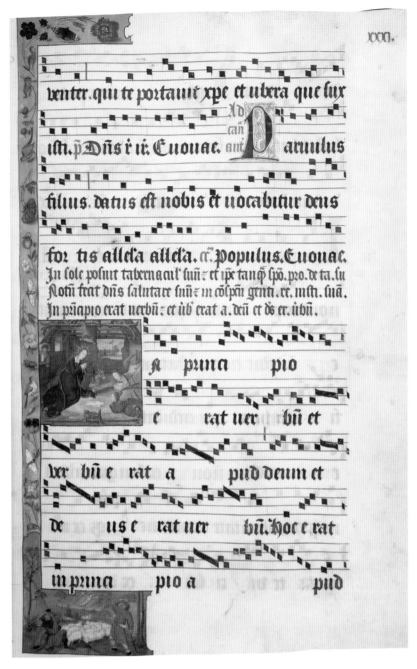

for example, echoes works and pictorial ideas that go back to paintings by Hugo van der Goes. The portrayal of the Christ Child lying face up on the ground, the sheaf of bundled wheat, and the facial type of Mary, with drawn features, swollen eyelids, and un-gathered hair, all recall works such as the Nativity of Hugo's Portinari Altarpiece (Florence, Uffizi). The shepherd kneeling in a striking contrapposto pose at the left foreground of the marginal illustration on the same page has an extremely close counterpart in a miniature from the circle of the Master of the Prayer Books of Around 1500 (the Da Costa Hours of c.1515, New York, Pierpont Morgan Library, M. 399, fol. 157v; Wolf 1982, fig. 10). Such figural motifs were doubtless disseminated through model drawings. The same probably holds for the figure of David in Penitence (fol. 61), which recalls a prototype

known in works in the style of the Vienna Master of Mary of Burgundy (for example, in the Rooklooster Breviary of 1477, Brussels, Bibliothèque royale de Belgique, MS IV 860, fol. 36; Los Angeles and London 2003–2004, no. 24). Works from these traditions were revised and recycled in Flemish illumination well into the sixteenth century. On stylistic grounds, Fitzwilliam MS 41 can be provisionally localized in Flanders or Brabant and dated c.1510.

PROVENANCE: acquired by Viscount Fitzwilliam in 1814; his bequest, 1816.

EXHIBITED: Cambridge 1993, no. 44.

LITERATURE: Searle 1876, no. 121; James 1895a, 93.

JHM

62

The Annunciation, the Visitation, the Ascension, Saints Peter and Paul

Four Leaves from a Gradual
In Latin
Brabant, probably Antwerp, c.1524

Parchment, 368–417 × 255–295 mm, text 307–312 × 212–216 mm, 9 lines each of music (4-line red staves) and text
SCRIPT: Gothic bookhand (textualis)

Fitzwilliam Museum, Marlay Cuttings Fl. 1–4

BECAUSE OF THEIR LARGE SIZE and their highly variable contents, which customarily reflect the liturgical specifications of the communities for which they were made, Choir Books were handwritten and decorated well into the sixteenth century and beyond, when many other traditional manuscript books were supplanted by printed editions. Many handmade Choir Books continued to be used well into the modern period; Marlay Cutting Fl. 3 includes a re-written Psalm verse in a more modern script, which reflects an updating of the liturgy in the community where it was used.

These four cuttings are from an illustrated Gradual. None of them contains obvious evidence of the place of their use or manufacture. Recently, however, Jan van der Stock suggested that they derive from the same codex as a set of eight illuminated cuttings now in Brussels (Bibliothèque royale de Belgique, MS II 3633: 1–8; St Petersburg and Florence 1996). A close comparison of text measurements, pen-flourishes and other decorative elements among the sets of cuttings in Cambridge and Brussels seems to confirm that hypothesis. Several of the leaves in Brussels bear the arms and motto of Marcus Cruyt, Abbot of the Cistercian monastery of St Bernard's at Hemiskem near Antwerp (1518–1536), ambassador of Emperor Charles V to Denmark, and a noted patron of manuscripts, paintings, and works of stained glass. According to a chronicle of the Abbey, Cruyt ordered the Gradual from which these leaves presumably derive in or around 1524 from the Louvain copyist Francis Weert. Other cuttings from the same Gradual are extant in private collections in Germany and New York, and possibly also in Paris, Musée Marmottan, Wildenstein Collection, Inv. M 6322 (Los Angeles and London 2003–2004, 509).

The decoration and illustration of the cuttings from the Gradual of Marcus Cruyt bear all the hallmarks of the Ghent-Bruges school of illumination, which by this date was the predominant style of richly illustrated manuscripts produced throughout large areas of the Low Countries. Characteristic features of this style include gilt or coloured panel borders decorated with foliage, flowers, insects, birds, figures and objects in *trompe-l'oeil* (portrayed as if three-dimensional forms that cast shadows on to the panels) and illustrations conceived as veritable pictures, with scenes set in expansive and atmospheric landscapes or interior settings. The picture style of the miniatures reflects the influence of the traditions of Flemish panel painting and manuscript illustration of the fifteenth and the early sixteenth centuries. There are echoes of pictorial prototypes from the fifteenth century, for instance, in the miniature of the Ascension, which reflects a composition attributed to the Vienna Master of Mary of Burgundy in the Breviary of Margaret of York, datable c.1475–1480 *(no. 50)*. The influence of Renaissance decorative vocabulary is also evident in such features as the columns and swags found in the miniature of Saints Peter and Paul, and the elegantly scalloped profiles of one or both ends on the panel borders in each of these cuttings. Similar stylistic features appear in a large and richly decorated Missal also made for Marcus Cruyt (private collection, formerly Sotheby's, London, 11 Dec. 1984, lot 55), which has been attributed variously to the Master of Charles V and the circle of a newly identified painter from his orbit, the Master of Cardinal Wolsey, prominent illuminators in Antwerp during this period (Los Angeles and London 2003–2004, no. 170). The miniatures in Cruyt's Gradual can be ascribed to painters from the same circle.

PROVENANCE: Marcus Cruyt, Abbot of St Bernard's at Hemiskem (1518–1536); Charles Brinsley Marlay (1831–1912); his bequest, 1912.

EXHIBITED: Cambridge 1993, no. 45.

LITERATURE: Wormald and Giles 1982, I, 96–97; St Petersburg and Florence 1996, 152.

JHM

1. The Annunciation. Fitzwilliam Museum, Marlay Cutting Fl. 1.

2. The Visitation. Fitzwilliam Museum, Marlay Cutting Fl. 2.

3. The Ascension. Fitzwilliam Museum, Marlay Cutting Fl. 3.

4. Saints Peter and Paul. Fitzwilliam Museum, Marlay Cutting Fl. 4

1

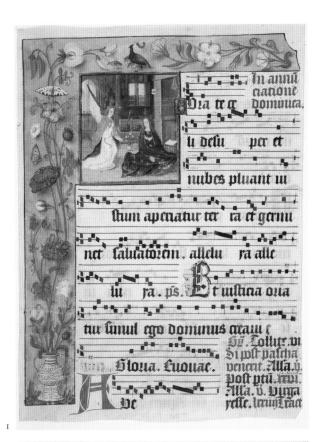

In annunciatione domine.

Ro te ce... li defu per et nubes pluant iu stum aperiatur ter ra et germi net saluatorem. allelu ra alle lu ia. ps. Et iustitia ona tur simul ego dominus creaui e Gloria. Euouae.

Hy. Colluc vi Si post pascha veneit. Alla. v. Post ptu. rvi. Alla. v. Virga resse. lvius Fract

Aue

2

gia mul off. Exultabut. rur. co. Ego vos elegi. rvi. ta in ple be. In visitatioe bte marie.

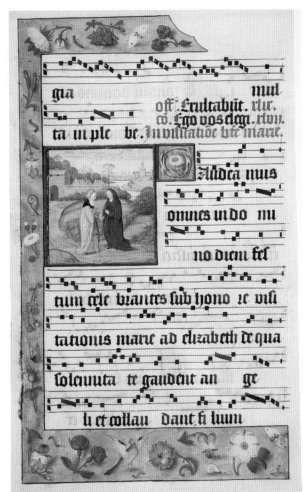

Gaudea mus omnes in do mi no diem fes tum cele brantes sub hono re visi tationis marie ad elizabeth de qua solennita te gaudent an ge li et collau dant fi lium

3

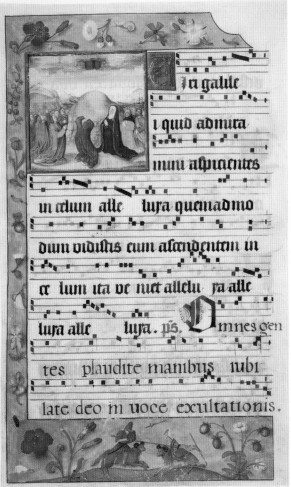

In galile i quid admira mini aspicientes in celum alle luia quemadmo dum vidistis eum ascendentem in ce lum ita ve niet allelu ia alle luia alle luia. ps. Omnes gen tes plaudite manibus iubi late deo in voce exultationis.

4

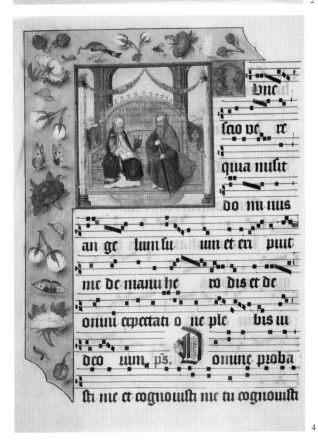

unc scio ve re quia misit do minus an ge lum su um et eri puit me de manu he ro dis et de omni expectati o ne ple bis iu deo rum. ps. Domine proba sti me et cognouisti me tu cognouisti

63

Noli me tangere

Historiated initial from a Gradual or Antiphonal
In Latin
Franconia, c.1514

Parchment, 190 × 206 mm

SCRIPT: Gothic bookhand (textualis) on reverse

Cambridge University Library, MS Add. 4165(7)

THE DRAMATIC LANDSCAPE, Christ's melancholic face and voluminous red robe, and the stylized berries folded within the bronze-like foliage shaping the letter A find parallels in contemporary painting from centres north of the Alps. They are particularly close to works of c.1517–1518 from the atelier of Albrecht Altdorfer (Paris 1984b; Merkl 1999, figs. 505, 507). The dating and area are also suggested by the Germanic nature of the script and musical notation on the reverse of the image. They are further supported by the style of twenty-five initials that seem to have been cut out of the same Choir Book and were pasted into an album which was sold at the Fountaine sale as the 'Property of a Lady' (Christie's, London, 6 July 1894, lot 146), now preserved in Toronto (Royal Ontario Museum, MS 997.158.157). Several of the Toronto initials show the

same liking for illusionistic, three-dimensional initials, for individualized, portrait-like features, and for atmospheric landscapes, especially at dusk or dawn, and they can be attributed to the master of the *Noli me tangere*. However, the majority are the work of one, or perhaps two, less capable assistants.

The Toronto album's title page announces that the initials came from an Italian Choir Book of c.1514. The date and a coat of arms with a trident, which feature in a modern inscription beneath the initial with the Assumption of the Virgin (fol. 12), may have been copied from the original volume. The *Noli me tangere* features another heraldic device, the sickle on a shield in the left-hand corner and probably on Christ's spade as well. Nicholas Rogers has suggested (in correspondence) an association with the Franconian family of Streitberg. The Toronto initials and their subject-matter reveal that the cuttings came from a multi-volume Gradual and Antiphonal set. It was commissioned for a Benedictine convent, since the feast of St Benedict received one of the most elaborate illuminations by the *Noli me tangere* Master (fol. 25). The Benedictine abbess who features prominently in three of the images (fols. 7, 14, 15) may well have been the patron.

The reverse of *Noli me tangere* contains the end of Vespers for Holy Saturday, including a reading from Matthew 28 as the Antiphon of the *Magnificat* for the Easter vigil: *Vespere autem sabbati*. This establishes that the initial *A* framing the *Noli me tangere* would have illustrated either the Antiphon for Saturday Vespers, *Alleluia*, or the first responsory for Matins on Easter Sunday, *Angelus Domini*. They shared the same text from St Mark's Gospel 16:1–7, beginning *Angelus Domini descendit* ('An Angel of the Lord came down'). Vespers of Holy Saturday was included not only in the Breviary, but also in the Missal because it followed directly the Mass of Holy Saturday. It is therefore hard to be certain whether the initial belonged to a Gradual or an Antiphonal. If it illustrated Saturday Vespers in the Gradual, the other Easter subject framed in an initial *A*, the soldiers asleep by the tomb in the Toronto album (fol. 8), may have introduced the first responsory for Sunday Matins in the Antiphonal volume. We are looking at illuminations from an astonishingly rich set of Antiphonals and Graduals. The original manuscripts would have contained many more images and some may resurface in public and private collections.

PROVENANCE: Edward Hailstone; his sale, Sotheby's, London, 4 Feb. 1891, part of lot 1465 or 1466; purchased by Samuel Sandars (1837–1894); his bequest, 1894.

LITERATURE: unpublished

SP

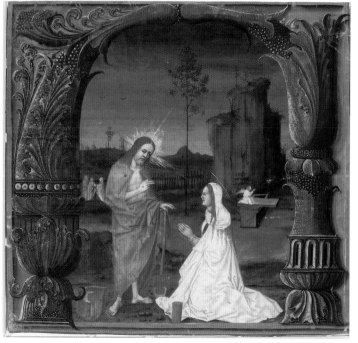

Noli me tangere. Cambridge University Library, MS Add. 4165(7)

64

Illuminated borders

Fragments from a Missal of Pope Leo X
Italy, Florence, 1513–1521
ARTISTS: Attavante (Vante di Gabriello di Vante
Attavanti, 1452–1524) and workshop

Parchment, MS Add. 4165(15a): 22 × 47 mm, 118 × 47 mm,
60 × 47 mm, 10 × 46 mm, 135 × 47 mm, 60 × 43 mm,
5 × 41 mm; MS Add. 4165(15b): 70 × 192 mm; MS Add.
4165(15c): 65 × 42 mm, 302 × 42 mm, 50 × 42 mm

Cambridge University Library, MS Add. 4165(15)

THESE FRAGMENTS came from one or more of the
three Missals illuminated by the workshop of
Attavante degli Attavanti, the last great Florentine illuminator *(see no. 104)*. They were made for Giovanni de'
Medici, Lorenzo de' Medici's second son, after his election as Pope Leo X (1513–1521). The Medici device, a
diamond ring with three feathers, and motto *Semper*
('always') dominate one of the vertical borders. The
other, made up of seven pieces, seems to lack a gold
medallion beneath the putto. It may have contained
another of Leo X's *imprese*, the yoke with a scroll inscribed *Suave* ('sweet'), referring to Matthew 11:30 ('For
my yoke is sweet and my burden light'). The Medici
arms surmounted by the papal insignia, and flanked by
two angels holding *cornucopiae*, would have decorated
the lower border of a magnificently illuminated page.

Numerous related fragments appeared in sales throughout the nineteenth and twentieth centuries, including
those of W.Y. Ottley, Samuel Rogers, W.H. Crawford,
Lord Northwick, and more recently at Sotheby's on
22 June 1993 and 21 December 1997. Two further fragments (BEL 1998, no. 15a and 15b) are particularly close
to the Cambridge borders. The largest sets of related
fragments are in the Samuel Rogers Album (Add. MS

Fragments with Leo X's arms and devices. Cambridge
University Library, MS Add. 4165 (15)

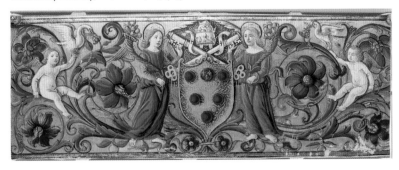

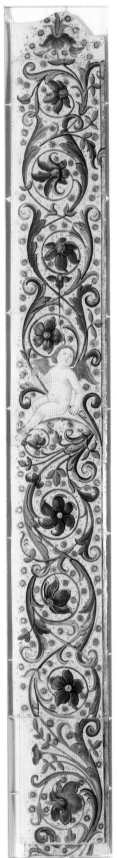
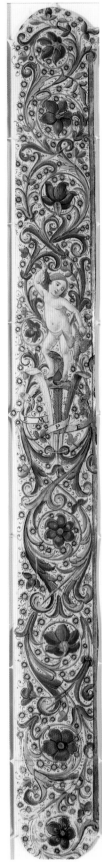

21412) and the Rothschild, or Ascott, Album (Add. MS 60630) in the British Library.

The manuscripts to which these borders belonged were among the 'ancient Papal books' kept in the Sistine Chapel and described in its 1714 inventory (Rome, Archivio di Stato, Camerale I, Inventari, Vol. 1560, Reg. 24; Talamo 1997). The inventory lists three Papal Missals with Medici arms. Two are associated with Leo X and all three are described as containing a Crucifixion miniature. Numerous fragments from these and other Sistine Chapel manuscripts, mutilated after the Napoleonic invasion in 1798, were brought to England by Abate Luigi Celotti. His sale at Christie's (26 May 1825) was a turning point in the history of manuscript collecting and scholarship (Evanston 2001, 53–59). The sale catalogue prepared by William Young Ottley offered descriptions of unprecedented detail, and presented manuscript illuminations as miniature paintings and 'the monuments of a lost art'. Borders very similar to those in Cambridge were pasted around two Crucifixion miniatures which appeared framed as paintings in the Celotti sale (lot 53, probably from Missal A.I.2, now Geneva, Comites Latentes Collection, and lot 51, from Missal A.I.3 or A.I.4, now New York, private collection, ex-Lehman Collection). During the nineteenth century, the fragments provided not only material for collages, but also inspiration for copies, such as the Crucifixion with the Papal Medici arms in the Victoria and Albert Museum (E. 4588–1910). It is important as evidence of what may have been the Crucifixion miniature in Leo X's third Missal, since it combines the salient features of the New York and Geneva compositions with new elements. This miniature also highlights one of the greatest challenges to students of Italian Renaissance illumination – the innumerable works of varying quality attributed to Attavante degli Attavanti and the need for a systematic analysis of his *oeuvre*.

PROVENANCE: Pope Leo X (1513–1521); Abatte Luigi Celotti (*c*.1768–*c*.1846); his sale, Christie's, London, 26 May 1825, lot 51 or 52; William Young Ottley (1771–1836); his sale, Sotheby's, London, 11 May 1838, lot 218; Edward Hailstone; his sale, Sotheby's, London, 4 Feb. 1891, lot 1465 or 1466; purchased by Samuel Sandars (1837–1894); his bequest, 1894.

LITERATURE: unpublished

SP

65

The Deposition from the Cross, the Vision of Pope Leo the Great, and border fragments from a Missal of Pope Clement VII

Italy, Rome, after 1523
ARTIST: Vincent Raymond (act. *c*.1515–d.1557)

Parchment, Marlay cutting It. 34: miniature 202 × 132 mm, left and right borders 312 × 58 mm, upper border 47 × 135 mm, lower border 66 × 135 mm; Marlay cuttings It. 35: miniature 203 × 143 mm, single piece forming left, upper and lower borders 314 × 200 mm, right border 325 × 60 mm.

Fitzwilliam Museum, Marlay cuttings It. 34, 35

IN THE EARLY NINETEENTH CENTURY these fragments were combined in collages and framed as paintings to satisfy a new fashion. Ironically, the awakening passion for manuscripts encouraged their destruction: the cutting up of manuscripts brought about an ever-growing appreciation for 'the lost art of illumination'. Crucial for these developments were the Sistine Chapel manuscripts, looted by Napoleon's troops in 1798, and Abate Luigi Celotti's collection (*no. 64*). Among the ninety-seven lots of fragments from Sistine Chapel volumes in Celotti's sale were the Fitzwilliam miniatures and borders, together with seventeen other composite lots now dispersed among public and private collections (New York 1992–1993, no. 90). They belonged to two magnificent volumes listed in the 1714 inventory of the Sistine Chapel manuscripts as Missals for saints' feasts: A.I.9 and A.I.10 (Rome, Archivio di Stato, Camerale I, Inventari, Vol. 1560, Reg. 24; Talamo 1997). Both Missals were commissioned by Giulio de' Medici shortly after he succeeded his cousin, Leo X, as Pope Clement VII (1523–1534). The borders advertise his election and links with his predecessor, and display the Medici arms and *imprese*, the yoke with the motto *Suave* ('Sweet') and the diamond ring with feathers and the motto *Semper* ('Always'). They also feature Clement VII's own mottos and emblems. *Vera Philosophia et cogitatio mortis* ('True philosophy and reflection on death'), is accompanied by symbols of death. *Candor ilesus* ('Whiteness/ innocence unharmed') is illustrated with sun rays passing through a crystal sphere and setting a tree on fire, but leaving the white banner with the Pope's motto undamaged. This device was inspired by the observations of Domenico Buoninsegni, Clement VII's treasurer, on the intensified effect of reflected sunlight, which spared only the whitest surfaces (Parry 1977). Scientific interests and moral philosophy blended into the emblem of a Pope who was one of the most discerning patrons of High Renaissance art.

The illumination of his two Missals is now generally accepted as the work of Vincent Raymond. The distinguished career of this French artist at the Roman Curia began under Leo X and culminated with his appointment as papal miniaturist in 1549, a position he held until his death in 1557 (New York 1992–1993, nos. 90, 91; London and New York 1994, nos. 127, 129, 130). The bright pigments and facial types in Pope Leo's Vision, and the busts of Prophets and Evangelists in the border of the Deposition miniature are characteristic of Raymond's early works. The Deposition miniature is by a different hand. The Renaissance ornament and putti in the borders of both miniatures are either modern or were crudely overpainted. Some of the original decoration survives in four of the border fragments (Marlay cuttings It. 33). One of Vincent Raymond's most engaging scenes is the medallion with Adam seated beneath the Tree of Knowledge (It. 34) and contemplating his sin redeemed by Christ, the Second Adam, on the Tree of Life. It anticipates the typological approach which will dominate the artist's later works, notably the double openings with Old and New Testament miniatures in the Hours of Eleanora Gonzaga (Oxford, Bodleian Library, MS Douce 29). The 'flash back' into the Old Testament episode invites the viewer to associate with different participants in the history of Salvation and opens up alternative vistas on the human condition, sinful or saved.

PROVENANCE: Pope Clement VII (1523–1534); Abate Luigi Celotti (*c.*1768–*c.*1846); his sale, Christie's, London, 26 May 1825, lot 63 (Marlay cutting It. 35) and parts of lot 74 (Marlay cuttings It. 33 and 34); Thomas Miller Whitehead; Charles Brinsley Marlay (1831–1912); his bequest, 1912.

EXHIBITED: London 1886, no. 9.

LITERATURE: D'Ancona 1962, 6, 21 n. 14; Wormald and Giles 1982, 119–20; New York 1992–1993, no. 90.

SP

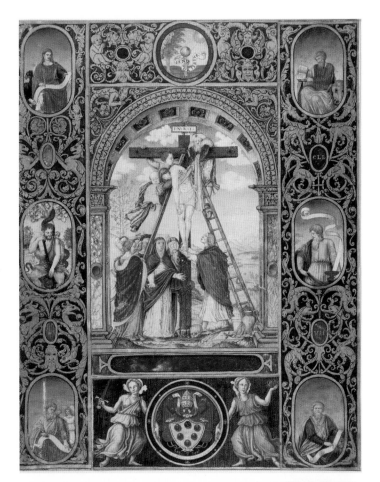

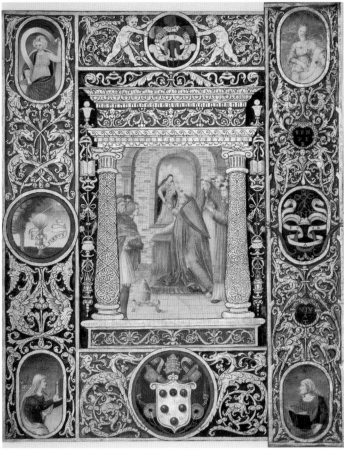

Deposition from the Cross. Fitzwilliam Museum, Marlay cutting It. 34

Vision of Pope Leo the Great. Fitzwilliam Museum, Marlay cutting It. 35

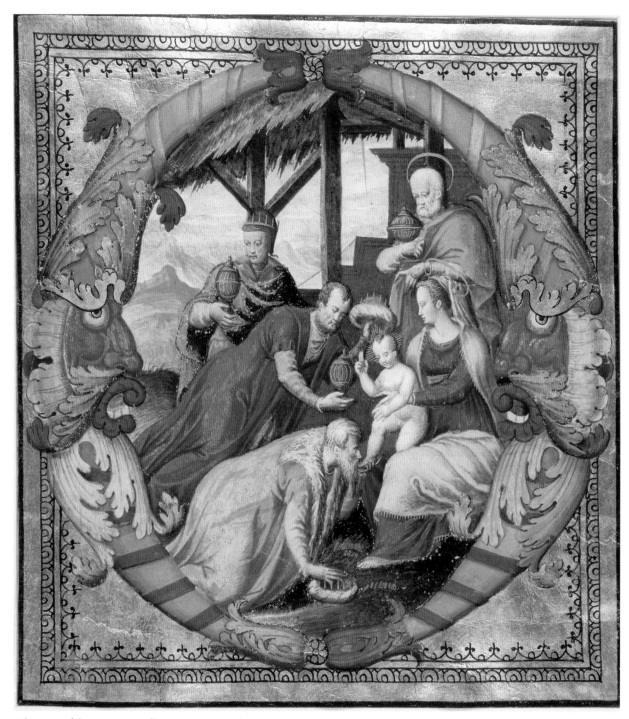

Adoration of the Magi. Fitzwilliam Museum, Marlay cutting It. 40

66

The Adoration of the Magi
Historiated initial from a Gradual

In Latin
Italy, Venice, *c.*1567–*c.*1572
ARTIST: Giovan Battista da Udine (doc. 1567–1576)
SCRIBE: Venturino Veneziano (doc. 1566–1572)

Parchment, 152 × 138 mm
SCRIPT: Gothic bookhand (textualis) on reverse

Fitzwilliam Museum, Marlay cutting It. 40

THIS DELICATE PAINTING once graced a de luxe manuscript in the Choir of San Marco in Venice. In the 1560s, the priest Giovanni Vitali led a major campaign of updating the liturgical books of the basilica (Venice 1995, 25–27, 141–48). An expert calligrapher in the Doge's service, he was personally responsible for the text and decoration of San Marco's *Orazionale*, *Kyriale*, and two of the four volumes in the *Graduale* set (Venice, Biblioteca del Museo Civico Correr, cod. Cigogna 1602; Venice, Museo Marciano, Inv. n. 15, Inv. n. 22, and Inv. n. 100). The other two volumes were copied by an equally accomplished scribe, Venturino Veneziano, a canon at San Salvador (Venice, Museo Marciano, Inv. n. 19 and Inv. n. 20). They are the only volumes in the set of Choir Books to boast a complete programme of illumination. Suzy Marcon identified the artist with Giovan Battista da Udine who received payments between 1567 and 1571.

In addition to the extant Choir Books, in 1572 Venturino was paid for an Antiphonal and Giovan Battista da Udine was involved in its illumination. Only seven miniatures are thought to have survived from this volume. Four are now in Venice (Biblioteca Nazionale Marciana, no shelf mark; Sotheby's, London, 4 Dec. 1994, lot 45; Venice 1995, no. 55, 56; BEL 1998, no. 19, 20); two were displayed in Paris in 2001 (Enluminures 2001, no. 43, 44); the Fitzwilliam Adoration of the Magi is the last. All of them have been associated with the missing Antiphonal, but some may have belonged to a Gradual. The Paris Ascension enclosed within a V initial would have introduced the *Introit* for the Mass on Ascension day: *Viri Galilaei* ('Men of Galilee'), while in an Antiphonal it would be found within the P initial of the first responsory for Matins, *Post passionem* ('After the Passion'). Likewise, in Antiphonals the Adoration of the Magi normally introduces the response for the feast of Epiphany, *Hodie in Jordane* ('Today in Jordan'). What appears as an O here is probably an initial E opening the

Introit for the Mass at Epiphany, *Ecce advenit dominator dominus* ('Behold, the lord, the ruler is come'). The standing king's gaze at the grotesque profile on the left invites the viewer to reconstruct the imaginary crossbar of the initial E by following the line of communication between the toothy monsters on the frame's surface. This is also suggested, in a more subtle way, by the gesticulations of the middle-aged king, the Christ Child, and the Virgin. Visual games like this one, teasing the viewer's eye with optical illusions and engaging the protagonists in a silent dialogue, are characteristic of Mannerism. This painted initial is amongst the most sophisticated Mannerist compositions of Venice, with its atmospheric landscape, radiant colour scheme, elaborately modelled garments, vigorous gesticulation, and delicate faces echoing contemporary works by Titian and Tintoretto.

PROVENANCE: Charles Brinsley Marlay (1831–1912); his bequest, 1912.

EXHIBITED: London 1886, no. 19.

LITERATURE: Wormald and Giles 1982, 122; Venice 1995, 27, fig. 111; BEL 1998, 59; Enluminures 2001, 100.

SP

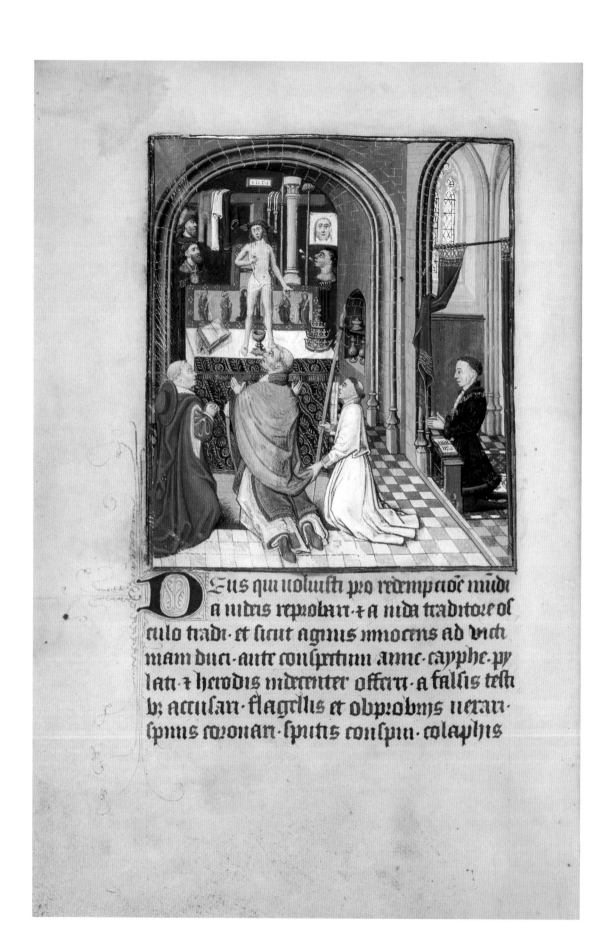

Eus qui noluisti pro redempcoe mudi
a iudeis reprobari · z a iuda traditore os
culo tradi · et sicut agnus innocens ad victi
mam duci · ante conspectum anne · cayphe · py
lati · z herodis indecenter offerri · a falsis testi
b; accusari · flagellis et obprobriis uexari ·
spinis coronari · spuitis conspui · colaphis

PRIVATE DEVOTION: HUMILITY AND SPLENDOUR

by Nigel Morgan and Paul Binski

THIS SECTION of the catalogue considers a broad class of manuscript more flexible in its definition than that of books assisting liturgy or public ceremony, namely devotional manuscripts. Interest in the nature of such manuscripts has grown significantly over the last two generations in part because of associated historical enquiry into the nature of the inner mental, emotional and spiritual life of the individual, and the idea of privacy: this most 'Catholic' aspect of medieval art provides evidence, for some, of proto-modern cultural attitudes. The public-private distinction is, in important respects, unhelpful: the 'private' life of the mind is not free from conventional thinking, and there is no inherent reason why devotion (from the Latin *vovere*, to make a vow or promise) cannot be a public activity. Again, the tendency to think of the devotional image as essentially a late-medieval phenomenon obscures the debt of devotional art not only to the public realm, but also to the religious life of the earlier Middle Ages. Thus, much of the language of Christian devotion had developed by the twelfth century; also, much of it had originated within the public liturgy of the Church and had been given formal shape, discipline and power by communal (whether monastic or secular) not private, experience. The history of the period from the thirteenth century is that of the general spread of public liturgical piety and associated works of art into lay, or extra-liturgical, life *(fig. 25)*. Devotions characteristically stand in relation to some object: devotion is, by its nature, *to* something or someone, and we must not forget that illuminated manuscripts were only one way in which devotional life was given shape and meaning. Another was provided by a large class of devotional art often concerning the Nativity or Passion of Christ which provides some of the most remarkable images made in the Middle Ages.

Private Devotional Books

To illustrate these ideas, we should recall that, while a large proportion of the illuminated books of the later centuries of the Middle Ages were of texts for private reading and devotion, above all those in Psalters and Books of Hours, both books derive their texts from the public liturgy of the Divine Office as contained in the Breviary.[1] Such private devotion was mainly that of the laity, but priests and members of the religious orders also used such books for extra-liturgical reading. Books of this sort received decoration in the form of full-page miniatures, historiated initials and decorative borders as frames to the text. These not only functioned as markers to the sections of the text, but as pictures to be viewed and meditated upon by the owners of the books.[2] Some of the pictures or historiated initials are attached to prayers which advise the contemplation of the image to accompany the reading of the prayer, or require such contemplation to obtain an indulgence for those prayers which are linked to indulgences. Another reason for the elaborate decoration of devotional books is doubtless the wish of often rich patrons to indicate

Fig. 25. Mass of St Gregory and Philip the Good in Prayer. Fitzwilliam Museum, MS 3–1954, fol. 253v

163

their wealth and social status. The many pictures in some of these books may have been used not only for meditation but also for teaching children the basic beliefs and stories from the Bible or the lives of the saints necessary for their religious education *(e.g. no. 105)*. The texts were also used for teaching reading, and for learning the Latin language and memorizing certain Psalms or prayers.

Psalters

The Psalter preceded the Book of Hours, which only emerged as a book in its own right in the middle years of the thirteenth century. Psalters for lay people with rich decoration and miniatures became common during the twelfth century, although examples from the Carolingian period in the ninth century show that such books were already made for lay people in this much earlier time. A Psalter contained the hundred-and-fifty Psalms, preceded by a Calendar, and followed by the Canticles and a Litany of the Saints. From the early thirteenth century Psalters also sometimes had after these texts the Office of the Dead *(no. 77)* and occasionally the Office of the Virgin *(no. 72)*. This last item was split off from the Psalter to form the major text constituent of the Book of Hours. In the twelfth century, Psalters began to have a series of prefatory full-page miniatures of Old and New Testament scenes set before the Psalms, and they also were given historiated initials at the liturgical divisions.[3] These liturgical divisions were for the first Psalm sung at Matins for the seven days of the week (Psalms 1, 26, 38, 52, 68, 80, 97 in the Vulgate numeration), and the first Psalm of Sunday Vespers (Psalm 109 in the Vulgate numeration). Very occasionally framed miniatures were used in addition to historiated initials at the liturgical divisions *(nos. 71, 79)*. In England also Psalms 51 and 101 of the three-part division of the one hundred and fifty Psalms received historiated or large ornamental initials. This was a result of a monastic practice of the Early Middle Ages in which sections of fifty Psalms were recited at a time as a devotional exercise. The prefacing of the Psalter with full-page miniatures continued into the fourteenth century but became rare after 1350 when only the historiated initials of the liturgical divisions formed the decoration.

Books of Hours

The ways that a private owner used the Psalter must have been diverse. The most devout might read the series of Psalms appropriate to the Breviary Offices of the hours of the day, or certain special Psalms such as the Gradual Psalms (119–33 in the Vulgate numeration) or Penitential Psalms (6, 31, 37, 50, 101, 129, 142 in the Vulgate numeration) were read as devotional exercises. The Psalms to be read for these various devotions were scattered among the hundred-and-fifty Psalms and the reader would have to know their opening words to find them. The Psalter therefore did not provide an easily structured text for private prayer. This structure of text was provided by the Book of Hours which became a separate book type in the mid-thirteenth century, even though its constituent elements had all originated much earlier in the Divine Office.[4] The Office of the Virgin Mary said daily was introduced into the daily Offices by the Benedictines and Cistercians in the first half of the twelfth century.[5] By *c.* 1200 this practice had spread to the secular church. A shorter version, the Little Office of the Virgin, became the standard text in a Book of Hours.

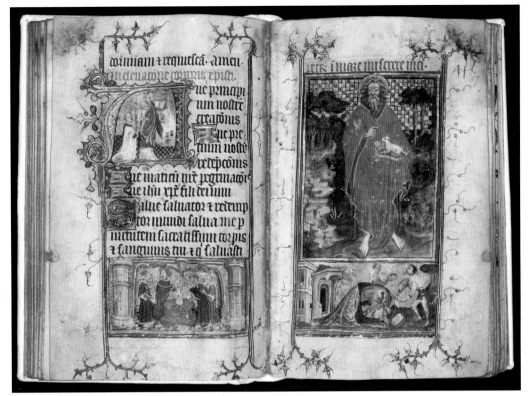

The Office of the Dead had been introduced as a monastic devotion much earlier, originating in the early ninth century.[6] This text too was incorporated in the Book of Hours, and so was that of the Office of the Commendation of the Soul, said immediately after a death.[7] In the Benedictine and Cistercian Office other forms of 'Hours' were added in the twelfth century to the daily Offices, or recited during certain seasons of the year. These included the Hours of the Holy Spirit, of the Trinity and of the Cross, and some or all were included in the texts of some Books of Hours (nos. 81, 85, 86, 87, 88, 90, 95, 96, 100, 102, 104, 106). In addition two series of Psalms were commonly included, the Gradual Psalms and the Penitential Psalms. The former are Psalms expressing trust in God's aid and the latter are Psalms of regret for sin. The Penitential Psalms are usually followed by the Litany of the Saints.

These various texts form sections of Books of Hours. Full-page miniatures and/or historiated initials are set at the beginning of each section.[8] The illustrations are often surrounded by or attached to elaborate decorative borders framing the minia-ture or the text of the page.

From the beginning, certain prayers were added to the Book of Hours, all orig-inating in previous centuries.[9] There were two famous prayers to the Virgin Mary Obsecro te and O intemerata,[10] and prayers to the face of Christ, Deus qui nobis signatis lumine vultus tui and Salve sancta facies.[11] Prayers referring to Christ's Passion or specifically to the Crucifixion were also included. A famous one cited the Seven Last Words on the Cross.[12] There were also devotions involving repeated prayers such as the Ave Maria, some of which became standardized in the mid-fifteenth century as the Rosary in the form it exists today.[13] Among such devotions were the Joys of the Virgin arranged as a group of seven or fifteen (nos. 88, 94).[14] Prayers to be said during Mass were also added, particularly those to be said when the conse-crated Host is elevated by the priest (fig. 26) or when it is exposed in a monstrance (nos. 83, 91). Some Books of Hours have the texts of select Masses for certain feasts of the year or Votive Masses (fig. 27).

Christ, the Passion and the Eucharist

Both Psalters and Books of Hours contain special images of Christ and scenes of his life. In Psalters having selected full-page miniatures before the Psalms, one often finds images of Christ in Majesty or the Crucifixion (*no. 68*). Some Psalters have narrative images of Christ's Life as prefatory illustrations to the Psalms (*nos. 69, 71, 73, 74*). Passion scenes are often used in Books of Hours for the sections of the Hours of the Virgin (*nos. 72, 82, 83, 85, 86, 87, 88, 89, 90, 91, 95, 96, 100, 102, 103*). They are sometimes combined with scenes from the early Life of Christ (*nos. 84, 94*). This arose from the interpolation of a short version of the Hours of the Cross with the Hours of the Virgin, involving a meditation on an event of the Passion.[15] Many Books of Hours have only the early Life of Christ for the sections of the Hours of the Virgin, sometimes ending with scenes of the Resurrection, Ascension and Coronation of the Virgin (*nos. 83, 85, 87, 89, 90, 91, 95, 96, 100, 102, 103*). The section of St John's Gospel narrating the Passion is included in some Books of Hours and illustrated with Passion scenes (*no. 96*) There are also vernacular narrative accounts of the Life and Passion of Christ with many pictures, as one in Anglo-Norman French (*no. 76*) and one in Dutch (*no. 93*).

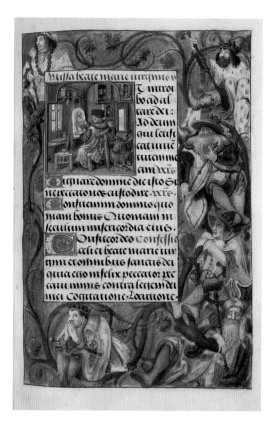

Fig. 27. St Luke painting the Virgin, Tree of Jesse, Votive Mass of the Virgin. Fitzwilliam Museum MS 1058–1975, fol. 36

The image of Christ as Man of Sorrows as a bust or standing figure is found in various contexts such as the Hours of the Cross (*nos. 103, 104*) or for Psalm 21 (Vulgate numeration), the Psalm of the Passion (*no. 94*).[16] The legend that St Gregory had a vision of Christ as Man of Sorrows standing on the altar during Mass, the Mass of St Gregory as it is called, is quite often illustrated in a variety of verbal contexts (*nos. 92, 95, 96 and fig. 25*). In some images of the Mass of St Gregory or the Man of Sorrows Christ is surrounded by the *Arma Christi*.[17] These are images of the objects or close-up action of the events of the Passion (e.g. whip of the Flagellation, Pilate's hands being washed, the hammer, the nails, the sponge, etc.) which acted as mnemonic devices for meditating on the Passion (*nos. 94, 105*).[18] Another special image of Christ is the Veronica Head, the image impressed on the handkerchief of St Veronica when she wiped the sweat from his face on the Way of the Cross.[19] This is usually associated with accompanying prayers to the Holy Face (*nos. 83, 95, 106*). Finally, some Books of Hours have prayers to the wound in the side and the other wounds of Christ, sometimes with small isolated images of the side, heart, hands and feet.[20]

Devotion to the Holy Trinity was very important. In Psalters this image accompanied Psalm 109 whose opening words, 'The Lord said unto my Lord', were interpreted in a trinitarian sense (*nos. 69, 77, 99*). In Books of Hours it was placed before the Hours of the Trinity or prayers to the Trinity (*nos. 81, 91, 95, 106*).

Eucharistic devotion, strengthened in the thirteenth and fourteenth centuries by ecumenical statements by the Catholic Church and by the acceptance of such feasts as Corpus Christi, is expressed in the images which accompany the prayers said at the Elevation of the Host or in front of the sacrament displayed in a monstrance. An exceptional example is the Miracle of the bleeding Host (*no. 83, fig. 26*), but more usual are people kneeling at Mass or before the Host in a monstrance (*no. 91*).

The Virgin Mary

The main text in a Book of Hours being the Hours of the Virgin, the illustrations in this section often show her with the Christ Child *(fig. 28)* or in scenes from the Life of Christ. She is also frequently represented in miniatures or historiated initials before the special prayers to her, *Obsecro te, O intemerata* and the Joys of the Virgin *(nos. 86, 88, 94, 100, 106)*. Various types of image show her with the Child, holding or suckling him at her breast. Images of her compassion also occur, above all the *Pietà* with the dead body of Christ across her lap. She is also represented in prefatory miniatures to Psalters.

The Virgin's apocryphal life beginning with her parents Joachim and Anne is occasionally found in a series of prefatory miniatures in Psalters, vernacular accounts of the Life of Christ *(no. 76)*, and also in various contexts in Books of Hours *(nos. 83, 88)*. It is also found in the picture-book 'Primer' of Claude of France *(no. 105)*.

The Saints

An important section of prayers in a Book of Hours is that at the end of Lauds of the Virgin in which prayers are said to the saints. In many late fourteenth- and fifteenth-century Books of Hours these are not placed in the Lauds but in a separate section either at the beginning or at the end of the book *(nos. 84, 87, 94)*. The number of *memoriae* or suffrages of the saints varies considerably, and the choice may often have depended on the book's commissioner. Exceptional numbers are found in some French Books of Hours *(nos. 85, 87)*. These prayers are illustrated by historiated initials or miniatures showing figures of the saints or in some cases events from their lives or their martyrdom *(fig. 29)*. The saints are also sometimes represented in prefatory miniatures to Psalters *(no. 78)*.

Fifteenth-century Books of Hours sometimes have a section of short readings from the four Gospels; each of them often received an Evangelist image *(nos. 88, 89, 95, 99)*.

Old Testament Subjects

In the Middle Ages the Psalms were all considered to have been written by King David, and thus pictures of him and his life are frequent in Psalters both as framed miniatures and within the historiated initials of the Psalms of the liturgical divisions *(fig. 30, nos. 73, 77, 79)*. He is often shown kneeling, harping, playing a psaltery or with his musicians at Psalms 1 and 80 *(nos. 70, 74, 77, 99)*. Other narrative images from the Old Testament sometimes occur as prefatory miniatures to Psalters *(e.g. nos. 69, 70, 72, 74)*. These picture stories of the patriarchs, heroes and heroines of the Bible served as moral exemplars of Virtue and Vice.[21] In Books of Hours, David before God is occasionally the illustration to the Penitential Psalms *(nos. 89, 90, 95, 100, 103, 104, 106)*, while Job on the Dungheap

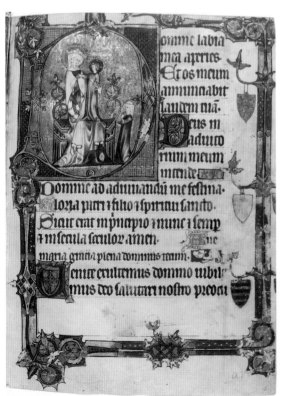

Fig. 28. Virgin and Child with Praying Woman, Hours, Matins of the Virgin, Cambridge University Library MS Dd.4.17, fol.19

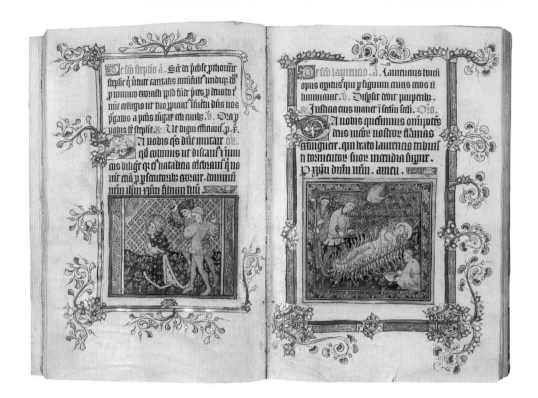

Fig. 29. Martyrdoms of Saints Stephen and Laurence, *Memoriae*, Trinity College MS B.11.7, fols. 24v–25

disputing with his friends often introduces the Office of the Dead *(nos. 84, 106)*. The choice of the latter image is based on the biblical readings for the nine lessons for Matins of the Dead, all taken from the Book of Job.

Prayers for the Dead and the Last Judgement

From *c.*1200 onwards many Psalters have the Office of the Dead added at the end of the book, and this text is also found in almost all Books of Hours. This consists of First Vespers, Matins and Lauds of the Dead. The Office originated as the prayers which started on the evening before the funeral and was followed by Matins and Lauds said before the funeral on the morning of the next day. Although originally composed for this function, the Office of the Dead came to be read on a regular basis as prayers for the dead that they should be released from their time in Purgatory. Another set of Psalms and prayers for the dead is found in some Books of Hours, the Commendation of the Soul. This originated as an Office said immediately following a death, but like the Office of the Dead came also to be used as a private devotional exercise of prayers for the benefit of the departed souls.

When it occurs in Psalters the Office of the Dead usually has only an historiated initial, but in many Books of Hours a full-page or part-page miniature precedes the text.[22] In both cases the subject is most commonly the Office of the Dead at the funeral or anniversary, showing the black-draped coffin surrounded by chanting figures *(nos. 84, 85, 88, 91, 93, 94, fig. 31)*. Occasionally the Requiem Mass or the Burial is depicted *(no. 90)*. Other subjects shown at the beginning of the text are the *memento mori* of the Three Living and the Three Dead, in which three fashionably dressed men or kings meet three skeletons *(nos. 95, 100, 104)*, or a man standing alone is threatened by a skeleton brandishing arrows *(no. 89)*.[23] The Commendation of the Soul often has a picture of angels taking souls in a white cloth up to Heaven or God holding the souls in a cloth *(nos. 84, 94)*.[24]

Inevitably prayers for the dead involved not only concern for the release of souls from Purgatory, but also thoughts of the final judgement at the Second Coming.

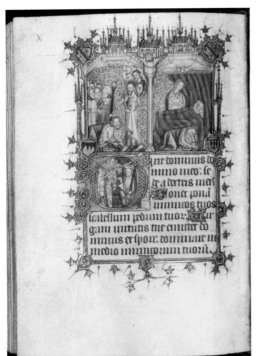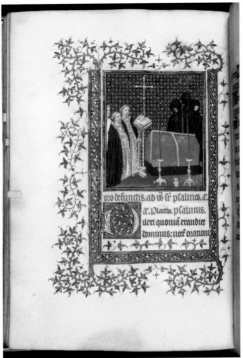

Fig. 30. David's penitence, Psalm. 109. Fitzwilliam Museum MS 38–1950, fol. 142v

Fig. 31. Funeral, Office of the Dead. Fitzwilliam Museum MS McClean 79, fol. 99v

In both Psalters and Books of Hours the image of the Last Judgement is often found, at the end of the sequence of prefatory miniatures in a Psalter *(nos. 69, 70, 74)*, or for the Penitential Psalms concerned with regret for sin in Books of Hours *(nos. 79, 83, 84, 91, 94)*.

REFERENCES

1   For Books of Hours and reading habits of the laity see Saenger 1985.
2   Lewis 1990 and Smith 2003 discuss the function of these images.
3   For the decoration of Psalters see Leroquais 1940–1941, Büttner 2005, and for the historiated initials of the liturgical divisions Haseloff 1938.
4   See Bishop 1918 for the origins of the Book of Hours and Wordsworth 1920 for the printed text of the Hours of York use.
5   For its introduction in England see Morgan 1999.
6   For the origins of the Office of the Dead see Ottosen 1993, 31–49.
7   Gougaud 1935.
8   See Leroquais 1927 – 1943 and Wieck 1988 for detailed discussions of the illustrations of Books of Hours. Good general accounts are Backhouse 1985, Harthan 1977, Wieck 1997, and Wieck 2001.
9   On the origins of many of these prayers see Wilmart 1932.
10 See Wieck 1988, 163–64 for translations of these prayers.
11 On the prayers to the Holy Face see Corbin 1947.
12 Wilmart 1935.
13 The commonly held belief that the Rosary originated at the time of St Dominic is a fiction.
14 Meersseman 1960.
15 Stadthuber 1950.
16 On the Man of Sorrows see Panofsky 1927 and Belting 1990.
17 On images of the Mass of St Gregory see Cologne 1982.
18 The origin and development of such images is discussed exhaustively by Robbins 1939, Berliner 1955, Suckale 1977, and Lewis 1996.
19 Lewis 1985.
20 Lewis 1996, Morgan 1993–1994, Morgan 2003.
21 On such narrative pictures in thirteenth-century England see Morgan 1992.
22 For images of the Office of the Dead see Wieck 1999b and Binski 1996.
23 On the Three Living and the Three Dead see Chihaia 1988, 43–126.
24 Sheingorn 1995.

67

Smaragdus, *Diadema monachorum*

In Latin
England, end of the eleventh or first quarter
of the twelfth century

Parchment, iii (modern parchment) + 75 (fols. 73–75 now only
stubs) fols., 307 × 197 mm, text 228 × 132 mm, 32 long lines,
ruled in hard point and crayon

SCRIPT: Caroline minuscule

BINDING: alum tawed skin over boards, 20th c.

Clare College, MS N1.2.2 (James no. 17)

THE *DIADEMA MONACHORUM* of the Carolingian monk Smaragdus of Saint-Mihiel was written as a commentary upon the Benedictine Rule and rapidly became a standard work of spiritual edification for both personal use and public reading at the evening gathering known as collation. This manuscript is one of the larger eleventh- or twelfth-century copies of English origin or provenance, and may have been intended for public reading since words that might have caused a reader to stress the wrong syllable have been supplied with accents.

Both the origin and provenance of the manuscript are unknown. It is written in a single idiosyncratic Anglo-Norman or perhaps Norman hand (apart from three short interventions in a second hand), which varies in size and appears on some pages too large in proportion to the space between the ruled lines. The textual divisions in the early part of the book are marked by deco-

Ornamental initial. Clare College, MS N1.2.2, fol. 2v, detail

rated initials which integrate the human, animal and foliate elements typical of Anglo-Norman illumination. Two of these initials, however (fols. 4 and 4v), are unusually small. The oddities of both script and decoration would appear to suggest that the book was made for local use within a community that lacked a well-established tradition of book production.

PROVENANCE: unknown.

LITERATURE: James 1905b, 35; Robinson 1997, 78; Gameson 1999, no. 48; Gneuss 2001, no. 31.

TW

68

Psalter

In Latin
England, probably Peterborough, *c.*1220–*c.*1225

Parchment, 236 fols., 310 × 198 mm, text 184 × 118 mm,
18 long lines, ruled in plummet

SCRIPT: Gothic bookhand (textualis)

BINDING: red leather over wooden boards, by S. Cockerell, 1979

Fitzwilliam Museum, MS 12

THE CALENDAR AND LITANY of this Psalter are of the Benedictine Abbey of Peterborough, and it may have been owned by its abbot. He is shown in the historiated initial of Psalm 101 in the company of a monk who is holding his crosier and genuflecting before the altar cross. The initial of that Psalm, which begins with the words 'O Lord hear my prayer', is quite often the place in Psalters where the owner or patron of the book is depicted. Following the Calendar and preceding the text of the Psalms is a full-page miniature of the Crucifixion (fol. 12). Some of the large illuminated initials of the Psalms of the liturgical divisions are ornamental (Psalms 26, 38, 51). Others have figural scenes: Christ (Psalms 1, 109), David and Goliath (Psalm 52), the possible abbot owner (Psalm 101) and fighting animals with a man fighting a lion (Psalm 80). Most other English Psalters of the period have a full set of historiated initials, and this may suggest that the manuscript was made at a monastic centre, away from the contemporary lay workshops of scribes and artists in Oxford and London. The other Psalms begin with much simpler initials in wash colours, with only rare touches of gold. This rather plain treatment of the page, with line endings only supplied for the first four pages (fols. 13–14v), contrasts with the much more luxurious appearance of the probable

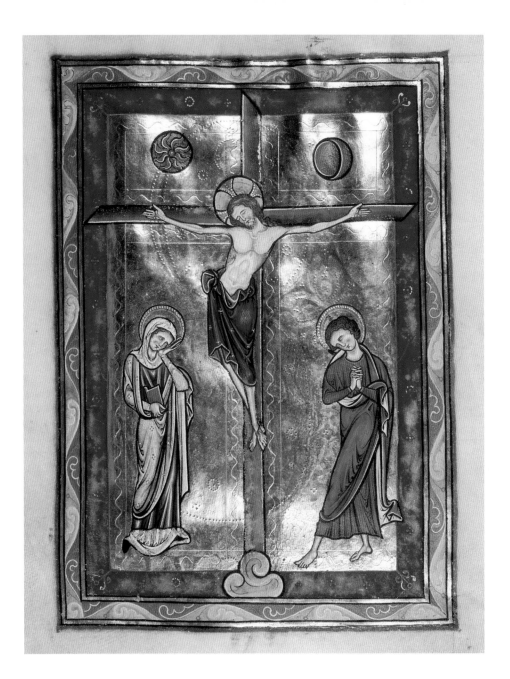

Crucifixion. Fitzwilliam
Museum, MS 12, fol. 12

London product, Trinity College MS B.11.4 *(no. 69)*
which has line endings in gold and colour as well as fully
illuminated opening initials and verse initials for each
Psalm. These differences may reflect monastic in-house
production, the patron's wish for a more austerely decorated book, or a distinctly Benedictine taste.

The Fitzwilliam volume is decorated by the same
artists as another Peterborough Psalter made for its
abbot, Robert de Lindesey (1214–1222), between 1220
and 1222 (London, Society of Antiquaries, MS 59). The
text pages of this second Psalter have a similarly plain
appearance, but it has five full-page miniatures and a full
series of historiated initials for the Psalms of the liturgical division. The Fitzwilliam Peterborough Psalter
may also have been made for Abbot Robert de Lindesey
or for his successor. It certainly must postdate 1220
because in the Calendar the feasts of the Translation of

Thomas of Canterbury (7 July) and Hugh of Lincoln
(17 Nov.), which were introduced in that year, are in
the hand of the original scribe.

The figure style of the artist is best seen in the full-
page Crucifixion miniature. The Christ on the cross is
a delicate figure with very thin arms and legs, his body
showing the features newly adopted by some artists in
the early thirteenth century, namely the curved pose of
the body and the single nail attaching the feet. Almost
all earlier crucifixes have two nails for the feet. The
Virgin and St John stand by, their gestures expressing
grief. John's tense pose is conveyed by the thrusting
forward of his front leg. The Crucifixion page of the
Society of Antiquaries manuscript shows similar characteristics but with iconographic differences such as
foliage sprouting from the cross and the presence of personifications of the Church and Synagogue, paralleled

by St Peter and Moses, in the surrounding frame. The Fitzwilliam Crucifixion with its plain frame and more dramatic poses of the three figures portrays a more emotional and meditative image. This may be the artist varying his iconography, if both are by the same man, or it may suggest a later development from the Society of Antiquaries Psalter. If so, it may be after 1222, and made for Robert de Lindesey's successor as abbot.

PROVENANCE: made for an abbot of the Benedictine Abbey of Peterborough c.1220–1225; acquired by Viscount Fitzwilliam in 1808; his bequest, 1816.

EXHIBITED: Cambridge 1966, no. 27.

LITERATURE: James 1895a, 22–23, pl. II; Frere 1894–1932, II, no. 1000; Haseloff 1938, 14, 100–101; Thoby 1959, 133, pl. XC; Cames 1966, 198, fig. 16; Sandler 1974, 136 n. 8, 140, 154–61; Morgan 1982–1988, no. 45, ills. 147–49; Morgan 2005, 211, 216, fig. 292.

NJM

69

Psalter

In Latin
England, probably London, c.1230

Parchment, ii + xi + 170 + i fols. (the manuscript originally was foliated ii + 181 + i, but was confusingly refoliated c.1985), 285 × 200 mm, text 203 × 118 mm, 18–19 long lines, ruled in plummet

SCRIPT: Gothic bookhand (textualis)

BINDING: gold-tooled calf over pasteboards, 17th c.; brown leather spine, 20th c.

Trinity College, MS B.11.4

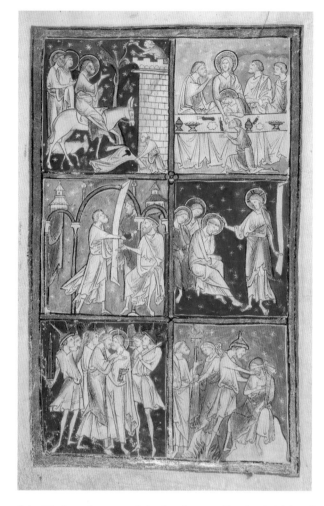

THE PSALTER is preceded by a Calendar and ten full-page miniatures with forty-eight narrative scenes of the Old Testament stories of Abraham, Jacob and Joseph, and New Testament scenes of the Life of Christ. The pictures end with the Last Judgement and the Torments of Hell. Unfortunately several other miniatures have been lost and the rebinding of those surviving has resulted in some of them being out of narrative order. The Psalms received sumptuously illuminated initials and line endings. The illuminator attempted to design a system of elaborate decoration for the whole page in which initials and line endings harmonize with the lines of script. There are large historiated initials at the liturgical divisions of the Psalms. This rich decoration continues up to fol. 122 (the painted line endings only to

fol. 68), but the rest of the book, save for the initials of the main Psalms, has simpler decoration by a less experienced artist. Such a programme of illustration and ornament places this manuscript at the highest level in the hierarchy of Psalter decoration. The placing of Old and New Testament narrative pictures before the Psalms had begun in the twelfth century and is found in the most luxurious Psalters of England, France and Germany in the thirteenth century, becoming less popular in the fourteenth century. It is difficult to understand the function of these pictures, which lack accompanying text and for the most part have no connection with the text of the Psalms. In Psalters for lay people they doubtless served to teach some of the basic stories of the Bible, but this Psalter was evidently made for an abbess of Augustinian canonesses who would have been well acquainted with them. She is represented in Psalms 101 and 109.

The Augustinian provenance is supported by the Calendar which has the characteristic feasts specially observed by that religious Order, e.g. the Octave of St Augustine (4 Oct). Some of the saints in the Calendar are characteristic of the Diocese of London, whereas a few are of the Winchester region. This might suggest

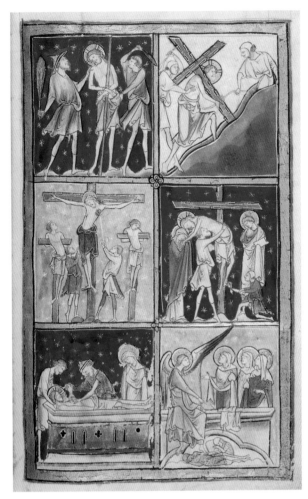

LEFT AND ABOVE: Scenes from the Life of Christ. Trinity College, MS B.11.4, fols. viii verso– ix (former fols. 8v–9)

the book was made in London but its London Calendar was adapted for a patron in the Winchester region.

The full-page miniatures have frames and details, such as haloes, executed in gold, but the figures are painted with flat colour washes set against coloured grounds ornamented with white patterns. The figures are tall and thin with somewhat angular stiff poses. Their emphatic gestures convey narrative meaning. This style is a more elegant version of that in the Chertsey Abbey Psalter (Cambridge, Emmanuel College, MS 252) and compares with stained glass of the miracles of St Thomas at Canterbury Cathedral. The historiated initials are painted by a second artist in a different manner, setting more carefully painted figures against gold grounds. His style is so close to that in the Glazier Psalter (New York, Pierpont Morgan Library, G. 25) that the same artist may have been responsible for both manuscripts.

PROVENANCE: Dame Ida de Ralegh, wife of Sir John de Ralegh of Beaudeport, Devon, who was mentioned as still living in 1346 (inscription on fol. 25v); she gave it to the Cistercian Walter

Hone, Abbot of Newnham, Devon, c.1338, during his lifetime and stipulated that it should pass to Dame Johane de Roches, nun of the Benedictine Abbey of St Mary, Winchester (Nunnaminster); in the library of Trinity College by 1614 when the catalogue recorded a *Psalterium cum picturis*.

EXHIBITED: Brussels 1973, no. 45; London 1987–1988, no. 255.

LITERATURE: James 1900–1904, I, 331–37; Haseloff 1938, 61, 118–19; Brieger 1968, 61, 92–94, pls. 23b, 25; Morgan 1982–1988, no. 51, ills. 167–74 (before refoliation); Henderson 1983, 408–409; Morgan 1992, 159–60, 168–70, 174–9, figs. 11–13; Kauffmann 2003, 151, 158, 167; Morgan 2005, 207, 210, 216, fig. 284.

NJM

70

The Fall of the Rebel Angels; Adam, Eve, Cain and Abel; the Last Judgement; the Wheel of Fortune; Christ and David; the Tree of Jesse

Six leaves from a Psalter
In Latin
England, probably Oxford, c.1240
ARTIST: William de Brailes (doc. 1238–1252)

Parchment, 250 × 170 mm, probably 18 lines of text

SCRIPT: Gothic bookhand (textualis) on reverse

Fitzwilliam Museum, MS 330

THE ART OF WILLIAM DE BRAILES, the thirteenth-century Oxford illuminator, is at once sombre and concentrated. His pictures are precise, carefully labelled, and a profound knowledge of Bible iconography is implicit in the modest-seeming compositions. His work, superficially in line with the decorative taste of the period favouring full-colour tempera painting on solid gold grounds, is relatively undemonstrative, the colours being dominated by dullish blues and oranges. Illuminated Bibles produced in France and England in this period tended to shrink, producing miracles of compression. De Brailes's art is manifestly part of the same trend. His Psalter and Bible pictures have a significant moralizing or homiletic tone (see no. 30). These leaves are the best demonstration of this mixture of narrative and pastoral intent in his art, and reward patient looking.

The leaves must come from a Psalter, to judge from the explicit content of leaves 5 and 6 showing Christ, David and Jesse, with the opening of Psalm 1 on leaf 6. How exactly they were arranged in this originally small-ish book is unclear; since the eleventh-century English

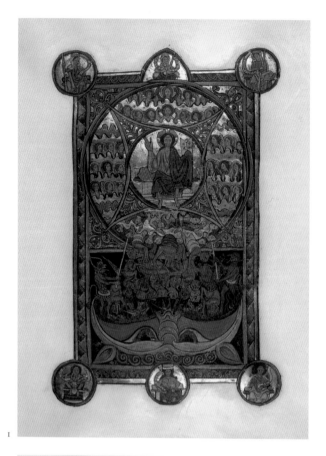

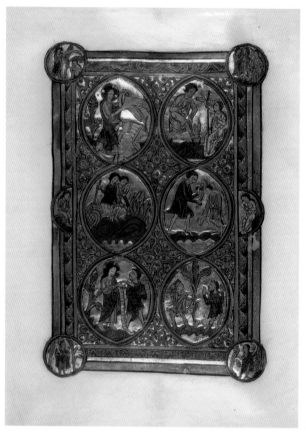

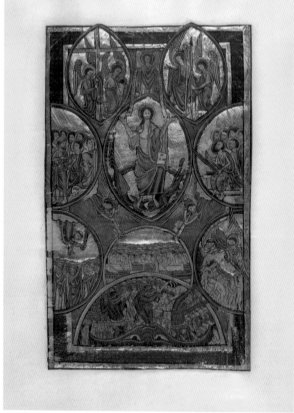

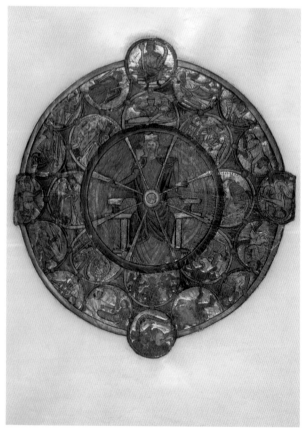

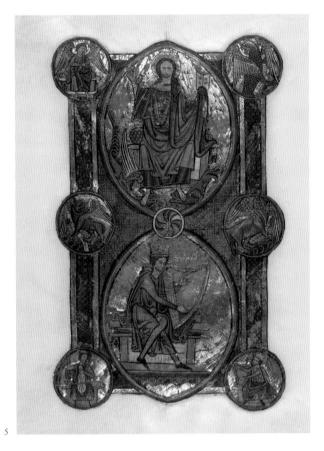

5

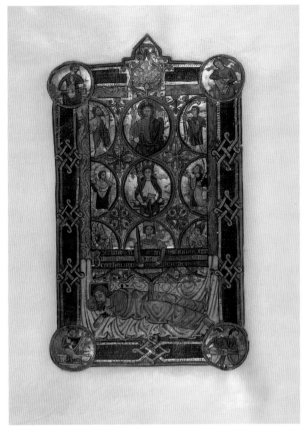

6

1. Fall of the Rebel Angels. 2. Adam and Eve, Cain and Abel.
3. Last Judgement. 4. Wheel of Fortune. 5. Christ and David.
6. Tree of Jesse. Fitzwilliam Museum, MS 330

Psalters had frequently been decorated with prefatory pictures drawn from the Bible, usually relating the story of the Fall and Redemption of Man.

Leaf 1 shows the Fall of the Rebel Angels, a popular topic in English Bible iconography, and is likely to have fallen very near the start of the prefatory pictures. Christ as alpha and omega presides over the fall of Lucifer into a spectacular Hell Mouth. Immediately de Brailes offers a commentary on Lucifer's pride preceding his fall by means of three personifications of the Virtues Charity, Humility and Patience along the top, and three Vices Avarice, Pride and Anger along the bottom. *Superbia*, Pride, is labelled as the *radix vitiorum*, Humility being its remedy *(compare no. 116)*.

Leaf 2 is taken from Genesis: God clothes Adam and Eve, they delve and spin; Cain and Abel make sacrifice and Cain murders Abel; God rebukes Cain, and Cain is shot by Lamech. Again, these are common enough themes in English Bible iconography, but, as with leaf 1, de Brailes volunteers a commentary. In medallions at the top, God rebukes Adam who in turn blames Eve; then God deals with Eve. The texts in the scrolls are based

upon Genesis 3. The Fall admits labour, pain and death into the world, 'for dust though art, and unto dust shalt thou return'. Below, Adam and Eve appear dejected to either side of the story of Cain and Abel. This idea is plainly a development of the rebuke and curse of God, Adam and Eve mourning both themselves and the fate of their children. The moral implications of the Fall have hit home. Enoch and Seth appear at the bottom.

Leaf 3 shows the Last Judgement, though it plainly did not follow the story of Adam and Eve. The material here is drawn from St Matthew's Gospel, 25. At the top are the instruments of the Passion, the text on the Cross concerning Christ's five wounds. Christ seated on a rainbow presides as Judge. To either side are the Apostles, with St Peter and Mary *mediatrix* to Christ's right, St Paul and the Apostles to the left. St Peter swoops down to rescue the saved while to the right St Michael grasps and lifts a tonsured man amongst the damned. This man is William de Brailes, labelled by the small scroll *W. de Brailes me fecit* (W. de Brailes made me) (fig. on p.413). William is saved in part by his art. The doctrines of intercession and good works (*Opus Dei*) are thus reinforced.

Leaf 4 shows a Wheel of Fortune. This picture is especially characteristic of de Brailes's cunning. Fortune herself turns the Wheel clockwise. It consists of two circuits of pictures also running clockwise. The outer one of

175

sixteen medallions reveals the Ages of Man. It starts at the lower left with a woman holding a banderole *Incipit rota fortunae* over a swaddled infant: we are prey to Fortune from birth. Man is enthroned in his prime at the top, and from the summit plunges towards death at the bottom in the form of a half-naked man from whose mouth issues a scroll. The inner circuit has eight medallions, starting top right with the inscription *Incipit ystoria Theophili*: this is the tale of the redemption by the Virgin Mary of the clerk Theophilus. Theophilus, like the dying man, is first shown half naked, as a model of *paupertas* and *desperatio*. He sells his soul to the Devil in the form of a sealed charter. He then appears in Hell, coincident with the dying man in the outer circuit: he has experienced spiritual death in return for the World. In misery he turns to the Virgin Mary for intercession; she wins it and his soul back, and he dies a good death, coincident with the prime of life above: he has regained spiritual life by renouncing the World. William de Brailes has created a clever homily on pride, ambition, intercession and penance. This image probably fell near the Last Judgement picture originally. The homiletic use of images of death at so early a stage in the history of pastoral illustration is remarkable, but implicit in the contents of Leaf 2.

Leaves 5 and 6 are Psalter material: in Leaf 5 Christ appears mightily in Majesty with harping David, accompanied by the Evangelists and musicians; in Leaf 6 the Tree of Jesse springs up via David, who embraces and guards the opening text of Psalm 1, Mary, Christ and the Seven Gifts of the Holy Spirit. This leaf was thus the last in the sequence before the Psalms.

Another leaf showing the Infancy of Christ has been noted as coming from the same manuscript (New York, Pierpont Morgan Library, M.913; Morgan 1982–1986, no. 72b).

PROVENANCE: Jean-Baptiste-Joseph Barrois (1784–1855); acquired by Bertram, 4th Earl of Ashburnham in 1849; his sale, Sotheby's, London, 10–14 June 1901, lot 404; purchased by Quaritch; George C. Thomas of Philadelphia; Dr A.S.W. Rosenbach; purchased from him by Sir Alfred Chester Beatty in 1920; included in his sale catalogue, Sotheby's, London, 7 June 1932, lot 11; withdrawn before the sale at Sydney Cockerell's initiative and given to the Museum by the National Art Collections Fund in 1932.

EXHIBITED: London 1923, no. 104; London 1930, nos. 145–150; London 1934, no. 7; London 1939, no. 135; Cambridge 1966, no. 29; London 1987–1988, no. 436.

LITERATURE: Millar 1926, no. 142; Millar 1927, I, no. 38, pls. LXXXI–XCI; Cockerell 1930, 3, 15–18, pls. XV–XVII; Rickert 1954, 114–15, pls. 98, 99a; Pollard 1955; Wormald and Giles 1982, I, 319–20; Morgan 1982–1988, no. 72a; Henderson 1991; Kauffmann 2003, 152, 185, Noel 2004, passim.

PB

71

Psalter

In Latin
Silesia, Breslau, *c.*1260

Parchment, i (parchment, 19th c.) + 147 + i (paper) + i (parchment, 19th c.) fols., 326 × 227 mm, text 203 × 132 mm, 23 long lines, ruled in brown ink

SCRIPT: Gothic bookhand (textualis)

BINDING: yellow morocco over wooden boards, 19th c.

Fitzwilliam Museum, MS 36–1950

THIS SUMPTUOUS BOOK combines every format of illustration and every pictorial approach to the text of the Psalms that could have been conceived by a thirteenth-century artist or patron. Surrounded by elaborate architectural designs and fantastical marginalia, the Calendar shows the Zodiac Signs, the Occupations of the Months, scenes dedicated to clauses of the Apostles' Creed, and a gallery of saints' portraits. Each Psalm has a marginal miniature illustrating its text in a literal sense, an ornamental initial, and a stunning array of marginal grotesques. The twenty-eight full-page miniatures distributed at the major text divisions narrate the lives of Christ and the Virgin, and support the liturgical and devotional use of the Psalms. The large historiated initials to the Psalms of the ten-fold division use either literal or christological illustration of the text. Perhaps the most complex and evocative of them is the *Beatus* initial to Psalm 1 shown here. It is the crowning achievement of the master who otherwise shared the work-load with three assistants.

The two compartments of the *Beatus* initial represent the Old and New Testaments. They are harmonized by the prophetic psalmody of King David on the left. Solomon on the right refers to God's Wisdom visualized at the top, while Isaiah predicts the Incarnation of the Word seen below. Interceding for humankind (and for the manuscript's owner), the Virgin and St John the Baptist introduce the theme of the Last Judgement through the Byzantine image of the Deësis. Uniting the two tiers of the image into a vertical Trinity, the dove is shown within an intersection, thus alluding to the double procession of the Holy Spirit. The composition is transformed into Christ's Baptism by the alignment of St John's figure with the Father's scroll: 'This is my beloved Son…' (Matthew 3:17). It takes a long string of words to describe the multi-layered meaning instantly conveyed by the image. It is a pictorial summary of Psalm 1, which according to medieval authorities summed up the entire Psalter.

Beatus initial.
Fitzwilliam
Museum,
MS 36–1950,
fol. 23v

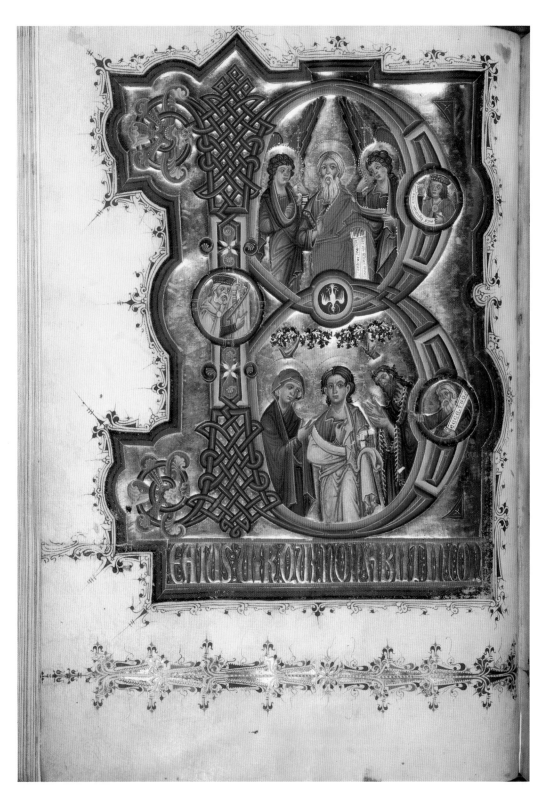

St Vincent, patron of the Premonstratensian monastery in Breslau, is prominent in the Calendar and the Litany, which includes St Clare (canonized in 1255), but not St Hedwig (canonized in 1267). A prayer on fol. 146 contains female forms and names God's 'servant Henry'. The

manuscript was made for a lady at the ducal court of Breslau between 1255 and 1267. It is one of the finest in a group of manuscripts centred round an Epistolary written in 1259 by the Paduan scribe Giovanni da Gaibana (Padua, Cathedral Sacristy). While emulating the style of the Epistolary, some of the most important manuscripts in this group were produced north of the Alps. The migration of the 'Gaibanesque' style from the Veneto to centres like Salzburg and Breslau has been linked to the patronage of the Dukes of Breslau and the Bohemian ruling dynasty of the Premyslids. A key figure in this migration was the brother of Henry III, Duke of Breslau (1241–1266), Vladislav, who was a student in Padua before being elevated to the archbishopric of Salzburg in 1265. The German saints present in the Psalter's Calendar and Litany have been interpreted as an indication that the manuscript was made for the daughter of Albert of Saxony, Helen, who married Duke Henry III after 1257. However, the presence of German saints may reflect the increasing German colonization of Silesia, particularly pronounced under Breslau's most notable bishop, Thomas I (1232–1268). Few patron saints of Saxony received the special treatment reserved in the Calendar and Litany for Saints Wenceslas, Vitus, and Adalbert of Prague.

An association of the prayer with another Duchess of Breslau, Anna Premyslid (1195–1265), sister of Wenceslas of Bohemia, seems more likely. Wife of Henry II of Breslau, and mother of Henry III and Archbishop Vladislav, Anna founded the convent of Poor Clares in Breslau. The graded feast of St Agnes, the only saint to be honoured with an Octave in the manuscript, may suggest particular devotion to the patron saint of Anna's sister, the devout Agnes of Bohemia, who founded the Franciscan convent in Prague. St Francis looms large in the Fitzwilliam volume. Another peculiarity is the importance of St Augustine, singled out in the Calendar and preceding even St Francis in the Litany. This may reflect the respect the Premonstratensians of St Vincent would have had for St Augustine's Rule or it may suggest a link with the Augustinian house in Breslau.

This sumptuous manuscript was hardly intended as a private devotional book. Its size and earlier covers, allegedly made of solid gold, but melted down at the Mint in Munich, are synonymous with a coffee-table book. Important visitors would have marvelled at the owner's wealth, status, and piety.

PROVENANCE: Duchess of Breslau; Bertram, 4th Earl of Ashburnham (Ashburnham 1853–1861, no. XXXIV in the Appendix); purchased from him by Henry Yates Thompson in May 1897; his sale, Sotheby's, London, 23 March 1920, lot 60; purchased by T.H. Riches who bequeathed it to the Museum in 1935.

EXHIBITED: London 1908, no. 174; Cambridge 1966, no. 42.

LITERATURE: James et al. 1902, 330–53; Thompson 1907–1918, V, pls. LVII–LXVI and VII, pl. X; Hänsel-Hacker 1952; Hänsel-Hacker 1954; Wormald and Giles 1982, 414–29, pls. 18–20; Soukoupová 1984; Corrie 1987; Robinson 1988, no. 208, pl. 113; Všetečkova 1995; Panayotova 2006.   SP

72

The Psalter and Hours of Isabelle of France

Use of Paris
In Latin
France, Paris, c.1255

Parchment, iv (20th century) + xiii + 296 + iv (20th century) fols., 190 × 140 mm, text 125 × 95 mm, 18 lines, ruled in plummet

SCRIPT: Gothic bookhand (*textualis*)

BINDING: Red seal skin over boards, c.1904, by Douglas Cockerell

Fitzwilliam Museum, MS 300

THIS BOOK is among the finest achievements of the artists, scribes and patrons who transformed thirteenth-century Paris into the leading European centre of manuscript production. The Calendar, highlighting feasts specific to the Sainte Chapelle and the obits of Philip Augustus, Louis VIII, Blanche of Castile, and their son, Robert of Artois, as well as the arms of France and Castile displayed in numerous line fillers, reveal that the manuscript's owner was a member of the French royal family. This and the female forms of prayers (fols. 240v, 241) allowed Sydney Cockerell to associate the book with the devout Isabelle of France (1225–1270), daughter of Louis VIII and Blanche of Castile, and sister of St Louis (r.1226–1270). She remains the likeliest owner, despite attempts to link the manuscript with St Louis' queen, Marguerite of Provence, or with their daughter, Isabelle. Mother and daughter would have demanded stronger allusions to Provence than are allowed for in this manuscript. Blanche of Castile's obit (27 Nov. 1252) and the feast of Peter Martyr, canonized in 1253, provide the *terminus post quem*. While the choice of a Sainte Chapelle Calendar may suggest a date before 1255 when Isabelle of France founded the Clarissan convent of the Humility of the Blessed Virgin Mary (later known as Longchamp), a date in the late 1250s is also acceptable. As the late Harvey Stahl pointed out (in correspondence), until her retirement to the convent in 1260, Isabelle may have been satisfied with a Parisian Calendar, Hours of the Virgin and an Office of the Dead following the Use of Paris.

The manuscript was conceived as a sister book to St Louis's own Psalter (Paris, Bibliothèque nationale de France, MS lat. 10525), whose Calendar reveals equally strong links with Sainte Chapelle and the royal family, and whose heraldic line fillers suggest a date after 1258

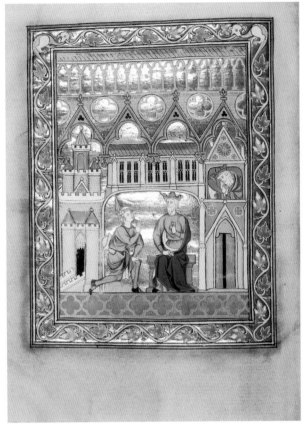 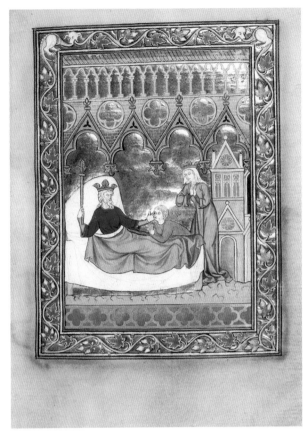

David grieves over Absalom's death. David recognizes Solomon as his successor. Fitzwilliam Museum, MS 300, fols. IIIv–IV

when St Louis' daughter Isabelle married Thibaut of Champagne, King of Navarre. The two manuscripts have often been studied together, as if one was copied from the other, but their precise relationship and order of execution remain elusive. While their almost identical size, layout, iconography, style, palette, and ornamental vocabulary demonstrate that they were planned simultaneously, substantial differences in their textual and visual content suggest strong personalization from the outset. The Parisian Calendar of the St Louis Psalter, penned in red and black, received additional feasts in Isabelle's manuscript and was written in blue and gold. The seventy-eight prefatory miniatures in the King's Psalter constitute half of the volume and amount to an Old Testament picture book, followed by the Psalms. The six miniatures in Isabelle's manuscript focus on David and Solomon, and introduce the ultimate devotional book, the Psalter-Hours. In addition to the eight historiated initials marking the main Psalm divisions in both manuscripts, Isabelle's prayer book received thirty-eight historiated initials for the Hours, suffrages, feasts of the Virgin, the Penitential Psalms, and the Office of the Dead (the last two now lost). The division of labour outlined by Sydney Cockerell requires only minor alter-

ations. The master of the six miniatures adheres to the frames and architectural backdrops used in the prefatory cycle of the St Louis Psalter, but replaces its dense and architecturally complex scenes with monumentally conceived narrative compositions in settings of calm, receding depth. At least four illuminators worked on the historiated initials. The artist responsible for the majority of illustrations in the Hours (fols. 177v–212v) was one of the two most influential masters in the St Louis Psalter (fols. 25v–28). But the most delicate modelling of textiles and facial expressions appears in the work of the last artist in Isabelle's Psalter-Hours (fols. 215–284v). Six illuminators collaborated on the ornamental initials and line endings in Isabelle's book. One of them was involved in the St Louis Psalter too. The artists often take over from each other within the same quire, even on the same page. This all-hands-on-deck approach implies a hurried campaign. The unfinished decoration and textual errors confirm it. They also reveal that the two manuscripts were copied side by side, but not from each other. Both volumes make mistakes – some are corrected in one manuscript, but in the other they are either ignored or have already been eliminated. The manuscripts do not share scribes except on a few replacement leaves correcting an error in the exemplar and penned by the same hand in both volumes (MS 300, fols. 71, 75, 76, 80; MS lat. 10525, fol. 157). It seems that work on the manuscripts progressed simultaneously, a likely solution since they were conceived as sister books. This may explain the large teams involved in each project and the insignificant overlap between them, a pragmatic approach to two equally ambitious and parallel, but strongly personalized campaigns. It is tempting to imagine brother and sister planning the set together to celebrate the devotional fervour and intimate bond they shared throughout their lives.

PROVENANCE: Isabelle of France (1225– 1270); Charles V, before 1380; John Boykett Jarman, by 1846; purchased from him by John Ruskin, 24 Feb. 1854; sold by Ruskin's heir, Joan Severn, to Henry Yates Thompson in 1904; purchased from him for the Fitzwilliam Museum by Sydney Cockerell, with subscriptions from Cambridge University members, 1919.

EXHIBITED: London 1908, no. 135; Cambridge 1966, no. 45; Paris 1968, 126.

LITERATURE: Cockerell 1905; Delisle 1907, I, 176; Dearden 1966, 134–135, no. 16; Backhouse 1967–1968, 89; Branner 1977, 132–137, 176–177, 238–239, no. 211, fig. 402; Wormald and Giles 1982, 280–284; Thomas 1985, 17–18; Robinson 1988, no. 202. pl. 111; Benett 2003, 56, 58, 63, 66–67, figs. 1, 5, 7; Panayotova 2005b; Panayotova 2006; entry by Harvey Stahl in Stones forthcoming.

SP

73

Psalter

In Latin
Northern France or Flanders, *c.*1290–*c.*1300

Parchment, 322 fols., 109 × 78 mm, text, 68 × 43 mm, 16 long lines, ruled in black ink

SCRIPT: Gothic bookhand (textualis)

BINDING: parts of blind-tooled fifteenth-century covers incorporated into a nineteenth-century brown leather binding

Cambridge University Library, MS Add. 4090

THE VERY SMALL SIZE of this Psalter is common for personal devotional books in the last three centuries of the Middle Ages. Its original destination can only be approximately defined from textual evidence because unfortunately in the fifteenth century, when it passed to the Benedictines of St Michael's Hildesheim, the texts of the Calendar, Litany and Office of the Dead were adapted to their use. A few of the original texts escaped

erasure. Aldegundis (30 Jan.), Gertrude of Nivelles (17 March), Marcellus (4 Sept.), Bavo (1 Oct.), Amandus (26 Oct.), and Winnoc (6 Nov.) are in the Calendar, Gertrude of Nivelles is also in the Litany. Fragmentary as these survivals are, they point to the dioceses of Tournai and Thérouanne, the border region between Northern France and Flanders. The rarest of these saints is Winnoc, whose relics were at Bergues near Dunkerque.

The Calendar (fols. 2–7v) is illuminated with scenes of the Labours of the Months characteristically set under large canopies with gables and pinnacles half the height of the page, and with frames ending in human or animal heads. Before some of the Psalms there are full-page miniatures set on gold grounds and under cusped arches in rectangular frames, having wide red borders with gold leaves, diamond shapes in their corners and surmounted by pinnacles: Christ before Pilate (fol. 61v), the Flagellation (fol. 81v), the Way of the Cross (fol. 101v). That on fol. 8 before Psalm 1 is, however, a nineteenth-century addition: it shows the kings of England and Scotland shaking hands. The Psalms of the liturgical divisions have historiated initials with border bar extensions which support grotesques involving humans, animals and birds: David harping and David beheading Goliath (Psalm 1, fol. 8v); David pointing to his eyes kneels before Christ (Psalm 26, fol. 40v); David pointing to his mouth kneels before Christ (Psalm 38, fol. 62); standing fool with a club holding a disc (Psalm 52, fol. 82); Christ above David in the water (Psalm 68, 102); David seated playing bells (Psalm 80, fol. 125); clerics singing at a lectern with an acolyte holding a candle (Psalm 97, fol. 147); God the Father seated with the Son (Psalm 109, fol. 171). The grotesques are of a humorous, even satirical nature, such as battling hybrids, a monkey in a cope reading a book ((fol. 8v), and a monkey musician (fol. 147).

The figure style and iconography of the full-page miniatures, as well as their frames with cusped arches surmounted by pinnacles, can be compared with two other Psalters from French Flanders of *c.*1300: Copenhagen, Kongelige Bibliotek, MS Ny.kgl.S.41.8° and Oxford, Bodleian Library, MS Laud lat. 84 (Carlvant 1982, 149; Bräm 1997, 81, 179, 224). The foliage borders in the Copenhagen manuscript are particularly close and the Way of the Cross is almost identical. The iconography of the Psalm initials is, however, different. These three manuscripts derive their ornamental frame types from the Psalter of Guy de Dampierre, Count of Flanders (1280–1305), which dates from *c.*1280–*c.*1285 (Brussels, Bibliothèque royale de Belgique, MS 10607; Stones 1996), although their quality is inferior and their date later, around or shortly after 1300. The Dampierre Psalter also has many marginal grotesques. The place of production and dating of the Psalter of Guy de Dam-

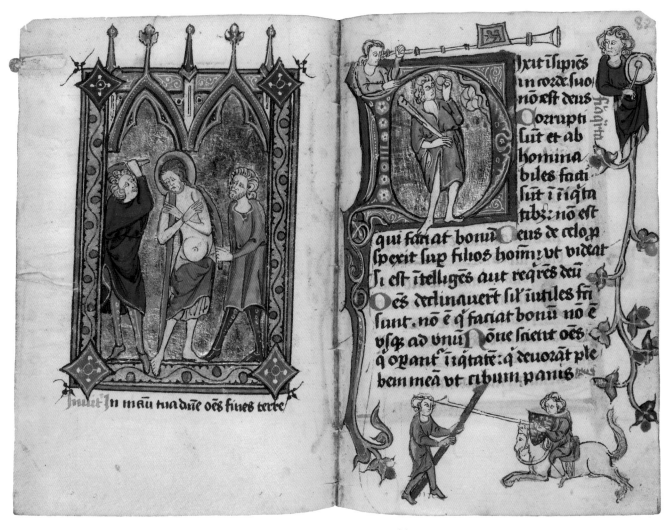

Flagellation and the Fool, Psalm 52.Cambridge University Library, MS Add. 4090, fols. 81v–82

pierre are controversial, with St Omer, Thérouanne and Bruges having been proposed, and some consider it was made before 1275. These places fall in the Dioceses of Thérouanne and Tournai to which the Calendar of the Cambridge Psalter points as well.

PROVENANCE: Benedictine Abbey of St Michael, Hildesheim, 15th c. (liturgical adaptation in Calendar, Litany, Office of the Dead, and an added Office of the Virgin); acquired by Samuel Sandars (1837–1894) in 1882; his bequest, 1894.

LITERATURE: Frere 1894–1932, II, no. 791; Krämer 1989, 353.

NJM

74

Psalter with Bible Pictures

In Latin
England, *c.*1270– *c.*1280

Parchment, 209 fols., 280 × 180 mm, text 185 × 115 mm, 21 lines, ruled in ink

SCRIPT: Gothic bookhand (textualis)

BINDING: blind tooled alum tawed goatskin over mill boards, D. Cockerell 1946

St John's College, MS K. 26 (James no. 231)

T HIS MANUSCRIPT is a composite, consisting of 25 folios of full-page Bible pictures added before a later fourteenth-century Psalter starting at fol. 26. The pictures were conceived on a bold scale and on leaves rather larger than the format of the Psalter, as indications of cropping (e.g. fol. 23v) show. These pictures may well have been planned for a Psalter such as this, since they are in the tradition of Bible pictures prefatory to the Psalms established in English manuscripts before the Conquest, and common in the twelfth and thirteenth centuries *(see no. 69)*. The aim of such images was to place the Psalms, as the principal liturgical and devotional texts of the Church, in their logical poetic and spiritual relation to the narrative of the Fall and Redemption of Man. This Psalter was owned by the Holland family and was evidently made around 1400, and can cast no obvious light on the origin of this very interesting series of pictures.

The images open with the Book of Genesis and God's creation of the birds and the animals, and continue up to the story of Abraham, before jumping to the Judgement of Solomon; they include a particularly massive and vivid image of King David with his harp and a cheerful little dog, as Psalmist (f. 25v), which certainly points to a Psalter context. The Sacrifice of Cain and Abel, and the murder of Abel, shown here, are common topics in such Psalter cycles *(see no. 70)*. To the left the brothers kneel before the holocaust, Abel with the lamb and Cain with the sheaf, with an angel above. Opposite, Cain clubs to death with a jawbone the strangely graceful, prostrate figure of Abel, grimacing in pain; an ape shoots at an owl in the engagingly-drawn trees beyond. Cain's head is shown both times in ugly profile, Abel's in comely three-quarters' aspect.

The Gospel pictures proceed from the Annunciation through the Nativity and Infancy of Christ, his Passion, the Last Judgement and the Death of the Virgin, ending with her Coronation. The small captions beneath the images are all in Latin and include a series of couplets in Latin beneath the Judgement of Solomon, which probably points to an early clerical or monastic readership or ownership. The lack of certain provenance is regrettable in so far as the pictures belong to a somewhat mysterious phase in the history of English illumination and painting beginning in the 1260s, which saw the production of the major late series of Apocalypse manuscripts (London, Lambeth Palace Library, MS 209; London, British Library, Add. MS 42555; Lisbon, Museu Calouste Gulbenkian, MS LA.139; Oxford, Bodleian Library, MS Douce 180; Morgan 1982–1988, nos. 126–128, 153), the Oscott Psalter (London, British Library, Add. MSS 50000, 54215; Morgan 1982–1988, no. 151), and the Westminster Retable in Westminster Abbey. Much controversy still surrounds the relative dates of these aesthetically outstanding and frequently mannered, learned and highly imaginative works of art. The St John's pictures were probably produced in the knowledge of the Westminster Retable and works in its circle, and yet it is itself markedly more strident in taste.

PROVENANCE: the Holland family, 14th century; given to the College by Charles Baker in 1672.

EXHIBITED: London 1908, no. 48; London 1923, no. 108; London 1930, no. 183; Brussels 1973, no. 56.

LITERATURE: James 1913, 264–70; Morgan 1982–1988, no. 179, ills. 381–88, fig. 4; Robinson 1988, no. 312, pl. 182; Kauffmann 2003, 174, 225, fig. 125.

PB

Cain murdering Abel.
St John's College, MS K.26, fol. 6

75

Picture-book of Saints

In Latin
England, *c.* 1290–*c.* 1300

Parchment, 9 fols., 184 × 135 mm
SCRIPT: Lombardic capitals in red and blue
BINDING: blind-tooled calf over boards, 1818; repaired by
S. Cockerell, 1981

Fitzwilliam Museum, MS 370

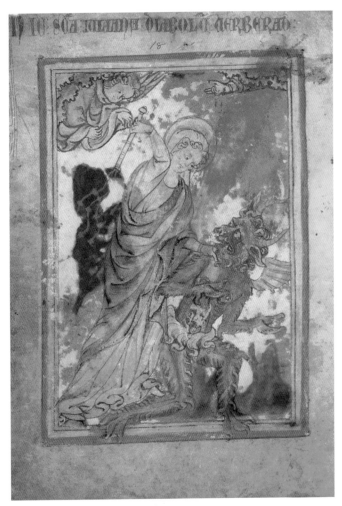

St Juliana and the Devil. Fitzwilliam Museum,
MS 370, fol. 10v

THE USE IN MANUSCRIPTS of single images of saints represented in their traditional guise developed significantly in the thirteenth century. The doctrine of intercession of the saints was widely established. The Lives of the Saints also provided models for imitation, their image offering a form of pastoral guidance for those in religious Orders, clergy and laity. Concision and instant recognizability were important in fulfilling these objectives; the period also witnessed the dissemination of vernacular epitomes of longer Saints' Lives, such as the South English Legendary. Manuscripts including sets of such images of individual saints were becoming increasingly common from around 1250. The tendency at first was to attach such images to some pre-existing book form, such as the Psalter, the principal devotional text (e.g. London, British Library, Royal MS 2.A.xxii), or the Apocalypse (e.g. London, Lambeth Palace Library, MS 209). In such cases the saints chosen indicate specific institutional or personal preferences and traditions. Soon, however, such images were to take on an independent life in the form of a new genre of book solely devoted to such pictures, in effect a saints' picture book, intended to focus prayer. A fine example is the late thirteenth-century picture-book of Madame Marie produced in the region of Mons (Paris, Bibliothèque nationale de France, MS nouv. acq. fr. 16251).

The manuscript displayed here is just such a book. It is executed in a lively supple pen and ink technique with blue, green and rose wash (*cf. no. 113*), the style indicating a date towards 1300. No other work by this artist is known. The eighteen images in the book have Latin titles in coloured capital letters. As presently bound, they are the Virgin Mary interceding before Christ, Christ the Judge, the Trinity, St John the Baptist (2), St Stephen martyred, Burial of the Virgin Mary, Coronation of the Virgin Mary, St Lawrence martyred, St Martin (2), St Nicholas, St Edmund of Abingdon, St Edward and St John, St Christopher, St Catherine, St Margaret martyred, and St Juliana enthusiastically flagellating a

terrified devil. It is likely that several leaves are missing, and that the Marian sequence originally started with her Burial, Coronation and Intercession, before Christ the Judge.

Because such images often occur in the context of devotional texts it is common to regard them as devotional aids rather than as elementary educational tools. However, this book is not in the vernacular, and its first intended user was monastic. The figure of a kneeling monk is to be seen below the Coronation of the Virgin. An inscription below the image of Mary interceding before Christ with the heading *Hic Maria virgo orat pro populo miserrime* ('Here the Virgin Mary prays for the wretched people'), mentions the monk's name, Richard: *Fili regna Patris Ricardo da prece matris* ('Oh Son, grant your Father's kingdom to Richard through the prayer of your mother'). Richard is unlikely to have needed elementary instruction in the theology of salvation. The

183

purpose of these images, for him at least, was devotional. The primary devotion here is clearly to the Virgin Mary. Male clerical use is also perhaps implied by the bishop and monk at the foot of Christ the Judge. But we should note that for a monk the images of female saints were absolutely appropriate role models. The stress on bishop-saints, such as Edmund of Abingdon, the Archbishop of Canterbury (canonized 1247), Martin and Nicholas, also reminds us that this was the great age of episcopal canonization in England. These three bishops were probably grouped together, along with St Edward, as examples of the virtue of charity.

PROVENANCE: M. Rashleigh, 1818 (signature on flyleaf); purchased from W.H. Robinson by the Friends of the Fitzwilliam Museum in 1935.

EXHIBITED: Cambridge 1966, no. 32.

LITERATURE: James 1936–1937; Wormald and Giles 1982, 374–76; Sandler 1986, no. 17.

PB

Crucifixion images. St John's College, MS K 21, fols. 52v–53

76

Canticles, Hymns, and Passion of Christ

In Latin and Anglo-Norman French
England, St Augustine's Canterbury, late thirteenth and early fourteenth century

Parchment, 96 fols., 317 × 230 mm, text 230 × 166 mm, 18 or 20 lines in one or two columns, ruled in plummet

SCRIPT: Gothic bookhand (textualis)

BINDING: blind tooled brown calf over pasteboard, J. Bowtell of Cambridge, 19th c.

St John's College, MS K. 21 (James no. 262)

THIS ALREADY SUBSTANTIAL MANUSCRIPT is a fragment lacking at least its first seventeen gatherings, over 204 leaves, which probably comprised a Psalter. It demonstrates the remarkable role the Psalter had as a focus for liturgically-based devotional material in the

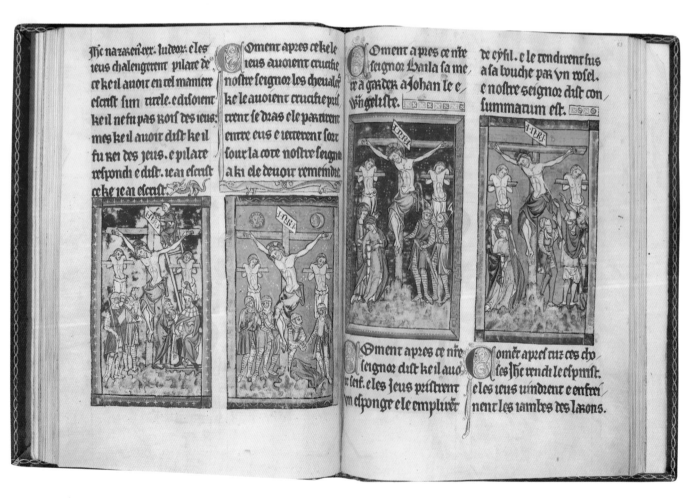

thirteenth century, because the surviving portion of the volume, consisting of Canticles and Hymns with illuminated initials, and an extended section of 100 images of the Passion of Christ with French texts, followed the Psalms. It is also notable for being a monastic book. Its Calendar is that for St Augustine's Abbey in Canterbury, and it also includes a hymn to St Augustine (fol. 94v). On fol. 9 is an image of a Benedictine monk praying to Christ with the text *Domine miserere*.

The function of the book is however somewhat more complex than that of *no. 75*, which is of the same period and type of patronage, in so far as the Passion illustrations between fols. 45v and 66 are clearly conceived as an extended series of contemplative prompts. Contemplation of the Passion of Christ at the liturgical hours had already become common in monastic and clerical devotions, and was starting to influence lay devotion too, not least in the new Books of Hours. Here, the French text with illustrations of the Passion is set between texts for Maundy Thursday and Easter, demonstrating the basis of devotional art in the public liturgy of the Church year. The Passion itself starts with the story of Lazarus, and proceeds very thoroughly by the standards of the Gospel picture-cycles common in Psalters of the time. To demonstrate this, the manuscript is displayed at fols. 52v–53 in the midst of the Passion narrative, with four representations of the Crucifixion of Christ. Very full images of Christ crucified on Golgotha were only starting to appear in English art at this time. Such images tend to compress several temporally separate incidents into one single image. Here on the contrary four separate images relate to four separate moments of the Passion: reading from the left, the nailing of the *titulus* of the Cross illustrates Pilate's sentiment 'What I have written I have written', the Jews speaking to Pilate below; the soldiers cast lots for Christ's garments; Christ commends Mary to St John's keeping as she faints into his arms; and the sponge is offered to Christ at the *consummatum est*, 'It is finished'. Narrative details act not in the service of a simple-minded realism, but as cues to deeper reflection on Christ's suffering which are governed by slow, methodical and disciplined meditation on all the possible textual and spiritual connotations of the image.

The extant sections of the manuscript were illuminated in two general styles by three or more artists. The first style, bold and somewhat coarse, occurs in the initials to the Canticles and Hymns, and, although later, it is somewhat similar to the Carrow Psalter (Baltimore, Walters Art Museum, MS W. 34; Morgan 1982–1988, no. 118) and to work in *no. 146*, both linked to East Anglia. It suggests that the book was begun in the last quarter of the thirteenth century. This style is found at the start of the Passion images to fol. 49v and is then replaced by a later, smoother idiom from fol. 50, which Sandler rightly sees as anticipating the Fenland Barlow Psalter (Oxford, Bodleian Library, MS Barlow 22, Sandler 1986, no. 91). Two hands seem to have worked in this style around 1300 or even later.

PROVENANCE: St Augustine's Abbey, Canterbury; given to the College by Edward Benlowes, Fellow Commoner, in 1621.

EXHIBITED: London 1908, no. 49.

LITERATURE: James 1913, 302–10; Sandler 1986, no. 8; Kauffmann 2003, 226, 231, 235, 257, fig. 172.

PB

77

Psalter (The Psalter of Simon de Montacute)

In Latin
England, Ely or Cambridge, *c.*1340–*c.*1345 and late fourteenth century

Parchment, 160 fols., 302 × 200 mm, text 270 × 120 mm, 22 lines, ruled in ink

SCRIPT: Gothic bookhand (textualis)

BINDING: gilt black morocco, 20th c.

St John's College, MS D. 30 (103★★)

THE PSALTER of Simon de Montacute is a fine example of a Psalter decorated at the principal Psalm divisions with historiated initials. The exhibited opening shows King David as Psalmist in the *Beatus* initial to Psalm 1, and David with Goliath at the bottom. Goliath falls backwards with his tongue lolling out as the full effect of David's slingshot is felt. In the border at the top is a hunting scene (*cf. no. 133*). A barbed quatrefoil between David and Goliath contains the arms of the presumed first owner of the book, Simon de Montacute, Bishop of Ely (1337–1345). Stylistically the book appears to be a product of the 1340s, the artist of this page painting borders further on in the book, as on fol. 107, but leaving the initials incomplete. Perhaps the death of Simon in 1345 interrupted the work for many decades until it was completed towards 1400 by the addition of the remaining initials. One of these, to the Office of the Dead on fol. 154v, is unexpected as it shows a group of nuns around a funeral bier. The Sarum-based Calendar of the Psalter however points unambiguously to the diocese of Ely, which would suggest that, if it is the original Calendar intended for Bishop Simon, the

185

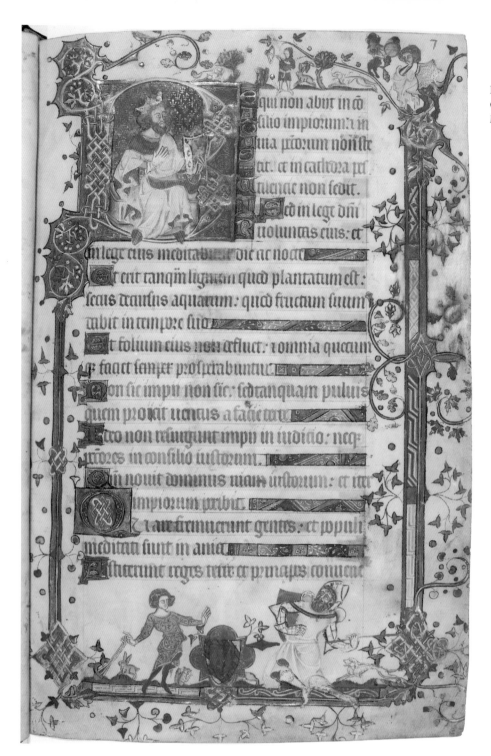

David as Psalmist, David and Goliath. St John's College, MS D. 30, fol. 7

book may later have fallen into the hands of female religious within the same diocese who had it finished.

The idiom of the first work represented by the *Beatus* page is typical of the showy, rather emphatic styles of the second quarter of the fourteenth century falling towards the end of the great era of East Anglian manuscript production and preceding the emergence of the workshops which produced the so-called 'Bohun' manuscripts (*no. 79*). It resembles Cambridge University charter Luard 33a★ dated 1343 (*no. 179*) and illuminated probably in Cambridge; it therefore poses the question as to whether it too may have been illuminated within the diocese, in Cambridge itself (Dennison 1986b).

PROVENANCE: Simon de Montacute, Bishop of Ely (1337–1345); Thomas Moyle, Wakefield, 18th c.; Rev. Henry Zouche, Swillington, Yorkshire, late 18th c.; Earls of Lonsdale, 19th–20th c.; Hugh Gatty, who gave it to the College in 1948.

EXHIBITED: Norwich 1973, no. 30.

LITERATURE: Sandler 1986, no. 112; Dennison 1986b, 52, 53–54; Robinson 1988, no. 300, pl. 144.

PB

78

Psalter (The Macclesfield Psalter)

In Latin
England, East Anglia, *c.*1330

Parchment, 252 fols., 170 x 108 mm, text 105 x 62 mm, 16 long
lines, ruled in brown ink
SCRIPT: Gothic bookhand (textualis)
BINDING: calf over pasteboards, 18th c.

Fitzwilliam Museum, MS 1–2005

N AMED AFTER ITS MOST RECENT OWNERS,
the Macclesfield Psalter is a discovery of
outstanding beauty and importance. It is the
missing link – textual, iconographic, and stylistic – between two of the finest East Anglian
manuscripts, the Gorleston Psalter of *c.*1220
and the Douai Psalter datable to the late 1330s
(London, British Library, Add. MS 49622 and
Douai, Bibliothèque municipale, MS 171;
Cockerell 1907; Sandler 1986, nos. 50 and 105;
Hull 1994; McIlwain 1999; Hull 2001). Both
are imposing volumes. The Macclesfield Psalter
is half their size, but more than matches their
richness and beauty. Its charming and provoca-
tive marginalia draw on motifs found in the
Gorleston Psalter, but supplement them with
new themes reinterpreted on a minuscule
scale. They re-appear at the main text divisions
of the Douai Psalter. The Macclesfield marginalia are unique in their density and profusion,
compelling the reader to re-examine text and
images page after page.

The historiated initials to the ten division
Psalms in the three manuscripts suggest the
same order of production. Their iconography
combines straightforward illustration of the
biblical text with allusions to the historical
context, Christological commentaries or liturgical use of the Psalms. This interpretative
approach draws on the illustrative programme
established in English Psalters *c.*1200 and is
suggestive of the iconographic sources for the
East Anglian manuscripts and the archaising
tastes of their makers and patrons.

Unlike the iconography, the style and technique of the Macclesfield Psalter are a new
departure. The adoption of classical motifs, the

three-dimensional volume and texture of fabrics, and the
rendering of the human body with the utmost anatomical precision make the Macclesfield Psalter one of the
earliest examples of the 'Italianate' tendencies in fourteenth-century English painting. Its most striking aspect
– and the salient feature of the Macclesfield Master – is
the unprecedented interest in human emotion and the
virtuoso depiction of its extremes. Yet, the gracefully
swaying figures with dainty features and the three-
headed monsters with hairy noses are equally characteristic of this versatile artist. His repertoire is so vast and
his juxtapositions of large and small, serious and ludi-
crous are so striking as to suggest the involvement of

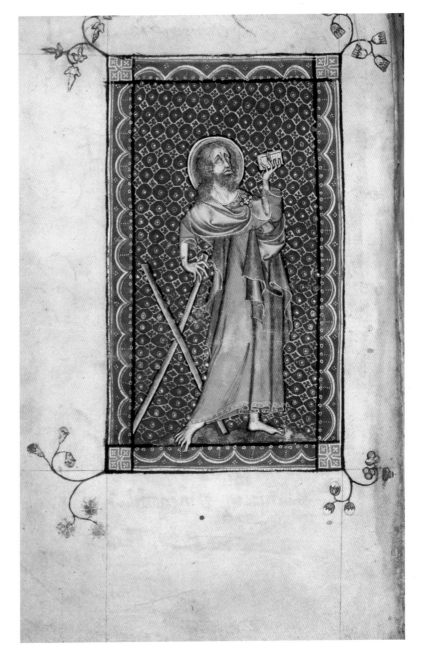

St Andrew. Fitzwilliam Museum, MS 1–2005, fol. 1v

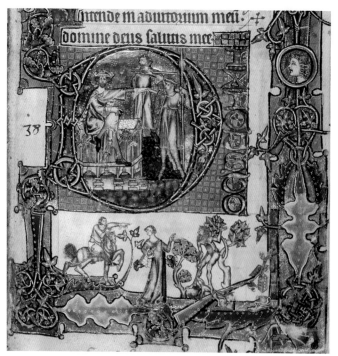

Saul sending Doeg to kill the priests of Nob, a horseman, a lady, and a wildman. Fitzwilliam Museum, MS 1–2005, fol. 58, detail

more than one artist. Indeed, several assistants decorated the manuscript, often painting designs sketched by the Master. The nature of this collaboration requires further research, but preliminary observations suggest a similar pattern of work in the Stowe Breviary of c.1322–1325, the earliest manuscript in which the hand of the Macclesfield Master may be detected (British Library, Stowe MS 12). The Stowe Breviary was the exemplar for the Calendars and Litanies of the Macclesfield and Douai Psalters. All three manuscripts, as well as the Gorleston Psalter, were probably copied by the same scribe who penned his catchwords in an elegant Anglicana. Frederica Law-Turner proposes a close link between the Macclesfield and Ormesby Psalters (Oxford, Bodleian Library, MS Douce 366; Law-Turner 2005).

Christopher de Hamel identified the Macclesfield Master with one of the two main illuminators of the Douai Psalter, the artist Caroline Hull named the Douai Psalter Assistant (Hull 1994). Another manuscript crucial for our understanding of the Macclesfield Master and his collaboration with the Douai Master is the copy of Bede's Ecclesiastical History in Cambridge, Trinity College, MS R.7.3. The Trinity Bede is a modest book copied by at least four hands after the example set by an expert scribe. Five of the six illuminated leaves were marked with inscriptions to ensure their return to the right place after they were sent out for illumination. This peculiar feature raises intriguing questions about the context in which the Macclesfield and Douai artists worked.

Various tempting suggestions about the patronage of the Macclesfield Psalter have been made, but the manuscript's internal evidence requires further examination. The Calendars of the Gorleston and Douai Psalters

(Sarum use with Norwich additions) contain the dedication of the Church of St Andrew in Gorleston (8 March). Crucial for the association of these two manuscripts with Gorleston, the dedication was not included in the Macclesfield Psalter – one of the two important differences between the nearly identical Macclesfield and Douai Calendars. The miniature of St Andrew in the Macclesfield Psalter may reflect a patron's association with one of the many churches dedicated to this popular saint. Among them was one of the richest parish churches in Norwich, the major artistic centre around which the Macclesfield and Douai Masters would have gravitated. The single coat of arms extant in the Macclesfield Psalter (fol. 37v) and identified by Anne Payne as that of the Gorges family, is not prominent enough to suggest direct patronage, but appears in the Stowe Breviary as well. Stronger evidence may have been lost with several of the missing or mutilated leaves, notably the excised initial to the Confession prayer (fol. 250). The bas-de-page shows a young layman praying at an altar, but the unusually detailed text mentions the handling of the sacred vessels with unclean hands and heart, and the neglect of the divine office, all matters pertinent to a religious. A Dominican in prayer is depicted beneath Psalm 107 (fol. 158), but St Dominic is absent from the Calendar and Litany – the second major difference with the Douai Calendar. This and many other aspects of the newly-discovered manuscript will challenge and reward generations of students.

PROVENANCE: Anthony Watson, bishop of Chichester (1596–1605); John Smeaton; sister Barbara, 15th c. (erased inscriptions on fols. 1, 8v); Library of the Earl of Macclesfield, Shirburn Castle; his sale, Sotheby's, London, 22 June 2004, lot 587; purchased with Museum funds, contributions from its Friends, grants from the National Heritage Memorial Fund, the National Art Collections Fund, the Cadbury Trust, and the Friends of the National Libraries, and donations from numerous trusts, foundations, and individuals following a public appeal launched by the National Art Collections Fund.

LITERATURE: Sotheby's 2004, lot 587; Law-Turner 2004; Law-Turner 2005.

SP

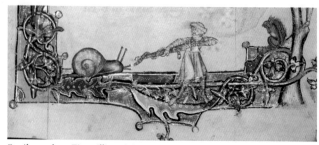

Snail combat. Fitzwilliam Museum, MS 1–2005, fol. 76 (bas-de-page)

79

Psalter

In Latin
England, London or Pleshey Castle, Essex,
c.1380–*c*.1385
ARTISTS: John de Teye (doc. 1361–1384) and others

Parchment, i + ii (paper) + iv + 243 + iv fols., 170 × 120 mm,
text 108 × 61 mm, 18 long lines, ruled in brown ink and
plummet

SCRIPT: Gothic bookhand (textualis)

BINDING: gold-tooled brown leather, sacred monogram and
Emblems of the Passion, two clasps (one modern), 17th c.

Fitzwilliam Museum, MS 38–1950

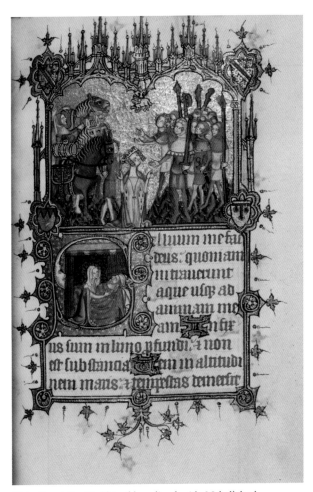

Abigail and David, Abigail kneeling beside Nabal's bed.
Fitzwilliam Museum, MS 38–1950, fol. 78

THIS PSALTER was probably made for Mary de Bohun (d.1394), daughter of Humphrey de Bohun (d.1373), Earl of Hereford and Essex. The heraldry on fols. 62 and 99 has the arms of Bohun and of Henry Bolingbroke, Earl of Derby, son of John of Gaunt. Mary married Bolingbroke in 1380 and perhaps the Psalter was produced for the marriage in that year. Other heraldry in the manuscript (of Butler, Courtenay, John of Gaunt and England) refers to those families into which past members of the Bohun family had married. Psalters and Books of Hours were made for the Bohun family between *c*.1355 and *c*.1385 by a group of artists who seem to have worked most of the time for the family at Pleshey Castle, Essex. One was John de Teye, an Augustinian friar. Some of these manuscripts were illuminated intermittently over a long period of time, but the Fitzwilliam Psalter was perhaps decorated in one campaign in the year or two before or after Mary's marriage in 1380. Other manuscripts made by these artists at the same time are the Psalter of Humphrey de Bohun completed after his death in 1373 (Oxford, Exeter College, MS 47, fols 9–19v), an Hours (London, British Library, Egerton MS 3277), and the Psalter-Hours also begun for Humphrey, but completed for Mary, perhaps also in connection with her marriage to Bolingbroke, since his arms are in that book (Oxford, Bodleian Library, MS Auct. D.4.4).

The Psalter has half-page miniatures set above historiated initials at the Psalms of the liturgical divisions, the first Gradual Psalm (119), and Psalm 137. As in other books made for the Bohun family the artists preferred narrative biblical illustrations. The life of David is depicted in thirty-five scenes, from his fighting the bear and the lion to the story of Seba's rebellion and the victory of Joab. These include the stories of David and Goliath, Saul, Abigail, Bathsheba and Absalom. The miniatures are surmounted by ogee arches and pinna-cles. Their pages have full borders of gold bars with gold foliage sprays and heraldry. The scenes have simple landscape or architectural backdrops on burnished gold grounds with elaborate punch-dot patterns. Some have crowds of people dressed in elegant courtly costumes, headgear and fashionable armour of the period. The Penitential Psalms and the Litany follow the Psalms and Canticles. The first Penitential Psalm has the Last Judgement depicted within a historiated initial. Most of the other pages have partial borders of gold bars with tendril foliate sprays coming from Psalm initials containing heads, animals and dragons.

The book ends with hymns and prayers followed by a Sarum Calendar. The obits of Henry VI, his wife Margaret of Anjou, and his son Edward were added to the Calendar, suggesting that the manuscript came into the possession of members of the royal family.

PROVENANCE: Mary de Bohun (d.1394) and/or her husband, Henry Bolingbroke; John Stafford, Archbishop of Canterbury (d.1452), arms on fol. 1; Henry VI or his wife, Margaret of

Anjou, arms on fol. 1; Burneby and Walton families, 15th and 16th c.; Henry Valentine Stafford-Jerningham, 9th Baron Jerningham acquired it before 1884 and gave it to his wife, Emma, Lady Stafford; given to her stepdaughter, Lady Chichele Plowden; sold in 1907 to Henry Yates Thompson (1838–1928); his sale, Sotheby's, London, 23 March 1920, lot 40; purchased by T.H. Riches; his bequest, 1935.

EXHIBITED: Cambridge 1966, no. 56; Brussels 1973, no. 70; London 1987–1988, no. 690; Paris 2004a, no. 63.

LITERATURE: Thompson 1912, 45–52; Thompson 1907–1918, IV, 33–35, pls. LII–LIX; James 1936, 53–59, pls. LXII–LXVIII; Wormald and Giles 1982, 431–36, pls. 31, 32; Alexander 1983, 148, 152; Sandler 1985, 367; Sandler 1986, I, 19, 21, 35, 45; II, 112, 151, 154, 156, 158, 159, 170, no. 139, ills. 369–70; Dennison, 1986c, 8, 9, pl. IIIA, fig. 4a; Dennison 1990b, 41, 47, 48, figs. 10, 13; Sandler 2002, 124; Sandler, 2003, 222–3, 225–26, pls. 50, 56; Sandler 2004, 11, 119, 121, 131, 145, 146, 152, 159 n.92, figs. 3, 8.

NJM

80

Book of Hours

Use of Sarum
In Latin and French
England, London or East Anglia, c.1320–1323

Parchment, ii + 135 + ii fols., 212 × 160 mm, text 146 × 101 mm, 16 long lines, ruled in brown ink

SCRIPT: Gothic bookhand (textualis)

BINDING: brown leather over wooden boards, by D. Cockerell, 1962

Cambridge University Library MS Dd.4.17

THE TEXT CONTENTS of this manuscript are typical of an early fourteenth century Book of Hours: Calendar, Hours of the Virgin, Hours of the Holy Spirit,

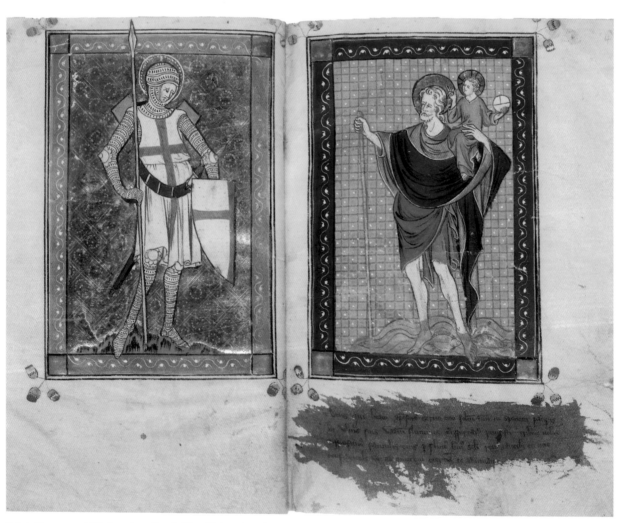

Saints George and Christopher. Cambridge University Library MS Dd.4.17, fols. 3v–4

Prayers in French, Penitential Psalms, Litany, Gradual Psalms, and Office of the Dead. They offer the reader devotional texts both for daily and for occasional use. The text is preceded by twelve full-page illustrations, each painted on only one side of the leaf: a female owner before an archbishop saint (fol. 1v), Saints Catherine and Margaret (fol. 2), St George (fol. 3v), St Christopher (fol. 4), Annunciation (fol. 5v), Nativity (fol. 6), Resurrection (fol. 7v), Ascension (fol. 8), Coronation of the Virgin (fol. 9v), Christ in Majesty (fol. 10), Standing Virgin and Child (fol. 11v), Crucifixion (fol. 12). These are neither in a narrative order nor systematically grouped, but were intended for devotional contemplation before reading the Life of Christ. Christ, the Virgin and Child, and the Crucifixion end the sequence. The Calendar has illustrations of the Signs of the Zodiac and Labours of the Months. Next, the text of the Hours of the Virgin opens on fol. 19 with a historiated initial showing the female owner kneeling before the seated Virgin and Child with a full decorative border surrounding the text including shields of England, Valence and one obliterated *(fig. 28)*. In the initial to Psalm 93 (*Venite exultemus*) is the shield of Reymes. This shield suggests that the woman depicted in the miniatures is Alice Reymes (née Reydon) who was married to Robert de Reymes of Eston Gosebeck in Suffolk. This identification is proven by the record in the Calendar of the death of Alice de Reydon on the 5th July. Unfortunately, the year of her death has been cropped away at some later date and goes as far as 'm°cccx'. A date after 1310 and before 1323 when she is definitely known to have been dead can thus be given for the manuscript. A further precision of the dating derives from the presence of St Thomas of Hereford, canonized in 1320, among the confessors in the Litany. The remainder of the text is elaborately decorated with ornamental initials and borders, but contains only one further figure illustration of a historiated initial of Christ blessing at the beginning of the Penitential Psalms (fol. 79).

There are four artists: the first painted the full-page miniatures, the second the Calendar pictures, and two others the opening pages of the Hours of the Virgin and the Penitential Psalms (fols. 19, 79). The decorative work of initials and borders in the text section may be by a fifth artist. The artist of the full-page miniatures is of a leading workshop operating *c*.1315–*c*.1335 and named after the Queen Mary Psalter, which later belonged to Queen Mary Tudor (London, British Library, Royal MS 2.B.vii; *see also nos. 117, 149 and fig. 1)*. The same artist worked on a Psalter made for a patron in the Norwich diocese *(no. 149)*, which later passed to Peterborough Abbey. The figure style of the artist responsible for fol. 19 is related to the Bardolf-Vaux Psalter (London, Lambeth Palace Library, MS 233). The border decoration by the artists of fols. 19 and 79, and that elsewhere

in the main text, relates to the Howard Psalter possibly made for John Fitton of Wiggenhall St German's, Norfolk (London, British Library, MS Arundel 83, pt. I), the Gorleston Psalter (London, British Library, Add. MS 49622), and the fourteenth-century part of the Alfonso Psalter (London, British Library, Add. MS 24686). It is not certain whether the Hours of Alice de Reydon was made in an East Anglian centre, as were some of these Psalters.

PROVENANCE: Alice de Reydon; Matilda or John Stranle in the late 14th c.; at the University Library by the mid-eighteenth century when it was entered in the 1754–1756 list (MS Oo.7.53).

EXHIBITED: Norwich 1973, no. 8; London 1987–1988, no. 571.

LITERATURE: University Library 1856–1867, I, 225–26; Raimes 1908, 317–18, col. pls.; Raimes 1939, 106–7, col. pls.; Oman 1950, 337–41; Michael 1981, 83, 86, 89; Sinclair 1982, nos. 4000, 4276, 4369, 5028, 5155; Sandler 1986, I, 31; II, 13, 73, 77, 78, no. 67, ills. 168–9, 170–1; Rézeau, 1986, no. 1991; Robinson 1988, no. 2; Dennison 1990a, 120–21, pl. XXVIIIB, XXXB; Gee 2002, 41–4, 139, pls. 3, 4; Kauffmann 2003, 230, Sandler 2004, 116 n. 117.

NJM

81

Book of Hours (The Grey-Fitzpayn or Clifford-Pabenham Hours)

Use of Sarum
In Latin
England, *c*.1315–*c*.1330

Parchment, 93 fols., 248 × 170 mm, text 160 × 95 mm, 19–21 long lines, ruled in plummet

SCRIPT: Gothic bookhand (textualis)

BINDING: oak boards, by D. Cockerell, 1980s

Fitzwilliam Museum, MS 242

THE SO-CALLED GREY-FITZPAYN HOURS is a fine example of the showy vigour of artwork in Books of Hours produced as independent Prayer Books for the lay market in England by the early fourteenth century. Its principal divisions are the Hours of the Virgin, Hours of the Trinity, Penitential Psalms, Hours of the Holy Spirit, Gradual Psalms and Office of the Dead. Of these, major illumination survives mostly from the first three, though the book is decorated throughout with border ornament and drolleries in profusion. The style is unique to this manuscript, and runs in parallel to the major workshops in the Midlands, London and East Anglian regions associated with the Queen Mary Psalter, London, British

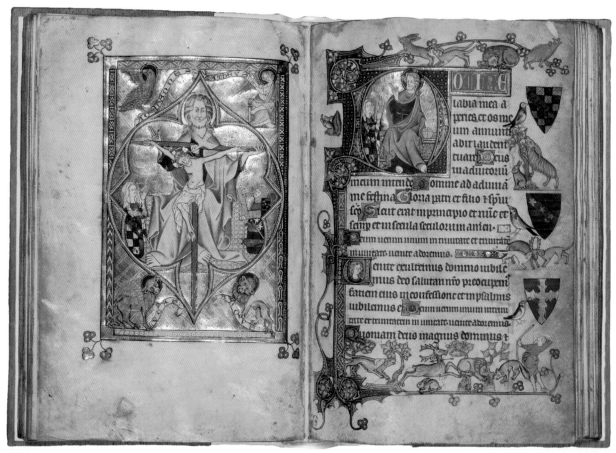

Throne of Mercy with patrons, Christ blessing with a patron. Fitzwilliam Museum, MS 242, fols. 28v–29

Library, Royal MS 2 B.vii (*see no. 80*) and the treatise of Walter de Milemete, London, British Library, Add. MS 47680 (Sandler 1986, nos. 56, 85). The Bardolf-Vaux Psalter suggests analogies, London, Lambeth Palace Library, MS 233 (Sandler 1986, no. 30). In fact there was more than one hand at work, as will be apparent from comparing the style and technique of the Annunciation on fol. 2v with the image of the Virgin and Child on fol. 3. The style of the Annunciation has a dry smooth quality, the facial features being inked in over white pigment creating the slightly blank complexion framed by carefully drawn curls common in the period; the modeling of the garments of the Virgin Mary on fol. 3 is notably softer and more supple. Discontinuities are normal in books of this type.

The images chosen are appropriate to the liturgical sections: the Annunciation and Virgin and Child for the Hours of the Virgin, the Trinity and Christ for the Hours of the Trinity exhibited here and the Crucifixion for the seven Penitential Psalms. The slightly slick grace of these pictures should not seduce us into thinking that they lack attention to text. Near the Crucifixion initial on fol. 55v we find in the border a small mammal sticking its nose and leg out of a hole, and a very fine bird, clear allusions to Matthew 8:20–21 'The foxes have holes and the birds of the air have nests; but the Son of man hath not where to lay his head'.

Considerable alertness is also necessary in using the copious heraldic evidence provided by the book. Key to the decoration is the inclusion of numerous images of the first patrons and users of the manuscript, a married couple shown as knight and lady who display their arms either on large shields, or on heraldic clothing. The fashion for donor 'portraits' of this type had been set in the previous century, and in fact little in the basic form of the book's decoration and taste for heraldry and fauna had changed much since high-art devotional manuscripts made from *c.*1280 onwards. The patrons are insinuated directly into the space of the religious images which jostle with marginalia: on fol. 3 they kneel below the Annunciation, and opposite they are to be found kneeling before the Virgin Mary and the Holy Face; on fol. 28v they kneel before the Trinity and on fol. 29 the lady is shown directly with a blessing image of Christ holding a globe; they reappear with the Crucifixion on fol. 55v. Formerly the man and woman were identified as Sir Richard Grey and Joan Fitzpayn, who were married by 1308. Following a suggestion of Cockerell, J.A. Goodall has recently re-identified them as John de Pabenham and Joan Clifford, who were married by 1314–1315; John died in 1331. If this identification holds true, the book dates to a later period (*c.*1315–1330) than has been customarily thought, and was also commissioned for a slightly lower-status couple whose marriage it perhaps celebrates. It is tempting to see the manuscript's vigorous display in the light of this last possibility, which has been accepted for the purpose of this entry.

PROVENANCE: Joan Clifford and John de Pabenham (d.1331); Sir Andrew Fountaine (1676–1753) of Narford Hall, Norfolk; fols. 37 and 55 were removed while the manuscript was at Narford Hall, sold at Puttick's, London, 16–18 July 1866, lot 865, and purchased by Samuel Sandars (1837–1894) who presented them to the Museum in 1892; the manuscript was sold at the Fountaine sale, Christie's, London, 6 July 1894, lot 143; purchased by William Morris who sold it to the Museum in 1895, where it came after his death in 1896.

EXHIBITED: London 1930, no. 215; Cambridge 1966, no. 53; Ottawa 1972, no. 35; Paris, 2004a, no. 42.

LITERATURE: James 1895a, 399–99; Egbert 1940, 90–94, 175–81; Wormald and Giles 1982, 157–60; Sandler 1986, no. 31; Goodall 1997, 180–81; Kauffmann 2003, 229.

PB

82

Book of Hours

Use of Sarum
In Latin
England, London and Bury St Edmunds,
*c.*1405 – *c.*1410 and *c.*1440

Parchment. iv (paper) + i + 140 + iv (paper) fols.,
212 × 150 mm, text 126 × 92 mm, 15 long lines, ruled in red,
purple and black-brown ink

SCRIPT: Gothic bookhand (textualis)

BINDING: marbled paper boards, brown leather spine, 1963

Cambridge University Library, MS Ee.1.14

THE BOOK contains the normal text of a Book of Hours: Calendar, Hours of the Virgin, Penitential Psalms, Office of the Dead and Commendation of the Soul, with historiated or ornamental initials with full

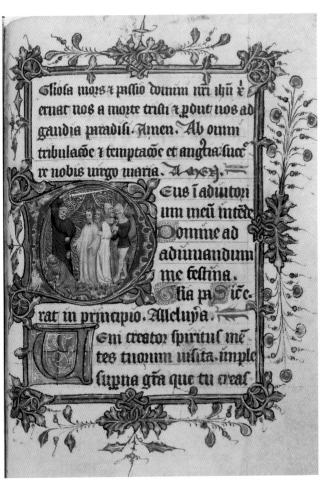

Betrayal. Cambridge University Library, MS Ee.1.14, fol. 32, detail

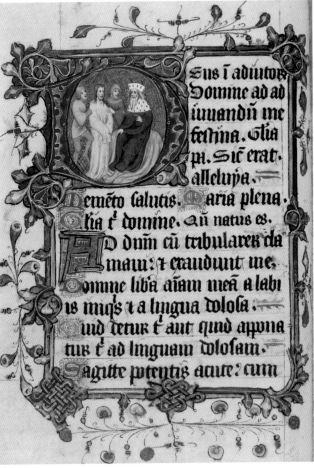

Christ before Pilate. Cambridge University Library, MS Ee.1.14, fol. 36v, detail

decorative borders of leaves and penwork sprays at the main sections of the text. Matins of the Virgin has the Virgin and Child, whereas the other Hours have Passion scenes from Gethsemane to the Entombment. Christ Judge is in the initial at the beginning of the Penitential Psalms. The Office of the Dead and the funeral Mass for the Commendation of the Soul (fol. 103) open with ornamental initials.

The decoration is of two widely separated periods: fols. 1–102v date to *c*.1405–1410 and fols. 103–139v to *c*.1440. The patron of this later section is suggested by a prayer on fol. 120 mentioning a man named Nicholas, and an addition to the Calendar on the 4th of October of the dedication of the church of St Mary, Bury St Edmunds, evidently made at the same time. The early part is in the style of two artists working in London from *c*.1405 onwards, Herman Scheerre and Johannes. The iconography of several of the Passion scenes is close to Herman Scheerre's work in the *c*.1405–*c*.1410 Neville Hours (Berkeley Castle, Gloucestershire, Trustees of the late Earl of Berkeley) and a *c*.1410 Book of Hours (Oxford, Bodleian Library, MS Gough liturg. 6). Stylistic influence from Johannes is evident in the image of the Virgin and Child at Matins and of Christ before Pilate at Terce. These are comparable with his work in *Li Livres du Graunt Caam* of *c*.1400–*c*.1410 (Oxford, Bodleian Library, MS Bodley 264). Kathleen Scott has pointed out the importance of the Cambridge Hours as evidence of interrelationships between the Johannes and Scheerre workshops in the early stages of their development. She attributes the initials on fols. 9, 41v, 44, 47, 53 to Herman Scheerre himself, and fols. 17v, 32, 39 to an assistant. The initial with Christ before Pilate is by a third artist influenced by Johannes. This may suggest that when Scheerre arrived in England around 1405 he initially worked with the Johannes workshop. The decorative borders incorporating symmetrical leaf pairs with intertwined stems, diamond leaves and clumps of interlace at the corners are in a style which is found in many manuscripts of the period 1385–1400, typified by those of the Litlyngton Missal (London, Westminster Abbey, MS 37).

This manuscript is also important for the second section made *c*.1440 because it compares with the few manuscripts perhaps made at Bury St Edmunds in this period. The only major decoration in this part of the book is the historiated initial and full border for the Commendation of the Soul. The figures are stocky and beady-eyed, and the border has acanthus and lobe-like leaves softly painted in pale blue, pink and green, similar to the type of border on fol. 177 of a Book of Hours (Cambridge, Fitzwilliam Museum MS3–1979), whose Calendar has the synodal feasts of the diocese of Norwich as well as the Translation of Nicholas on the 9th of May, also added in red to the Calendar of MS

Ee.1.14. This interest in Nicholas probably relates to the important gild of the Translation of Nicholas patronized by the leading merchants of Bury St Edmunds. The Hours at the Fitzwilliam Museum is another Bury St Edmunds product of *c*.1440. The origins of this characteristic border decoration is in Bury work of over twenty years earlier in the Psalter with a Litany of Bury St Edmunds Abbey belonging to Bury Grammar School, but now kept at the Suffolk Record Office.

PROVENANCE: Nicholas of Bury St Edmunds, possibly living in the parish of St Mary there, *c*.1440; John Moore, Bishop of Ely (1707–1714); presented to the Library by George I in 1715.

LITERATURE: University Library 1856–1867, II, 14–15; Rogers 1987, 232 n. 14, 237–8, 239, 241; Scott 1996, no. 16.

NJM

83

Book of Hours (The Carew–Poyntz Hours)

Use of Sarum

In Latin

England, third and fourth quarters of the fourteenth century; first and third quarters of the fifteenth century

Parchment, 189 fols., 180 × 118 mm, text 100 × 80 mm, 14 long lines, ruled in pink ink

SCRIPT: Gothic bookhand (textualis)

BINDING: alum tawed skin over oak boards, by Robert Proctor, 2004

Fitzwilliam Museum, MS 48

THE CAREW-POYNTZ HOURS (so called after a fifteenth-century inscription in the book in the hand of Elizabeth Poyntz referring to her half-sister, the wife of Edmund Carew) is an enigmatic and complex manuscript with an extremely rich programme of illumination. It casts much light on the eclecticism of English book production in the second half of the fourteenth century, and the potential of book design to incorporate proximate yet not always related strands of picture-making. The relatively small scale of the book and general character of the illumination immediately bring to mind high-quality fourteenth-century French work. One sign of this is the general use of thin frames which bifurcate and sprout into dainty, sparkling, gilt ivy-leaf foliage, on the whole a French method of border design throughout much of the century and uncommon in all but a few English works of the period, notably some of the so-called 'Bohun' manuscripts. Other indices of an aspiration to mimic the best French work are the common use of grisaille, i.e. grey and white painting, popular in Paris since the early part of the century, and the use of small sequential narrative images at the bottom of the page, i.e. bas-de-page. For the last format, precedents existed in English illumination too, as in the Queen Mary Psalter (London, British Library, Royal MS 2.B.vii), the Tickhill Psalter (New York, Public Library, Spencer MS 26) and, above all, the Taymouth Hours of the second quarter of the century (London, British Library, Yates Thompson MS 13; Sandler 1986, nos. 56, 26, 98). The Taymouth Hours, a similarly eclectic work, seems especially to herald the form of this manuscript, but it lacks its self-conscious allusion to French book-painting.

The decoration can only be summarized here briefly. The Hours are prefaced by a set of prayers with a long bas-de-page sequence illustrating rather fully the Old Testament, and opening with lively and quite distin-

guished drawing in a sub-Pucellian manner, which is joined by another hand related to the Fitzwarin Psalter (Paris, Bibliothèque nationale de France, MS lat. 765; Sandler 1986, no. 120). This restlessness is absolutely typical of the book, and we may note that the illumination is not always complete, indicating perhaps that the manuscript was illuminated piecemeal, but according to one basic scheme. There are in this part distinct signs of familiarity with the French artist known as the *Maître aux Boqueteaux*; other French works which compare are the Hours decorated by the 'Parement' workshop (Paris, Bibliothèque nationale de France, MS nouv. acq. lat. 3093) and the Hours from the circle of the so-called Pseudo-Jacquemart (Paris, Bibliothèque nationale de France, MS lat. 18014). Yet other Bible pictures were executed around 1400 or later. The delicate grisaille of these early pictures is gradually displaced by a relatively coarse full-colour technique. On fols. 39v and 47 devotional images, namely the Holy Face and St Andrew, occupy the larger panels above the bas-de-page with

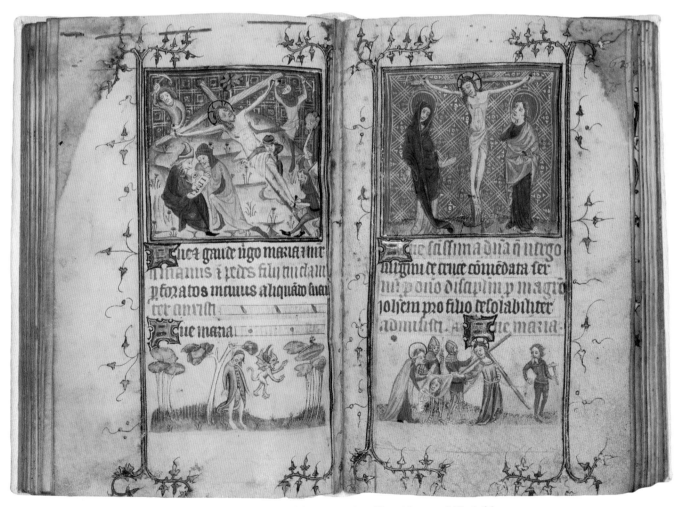

Nailing to the Cross, Judas' suicide, Crucifixion, Carrying of the Cross. Fitzwilliam Museum, MS 48, fols. 74v–75

absolute indifference to the Bible action below. Two female donors are shown with a bishop on fol. 58, work dating to a campaign around 1400. From fol. 58v onwards the illustrations pertain to the Lives of the Virgin Mary and Christ, together with 49 salutations to the Virgin; those in the main frame and the bas-de-page now (more or less) coordinate, as if footnotes were being added to a pictorial text: thus on fol. 64v the image of the Nativity of Christ has the martyrdom of St Anastasia, one of the holy midwives, below it. As a rule the more liturgically central images are the larger ones. This section of the book (fols. 56–70v) has been thoroughly overpainted.

Curious illogicalities appear in the ordering of images within this top-and-bottom scheme, as in the case of the Ascension images. In the opening chosen for the exhibition, fols. 74v–75, we see the nailing of Christ to the Cross on the ground, *jacente cruce*, i.e. according to the Pseudo-Anselm. Pilate writes out the *titulus*. Below, Judas hangs himself, his entrails dropping out. Next, above, is the Crucifixion, with the Carrying of the Cross below and the impression of Christ's face taken on the cloth by St Veronica, which should precede the image above in time. Elsewhere, devotional themes emerge, as in the case of the images relating to the Cross, notably St Helena (fol. 84) and the Stigmatization of St Francis (fol. 85), later reworked into St George and the Dragon, but just apparent in the underdrawing. The Hours of the Virgin initiated by the fine image of a female patron before the Virgin Mary (fol. 86) include an image of St Edmund of Abingdon with the Virgin opposite the Last Judgement (fols. 151v–152). The last, and remarkable, sequence consists of bas-de-page images of the Miracles of the Virgin with her Litany (fols. 152–189). The insistence on images of female devotees, including three women at an altar preceding the Gradual Psalms (fol. 164v), render it certain that a female audience was intended, and one which laid emphasis on such saints as Edmund and Francis. This early ascetic strand, pushed aside with the reworking of some of the saints' images, may also explain the remarkable miniature on fol. 189 showing a king assaulted by Death with an arrow, with devils cavorting beneath.

The complexity and sense of challenge to 'order' apparent in the Carew-Poyntz Hours may illustrate haphazard methods of execution. But they may also help us to understand the anti-naturalistic tendencies of much devotional art, its conscious breach of rational temporal and spatial relationships in order to set up new ones, which belong to a quite separate religious-imaginative order. This new pattern had been emerging in devotional image making and texts since at least the twelfth and thirteenth centuries, and its still poorly understood multivalency warns us against imposing on such compilations a post-Enlightenment epistemology, of which

(perhaps ironically) 'centre and margin' is a recently fashionable example.

PROVENANCE: Elizabeth Poyntz, 15th c.; purchased by the Museum from Quaritch, 1889.

EXHIBITED: Cambridge 1966, no. 57; Paris 1968b, no. 254.

LITERATURE: James 1895a, 100–20; Sandler 1986, no. 130; Wormald 1988, 88, 92, 101–102; Despres 1998; Rogers 2001, 205–9, pls. 41–44; Kauffmann 2003, 211, 214, 215, 226–30, figs. 159–64.

PB

84

Book of Hours

Use of Sarum
In Latin
England, London, *c.*1415–*c.*1420

Parchment, ii (paper) + ii + 120 + iii + ii (paper) fols., 268 × 184 mm, text 182 × 104 mm, 20 long lines, ruled in brown-black ink

SCRIPT: Gothic bookhand (textualis)

BINDING: Green velvet, probably 18th c.

Trinity College, MS B.11.7

THIS IS ONE of the most richly decorated English Books of Hours of the early years of the fifteenth century. It has been thought to be a royal book because a king kneels at Mass in the framed miniature accompanying the Collect for peace at the end of Lauds (fol. 31v), and a princess kneels before Christ crucified in the miniature for the *memoria* of the Holy Cross, also at Lauds (fol. 21). A third image of ownership is a man kneeling before the standing Virgin and Child in a full-page miniature preceding the *memoriae* at Lauds (fol. 20). Also there are two mottoes providing evidence of ownership in the backgrounds of the miniatures on fols. 45, 57v. Nicholas Rogers has identified one of the mottoes with Sir John Cornwall and his wife, the Princess Elizabeth, sister of Henry IV. The couple was well known to King Henry V, Elizabeth being his aunt, and John being a leading soldier at Agincourt in 1415 and at the siege of Rouen in 1419. The depiction of Henry V kneeling at Mass in the prayer for peace could reflect the petition in the Litany, 'grant our king and princes peace and true concord and victory'. It would have been appropriate in the political context of the Treaty of Troyes and the king's marriage to Catherine of France in 1420, the time at which the manuscript was probably made. The Calendar has the synodal supplements for the diocese of Norwich, and the *memoriae* at Lauds include

Betrayal and Visitation.
Trinity College,
MS B.11.7, fol. 32v

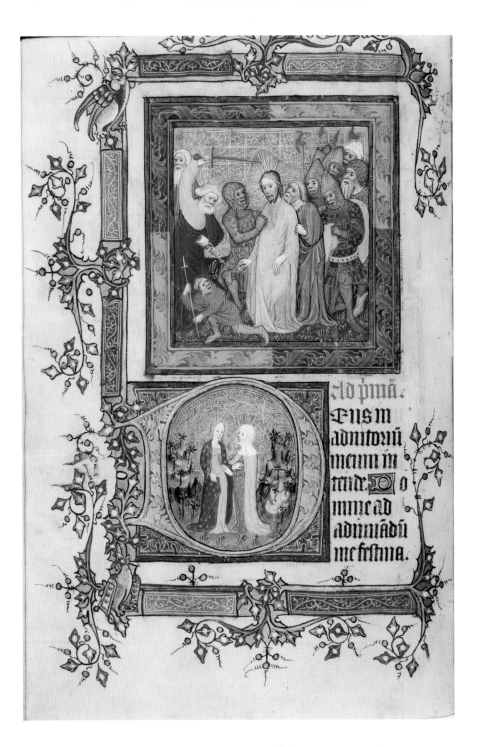

Saints Edmund and Etheldreda, both features suggesting that the patrons had connections with East Anglia. This seems not to have been the case for Sir John or his wife, Elizabeth, so it is possible that the book was originally commissioned for another patron, but was completed for them.

The Calendar has roundels of the Labours of the Months and the Zodiac Signs. Each of the Hours of the Virgin begins with an historiated initial of the early life of Christ from the Annunciation to the Massacre of the Innocents accompanied by heavy decorative borders, and from Prime to Compline with a series of miniatures of the Passion from the Betrayal to the Entombment.

The juxtaposition of these two narrative sequences reflects the text in which the Hours of the Cross are intercalated with the Hours of the Virgin, requiring a reading on the events of the Passion to precede the Hours. A notable feature of the illustrative programme is the many half-page miniatures of saints for the *memoriae* at Lauds. A particular devotion to Saints Christopher and Anne is indicated by full-page miniatures for them. Anne is shown teaching the young Mary to read. The remaining decoration consists of historiated initials for the final sections of the book: the Last Judgement for the Penitential Psalms, Susanna and the Elders for the Gradual Psalms, the Funeral Mass and Job on the

Dungheap for the Office of the Dead, and God holding souls in a napkin for the Commendation of the Soul.

There are three artists. The first decorated the Calendar and several of the full borders working in a late fourteenth-century manner, close to that of the *c.*1390–*c.*1395 Coronation Order in Pamplona (Archivo de Navarra, MS 197). He was of an older generation, whereas the other two artists of the miniatures and historiated initials are under stylistic and iconographical influences from the three leading London artists of the period 1410–1430, Herman Scheerre, Johannes Siferwas, and Johannes.

PROVENANCE: Sir John Cornwall and his wife, Princess Elizabeth, sister of Henry IV; Sir John Leigh (d.1564), his arms on fol. 45; Thomas Coppinger who gave the book to the College in 1662.

LITERATURE: James 1900–1904, I, 342–46; Alexander 1972, 169, pl. 6; Alexander 1983, 149, pl. 9; Morgan 1993–1994, 514, 820 fig. 7 but caption as for fig. 8; Rogers 1994; Orr 1995; Scott 1996, I, 29, 39, 41, 48, 54, 56, 57, 65 n. 5, 72 n. 31, figs. 194–96, col. pl. 9; II, no. 47, 38, 56, 72, 95, 120, 135, 150, 156, 158, 163, 168, 169, 177, 212, 213, 214, 218, 335, 338, 342, 345, 351, 382–83; Morgan 2002, 97, fig. 2

NJM

85

Book of Hours (The *Grandes Heures* of Philip the Bold)

Use of Paris
In Latin and French
Paris, 1376–1379; Paris 1390; Brussels, *c.*1450
ARTISTS: Master of the Bible of Jean de Sy (act. *c.*1350–*c.*1380); Master of the Coronation Book of Charles V (act. *c.*1355–*c.*1380); miniatures added *c.*1450 by Marc Caussin (doc. 1432–1479), Willem Vrelant (act. *c.*1449–*c.*1481), the Master of Wauquelin's Alexander (act. *c.*1445–*c.*1460), Jan Tavernier (act. *c.*1434–*c.*1460), Dreux Jean (the Master of the Girart de Roussillon, act. *c.*1430–*c.*1467) and others
SCRIBE: Jean L'Avenant (act. *c.*1350–*c.*1386)

Parchment, 275 fols., 253 × 178 mm, text 165 × 104 mm, 24 long lines (20 for the Canon of the Mass) ruled in red or purple ink

SCRIPT: Gothic bookhand (textualis) and Gothic bookhand (hybrida)

BINDING: native-dyed niger morocco over oak boards, by S. Cockerell, 1980s

Fitzwilliam Museum, MS 3–1954

THIS IS THE CENTRAL and the only extensively illustrated portion of an unusually complex Book of Hours with Masses and prayers made for Philip the Bold, Duke of Burgundy (1363–1402). Surviving documents refer to this book as Philip's *Grandes Heures* and provide precious information about the dates of its production. The Parisian scribe Jean L'Avenant, *escrivain du roi*, was responsible for writing both the original portions of the book and an accompanying Book of Prayers that is also extant (Brussels, Bibliothèque royale de Belgique, MS 10392; Dijon and Cleveland 2004–2005, no. 32). The additions and alterations made to it by Philip the Bold in 1390 and by his grandson, Philip the Good, Duke of Burgundy (1419–1467), in the 1450s are also documented and so are the payments for some of the early bindings (de Winter 1982 and 1985; van Buren 2002). These include a record of the rebinding of the manuscript in two volumes for Philip the Good in 1451, which is related to the survival of part of the original *Grandes Heures* in a separate volume in Brussels (Bibliothèque royale de Belgique, MS 11035–37; Dijon and Cleveland 2004, no. 33).

Books of Hours do not normally contain the texts of Masses and extensive series of rarely encountered prayers. The presence of these elements in the *Grandes Heures* of Philip the Bold anchors this book in his own dynastic history. Many of these texts replicate those known to have been included in a Book of Hours (apparently not extant) that was made for Philip's father, Jean le Bon (d.1364). Philip's manuscript also replicates texts and some of the cycles of illustration of the Savoy Hours, a sumptuous book written in the 1330s for Blanche of Burgundy, Countess of Savoy and granddaughter of King Louis IX of France (formerly Turin, Biblioteca Nazionale e Universitaria, MS E.V.49, destroyed by fire in 1904, with parts extant in New Haven, Yale University, Beinecke Library, MS 390). The Savoy Hours belonged subsequently to Philip's older brother, Charles V, who enhanced it with new texts and miniatures, including depictions of him at prayer that have counterparts in the *Grandes Heures*. Finally, texts found in the Savoy Hours, Jean le Bon's Book of Hours and the *Grandes Heures* of Philip the Bold are replicated in two of the earliest Books of Hours made in the 1370s or 1380s for Jean, Duc de Berry, another of Philip the Bold's older brothers and by far the greatest patron of illuminated manuscripts of his day, namely his *Petites Heures* (Paris, Bibliothèque nationale de France, MS lat. 18014) and his *Très Belles Heures de Notre Dame* (major portions in Paris, Bibliothèque nationale de France, MS nouv. acq. lat. 3093, formerly Turin, Biblioteca Nazionale e Universitaria, MS K.IV.29 (burnt in 1904), and Turin, Museo Civico d'Arte Antica, Inv. no. 47; Marrow 1998). The shared contents of these distinctive books establish a chain of connections among manuscripts made for members of the French royal family over a span of nearly seventy years: from a Book of Hours made for a Capetian princess who was a granddaughter of Louis IX, to one made for a Valois king, Jean le Bon, to Books of Hours made for two of Jean le Bon's sons, the Dukes of Berry and Burgundy. This period of six decades was one of significant unrest for the French royal family, marked by challenges to the Valois succession, the Hundred Years' War, and persistent social and economic disruptions that threatened the cohesion and continuity of the realm. If only for these reasons, one can appreciate the special appeal to members of the Valois family of including the same texts in their books of private piety. In so doing, they established a community of devotion among one another as well as continuity between past and present. Philip the Bold's *Grandes Heures* is linked to a group of related Books of Hours made for the Duke's forebears and members of his immediate family, and binding the owners individually and dynastically.

The illustrations of the original part of the manuscript consist of twenty-four small miniatures of the Occupations of the Months and Signs of the Zodiac, eleven large miniatures demarcating major texts or their parts, and a hundred and five small rectangular column miniatures. They are by painters still working in pictorial traditions going back to the activity of the French royal illuminator, Jean Pucelle (act. *c.*1310–*c.*1334), and who are best known for their contributions to other books made for King Charles V. In regard to its picture style as well as well as its texts, therefore, Philip's *Grandes Heures* is closely linked to manuscripts belonging to the traditions of the French royal family. Formerly known by the collective appellation of the 'Masters of the Umbrella Trees' *(Maîtres aux Bouqueteaux)* after the distinctive small trees found in many of their landscapes, these illuminators have been more fully individualized and re-named in recent years. Most of the original illustrations of Philip's *Grandes Heures* are nowadays ascribed to two painters, the Master of the Bible of Jean de Sy and the Master of the Coronation Book of Charles V.

Philip the Good inherited the *Grandes Heures* from his grandfather and eventually found his own way of inscribing himself into the traditions of dynastic affiliation and continuity embodied in Philip the Bold's manuscript. Around 1450 he revised and enlarged it through the addition of prayers written by Jean Miélot, his secretary and frequent translator of devotional works; suffrages of saints venerated especially in the southern Low Countries, such as Adrian, Aldegundis, Eligius, Gertrude and Waldetrude; and a virtual gallery of illuminated and illustrated leaves and cuttings, including one that portrays Philip the Good in prayer as if attending the Mass of St Gregory and others that contain his

emblems. Most of the illustrated additions come from disparate manuscripts by as many as twenty different miniaturists, including illuminators of other manuscripts made for Philip the Good during this period. The Duke's aim may have been to collect a kind of souvenir book or catalogue of works by many leading illuminators of the day. The additions, which also include imprints of religious medals that were subsequently removed from the volume (Köster 1979; Köster 1984), demonstrate the continued importance of this book as a focal point of Burgundian ducal devotion. Philip the Good cherished and used the *Grandes Heures* that he had inherited from his grandfather, the first Duke of Burgundy. In revising and personalizing it, he also invested it with distinctive traces of his own historical memory.

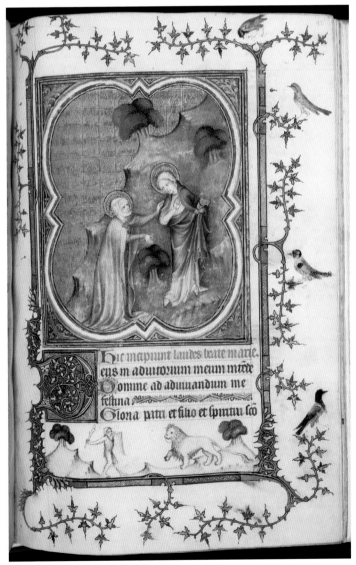

Visitation. Fitzwilliam Museum MS 3-1954, fol. 92

PROVENANCE: Philip the Bold, Duke of Burgundy (1342–1402); Philip the Good, Duke of Burgundy (1396–1467); Mrs W.F. Harvey of Purbrook Heath House, Hampshire, 1867; Viscount Lee of Fareham (1868–1947); his bequest, 1947; presented to the Museum by his widow in 1954.

EXHIBITED: London 1953–1954, no. 570; Cambridge 1966, no. 67; Cambridge 1993, no. 46; Dijon and Cleveland, 2004–2005, no. 34.

LITERATURE: Meiss 1967, 109, 128, 156, 175, 188, figs. 546, 609–608; Harthan 1977, 94–97, 180; Köster 1979; de Winter 1982; Wormald and Giles 1982, 479–99; Köster 1984, 535; de Winter 1985; Robinson 1988, no. 209, pl. 161; Avril, Dunlop and Yapp 1989, 69, 72, 86, 89, 97–98, 207–208, 252, 269, 275, 295, 304, 340, 348; Maddocks 1991, 6; Naughton 1991, 112 n. 10; van Buren 1996, 443, 448, 479, 481–85, 521, 533, 539, 548, 550; Bousmanne 1997, 242–46, figs. on pp. 313–14; Marrow 1998, 2; Smeyers 1999, 297, fig. VI.11; Bousmanne and Van Hoorebeeck 2000, 229–42, 264–72; van Buren 2002; Los Angeles and London 2003–2004, 212–13.

JHM

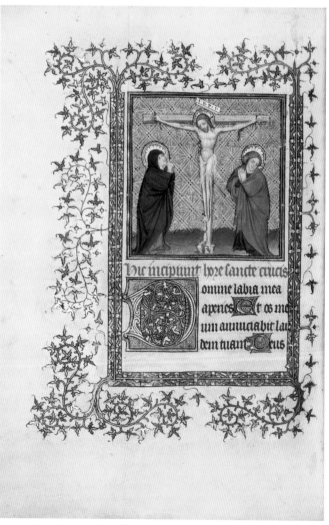

Crucifixion. Fitzwilliam Museum, MS McClean 79, fol. 89v

86

Book of Hours

Use of Rome
In Latin and French
France, Paris, *c*.1405–*c*.1410
ARTIST: Virgil Master (act. *c*.1400–*c*.1420)

Parchment, iii + 148 fols., 235 × 165 mm, text 114 × 74 mm, 14 long lines, ruled in red ink

SCRIPT: Gothic bookhand (textualis)

BINDING: gold-tooled brown leather, by Zaehnsdorf, 19th c.; inside both covers are pasted fragments of the 1561 brown leather binding stamped with biblical scenes

Fitzwilliam Museum, MS McClean 79

THIS IS A RARE EXAMPLE of a Book of Hours made for a brother of the Order of St Anthony of Vienne who is shown kneeling before his patron, St Anthony Abbot, on fol. 144. He wears the black habit with a blue Tau cross common to his Order. The Order was founded to serve hospitals, and its mother house at Vienne possessed the body of St Anthony (Ladner 1973; Mischlewski 1995). They had a house in Paris, and the Paris origins of the artist may suggest that the book was made for a member of that house. The Anthonites followed the Use of Rome, and that is the Use of the Office of the Virgin and Office of the Dead in this manuscript. The Calendar is not Anthonite. It is of a general martyrological type, with a saint on nearly every day, which is commonly found in Parisian fifteenth-century Books of Hours. The rather short Litany possibly suggests the Paris house of the Anthonites, as Denis is the only French saint among the martyrs, and Anthony heads the monks and hermits section of the confessors, which include the French saints Ivo and Louis. Although the Penitential Psalms which precede the Litany are entitled with the rubric *secundum usum curie romane* ('following the use of the Roman Curia') the Litany is not of the Use of Rome.

The text and pictorial contents are normal for a Parisian Book of Hours of the early fifteenth century: Calendar, Readings from the Four Gospels, Hours of the Virgin, Penitential Psalms, Litany, Hours of the Cross, Hours of the Holy Spirit, the two Marian prayers, *Obsecro te* and *O intemerata*, and a *Memoria* to St Anthony. It is unusual to find only one *Memoria* for a saint, but the single text for St Anthony is all the more significant in view of the ownership of the book. The decoration is limited, and several blank pages facing the beginning of texts suggest more images were planned but never executed. There are even blank leaves after the *Memoria* of St Anthony, suggesting that more *Memoriae* might have been intended. The miniatures are accompanied by full decorative borders: Annunciation (Matins of the Virgin, fol. 11), Christ blessing (Penitential Psalms, fol. 71), Crucifixion (Hours of the Cross, fol. 89v), Pentecost (Hours of the Holy Spirit, fol. 95), Requiem Mass (Office of the Dead, fol. 99v), Virgin and Child (*Obsecro te*, fol. 137), and St Anthony with a kneeling Anthonite brother for his *Memoria*. *O intemerata* has an ornamental initial with a full decorative border (fol. 143v). The full decorative borders on these pages have tendrils of gold pink and blue ivy leaves. The miniatures have either small chequer pattern grounds or larger diaper patterns of gold on orange-pink with gold and blue ornament.

These backgrounds, the figure style, the pale grey modelling of the faces, and the colour palette dominated by slate-blue, pale rose-orange, light green, and violet, are features of the Virgil Master who also works on Trinity College MS B.11.31 *(no. 87)*. The Fitzwilliam Hours, however, is an early work before his contact with the Boucicaut workshop, whereas the Trinity Hours is late in the artist's career. The origins of his style seem to come from the circle of Jacquemart de Hesdin and his followers. The miniature of Christ blessing shows him flanked by an altar with chalice and paten (or Host), and a table with the Tablets of the Law, as in the same subject for the Penitential Psalms in *(no. 87)*.

PROVENANCE: Anthonite brother, represented on fol. 144; Anthonite house in Cologne, 16th c.; Sir J.L. Goldsmid; his sale, Puttick and Simpson's, 11 April 1889, lot 376; purchased by Frank McClean (1837–1904); his bequest, 1904.

LITERATURE: James 1912a, 163–64; Meiss 1967, 360; Meiss 1974, 409.   NJM

87

Book of Hours

Use of Paris
In Latin and French
France, Paris, *c*.1410–*c*.1420
ARTISTS: Virgil Master (act. *c*.1400–*c*.1420) and workshop, artists of the 'Bedford trend'
(act. *c*.1410–*c*.1420)

MS B.11.31: Parchment, v (paper) + 129 + iv (paper) fols., 222 × 180 mm, text 116 × 80 mm, 16 or 17 long lines, ruled in pink-red ink

MS B.11.32: Parchment, v (paper) + 104 (continuing numeration from vol. I beginning fol. 130) + ii (paper) fols, 221 × 180 mm., text 114 × 80 mm., 16 long lines, ruled in pink-red ink

SCRIPT: Gothic bookhand (textualis)

BINDING: white vellum, semée fleur-de-lis and arms of Anne of Austria in centre of both covers; MS B.11.31 has *Office de la Vierge* in gold on the spine and MS B.11.32 *Memoir de plus(ieurs) Saints*, 17th c.

Trinity College, MSS B.11.31 and B.11.32

THIS LITTLE-STUDIED, profusely illuminated Book of Hours is the product of two Parisian groups of artists in the second decade of the fifteenth century. The first volume has eighteen miniatures, and the second volume (not discussed by Meiss, 1974) no less than a hundred miniatures. There are more than two artists involved, but two styles are evident: that of the Virgil Master and that of the so-called 'Bedford trend'. The latter was associated with a group of artists, including the Bedford Master himself, who worked *c*.1410–*c*.1420 before the Bedford Master's workshop was established by *c*.1420 in works like the Hours of Isabelle of Brittany, or Lamoignon Hours (Lisbon, Museu Calouste Gulbenkian, MS LA.143) and the *c*.1422 Hours of Charles VII (Vienna, Österreichische Nationalbibliothek, MS 1855). The book is now bound in two volumes, but originally was probably a single manuscript. Folios. 13–54 in MS B.11.31 are by the workshop of the Virgil Master, and the Calendar (fols. 1–12v) and fols. 59v–129 by the 'Bedford trend' artists. The illumination of MS B.11.32 is entirely by the 'Bedford trend' artists. The work in the style of the Virgil Master was by two hands, and there seem to be at least three 'Bedford trend' artists, difficult to distinguish from each other.

The Hours of the Virgin has seven miniatures of the early life of Christ from the Annunciation to the Flight into Egypt for Matins to Vespers, but has the Coronation of the Virgin for Compline (fol. 59v). Then follow the Hours of the Cross with Passion scenes from the Betrayal to the Entombment, and the Office of the Holy Spirit with a miniature of Pentecost (fol. 77). The Penitential Psalms have Christ blessing surrounded by the four Evangelists (fol. 85), and the Office of the Dead has the Requiem Mass (fol. 103). As usual in French Books of Hours of this period the *Memoriae* of the saints are gathered together at the end, now in vol. II. They are exceptionally numerous, starting with the feasts of the Annunciation, Christmas, Circumcision, Good Friday, Easter Sunday and Ascension, and continuing with the more usual series, which begins with the Holy Spirit, the Trinity, and the Virgin Mary, and contains over eighty saints.

This is a late work of the Virgil Master's workshop. Their early work of *c*.1400–*c*.1405 is represented in *no. 86*. In his later period the Virgil Master was influenced by the Boucicaut workshop. His colours are dominated by a blue-grey, pale rose-orange, light green and violet,

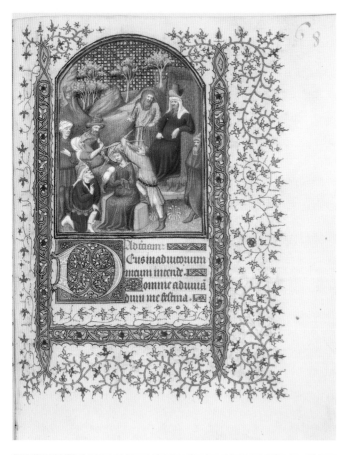

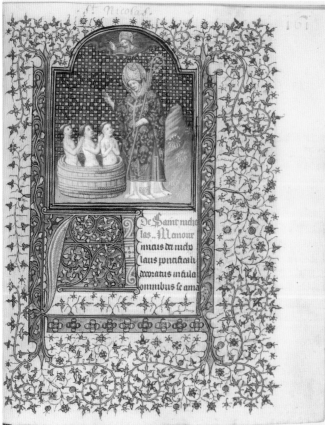

Mocking of Christ. Trinity College, MS B.11.31, fol. 68
St Nicholas baptizing three boys. Trinity College, MS B.11.32, fol. 161

with balanced integration of his figures with their landscape background. The 'Bedford trend' artists used a wider range of brighter colours, and the figures are lively and expressive in pose, gesture and glance. Many artists were involved in the 'Bedford trend' workshop and individual hands remain to be identified.

The *Memoriae* show a choice of saints widely venerated in France, but some are less usual: Ligier (fol. 170), Thibault (fol. 176), Leu (fol. 190), Aubin (fol. 193), Aignan (fol. 194), Genevieve (fol. 214), Juliana (fol. 219), Radegund (fol. 225), Batildis (fol. 231). These do not suggest any particular diocesan Use, not even Paris. The Hours of the Virgin and the Office of the Dead are of the Use of Paris. The Calendar is martyrological with a saint on almost every day. It resembles Calendars found in printed books of the Use of Paris, but these are variable and are not reliable for localizing a place of production or destination.

PROVENANCE: Anne of Austria (1601–1666), wife of Louis XIII of France and mother of Louis XIV; given by A. Vansittart, fellow of the College, in 1861.

LITERATURE: James 1900–1904, I, 379–87 and IV, pl. XVII; Meiss 1968, 142; Meiss 1974, 366, 409.

NJM

88

Book of Hours (Hours of Isabella Stuart)

Use of Paris
In Latin and French
Northern France, probably Angers, *c*.1431
ARTISTS: Masters of the Grandes Heures de Rohan (act. *c*.1410–1440)

Parchment, ii + 232 + i fols., 248–251 × 184 mm, text 118–120 × 75 mm, 15 long lines ruled in red ink

SCRIPT: Gothic bookhand (textualis)

BINDING: calf over pasteboard, gold-stamped corner pieces and central oval with the Crucifixion, 17th c.

Fitzwilliam Museum, MS 62

THIS IMPOSING BOOK OF HOURS – certainly one of the best known and the most extensively illuminated examples of the genre in Cambridge – was illustrated by the Rohan Masters, distinctive painters thought to have been active in Troyes, Paris and Angers from *c*.1410–1440. They take their name from a sumptuously illuminated Book of Hours known as the *Grandes Heures de Rohan* because of the added coats of arms of an unidentified member of the Rohan family (Paris, Bibliothèque nationale de France, MS lat. 9471). The style of these painters is characterized by decorative richness and complexity, crowded compositions, bright and intense colour contrasts, highly patterned surfaces, and sometimes incongruously deployed perspective and figural proportions. Their painting style lends itself to narrative profusion, dramatic expression, and the evocation of the supernatural. Their penchant for narrative elaboration and complexity can be seen in the subsidiary figures and scenes depicted in the backgrounds and the architectural superstructures of some of their miniatures, and especially in marginal illustrations that either complement the larger miniatures they accompany or belong to independent cycles of illustration.

Every page of this manuscript is decorated and illustrated. In addition to the twenty-four large miniatures that demarcate text divisions, there is an unusually extensive complement of marginal illustrations, making for a full pictorial programme of five hundred and twenty-eight miniatures. Among its most novel features are the four cycles of marginal miniatures illustrating the visionary narratives of the Apocalypse of St John and the fourteenth-century French poems of the 'Three Pilgrimages' of Guillaume de Deguilleville. The four series of marginal illustrations cut across the texts of the Book of Hours, grafting secondary layers of meaning on to the traditional contents of this type of book. Unlike the few analogous picture cycles in other *Horae* of the period, including the *Grandes Heures de Rohan*, the marginal cycles here are unaccompanied by explanatory captions. Either the owner of the manuscript was familiar enough with the contents of the Apocalypse and the 'Three Pilgrimages' to follow the picture stories on her own, or, one imagines, the book was intended to be used with a learned advisor, such as a confessor or another teacher, who would have expounded their meaning.

The four visionary marginal cycles are related to the portions of the manuscript they accompany. The cycle of the *Pilgrimage of Jesus Christ* comes first, accompanying the Gospel Sequences, which treat the life of Christ from the Incarnation to the Resurrection, and the Prayers to Mary that celebrate her part in the scheme of Redemption. The cycle of the Apocalypse accompanies the Hours of the Virgin, echoing exegetical interpretations of the Apocalyptic Woman as Mary and adding an eschatological dimension to the review of salvation history traced in its primary picture cycle, which culminates in a large miniature of the Coronation of the Virgin in Heaven. The images from the *Pilgrimage of Human Life* accompany the Seven Penitential Psalms and Litany, the Short Hours of the Cross and the Holy Spirit, and the Passion according to St John. The *Pilgrimage of*

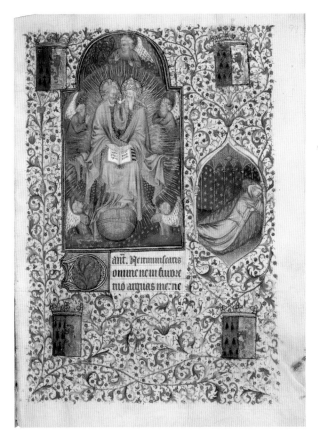

Trinity adored by Angels. Fitzwilliam Museum, MS 62, fol. 99

the Soul fittingly accompanies the Office of the Dead. As has recently been observed, these marginal cycles depart from the textual narratives and the conventional pictorial traditions of their sources: they were excerpted and reordered 'to create a coherent visual narrative, staged by paired images, articulated by repeated motifs and visual echoes, and unified by an overarching theme' so as 'to provide a visual deep structure connecting disparate elements of the Isabella Hours' (Emmerson 2004).

Some of the miniatures found in this and other of the most elaborately illustrated manuscripts ascribed to the 'Rohan Master' are more monumental in conception and more refined in finish than the majority of the illustrations in the same books. Examples in Fitzwilliam MS 62 include the large miniatures of the Apocalyptic Madonna and Child with Saints Peter and Paul (fol. 136v), the Virgin and Child in a Gothic Building (fol. 141v), and the Man of Sorrows (fol. 199). Some manuscripts in the less monumental and less polished styles seem to pre-date those of the so-called 'Rohan Master'. These stylistic discrepancies may not reflect the participation of a master, who would have established the shop where these works were made and supervised the design of all the books, and of his assistants, as has usually been assumed. They could point instead to the activity of a family of painters, one of whose younger members, presumably active predominantly as a monumental painter, would have contributed the highly polished miniatures (Paris 2004b, 371).

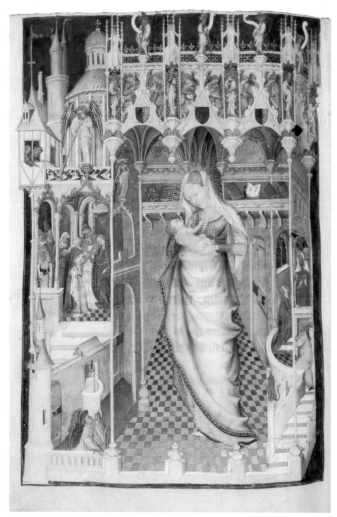

Virgin and Child with subsidiary scenes from the Life of the Virgin. Fitzwilliam Museum, MS 62, fol. 141v

In this book, as in other manuscripts by the Rohan Masters, miniatures of differing degrees of refinement echo works by other leading illuminators of the period. Noteworthy examples in Fitzwilliam MS 62 include the miniature of the Annunciation, which has close compositional counterparts in manuscripts by or from the circle of the Boucicaut Master (Meiss 1974, 263), and also the full-page miniature of the Virgin and Child in a Gothic Building – the largest and most intricate illustration in the book – which reflects prototypes associated with the Limbourg Brothers (Meiss 1974, 265).

This manuscript is known as the 'Hours of Isabella Stuart' from the coats of arms added in the borders of many of the large miniatures and over-painted on the garment of the donor's figure kneeling before the Virgin and Child (fol. 20). Isabella, daughter of James I of Scotland, was not the original owner of the manuscript. The clumsily added arms are those she bore after her marriage in 1442 to Francis I, Duke of Brittany. The manuscript was most probably made for Yolande d'Anjou, first wife of Francis I, possibly at the time of their marriage in 1431, or for her mother, Yolanda of Aragon, Queen of Sicily and wife of Louis II of Anjou. Yolanda of Aragon owned some manuscripts used as models by the Rohan Masters and may well have commissioned works from them, including the *Grandes Heures de Rohan* and the Hours that belonged to her son, René d'Anjou (Paris, Bibliothèque nationale de France, MS lat. 1156A).

PROVENANCE: made for the young woman portrayed kneeling before the Virgin and Child on fol. 20, possibly Yolande d'Anjou (d.1440) or her mother, Yolanda of Aragon; Isabella Stuart, daughter of James I of Scotland (d.after 1495); Isambert family of Paris, whose family register from 1578–1619 is on fols. 231v–233; acquired by Viscount Fitzwilliam in 1808; his bequest, 1816.

EXHIBITED: Cambridge 1966, no. 68.

LITERATURE: Searle 1876, 35–37, no. 21; James 1895a, 156–74; Fry 1905; Durrieu 1912a, 16, 20, 21; Durrieu 1912b, 85, 87, 92–93, 167–70, 177, fig. 14; James 1931, 17, 72, no. 75; Heimann 1932, 5–12, 16, 22, 24, 58, 60, figs. 6–9; Toynbee 1946, 303–304, pls. C, D; Ring 1949, 203–204; Porcher 1959, 5, 11; Meiss 1963, 152–53, fig. 4; Pächt 1963, 135, fig. 2; Meiss and Thomas, 1973, 14, 15, 25, 26, 27, 246; Meiss 1974, 263–66, 306–307, figs. 857, 862, 863, 865–67; Harthan 1977, 114–117; Büttner 1983, 10, 127 n. 196, 146 n. 54, 167, 210, fig. 190; Camille 1985c, 227–46; Emmerson and Lewis 1986, 468, no. 168; Naughton 1991, 113–15, pl.3; Paris 1993, 26; Emmerson 2004; Legaré 2004, 175, figs. 4–5; Paris 2004b, 316, 371.

JHM

89

Book of Hours

Use of Coutances
In Latin and French
France, Normandy, probably Rouen, *c*.1440–*c*.1445
ARTIST: Fastolf Master (act. *c*.1415–*c*.1450) and assistant

Parchment, ii (paper) + i + 179 + ii (paper) fols., 210 × 154 mm, text 102 × 68 mm, 15 long lines, ruled in brown ink

SCRIPT: Gothic bookhand (textualis)

BINDING: brown leather, 20th c.

St John's College, MS N. 24 (James no. 264)

THE LITURGICAL USE of this Book of Hours, in its Hours of the Virgin and Litany, is that of the diocese of Coutances in Normandy. The Feast of the Relics of Coutances is recorded in the Calendar on the 30th of September and on the 21st of September Laudus

(Lô), the principal patron of the diocese, is entered in gold. Laudus is also among the confessors in the Litany. Although its first recorded owner is Lady Margaret Beaufort, foundress of St John's College, she is unlikely to have been the original patron. The manuscript may have been acquired by her father, John, Duke of Somerset (d. 1444), when he was in Normandy as captain-general of the English army in 1443.

There are miniatures before each of the main sections of the text, but some pages have been removed. The readings from each of the Gospels have the Evangelists writing: John (fol. 13), Luke (fol. 14), Matthew (fol. 15v), and Mark (fol. 17v). The Hours of the Virgin received a cycle of the Early Life of Christ: Annunciation (Matins, fol. 28), Nativity (Prime, fol. 51), Adoration of the Magi (Sext, fol. 62), Presentation in the Temple (None, fol. 66). Then follow David kneeling before God (Penitential Psalms, fol. 88), Death as a corpse threatens a young man (Office of the Dead, Vespers, fol. 120), Requiem Mass (Office of the Dead, Matins, fol. 128), and the Last Judgement (Prayer of the Seven Requests to Our Lord, fol. 175). The last text, common in French fifteenth-century Books of Hours, is a prayer to Christ on the Cross, and is frequently accompanied by a miniature of the Last Judgement. As in many French fifteenth-century Hours (e.g. no. 87) the *Memoriae* of the saints are not placed in their liturgical position at Lauds, but at the end of the book: St John the Baptist (fol. 166) and St George (fol. 168). The pages with miniatures have full borders and those with illuminated initials for the sections of the text or for special prayers, such as *Obsecro te* (fol. 18v) and *O intemerata* (fol. 23), have partial borders. These borders have black tendrils terminating in gold ivy leaves and other leaf types, interspersed with acanthus leaves, flowers and fruit. This ornament is typical of the Fastolf Master's work in Rouen such as in Hours of the Use of Rouen (New York, Pierpont Morgan Library, M. 27).

The decoration is by two artists. Most of it is by an artist very close to the Fastolf Master, if not the Master himself (fols. 13, 14, 15v, 17v, 51, 62, 66, 88, 128, 175). He worked in Rouen from c.1420–c.1445 and in the final stages of his life in England. He is named after a manuscript he made for Sir John Fastolf (1378–1459), a copy of the *Epitre d'Othéa* (Oxford, Bodleian Library, MS Laud misc. 570). He was probably trained in Paris c.1415– c.1420 in the workshops of the Boucicaut and Bedford Masters. Another Book of Hours he illuminated for the Use of Coutances is Paris, Bibliothèque de l'Arsenal, MS 560. His work is characterized by bright colours, strongly delineated outlines, modelled faces, angular modelled draperies and stylized landscapes, often with golden stars in the skies. The second artist (fols. 28, 120, 166, 168) may have come out of his

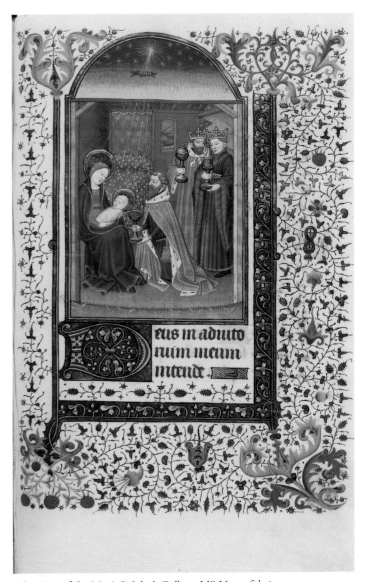

Adoration of the Magi. St John's College, MS N. 24, fol. 61

workshop but used softer colours and although his figures are precisely defined, their outlines are not so sharp as in the work of the Fastolf Master.

PROVENANCE: Lady Margaret Beaufort, Countess of Richmond and Derby (1443–1509); on fol. 12v, in Lady Margaret Beaufort's own handwriting, is recorded the gift of the book to Lady Shirley, *i.e.* Anne, perhaps when she married Sir Ralph Shirley in 1502 (formerly considered to be the wife of Richard Shirley, Lady Margaret's bailiff); Francis Belo (Beale?), 17th c.; Fountaine family of Narford Hall, Norfolk, who sold it in 1895 to Alexander Peckover, Lord Peckover of Wisbech (1830–1919); given by him to the College in 1902.

LITERATURE: Scott 1911, pl. XIV; James 1913, 311–13; Alexander 1971, 249; New York 1982, 15, no. 21; Harris 1983, 300; Jones and Underwood 1992, 160, 284, pl. 7; Powell 1998, 203; Wüstefeld 2003, 243.   NJM

90

Book of Hours

Use of Paris
In Latin and French
France, Paris, *c.*1440 – *c.*1450

Parchment, ii + 205 + ii fols., 196 × 140 mm, text 92 × 60 mm,
13 lines, ruled in red ink

SCRIPT: Gothic bookhand (textualis)

BINDING: gold-tooled brown morocco, lozenge-shaped
compartments containing two C's interlaced (supposed by
former owners to be the device of Charles II), 17th c.

Fitzwilliam Museum, McClean MS 81

THE THIRTEEN HALF-PAGE MINIATURES of this handsome Book of Hours are by two associates of the
Bedford Master, who was among the most prominent

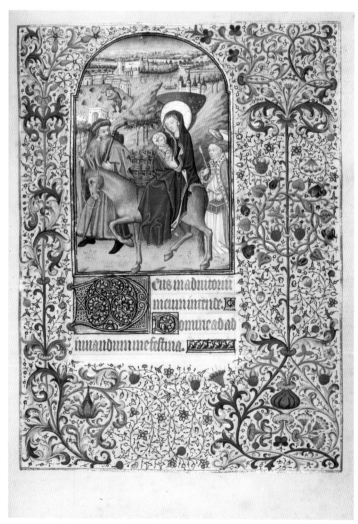

The Flight into Egypt. Fitzwilliam Museum, McClean MS 81, fol. 77

illuminators working in Paris during the first and second
quarters of the fifteenth century. Active from *c.*1410 into
at least the 1430s, the Bedford Master derives his name
from two sumptuous and copiously illustrated manuscripts, a Book of Hours (London, British Library, Add.
MS 18850) and a Breviary of Sarum Use known as the
Salisbury Breviary or the Breviary of John, Duke of
Bedford (Paris, Bibliothèque nationale de France, MS
lat. 17294). They were produced in Paris for John of
Lancaster, Duke of Bedford, brother of Henry V and
regent in Paris during the English occupation following
the victory at Agincourt. Both manuscripts, like others
attributed to the Bedford Master, are characterized by
the decorative richness of their miniatures, their bright
and colourful palette, and their complex and lively
narrative style. The two miniaturists who collaborated
in McClean MS 81 also contributed scores of illustrations – primarily small rectangular marginal vignettes –
to the Salisbury Breviary thought to have been produced
for John, Duke of Bedford, but completed only after his
death in 1435. The more incisive painter of
the two, whose miniatures are more spatially
developed and whose forms are more precise
and finely modelled, has been identified as the
painter of the St Stephen page of the Salisbury Breviary (Paris 1993, 24; Reynolds
2005); he contributed five miniatures to the
present book (fols. 44v, 56v, 72v, 77r, and
84v). The other painter, responsible for eight
miniatures including all those commencing
major texts in the manuscript (fols. 19r, 63r,
68r, 91, 111, 118, 124, 186), paints more
broadly and employs more crowded compositions of greater decorative richness, the
majority dominated by larger figures portrayed closer to the picture plane. His style is
reminiscent of that found in the marginal
illustrations of gatherings alternating with
those by the St Stephen Master in the latter
parts of the Salisbury Breviary (*e.g.* fols. 508–
515), and recalls that of works attributed to the
'Chief Associate of the Bedford Master', now
re-named the Dunois Master (Paris 1993,
36–37).

Several of the miniatures derive from
compositional prototypes by leading Parisian
illuminators of the first quarter of the century.
The figures of the Virgin holding the swaddled Child and the angel who carries a small
casket and holds a sceptre in the Flight into
Egypt echo analogous figures (in reverse
orientation) in the Boucicaut Hours (Paris,
Musée Jacquemart-André, MS 2, fol. 90v),
and elements of the miniatures of the

Nativity, the Presentation in the Temple and the Coronation of the Virgin reflect compositions found in the celebrated *Très Riches Heures* of Jean de Berry (Chantilly, Musée Condé, MS 65, fols. 44v, 54v, and 60v, respectively), the masterpiece of the Limbourg Brothers. There are also traces of the influence of decidedly newer artistic currents: the panoramic views of distant riverscapes with their suggestions of reflective water and distant horizons in the backgrounds of the miniatures of the Visitation, the Nativity and the Flight into Egypt echo details of the background of Jan van Eyck's *Rolin Madonna* (Paris, Musée du Louvre), painted in the 1430s for the chapel at Autun of Nicholas Rolin, Chancellor of Burgundy under Philip the Good (van Buren 1999).

The manuscript has some features that distinguish it from the large body of works from the entourage of the Bedford Master. The border decoration is finer and more restrained than that found in most manuscripts in this style. Miniature leaves have fine networks of ink sprays and understated foliage, and all text leaves are decorated with delicate networks of gold ivy leaves. The decorative palette is also unusual in that all the painted initials after the first two gatherings are executed in blue with white tracery on gold grounds, rather than in alternating blue and red as is typical in most works. This uncommon decorative scheme lends the book an unusually harmonious and refined feel. The decorated borders on miniature pages are framed with thin gold fillets, as in some other manuscripts in similar styles, but five of the miniature leaves also have elegantly looped corner pieces that we have not yet encountered in related works.

Although the manuscript lacks signs of personalization in either its contents or its decoration, it is missing a single leaf commencing the French prayers to the Virgin that presumably had a half-page miniature of the Virgin and Child and that might also have contained a donor portrait or other evidence of its original ownership. Despite its relatively modest size and number of miniatures, it seems sufficiently refined to have been produced on commission.

PROVENANCE: Samuel Rogers; his sale, Christie's, London, 28 April 1856, lot 1015; purchased by William Goldsmid; André B. Knox; sale at Sotheby's, London, 12 August 1872, lot 253; Alexander Bain; sale at Sotheby's, London, 1 July 1901, lot 1086; Frank McClean; his bequest, 1904.

LITERATURE: James 1912a, 167–68; Paris 1993, 24; Comblen-Sonkes and Lorentz 1995, 55, no. 19; van Buren 1999, 158, fig. 5; Reynolds 2005.

JHM

91

Book of Hours

Use of Utrecht (compilation and translation of Geert Grote)
In Dutch (a few rubricated *incipits* in Latin)
Northern Netherlands, Utrecht, *c.*1430
ARTISTS: Masters of Zweder van Culemborg (act. *c.*1415–1445)

Parchment, ii (original, frame-ruled leaves) + 237 (fols. 1–235 [236–237 unnumbered]) fols., 161–164 × 122 mm, text 84 × 53 mm, 15 lines, ruled in purple ink

SCRIPT: Gothic bookhand (textualis)

BINDING: blind-tooled reddish-brown calf over boards, two brass clasps and catchplates on leather hinges, 15th c.

Fitzwilliam Museum, MS 141

THE TWENTY-FOUR large historiated initials that illustrate this manuscript are all in the style of the Masters of Zweder van Culemborg, the leading illuminators in Utrecht from *c.*1415 to 1445. The miniatures display the new interest in pictorial naturalism introduced into Dutch illumination by these painters, evident in their concern to depict interior scenes in habitable settings and to portray many exterior scenes in detailed and panoramic landscapes set beneath atmospherically luminous skies. The naturalistic spatial and lucent effects cultivated by the Zweder Masters are achieved not only through compositional and colouristic means, but also through a new subtlety of modelling. Forms are built up from minuscule dabs of paint, overlaid to create an illusion of materiality in textured surfaces and simulating the appearance of objects in light. The painters also use metallic gold and silver to suggest the reflective qualities of some costumes and details of furnishings, silver particularly for windows and gold to decorate the somewhat old-fashioned ornamental backgrounds found here in six of the miniatures. The painters add visual interest and suggest pictorial depth in many of their landscapes by depicting very small animals in the countryside and portraying the towers of distant cityscapes jutting up from behind hills at the horizon. They animate some pictorial narratives by using subtle gestures and directed gazes among the protagonists or by introducing domestic elements, such as the portrayal of Joseph warming a cloth for the Christ Child by a fire in the foreground of the Nativity.

The cycle of illustration of the Hours of the Virgin is unusual in its scope and in elements of its subject matter: it forgoes an illustration at Lauds and includes illustrations of two subjects in temple settings, a Circumcision,

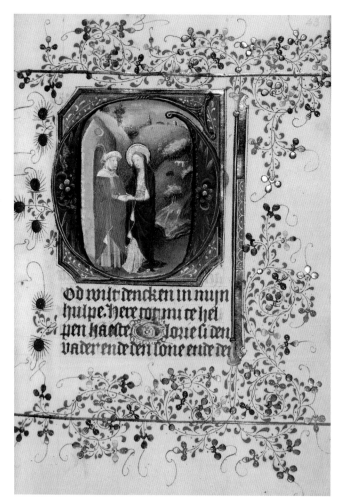

Visitation. Fitzwilliam Museum, MS 141, fol. 43

at None, where Christ is presented by Mary to a priest in a manner similar to that found in portrayals of the Presentation in the Temple (only a knife on the table top alludes to the Circumcision), and a Presentation in the Temple at Compline.

The manuscript is one of only four known Dutch *Horae* containing an exceedingly rare version of Short Offices for the Days of the Week (fols. 82–149v), and it is the earliest of this group. Four of its elements are familiar from other versions of the Offices of the Days of the Week (i.e., the Sunday Hours of the Trinity, Thursday Hours of the Sacrament, Friday Hours of the Passion, and Saturday Hours of the Virgin – the last lacking its first page before fol. 142, which was excised and presumably contained a historiated initial); the texts that distinguish this small group are the Monday Hours of All Souls, the Tuesday Hours of the Baptism and the Wednesday Hours of the Betrayal. The miniature illustrating the Monday Hours of All Souls is unusual in its iconography: it portrays three nude figures being dragged into a hell-mouth by three devils, one of whom dramatically pours blood on one of the figures.

The patrons of other works by the Masters of Zweder van Culemborg include members of many of the leading families of the Northern Netherlands, both in

Utrecht and in Guelders. The original owner of the present manuscript is unfortunately not identified; she is the women dressed in black portrayed at prayer in the margin adjacent to the miniature of the Annunciation (fol. 14) and probably also together with a praying man in the miniature of the Adoration of the Host (fol. 162v). One or more later owners apparently asked friends to autograph the book, for there are inscriptions of different names, mottoes or emblems on fols. 48v, 151v, 157, 157v, 160 and 161.

PROVENANCE: made for the unidentified woman portrayed at prayer in the margin of fol. 14 and possibly also with a praying man in the miniature on fol. 162v; Viscount Fitzwilliam (1810); his bequest (1816).

EXHIBITED: Cambridge 1966, no. 81; Cambridge 1988–1989, no. 91.

LITERATURE: Searle 1876, 130–31, no. 110; James 1895a, 323–25; Byvanck and Hoogewerff 1922–1926, no. 38, pls. 127–28; Byvanck 1923b, 78; de Wit 1926, 123, 124; de Wit 1927, 71–72, 100; de Wit 1929b, 276, fig. 2; Byvanck 1930, 130; Hoogewerff 1936, 439–40, figs. 226–27; Byvanck 1937, 57, 128, figs. 128–29; Delaissé 1968, 20, fig. 14.

JHM

92

Book of Hours

Use of Utrecht (compilation and translation
of Geert Grote)
In Dutch
Eastern Netherlands, probably Zwolle, *c.*1470
ARTISTS: Masters of the Zwolle Bible (act. *c.*1460 –
*c.*1480)

Parchment, ii + 210 fols. (ff. 1, 3–211), 182 × 133 mm, text
92–95 × 66 mm, 18 lines, ruled in brown ink

SCRIPT: Gothic bookhand (textualis)

BINDING: contemporary blind-tooled brown calf over wooden
boards, sewn on five sewing supports, two silver-gilt modern
clasps fitted with chain lockers

Cambridge University Library, MS Add. 4103

THIS MANUSCRIPT is among the finest localized to Zwolle, in the eastern Netherlands, from the third quarter of the fifteenth century. The painter of the miniatures and border decoration is one of the 'Masters of the Zwolle Bible', so-named because of their contributions to a monumental, six-volume Bible from the collegiate church at Utrecht that was written between

1464 and 1476 at the community of the Brethren of the Common Life, the *Domus Fratrum seu Clericorum*, at Zwolle (Utrecht, Universiteitsbibliotheek, MS 31). More than sixty other manuscripts survive, predominantly Books of Hours, that are executed in related styles and that echo some of the compositional types found in the Cambridge Hours. Most of the related works are Books of Hours produced apparently for the open market, rather than on commission. Known collectively as the 'Sarijs manuscripts' after a scribal error that appears in many of the Calendars of the group ('Sarijs' written incorrectly in place of 'Marijs' on 19 January, including the present manuscript), they may have been written by students of the Brethren of the Common Life at Zwolle (Wierda 1995). The Cambridge Hours, in contrast, must have been specially commissioned, for it includes a text of the Mass of the Virgin that occurs in only one other *Horae* belonging to the group; its cycle of illustration is more extensive and complex than those found in most of the other 'Sarijs' Hours; its miniatures are spatially more complex and atmospheric, and its border decora-

tion more precise and refined than in other works of the group. Considering the high quality of its script, decoration and illustration, this manuscript as well as a few others most closely related stylistically to the Zwolle Bible (Utrecht/New York 1989–1990, nos. 86, 88 [inserted miniatures only]) may have been illuminated by secular craftsmen rather than by members of the Zwolle Brethren as has been suggested.

The subjects and compositions of many of the miniatures are unique among works of the 'Sarijs group' and rare also in the wider tradition of Dutch illumination. Many compositions derive in whole or part from works in other media. Woodcuts from the block book editions of the *Biblia Pauperum* and the *Speculum Humanae Salvationis* inspired the marginal illustrations of Old Testament prefigurations that accompany miniatures of the Annunciation and the Crucifixion. Other miniatures that depend in part or whole on woodcuts or engravings include: the figure of Jesse in the Tree of Jesse (block book of the *Speculum Humanae Salvationis*); the Expulsion of the Money Changers (Israhel van Meckenem),

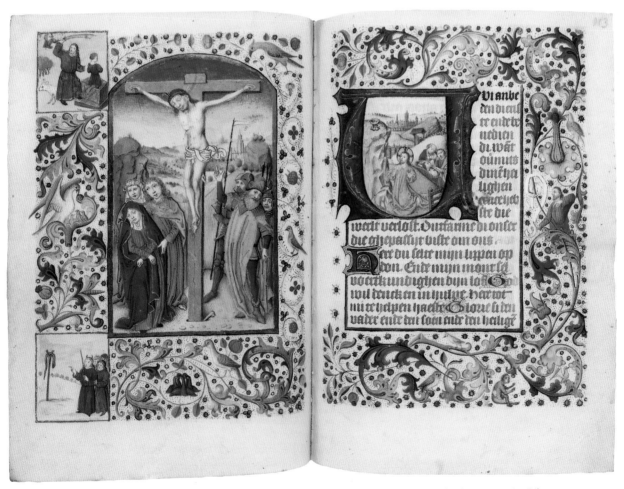

Crucifixion with Old Testament prefigurations and Christ in the Garden of Gethsemane. Cambridge University Library, MS Add. 4103, fols. 112v–113

a very rare subject at Matins of the Eternal Wisdom; the Sacrifice of Elias on Mount Carmel and the Crucifixion (block book of the *Biblia Pauperum*); the Agony in the Garden of Gethsemane and the Arrest of Christ (Master E.S.); the Mass of St Gregory (Master IAM of Zwolle); and the vaulted settings of the Trinity and Pentecost (Master W with the Key). There are also echoes of works of early Netherlandish painting: the figural composition of the Trinity goes back to a model ascribed frequently to the Master of Flémalle, and the miniature of the Annunciation recalls aspects of the setting of Jan van Eyck's *Madonna in a Church* (Berlin, albeit in reversed orientation), and of his figures of Gabriel and Mary in the *Ghent Altarpiece*. The considerable dependence on models from other media in this manuscript can be attributed to a presumed lack of a highly developed prior tradition of manuscript illumination in Zwolle and to the high esteem in which some of these exemplars were held in the Lowlands.

PROVENANCE: 'Marie Cornelisdochter, [15]70' (ownership inscription inside upper cover); Col. Everett, M.F.H., of Warminster; his (anonymous) sale at Christie's, London, 22 January 1884, lot 161; purchased by Samuel Sandars (1837–1894); his bequest, 1894.

EXHIBITED: Utrecht and New York 1989–1990, no. 85.

LITERATURE: Jenni and Thoss 1982, 119, fig. 95; Marrow 1991, 61, fig. 42; van der Hoek 1991, 280; Wierda 1995, 202 (index); Obbema 1997, 28; Marrow 2003, 317, fig. 421; Hermans 2004, 36, fig. 17.

JHM

93

Life of Christ (the 'Pseudo-Bonaventura-Ludolfiaanse Leven van Jesus')

In Dutch
Northern Netherlands, Delft, *c.*1470–*c.*1480
ARTIST: Master of Beatrijs van Assendelft's Leven van Jesus

Parchment, iii + 195 fols., 268 × 190 mm, text 172 × 117 mm, 2 columns, 30 lines, ruled in brown ink

SCRIPT: Gothic bookhand (textualis)

BINDING: contemporary brown calf over wooden boards, blind-stamped with diaper patterned rectangle and roundels enclosing the *Agnus Dei*.

Fitzwilliam Museum, MS 25

THE TEXT of this manuscript is a compilation of two of the most extensive and important Latin lives of Christ from the late Middle Ages, Pseudo-Bonaventura's *Meditationes vitae Christi* and Ludolph of Saxony's *Vita Jesu Christi*. Produced probably during the late fourteenth century by an unknown Carthusian active in the Rhineland, the compilation offered pious readers a relatively concise account of the Life and Passion of Christ for devout meditation. The Latin text was translated into Middle Dutch by the turn of the fifteenth century and enjoyed considerable success, especially in circles of the religious reform movement known as the *Devotio Moderna* (Modern Devotion). In addition to the 44 extant manuscript copies of the Middle Dutch translation, the text was printed at Delft in 1479 and it also circulated in Low German, Ripuarian (Cologne dialect) and Franconian dialects.

Intended for private meditation by lay as well as monastic readers, the *Pseudo-Bonaventura-Ludolfiaanse Leven van Jesus* owes its popularity to the emphasis upon Christo-centric devotion that was a hallmark of the *Devotio Moderna* and to the widespread use of the vernacular in its circles. Only two copies are illustrated: this one and another in Wolfenbüttel (Herzog August Bibliothek, Cod. Guelf. 46.2 Aug.4°). Both were written in Delft in the last quarter of the fifteenth century, as is shown by the distinctive pen-flourish decoration on text pages in the volumes. But the Cambridge and Wolfenbüttel copies contain different redactions of the text (Cambridge, for example, begins with the translator's prologue, which is lacking in Wolfenbüttel) and they differ also in the number, placement, subjects and compositions of the illustrations as well as in their miniature styles.

The thirty full-page miniatures in the Cambridge manuscript – all on the versos of inserted single leaves with blank rectos – are by a painter named after this book as the 'Master of Beatrijs van Assendelft's Leven van Jesus'. He is the most skilled of the so-called 'Masters of the Delft Half-Length Figures' who were active in Delft from *c.*1450–1480 and are named after the half-length figures of angels, prophets and saints in the margins of their miniature pages. Another characteristic feature of many manuscripts in this group are elaborate architectural canopies above the miniatures, which invest them with qualities of monumentality and ecclesiastical reference. The miniatures in the present book stand out from all others in the style because of their large size, the monumentality of their figures, the crispness of their modelling and the richness of their colouration. The full-page miniatures are accompanied by half-length figures of saints or other haloed figures in the lower margin, prophets or angels emerging in half-length from flowers in the centre of the left margin, and birds or grotesque figures in three corners of the margins. The

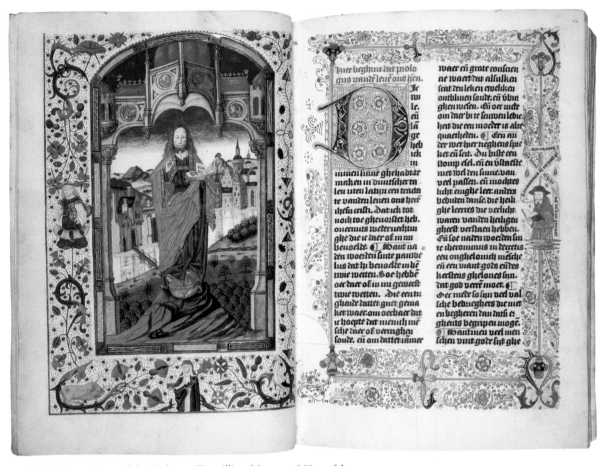

God the Father and text of the Prologue. Fitzwilliam Museum, MS 25, fols. 3v–4

facing text pages are richly decorated with dense red and blue pen-flourishes and incorporate small depictions of animals, angels, saints or other religious figures in the centre of the right margin, some of them accompanied by scrolls inscribed in blue ink with pious legends or sayings in Dutch. The miniature of Pentecost derives from an engraving of the same subject by the Master E.S. (Lehrs 35); the remaining miniatures of the cycle appear to be largely original compositions by the painter. These include some rare subjects, such as a depiction best known from French mystery plays and art as the *Procès de Paradis,* in which female personifications of Mercy, Peace, Truth and Justice kneel in prayer to beseech God the Father to redeem mankind (fol. 13v); the depiction appears to be unique in Dutch illumination and to differ compositionally from those current in neighboring artistic traditions.

Notes on the flyleaves state that the manuscript belonged to Beatrijs van Assendelft and that she donated it to the convent of Ter Zijl in Haarlem. Four illustrated manuscripts survive that were made for Beatrijs, her parents and other members of her family, all apparently produced in Delft (Wüstefeld 1992). Beatrijs was a nun

in The Hague prior to entering the convent of Regular Canonesses of Ter Zijl in 1485, and the Cambridge *Leven van Jesus* probably dates from the time she was resident at The Hague. Beatrijs also owned a sumptuously illustrated Breviary dating from the period of her residence at Ter Zijl (Utrecht, Museum Het Catharijneconvent, MS OKM h 3).

PROVENANCE: Beatrijs van Assendelft who donated it to the convent of Regular Canonesses of Ter Zijl in Haarlem, which she entered in 1485; Marytghen Jans of Haarlem, bequeathed to an unidentified owner in 1635; Viscount Fitzwilliam (1813); his bequest (1816).

EXHIBITED: Cambridge 1966, no. 115; Cambridge 1988–1989, no. 85

LITERATURE: Searle 1876, 131–32, no. 112; James 1895a, 60–65; Priebsch 1896, 34–6; Byvanck 1923a, 200; Byvanck and Hoogewerff 1922–1926, 56, no. 128, pls. 133–135, figs. 92–93; de Vreese 1931, xxvii–xxix, 171, frontispiece; Byvanck 1937, 102, 127, fig. 132; Hoogewerff 1937, 338–339, figs. 163–164; Byvanck 1943, 70–71, fig. 62; de Bruin 1980, xix; Biemans 1984, 300 (cited as MS 6 G 8); Pächt 1987,187–188, fig. 8; Utrecht and New York, 1989–1990, 196, 204, 274; Pächt and Thoss 1990, text vol., 111, fig. 119; Wüstefeld 1992, 9, 28–31.   JHM

94

Book of Hours

Use of Sarum
In Latin
Flanders, Bruges, *c.*1460–1470

Parchment, iv + 186 + iv fols., 235 × 173 mm, text
135 × 85 mm, 20 long lines, ruled in red ink

SCRIPT: Gothic bookhand (textualis)

BINDING: gold-tooled brown morocco, traces of two ties on
fore edge, gilt edges, 17th c., rebacked.

Fitzwilliam Museum, MS 53

THIS IS A CLASSIC and imposing example of what
can be characterized as an 'Anglo-Flemish Book of
Hours', that is, a manuscript produced in Flanders for
use in England. Although manuscripts were made in
Flanders for the English market virtually throughout the
fifteenth century, the great majority of the Books of
Hours produced for this market are humdrum examples,

rarely distinguished in their contents, cycles of illustration, or artistic quality. Fitzwilliam MS 53 is profusely
decorated and illustrated in styles that point unmistak-
ably to Flanders. A number of the miniatures have red
backgrounds decorated with foliate designs in liquid
gold, which recall works in one of the most popular
styles current in Bruges and other centres in Flanders
from *c.*1415–1450, namely those ascribed to the so-
called Masters of the Gold Scrolls. The miniatures are
by one or more painters working in colourful and linear
styles derived from that of Willem Vrelant, one of the
leading illuminators in Bruges during the third quarter
of the fifteenth century.

MS 53 belongs to a distinct sub-group of Anglo-
Flemish *Horae* illustrated with Vrelantesque miniatures.
The three books of this group known to us are larger in
size than most of the *Horae* produced in the Low
Countries for English patrons and also contain unusually extensive and complex picture cycles (Marrow
2002). The other two manuscripts are a Book of Hours
in Rio de Janeiro (Biblioteca Nacional, MS 50.1.1) and
the Pembroke Psalter-Hours (Philadelphia Museum of
Art, Acc. no. 45-65-2). In addition to having similar
border decoration and stylistically related miniatures

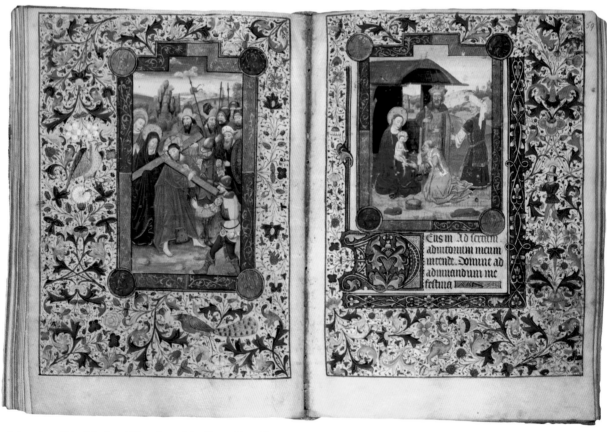

Adoration of the Magi and Carrying of the Cross. Fitzwilliam Museum, MS 53, fols. 58v–59

(painted, however, by different collaborators), the three books share the same type of three-line initials, all apparently from the same centre or shop and apparently unique to this group. They are in colour or gold, enclosing red or blue fields decorated with distinctively rendered flowers, birds, other animals, figures or objects drawn in yellow-gold outline. All three manuscripts illustrate the Hours of the Virgin with ensembles of full-page miniatures of the Passion facing half-page depictions of scenes from the Infancy of Christ, as are found in many richly illustrated *Horae* made for export to England. All contain secondary pictorial cycles, such as historiated initials illustrating Suffrages after Lauds of the Virgin. The Cambridge Hours and that in Rio also include cycles of historiated initials illustrating the Short Hours of the Cross, intercalated at the end of each of the Hours of the Virgin from Lauds onwards. In the Rio Hours these consist of depictions of the Fall of Man followed by subjects related to the Passion, while in the Cambridge Hours, only the first, showing Mary and St John standing at the left of Christ on the Cross, is drawn from the Passion, and the remaining six are Old Testament pre-figurations of the events portrayed in the full-page miniatures commencing each of the relevant hours. The subjects of the Old Testament scenes derive from the *Speculum humanae salvationis*, an illustrated typological compendium popular in the later Middle Ages *(see no. 36)*. The Cambridge and Rio Hours share some similar compositional types (e.g., their full-page depictions of John the Baptist and the Martyrdom of St Catherine), and both have circular corner pieces at the corners of many of their large miniatures, consisting of monochromatic depictions of angels, saints or prophets in the Cambridge Hours and full-colour depictions of saints in the Rio Hours.

Some images in the Cambridge Hours are highly distinctive. Examples include the full-page miniature of an angel standing behind an open grave and holding a mirror with a reflection of a skull that prefaces the first prayer in the book, addressed to one's guardian angel, and the second large miniature, introducing prayers to the Apostles, which portrays all twelve Apostles, two each in six compartments arranged side-by-side in vertical files of three. Each of these miniatures and their facing text pages are also distinctive in having opulent border decoration of painted foliage, flowers, birds and some figures on gold panel borders, which differs from the scheme of border decoration on unpainted vellum found in the remainder of the manuscript. The decoration on these miniature pages differs from that on the facing text pages, and the miniatures have plain rectangular frames rather than the stepped frames with circular corner pieces found elsewhere in the book. These departures from the overall decorative scheme should

probably be understood as efforts to add special lustre and visual interest at the beginning of the manuscript's programme of illustration.

PROVENANCE: acquired by Viscount Fitzwilliam in 1812; his bequest, 1816.

EXHIBITED: Cambridge 1993, no. 40.

LITERATURE: Searle 1876, 72–73, no. 62; James 1895a, 131–34; Rogers 1982, 312–17; Philadelphia 2001, 61, 64, n. 6 (erroneously cited as Ms. 153); Marrow 2002, 879, 882–83, 889.

JHM

95

Book of Hours

Use of Rome
In Latin
Flanders, Bruges or Ghent, *c.*1490
ARTISTS: Master of the Dresden Prayer Book (act. *c.*1470–*c.*1520), Master of James IV of Scotland (act. *c.*1485–*c.*1525), Painter of Add. MS 15677 (act. *c.*1490–*c.*1500), and Master of St Michael (act. *c.*1490–*c.*1500)

Parchment, i (paper) + 190 + i (paper) fols., 195 × 135 mm, text 102 × 60 mm, 20 long lines, ruled in red ink

SCRIPT: Gothic bookhand (hybrida)

BINDING: red velvet over wooden boards, two gilt clasps with catch plates, gilt and gauffered edges, 19th c.

Fitzwilliam Museum, MS 1058–1975

LIKE THE MOST sumptuously illustrated Books of Hours of the late fifteenth century, this volume is a collaborative project between four highly accomplished artists. Bodo Brinkmann has outlined the contribution of each of them (Brinkmann 1992).

The composition of Christ's prayer and Betrayal (fol. 15) is a mature work by the Master of the Dresden Prayerbook, named after one of his earliest manuscripts (Dresden, Sächsische Landesbibliothek, MS A. 311) and credited with some of the most ground-breaking innovations in fifteenth-century Flemish illumination: the illusionistic strewn-flower borders, the full-page Calendar miniatures previously known only from Duc de Berry's *Très Riches Heures*, and the integration of miniature and border into a continuous narrative space (Brinkmann 1997; Los Angeles and London 2003–2004, 207–208).

The images of Saints Peter and Paul (fol. 166) and of Saints Philip and James (fol. 168v) have been associated with another leading artist, the Master of James IV of

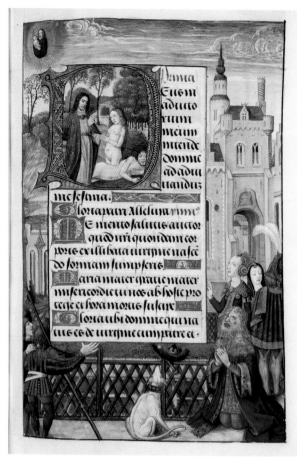

Creation of Eve and Octavian's vision. Fitzwilliam Museum, MS 1058–1975, fol. 74

Scotland (Brinkmann 1992; Cambridge 1993, no. 28). They and the miniature of St Catherine (fol. 180) are among his most captivating portraits. The male saints are remarkably close to the representation of St Andrew in the artist's eponymous manuscript (Vienna, Österreichische Nationalbibliothek, MS 1897, fol. 24v). The small miniature of St Luke painting the icon of the Virgin in the Cambridge Hours (fol. 36, *fig. 27*) finds its 'zoom-in' reversed image, a contracted mirror reflection, in the same subject depicted by the Master of James IV of Scotland in the Breviary of Isabella of Castile some time before 1497 (London, British Library, Add. MS 18851, fol. 473; Backhouse 1993, frontispiece and fig. 64; Los Angeles and London 2003–2004, no. 100).

The third artist in the Cambridge Hours, responsible for the Tree of Jesse border (fol. 36, *fig. 27*) and for the image of St Michael defeating the Devil (fol. 165), remains elusive. His identification with the Master of the Lübeck Bible is hard to justify (Cambridge 1993, no. 28). Until other works by him come to light, he may be called the Master of St Michael. His unique combination of light and subtle hues with painfully contorted

postures imbues his work with drama and explosive energy. His dynamic, expressionistic, and liberated idiom is well ahead of his time. It appears both highly idiosyncratic and strikingly modern.

Finally, the artist whom Brinkmann named the Painter of Add. MS 15677 after a manuscript in the British Library was responsible for the vast majority of miniatures in the Cambridge volume. With the solemn Eyckian image of *Salvator mundi*, facing a luxurious border of peacock feathers, he paid tribute to the Vienna Master of Mary of Burgundy (cf. Oxford, Bodleian Library, MS Douce 219–220, fols. 97v–98). It was from his most gifted successors, the Master of the Dresden Prayerbook and the Master of James IV of Scotland, that the Painter of Add. MS 15677 learned his art. He seems to derive his architectural visions directly from works by the Master of James IV. It is his characteristic use of liquid gold against a deep blue sky to designate a glimpse into heaven that the Painter of Add. MS 15677 employed in the border scene of Jacob's dream (fol. 85). He also emulated the James IV Master's innovative combination of New Testament miniatures with Old Testament typological borders and the unfolding of the narrative in integrated miniatures and borders across a double opening (Los Angeles and London 2003–2004, 366–67). The Passion story in the Cambridge Hours spreads over folios 24v and 25, but instead of integrated borders uses the narrative medallions typical of the Master of the Dresden Prayerbook. It was also the Dresden Master who provided a model for one of the more unusual borders. The branches and acanthus painted in gold ink on fol. 65 repeat a pattern used in the Breviary of Isabella of Castile in which the Dresden Master collaborated with the Master of James IV of Scotland (London, British Library, Add. MS 18851, fol. 63; Backhouse 1993, pl. 10). Executed between the late 1480s and 1497, Queen Isabella's Breviary provides numerous parallels and suggests a similar date for the Cambridge Hours. Another of the Dresden Master's penchants, the Calendar illustrations of the changing seasons, inspired the Painter of Add. MS 15677 to create the snow games and boating parties in the Cambridge Calendar, which are among the most enchanting landscape genre paintings to be found in contemporary manuscripts.

It is in the unusual and thoughtful combination of stock motifs from his masters' repertoire that the Painter of Add. MS 15677 holds his own. The opening of Prime shown here is a good example. Though modelled on the depiction of David praying in a courtyard, a common opening for the Penitential Psalms in contemporary Books of Hours, the Cambridge border depicts Emperor Octavian's vision of the Virgin and Child. The Sibyl, clad in an exotic costume and headgear, reveals the apparition by pulling the text page away – an illusionistic trick favoured by Renaissance artists. The account of Octavian's vision and the Sibyl's prophecy accompanies the Nativity story in the *Golden Legend* as in the richly illustrated Fitzwilliam copy *(see no. 128)*. It also features in fifteenth-century Hours as a border scene accompanying the Nativity image at the beginning of Prime. The Painter of Add. MS 15677 chose to open Prime with the Creation of Eve, an Old Testament reference to Mary and her virginal birth of Christ. The image contained within the initial seems to recede into the distance of the biblical past, adding a third plane of vision to those of the written page and the border. But it also intercepts Octavian's line of vision. It is his gaze that unifies the story of Creation and Redemption through the hope for personal salvation. Unlike the generalized and bland faces for which the Painter of Add. MS 15677 has been justly criticized, (Brinkmann 1992) Octavian's features have the immediacy and intensity of a portrait. He may well represent the individual whose arms were overpainted on the front fly-leaf, but whose voice echoes in the male forms of the *Obsecro te* prayer (fols. 47–49v). His status, wealth, and piety are demonstrated by the explicit association with King David and Emperor Octavian in his manuscript, the work of artists who painted the most opulent Books of Hours for the ruling houses of Europe.

PROVENANCE: John Malcolm of Poltalloch (d.1893); purchased from the executors of his son, Lord Malcolm of Poltalloch, by C.W. Dyson Perrins in 1906; his sale, Sotheby's, London, 9 Dec. 1958, lot 38; purchased by Henry Davis who presented it to the Museum in 1975.

EXHIBITED: London 1908, no. 166; London 1953–1954, no. 605; Cambridge 1993, no. 28.

LITERATURE: Wormald and Giles 1982, 590–95, figs. 88–91; Brinkmann 1987–1988; Brinkmann 1992; Brinkmann 1997, 279, 318–25, 328, 345, figs. 334–37, pl. 60.

SP

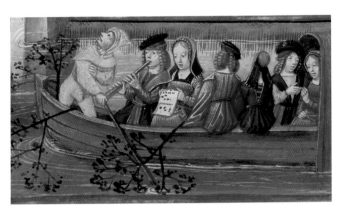

Boating party. Fitzwilliam Museum, MS 1058–1975, fol. 5v, detail

96

Book of Hours

Use of Rome
In Latin and Spanish
Flanders, Bruges, *c.*1490
ARTISTS: Master of the Prayer Books of around 1500 (act. *c.*1490–*c.*1515) and workshop

Parchment, iii (paper) + ii + 218 + ii + iii (paper) fols., 190 × 131 mm, text 103 × 69 mm, 17 long lines, ruled in pink ink
SCRIPT: Gothic bookhand (textualis)
BINDING: gold-tooled red morocco over pasteboards, gilt and gauffered edges, 18th c.

Cambridge University Library, MS Add. 4100

ALTHOUGH a richly illustrated collaborative project like the previous manuscript *(no. 95)*, this is a homogeneous workshop product. The only exception is the miniature of the Adoration of the Child (fol. 71v), inspired by Gerard David's work and related to his Adoration of the Child in the Breviary of Isabella of Castile (London, British Library, Add. MS 18851, fol. 29; Backhouse 1993, fig. 7; Los Angeles and London 2003–2004, no. 100). The artist of the Cambridge miniature has not been identified, but the modelling of fabrics and the facial type of Joseph in particular are paralleled in the miniature of St John on Pathmos in Isabella's Breviary (Backhouse 1993, fig. 46), whose painter is still unknown.

The remaining miniatures are by the workshop of the Master of the Prayer Books of around 1500. Named after a group of devotional manuscripts, but also appreciated for his innovative illustration of secular texts, this artist led a prolific workshop in late fifteenth- and early sixteenth-century Bruges (Los Angeles and London 2003–2004, 394–95). While its output varies in quality, its overall stylistic consistency and the frequent collaboration of master and assistants within the same image have discouraged scholars from distinguishing between the various hands. The only attempt was made in a study focusing on the Cambridge Hours (de Kesel 1992). The division of labour outlined by de Kesel could now be expanded to cover all miniatures. The Master of the Prayer Books of around 1500 painted the Annunciation, the Annunciation to the Shepherds, and the Presentation in the Temple (fols. 43v, 76v, 85v). He was also responsible for the figure of the Virgin in the Visitation (fol. 60v), but the rest was painted by an assistant who also worked on the Massacre of the Innocents (fol. 98v), on the Crucifixion to the *Stabat mater* prayer (fol. 194*v), and on four

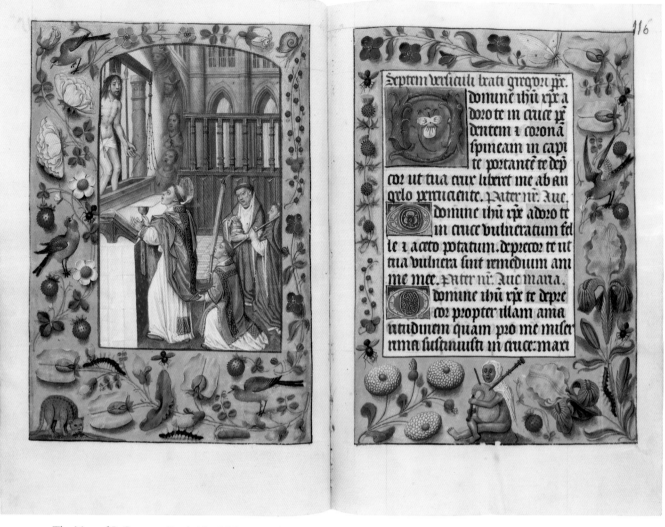

The Mass of St Gregory. Cambridge University Library, MS Add. 4100, fols. 115v–116

of the miniatures illustrating the Passion according to St John (fols. 181v, 189v, 190v, 193v). The fifth of the Passion miniatures, the Flagellation and Crowning with Thorns (fol. 186v), was by an accomplished associate, who also illuminated the Raising of Lazarus (fol. 142v) and the Mass of St Gregory shown here. The raised angle of vision is skilfully combined with the intersecting planes of the altar and the aisle to create a dynamic composition and convey the mystery of the Eucharist through Christ's dramatic appearance. An artist who favoured large and rounded faces, with puck noses and wide-open eyes, executed the Pentecost miniature (fol. 22v) and the image of David in prayer (fol. 122v). The Crucifixion to the Hours of the Cross (fol. 15v) and the Flight to Egypt (fol. 90v) are by the illuminator responsible for the Calendar scenes and the small miniatures to the suffrages.

The patronage of this manuscript seems as problematic as the division of labour. Pächt suggested that the original owner was Isabella of Aragon (c.1465–1524), granddaughter of Ferdinand I of Aragon and wife of Gian Galeazzo Sforza, Duke of Milan, and that she sent the volume to Queen Isabella of Castile. A letter previously enclosed with the volume (MS Add. 4100(2)), dated September 1500 or 1501, and signed by 'your obedient servant and niece Isabella of Aragon', refers to the Queen of Hungary, and emphasizes a mutual belonging to the House of Aragon. Lieve de Kesel pointed out that the recipient must have been Beatrice (1457–1508), daughter of Ferdinand I of Aragon and widow of Matthias Corvinus. Yet, the letter makes no mention of the manuscript and does not prove Beatrice's or Isabella's ownership. The volume contains no heraldic evidence and the Bruges Calendar would have been irrelevant to a Duchess of Milan or a Queen of Hungary. Yet, the manuscript was certainly made for a Spaniard, since the original scribe wrote two Spanish rubrics (fols. 196★, 197) among the Latin ones. The letter finishes with a recommendation of Antonio de Cardoña, Isabella's ambassador, and an eighteenth-century inscription on the flyleaf records that he brought the manuscript from Gran, or Esztergom in Hungary. This, together with the Spanish rubrics and the masculine forms in the *Obsecro te* prayer (fol. 39v), suggests that Antonio, the bearer of the letter, may have also been the owner of the manuscript. The acronyms inscribed in capitals formed of branches within the border on fol. 206v still keep their secret: 'NSMO.AONEH' and 'NSAIKVS'.

PROVENANCE: inspected by the Inquisition in Valladolid on 7 Dec. 1573 (fol. i); Cardoña family until the 19th c.; purchased from Ellis and Scrutton by Samuel Sandars (1837–1894) in 1886; his bequest, 1894.

EXHIBITED: London 1953–1954, no. 607; Bordeau 1954, no.152; Cambridge 1993, no. 52.

LITERATURE: Frere 1894–1932, II, 121; Dogaer 1987, 159; de Kesel 1992.   SP

97

Miniatures from the Hours of Albrecht of Brandenburg

Flanders, Bruges, *c.*1522–1523
ARTIST: Simon Bening (1483–1561) and assistants

(a) The Crucifixion, The Annunciation, The Virgin and Child with St Anne, The Last Judgement, The Assumption of the Virgin

Parchment, 180 × 130 mm

Fitzwilliam Museum, MS294a–e

(b) The Crucifixion

Parchment, 187 × 135 mm

Fitzwilliam Museum, MS 3–1996

The five miniatures (MS 294a–e) derive from a sumptuously illustrated Book of Hours made for Cardinal Albrecht of Brandenburg (1490–1545), Archbishop and Elector of Mainz, Primate of Germany, and one of the foremost patrons of the arts of his time. They form part of the ensemble of full-page miniatures excised from this celebrated manuscript at an uncertain date, of which the largest known group, including these leaves, emerged in Rome in 1856, where they were acquired by the Marquess of Londonderry. While many of the full-page miniatures from Albrecht's Hours have entered public collections, the manuscript from which they were excised was and still is in private hands, and has long been inaccessible. Only relatively recently has it been possible to confirm earlier hypotheses that the excised full-page

miniatures derive from the Hours of Albrecht of Brandenburg and to establish their original locations in the book. According to the reconstruction by Hindman (1997), the Cambridge miniatures of the Annunciation, the Crucifixion, the Last Judgement, the Virgin and Child with St Anne, and the Assumption of the Virgin prefaced the Hours of the Virgin, the Hours of the Cross, the Seven Penitential Psalms, a Suffrage to St Anne, and a Prayer for the Feast of the Assumption, respectively. The miniature of Christ on the Cross with Mary and St John, originally faced the text of the *Stabat Mater* (rubricated as the *Planctus beatae Mariae virginis*).

The miniatures of the Hours of Cardinal Albrecht of Brandenburg are universally ascribed to Simon Bening and assistants. Born in 1483 or 1484, Simon was the son of the Ghent illuminator Alexander (or Sanders) Bening (act. *c.*1469, d.1518). Simon was active from the turn of the sixteenth century, primarily in Bruges, where he became a citizen in 1519; he enjoyed an international reputation as the most widely admired illuminator from the Netherlands, illuminating no less than three manuscripts for Albrecht of Brandenburg, a patron also of such distinguished painters as Albrecht Dürer, Lucas Cranach the Elder, and Matthias Grünewald. Bening was prized, among others, for his fine, resonant colouristic sense which enhanced his depictions of nocturnal scenes, and for the atmospheric qualities of his landscape settings, achieved through flecklike brushwork. His compositional and expressive range extended from hieratically conceived devotional images and sweetly idealized figures to works of vivid narrative and dramatic expressive intensity.

Part of the success enjoyed by Bening and his best contemporaries can be attributed to their facility in recycling compositional prototypes by distinguished Flemish miniaturists active in the 1470s and 1480s, such as the Vienna Master of Mary of Burgundy, painters of his circle, and important Bruges painters such as Jan van Eyck and Gerard David, as well as emulating some printmakers (Martin Schongauer, Albrecht Dürer). Bening also revised and consistently refined many of his own compositional types, which invested them with qualities both of familiarity and fresh visual interest. To cite only a few such examples from the set of miniatures in the Fitzwilliam Museum: the compositions of the Crucifixion, the Annunciation and the Assumption of the Virgin echo prototypes of the 1470s and 1480s by the Vienna Master of Mary of Burgundy; the figures of the Annunciation have close counterparts in one of a set of miniatures from a Rosary Prayer Book by Bening sold at Christie's (New York, 9 June 1993, lot 6), and its setting is closely emulated in Bening's Annunciation in the Holford Hours, dated 1526 (Lisbon, Museu Calouste Gulbenkian, MS LA.210, f. 1v, in reversed orientation). The composition of the Last Judgement replicates many features of

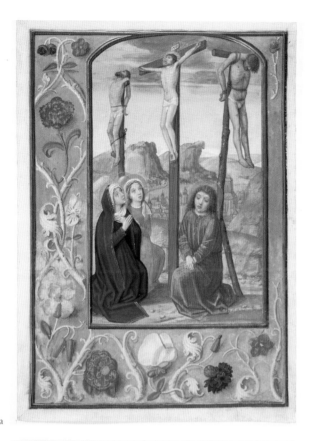

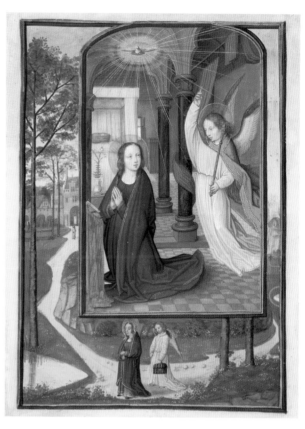

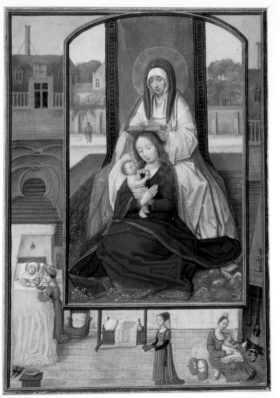

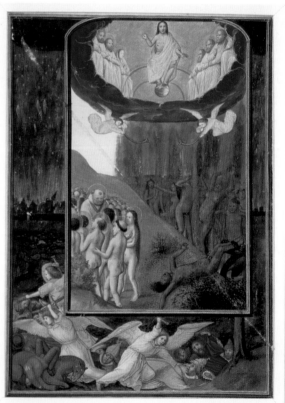

a. The Crucifixion between the two Thieves; b. The Annunciation. Fitzwilliam Museum, MS 294a & b
c. The Virgin and Child with Saint Anne; d. The Last Judgement. Fitzwilliam Museum. MS 294c & d

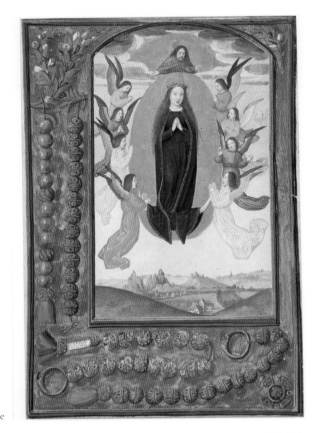

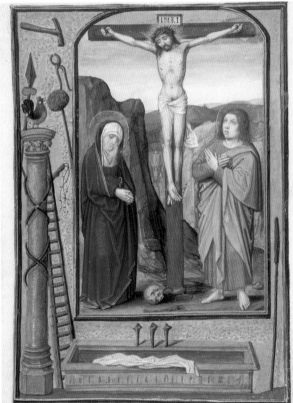

e. The Assumption of the Virgin. Fitzwilliam Museum, MS 294e
The Crucifixion. Fitzwilliam Museum, MS 3-1996.

Bening's miniature in the same Rosary Prayer Book sold at Christie's in 1993, while many figures in its illustrated border derive from the depiction of the Massacre by the Four Angels in Albrecht Dürer's woodcut of *c.*1498 from the Apocalypse (Ch. IX; Meder 171); the figural arrangement of St Anne, the Virgin and Child, is replicated in a small miniature in the Holford Hours of 1526, cited above (f. 181v), and its border scene of the Birth of the Virgin appears in a slightly revised version in one of Bening's miniatures in the Musgrave Hours of 1524 (Upperville, Virginia, Collection of Mrs Paul Mellon, f. 114v).

(a) PROVENANCE: Cardinal Albrecht von Brandenburg (1490–1545); Frederick, Marquess of Londonderry, acquired in Rome in 1856; Rev. E.S. Dewick; given by the Friends of the Fitzwilliam Museum in 1918.

EXHIBITED: London 1908, no. 120; London 1953–1954, no. 620; Cambridge 1993, no. 31.

LITERATURE: Wolf 1982, 50–53, figs. 39–43; Wormald and Giles 1982, 1, 270–73; Hindman et al. 1997, 99–112; Challis 1998, 263.

(b) PROVENANCE: Cardinal Albrecht von Brandenburg (1490–1545); Frederick, Marquess of Londonderry, acquired in Rome in 1856; Captain G. Pitt-Rivers sale, Christie's 14 March 1929, lot 130; purchased A. Horace Buttery; Phyllis Giles, Keeper of Manuscripts and Printed Books at the Museum (1947–1974); her bequest, 1996.

LITERATURE: Christie's Season 1929, 55; Hindman et al 1997, 102–3, 111, fig. 13.10. JHM

98

Two Leaves from a Rosary Psalter

In Spanish and Latin
Flanders, Bruges, c.1525
ARTIST: Simon Bening (1483–1561)

Parchment, 2 fols., 100 × 80 mm, text 75 × 48 mm, 16 lines, ruled in red

SCRIPT: Gothic bookhand (textualis) on reverse

Fitzwilliam Museum, MS 257a–b

THESE TWO LEAVES are part of a set from a dismembered Rosary Psalter. Fourteen single leaves from the same manuscript are in the Boston Public Library (MS q Med. 35). All but two of them contain, like the Fitzwilliam leaves, text in Spanish and Latin on the reverse of leaves with full-page miniatures (Kupfer-Tarasulo 1979, discussing twelve leaves then in Boston;

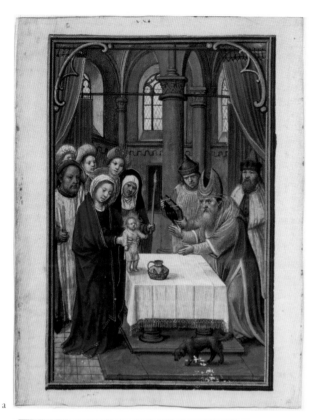

a

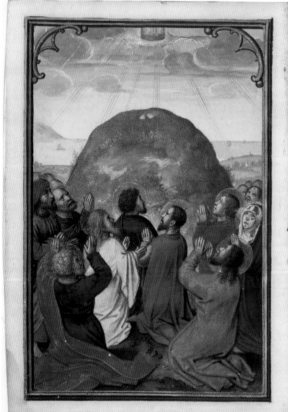

b

a. Presentation in the Temple. b. Ascension.
Fitzwilliam Museum, MS 257a–b

another two were acquired after a sale at Christie's, London, 22 May 1981, lot 12). One of the leaves without text contains a miniature of the Annunciation that would have commenced the narrative cycle. The other, portraying the Empty Cross, may well have served as its tailpiece, as may be gauged from the location of a similar depiction in another Rosary Prayer Book, dated 1545, that contains the same Spanish text and was also illustrated by Simon Bening or members of his shop (Sotheby's, London, 6 July 2000, lot 57; Private collection). In the later copy, the miniature of the Empty Cross comes at the end of the Rosary cycle and serves as a frontispiece to a following text of the Psalms of the Passion. The Boston miniature of the Empty Cross is inscribed SPALTERIUM (sic) CRUCIS, which would be an apt title for a text, now lost, of the Passion Psalms.

In addition to the miniature of the Empty Cross, the Boston-Cambridge Rosary Psalter contains fifteen leaves with miniatures and text corresponding to the Fifteen Mysteries of the Virgin. The prayers and miniatures form three groups of five subjects defined by different stages in the life of Mary and Christ. The first set, known as the joyful mysteries, recounts the Infancy of Christ: Annunciation, Visitation, Nativity, Presentation in the Temple (Fitzwilliam 257a), and Christ among the Doctors. The second, of sorrowful mysteries, treats the Passion: Agony in the Garden, Flagellation, Crowning with Thorns, Carrying of the Cross, and the Crucifixion. The third, glorious mysteries, consists of events after the Passion: Resurrection, Ascension (Fitzwilliam MS 257b), Pentecost, Assumption of the Virgin, and Coronation of the Virgin. The book was designed to maintain a regular alternation of miniature and text leaves, with miniatures on versos facing the texts that accompanied them on rectos. In this manner, they sustain a regular rhythm of pictorial and prayerful devotion. The text consists of short meditations in Spanish on each of the events celebrated in the Fifteen Mysteries, accompanied by Latin *incipits* of the *Pater noster* (Our Father) and abbreviated rubrics instructing the petitioner to recite ten *Ave Marias* (Hail Marys). This type of devotional exercise is known as a Rosary Psalter because the fifteen groups of ten Hail Marys make for a total of 150 prayers to Mary, which corresponds to the number of Psalms in the Psalter.

The miniatures are characteristic works by Simon Bening of Bruges, produced at the height of his powers, *c.*1525. They display the extraordinary command of detail, atmospheric effects and polish for which he was well known and which made him one of the most esteemed illuminators in Europe during the first half of the sixteenth century *(see nos. 57 and 97)*. It is a measure of Bening's considerable success that his works were commissioned and collected by buyers from different countries in Western Europe, including Germany, Italy,

Spain and Portugal. The largest group of works known to have been made by Simon Bening for Spanish patrons are Rosary Prayer Books of the type represented by the Boston-Cambridge leaves. In addition to the copy of the Rosary Prayer text of 1545 cited above, which is also written in Spanish but is unfortunately incomplete, Bening was the author of a single leaf of the Resurrection in Washington from yet another copy of the same Spanish text (National Gallery of Art, Rosenwald Collection, B-22, 897). Other genres of Rosary Prayer Books made for Spanish patrons and illustrated by Bening include the Beatty Rosarium (Dublin, Chester Beatty Library, MS W. 99), with thirty-three miniatures, and an incomplete book offered on the art market in 1993 (Christie's, New York, 9 June 1993, lot 6). The latter contained eleven miniatures and text sides with decorated initials 'P' or 'A' (presumably for *Pater noster* and *Ave Maria*), but lacked their prayers, which were apparently never written. Their absence makes it impossible to prove conclusively that this book was also destined for a Spanish owner. Simon Bening need not have travelled to Spain to have received or executed these and other commissions for Spanish patrons. During his lifetime, Bruges boasted a large colony of foreign merchants, including collectors, agents active in commissioning and exporting luxury goods, and those capable of writing fine manuscripts in most major European languages, including Spanish.

PROVENANCE: Henry Yates Thompson (1838–1928); his gift, 1895.

EXHIBITED: Cambridge 1993, no. 29; Los Angeles and London 2003–2004, no. 144.

LITERATURE: Kupfer-Tarasulo 1979; Wormald and Giles 1982, 186–87; Marrow 1984, 541; Hindman 1989, 17; Testa 1994, 418.

JHM

99

Psalter

In Latin
Italy, Naples, *c.*1460–*c.*1470
ARTIST: Matteo Felice (act. *c.*1455–*c.*1495)
SCRIBE: Pietro Ursuleo of Capua (act. *c.*1440–d.1483)

Parchment, iii (paper, 19th c., unfoliated) + 167 + i (paper, 19th c., unfoliated) fols., 180 × 140 mm, text 132 × 95 mm, 19 long lines, ruled in pink ink

SCRIPT: Humanistic minuscule

BINDING: paper over pasteboards, vellum spine, 18th c., gilt and gauffered edges from an earlier binding

Trinity College, MS O.7.46

ALL ASPECTS of this Psalter, from its liturgical apparatus to its script and decoration, point to the most refined examples of Neapolitan illumination of the 1460s. The Calendar, though exceedingly sparse, singles out the patron saint of Naples, San Gennaro (19 September), together with two Neapolitan bishops, St Severus (30 April) and St Anellus (14 December), and the dedication of San Salvatore, the basilica built in the fourth century by bishop Severus and later re-dedicated as San Giorgio Maggiore (9 November). The confident humanistic minuscule is the work of Pietro Ursuleo, who signed the manuscript on fol. 167v. One of the most prolific and famous Neapolitan scribes, he enjoyed a long career at the courts of three Neapolitan rulers, René of Anjou, Alfonso the Magnificent, and Ferrante I of Aragon, as well as the patronage of Cardinal Oliviero Carafa and Pope Sixus IV. Most importantly, he was a frequent collaborator of the artist who made the Trinity Psalter a masterpiece of Neapolitan illumination (Toscano 1995; Naples and Valencia 1998, 417–36). Matteo Felice, trained in the workshop of Cola Rapicano, which served mainly the kings of Naples and their courtiers, was among the artists who equipped the Aragonese royal

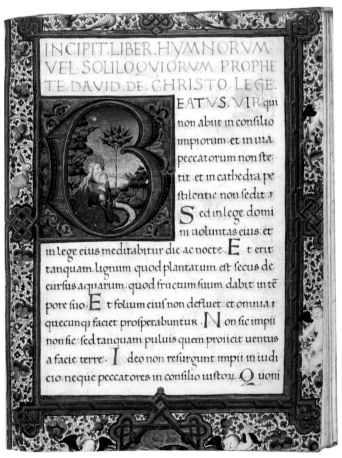

Beatus initial with David playing the psaltery. Trinity College, MS O.7.46, fol. 11

library with its most splendid manuscripts during the second half of the fifteenth century. While another Cambridge manuscript characterizes Matteo Felice's late career *(no. 164)*, the Trinity Psalter shows the young artist in his prime. The historiated initials to the eight division Psalms (fols. 11, 29, 40v, 51, 62, 75, 87, 100), the conventional diapered backgrounds in the four Evangelists' miniatures to the accounts of the Passion (fols. 140v, 148v, 155v, 162v), the white vine-scroll initials to the Passion narratives, ordinary Psalms, Canticles and prayers, and the Neapolitan borders with flowers, broad-faced putti, and spiky gold-leaf sprays at the major text divisions combine local, Flemish, and Florentine features. Two of the devotional books on which Felice concentrated are particularly close to the Trinity volume. A Psalter in the Hague (Koninklijke Bibliotheek, MS 131 F.18) and a Psalter-Hours in Geneva (Bibliothèque publique et universitaire, Comites Latentes Collection, MS 198; Toscano 1995, figs. 12–15; Naples and Valencia 1998, 420–21, figs. 3–8) show the cusped haloes, raised eyebrows, massive beards, heavy noses, and trees 'spinning' in a vertigo that can be seen here. The compositions within the Geneva and Trinity *Beatus* initials, and their borders are almost identical.

Although the arms of the original patron of the Trinity Psalter were trimmed (probably in the sixteenth or seventeenth century when the manuscript received its elaborately gilt edges), we may suspect that he was closely associated with the Aragonese royal family. Gennaro Toscano has pointed out that a large number of contemporary devotional manuscripts were produced by Matteo Felice and his colleagues at Rapicano's workshop for prominent members of the Neapolitan court, such as the Avalos family for whom Pietro Ursuleo copied the Psalter in the Hague. The man who had his personal prayers recorded before and after the Litany in the Trinity Psalter (fols. 137v, 140) asked for the Psalms to be listed at the beginning of his book in the order in which he was to read them throughout the week (fols. 1v–2). He also requested a list of Psalms to be recited on specific occasions (fol. 1). Together with the Medici manuscript *(no. 101)*, this volume attests to the enduring popularity of the Psalter as a devotional text and a de luxe status symbol among wealthy bibliophiles in Renaissance Italy.

PROVENANCE: Ser Capon Galdi (ownership inscription, fol. 2); Thomas Gale (1635/1636–1702); Roger Gale (1672–1744) who presented it to the College in 1738.

LITERATURE: James 1900–1904, III, 384–85.

SP

100

Book of Hours

Use of Rome
In Latin
Italy, Naples, 1478
ARTIST: Cristoforo Majorana (doc. 1480–1494)
SCRIBE: Alexander Antonii Simonis (fl. *c.*1475)

Parchment, ii + 325 fols., 175 × 120 mm, text 85 × 52 mm, 12 long lines, ruled in black ink

SCRIPT: Humanistic minuscule

BINDING: contemporary brown leather over birch boards, blind-tooled frame and central panel of interlaced ropework, sewn on four double tawed skin sewing supports, endbands at head and tail, traces of two pins on upper cover, gilt and gauffered edges.

Fitzwilliam Museum, MS 153

Few BOOKS OF HOURS received a richer illustrative cycle than this manuscript, boasting twenty-six miniatures with architectural frames, panoramic landscapes, and peculiar iconography, which deserves a detailed examination. Even fewer Hours reveal so much about the people who commissioned and made them. The scribe, Alexander Antonii Simonis, signed and dated the manuscript. His page-long colophons describe him as an Augustinian hermit, who visited Rome and Bologna frequently, and who was educated in theology in his native Florence and in Naples where he completed this manuscript in the twenty-third hour on 7 September 1478 (fols. 126v, 270–270v, 314).

The patron was just as eloquent. His arms, though effaced on the first miniature shown here, left an offset on the facing page and survived on the elaborate opening to the Penitential Psalms *(fig. 42)*. St Augustine's prayer and the *Obsecro te* reveal his name, Lorenzo Strozzi. Member of the wealthy Florentine merchant class, Lorenzo di Matteo was employed in branches of the Strozzi firm in Valencia and Avignon, then in Bruges in the 1450s, and finally, from 1461, in Naples where he died in 1479. His early passion for collecting and trading in paintings, documented during his Bruges sojourn (Nuttall 2004, 34, 45, 121–22), probably developed further in Naples. Both he and his brother Filippo, who built one of the most extravagant palaces in fifteenth-century Florence, indulged their taste for art through their close contacts with the Aragonese court.

This Book of Hours was illuminated by Cristoforo Majorana, one of the leading Aragonese artists of the 1480s and 1490s (Naples and Valencia 1998, 441–52). He enriched the eclectic nature of fifteenth-century

Neapolitan illumination, already a blend of Catalan, Franco-Flemish, Ferrarese, and Florentine styles, with the Veneto-Roman predilection for architectural frontispieces. They feature in twenty-four of the twenty-six miniatures. The majority show Majorana's collaboration with a competent assistant, but the three major text divisions, the Hours of the Virgin, the Penitential Psalms, and the Office of the Dead (fols. 15, 144, 176) are by the master himself. They open with spectacular monuments set in landscapes, hung with antique trophies, and partially obscured by the text suspended from their arches and columns by busy putti. None of the manuscripts in which Majorana displayed this lavish, three-dimensional treatment of architecture predate the Fitzwilliam Hours. The closest parallels are found in King Ferrante's Pliny and Aesop of c.1481 (Valencia, Biblioteca Universitaria, MS 758; El Escorial, Monasterio de San Lorenzo de El Escorial, Biblioteca, MS h.I.9; Naples and Valencia 1998, no. 31, 33).

The new Veneto-Roman fashion was brought to Naples with the manuscripts Gaspare da Padova illuminated for Giovanni d'Aragona and his brother Alfonso, Duke of Calabria and close friend of Cardinal Francesco Gonzaga. Gaspare only passed into Giovanni's service after the death of Cardinal Gonzaga in 1483, but was already illuminating manuscripts for Alfonso of Calabria in the mid-1470s. One of them, Alfonso's copy of Josephus of c.1475–1480 (Valencia, Biblioteca Universitaria, MS 836; Naples and Valencia 1998, no. 53; Padua 1999, no. 132), offers close parallels for the bronze pillars of the monument in the Cambridge Hours, while others provide models for the antique trophies and receding, moon-shaped arches. Lorenzo Strozzi's Hours demonstrate that by 1478 Cristoforo Majorana had established the *all'antica* style in Naples. He was the preferred Neapolitan artist of Cardinal Giovanni and Alfonso of Calabria, who otherwise favoured Florentine scribes and their disciples. Lorenzo Strozzi's choice of both artist and scribe reflects the tastes of the most discriminating art patrons at the Aragonese court.

PROVENANCE: Lorenzo Strozzi (d.1479; arms on fol. 144 and prayers on fols. 261, 275v); acquired by Viscount Fitzwilliam in 1811; his bequest, 1816.

EXHIBITED: Cambridge 1966, no. 104; Cambridge 1989–1990, no. 99.

LITERATURE: James 1895a, 346–48; de Marinis 1947–1952, I, 88, 96 n. 34, 153; Robinson 1988, no. 195, fig. 317.

SP

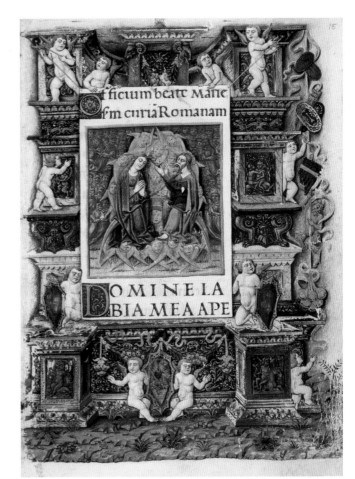

Architectural frontispiece, Coronation of the Virgin. Fitzwilliam Museum, MS 153, fol. 15

101

Psalter and Hymnal

In Latin
Italy, Florence, c.1475–c.1480
ARTIST: Gherardo di Giovanni del Fora (1446–1497)
SCRIBE: Antonio di Francesco Sinibaldi da Carmignano (1443–1528)

Parchment, i (paper) + 209 + ii (paper) fols., 193 × 125 mm, text 113 × 60 mm, 20 long lines, ruled in hard point

SCRIPT: Humanistic minuscule

BINDING: gold-tooled dark blue morocco over pasteboards, gilt and gauffered edges with Medici arms on fore-edge, arms of Nicholas Fouquet (1615–1680) on spine, 17th c.

Fitzwilliam Museum, MS 37–1950

THIS SPLENDID MEDICI COMMISSION brought together one of the most accomplished humanistic scribes and one of the leading Florentine artists of the late fifteenth century. Albinia de la Mare attributed the elegant script to the young Antonio Sinibaldi whose work would be sought after by the most discriminating collectors of the 1480s and 1490s, including Cardinal Giovanni of Aragon and King Matthias Corvinus of Hungary. In the 1470s, Sinibaldi copied manuscripts for Lorenzo de' Medici and Albinia de la Mare suggested that the Fitzwilliam Psalter-Hymnal might have been one of them. Indeed, one of Lorenzo's most personal devices, the *broncone*, or lopped branch, features prominently in the title page borders and forms the initials to every Psalm, Canticle and hymn. Another Medici device, the flaming branches, is used even more emphatically on the double opening shown here and throughout the volume. Yet, the Medici arms with the nine red balls seen here were not associated with the main branch of the family after 1465 and Grazelli has suggested a patron from one of the side branches who remains elusive.

By contrast, the artist has been firmly identified. The full, rounded faces with massive, stubby noses, the rich modelling of fabrics in gold ink highlights, the calm, noble figures, the refined details of the landscape, and the exquisite jewelled borders are the work of Gherardo di Giovanni del Fora *(see also no. 56)*. Together with his brother Monte, he enjoyed the patronage of the Strozzi, the Medici, and King Matthias Corvinus, as well as of the leading religious institutions in Florence (Garzelli 1985, 267–330). One of the most famous and versatile artists in late fifteenth-century Florence, Gherardo was praised by Vasari as a painter and master of mosaics, but above all as an illuminator. He excelled in the depiction of topical architecture and landscapes in which the delicate nuance of gradually fading colours shapes the receding depth of space, while the realistic details, such as the birds on the lake seen here and the water mill at the foot of the hills, suggest familiarity with contemporary Northern painting. Indeed, Vasari records that Gherardo sought engravings by Schongauer and Dürer, and copied their designs with great interest (Nuttall 2004, 140). There would have been no shortage of Flemish models either, since the commercial and artistic exchange with Bruges was promoted by leading Florentine businessmen such as Filippo Strozzi for

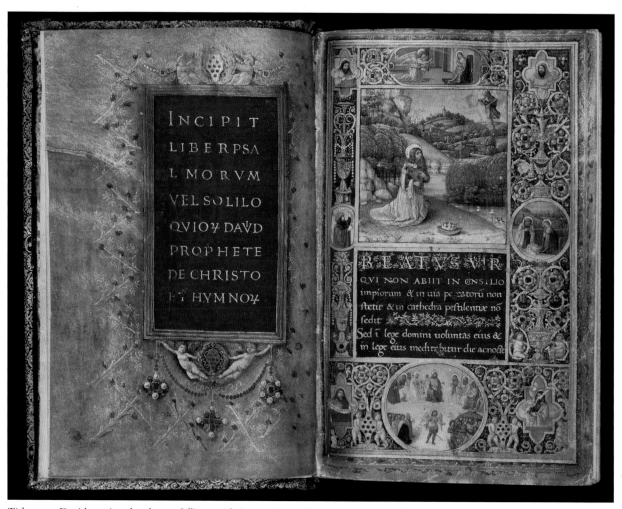

Title page, David praying, border medallions with Annunciation, Nativity, and Last Judgement. Fitzwilliam Museum, MS 37–1950, fols. IV–2

whom Gherardo and Monte illuminated a celebrated printed Pliny in 1479–1483 (Oxford, Bodleian Library, Arch. G.b.6; London and New York 1994–1995, no. 85). Consistent with the ornamental vocabulary and page layout of the Strozzi Pliny, though perhaps slightly earlier, the Medici Psalter-Hymnal may well be among Gherardo's first responses to the art of the Northern Renaissance. Nevertheless, its de luxe double opening on green-stained vellum, the illusionistic treatment of its title page, and the borders designed in the fashionable *all'antica* style are all representative of Italian humanistic manuscripts conceived at the highest level of artistic accomplishment and patronage.

PROVENANCE: Medici family; Nicholas Fouquet (1613–1680) whose collection was sold in Paris in 1668; Phillip Carteret Webb; his sale, 25 Feb.–14 March 1771, probably lot 2796; Michael Wodhull, 28 June 1797; C.W. Loscombe of Clifton; his sale, Sotheby's, London, 19 June 1854, lot 1173; purchased by Sir William Tite; his sale, Sotheby's, London, 30 May 1874, lot 2416; B. Quaritch, catalogues 1880, no. 84 and 1886, no. 35764; purchased by H.Y. Thompson in 1894; his sale, Sotheby's, London, 23 March 1920, lot 62; purchased by T.H. Riches who bequeathed it to the Museum in 1935.

EXHIBITED: London 1862, no. 6876; London 1874, no. 146; Cambridge 1966, no. 97; Cambridge 1989–1990, no. 81.

LITERATURE: James 1898, 140, no. 30; Thompson 1907–1918, V, pls. LXIX, LXX; D'Ancona 1914, II, 1676; Wormald and Giles 1982, 429–31, figs. 71, 72; Garzelli 1985, 282, 301, 327–28, figs. 977, 978; de la Mare 1985, 453, 486.

SP

102

Book of Hours

Use of Rome
In Latin and Italian
Italy, Milan or Cremona, *c.*1490

Parchment, 112 fols. (foliated 1–9, 11–57, 59–114),
154 × 109 mm, text 89 × 62 mm, 19 long lines, ruled in crayon

SCRIPT: Gothic bookhand (textualis)

BINDING: black leather over wooden boards, gilt edges, 19th c.

Cambridge University Library, MS Add. 4104

THIS RICHLY ILLUMINATED devotional book exemplifies the final and most glorious period in the development of Lombard manuscript illumination. The last two decades of the fifteenth century witnessed the self-aggrandizing art patronage of Lodovico il Moro (1451–1508), second son of Francesco Sforza (r.1450–

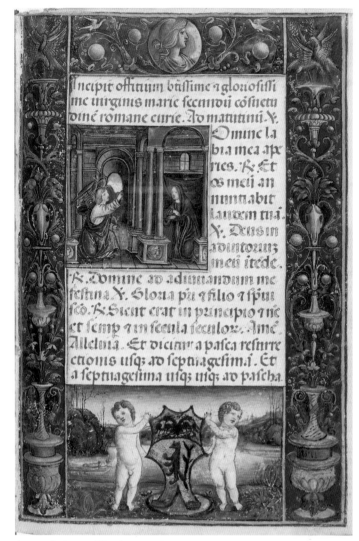

Annunciation and Putti supporting arms.
Cambridge University Library, MS Add. 4104, fol. 11

1466) and uncle of Gian Galeazzo Sforza (1469–1494) after whose early death he usurped the ducal crown. The leading court illuminator of his time was Giovan Pietro Birago (doc. 1471–1513), a priest who worked in Brescia in the 1470s and probably in Venice in the 1480s before settling down in Milan around 1490. It is Birago's work of around 1490 that provides the closest parallels to the Cambridge manuscript, notably his celebrated Hours of Bona Sforza (London, British Library, Add. MSS 34294, 45722, 62997, 80800; Evans 1992; Evans and Brinkmann 1995) and the four vellum copies of the 1490 edition of the *Sforziada* (London, British Library, G. 7251 [IB. 26059]; Florence, Galleria degli Uffizi, Inv. nos. 843, 4423–4430; Paris, Bibliothèque nationale de France, Vélins 724; Warsaw, Biblioteka Narodowa, Inc. F. 1347; Evans 1987; London and New York 1994–1995, no. 16). Like these volumes, the Cambridge Hours feature borders composed of antique vases, candelabra, cameos, and cornucopiae surmounted by eagles, flanked by symmetrically positioned pearls, and executed in a combination of gold ink and striking red, blue and green pigments. The page layout at the major text divisions, balancing the all'antica borders with bas-de-page scenes and small miniatures instead of historiated initials, the use of bold colours covering large areas, the vigourous figures, the firm outlines, the crisp tangibility of fabrics, the segmented treatment of hair, and the deep landscapes with sky and water rapidly fading from saturated blue in the foreground to pale yellow in the horizon are all typical of Birago's style. They were painted by an artist closely associated with him. His most accomplished miniatures open the Hours of the Virgin shown here (fol. 11) and the Penitential Psalms (fol. 59). The rest of the major text divisions, published here for the first time, were illuminated by at least two assistants: Visitation (Lauds, fol. 17v), Nativity (Prime, fol. 24v), Annunciation to the Shepherds (Terce, fol. 27v), Adoration of the Magi (Sext, fol. 30), Presentation in the Temple (None, fol. 32v), Massacre of the Innocents (Vespers, fol. 35), Burial of the Virgin (Compline, fol. 39v), landscape with two deer (Salve sancta parens, fol. 54), skeleton beside tomb, putto with skulls and bones in landscape (Office of the Dead, fol. 73v), Crucifixion, Carrying of the Cross (Hours of the Cross, fol. 100v); initial with the dove of the Holy Spirit, Pentecost (Hours of the Holy Spirit, fol. 108).

The unidentified arms on fol. 11 are a later addition, but the prominence of St Homobonus in the Calendar (13 Nov.) and Litany (fol. 68) suggests a patron associated with Cremona. This manuscript witnesses the tastes and patronage of local nobility, which aspired to the art favoured by the Duke of Milan and his immediate court circle.

PROVENANCE: given to Edward Jacob (d.1788) by John White in 1756; W. Herbert, 1780; T. Shadford Walker; his sale, Sotheby's, London, 23 June 1886, lot 308; purchased by Quaritch, his general catalogue 1887–1898, no. 35763; purchased by Samuel Sandars (1837–1894) on 15 Dec. 1886; his bequest, 1894

EXHIBITED: London 1893–1894, no. 115–3; Cambridge 1989–1990, no. 45.

LITERATURE: Frere 1894–1932, II, 121.

SP

103
Book of Hours

Use of Rome
In Latin
Italy, Naples, c.1490
ARTISTS: Cristoforo Majorana (doc. 1480–1494) and a colleague

Parchment, 259 fols. (foliated 1–23, 25–68, 70–113, 115–118, 121–122, 125–130, 132–203, 205–233, 235–269), 175 × 120 mm, text 103 × 67 mm, 15 long lines, ruled in faint red ink

SCRIPT: Humanistic minuscule

BINDING: gold-tooled red morocco over boards, gilt edges with traces of marbling, 18th c.; repaired by W.H. Smith & Son, London, October 1960.

Cambridge University Library, MS Add. 4105

THIS BOOK OF HOURS demonstrates the consummate skills and eclectic vocabulary of Neapolitan illuminators in the last quarter of the fifteenth century. The miniature of the Virgin and Child, which opens the Hours of the Virgin (fol. 13), exemplifies the late, sketchy and loose style of Cristoforo Majorana (see no. 100). With the assistance of a close follower, he was responsible for all of the small miniatures with initials suspended from their frames and floral or antique borders: Annunciation (Lauds, fol. 25), Nativity (Prime, fol. 45), Adoration of the Magi (Terce, fol. 51), Resurrection (Sext, fol. 57), Ascension (None, fol. 63), Assumption of the Virgin (Compline, fol. 77), Isaiah (Saturday Vespers before first Sunday of Advent, fol. 82), Man of Sorrows (Hours of the Passion, Matins, fol. 93), Flagellation (first lesson, fol. 99), Vernicle (Lauds, fol. 102), Mocking of Christ (Prime, fol. 107), Carrying of the Cross (Terce, fol. 111), Nailing to the Cross (Sext, fol. 115), Entombment (Compline, fol. 130), David praying (Penitential Psalms, fol. 135), two souls praying in Hell (Office of the Dead, first nocturn, fol. 164v), saint-bishop (suffrages, fol. 219v). Among the missing leaves were similar miniatures and borders for Vespers of the Virgin, and for None and Vespers in the Hours of the Passion. Many of the extant miniatures share iconographic peculiarities with contemporary Neapolitan Books of Hours (see no. 100) and deserve further examination.

The only illumination in the manuscript to depart from Majorana's style is the beginning of the Office of the Dead shown here. Although the putti's rounded, plump faces draw on Nardo Rapicano's and Matteo Felice's work (see no.99), the exuberant liquid gold border is a new departure in Neapolitan illumination. Neither Matteo Felice nor Nardo Rapicano and Cristoforo

Majorana showed interest in the Veneto-Paduan 'jewelled' style which the Master of the London Pliny brought to Naples in the 1480s *(see no. 174)*. The artist of the Cambridge Office of the Dead seems fluent in it. This suggests a date in the late 1480s or early 1490s, which is compatible with the time frame established by the reference to Innocent VIII (r.1484– 1492) in a prayer on fol. 154.

The invocation to St Gennaro, the patron of Naples, in the Litany as well as the feast of St Louis of Toulouse, son of Charles II of Naples (19 Aug.), and the dedication of San Salvatore (9 Nov.) in the Calendar confirm the Neapolitan origin of the manuscript. The feast of St Louis would have been particularly relevant to the manuscript's original owner. He recorded his name *Loisius* or initial *L* in many of the prayers. His arms were erased from fol. 13, but the medallion in the border to the Office of the Dead seems to preserve his portrait. Patrick Zutshi suggested (in conversation) that *Loisius* may be read as Aloysius, a tempting hypothesis. The nineteenth-century identifications with Louis XII (r.1498–1515), whose engraved portrait was inserted among the front paper flyleaves in the eighteenth century, or with Louis de Tremoille, the French commander defeated at Novara in 1513, may seem too late in view of Majorana's involvement in the manuscript. Jonathan Alexander remarked that Louis XI (r.1461–1483) would be more appropriate. Yet, the internal *terminus post quem* of 1484 excludes this possibility. An association with the future Louis XII as Duke of Orleans should be reconsidered. King Ferrante's second son, Federico d'Aragona (1451–1504) spent the period between 1478 and 1482 in the French court, and was exiled in Tours in 1501–1504. His patronage of Louis XII's painter Jean Bourdichon (Naples and Valencia 1998, 299–303) stimulated an exchange between French and Neapolitan artists and bibliophiles, of which the Cambridge Hours may be another manifestation.

PROVENANCE: original owner's name *Loisius* or initial *L* in prayers (fols. 220, 235, 235v, 236v, 239v, 261v, 266v); William Hamper (1776–1831); purchased at his sale (R.H. Evans, London, 21 July 1831, lot 493) by Thomas Rodd (1796–1849); Samuel Sandars (1837–1894); his bequest, 1894.

EXHIBITED: London 1893–1894, no. 115; Cambridge 1989–1990, no. 101.

LITERATURE: Frere 1894–1932, II, 121; Alexander 1985, 114.

SP

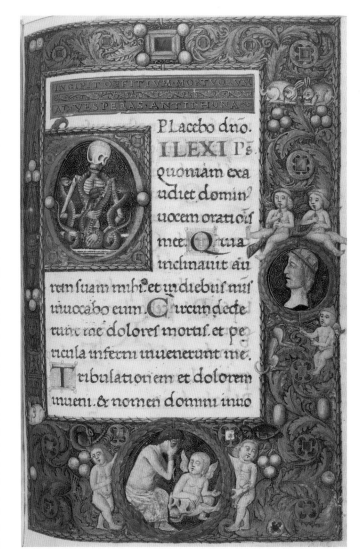

Opening to the Office of the Dead. Cambridge University Library, MS Add. 4105, fol. 157

104

Book of Hours

Use of Rome
In Latin
Italy, Florence, *c.*1490
ARTISTS: Attavante (Vante di Gabriello di Vante Attavanti, 1452–1520/1525) and assistants

Parchment, iii + 195 + iii fols., 142 × 102 mm, text 67 × 47 mm, 12 long lines, ruled in red ink

SCRIPT: Gothic bookhand (textualis)

BINDING: red velvet over paste boards, 19th c.

Fitzwilliam Museum, MS 154

THIS OPENING was painted by Attavante, one of the most celebrated illuminators in High Renaissance Florence. Enjoying an international clientele of ecclesiastical

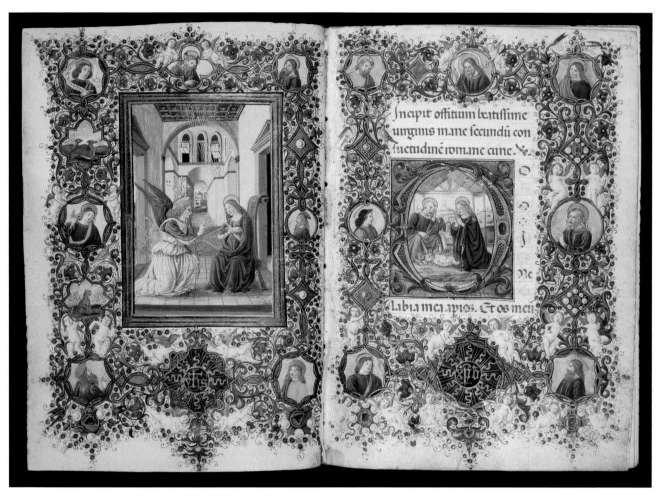

Annunciation and Adoration of the Child. Fitzwilliam Museum, MS 154, fols. 13v–14

and royal patrons, including King Matthias Corvinus of Hungary and Pope Leo X *(see no. 64)*, Attavante worked on volumes as diverse in medium, content and design as the Choir books of Santa Maria degli Angeli, Leonardo Bruni's *Florentine History*, and the splendid edition of Dante's *Divine Comedy* printed by Niccolò di Lorenzo in 1481 (Garzelli 1985, 220–45; London and New York 1993–1994, 39–40; D'Ancona 1994, 74–78). Of the Books of Hours firmly attributable to him, this is one of the most accomplished. It shows Attavante at an early stage of his independent career. Its compositions and ornamental vocabulary betray workshop patterns, which he adopted while apprenticed to Francesco di Antonio del Chierico in the early 1470s. They recur in manuscripts attributed to another of del Chierico's assistants, who collaborated with Attavante in the 1470s and 1480s and was named the Master of the Hamilton Xenophont after a manuscript in Berlin (Kupferstichkabinett, MS 78 C.24; Garzelli 1985, 157–62). The Virgin Annunciate seated on a high chair and the Archangel's flowing ribbons feature

in numerous works from the 1480s by Antonio del Chierico's anonymous followers (e.g. Cambridge University Library, MS Add. 4106), as well as in Books of Hours attributed to Attavante and to the Master of the Hamilton Xenophont (Garzelli 1985, figs. 492–493, 840–860). Attavante transformed these common motifs into a magnificent Renaissance composition. Centred within a neo-classical building and opening up to a distant landscape, it followed Alberti's principles of geometry and vanishing point perspective prized by Renaissance architects and painters. Attavante presented the interior of Mary's chamber as the meeting point of man-made and God-sent, the *inner sanctum* of the Incarnation, thus creating a three-dimensional ensemble of architecture and nature permeated by the divine presence.

His Annunciation became an influential model, especially in combination with the Adoration of the Child on the facing page. Both were adopted in Florentine Books of Hours of the 1490s, challenging the earlier page layout for Matins, which showed the Virgin standing in a portico, filled the facing initial with the Virgin and Child, and relegated the Adoration of the Child to a border medallion (London and New York 1994–1995, no. 31–33). These parallels and contrasts, as well as the appearance of the Adoration of the Child in Attavante's earliest dated work, the 1483 Missal of Thomas James (Lyon, Bibliothèque municipale, MS 5123, fol. 16; London and New York 1994–1995, no. 3), may suggest a date for the Fitzwilliam Hours in the late 1480s. By then, Attavante was already an established master with his own assistants, as the division of labour in this manuscript confirms. He painted the double openings at Matins for the Hours of the Virgin and the Penitential Psalms (David beheading Goliath and praying in the wilderness, fols. 84v–85), but entrusted an assistant with the initials for the remaining Hours of the Virgin and of the Passion. The other major text divisions, the Hours of the Cross, the Hours of the Passion, and the Office of the Dead, were illustrated by a third artist. Annarosa Garzelli identified him with the Master of the Hamilton Xenophont. If the second part of the manuscript was illuminated by him, it shows Attavante's long term colleague and collaborator in a subordinate role. The stylistic comparison with other works attributed to him does not seem conclusive and a detailed study of his artistic personality, as well as of Attavante's numerous assistants and followers, is much needed.

It is tantalizing that a manuscript of such exceptional quality bears no evidence of patronage. However, there may have been a change of plan fairly early in the

campaign. The numerous border medallions at the main text divisions, flanked by putti and perhaps intended for an owner's arms and devices, were either overpainted with the Sacred Monogram at the beginning of the manuscript or filled with busts of Christ, prophets, and Apostles in its later parts. It is possible that a change of patron prompted Attavante to hand the commission over to his colleague.

PROVENANCE: Acquired by Viscount Fitzwilliam in 1812; his bequest, 1816.

EXHIBITED: Cambridge 1966, no. 98.

LITERATURE: James 1895a, 349–50; D'Ancona 1914, 650; Garzelli 1985, 161, 242, figs. 499, 839, 843.

SP

105

The Primer of Claude of France

In Latin
France, *c.*1505–*c.*1510
ARTIST: Guido Mazzoni of Modena (act. 1473–1518)

Parchment, v (paper, 19th c.) + 10 (fols. 2v–9 paginated 1–14) + v (paper, 19th c.) fols., 260 × 175 mm, text 11 × 65 mm, 12 lines, ruled in red ink

SCRIPT: Gothic bookhand (textualis)

BINDING: red leather over wooden boards, 19th c.

Fitzwilliam Museum, MS 159

CHILDREN'S BOOKS are among the rarest medieval survivals. Most children learned to read from Psalters and Books of Hours (hence their English name 'Primer'), but some had specially designed Primers. This is one of the few extant examples. It contains everything the girl who voiced her prayers on pp. 10–11 needed to rehearse her Latin, learn her Bible, and practice her daily devotions. It opens with the alphabet, carefully penned and including variant shapes of letters and the three most common abbreviations. The scribe used them consistently in the text. The universal prayers of the Christian Church (*Our Father*, *Hail Mary*, Apostles' Creed, Grace before and after meals, Act of Confession, and Mass prayers) were clearly written on the fourteen pages of what is, essentially, a picture book. The story of the Creation, Fall, and Redemption unfolds in the miniatures which frame the short columns of text and dominate the page layout.

The opulent illumination and rich heraldry reveal the original owner. The girl presented by Bishop St Claude

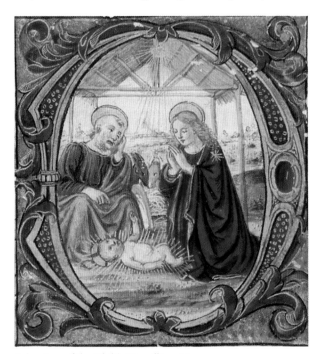

Adoration of the Child. Fitzwilliam Museum, MS 154, fol. 14, detail

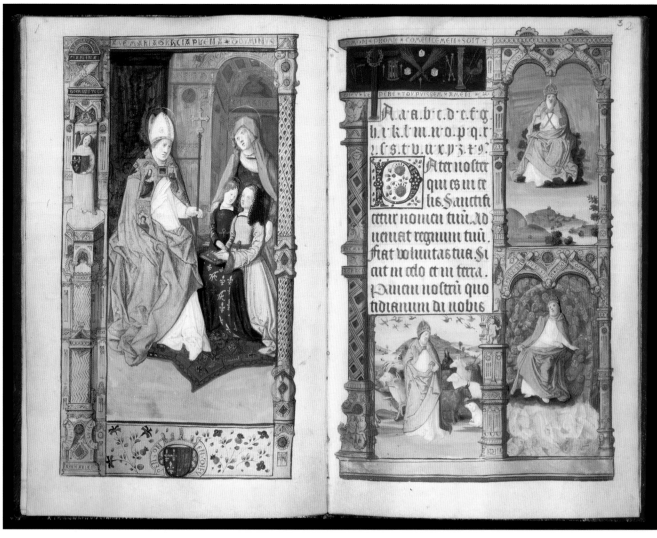

Anne of Brittany presented to St Claude and Creation scenes. Fitzwilliam Museum, MS 159, pp. 1–2

to St Anne and the Virgin in the miniature on p. 14 is Louis XII's and Anne of Brittany's eldest daughter, Claude (1499–1524). The fabric covering her prayer-desk is embroidered with her initial C. Like the angel's shield on the right and that in the lower margin, it impales the arms of France and Brittany. Claude's black gown and Breton headdress display the fashion Anne of Brittany introduced in the royal court. It may also represent an attempt to clothe the young girl in her mother's role, in anticipation of her future as planned around 1504–1505. In 1504, Claude's earlier engagement to Charles of Luxembourg, the future Holy Roman Emperor, was renewed, but in 1505 she was formally engaged to Francis, Duke of Angoulême, whom she married in 1514. The following year they were crowned King and Queen of France.

Previously named the Master of Antoine de Roche after one of his patrons, the illuminator was recently identified by Eberhard König as Guido Mazzoni of Modena. Impressively versatile in his command of different media, he was appreciated by aristocratic patrons throughout Italy (Verdon 1978). In 1496 he left for France with Charles VIII and was recorded among his Italian artists. After the king's death in 1498, Mazzoni remained closely associated with his widow, Anne of Brittany, working on the equestrian statue of Anne's third husband, Louis XII, and on manuscripts for the queen and her circle. Around 1500, he illuminated two Books of Hours (Oregon, Mount Angel Abbey, MS 6; Heribert Tenschert 2001, no. 44), which share the Primer's devotion to St Claude and display similar designs, inscriptions, and iconographic details. They show the idiosyncratic orthography of prayers and captions inscribed within the architectural frames in which König detected Italianate elements and which also appear in the Primer.

It was Anne who entrusted Guido Mazzoni with the illustration of the Primer and who decided on its content. Its prayers already featured, although in abbreviated form, in Anne's Prayer Book (New York, Pierpont Morgan Library, M. 50), which doubled as an ABC for her son Charles-Orland (1492–1495). They reappeared in the Primer of Renée, Claude's younger sister (Modena, Bibliotheca Estense, MS lat. 614), which postdates Anne's death in 1514. While neither of these manuscripts was illuminated by Mazzoni, Claude's Primer provides the link between them. It was made for Claude's own use, but Anne's involvement is unmistakable. She is depicted in the frontispiece shown here, introduced by St Anne and blessed by the saintly bishop after whom she named her daughter. Upon the prayer-desk embroidered with her initial rests the Primer, a most fitting gift from a royal mother to the future Queen of France.

PROVENANCE: Claude of France, before 1514; acquired by Viscount Fitzwilliam in 1808; his bequest, 1816.

LITERATURE: James 1895a, 356–59; Harthan 1977, 134–37; Sterling 1987–1990, I, 206; Paris 1993, 397; Wieck 1999, 151; König 2001, 8, 134, 141–42, 184; Wieck 2002, 1630.

SP

106

Book of Hours

Use of Rome
In Latin
France, Paris, c.1525–1530
ARTIST: Noël Bellemare (doc. 1512–1546)
and assistants ('Doheny Master')

Parchment, iii + 126 (paginated 1–252) + iii fols., 146 × 85 mm, text 95 × 48 mm, 20 long lines, ruled in red ink

SCRIPT: Humanistic minuscule

BINDING: red morocco over pasteboards, gold tooled *pointillé* leaf and dot pattern on outer margins, pewter clasps, 18th c.; rebacked by Robert Proctor, 2003.

Fitzwilliam Museum, MS 134

THIS BOOK OF HOURS is a splendid example of French Renaissance manuscript illumination and a representative specimen of one of the finest groups of manuscripts produced in Paris during the second quarter of the sixteenth century. Fitzwilliam MS 134 belongs

to a group of fourteen luxurious *Horae* produced in the same workshop during the 1520s and 1530s. Features common to most books in this group include humanistic script and epigraphic capitals, marginal illustration of gold panel borders with depictions of foliage, flowers and insects in *trompe-l'oeil*, Italianate tabernacle borders framing large miniatures, and miniatures that draw creatively on works of Antwerp Mannerist painting, German prints (particularly those of Albrecht Dürer), and Italianate decorative and figural vocabulary.

Originally assigned to a '1520s Hours Workshop' because of examples dated in that decade (Orth 1976; Orth 1988; Orth 1989), the works in this style have now been linked with the activity of Noël Bellemare, a painter and illuminator documented in Antwerp in 1512 and in Paris in 1515–1546, where he lived on the bridge of Notre-Dame, an established centre for Parisian illuminators, printers and *libraires* (Leproux 2001, 111–140). Although no signed manuscripts or documentary evidence connects Bellemare with the group of manuscripts formerly assigned to the '1520s Hours Workshop', he was active as a designer of works of stained glass, some of which are documented, and which serve as the nucleus of an oeuvre comprising paintings and illuminated manuscripts. Different painters appear to have collaborated on the manuscripts in Bellemare's style, suggesting that he was the head of the workshop where these works were made. Bellemare may well have painted some of the extant works, but because of the absence of evidence to establish which ones might be assignable to him and which to collaborators presumably working under his direction, the manuscript oeuvre is characterized as belonging to the 'Bellemare Group'.

One of the hallmarks of works of the Bellemare Group is the shared use and re-use of a number of common compositional and figural models among different painters. Shared motifs are particularly prominent in *Horae* associated with Bellemare's shop, which the late Myra Orth assigned to five miniaturists (Orth 1988, 58–9). Fitzwilliam MS 134 belongs to the largest such group, ascribed by Orth to the Doheny Master, whom she named after a manuscript formerly in the collection of Estelle Doheny in Camarillo, California (sale at Christie's, London, 2 December 1987, lot 174, now in a Private collection). Among works attributed to the Doheny Master, the Dutuit Hours (Paris, Petit Palais, Dutuit Collection, MS 37) bears the closest and the widest range of similarities to Fitzwilliam MS 34. Although their page sizes differ, the measurements of their written areas are identical. Ordinary text pages in both manuscripts have frames of gold fillets in the form of sticks, bars or knotted *cordelières* terminating in the lower margins in a variety of stylized knots. Seven of the fourteen full-page miniatures in the Fitzwilliam

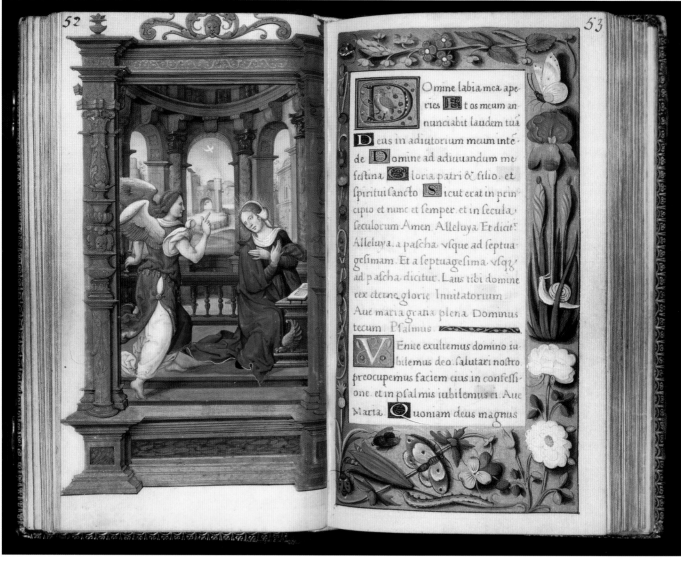

Annunciation and Matins of the Virgin, Fitzwilliam Museum, MS 134, pp. 52–53

Hours (of an original complement of fifteen; it lacks a Crucifixion at the beginning of the Hours of the Cross) are replicated in the Dutuit Hours: *Ego Sum*, the Annunciation, Visitation, Nativity, Adoration of the Magi, Presentation in the Temple and Job Mocked, and the first four of these also have identical architectural frames (Orth forthcoming, cat. no. 45). These and other of the miniatures have counterparts in additional *Horae* belonging to the Bellemare Group, including some ascribed to different painters.

The miniaturists, border decorators and the painters of miniature frames in these books appear to be different craftsmen. They drew from a common stock of models, replicating them in a variety of permutations and combinations, and gradually altering and updating them in accord with the changing taste and style of the

presumed director of the shop, Noël Bellemare. Early works in the group show the greatest debt to Antwerp Mannerist paintings, which were known to collaborators in the Bellemare Group primarily through the intermediary of model drawings (Orth 1989). Since Bellemare began his known career in Antwerp, he presumably brought a cache of such drawings back to Paris with him. In later works, the calligraphically complicated compositions, elongated and improbably posed figures, and theatrical costumes inspired by Antwerp Mannerist paintings yielded to works demonstrating greater restraint and increased influence from the traditions of Italian Renaissance art. Fitzwilliam MS 134 is an intermediate work, still demonstrating influence from the traditions of Antwerp Mannerism in such details as the implausibly complex pose of the figure at the left foreground of the Annunciation to the Shepherds, or the fanciful architecture of the Adoration of the Magi, but also including miniatures, such as the Visitation or David in Penitence, of noteworthy classical balance, order and grace. The works of the Bellemare Group demonstrate no substantive connections with Flemish manuscript illumination of the same period, which in addition to local patronage, enjoyed conspicuous success among leading patrons in Germany, Italy, Spain and Portugal. The mix of stylistic elements found in manuscripts belonging to the Bellemare Group constitutes a distinctly French idiom of Renaissance manuscript illumination, which has counterparts in other French works of art from the period of Francis I.

Like most other *Horae* in the Bellemare Group, Fitzwilliam MS 134 lacks any apparent signs of personalization or of its original ownership. The majority of the Books of Hours in this style may well have been produced seriatim for the open market, albeit for a class of moneyed and discriminating buyers.

PROVENANCE: acquired by Viscount Fitzwilliam in 1808; his bequest, 1816.

LITERATURE: Searle 1876, no. 93; James 1895a, 315–17; Orth 1976, 348–63, 371, 444, 449–50, figs. 157, 165, 193, 197, 228; Orth 1980, 46–47; Orth 1988, 46, 47, 58, 59; Orth 1989, 84; *Diminuto devocionario* 1995, 116; Buck 1997, 296, 301; Orth 2005, no. 45.

JHM

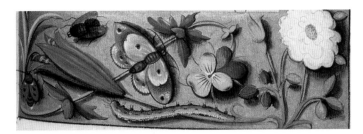

Detail of border, Fitzwilliam Museum, MS 134, p.53

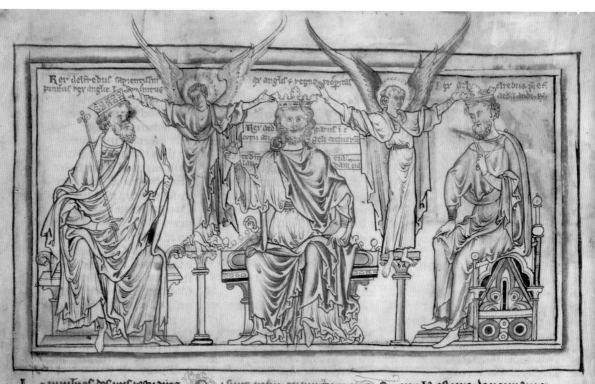

r numbres des rois regnaiez
eis chreitureus e cunquerranz
e fiz e freres de autre part
urol autre gesta aedwiard.
unt sun estoit Aedgar numez
ois fu de tuz bons estorez
eu tens de sa nescance.
l augre par signifiance.
mistrent pres en chantant.
l tens ke il seroit regnant
unt apres auoit le fiu
ois peisibles cum Salamun
ar cunal de sun barnage
alie par mariage.
u duc richard de normenche
t flur fu de chiualerie
une fille auoit mur bele
en entriehec damaisole
rois aedgard auoit un fiz
ert de force e seus garniz
aelfred hout nun bon iusticers
en pes peisible en guerre en fens
egne tint par uasselage

i sunt peinz en purttiure
t seint rois chint la same dire
rois sureint ia terrens
ore sint rois celestiens
e lur lignage fu estrait
diuuard de ki eist luie s fait
un eist ki ert peisible e sage
mez tremuz. Eist la femme
spusa. kauoit nun enme
nut li euples fu auenant
un de satu e ol luscaut
de lis e rose espanie
en tiue cuple e cumpainnie
lun fu de sane real
autre eim lru naturel
one fu de la reine
seiute tute la orine
eo pruua li nies e frere
a reine ke bone ere
eo fu richardz edut robert
un la estoire ni en fait terez
kar lur uie glorinse
lur mort fu preciuse

um la estoire de normantz
u latin eut e en romance
ore re pairum ala matire
chint iuis en en purpos dire
eldred hout auant un fiz
e la fille cunte theodrir
edmund ferru coste hout nun
archi e fort cum est leun
uis de la secunde femme
ille richard hout mueunme
il fred ki trop tost murut
ais aedmundz tai e crut
passa par uasseldage
ur le meuz de sun lignage
auoit mils uers ki atente
uis fu la reine en ceinte
un enfant kauenir fu
ar grace de deu e sa uertu
uant de poer serrot eage
i plus prudume de sun lignage
o fu aedward chint dire doi
i puis fu dengletere roi
tel tens uint en engletere

HISTORY AND LITERATURE: SACRED AND SECULAR

Rosamond McKitterick and Paul Binski

THE EMERGENCE of the European vernacular languages in the Middle Ages and their coexistence with Latin, the official language of the Church and of education, represent a dramatic enrichment of European culture. Most of the languages of medieval Europe still exist in modern forms, though some, such as Cornish or Occitan have become extinct as a consequence of communities being integrated into groups speaking a language that became more dominant. Old Irish is found in texts as early as the seventh century and Welsh, Breton and Cornish are also found in medieval manuscripts. In Europe the written form of many languages is associated with the conversion to Christianity. Thus Anglo-Saxon missionaries to Germany, and English and German missionaries in Scandinavia appear to have provided the initial impetus for written forms of Old High German and Old Norse respectively. Throughout Christendom, the dominance of the liturgical and biblical languages gradually gave way before the emergent local vernacular, especially in the Romance regions where French, Italian, Spanish, Portuguese and Romanian developed out of Latin. Although initially most vernacular texts were religious in nature, or even translations of Christian Latin works, it was not long before wonderful new literary works were composed, with versions and adaptations of old stories known from Latin texts, such as the story of the Trojan War or Chaucer's *Troilus and Creseyde (no. 129)*, as well as entirely new works. The *Roman de la Rose (no. 123)* and the works of Christine de Pizan in France *(no. 125)*, Chaucer's *Canterbury Tales (no. 130)* and poems and stories from other great writers such as John Lydgate in England are but a tiny sample of the wealth of creativity in vernacular literature in Europe from the twelfth century onwards. Vernacular literature, both secular and sacred, assumed a place side by side with the vast existing corpus of Latin literature from Antiquity and the earlier Middle Ages; each enriched the other.

Much of the interaction between Latin and the vernaculars accompanied a simultaneous interaction between sacred and secular concerns and between the clergy and laity. Bi- or even tri-lingualism was common. In England for much of the period after the Norman Conquest, for example, English, French and Latin were in use in different contexts but often by the same people. The presence of clerics in noble households as chaplains, secretaries or tutors, the daily communications associated with town life, and the interests of the lay elites in the arts and patronage of culture meant that there was a considerable intertwining of interests and Latin and vernacular traditions in non-ecclesiastical contexts throughout Europe.

These social contexts included royal and noble courts, townhouses of the civic dignitaries and private households. Secular literature and stories were produced for members of the educated upper classes who might have read the books as individuals, or to small groups informally. So, too, devotional works, guides to governance and moral behaviour, and didactic treatises on a variety of subjects were commissioned by, or presented to, members of the lay elites. Some of the books included in this category and exhibited here are René of Anjou's *La Mortifiement de Vaine Plaisance*

Fig. 32. Kings Alfred, Edgar and Ethelred with angels. Cambridge University Library, MS Ee.3.59, fol. 3v

235

(no. 121), the *Somme le Roi*, Jehan Robertet's *Les Douze Dames de Rhétorique (no. 127)*, Gower's *Confessio Amantis (no. 131)* and Roger Dymmok's tract against the Lollards.

Many of the books included in this necessarily miscellaneous section cannot be understood simply in terms of modern categorization: they illustrate the porous boundaries of medieval thinking about the historical, the spiritual, the mythological and the pastoral. Genres were not necessarily distinct, and works of literature and history could also have additional didactic, religious or moral functions. Thus in his *Memorable Deeds and Sayings (no. 120)*, the Roman historian Valerius Maximus made it clear that conventions of personal and public morality and conduct within public affairs were communicated through rhetorical examples. Yet he also presented a concern for the excesses of civilization. He offered moral reflections on the very monuments, political symbols of power, statues, public buildings and the ostentatious display of wealth in the form of marble, gold and paintings that would undoubtedly have impressed visitors to Rome. His text could certainly provide historical examples and information, but with his perception of the past as a moral warning and set of historical precedents, Valerius Maximus provided a model for subsequent reinterpretations of the classical ideas of Rome and more generally, for perceptions of the past. Similar techniques for instruction by persuasion and example characterize such Christian pastoral works as the *Somme le Roi (no. 116)*.

Valerius Maximus also serves as a representative example of further cross fertilization between the Latin and vernacular traditions, for his writings were translated into a number of the European languages which circulated alongside the fine Latin versions disseminated throughout the Middle Ages. A French version made by Simon de Hesdin, for example, was presented to King Charles V of France and a Latin version produced in the Low Countries in the fifteenth century is included in this exhibition *(no. 120)*. The massive *Historia scholastica* of biblical history up to Christ's Ascension, completed with a history of the Apostles by Peter of Poitiers, was translated into French, Dutch, Portuguese and Czech, and versified and dramatized. The story of Alexander the Great, represented here in the Trinity copy of the Alexander Romance *(no. 122)*, was presented to medieval audiences in many forms and languages – Greek, Latin, French, Spanish, Italian, German, Dutch, Middle English, Old Norse and even medieval Arabic – with a strong emphasis on its moral lessons about power and pride (Ross 1963).

Further, familiar works might be adapted into a new literary form for communication to a different audience. This appears to have been the function of William Caxton's rendering of the moralized Ovid *(no. 169)* and Arator's versified transformation of the Acts of the Apostles *(no. 12)*. Arator's work was designed for recitation; it serves as a further reminder that the written text could also be a performed text and thus play a large role in oral communication (Green 1994).

The audiences for history and for literature throughout the Middle Ages were more often than not one and the same (Gransden 1974–1982; Innes and McKitterick 1994; Morgan 1996; McKitterick 2004). History can indeed be regarded as a form of literature, yet with the overriding purpose of keeping alive the memory of those dead and gone and to bring them to the attention of future generations. History could also have a moral and didactic function. Bede, in his *Ecclesiastical History*, thought that his history could provide good examples as well as a record of the deeds of wicked men to encourage the reader or hearer to avoid what was sinful or perverse. Hagiography could serve a similar purpose and draw on related ideas and sources. The degree to which history set out to portray a true record or a selective and dramatic presentation of events for particular purposes implicated it in styles and methods of interpretation commonly associated with rhetoric and literature (Morse 1991). Nevertheless, the written modes of memory-keeping took many forms. One of the most striking characteristics of the literature and historical writing of medieval Europe is how much variety there was in the forms of historical records of past actions and deeds.

Those writing in Europe in the Middle Ages certainly inherited a number of written precedents for historical writing from Antiquity. These included, first, the historians of classical and Late Antiquity such as Caesar, Livy, Sallust, Tacitus, Suetonius, Velleius Paterculus, Eutropius and Justinus. These so-called pagan historiographers focused on war and politics, emphasized the political and moral function of their writing and deployed the rhetorical tradition in their texts, not least in putting invented speeches into the mouths of their protagonists *(i.e. ethopoiia)*. Not surprisingly such an approach to historical narrative continued to find favour in later centuries, whether in later copies of its original form, or in histories that emulated this style of writing.

Secondly, the development of Christian historiography in the fourth century has been regarded as a direct challenge to the pagan view of the past. Augustine's conception of history is key to this. Conversion to Christianity entailed the discovery of, and realignment with, a new past that embraced the Old Testament in its entirety and propagated the Jewish vision of God's providence revealing itself in history. Christian history was added to Jewish history as part of one long teleologically-connected scheme of Redemption. Josephus' histories of the Jews in his *Antiquities* and the *Jewish Wars (nos. 108, 109)* as well as the Bible were of great importance in the formation of the Christian view of the past. Eusebius, the most prominent of the early Christians to put together a history of the Christian Church, offered accounts of religious beliefs and practices, battles against persecution and heresy, struggles against evil and the devil, and a narrative which incorporated many documents, synodal proceedings and imperial letters. Eusebius also compiled a Chronicle, subsequently translated and extended by Jerome. It took the form of chronological tables constructed from Abraham to the twentieth year of the reign of the Emperor Constantine I. Olympiads are cited alongside the years since Abraham by way of chronological orientation, as, where appropriate, were the regnal years of kings, judges, archons and emperors. Columns were provided to indicate events under the headings of Medes, Persians, Athenians, Hebrews, Macedonians and Romans. Eusebius-Jerome did not tell the Hebrew story alone, therefore, for the fortunes of Jews and Christians are intertwined with the histories of the Assyrians, Persians, Greeks, Romans and others.

It was the ecclesiastical history of Eusebius, together with the Chronicle of Eusebius-Jerome, which proved to be the most influential model for Christian forms of historiography. Eusebius was emulated by many subsequent historians, not least Bede himself, for Eusebius-Jerome had demonstrated how local or national history could be placed in the context of God's time. By this means authors were able explicitly to link their present to the whole course of Christian history. Similarly, the focus on Christians as a group was also influential for subsequent historians who wrote the histories of particular people, e.g. the Franks, and portrayed them as successors of the Jews and early Christians as the chosen people of God.

In addition to emulating and continuing types of historical narrative inherited from the classical and early Christian periods, new forms of historical writing such as annals, historical epics, secular biographies and Saints' Lives were developed in the course of the Middle Ages, especially in France and Germany and, in their wake, England. Among these, histories of institutions such as monasteries (themselves often organized as serial biographies) and sacred biographies of individuals, characterized as hagiography, are prominent. Many of the former, such as the History of St Augustine's Canterbury *(no. 115)*, demonstrated how the past of a particular institution or of a people was crucial for the formation of that community's identity. Thus written history acted as an expression of identity as well as a record of collective memory. Similarly the Life of Edward the Confessor is an instance of the combining of sacred and secular concerns and of different narrative conventions to create a very distinctive and influential work, one of whose purposes is to promote not only kingship, but also Westminster Abbey *(fig. 32, no. 113)*.

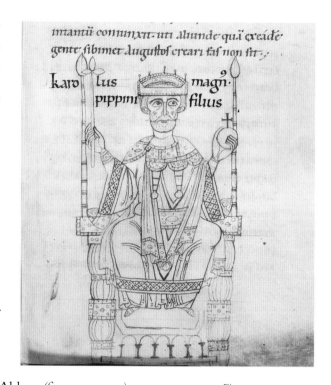

Fig. 33. Charlemagne. Corpus Christi College, MS 373, fol. 24, detail

A further important successor of the Chronicle of Eusebius-Jerome was the genre of world chronicle or universal history. This contrived to combine aspects of both the pagan and the Christian historiographical methods and scope. Universal history was sacred history; histories which traced the rise and fall of empires from the time of Abraham were by implication directed conceptually towards the Last Judgement and the working out of God's providence in time. Yet many historians in the Middle Ages sought to identify or define the position of their own times in relation to this larger scheme of events. Time and chronology thus could also play a role in defining a people. It was not until the eighth century AD that the Christian era began to play a role as an organizing principle in historical narratives. Histories began with the foundation of Rome, with Abraham – as Eusebius-Jerome had done in their Chronicle – or with the creation of the world itself as the fifth-century writer Orosius had advocated in his *Seven books of history against the pagans*. Thereafter the chronology might be orchestrated in terms of the years of the world, or more imprecisely as a succession of events with occasional reference to the reign of current rulers. From the eighth century, however, histories in the form of yearly annual entries start to be produced. Yet as can be seen from the manuscript of the 'Imperial Chronicle' in this exhibition *(fig. 33, no. 107)*, the author oriented himself more in relation to the Frankish than to a Christian or Roman past, despite a superficial resemblance to the genre of universal history which flourished in late medieval France in particular. In England, a number of writers also adopted the framework of universal history. One of the most famous of the English historians was Matthew Paris, whose *Chronica Majora (no. 114)* covered the period from the Creation to the affairs of England in 1259. Matthew Paris, in his versatility and crossing of conventional boundaries in terms of language, craftsmanship, literary genre and social involvement, is a figure that in many ways combines all the themes addressed in this essay: he was a monk, yet had travelled to Norway as well as other places in England; he wrote in both prose and verse; he wrote in both Latin and Anglo-Norman; he was concerned with political and secular affairs; he illustrated many of his own texts (Vaughan 1958; Lewis 1987).

The unusual nature of Matthew Paris's art draws attention to the fact that surviving early medieval works of literature and history are rarely illustrated. Although there is a handful of Late Antique codices with picture cycles, generally the books chosen for embellishment in late Antiquity and the early Middle Ages were primarily liturgical books, and these were rarely narrative pictures. It is possible that wealth might have been the simple determinant of whether or not a book was illustrated. Attitudes towards the appropriateness or even necessity of illustration may also be relevant. There is no evidence that classical or early Christian histories were illustrated and all our earliest copies are almost entirely without adornment apart from headings and display capitals, and occasionally a fine initial. Some used the visual medium to provide pictorial exegesis on the text. Yet from late Antiquity we also have resplendent illustrated copies of Virgil's great historical epic, the *Aeneid* (Wright 2001). In sculpture, historical scenes are known from Antiquity from triumphal arches and columns such as Trajan's column in Rome. It is not until the twelfth century that illustrations begin to appear in historical texts, at first in the form of small drawings inserted into the margins or within the text. Only in the later Middle Ages are universal histories and Chronicles produced with extensive and lavish illustration.

With the works of history and literature of all kinds we need to remember that although these survive in book form they should also be seen in terms of visual impact and performance. The texts were most probably intended for individual use as well as for a listening public. The illuminations and narrative illustrations served to highlight particular episodes and to draw the attention, understanding and admiration of those who owned them, quite apart from their function as displays of wealth and social standing. The decoration of books, moreover, was extended to the illumination of laws and documents which individuals and institutions of great wealth and social standing were in a position to commission. The richly ornamented copies of documents such as the Statutes of the Order of the Golden Fleece *(no. 138)*, the charter of King Edward I *(no. 133)*, the Statutes of the Order of the Garter *(no. 137)*, the *Statuta Angliae (no. 134)*, and *La anatomia de España (fig. 34, no. 142)* are eloquent witnesses to the devotion or artistic and scribal resources to make statements about political power and authority. Equally the Medinilla patent of nobility from Valladolid *(no. 141)* is a clear indication of the high expectations of members of the aristocracy and their access to literacy and the skills of artisans in order to make osten-

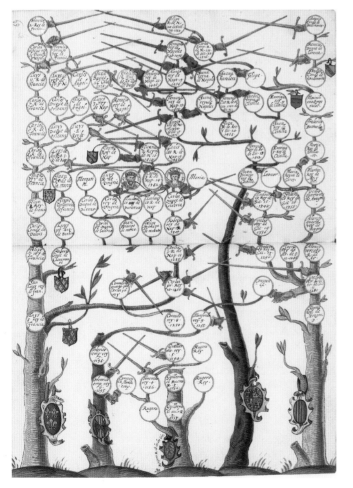

Fig. 34. European dynasties. Cambridge University Library, MS Gg.6.19, fols. 36v–37 *(shown here as upright image)*

239

tatious statements about their social rank. Therefore everyone involved in the production and reception of these books, whether author, scribe, artist, reader or audience, was contributing to the communication of the texts. Our reception of them as works of art should not be at the expense of a recognition of the meaning of the texts and of the social and cultural milieu in which these manuscripts and illuminated documents were produced.

The examples of book art which follow demonstrate the developments outlined in this essay. First, we find chronicle writing devoted to the history of peoples, specifically the Franks and the Jews *(nos. 107, 108, 109)*; biblical and secular history in the twelfth-century writings of Peter of Poitiers and Petrus Comestor follows *(no. 110)*. Three works of hagiography concerning Cuthbert, Guthlac and Edward the Confessor, demonstrate the proximity of this genre to history writing *(nos. 111, 112, 113)*. The bridge from the Cambridge Life of St Edward *(no. 113)* to the great *Chronica Majora* of Matthew Paris *(no. 114)* is inevitable; Matthew Paris also used at least one other book in this collection *(no. 28)*. His generous conception of institutional history is continued in the St Augustine's chronicle *(no. 115)* which, like Matthew's, includes mapping, again enabling a connection to another book in the exhibition *(no. 1)*. The emphasis then shifts towards the considerable body of writings of Christian pastoral instruction on the fundamental tenets of the faith and the nature of virtue and sin. The universalist reforming policies of the Catholic Church were stimulating the production of texts of pastoral instruction for the laity, often in the vernacular, which attracted illustration. For all their moral subtlety there is a touch of the schoolroom about such texts as the *Somme le Roi*, reflecting the widespread efforts of the Church to promulgate and, if necessary, enforce proper doctrine evidenced in the great ecumenical councils of the Lateran in 1179 and 1215. Though often very modest works produced in thousands for lay instruction, a minority received fine illumination for royal or seigneurial patrons such as the late thirteenth-century *Somme le Roi* written for Philippe III by a Dominican, and its unique English illuminated counterpart *(nos. 116, 117)*. The role of bishops in pastoral instruction was as important as that of the preaching orders, as we see from the later compendium of works by St Augustine and the major English bishop and pastoral writer, Robert Grosseteste, Bishop of Lincoln (d.1253) probably made for the young Henry Bolingbroke *(no. 118)*. Works such as Valerius Maximus's *Memorable Deeds and Sayings* *(no. 120)* and Guillebert de Lannoy, *L'Instruction d'un Jeune Prince (no. 120)* belong to a parallel tradition of secular advice literature for rulers or aristocrats, and rooted in classical, ethical and rhetorical traditions. A high proportion of works in this section were instrumental in influencing notions of civilized conduct which have until recently formed the bedrock of Western conceptions of courtliness, or courtesy.

Literary entertainment in the vernacular includes the Anglo-Norman Alexander Romance *(no. 122)*, a commercial Parisian copy of the *Roman de la Rose (no. 123)*, the remarkable collection of the complete works of Guillaume de Machaut *(no. 124)*, Christine de Pizan's *L'Epistre d'Othéa (no. 125)* and an exceptional copy of the *Légende Dorée*, a French translation of Jacobus de Voragine's *Legenda aurea* based on the translation of Jean de Vignay, produced for Jeanne de Bourgogne, wife of King Philippe VI of France *(no. 128)*. The manuscripts of the works of Chaucer, Gower and Lydgate include the remarkable *Troilus and Creseyde* frontispiece *(no. 129)* almost certainly showing Chaucer himself. A group of fine English, Netherlandish, Venetian and Spanish manuscripts concerning ritual, rank and territory completes this section.

107

Imperial Chronicle

In Latin
Germany, 1112–1113

Parchment, ii + 96 + ii fols., 215 x160 mm, text
160 × 85–90 mm, 24 long lines, ruled in hard point

SCRIPT: late Caroline minuscule / early Gothic bookhand
(textualis)

BINDING: full undyed goatskin over millboards, by J.P. Gray,
1954.

Corpus Christi College, MS 373

THIS TEXT is the autograph of an anonymous author working in Würzburg in 1112–1113. It recounts the history of the Franks, clearly presented as the ancestors of the Emperor Henry V at whose request it was written. It provides the history from the origins of the Franks in Troy to the twelfth century, and associates the illustrious Carolingian rulers of the Frankish Empire, not least Charlemagne, with the Saxon and Salian emperors of the German regions. The Trojan origins of the Franks were first claimed in the seventh century by the Frankish historian Pseudo-Fredegar. A different version of the Trojan story was provided by an anonymous author of a text known as the *Liber historiae francorum*. In this work Book I covers the period from the beginnings to Charlemagne; Book II the period from *c.*800, the year in which Charlemagne was crowned Emperor of the Romans in Rome by Pope Leo III, to 1100. Book III gives the story from 1106–1113. A continuation has been added which takes the narrative to 1125. The third quire with the account of the years 760–784 is missing.

This Chronicle used to be attributed to Ekkehard of Aura (Buchholz 1888; von den Brincken 1957). However, it is now widely accepted that Ekkehard's Chronicle was not only a reworking and continuation to 1106 of an earlier universal Chronicle by Frutolf of Michelsberg, but that he had made use, while resident in Würzburg, of the anonymous imperial Chronicle whose sole witness is this autograph. The complex text history of this important historical work is indicated by the fact that the anonymous author worked in part from a first draft of Ekkehard's reworking of Frutolf and made various improvements which Ekkehard incorporated into his own final version made for Erkembert, Abbot of Corvey before 1116–1117 (Schmale and Schmale-Ott 1972). Unfortunately nothing has been established about the author of the Corpus Chronicle apart from what is indicated in his text. It is written in good Latin and is more sympathetic to imperial power than to the papacy.

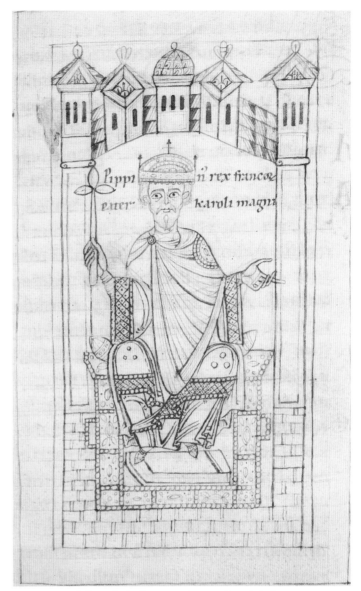

King Pippin, father of Charlemagne. Corpus Christi College, MS 373, fol. 14

The book is illustrated with pen drawings outlined in brown and red. They mostly comprise a series of kings and emperors portrayed enthroned and full face, with crown and sceptre. The marriage feast in 1114 of Henry V and the English princess Matilda is described and depicted in the Chronicle on fol. 95v. The portrayal of the king exhibited here is typical of the collection, with the royal regalia in the form inherited from Carolingian ruler portraits. Pippin III, depicted here, was the father of Charlemagne. Pippin usurped the throne of the Merovingian kings of the Franks in 751. He is given a full page, whereas his more famous son is squeezed into the lower half of fol. 24 *(fig. 33)*. Each book is introduced by an *incipit* in Rustic capitals and a six-line pen-drawn foliage initial with animal head finials. The work was dedicated to Henry V of Germany who was married to the English princess Matilda, daughter of Henry I of England.

PROVENANCE: the flyleaves include a ninth-century charter donation to St Kylian, Würzburg from the diocese of Würzburg which refers to a Count Egino and his wife Ventilgart as well as Bishop Wolfger of Würzburg (d.832); possibly brought to England by Henry V's widow Matilda and certainly in England by the late fourteenth century; Matthew Parker (1504–1575); his bequest, 1575.

EXHIBITED: Cambridge 1975, no. 16.

LITERATURE: James 1912b, II, 215–18; Schmale-Ott 1971; Robinson 1988, no. 155, pl. 41.

RMCK

108

Josephus, *Antiquitates iudaicae*, Books I–XIV

In Latin
Christ Church, Canterbury, first quarter of
the twelfth century

Parchment, iii (i modern paper, ii–iii medieval parchment) + 235 (foliated 5–239) + v (i–iv medieval parchment, v modern paper) fols., 406 × 280–290 mm, text 303 × 192 mm, 2 columns, 39 lines, ruled in plummet.

SCRIPT: late Caroline minuscule

BINDING: quarter niger morocco with marbled paper sides, by S. Cockerell, 20th century.

Cambridge University Library, MS Dd.1.4

THIS AND THE NEXT MANUSCRIPT *(no. 109)* comprise a two-volume copy of the two major historical works of the first-century Jewish historian, Josephus Flavius. In the medieval Latin West, these texts were read primarily as adjuncts to biblical study and the patristic exegesis that accompanied it. They enjoyed renewed popularity from the early twelfth century, and were accorded the same kind of visual presentation as the major patristic texts that were also being copied in considerable numbers during this period.

The two volumes are among the largest and most handsome books produced at Christ Church, Canterbury during the early twelfth century, and display as full and elaborate an apparatus of major initials, minor initials, display script and rubrics as any of the Christ Church books of this date. The text was evidently studied closely at Christ Church during the twelfth century, since marginal annotations were supplied that added precision to Josephus's own internal cross-references. In the fifteenth century, it was one of a number of manuscripts that was heavily annotated by a Christ Church monk with a series of heavy dots and ice-cream cone-

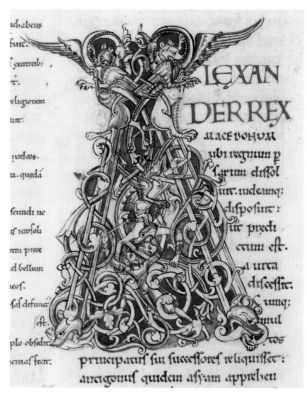

Inhabited initial. Cambridge University Library, MS Dd.1.4, fol. 184v, detail

shaped marks drawing attention to passages he considered of special importance.

Both volumes are the work of different artists but a single Christ Church scribe who wrote an excellent mature version of the distinctive variety of Caroline minuscule developed at Christ Church during the late eleventh and early twelfth centuries. In this volume, the major initials were supplied by three artists whose work displays different phases in the development of Anglo-Norman manuscript art at Christ Church. The artist of the inhabited initials on fols. 64v, 100v, 121, 170 and 184v designed initials that still reflect the late Anglo-Saxon style of figure-drawing. The artist of the initial on fol. 220, however, was already working within a stylistic tradition that is more obviously Romanesque. His work has been identified not only in other Christ Church manuscripts, but also in books written by scribes at nearby Rochester Cathedral Priory (including Trinity O.4.7, *no. 23*). The inclusion of these Rochester books in a catalogue probably datable to 1122–1123 provides valuable dating evidence for the activity of this artist and for the use of a more fully-developed Romanesque style of manuscript illumination at Christ Church before the end of the first quarter of the twelfth century.

PROVENANCE: Christ Church, Canterbury: no. 339 in early 14th-century catalogue of Prior Eastry; 15th-century Christ Church *ex libris* inscription, fols. 114, 227; no. 149 in Ingram's list of 1508; Richard Holdsworth, Master of Emmanuel College (d.1649); his bequest, 1649; received by the University Library in 1664.

EXHIBITED: London 1984b, no. 43.

LITERATURE: University Library 1856–1867, I, 6–7; James 1903, 51, 157; Dodwell 1954, 22, 29, 39, 68, 73, 78, 120; Kauffmann 1975, no. 43; Heslop 1984, 200; Gameson 1995, 130; Gameson 1999, no. 17.

TW

109

Josephus, *Antiquitates iudaicae, Books XV–XX; De bello iudaico*

In Latin
Christ Church, Canterbury, first quarter of the twelfth century

Parchment, iii (i–ii paper, iii medieval parchment) + 217 (numbered sporadically and inaccurately to give the following sequence: 1–20, 31–106, 123–26, 128–245, and followed by an early 16th-c. printed book) fols., 377 × 280 mm, text 306 × 193 mm, 2 columns, 39 lines, ruled in plummet

SCRIPT: late Caroline minuscule

BINDING: gold-tooled brown leather over boards, with arms of William Crashaw, early 17th century.

St John's College, MS A. 8 (James no. 8)

THIS IS THE SECOND of a two-volume copy of the works of Josephus *(see no. 108)*. Its major initials were executed by a different group of three artists, indicating the richness of the artistic as well as scribal resources available at Christ Church during the early decades of the twelfth century.

Some doubt surrounds the iconography of the initials to Book XV and Book XVII, which Dodwell argued had been mistakenly included in the wrong volume, since he believed that their subject-matter applied to Books I and III. This presumed error, together with the comparative paucity of historiated initials in Christ Church manuscripts might, therefore, indicate a lack of experience in pictorial illustration on the part of artists at Christ Church. But it has subsequently been suggested that the initial to Book XV can be interpreted in a way that makes more sense of its position.

The iconography of the initial to the first book of the *Jewish Wars* also raises questions that are difficult to resolve. It depicts not only the author, Josephus, but also a seated scribe named in an inscription, Samuel. Since no Samuel has been identified in connection with

Josephus, it is tempting to interpret this as a scribal portrait. A Samuel '*leuita*' is recorded in an extensive early fifteenth-century Christ Church obituary list, which includes the names of monks and other persons associated with the priory from the pre-Conquest period onwards (London, British Library Arundel MS 68, fol. 47). The simple form of the name might suggest an early date, but no evidence survives to date this Samuel more closely to the early twelfth century.

PROVENANCE: late twelfth-century Christ Church library mark, fol. 1; no. 340 in the early fourteenth-century catalogue of Prior Eastry; fifteenth-century Christ Church *ex libris* inscription, fols. 2, 243; no. 148 in Ingram's list of 1508; William Crashaw (1572–1626); c.1615 Henry Wriothesley, Earl of Southampton; given to the College by his son Thomas Wriothesley in 1635.

EXHIBITED: London 1984b, no. 43a.

LITERATURE: James 1903, 51, 157; James 1913, 9–10; Dodwell 1954, 22, 32, 36, 63, 70, 77, 121; Kauffmann 1975, no. 44; Deutsche 1986, 61, fig. 6; Gameson 1999, no. 118; Kendrick 1999, front cover, 131, fig. 62.

TW

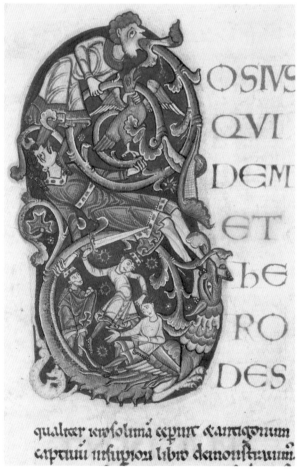

Cain's sacrifice; Cain slaying Abel. St John's College, MS A.8, fol. 1v

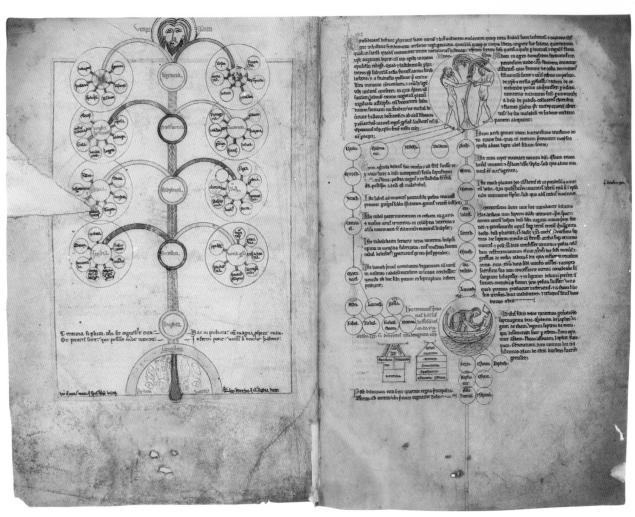

Tree of Vices, Temptation of Adam and Eve, Noah building the Ark. Christ's College, MS 5, fols. 1v–2

110

Peter of Poitiers, *Compendium in genealogia Christi*; Peter Comestor, *Historia scholastica* and *Allegoriae*

In Latin
France or England, *c.*1210– *c.*1230

Parchment, ii (paper, 19th c.) + 154 + ii (paper, 19th c.) fols., 320 × 220 mm, text 230–235 × 140–155 mm, 2 cols., 58 lines, ruled in crayon and plummet

SCRIPT: Gothic bookhand (textualis)

BINDING: brown leather over pasteboards, 19th c., rebacked; the chain of a previous binding left holes and rusty stains in the lower margins.

Christ's College, MS 5

PETER OF POITIERS, Chancellor of the University of Paris (1193–1205), was as interested in sacred history as in speculative theology, and also famous for his eloquent preaching and effective teaching of *sacra pagina* (Moore 1936, 118–22). These multifarious interests, but mostly his concern for poor students, gave rise to his *Compendium*, a sequence of genealogical tables with brief entries on Christ's ancestors, biblical characters, and historical rulers. It provided an indispensable tool for the study of the Bible, together with Peter Lombard's *Magna Glossatura* and Peter Comestor's *Historia Scholastica*, to which it was often appended, as in this manuscript and other Cambridge copies (Corpus Christi College, MS 29, Cambridge University Library, MSS Dd.1.16 and Ff.3.7). Its immediate success and long-lasting popularity led to the wide dissemination of numerous versions of the text. They range from sporadic *ad hoc* additions, excerpted from biblical paraphrases and versifications such as the *Historia Scholastica* or Peter Riga's *Aurora*, to heavy interpolations, which reduced the original *Compendium* to only one part of a large world chronicle. Cambridge is rich in copies preserving various recensions and dating from the twelfth to the fifteenth century. Some fifteenth-century copies, such as a scroll in

244

Cambridge University Library, MS Dd.3.56, contain fewer interpolations than manuscripts dating from as early as the end of the twelfth century, for instance MS Dd.1.16 at the University Library. The Christ's College copy preserves one of the purest versions and features of the *Compendium*'s original format, the animal skins which Peter of Poitiers used to hang in the classroom. It is also representative of the *Compendium*'s pictorial content.

The diagrams of Noah's ark, the mansions in the desert, the Tabernacle, and *habitatio regis et sacerdotum*, all present in this volume (fols. 2, 3v, 6), were designed by Peter of Poitiers as mnemonic devices. They structured and elucidated the large body of factual material summarized in the genealogical tables (Evans 1980; Di Mauro 1992). Simply informative or aesthetically pleasing, they reveal a highly developed appreciation among medieval readers for the pedagogical advantages of diagrammatic images. By contrast, the illustrations of biblical personages and scenes, and of world rulers were probably not among the components which Peter of Poitiers considered essential: though a feature of many interpolated copies, they are found in very few manuscripts of the original version. Christ's College MS 5 is one of them. In addition to the images seen here, the volume contains medallions with Isaac's Sacrifice (fol. 2v), David playing his harp (fol. 4), the Nativity and the Flight to Egypt (fol. 7), the Crucifixion and the Ascension (fol. 7v). The drawings are tinted in green and ochre. Their details are enhanced in the red and blue pigments used for the penwork capitals, diagram frames, and lines between the names' annulets. This and the division of labour throughout the volume, with changes of scribal hands and decoration coinciding but not corresponding neatly to the quire structure, suggest that the manuscript was produced in a religious house. At some stage the volume was clearly chained for communal use in a monastic or cathedral library.

Yet, in its capacity as a reference tool on biblical and secular history, the *Compendium* entered other realms, those of cosmology, divination, preaching, and moral theology (Hilpert 1985; Carlino 1996–1997; Panayotova 2001). It was disseminated together with sermons. Its textual and visual content was extended to cover the elements of Creation or devices for prognostication (Cambridge University Library, Dd.3.56). It also received additional images associated with other works by Peter of Poitiers, the seven-branched candlestick (Cambridge, Corpus Christi College, MS 29 and Fitzwilliam Museum, MS 253) or trees of Virtues and Vices. The Tree of Vices seen here was by a hand not otherwise found in the manuscript. Although an abstract theological diagram with a strong devotional and ethical bias, very different from the seemingly pragmatic purpose of the *Compendium*'s drawings, it introduces the theme of

Salvation with which the historical and genealogical progression in the *Compendium* culminates.

PROVENANCE: Edward Wilde (ownership inscription, 17th c., fol. 1) who had been a student at Christ's (Peile 1910, I, 269) and probably gave or bequeathed the manuscript to the college.

LITERATURE: James 1905c, 5–6 ; Panayotova 2001, 332 n. 27, 335 n. 34, 336 n. 38, 340, 341.

SP

111

Bede, Lives of St Cuthbert, etc.

In Latin
Southern England, 934–939

Parchment, 96 fols., 292 × 197 mm, text 212 × 122 mm, 26 long lines, ruled in hard point

SCRIPT: Insular minuscule (Anglo-Saxon square minuscule)

BINDING: undyed goatskin over boards, 20th c.

Corpus Christi College, MS 183

FEW MANUSCRIPTS are as expressive of the historical context within which they were produced as Corpus 183. Its illustration and contents reveal that it was an instrument of King Æthelstan's patronage of the most powerful Northumbrian religious community as he sought to maintain control over Northern England, only recently brought under the rule of the West Saxon dynasty. The manuscript is a superb witness to the revival of intellectual and religious life, including high standards of book production, achieved between the reigns of Alfred and his grandson, Æthelstan. It is also an early example of the fruitful combining of Continental and native traditions of book arts that would culminate in the achievements associated with the tenth-century monastic reform.

Gifts of books and relics were important tools in Æthelstan's patronage of religious houses. Corpus 183 is the only surviving example of books that were wholly made in England during his reign. It was designed from the outset as a presentation copy for the community of St Cuthbert at Chester-le-Street. The superb full-page, framed frontispiece depicting a crowned king with an open book and a saint standing before a church, one hand raised in blessing, the other holding a book, is widely accepted to represent Æthelstan himself and St Cuthbert, the most important saint of the north of England. This is followed by a carefully planned collection of texts about the saint: Bede's prose and metrical lives, and a liturgical Office. The two lives are separated by an assemblage of material including a number of lists

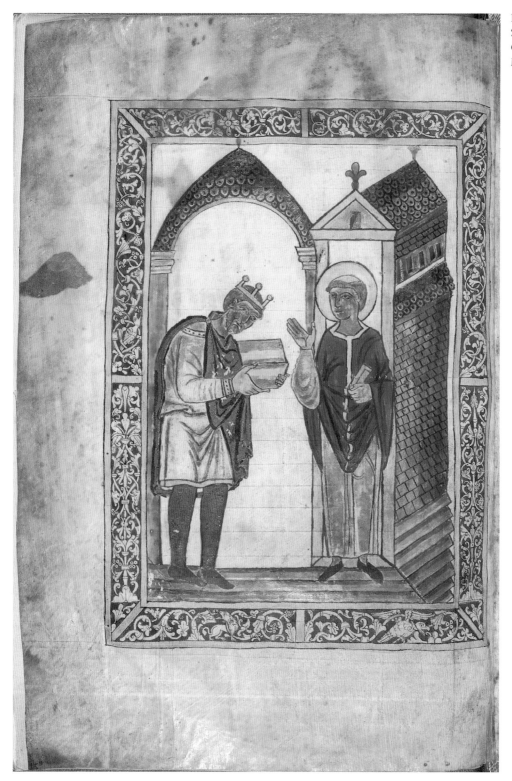

King Æthelstan with
St Cuthbert. Corpus
Christi College,
MS 183, fol. 1v

of popes, bishops and kings of Anglo-Saxon dioceses and kingdoms, and royal genealogies. It has been suggested that the inclusion of this material may have made the gift more than an act of patronage from a member of the West-Saxon dynasty to the community of a Northumbrian saint to secure their favour. It may have also been a politically pointed reminder 'of the essential unity of the Anglo-Saxon church and ... the ancient links which bound the various Anglo-Saxon kingdoms together.'

The papal and episcopal lists on fols. 59–64v do not offer straightforward clues as to when the book was produced and presented to the community at Chester-le-Street. They include Bishops Ælfheah of Winchester and Æthelgar of Crediton who became bishops some time between June and December 934, yet according to the late Anglo-Saxon *Historia de Sancto Cuthberto*, a Life of St Cuthbert in verse and prose was given by Æthelstan on the occasion of his visit en route to Scotland, a visit which took place in May 934. There are, however, good grounds for regarding this part of the *Historia* as representing a conflation of information, and hence tradition rather than fact. The book may have been given at any time between June 934 and October 939, when Æthelstan died.

The manuscript is one of a small group of related books that M. Gretsch has used to demonstrate the character of religious life and Latin learning in southern England and its importance for the achievements associated with the Benedictine reform in the latter half of the tenth century. It is written on very well prepared parchment by a single, superb scribe, who also collaborated in writing a copy of Aldhelm's prose *De virginitate* (London, British Library, Royal MS 7.D.xxiv, part II: fols 82–162). The two books may also share an artist. The presentation miniature, the earliest such image known from England, reflects the close Continental contacts fostered during Æthelstan's reign, the vine-scroll motifs in the border and the iconography deriving from Carolingian precedents. This is also true of the ornament in the major decorated initial P on fol. 6. The numerous smaller colourful initials that articulate the texts, however, also draw upon and develop the earlier Insular repertoire of decorative motifs.

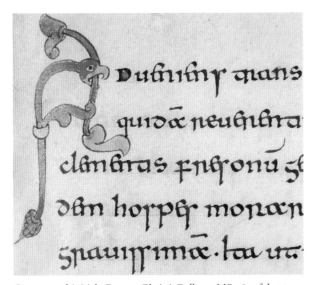

Ornamental initial. Corpus Christi College, MS 183, fol. 53

PROVENANCE: additions on fols. 93–94 and 96v demonstrate ownership by the community of St Cuthbert perhaps from the late tenth century and certainly by the last quarter of the eleventh, by which time it was established at Durham; Matthew Parker (1504–1575); his bequest, 1575.

EXHIBITED: London 1984, no. 6.

LITERATURE: James 1912b, I, 426–41; Temple 1976, no. 6; Keynes 1985, 180–85; Robinson 1988, no. 137; Budny 1997, no. 12; Gretsch 1999, 352–59; Gneuss 2001, no. 56.

TW

112

Jerome, Life of St Paul the Hermit; Felix, Life of St Guthlac

In Latin
Southern England, second half of the tenth century

Parchment, ii (modern paper) + 160 + ii (modern paper) fols., 230 × 142 mm, text 146 × 92 mm, 19 long lines, ruled in hard point

SCRIPT: Insular minuscule

BINDING: undyed goatskin over boards, 20th c.

Corpus Christi College, MS 389

THIS WELL EXECUTED VOLUME contains the lives of two eremitical saints – Paul of Thebes, the first Christian hermit according to tradition, and Guthlac (*c*.674–714), a Mercian nobleman who became an anchorite in the Fens at Crowland. The Lives were intended as a pair, with similarly elaborate pen-drawn ornamented initials and coloured display scripts marking the beginning of each text, each of which begins on the second leaf of a new quire. The pairing of the Life of an early Anglo-Saxon saint with that of an early Christian Desert Father may have been prompted in part by the extent to which Felix's text is influenced by Athanasius Life of St Anthony. Both texts were considered suitable reading for spiritual edification; indeed, the final chapter of the Benedictine rule specially recommended texts that gave accounts of the lives and teachings of the Desert Fathers as 'tools of virtue for good-living and obedient monks'. The small format might indicate a book intended for personal perusal, for devotional and perhaps also scholarly purposes, to judge from the glosses to the highly difficult prose of Felix's prologue. Fols. 57v–63v, however, have been marked up, perhaps in the late tenth or early eleventh century, as eight lections for the Octave of St Guthlac, which might suggest that it was also used for public reading in the refectory or at collation.

It was written by a single, skilled scribe in a late version of the distinctive variety of Insular minuscule developed in tenth-century England, Anglo-Saxon Square minuscule. His hand has also been identified in a copy of Gregory's *De cura pastorali* (Oxford, St John's College, MS 28). The expertly drawn pen initials, ornamented with intricate interlace and dragons' heads, together with the scheme of display capitals, rustic capitals and minor coloured initials that articulate the texts, bear witness to an increasing sophistication in book arts in tenth-century England, and the development of distinctive traditions of manuscript decoration. In common with other well-made late Anglo-Saxon books, its illumination was supplemented during the eleventh century. The first leaf of the opening quire of each text was originally left blank, a full-page framed ink-drawing of Jerome, seated as a scribe before a lectern, receiving inspiration from the Holy Spirit, was added on fol. 1v as a frontispiece to the Life of St Paul, and a similar frontispiece was begun on fol. 17v. This latter drawing was never completed, but was probably intended to depict Felix presenting his Life to its dedicatee, King Ælfwold.

As with so many late Anglo-Saxon books, the place of origin of Corpus 389 cannot be determined, although St Augustine's, Canterbury is likely. Its later medieval provenance there would not be sufficient evidence on its own, but St Augustine's was a centre at which both Square minuscule and the recently imported Continental Caroline minuscule were being written during the later tenth century, and which followed the, by then, more conservative Insular practice of quire arrangement whereby at each opening apart from the central one, the flesh-side of the leaf faced the hair-side of the next leaf, as opposed to like-facing-like.

PROVENANCE: St Augustine's, Canterbury, *ex libris* inscription, 14th c.; Matthew Parker (1504–1575); his bequest, 1575.

LITERATURE: James 1912b, II, 239–40; Bishop 1971, 3; Temple 1976, no. 36; Dumville 1994, 138, 142; Budny 1997, no. 23; Gneuss 2001, no. 103.

TW

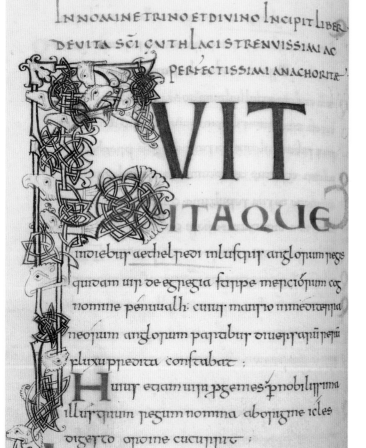

Ornamental initial. Corpus Christi College, MS 389, fol. 22v

113

Life of St Edward the Confessor
(*La Estoire de Seint Aedward le Rei*)

In Anglo-Norman French with some Latin captions
England, Westminster, *c.* 1255

Parchment, 37 fols., 279 × 193 mm, text 102–177–112 × 165 mm, 3 columns (2 on fol. 36), 48 lines to a full column, 13–26 lines below miniatures, ruled in plummet

SCRIPT: Gothic bookhand (textualis)

BINDING: full nigger morocco, by S. Cockerell, 20th c.

Cambridge University Library, MS Ee.3.59

THIS MANUSCRIPT belongs to a class of smaller book that continued to enjoy great popularity in the Middle Ages, the Saint's Life. Its subject is the life and miracles of St Edward the Confessor (d. 1066, canonized 1161), the most important royal saint of the English besides St Edmund of Bury. It is the finest pictorial monument of the royal cult in existence. St Edward enjoyed particular popularity in the thirteenth century, having been promoted as a patron saint of King Henry III. Henry greatly favoured images of St Edward in his royal residences and ecclesiastical foundations, not least at Westminster, where the saint lay enshrined. The text is in Anglo-Norman verse, and is based in part upon the Latin Life of St Edward composed in the twelfth century by Ailred of Rievaulx. Many aspects point strongly to Matthew Paris's authorship of the verses. Matthew was engaged in translating and illustrating Saints' Lives for highly-placed aristocratic women. This text is dedicated to Queen Eleanor of Provence, whom Henry III married in 1236. The objective of the poem is to introduce the Life of this most important royal saint to Eleanor. Numerous textual details are drawn from the historical works of Matthew Paris, who had contacts at court and whose talents as versifier, historian (see no. 114) and artist were widely recognized. The text ends with the Norman Conquest and the first recognition of St Edward's sanctity. The fact that it is called an *Estoire* reminds us of the role of history as a form of moral instruction. The text must date to after 1236, but several features indicate that it cannot have been composed much after 1245.

The present manuscript, consisting of sixty-four tinted illustrations at the head of most pages, was not produced or illuminated by Matthew, but rather by a later generation of at least three artists working for the English court. Their style corresponds very closely to wall paintings at Windsor Castle executed around 1250 and to drawings in the Westminster Psalter of the same period (London, British Library, Royal MS 2.A.xxii). Tinted drawings of this sort were very fashionable in the middle of the thirteenth century; whoever illuminated this manuscript was also engaged in the production of illustrated Apocalypses (e.g. Los Angeles, J. Paul Getty Museum, Ludwig MS III.1; Morgan 1982–1988, no. 122, 124–125, 107). The soft delicate restraint of this form of decoration, with no full colour and little or no gilding, points to a sophisticated scale of values on the part of highly-placed patrons who accorded importance to subtlety and temperance as well as show. We might contrast the bold effects of the Trinity College Apocalypse (no. 40). The crisp French-inspired elegance of many of the drawings in the *Estoire* points to a date of execution of this manuscript in the 1250s. This suggests that it is a copy of the original illustrated poem presumably presented by Matthew to Eleanor of Provence in the years 1236–1245. For whom this copy was made is unclear. One possible recipient, given the date, character and purpose of the book, could have been Eleanor of Castile, who married the future Edward I in 1254 and arrived in England shortly afterwards. She, like her mother-in-law, would have needed instruction in the lives of the great English saints. In 1288, according to a wardrobe account of items held at the Tower of London, Eleanor possessed a book of the Lives of Saints Thomas of Canterbury and Edward. Matthew Paris had produced a single volume of Lives of Saints Thomas and

Edward in the 1240s. The likelihood that these books were connected is quite strong.

The book is open at the celebrated illustrations of miracles at St Edward's tomb in Westminster Abbey. The left hand illustration shows Edward being buried with much ceremony; the sick and lame are already gathering and entering the space below the tomb chest, putting their crutches to one side. The right hand picture shows a row of blind men led gingerly towards the now more richly adorned tomb, St Edward's typical healing miracle being the granting of sight. At the centre, sighted men kneel at the tomb or crawl in to the round openings or 'squeezing places' in its base, to pray and touch the tomb of the saint. Above rises a metalwork shrine with figurines, seen end-on. Statues of St John the Evangelist as pilgrim, and St Edward, stand to either side on colonettes, and a monk chants the *Te Deum* at a lectern to the right. The image is a fantasy-representation of a shrine that Henry III was constructing for the Abbey, itself rebuilt from 1245. It is also a fantasy representation of the cult itself, for St Edward was not a popular saint, an object of mass pilgrimage or a great healer, but the emblem of a tiny political elite. The tacit myth promoted here is that he was in fact as great as St Thomas of Canterbury, a truly popular wonderworker. This promotion of the shrine would make sense if this Life had been coupled to a similar but now-lost Life of St Thomas himself. One further pastoral objective of the text was to support the shrine, rights and privileges of Westminster Abbey.

PROVENANCE: Eleanor of Castile (d.1290); Laurence Nowell, 1563, who may have acquired it from William Bowyer, Keeper of the Records in the Tower, who made numerous manuscripts available to Nowell; William Lambarde, Nowell's friend; Mr Cope (probably Michael Cope); William Cecil, Lord Burleigh (sold 1687); John Moore, Bishop of Ely (1707–1714); presented to the Library by George I in 1715.

EXHIBITED: Ottawa 1972, no. 19; London 1987, no. 39.

LITERATURE: University Library 1856–1867, II, 98–99; James 1920; Henderson 1967; Wallace 1983; Morgan 1982–1988, no. 123; Robinson 1988, no. 24, pl. 107; Binski 1991; Kauffmann 2003, 194.

PB

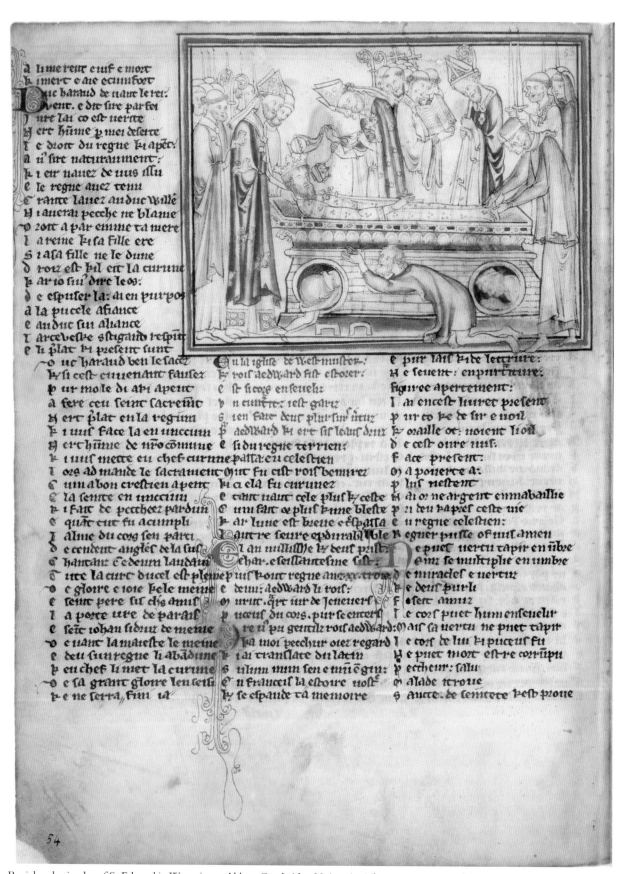

Burial and miracles of St Edward in Westminster Abbey. Cambridge University Library, MS Ee.3.59, fol. 29v

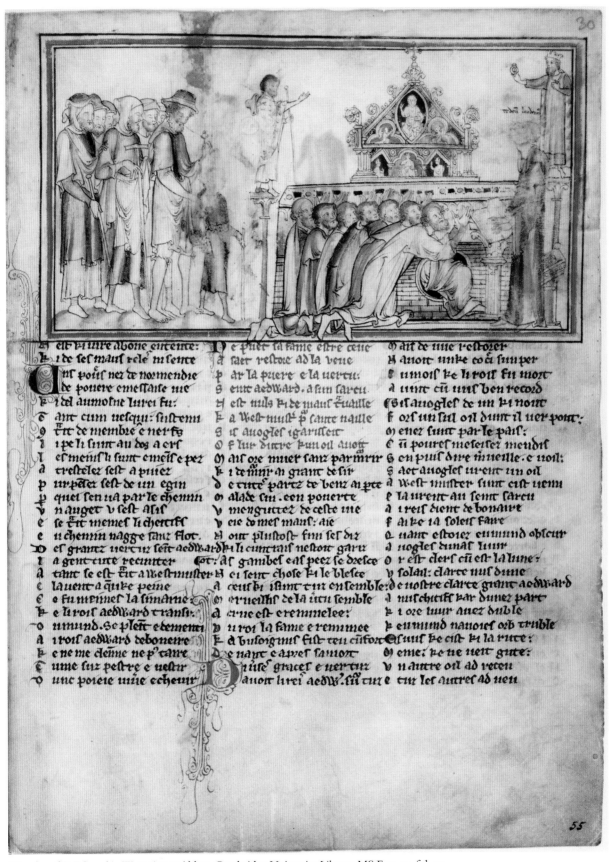

Miracles of St Edward in Westminster Abbey. Cambridge University Library, MS Ee.3.59, fol. 30

114

Matthew Paris, *Chronica Majora*, vol. 2

In Latin
England, St Albans, 1236–1259
ARTIST AND SCRIBE (partly): Matthew Paris (d.1259)

Parchment, 284 fols. (281 according to the medieval ink foliation followed here), 360 × 245 mm, text 270 × 178 mm, 2 columns, 49–56 lines, ruled in plummet
SCRIPT: Gothic bookhand (textualis)
BINDING: white calfskin over oak boards, 2003

Corpus Christi College, MS 16

THE *Chronica Majora* of Matthew Paris is one of the most celebrated of all English medieval literary manuscripts. By virtue of the quality of its text and its illustration, it is the most enduring and extraordinary monument of the Benedictine tradition of historical compilation. Matthew succeeded the previous St Albans' historian Roger of Wendover in 1236, almost certainly because he had already shown literary or artistic competence. Though nothing for certain is known about his early mental preparation, Matthew (born perhaps in 1189 or *c.*1200) would not have been the first trained artist, scribe or writer who professed at St Albans having already had an earlier career in the lay world. The *Gesta Abbatum* or 'Deeds of the Abbots', which Matthew compiled, notes that his artistic precursor at the house, Walter of Colchester, had precisely this sort of career. St Albans was sufficiently near London and other hubs of artistic, social and intellectual activity for it to remain an attractive option for the talented, one of whom Matthew undoubtedly was. If Matthew was indeed born as early as 1189 (the date of the commencement of vol. 2 of the *Chronica Majora*, as commented by Christopher de Hamel in conversation), he might equally have received

the training and patronage of some episcopal or seigneurial household: such a background could explain his evident gifts of diplomacy and sensitivity to the pastoral needs of the upper-class laity, for whom he made some of his Saints' Lives. Having entered the house in 1217 he clearly ransacked the Abbey's distinguished library for images, using, for instance, the Trinity College Glossed Gospels *(no. 28;* Lewis 1987, 31, figs. 9–10). Matthew presumably assisted Roger of Wendover and showed independent flair for the production of texts with illustrations. Of these the most obviously attractive were the Lives of such English saints as Alban, Thomas and Edward. Matthew's autograph illustrated Life of St Alban (Dublin, Trinity College, MS 177; Morgan 1982–1988, no. 85) may have been amongst the first of these to be put together in the 1230s or earlier, with Thomas and Edward following. The text of St Edward's Life, the sole copy of which is in Cambridge *(no. 113),* indicates an early compilation around 1236–1245. There are important stylistic and technical points of contact between the Alban manuscript and MS 16 (e.g. fol. 49v), such as the use of pasted-in painted insertions. Matthew's contacts with Henry III and diplomatic work with King Haakon IV of Norway point to something evident anyway from his talent, industry and insight, namely that he had remarkable personal and intellectual qualities. His historical compilations indicate his generous conception of universal history, and remind us that in this conception the boundaries between the secular and religious were porous: map-making, for example, fell into both categories, and so did a saintly *Estoire (no. 113).* Much in Matthew's career indicates that he too moved between these spheres with ease unusual for someone in monastic orders.

The *Chronica Majora* forms two manuscript volumes at Corpus Christi College, MS 26 covering the period from the Creation to 1188 and MS 16 from 1189 through the remainder of Matthew's life. A third part continued to 1259 is to be found in London, British Library, Royal MS 14 C.vii, together with the *Historia Anglorum* (Morgan 1982–1988, no. 92; Lewis 1987,

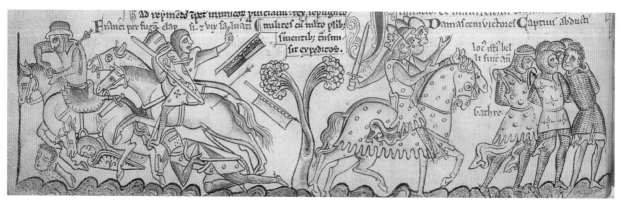

Defeat of the French at Gaza. Corpus Christi College, MS 16, fol. 133v, detail

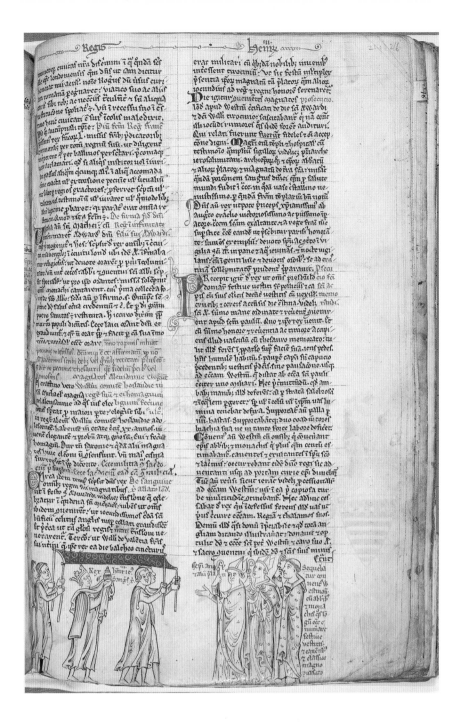

457–67). Some prefatory material has recently been removed from MS 16 and bound separately, including an itinerary, a map, and the drawing of the elephant sent to Henry III in 1255 (Morgan 1982–1988, no. 88, at 137; Lewis 1987, 446–47). MS 16 comes nearest to eye-witness reportage of material dating to after 1236. The text was not written in its entirety by Matthew but in part by a professional scribe, though Matthew's open and deft hand is usually much in evidence after fol. 36. At the head of the first folio is the note *Hunc librum dedit Frater Matheus de Parisius Deo* and the date 1189. Matthew's outlook on the reigns of Henry III, Louis IX, Frederick II, the Crusades, the deeds of the Tartars and Saracens, the misfortunes of the aristocracy and reli-

gious developments is at once cosmopolitan and rabidly xenophobic. Even the first few quires give some indication of the remarkable and generally positive panorama of Matthew's interests and of his acute and swift assimilation of the new. The outcome is a recitation of 'great events' of the times. On fol. 43v he shows the gathering of the Fourth Lateran Council in 1215; on fol. 49v the events in Rome in 1216 relating to the relic of the Veronica, accompanied by what may be the earliest surviving representation of the image in Western art; on fol. 66v are St Francis preaching to the birds and an account of his stigmatization in 1226, again, though depicted somewhat after 1236, one of the earliest representations of this event. On fol. 26, next to a drawing

253

of a Franciscan, Matthew includes an approving note regarding the apostolic poverty and excellence of life of the new Franciscans – a view he was soon to abandon. Matthew was swift to praise and to condemn, his history having a strong sense of moral purpose. He was especially suspicious of the papacy and the English Crown, and yet sufficiently close to Henry III to honour the King's request that the events of 1247, in which Henry processed a relic of the Holy Blood of Christ through London and Westminster, might be set down by him (fol. 215). Such illustrations of dated events provide useful markers for the development of Matthew's style here and in other works; for example the drawing of the elephant, which arrived in London in 1255, was manifestly made in the period 1255–1259, and is close in style to the *Lives of the Offas* (London, British Library, Cotton MS Nero D.i; Morgan 1982–1988, no. 87a). It is still unclear how Matthew envisaged this Chronicle to be used, and whether he compiled it as much for his own amusement as for the glory of St Alban.

PROVENANCE: given by Matthew Paris to the Abbey of St Albans; Robert Talbot of Norwich (d.1558); Sir Henry Sidney (d.1586); Matthew Parker (1504–1575); his bequest, 1575.

EXHIBITED: Cambridge 1975, 13, pls. 20–22.

LITERATURE: James 1912b, I, 54–58; Vaughan 1958, 21–22, 49–77; Morgan 1982–1988, no. 88; Lewis 1987; Robinson 1988, no. 125, pl. 106; Kauffmann 2003, 182.   PB

115

Thomas of Elmham, *Speculum Augustinianum*

In Latin
England, Canterbury, St Augustine's Abbey,
*c.*1410–*c.*1413
SCRIBE AND ARTIST: Thomas of Elmham, fl. *c.*1410

Parchment, 116 + i fols., 547 × 385 mm, text 320 × 220 mm, 2 columns, 40 lines, ruled in red ink

SCRIPT: Gothic bookhand (textualis)

BINDING: red morocco over pasteboard, 1968

Trinity Hall, MS 1

THOMAS OF ELMHAM'S CHRONICLE concerns the very considerable history of St Augustine's Abbey and its antiquities. Based in part on Bede and William of Malmesbury, the text is an exemplification and defence of the privileges of this ancient English monastic

establishment. It was compiled by a monk of St Augustine's, Thomas of Elmham, who showed some interest in his place of origin in Norfolk and included his name in an acrostic. Internal evidence, not least the chronological tables which start the book, shows that Thomas was working on this manuscript shortly before 1414 when he left the Abbey for another post (late entries in his hand include the election of the antipope John XXIII in 1410 and the deposition of Richard II in 1399). The tables were planned for the period through to 1453, but left blank (Hardwick 1858, xix, xxii).

In common with, for example, Matthew Paris's *Chronica Majora (no. 114)* the work is at once a compilation of dates and events and in this case especially documents and other proofs relevant to the house's history. It includes very striking efforts to reproduce not only the text of early charters but also the appearance of their Anglo-Saxon manuscript hands (fols. 21v–23); and near them are good pen-drawn reproductions of early seals of the Abbey (fol. 24) and of papal bulls (fol. 26v). These are a very early instance of 'antiquarianism' (Gransden 1974–1982, II, 206, 345–55).

Thomas of Elmham was also an important maker of maps or plans, this manuscript containing two remarkable ones. The first is a map of the island of Thanet in Kent (fol. 42v), illustrating the legend of how the pet hind of Queen Dompneva of Mercia traced out the boundary of the abbey's manor there. It shows several landmarks and features of note, including the figures of a man carrying a passenger pick-a-back to a ferry linking the island to Kent. The second is a plan of the interior of the east end of St Augustine's Abbey (fol. 77), an admirable example of the Abbey's concern with its ancient relics. The plan is dominated by a view of the high altar screen of the church, which shows two square doors, or *ostia*, leading to the relics beyond. These are presumably north and south aisle doors from the nave to the east end. In between is the altar screen itself. It has a pair of doors at either end with closed wrought-iron gates, like those made for the choir at Christ Church Canterbury under Prior Eastry around 1300. The screen is crenellated and has rows of framed quatrefoils, indicating a fourteenth or fifteenth-century date. Shafts with spiral decoration in turn support a large red beam decorated with scrollwork, which supports two angels and a Majesty of Christ. Gervase of Canterbury, writing in the late twelfth century, describes a similar high altar beam with a Majesty in Christ Church before the fire of 1174. Both high altars were display-points for shrines. Along the top of the screen in this manuscript we can see two arm reliquaries, two crosses and a house shrine, as well as six books, identified by a small inscription as the books sent from Pope Gregory (the Great) to Augustine. It is intrinsically probable that they included

Plan of the east end of
St Augustine's Abbey.
Trinity Hall, MS 1,
fol. 77

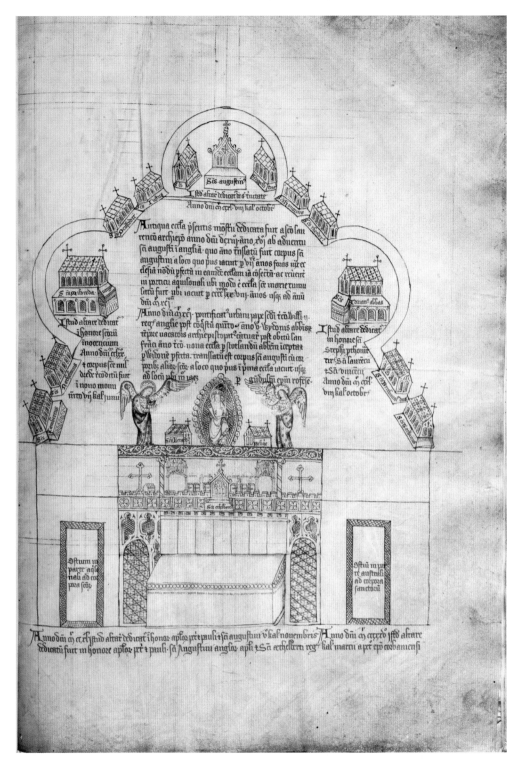

the St Augustine's Gospels *(no. 1)*. A long inscription below notes that the altar was dedicated in 1240 to Saints Peter, Paul and Augustine, and again in 1325 to Saints Peter, Paul, Augustine and Ethelbert. This text probably reproduces dedication inscriptions around or near the altar in question. Beyond the screen are indications of the chapels containing the reliquaries of saints headed by St Augustine, and including large shrines of St Mildred and St Adrian. The lengthy inscription relates the history of the various locations of the relics. Early ecclesiastical plans such as this are rare, though an early one showing the waterwork systems of Christ Church is to be found in the Eadwine Psalter *(no. 25)*, also a Canterbury product.

PROVENANCE: St Augustine's Abbey, Canterbury; given to the College by Robert Hare (*c.*1530–1611) (inscription on fol. 1).

LITERATURE: Hardwick 1858; James 1907, 1–4; Skelton and Harvey 1986, 107–26; Robinson 1988, no. 390, pl. 200; Henderson 1999, 66.

PB

116

Leaves from Frère Laurent, *La Somme le Roi*

In French
France, Paris, *c*.1290–*c*.1300
ARTIST: Master Honoré (doc. 1289–1312)

Parchment, 170 × 120 mm

Fitzwilliam Museum, MSS 192, 368

THE THIRTEENTH CENTURY witnesses an enormous surge in the production of improving pastoral literature, developed first by and for churchmen, but then propagated amongst the laity. Such literature was preoccupied with the fundamentals of Christian belief, notably the Seven Sacraments and the doctrine of penance. Penitential literature was often focused on the disposition of man to sin (i.e. vice) and the actual act of sin itself. To remedy the disposition was to ward off the

act. Hence the stress in the thousands of treatises written in later Middle Ages on Virtue and Vice, preferably rendered vivid by telling examples from the Bible or elsewhere. Most such texts were utilitarian, even dreary, little works. The *Somme le Roi* fell into a small and exceptional category, for it was beautifully illuminated. Patronage was everything: the *Somme le Roi* was compiled in 1279 by the Dominican royal confessor Frère Laurent for King Philippe III of France, and was probably conceived to have illustrations from the start. The text enjoyed wide circulation throughout Europe in the next century, and was eventually printed. It consists of a series of catechetical tracts before a treatise on the Seven Gifts of the Holy Spirit, its most original part.

These leaves are two of the most beautiful ever made in Gothic Paris, but their beauty is an aspect of their utility. In keeping with its much more modest grassroots cousins, the aim of the aristocratic *Somme* was practical, remedial and deliberative: the Seven Deadly Sins find their remedies in Seven Virtues which spring from the seven petitions of the *Pater noster*, which in turn spring from the Seven Gifts of the Holy Spirit: thus Pride is remedied by Humility which springs from Fear

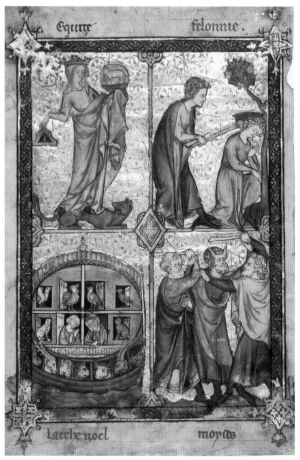 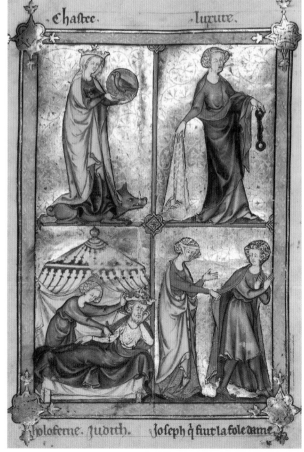

The Virtues and Vices: Equity and Felony; Chastity and Luxury. Fitzwilliam Museum, MSS 192, 368.

of God, and so on. The stress on sevens in such works was partly symbolic, partly mnemonic. Here, then, the systems and subdivisions of scholasticism come to the fore, with the aid of images. The aim of the pictures is to offer remedy through example and counter-example. In MS 368 the virtue to be inculcated is chastity, the vice to be extirpated is luxury, or unchastity, here personified as *chastee* and *luxure* in the form of two women. Crowned Chastity holds a bird-emblem, a symbol of purity; she tramples on a hog. Uncrowned Luxury in contrast holds a manacle and towel, and spits blood. The personifications are accompanied below by *exempla* or figures of the sort that might be cited in a sermon: Judith, shown with Holofernes, is a figure for chastity since she exhibits the Virtue's root idea, namely fidelity; and Joseph, also a figure for chastity, escapes the advances of Potiphar's wife. We note how the vicious women resemble each other. In MS 192 the Virtue in question is *Equite*, treading a wolf and holding a plummet, and the Vice *Felonnie*. Here only Virtue is personified, its figure being the two-by-two balance of Noah's Ark below; the Vice of Ire is exemplified by Cain murdering Abel and by men contending with sticks, separated by Moses.

The doctrines implicit in such Christian-moral images were sophisticated, revealing knowledge of Aristotle's ethical doctrine of the mean as propounded in his *Ethics*. So too is the style of representation. These two small leaves were detached from a manuscript which is now London, British Library Add. MS 54180. The book was illuminated in Paris at the end of the thirteenth century by, or in the immediate circle of, its most famous documented illuminator of the period, Master Honoré. The high-point of Parisian Gothic elegance stresses softness, delicacy and subtlety of tone as well as colour. One might say the refinement of style was an aspect of the refinement of moral sensibility apparent in the ideas. Note the delicate *rinceaux* or foliage scrolls on the gilded backgrounds of the scenes.

PROVENANCE: MS 192 given to the Museum by Samuel Sandars in 1892; MS 368 given by the Friends of the Fitzwilliam Museum in 1934.

EXHIBITED: Ottawa 1972, no. 5; London 1987–1988, no. 356.

LITERATURE: James 1895, 399–400; Cockerell 1906; Millar 1953; Millar 1959; Tuve 1964, pl. 8c; Turner 1968–1969; Kosmer 1973; Wormald and Giles 1982, 369–70; Paris 1998, no.183.

PB

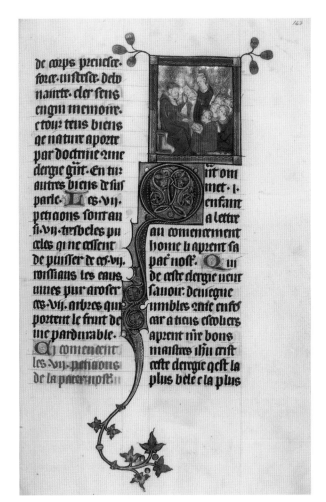

Doctor instructs boys about the Lord's Prayer.
St John's College, MS S. 30, p. 143

117

Somme le Roi and miscellaneous texts

In Anglo-Norman French and English
England, *c.*1320–*c.*1330

Parchment, 270 pages, 275 × 185 mm, text 175 × 115 mm, 2 columns, 22 lines, ruled in ink

SCRIPT: Gothic bookhand (textualis)

BINDING: red morocco with gold tooled border, over pasteboard, 19thc.

St John's College, MS S. 30 (James no. 256)

THIS UNIQUE English illuminated copy of the *Somme le Roi* (on pp.1–233) produced in early fourteenth-century England illustrates a very different didactic strategy, suggesting that it was not a straightforward copy of illuminated French versions *(see no. 116)*. Thus the key text of the *Somme*, the section on the Seven Gifts of the Holy Spirit, is largely omitted. Here instead we find ten historiated initials or column-miniatures at various divisions of the first texts of the *Somme*, starting with the

Ten Commandments and Christ in Majesty, the Creed or Articles of the Faith, warnings against sin, admonitions to accept Death (with an early instance of Death personified), material gain and the Wheel of Fortune, the *Pater Noster* or Lord's prayer, Christ preaching to his disciples, and St Paul preaching. The outlook is catechetical, stressing the basic tenets of the faith and the necessity of teaching and learning them. The book is open at the illustration on p. 143 treating the Seven Requests of the *Pater Noster*: a doctor robed in blue and holding a birch rod addresses five seated boys, a sixth one holding a tablet inscribed with the ABC. This pedagogy is in line with the reforming programme of diocesan legislation in the previous century, which laid special emphasis on the instruction of the boys of the parish in the catechism. Despite this objective, the text of this particular manuscript is significantly disordered.

The very delicate style of the illustrations reflects at least in part the impact in England of high-quality French illumination such as that in the previous copy *(no. 117)*. The manuscript was illuminated by the very active workshop associated with the Queen Mary Psalter (London, British Library, MS Royal 2.B.vii; Sandler 1986, no. 56), the output of which includes another manuscript of pastoral nature, Paris, Bibliothèque nationale de France, MS fr. 13342 (Sandler 1986, no. 58; Dennison 1986; *see also nos. 80, 149*). Its two main texts are the Anglo-Norman French version of St Edmund of Abingdon's very influential pastoral treatise *Speculum ecclesie*, or Mirror of the Church, and a short tract on the mass in Anglo-Norman French beginning *Ceo qe vous deuez fere e penser a chascon point de la Messe* ('What you should do and think at each point of the Mass'), which contains a series of pictures giving very general guidance as to conduct and deportment in church. The high quality and the content of both books indicates lay patronage and styles of instruction that are unlikely to have been open to more than a very few. The present manuscript contains no obvious signs of medieval provenance aside from a fragment of an early fourteenth-century account roll used as its first flyleaf which includes at least eight place names pertinent to the area between Cambridge, Peterborough and Lincolnshire, i.e. the Fens. Since the date of the flyleaf's association with the bulk of the book is unknown this evidence remains only suggestive.

PROVENANCE: Thomas Pyerpount, 15th–16th c.; Thomas Leech; inscription on flyleaf recording Thomas Baker (d.1740); presumably his bequest, 1740.

LITERATURE: James 1913, 291–93; Sandler 1986, no. 60; Dennison 1986a, 289–90.

PB

118

Compendium of devotion and moral instruction; Augustine, *De mendacio*

In Latin
England, last quarter of the fourteenth century; 1399–1406

Parchment, ii (paper, 17th c.) + 270 (Part I) + 19 (Part II, numbered 271–89) + ii (paper, 17th c.) fols., Part I: 275 × 195 mm, text 190 × 120 mm, 42 long lines, ruled in plummet; Part II: 275 × 190 mm, text 194 × 133 mm, 2 columns, 44 lines, ruled in plummet.

SCRIPT: Gothic bookhand (textualis)

BINDING: gold-tooled brown leather over boards, arms of George Willmer on upper cover, 17th c.

Trinity College, MS B.2.16

THIS VOLUME is a composite of two originally independent elements, both of which may have been made for, or associated in some way with, Henry IV of England.

Part I comprises a carefully produced compendium of Latin texts of devotion and moral instruction, almost certainly made for Henry IV before he became king. His arms form part of the lower border of fol. 4. It is an important addition to our knowledge of the non-liturgical books owned by Henry, which are otherwise known only from the list of nine volumes allegedly appropriated by the London stationer Thomas Marleburgh, with the connivance of the former keeper of Henry's books, Ralph Bradfield.

The contents no less than the decoration were carefully compiled and designed with the owner in mind. The book opens with Geoffrey of Beaulieu's Latin translation of the so-called 'Teachings' of Louis IX (the moral advice written near his death for his son Philip III), which acts as a preface to the entire compendium, preceding a detailed list of contents. Elaborate fully-painted or pen-drawn borders divide the compendium into four sections, the first comprising treatises and sermons by or attributed to Augustine on aspects of Christian morality and behaviour, the second and third containing primarily devotional texts attributed to Augustine and by or attributed to Anselm, and the fourth, Grosseteste's *De meditatione*, followed by further Augustinian sermons of moral instruction. The devotional theme of the second section is reinforced by an image of a kneeling knight in the left-hand border, praying to a depiction of a Trinity Crucifix within the opening initial.

The book is carefully rubricated, and was ruled to accommodate marginal annotations and headings to draw attention to important subject-matter, and to break up some of the lengthier devotional texts into smaller portions for the purposes of meditation. The scribe employed comparatively few abbreviations for a Latin manuscript of this date, as well as unusually well separated letters and words, perhaps with the needs of a non-professional reader in mind.

Some of the contents are textually closely related to an early fourteenth-century manuscript from the Augustinian Abbey of Leicester (Cambridge, Trinity College, MS B.14.7), a community with very close ties to the house of Lancaster during the fourteenth century. Philip Repyngdon, Abbot of Leicester (1394–1404), was one of Henry's chaplains and confessors, and it is tempting to see his guiding hand behind this compendium.

Fols. 271–89 did not originally form part of the same volume, to judge from their different dimensions, script, layout and decoration. Nevertheless, they too may have been associated in some way with Henry IV after he seized the throne, since the royal arms in their pre-1406 form are presented in the lower border to fol. 271, and the style of the border is consistent with a date around

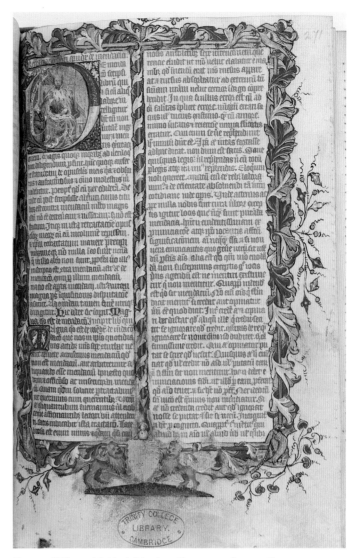

Crowned King with black Monk or Canon, royal arms of England. Trinity College, MS B.2.16, fol. 271

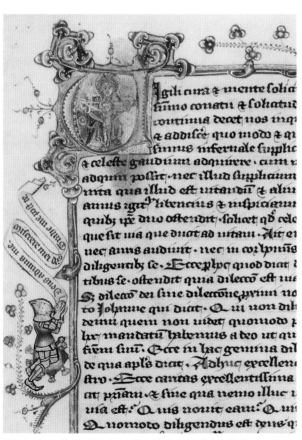

Trinity Crucifix with a Kneeling Knight. Trinity College, MS B.2.16, fol. 107, detail

1400. Augustine's *retractatio* on the *De mendacio*, which acts as a preface to the work, begins with an historiated initial of a seated king, with a black monk or canon quoting a verse of Psalm 5 taken from the *De mendacio*: 'Thou hatest all the workers of iniquity; thou wilt destroy all that speak a lie'. Given the circumstances of Henry's accession and the criticism it provoked, the choice of text is intriguing. But without further evidence to confirm Henry's association with this part of the manuscript, it might be unwise to speculate further.

PROVENANCE: given to the College by George Willmer (d.1626).

LITERATURE: James 1900–1904, I, 70–73; Scott 1996, II, 21; Webber 1997, 34, 39; Stratford 1999, 260–61.

TW

119

Thomas Chaundler, *Liber Apologeticus de omni statu humanae naturae*

In Latin.
England, Oxford, 1457–1461

Parchment, ii + 67 + i fols., 265 × 223 mm, text 225 × 150 mm, 36 long lines, ruled in crayon

SCRIPT: Humanistic minuscule

BINDING: blind-stamped brown calf over pasteboards, late 17th c., rebacked.

Trinity College, MS R.14.5

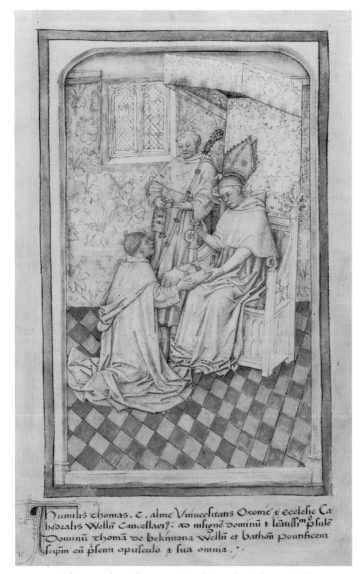

Thomas Chaundler presenting his work to Thomas Bekynton. Trinity College, MS R.14.5, fol. 9v

THOMAS CHAUNDLER'S *Liber Apologeticus* takes the form of a Latin play on the subject of the Fall and Redemption of man, and while it shares certain features with the vernacular mystery cycles and allegorical morality plays of the time, its verbosity and lack of dramatic action militate against the idea that it was ever performed *par personnages*. At the time he composed it, Chaundler was Chancellor of the University of Oxford and of Wells Cathedral, which dates the production of the manuscript to somewhere in the years between 1457 and 1461. Its dedicatee was Thomas Bekynton, Bishop of Wells, to whom a fulsome panegyric is addressed at the beginning of the text. Both Bekynton and Chaundler were at the forefront of the development of academic Humanism in England in the fifteenth century, and the *Liber Apologeticus* reflects their shared interests, both textually and in its physical appearance. The hands of the two scribes who contributed to the manuscript provide early examples of the appearance of humanistic script in England, and the text itself, though doctrinally orthodox, has marked humanistic leanings. Man's Fall is depicted as a conflict for the possession of his soul between Reason and Sensuality (personified as two female figures), and his redemption is effected with virtually no reference to the conventional apparatus of late medieval Catholicism (Church, Sacraments, Christ's Passion, the Trinity etc.). Instead, Mercy and Peace debate with Justice and Truth before God as to whether Man should be saved, and he, armed with the virtues of Fortitude, Justice, Temperance and Prudence, goes on to confront and overcome Death.

Despite the use of dramatic form, it seems likely that Chaundler's book was designed in the first instance for Bekynton's private contemplation, and, as if to compensate for the play's lack of conventional dramatic appeal, the text is prefaced by a series of fourteen very skilfully coloured line drawings which depict the principal episodes. Several of the illustrations depict Man naked, and constitute early and unusual studies of the male nude figure in various postures. At the end of the sequence, and *en face* with the panegyric to Bekynton, is a portrayal of Chaundler presenting his book to the bishop. The illustrations have few close English parallels; some features, such as the fall of drapery, have much in common with Flemish art of the time.

PROVENANCE: Thomas Bekynton, bishop of Bath and Wells (1443–1465); given to Wells Cathedral by Bekynton (inscription fol. 1v); ownership inscription: 'Steuyn Carslegh ys boke' (16th c., fol. 1); given by Thomas Nevile (1548–1615), Master of Trinity College (1593–1615).

LITERATURE: James 1900–1904, II, 285–88; James 1916; Enright-Clark Shoukri 1974; Oxford 1970, 20–21; Robinson 1988, no. 353, pl. 273; Scott 1996, II, 285–88.   RB

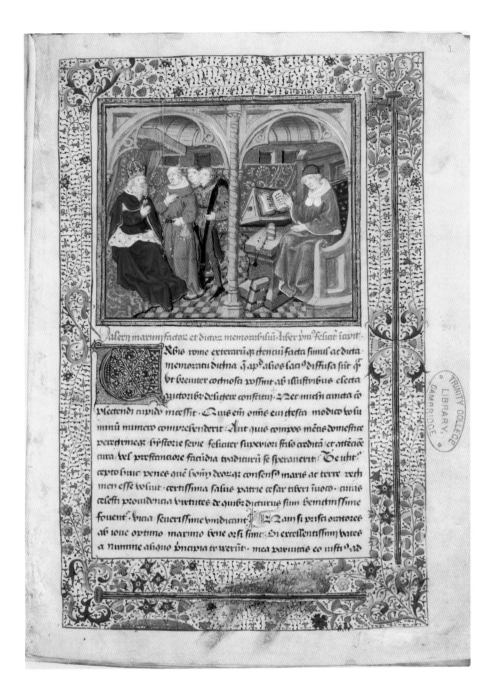

120

Valerius Maximus, *Factorum ac dictorum memorabilium Libri IX*

In Latin
Southern Netherlands, fifteenth century

Parchment, 143 fols., 280 × 120 mm, text 193 × 120 mm,
30 long lines ruled in black ink

Script: Gothic bookhand (cursive)

BINDING: calf over wooden boards, metal corner-pieces, remains
of clasps, blind-tooled shield in centre: a saltire engrailed and a
griffin's head for crest, 16th c.

Trinity College, MS O.4.45

VALERIUS MAXIMUS dedicated his nine books of examples of 'memorable deeds and sayings' to the Emperor Tiberius (14–37) possibly soon after the year 31 (Briscoe 1998; Wardle 1998; Shackleton-Bailey 2000). Valerius insists in his preface that his work had a practical purpose to save everyone else the trouble of scouring all the available literature for good examples of events and customs in both the Roman and non-Roman world (Maslakov 1984). Nevertheless, there is a strong moral emphasis, with headings such as Gratitude, Chastity, Cruelty and Moderation, as well as moralizing comments inserted by the compiler. His themes are illustrated with historical examples taken from the works of the great classical writers Livy, Varro, Cicero and Pompeius Trogus. This collection of 'memorable doings and sayings' was a kind of antique version of the Reader's Digest. It enjoyed

261

some success in Antiquity and the collection appears to have survived into the Carolingian period. Later medieval descendants of the text are from a ninth-century codex produced in northern France and now in Bern, Burgerbibliothek, MS 366. This was a book used by the Frankish scholar, Lupus of Ferrières (d.860), who inserted passages from an epitome of Valerius Maximus compiled in late Antiquity by Julius Paris, which survive in a manuscript compiled by Heiric of Auxerre, one of Lupus's pupils. Thus descendants from the 'pre-Paris' and 'post Paris' text of Lupus proliferated thereafter with the numbers beginning to grow appreciably in the twelfth century. The text had reached Italy again by the thirteenth century.

The full text and the Julius Paris epitome were immensely popular throughout Europe during the later Middle Ages (Bloomer 1992). What has been described as 'Practical ethics for Roman gentlemen' was clearly felt to be a useful sort of book for late-medieval gentlemen to own as well (Skidmore 1996). An astonishing number of extant manuscripts has survived, with well over six hundred fourteenth- and fifteenth-century copies of the text or commentaries, in addition to the large number of translations. In Cambridge alone there are eleven copies of the text: four from the fifteenth century (Cambridge University Library, MS Gg.6.2, Peterhouse, MSS 249 and 258, in addition to this Trinity manuscript); three from the fourteenth century (St John's College D.22 (James no. 97); University Library, MS Mm.2.18, and Queens' College, MS Horne 22 (James no. 10); three dating from the twelfth and thirteenth centuries (University Library, MS Kk.3.23, Pembroke College, MS 105, and Trinity College, MS O.3.34); and one set of excerpts from the late eleventh or early twelfth century (Trinity College, MS R.16.34). Valerius Maximus was commented on by a number of late medieval French, German and especially Italian scholars, and translated into many European vernaculars in the fifteenth century. The French and the Italian translations were particularly in demand. Copies of the text from Flanders are less common and it is likely that a wealthy and well-educated lay patron commissioned this book.

Within a decorated border at the beginning of the text a man reads a book at a lectern and an emperor is depicted. This may show Valerius Maximus presenting his book to the Emperor Tiberius or the presentation of this very copy to its patron. Each of the nine books begins with a very fine initial and decorated border, as on fol. 112v. Neither the artist nor the scribe has been identified.

PROVENANCE: acquired on the Continent by Thomas Gale and given to Trinity College by his son Roger Gale in 1738.

LITERATURE: Schullian 1981; Reynolds 1983, 290–92, 429–30.

RMCK

121

Guillebert de Lannoy, *L'Instruction d'un jeune Prince*; René d'Anjou, *Le Mortifiement de Vaine Plaisance*

In French
North France, Hesdin or Valenciennes, c.1465–c.1468
ARTISTS: Simon Marmion (c.1425–1489), Loyset Liédet (c.1420–1479)

Parchment, 65 + i (paper) fols., 308 × 220 mm, text 190 × 131 mm, 35 long lines, ruled in pink-red ink

SCRIPT: Gothic bookhand (hybrida)

BINDING: red velvet over wooden boards, brass bosses and clasps, horn-covered *fenestra* with the titles of the two treatises on lower cover, probably 16th c.

Fitzwilliam Museum, MS 165

IN FIFTEENTH-CENTURY FRANCE and Flanders illustrated books for the moral, spiritual and political education of the nobility were produced in richly illustrated editions with texts in French. This book contains two such texts. The first (fols. 6–29) was written c.1435–c.1442 by the ambassador and counsellor Guillebert de Lannoy (1386–1450) under the name of Feuillant de Jonal, supposedly for a thirteenth-century fictitious king, Rudolph of Norway, but intended for the use of Philip the Good, Duke of Burgundy. The first part of the treatise discusses the authority and actions of the prince in relation to God and chivalric values. The second part advises the prince on the choice of counsellors and the dangers of having favourites. The third part is concerned with the issue of war and how it can be justified. There is only one illustration of the author, kneeling and presenting his book to the enthroned prince surrounded by his counsellors (fol. 10v). In the lower border are the arms of Jacques de Luxembourg and a monogram (I H?) which has not been identified. Jacques' arms are also found in a Flemish Book of Hours (Los Angeles, J. Paul Getty Museum, MS Ludwig IX 11). The borders are similar to the simpler borders in the Breviary of Margaret of York *(no. 50)*. The artist of the miniature is the panel painter and illuminator, Simon Marmion, who was based in Valenciennes. His work is characterized by subtle tones of soft colours and individual portrait heads with solemn expressions.

The second treatise (fols. 30–64) is an allegorical romance about the soul and the heart written in 1455 by René, Duke of Anjou, Count of Provence and King of Naples (1409–1480) (Bubenicek 1980). The lost original illustrated copy of the *Mortifiement* was perhaps made by

The Heart nailed to
the Cross. Fitzwilliam
Museum, MS 165,
fol. 59v

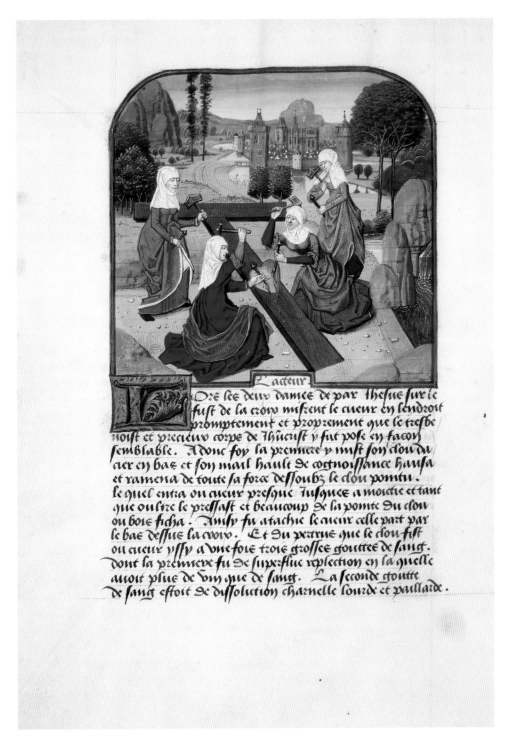

the Master of the *Coeur d'Amours epris*, and this version
illustrated by Loyset Liédet follows its iconography with
some modifications. Nine framed pictures fill a large part
of the page, the characters all shown as female personifications: Soul sits holding her heart (fol. 31), Fear of God
and Contrition speak to the Soul (fol. 34v), Fear of God
advises the Soul (fol. 41), a parable of a chariot drawn by
two horses, one blindfolded (fol. 46), a parable of a poor
woman (fol. 48v), a parable of a besieged city (fol. 51v),
Soul gives her heart to Fear of God and Contrition (fol.
54v), *Heart is nailed to the Cross* by Fear of God, Faith,
Love and Grace (fol. 59v), Soul, accompanied by Fear of
God and Contrition, holds the Cross on which is her
Heart (fol. 61v). The scenes are set in rural landscapes or
in a courtyard, garden or interior of a house. Liédet uses
bright strong colours and clearly defined figure contours.

The date of before 1468 is based on the absence of the collar of the Order of the Golden Fleece to which Jacques de Luxembourg was admitted in 1468. Also, until his move to Bruges in 1469, Liédet was active in Hesdin, near Valenciennes, where Marmion was based. Some consider a date after 1470 to be more appropriate in regard to the style of the two artists.

PROVENANCE: Jacques de Luxembourg, Seigneur de Fiennes (c.1426–1487); Hermann de Bourgogne (1570–1626), Count of Falais-sur-Méhaigne; acquired by Viscount Fitzwilliam in 1814; his bequest, 1816.

EXHIBITED: Cambridge 1966, no. 107, pl. 28; Cambridge 1993, no. 50.

LITERATURE: James 1895a, 365–66; Lyna 1926, xli, lxviii–lxx, 1–61, pls. 1–10; Lyna 1928, 179, 181; Hoffman 1969, 245; Hoffmann 1973, 273–75, pl. 19a; van Leeuwen 1975, II–III, VI, VIII–IX, XV, 1–54, 211, 221, 235; Hindman 1977a, 191–93, 204, fig. 10; Pächt 1977, 18; von Euw and Plotzek 1982, 195; Robin 1985, 177–81; Los Angeles and London 2003–2004, 109.

NJM

122

Thomas of Kent, *Roman de toute chevalerie*

In Anglo-Norman French
England, c.1240–c.1250

Parchment, iii (paper) + 46 + iii (paper) fols., 280 × 196 mm, text 219 × 153 mm, 2 columns, 46 lines, ruled in crayon

SCRIPT: Gothic bookhand (textualis)

BINDING: quarter goatskin, 20th c.

Trinity College, MS O.9.34

THIS VERSE ROMANCE tells the story of the life and travels of the Greek hero, Alexander. It was written by Thomas of Kent in the second half of the twelfth century. He may have been a Benedictine monk, because an illustration of the author in a later copy shows him in a Benedictine habit. A copy of c.1308–1312 (Paris, Bibliothèque nationale de France, MS fr. 24364) has a set of pictures very similar to the Trinity manuscript, but it is complete, whereas the Trinity copy has lost over half of its text with the accompanying pictures. In its present state there are one hundred and fifty two framed pictures set in various positions in the two-column text. These are drawings tinted in green, brown, blue and red. The total number of illustrations can be reconstructed from the Paris manuscript, which has

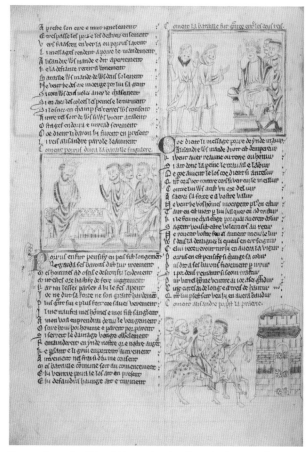

Scenes from the life of Alexander the Great. Trinity College, MS O.9.34, fol. 33v

three hundred and eleven miniatures. These were all intended to be fully coloured rather than in tinted drawing, although in part of the manuscript drawings never received their colouring. There is also a c.1350 copy (Durham, Cathedral Library, MS C.IV.27 B) which never received illustration but has two hundred and ninety-seven picture titles.

The pictures illustrate the battles of Alexander against Darius and the Persians, and many show the exotic peoples he met in the East. The figures are in lively positions with jerky postures and expressive gestures. The tinting is decorative rather than being used to define the three dimensional form of the figure as in most contemporary works in this technique. Although the tinted drawing style of this manuscript has often been compared with that of the St Albans monk, Matthew Paris *(e.g. no. 114)*, it was widespread in England in the first half of the thirteenth century. The figure style of the Alexander romance is completely unlike that of Matthew Paris and there seems no reason at all to assume any connection with St Albans Abbey. The manuscript was certainly not made there, despite repeated sugges-

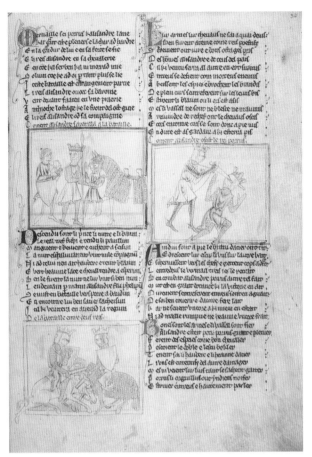

Scenes from the life of Alexander the Great. Trinity College, MS O.9.34, fol. 34

PROVENANCE: Thomas Gale (1636–1702); Roger Gale (1672–1744) who presented it to the College in 1738.

EXHIBITED: Brussels 1973, no. 50; London 1987–1988, no. 313.

LITERATURE: James 1900–1904, III, 482–91, IV, pl. XV; Ross 1969, 690–94, fig. 2; Secomska 1975, 60, 66, pls. 8h, 8i; Foster 1976–1977 (edition of text); Secomska 1977, 128, 145, 146, 153, 155, 158, 176, 177, 179, 181–3, 288, 292, 294–5, figs. 89–93; Morgan 1982–1988, no. 81, ills. 271–74; Avril and Stirnemann 1987, 126–38, no. 171; Ross 1988, 25, 26, 110 n. 98; Busby 2000, 322–28.

NJM

123

Guillaume de Lorris and Jean de Meun, *Le Roman de la Rose*

In French
Paris, c.1330
ARTISTS: Richard and Jeanne de Montbaston
(doc.1325–1353)

Parchment, 141 fols., 320 × 228 mm, text 234–245 × 164 mm, 2 columns, 40 lines, ruled in ink

SCRIPT: Gothic bookhand (textualis)

BINDING: gold-tooled brown mottled calf over pasteboards, 17th c.; rebacked by J.P. Gray, 20th c.

Cambridge University Library, MS Gg.4.6

THE ROMAN DE LA ROSE was one of the most celebrated and popular products of the medieval culture of courtly love. Its text is generally understood to have been composed in two phases, the first 4,000 or so lines being written by Guillaume de Lorris probably in the 1220s, the rest by Jean de Meun between 1269 and 1278. The evidence for this is provided in the text by Jean himself. Numerous manuscript copies survive, far more so than the Canterbury Tales. The text (or texts) are an allegory of a love affair which opens with Guillaume's account of the dream vision of a young man, Lover. It is conducted according to the conventions of courtly love, of which the most well known is the idea of love of the unattainable. Jean's section is more in the learned character of a university disputation between various characters (Reason, Friend, Rebuff etc.), but this seems not to have deterred a general readership alert to the didactic character of the text.

The poem was well established by the time that MS Gg.4.6. was executed towards the middle of the fourteenth century. The scene shown here is Guillaume's Garden of Pleasure, during May. In Lover's dream, the

tions by literary scholars. The jerky postures and lively gestures are a later and somewhat cruder version of a tinted drawing style occurring in a *c.*1220–*c.*1230 Psalter fragment made for Chertsey Abbey (Cambridge, Emmanuel College, MS 252), and this style probably can be attributed to lay artists working in London who are quite apart from Matthew Paris's tinted drawing at St Albans. A date nearer the mid-century is suggested for the Trinity Alexander on the basis of the elaborate penwork.

The story of Alexander was evidently popular in mid-thirteenth-century England, not only in illustrated manuscripts such as this but in wall paintings as recorded in 1247 in Henry III's palace at Clarendon, and in 1252 in the Queen's Chamber at Nottingham Castle. The extensive cycle of pictures in the Trinity manuscript has some parallels with the life of Alexander pictures in the *Pantheon* of Godfrey of Viterbo written *c.*1185–1190 which exists in several thirteenth- and fourteenth-century copies made in Italy and Poland (e.g. Sandomierz, Chapter Library, MS 114 made in 1335).

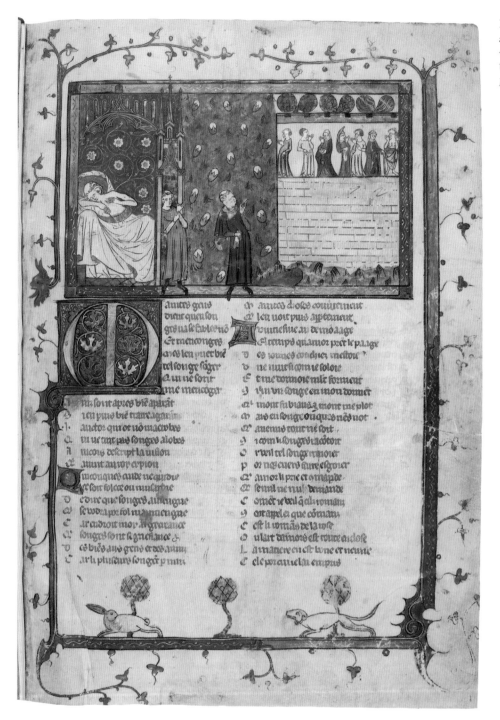

Lover's dream, awakening and encounter of the walled garden. Cambridge University Library, MS Gg.4.6, fol. 3

Rose-bush appears behind him like an emanation. He awakes and dresses in a bright orange tunic by tying up his sleeve, until then the usual method of fastening (buttons are not commonly mentioned until the 1330s). Suddenly transvested into a blue tunic he sets off and encounters a garden surrounded by a high wall adorned with painted images. These depict a series of unpleasant characters: Hate, Cruelty, Covetousness, Avarice, Envy, Sorrow, Old Age, Hypocrisy, and Poverty. All of them are characterized very vividly in the text, though scarcely so in the illumination, despite the fact that each figure is shown in slightly more detail on the following folios. At the foot of the folio the thrill of the chase is represented by a dog pursuing a hare. The pictures proceed to relate how Idleness led Lover into the garden to the spring of Narcissus. MS Gg.4.6 has nearly thirty images, including one of Jean de Meun as author (fol. 30).

In style, the manuscript is comparatively simple and

direct, even formulaic. Its principal colours are blue, orange, tan, rose and green, with little use of gold. This shorthand quality is not uncommon in vernacular romances made for lay reading. The artists may be identified as Richard de Montbaston and his wife Jeanne, who ran a family firm involved in the commercial illumination of numerous manuscripts in Paris, including texts of the *Roman de la Rose* (Rouse and Rouse 2000, II, 202–6). Their general artistic idiom is one we encounter in northern French or Flemish illumination in the second quarter of the fourteenth century, and also in Paris; it somewhat resembles for example a *Bible historiale* of the 1330s or so (Paris, Bibliothèque Sainte-Geneviève, MS 22; Paris 1981, no. 244). Of the original patron or readership of this manuscript nothing is known.

PROVENANCE: R. Smith; John Moore, Bishop of Ely (1707–1714); presented to the Library by George I in 1715.

LITERATURE: University Library 1856–1867, III, 145; Langlois 1910, 148; Fleming 1969, 40, 95; Rouse and Rouse 2000, II, 202–6.

PB

124

Guillaume de Machaut,
Oeuvres complètes

Mostly in French
Northern France, probably Paris, *c.*1370–1372
ARTISTS: Master of the Bible of Jean de Sy (act. *c.*1350–*c.*1380); Master of the Coronation Book of Charles V (act. *c.*1355–*c.*1380); and others

Parchment, i (medieval parchment) + 390 + i (modern parchment) fols., 314 × 220 mm, text 220 × 163 mm, mostly 2 columns, 40 lines, ruled in ink

SCRIPT: Gothic bookhand (textualis)

BINDING: Spanish or Italian goatskin over wooden boards, blind-stamped central compartments with gilt plugs and traces of an inlaid coat of arms, 15th c.

Corpus Christi College, on deposit from the collection of James E. and Elizabeth J. Ferrell

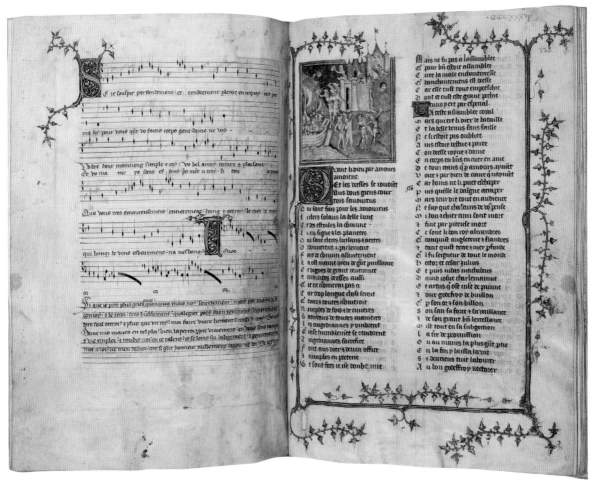

Knights attacking a Saracene castle. Corpus Christi College, on deposit from the Collection of James E. and Elizabeth J. Ferrell, fols. 334v–335

THE FRENCH COURT POET and musician Guillaume de Machaut (*c.*1300–1377) is generally regarded as the most important composer of the late Middle Ages. This is the oldest and most textually accurate manuscript of his complete works, probably prepared for presentation by the author himself under his own supervision. It comprises all of Machaut's principal compositions in verse and music, including the ballads, lays, motets and the earliest great polyphonic setting of the Mass, the four-part *Messe de Notre-Dame*. It includes 235 pages with music. This is one of several composite anthologies of Machaut's work made in the author's lifetime. The earliest, with fewer texts, is Paris, Bibliothèque nationale de France, MS fr. 1586, with magnificent miniatures, including two by the principal painter of the present volume. It dates from about 1350–1356. The present manuscript is the second, datable on internal evidence to between 1362 and 1377, but probably made in or soon after 1370. It became, in turn, exemplar for a third copy, Paris, Bibliothèque nationale de France, MS fr. 1585, doubtless also from the 1370s. Other copies dating from within the fourteenth century include Paris, Bibliothèque nationale de France, MS fr. 9221, owned by the Duc de Berry. All were apparently made for the family of Charles V or for members of the royal household.

The manuscript has one hundred and eighteen miniatures, including scenes of romance, mythology and natural history. Several are framed by the tricolour borders of the French royal family. The principal painter here is the Master of the Bible of Jean de Sy, named after Paris, Bibliothèque nationale de France, MS fr. 15397, made for Jean le Bon (d.1364). The artist was once known as the *Maître aux bouqueteaux* from his use of little copses on hillsides in the backgrounds of pictures. Further miniatures here include work by the Master of the Coronation of Charles V, the Master of Jean de Mandeville and the Master of the *Grandes Chroniques* of Charles V, each named after their respective work in London, British Library, Cotton MS Tiberius B.viii, Paris, Bibliothèque nationale de France, MS nouv. acq. fr. 4515, and fr. 2813, and all painted for Charles V. The division of hands in the Machaut manuscript mostly corresponds to the various gatherings from which the book is assembled, suggesting that sections of the unbound book were divided up to be illuminated simultaneously among the painters in the royal court.

This copy may have been intended for Charles of Navarre (1332–1387), the King's cousin and dedicatee of several of the poems. Soon afterwards, however, it almost certainly belonged to Gaston Fébus (1331–1391), Count of Foix, author of the *Livre de Chasse* and nephew by marriage of Jeanne de Bourbon, Queen of Charles V. It contains the family motto of the counts of Foix on the flyleaf, *Jay belle dame*. In a letter of June 1389 Yolande de Bar (1365–1431), Queen of Aragon, wrote to Gaston Fébus to thank him for lending her his manuscript of Guillaume de Machaut. Further letters of 1390 and 1391 suggest that the queen never returned it. There is a detailed description of what must be the present volume in Valencia in 1417 as no.17 in the inventory of Alfonso the Magnanimous (1396–1458), King of Aragon and Sicily. The traces of arms on the cover are also consistent with those of Aragon. It perhaps remained in Valencia until the residue of the ancient royal collection there was dispersed by French troops in 1811. It may have come then into the possession of the Napoleonic marshal, the Comte de Vogüé (1769–1839), whose descendants owned it in the late nineteenth century. It is known in the musical literature as the 'Codex Vogüé', or '*Vg*'. It was bought from the Vogüé family probably by Nathan Wildenstein (1851–1934) and it remained in the family possession in New York, famous but notoriously inaccessible, until its recent acquisition by the present owners, who have generously placed it on deposit at Corpus Christi College.

PROVENANCE: perhaps Charles of Navarre (1332–1387); probably Gaston Fébus (1331–1391); Yolande de Bar (1365–1431); Alfonso the Magnanimous (1396–1458); the royal library of Navarre; the Vogüé family; the Wildenstein family.

LITERATURE: Latrie 1877, xxviii–ix; Reaney 1969, 342–68; Keitel 1982, 81–82; Avril 1982, 125–26; Bent 1983; Earp 1989; Earp 1995, 84–85, no.3, 134–35.

C DE H

125

Christine de Pizan, *L'Epistre d'Othéa*

In French
France, second quarter of the fifteenth century

Parchment, ii (paper) + 52 + ii (paper) fols., 295 × 220 mm, text 210 × 175 mm, 3 columns, 43 lines, ruled in crayon
SCRIPT: Gothic bookhand (cursive)
BINDING: gold-tooled red morocco over boards, 18th c.

Newnham College, MS 5

CHRISTINE DE PIZAN'S *Epistre d'Othéa* composed *c.*1400, has been described as a work of 'chivalric mythography', and during the fifteenth and early sixteenth centuries it attained widespread popularity in France and England. The earliest manuscripts were prepared under Christine's direct supervision as presentation copies for noble patrons such as Jean, Duc de

Berry, and are furnished with copious schemes of high-quality painted miniatures, one to each of the one hundred classical fables which the goddess Othéa expounds (with a moralized 'Glose', and a spiritual 'Allegorie') to the young knight Hector. Newnham College MS 5 belongs to a second, more popular phase of the work's dissemination, and contains an equal number of skilfully drawn pen-and-ink miniatures, approximately 70 × 60 mm, whose colouring is restricted to washes in yellow, green and blue. The artist's style was swift and sketch-like, so that the faces and gestures of the human figures are often animated and expressive. Numerous good two-line gold initials on a blue and purple ground with white filigree work add to the quality of the book.

Folio 37 verso is devoted to the story of Orpheus's descent to the infernal regions in search of Eurydice, which Christine moralizes and allegorizes as an anti-type of proper chivalric behaviour, and thus a bad example to Hector. It is not a true knightly 'aventure', since the hero, prompted by love alone, ventures forth armed with only a harp, and from Christian perspective his quest to bring back Eurydice from the dead implies a dangerous error in demanding a miracle in defiance of the divine will. The illustration of the fable in Newnham MS 5 is one of several examples where text and image appear to be at odds. Normally, Eurydice is shown in the opening of Hell Mouth, being physically restrained from joining her lover by grasping devils. In some cases, however, as here, she seems to have emerged to re-join him, and the picture belongs to an earlier iconographic tradition (represented by illustrations of the scene in manuscripts of the *Ovid Moralisée* and Machaut's *Dit de la Harpe*) where Orpheus and Eurydice are reunited and resume their former lives. As Serena Marcolini has suggested, there may here be a faint echo of the Celtic oral and literary version of the story, where Orpheus succeeds in rescuing Eurydice from the Other World, best known in the fourteenth-century English translation of a lost Breton *lai*, *Sir Orfeo*.

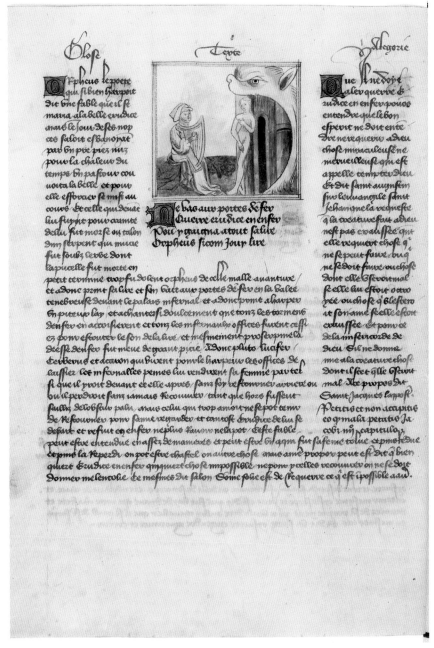

Orpheus and Eurydice. Newnham College, MS 5, fol. 36v

PROVENANCE: Baron Seillière sale, Paris, 1890 (Porquet 1890, lot 1222); Damascène Morgand (Morgand 1893, 548, item 2.827); sold by Edouard Rahir to Henry Yates Thompson, 1904; given to Newnham College in memory of H. Y. Thompson, 1929.

LITERATURE: Thompson 1907, 33–38; Ker 1977, 240; Mombello 1967, 242–45; Hindman 1986, 141–42; Marcolini 1999; Parussa 1999.

RB

269

126

Stephen Scrope, *The Epistle of Othea to Hector*

In English
England, *c*.1450–*c*.1460
ARTISTS: William Abell (act. 1446–1474) and the
Abingdon Missal Master (act. 1450–1461)
SCRIBE: Ricardus Franciscus (act. 1447–1456)

Parchment, ii + 61 + ii fols., 283 × 220 mm, text 190 × 130 mm,
28–29 long lines, ruled in hard point

SCRIPT: Gothic bookhand (cursive)

BINDING: blind-stamped brown calf over boards, 17th c.

St John's College, MS H. 5 (James no. 208)

STEPHEN SCROPE'S *Epistle of Othea to Hector* is one of
three independent English translations from the
French original of Christine de Pizan, and the only one
to include illustrations, which derive from a scheme
devised by the author herself *(see no. 125)*. The translation's original dedicatee was the career soldier and
administrator Sir John Fastolf. His stepson, Scrope, was

Perseus (labelled 'Percyvalle' in the margin) upon Pegasus,
rescuing Andromeda from the sea-monster Bellue. St John's
College, MS H.5, fol. 9, detail

a member of his household after Fastolf's retirement to
his London mansion in Southwark in about 1440, and
later at Caister Castle in Norfolk. Long service in France
with John, Duke of Bedford, had left Fastolf with,
amongst other things, a taste for de luxe illustrated books
of the type produced for the French court and nobility
in the late fourteenth and early fifteenth centuries
(Beadle 2004). Included in his collection was an exceptionally fine illuminated copy of the French *Othéa* made
in England in 1450 (Oxford, Bodleian Library, MS
Laud. misc. 570), which Scrope undoubtedly knew,
since it clearly provided the illustrative model, though
not the precise text, for the English version in the St
John's manuscript. Fastolf died in November 1459, and
his original presentation copy has not survived. The St
John's *Othea* was directed to Humphrey Stafford, Duke
of Buckingham, who was killed at the battle of North-
ampton in July 1460. The first miniature on fol. 1, showing Scrope presenting his book to Buckingham, has
been attributed by Jonathan Alexander and Kathleen
Scott to the noted English artist William Abell. The relationship between the Laud French *Othéa* and the St
John's manuscript is especially close. They are both the
work of a prolific scribe signing himself 'Ricardus
Franciscus' (perhaps a Frenchman), whose stylish secretary hand, anticipating the flamboyant *lettre bâtarde* fashionable in the best manuscripts later in the century, was
much in demand in London in the 1440s and 1450s
(Jefferson 1995).

The artist responsible for the five grisaille miniatures
following fol. 1 has not yet been identified. Kathleen
Scott argued that his work is to be found in several other
manuscripts, notably in the Abingdon Missal (Oxford,
Bodleian Library, MS Digby 227 and Oxford, Trinity
College, MS 75) and in the frontispiece to the important collection of English poetry in Oxford, Bodleian
Library, Fairfax MS 16 (Norton-Smith 1979; Scott
1996). On a flyleaf at the end of the St John's copy is his
workshop's computation of not only the miniatures, but
also the very numerous small illuminated initials and
other decorative features that give the manuscript its
general impression of quality: 'vj pagentis / .ij. C [200]
champis xj. / iij C [300] paragraffis x.'; the term 'pageants'
to describe the illustrations is unusual, but not without
parallel.

PROVENANCE: Humphrey Stafford, Duke of Buckingham
(d.1460); Bremschet family, London, late 15th century; St John's
College, Cambridge from an unknown date.

LITERATURE: James 1913, 238–40; Alexander 1972; Bühler 1949;
Bühler 1970, xiv–xv, xviii–xxi; Norton-Smith 1979, xii;
Robinson 1988, no. 308, pl. 244; Jefferson 1995; Scott 1996, I,
263–66, 280–81; Beadle 2005.

RB

127

Jean Robertet, Georges Chastellain, and Jean de Montferrant, *Les douze dames de rhétorique*

In French
Flanders, Bruges, 1467–1468
ARTIST: Master of Anthony of Burgundy
(act. *c.*1460–1480)

Parchment, 58 fols. (foliated 2–61), 275 × 203 mm,
172 × 115 mm, 35 long lines, ruled in red ink

SCRIPT: Gothic bookhand (hybrida)

BINDING: gold-tooled brown leather over wooden boards, 18th
c.; sewn on five sewing stations; clasps closing back to front and
enamelled with Montferrant's arms survive from the original
binding, but were turned upside down when attached to the
lower cover of the present binding.

Cambridge University Library, MS Nn.3.2

FEW OWNERS of de luxe illuminated manuscripts
could claim to be both their commissioners and
authors. Jean de Montferrant, whose arms were painted
on the first page and enamelled on the clasps, was the
key link in the debate on poetry preserved on the pages
of this volume. His positions as chamberlain of Philip
the Good and tutor of the young Jacques de Bourbon,
recorded in the rubricated title shown here, made him
the ideal intermediary and arbiter in the exchange
between the two poets, Jean Robertet, secretary of
Charles I, Duke of Bourbon, and Georges Chastellain,
chronicler of Philip of Burgundy. While the exchange
took place in 1463 or 1464, this manuscript was made
for Montferrant between his appointment as chamberlain in 1467 and Jacques de Bourbon's death in 1468.

Two other contemporary illuminated copies of the
correspondence survive: one was made for Louis of
Gruuthuse (Paris, Bibliothèque nationale de France,
MS fr. 1174) and the other belonged shortly after its
completion to Philip of Cleves (Munich, Bayerische
Staatsbibliothek, MS Gall. 15). All three were the work
of distinct scribes and artists, but shared a common
model (Chavannes-Mazel 1992, Bruinsma 1992). The
Cambridge copy, by far the most accomplished, was illuminated by the Master of Anthony of Burgundy. Named
after manuscripts he painted for Anthony (1421–1504),
the most famous of Philip the Good's many illegitimate
children, the artist specialized in the illustration of secular texts. Since few of them had established iconographical programmes, he created some of the most
innovative compositions in Bruges during the late 1460s

and early 1470s (Los Angeles and London 2003–2004,
264, no. 69, 70). *Les douze dames de rhétorique* would have
presented him with an unusual challenge. The Cambridge
volume preserves his unique response.

Hopeful to engage Chastellain in a poetical discussion, Robertet approached him through Montferrant.
The manuscript opens with Robertet's first letter and
the miniature captures the very moment when it is
delivered to Montferrant.

Chastellain ignored Robertet's approaches until Montferrant reported an extraordinary event, the appearance
of twelve ladies, the delightful companions of Rhetoric,
who intervened in favour of Robertet. The account of
their apparition and Montferrant's response illustrated
in two miniatures (fols. 19, 22v) leads on to their solo
acts. With the exception of Florie Memoire which has
been cut out, each lady makes an individual appearance
with a poetical speech and a portrait: *Science, Eloquence,
Profundité, Gravité de sens, Vielle Acquisition, Multiforme*

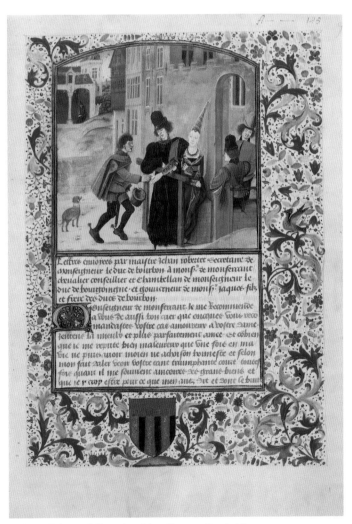

Robertet's letter delivered to Montferrant. Cambridge
University Library, MS Nn.3.2, fol. 9

Richesse, Noble Nature, Clere Invention, Precieuse Possession, Deduction Loable, and *Glorieuse Achevissance* (fols. 26v, 27v, 28v, 29v, 30v, 31v, 33v, 34v, 35v, 36v, 37v). Eloquence is shown in the garden of a stately home overlooking the streets and canals of Bruges *(see back cover)*. Neither the setting with its unique blend of a landscape and cityscape, nor Eloquence's attribute, the compass, nor her biblical motto *Diffusa est gracia in labiis meis* ('Grace is spread through my lips') are accounted for by the text. The discrepancy between the images and the rhetorical, highly abstract verses has been explained by models designed for monumental paintings, the influence of mime and drama, suggested by the stage-like curtains in some of the miniatures, or further discussions between the participants in the poetical exchange. Whatever the explanation, the images testify to the artist's imaginative response to the sophisticated demands of the patron-author.

PROVENANCE: Jean de Montferrant, Lord of Bugey (arms on clasps and fol. 9); John Moore, Bishop of Ely (1707–1714); presented to the Library by George I in 1715.

EXHIBITED: London 1953–1954, no. 587; Cambridge 1976, no. 2; Bruges 1981, no. 110; Cambridge 1993, no. 51; Los Angeles and London 2003–2004, no. 70.

LITERATURE: University Library 1856–1867, IV, 473–74; Zsuppàn 1970, 23, 37, 112–35; Jenni and Thoss 1982, 104, 107, 108, figs. 63, 64; Jung 1982, 238; Lemaire 1983, 11–15, ill. 4; Muhlethaler 1985; Dogaer 1987, 124; Chavannes-Mazel 1992; Bruinsma 1992; Cowling 2002.   SP

128

La Légende dorée

In French
Flanders or Northern France, Bruges or Amiens, *c.*1490 and Hainaut, *c.*1510
ARTISTS: Master of the Dresden Prayer Book (act. *c.*1470–*c.*1515); Master of Marguerite de Liedekerke (act. *c.*1480–*c.*1510)

Parchment, iii + 269 + iii fols., 392 × 298 mm, text 279–282 × 194–208 mm, 2 columns, 38 lines, ruled in purple or red ink.
SCRIPT: Gothic bookhand (hybrida)
BINDING: red velvet and calf over wooden boards, traces of four circular bosses on each cover, probably 16th c.

Fitzwilliam Museum, MS 22

THIS LITTLE-KNOWN MANUSCRIPT is an exceptional copy of the *Légende dorée*, a French translation of Jacobus de Voragine's *Legenda aurea*. The Latin *Golden Legend* was a compilation of abbreviated lives of the saints arranged in liturgical sequence. The basis of the French text of MS 22 is the translation of Jean de Vignay, produced around 1333–1348 for Jeanne de Bourgogne, wife of King Philippe VI of France. By at least 1402, Vignay's text was supplemented by the addition of some forty-two *festes nouvelles*, and that version served as a basis for later revised and expanded French redactions. Fitzwilliam MS 22 is a partial copy of the most distinctive of the revised versions. Known in only three manuscript copies and a rare printed edition (Russell 1986, 132), this redaction departs from the liturgical sequence of texts found in Voragine's Latin original and Vignay's translation, and it presents chapters on the principal events of Christ's life in narrative sequence at the beginning of the text. It includes new texts of catechetical and devotional character – an Exposition of the Mass (Frere 1899) and texts on the Ten Commandments and the Twelve Articles of the Faith – and it also incorporates a new series of Saints' Lives, among them a group venerated especially in the border region of northern France and Flanders (e.g., Saints Waudrud, Piat, Lievin, Bavon, Ghislain and Géry). This version was probably composed in that region, possibly close in date to the printed edition, which has been dated *c.*1475–1477 and assigned to the 'Printer of Flavius Josephus', provisionally localized at an unidentified site in present-day Belgium.

Unlike the Latin original of Voragine's text, which circulated primarily in un-illustrated manuscripts held in the libraries of religious institutions, most of the extant copies of the versions of Jean de Vignay's French translation were produced in illuminated copies for secular patrons (Maddocks 1986). The French copies typically include frontispiece illustrations, supplemented in richly illustrated examples by miniatures at individual chapter headings. Fitzwilliam MS 22 is the only known copy of the *Légende dorée* for which an extensive cycle of narrative depictions was planned. Despite its impressive size, the manuscript is fragmentary, containing only eighty-seven chapters out of a total of two hundred and thirty eight. If complete, it would have included two more volumes of comparable size. The eighty-seven chapters were to be illustrated with a cycle of no less than three hundred and ninety four miniatures, comprising frontispiece illustrations, miniatures at the headings of chapters (usually extending across the two columns of text), and cycles of narrative illustration within the chapters. The programme of illustration was never completed: only one hundred and forty-six of the planned three hundred and ninety-four miniatures were executed, but some of the other spaces reserved for miniatures preserve sketches and marginal notes that appear to be instructions for illuminators.

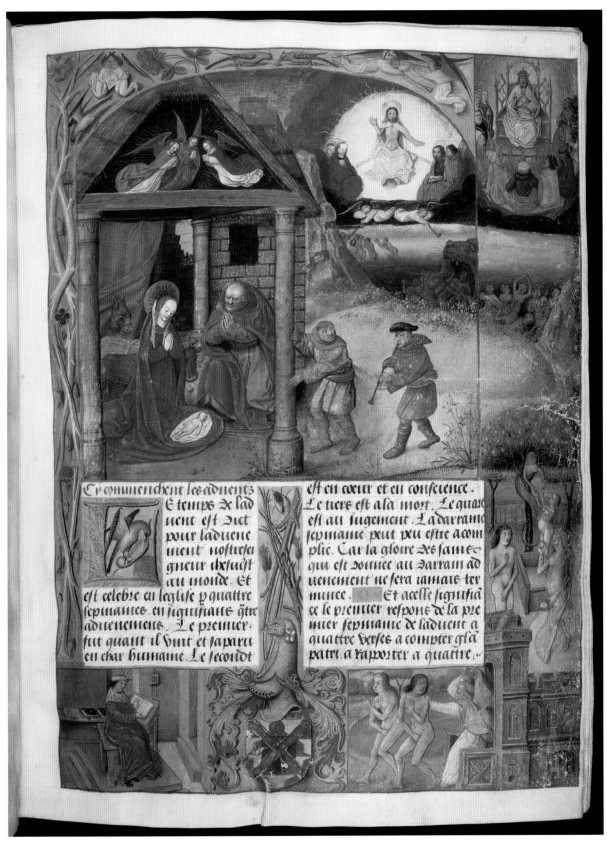

Nativity and Last Judgement with marginal scenes of God Enthroned, Souls in Limbo, the Fall and Expulsion from Paradise, and a writer, perhaps Jacobus de Voragine. Fitzwilliam Museum, MS 22, fol. 2

The illustrations belong to two campaigns of illumination. The first, comprising the frontispiece illustration of Jean de Vignay's preface (fol. 1), the two-column miniature of the Nativity and the Last Judgement at the beginning of Advent (fol. 2), and most of the other miniatures in gatherings 1–3 and 10, is characteristic of the Master of the Dresden Prayer Book, a leading illuminator in Bruges, and possibly other centres in northern France and Flanders, c.1470–1515. As the great majority of this original and distinctive miniaturist's works appear in Books of Hours, the addition of more than sixty miniatures to his oeuvre in this large-format manuscript adds significantly to our knowledge of the range of his activity. His brilliant atmospheric and colouristic effects, loose painting style, and expressive use of ordinary or common figural types are displayed to fine advantage here in depictions of nocturnal scenes and landscapes, including a memorable cycle of depictions of the Fifteen Signs of the Last Judgement (fols. 6v–8; Simon 1978, 185–88). This campaign probably dates to c.1490.

Around 1510, a second miniaturist added more than eighty miniatures to the unfinished cycle of illustration. His work can be seen on the frontispiece to Advent (fol. 2), where he added the marginal decoration surrounding and partly extending the miniature of the Nativity by the Master of the Dresden Prayer Book. The coat of arms in the added decoration in the lower part of this page and the motto included in one of the added miniatures in the same style (fol. 86) identify the patron of this campaign of illumination. This was Jean II, Lord of Oettingen and Flobecq (d.1514), who lived in Hainaut and from whose library seven other illuminated manuscripts in French have been identified (Lemaire 1993). The miniatures of this campaign have been attributed to the Master of Marguerite de Liedekerke (Legaré 2003), whose earliest datable work was commissioned in 1482 and who has been named after the patron of an extensively illustrated Antiphonal made c.1500–1502 for the Benedictine convent of Forest (Westmalle, Abdij der Trappisten, MS 9).

PROVENANCE: Jean II, Lord of Oettingen and Flobecq (coat of arms, fol. 2r; motto, *Ou que ie soie*, on a scroll in the miniature, fol. 86r); acquired by Viscount Fitzwilliam in 1803; his bequest, 1816.

LITERATURE: Searle 1876, 121–22, no. 105; James 1895a, 43–51; Frere 1899; Knowles 1954, 380; Simon 1978, 185–88; Russell 1986; Maddocks 1986, 159; Maddocks 1991, 13; Hamer 1993; Legaré 2003; Los Angeles and London 2003–2004, 339.

JHM

129

Geoffrey Chaucer, *Troilus and Creseyde*

In Middle English verse
England, perhaps London, c.1415–c.1425
ARTIST: The Master of the Corpus Troilus (act. c.1410–c.1430)

Parchment, v (modern) + ii (medieval pastedown and flyleaf) + 150 + i (medieval pastedown) + iv (modern) fols., 314 × 220 mm, text 214 × 120 mm., 35 lines (5 stanzas of 7 lines, plus intermediary blank lines), ruled in plummet

SCRIPT: Gothic bookhand (textualis)

BINDING: modern red goatskin over wooden boards, by the Cambridge Colleges Conservation Consortium, 1994

Corpus Christi College, MS 61

THE MAGNIFICENT ILLUMINATED FRONTISPIECE to the Corpus Christi College *Troilus* is probably the most famous image in the history of English medieval literature. There is a haze of thumbing before the figure of a bearded man declaiming from a pulpit where countless admirers of the book have stubbed their fingers and have declared that this must be Chaucer himself. Before the poet is a seated prince, dressed in gold and white fur, listening attentively. The scene is set in a wonderful open-air glade at the foot of a hill among a party of noble men and women seated and standing, listening and making conversation. In the upper background are two fairy-tale castles on hilltops, with further groups of nobles descending and greeting each other. They may be figures from the story of *Troilus*, such as Creseyde being escorted from Troy to be handed over to Diomede and the Greeks on the left, the major event of Book V of the poem, or it may allude to the beginning of Book I where Troilus and Creseyde emerge from the temple of Pallas in Troy to join the Trojan nobles in attending the feast of the Palladium. It may simply show more people descending to the valley to listen to Chaucer.

This is by far the most spectacular painting in any Middle English manuscript but it is only a foretaste of what was designed to be a manuscript of almost inconceivable opulence, for there are spaces carefully left for about ninety further illustrations never added. By any definition, this was a princely commission, evidently abandoned unfinished. The question of who the patron was, however, has worried Chaucer scholars for centuries. The book is too late for Richard II (r.1377–1399), Chaucer's own king. The prince could be Henry V (r.1413–1422) but his copy of *Troilus* survives in New York, a much humbler book (Pierpont Morgan Library, M.813). Scott has proposed Charles d'Orléans (1394–1465), the

French royal aesthete and poet, nephew of Charles VI, who was taken prisoner at the Battle of Agincourt in 1415 and spent the next twenty-five years as a hostage in England, living in some style (originally at the king's expense), fluent in English, collecting and commission-ing manuscripts. This makes good sense. The tradition of richly illustrated literary texts was as common in the French court as it was unknown in England. Even the script, in a formal display hand, is characteristic of the grandest copies of French vernacular texts, such as the

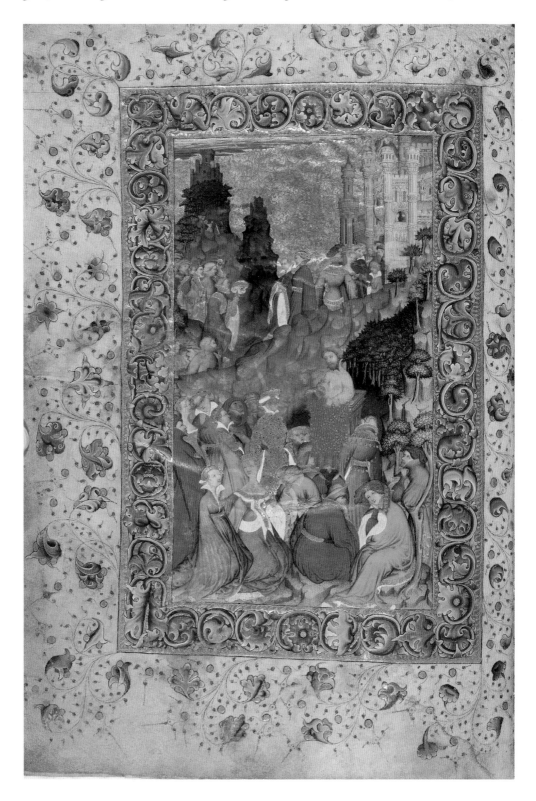

Chaucer addressing a noble audience. Corpus Christi College, MS 61, fol. 1

Roman de la Rose, and it might easily have been requested by a French-speaking patron for whom the English bookhands were less easy to read.

The frontispiece seems to be by two illuminators. The border is completely English and the same hand occurs in several other books, probably including the Prayer Book of Charles d'Orléans, now in Paris (Bibliothèque nationale de France, MS lat. 1196). The central miniature is evidently by a different artist. The hand apparently occurs in only one other book, a beautiful but enigmatic copy of John de Burgh at Longleat House, MS 24, probably made for a member of the Scrope family of York (Charles d'Orléans was held in Yorkshire from 1417). The Chaucer frontispiece is extraordinarily French in style, and it seems almost inconceivable that the painter has not studied something like the *Belles Heures* of the Duc de Berry, which the Limbourgs illuminated in Bourges around 1408. It has also been argued by Schmidt that the technique is Milanese, and that the artist was equally intimate with luxury manuscripts of the Visconti court. The question must at least be asked (as it probably has not) whether the painter could conceivably be Charles d'Orléans himself, multi-talented and over-educated. He was the great-nephew of the Duc de Berry, whom he had visited in Bourges in 1411, and he was the son of Valentina Visconti, who left him her own library in 1408. Some poets, and kings too (if we include René d'Anjou), were also illuminators.

The manuscript was evidently back on the market before it was finished, perhaps when the assets of Charles d'Orléans were sold to meet his debts, and there are small additions in the hand of John Shirley (d.1456), London bookseller. Except for one much-debated inscription, the book has no secure provenance before its acquisition by Stephen Batman in 1570, chaplain to Matthew Parker. The controversial fifteenth-century inscription is in the middle, fol.101v, 'nev[er] foyeteth Anne nevyll'. It has always been assumed that an Anne Neville owned the book, and the candidates usually proposed are Anne (d.1492), wife of Richard Neville, or Anne (d.1480), daughter of Ralph Neville, Duke of Westmorland. There might be a better explanation. There was a custom, probably originating in the court of Burgundy, that when a member of the royal family visited a private house, he or she would be asked to write an inscription in the family's most precious book, usually along the lines of 'remember me' or 'pray for me' and a signature. There are many examples in England from about the 1470s onwards, including, for example, Richard III as Duke of York who wrote a similar inscription in a margin in the middle of another Chaucer, Longleat House MS 257, fol.98v, but certainly did not own it. The simplest identification here would be his wife, Anne Neville (d.1485), who married Richard in 1472 and was Queen of England from 1483.

She did not own the Corpus *Troilus* but she evidently visited someone who did.

PROVENANCE: probably Charles d'Orléans (after 1415); John Shirley (d.1456); Stephen Batman, acquired in 1570 from 'Mr Cari', probably William Carye; Matthew Parker (1504–1575); his bequest, 1575.

EXHIBITED: Cambridge 1975, no. 28; London 2003–2004, no.171.

LITERATURE: James 1912b, I, 126–27; Parkes and Salter 1978; Boffey 1995, 2, 10, 13; Seymour 1995, 59–60, 160; Scott 1996, no. 58; Hardman 1997; Connolly 1998, 41, 63, 108–10, 112, 113, pl.3.x; Kendrick 1999, 196–98; Harris 2000; Scott 2000; Schmidt 2001; Helmbold 2002; Scott 2002, 45.

C DE H

130

Geoffrey Chaucer, Poetical Works

In English

England, East Anglia, first quarter of the fifteenth century

Parchment, 517 fols. (some now represented by modern parchment inserts attached to stubs) + 37 fols. (added *c.*1600), 310 × 182 mm, text 195 × 105 mm, 38–40 long lines, ruled in crayon and hard point

SCRIPT: Gothic bookhand (with anglicana formata and bastard secretary elements)

BINDING: alum tawed skin over wooden boards, 1995

Cambridge University Library, MS Gg.4.27(1)

CAMBRIDGE UNIVERSITY LIBRARY MS Gg.4.27 is an important but sadly mutilated early fifteenth-century compilation containing most of the major poems of Geoffrey Chaucer (d.1400), including the *Canterbury Tales*, *Troilus and Criseyde*, the *Parlement of Foules* and the *Legend of Good Women*, with a unique version of its *Prologue*. No other attempt to collect Chaucer's 'poetical works' survives from the period before the introduction of printing, and only the Ellesmere manuscript of the *Canterbury Tales* (San Marino, Huntington Library, MS EL 26 C9) possesses a comparable scheme of decoration and illustration. In its original form MS Gg.4.27(1) probably included upwards of twenty pictures of the Canterbury pilgrims to whom Chaucer attributes his narratives, but the leaves bearing most of them were removed, probably in the sixteenth century, leaving only those featuring the Reeve, the Cook, the Wife of Bath, the Pardoner, the Monk and the Manciple, who is shown here. Whoever mutilated the manuscript also left behind three of the seven

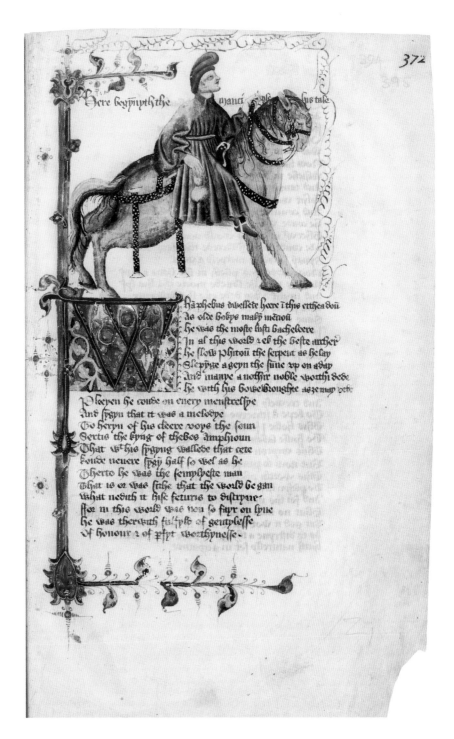

The Maniple and the beginning of his Tale. Cambridge University Library, MS Gg.4.27(1), fol. 395

pictured pairs of Vices and Virtues – unusual in manuscript illumination, and unique in extant Chaucer manuscripts – which illustrated the Parson's sermon at the end of the *Canterbury Tales*: Envy and Charity, Gluttony and Abstinence, Lechery and Chastity. Another most unfortunate loss from the scheme of illustration are the two full-page miniatures which apparently stood between the ending of the *Canterbury Tales* and the beginning of *Troilus and Criseyde*, traces of whose existence were noted by Henry Bradshaw of the University Library in the course of his reconstruction of the original quire structure during the 1860s.

The idea of marking the beginning of each of the

Canterbury Tales with a picture of its pilgrim-teller probably originated with the design of the Ellesmere manuscript, copied in London not long after Chaucer's death by a scribe who had been closely associated with the poet. The present book by contrast is a somewhat later provincial product. To judge by the East Anglian dialect into which Chaucer's London English has here been 'translated' (presumably for the convenience of local readers), the scribe is likely to have hailed from the general area within which Cambridge, Bury St Edmunds and Thetford were the larger towns. Kathleen Scott has recently argued that the artist who was responsible for the miniatures and the two illuminators who added the numerous

277

decorative borders and initials were also from East Anglia, though the latter seem to have worked in a style more characteristic of the turn of the fourteenth century, rather than the 1420s–1430s, when the manuscript was made. Many textual and decorative features of the manuscript, discussed in detail by Parkes and Beadle in the introduction to the facsimile published in 1980, have a makeshift or *ad hoc* air, as if it were the work of craftsmen commissioned to imitate a more sophisticated model of vernacular book production with which they were unfamiliar.

Whereas the Ellesmere pilgrim miniatures were imaginatively and dynamically placed in the margins near the beginnings of the relevant tales, those in the present book have been taken into the text column. There they sit without the addition of any of the background features one might expect, sometimes within a hastily added penwork frame, as is the case here with the Manciple, whose horse has been distorted to fit the column width. Unlike some of the pilgrims, the Manciple is not described physically in the General Prologue to the *Canterbury Tales*, leaving the artist free to imagine his appearance. The object that he holds is a wine-gourd, which features in his encounter with the drunken Cook in the prologue to his tale.

PROVENANCE: no early marks of ownership; Joseph Holland, antiquary *c*.1600; may subsequently have been in the library of Richard Holdsworth, Master of Emmanuel College (d.1649); his bequest, 1649; received by the University Library in 1664.

LITERATURE: University Library 1856–1867, III, 172–74; Parkes and Beadle 1980; Scott 1996, I, no. 43.

RB

131

John Gower, *Confessio Amantis*

In English
England, London, *c*.1450–*c*.1470

Parchment, i (paper) + i (originally the final leaf of the text, now misplaced at the beginning) + 188 + i (paper) fols., 457 × 310 mm, text 312 × 195 mm, 2 columns, 45–47 lines (occasionally 38 lines), ruled in purple, red and black ink

SCRIPT: Gothic bookhand (anglicana)

BINDING: gold-tooled calf over pasteboards, 18th c.

St Catharine's College, MS 7

THIS VERY LARGE BOOK, which is difficult to read without a lectern for support, was doubtless designed for a reading of John Gower's poetry to a group of people, in the same way as Chaucer recites his poem before the courtly assembly of lords and ladies in the frontispiece to the Corpus *Troilus and Criseyde (no. 129)*. Such very large format books of Middle English verse and prose either gathered together a diverse selection of works, such as the Vernon manuscript (Oxford, Bodleian Library, MS Eng. poet. a.1), or contained a work or works by a single author such as this copy of Gower's *Confessio Amantis*, or Lydgate's *Romance of Generydes*, *Troy Book* and *Siege of Thebes (no. 132)*.

The earliest version of Gower's poem can be dated to 1390. The version in this manuscript is in East Anglian dialect. After a long Prologue concerned with the moral state of society in the past and present, the poem is arranged in eight sections of stories grouped under the sins of Pride, Envy, Wrath, Sloth, Avarice, Gluttony and Lechery, with the addition of a section on the education of a king. These stories are set in the context of a dialogue between the confessor, Father Genius, and the poet. Illustrated manuscripts of the poem appeared certainly within two years of its composition in 1390, that in San Marino, Huntington Library, MS 150 being datable *c*.1392–1399. The iconography, number of pictures and the position in the text where they are placed vary considerably between the manuscripts. The textual and pictorial traditions of Gower's *Confessio Amantis* are very complex. This manuscript has only two images which are 'standard' pictures found in the earliest illustrated manuscripts, and which may have been authorized by Gower. The first is in the Prologue in an adaptation in English verse of the part of the book of Daniel which deals with Nebuchadnezzar's dream to illustrate division as a cause of evil: Nebuchadnezzar in bed has a dream-vision of a statue with a gold head, body of silver, belly and thighs of brass, legs of iron and the feet partly of iron and partly of clay. This is set as a framed miniature in the text, and a space has been provided for it between the lines of verse. The second picture in Book I seems to have been an afterthought without space provided, so that it penetrates extensively into the margin: the confessor seated with the penitent kneeling before him and the head of God above. The figure style is rather flat and linear with the figures quite large in proportion to the frames. At the beginning there may have been a plan to illustrate it more fully, but this was abandoned after the first two pictures and no more spaces were left for illustration. This lack of miniatures is compensated by handsome illuminated foliage initials and full borders at the beginning of the Prologue and each of the eight books. Among the acanthus foliage are blossoms with large pointed dotted stamens. This 'overblown' foliage with blossoms is characteristic of the third quarter of the fifteenth century in England.

The St Catharine's *Confessio Amantis* has some connec-

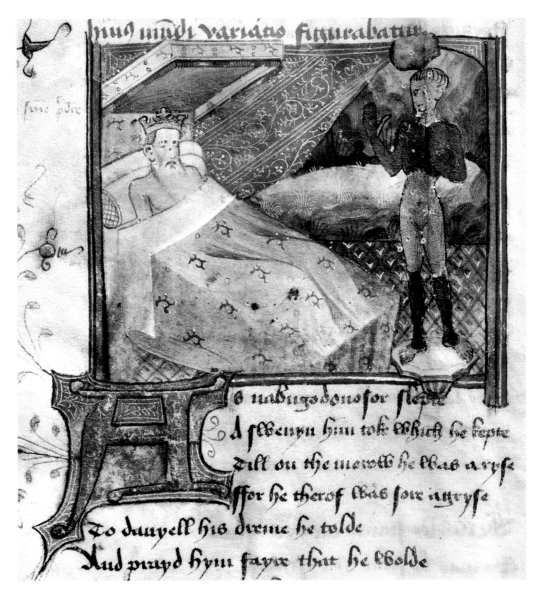

tion with another copy of *c.*1460–*c.*1470 (New York,
Pierpont Morgan Library, M.126), but in that case the
poem is given seventy-nine illustrations. The Nebuchadnezzar miniature, however, is placed at exactly the
same point in the text in both manuscripts. The two
pictures in the St Catharine's manuscript are insufficient
for adequate comparison with the Flemish-influenced
style of the Morgan manuscript.

PROVENANCE: Baxter Bohun (1616–1658), a gift from his
grandmother Lany in 1652; Edmund Bohun (1645–1699); given
to the College by William Bohun of Beccles, Suffolk, in 1740.

LITERATURE: Macaulay 1900–1901, I, cxlvi–cxlvii; James 1925,
14–15; Griffiths 1983, 169, 177; Scott 1996, I, 70 n. 4, 72 n. 10;
II, 324; Emmerson 1999, 147 n. 12, 185; Pearsall 2004, 74, 82, 90.

NJM

132

The Romance of Generydes, John Lydgate, *Troy Book* and *Siege of Thebes*

In English
England, East Anglia, third quarter
of the fifteenth century

Parchment, 211 fols., 443 × 315 mm, text 295 × 215 mm,
48 long lines, ruled in black ink

SCRIPT: Gothic bookhand (cursive)

BINDING: contemporary alum tawed skin over wooden boards;
arms painted on edges.

Trinity College, MS O.5.2

THE DECORATION of Trinity College MS O.5.2 is
distinctive and revealing of its origins. It consists
of several full-page borders, a number of miniatures

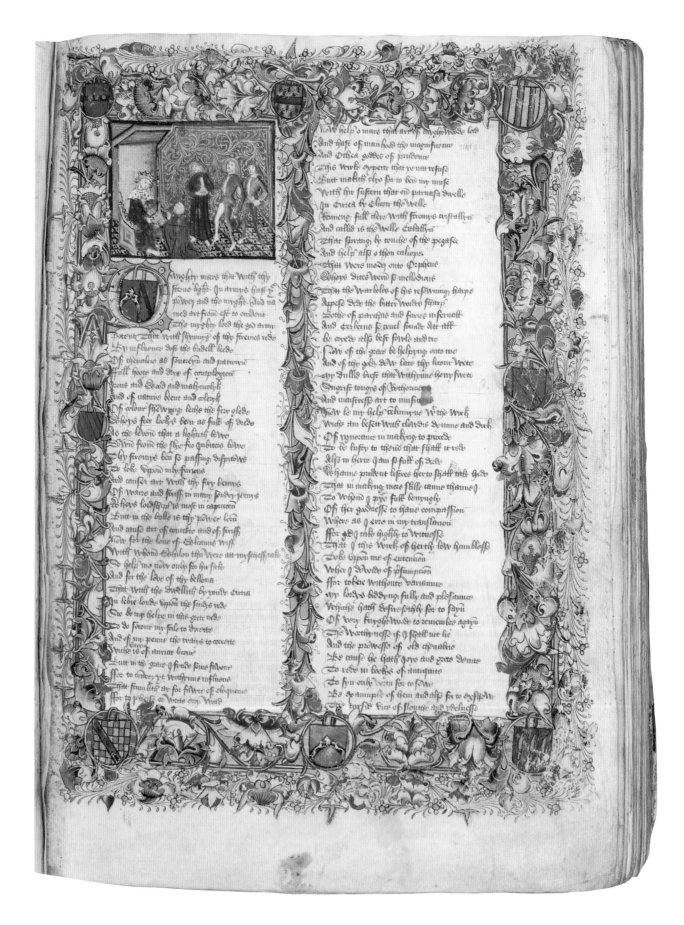

illustrating John Lydgate's *Troy Book*, and numerous coats of arms, which are not only incorporated into the decorative scheme and scattered randomly in the margins, but are also painted on the fore-edges of the book. These were partly deciphered by Aldis Wright and analysed more thoroughly by Pearsall who showed that the manuscript reflects the close connection of two Norfolk families, the Knyvetts of Buckenham and the Thwaites of Hardingham. Specifically, the present form of the volume seems to celebrate their union through the marriage of John Thwaites (1457–1507) and Anne Knyvett (d.1541), which probably took place in the 1480s or 1490s. Though evidently all the work of a single scribe, the manuscript is a composite volume. The section containing *Generydes* previously belonged to the Knyvetts and that containing the *Troy Book* and the *Siege of Thebes* to the Thwaites. The bringing together of these two parts of the manuscript and of the two families was marked by a second phase of decoration in which more escutcheons were painted at irregular intervals in the margins of many pages 'presumably to certify ownership, much as a modern library will stamp a number of pages of a book' (Pearsall 1961, 208). In the sixteenth century, Anthony Thwaites (probably the son of John) and a Henry Thwaites wrote their names in the book (fols. 190v, 211v).

The poems of John Lydgate, monk of Bury St Edmunds (d.1449), who is shown here presenting his *Troy Book* to King Henry V, were popular amongst East Anglian gentry of the type represented by the Knyvetts and Thwaites. Their copies were no doubt made and decorated locally. The *Troy Book*, of which there are several other illustrated copies, was completed in 1420, and the artist of the Trinity manuscript, working some fifty years later, presumably derived his presentation miniature from an exemplar of rather earlier date.

PROVENANCE: the families of Knyvett and Thwaites, Norfolk, late 15th to 16th century; it is not known how the manuscript reached Trinity College.

EXHIBITED: Norwich 1973, no. 70.

LITERATURE: Aldis Wright 1873–1878, v–vi; James 1900–1904, vol. III, 298–300; Pearsall 1961; Scott 1996, II, 261, 283.

RB

John Lydgate presenting the *Troy Book* to King Henry V. Trinity College, MS O.5.2, fol. 38

133

Free Warren Charter (the Pilkington Charter)

In Latin
England, 1291

Parchment, 191 × 285 mm, text 100 × 240 mm, 13 lines; fragment of Great Seal of England in green wax attached by cord

SCRIPT: Charter hand

Fitzwilliam Museum, MS 46–1980

THIS CHARTER was issued by Edward I in June 1291. It confirms to Roger de Pilkington that he and his heirs shall have free warren in his demesne lands in Pilkington and elsewhere in Lancashire, without encroachment on the royal forests. 'Warren', from the Old French *garenne* or game-park, means the right to keep or hunt game, and is a term associated only secondarily with rabbits. The charter was issued at Norham near Berwick while Edward was in the north of England negotiating between the claimants to the throne of Scotland. The witnesses to the charter include some of the most substantial administrators of the day: John le Romeyn, Archbishop of York, Robert Burnell, Bishop of Bath and Wells and Anthony Bek, Bishop of Durham. The Great Seal, showing King Edward seated on a fine throne with leopards or lions at its side, is of a form established late in the reign of his father Henry III.

The document is decorated in a cheerfully appropriate way with a frame of curiously inert but sometimes beautifully-observed creatures, some of which were natural targets for hunting. To the lower left is the alert figure of a crossbowman with his dogs. From top left reading clockwise, the creatures are: a rabbit and hare, roller, peacock, merlin, hobby, woodlark, bullfinch, crossbill, woodcock and hooded falcon, with a quail, cow and sheep below the line; a kingfisher, tree creeper, squirrel, wild cat, boar, fox, roe doe, roe buck, fallow doe, fallow buck, hind, red stag, waxwing, snowbunting, hawfinch and jay. From some point around 1280 fauna began to find great popularity in English illumination, notably in the Alfonso Psalter (London, British Library, Add. MS 24686) and in the Bird Psalter (Fitzwilliam Museum, MS 2–1954; Sandler 1986, nos. 1, 10). The style of this charter is somewhat similar to a copy of Petrus Comestor's *Historia scholastica* given by Edmund, Earl of Cornwall to his foundation at Ashridge in 1283 (London, British Library, Royal MS 3.D.vi; Sandler 1986, no. 2). The clearly written text will almost certainly have been prepared and sealed in the Chancery

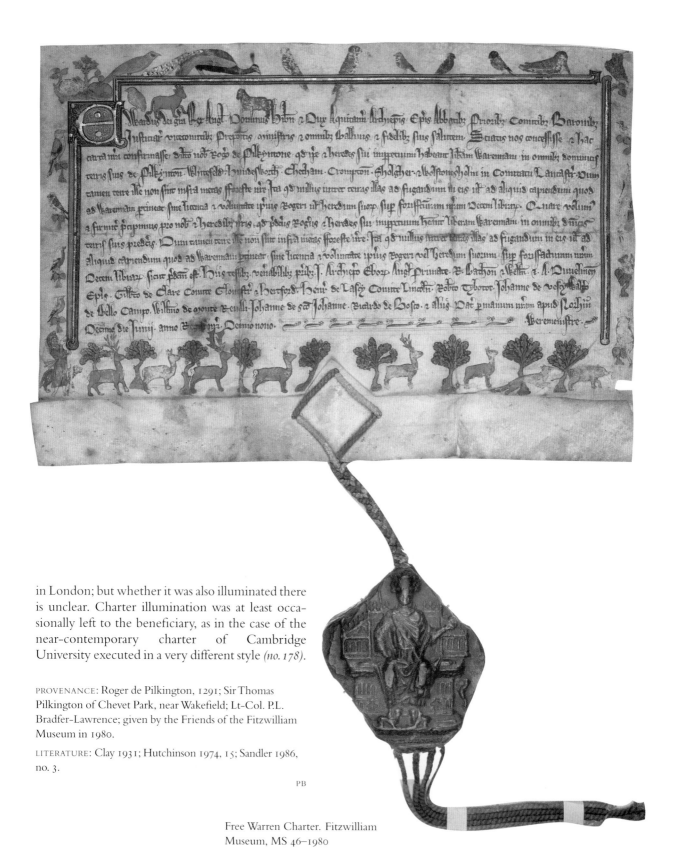

in London; but whether it was also illuminated there is unclear. Charter illumination was at least occasionally left to the beneficiary, as in the case of the near-contemporary charter of Cambridge University executed in a very different style *(no. 178)*.

PROVENANCE: Roger de Pilkington, 1291; Sir Thomas Pilkington of Chevet Park, near Wakefield; Lt-Col. P.L. Bradfer-Lawrence; given by the Friends of the Fitzwilliam Museum in 1980.

LITERATURE: Clay 1931; Hutchinson 1974, 15; Sandler 1986, no. 3.

PB

Free Warren Charter. Fitzwilliam Museum, MS 46–1980

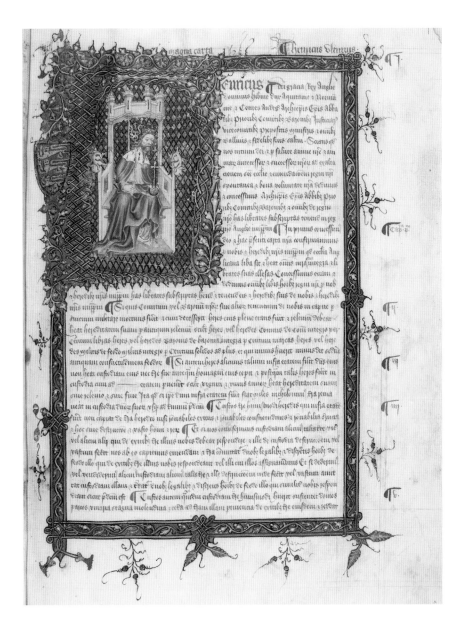

King Henry III with the ancient arms of England. St John's College, MS A.7, fol. 1

134

Statutes of England, Henry III to Richard II

In Latin and French.
England, c.1388–1389

Parchment, iii + 206 fols., 345 × 245 mm, text 222 × 144 mm, 39 long lines, ruled in brown ink

SCRIPT: Gothic bookhand (anglicana formata)

BINDING: reverse brown calf, blind stamped, 17th c.

St John's College, MS A.7 (James no. 7)

LEGAL MANUSCRIPTS such as those containing lists of statutes are often utilitarian in appearance, but St John's College MS A.7 is an example of a de luxe copy produced during the reign of Richard II. Its miniatures are the work of an artist with court connections and a knowledge of the International Gothic style. It is a manuscript designed to be admired for its appearance rather than consulted for its contents, which are merely statements of the principal royal laws passed during the previous two centuries. The beginnings of the lists of statutes for the reign of each successive king from Henry III to Richard II are marked by an elaborately ornamented page consisting of a full border and a large, richly decorated initial showing the king enthroned. Within the text, each individual statute begins with a gold, blue and pink four-line initial with sprays extending up and down the margin. The last statute (fols. 154–56v) is dated to the twelfth year of the reign of Richard II, i.e. 22 June 1388 to 21 June 1389, and the manuscript is thus likely to have been written at or soon after that time. The scribe then left a series of blank leaves ruled ready to receive the texts of more statutes as they were passed in subsequent years.

As Lucy Sandler has pointed out, the closest stylistic relative to the paintings of the kings in the St John's

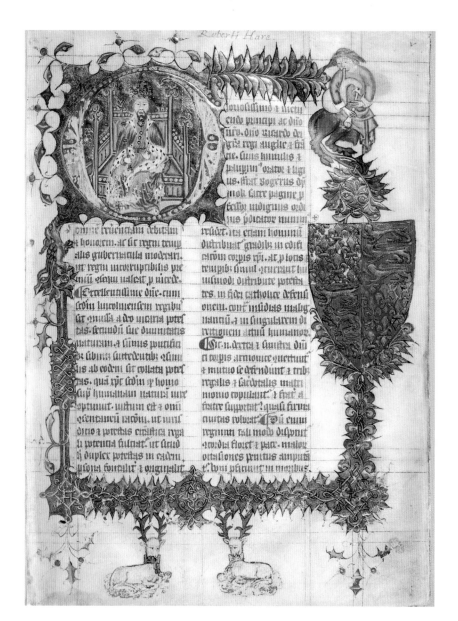

Richard II. Trinity Hall,
MS 17, fol. 1

Statutes is to be found in the miniatures of the Westminster *Liber Regalis*, which was also produced in
Richard II's time and in which the Orders for the
coronations and funerals of English monarchs are
described and illustrated (London, Westminster Abbey,
MS 38; Sandler 1986, no. 155; Binski 1997). Richard's
taste for lavish material objects and ostentatious display
is well attested, and it would not be surprising if this
manuscript were directly connected with him, or with
a member of his immediate circle.

PROVENANCE: unknown.

LITERATURE: James 1913, 8–9; Rickert 1952, 79–80; Sandler
1986, no. 155; Binski 1997, 239.

RB

135

Roger Dymmok, *Liber contra XII Errores et Hereses Lollardorum*

In Latin and English
England, probably London, *c*.1395

Parchment, ii + 158 + iii fols., 265 × 195 mm, text
167 × 50+9+49 mm, 2 columns, 30 lines, ruled in red ink

SCRIPT: Gothic bookhand (textualis)

BINDING: alum tawed calfskin, by Melvin Jefferson, 20th c.; edges
painted with shields of arms of England and France Ancient, *c*.1395

Trinity Hall, MS 17

IN JANUARY 1395 Lollards posted a declaration of their
beliefs on the doors of Westminster Hall and St Paul's
Cathedral. As well as causing a political panic, this action

prompted a refutation of their propositions by the Dominican Roger Dymmok. Dymmok, who came from Scrivelsby in Lincolnshire, had been Prior of the Black Friars at Boston, but at the time of the composition of this tract he was Regent Master in charge of theological studies at the London convent (Emden 1957–1959, I, 617). He gives each of the Lollards' twelve Conclusions in English, followed by a translation into Latin, and then proceeds to demolish systematically their heretical positions on such matters as ecclesiastical authority, the priesthood, religious vows, the sacrifice of the Mass, prayers for the dead, pilgrimage and the use of images.

Dymmok's response to the Lollards was addressed to Richard II. This manuscript is the presentation copy made for King Richard himself. The opening folio has a historiated initial of Richard enthroned, and a large shield of France Ancient and England quarterly in the right border. At the bottom of the page is a pair of lodged white harts, with chained crowns round their necks. The white hart was Richard's badge, and appears prominently on the Wilton Diptych. The bagpiping hybrid in the top right-hand corner is reminiscent of the large drolleries in the borders of the third campaign of the Exeter Bohun Psalter (Oxford, Exeter College, MS 47), by a London-based workshop of the 1390s (Dennison 1990b).

The prologue is illustrated by an initial of St John the Baptist addressing six men, identified as Pharisees and Sadducees by the text from St Matthew's Gospel, 'Ye brood of vipers, who hath shewed you to flee from the wrath to come?', with which the prologue begins. St John the Baptist was regarded as a precursor of the Order of Preachers and the Pharisees and Sadducees are therefore to be seen as the spiritual ancestors of the Lollards. The third historiated initial, on fol. 14, showing Constantine the Great and St Sylvester supporting a model church, is both an illustration of the donation of temporal possessions to the Pope by the first Christian Emperor and also symbolic of the union of spiritual and temporal authority in upholding the Church. Although Cronin's claim that the Emperor resembles Richard II cannot be sustained, Constantine is here presented to Richard as a model of the orthodox ruler, collaborating with the Church.

Stylistically the work is closest to a Psalter-Hours made for Eleanor de Bohun (Edinburgh, National Library of Scotland, Adv. MS 18.6.5), and to other works by Hand C of the Carmelite Missal (London, British Library, Add. MSS 29704, 29705, 44892). This suggests that the artist, whose hand has not yet been identified elsewhere, was based in London. The borders, with their symmetrically disposed foliage elements, are also characteristic of London work of the 1390s. Trinity Hall MS 17 is usually discussed in the context of the patronage of Richard II, but it is instructive to consider it as an example of Dominican book production. It is probable

that there was a symbiotic relationship between 'in house' scribes and 'professional' stationers similar to that documented in Paris (Rouse and Rouse 2000, I, 81–97). However, although the illuminator was most likely a layman, there remains the possibility that John Siferwas was not unique as an illuminator in the Order.

Trinity Hall 17 was most probably discarded from the Royal Library at the Reformation, acquired by Sir Thomas More's grandson and given by him to the recusant antiquary Robert Hare who presented it to Trinity Hall.

PROVENANCE: Richard II; Sir Anthony Roper of Farningham, Kent (d.1597); Robert Hare (1588) who presented it to Trinity Hall.

EXHIBITED: London 1993, no. 15.

LITERATURE: James 1907, 34–36; Cronin 1922; Rickert 1952, 92; Rickert 1965, 153; Sherborne 1983, 22; Scattergood 1983, 33; Alexander 1983, 146; Doyle 1983, 170; Cavanaugh 1988, 314; Robinson 1988, no. 394, pl. 178; Saul 1997a, 303, 356, 451, pl. 10; Saul 1997b, 28; Watson 2000, 213, 219; Scott 2002, 22–25, pls. Ia–b, col. pl. on p. 17.

NR

136

Procession at the opening of Parliament, 1512

England, London, c.1512
Parchment roll, 5490 × 273mm, on eight skins

Trinity College, MS O.3.59

THIS ROLL depicts the procession to the House of Lords at the opening of Henry VIII's second parliament, on 4 February 1512. At the head are the Lords Spiritual: first the abbots and priors of the major houses, beginning with the Abbot of Tewkesbury and ending with the Abbot of Westminster, who are followed by the bishops, beginning with the Bishop of Bangor. In the centre, under a canopy carried by four small tonsured figures, walks Henry VIII, immediately preceded by the Archbishop of Canterbury (William Warham), Garter King of Arms (Sir Thomas Wriothesley), the Duke of Buckingham and an unidentified person, probably the Lord Chamberlain of the Household. The final group is headed by the prior of the Order of St John of Jerusalem, who is followed by the other Lords Temporal. Over the heads of most people are their heraldic shields. These have not been completed for the bishops, and for some people no shield has been included: there is also some confusion over the Duke of Buckingham, whose shield has been included twice, albeit sketchily. The roll

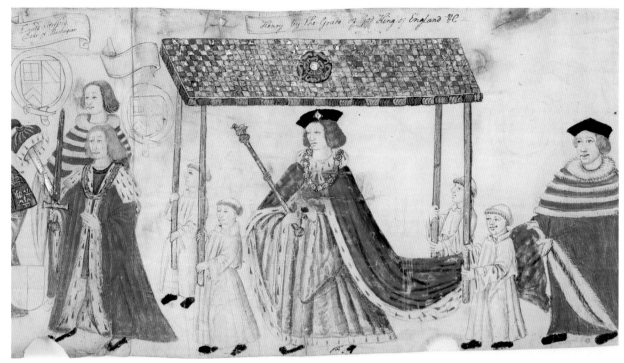

Procession to the House of Lords at the opening of Henry VIII's second parliament, 4 February 1512. Trinity College, MS O.3.59

was evidently never quite finished, and some captions were added many years later. The faces, generally very uniform, cannot be regarded as portraits.

The roll is the work of at least two artists, who drew the figures in brown ink and added shading in short strokes. Most colour was added after this: the colours are predominantly red, blue, black and gold, with appropriate additions for the heraldry. The canopy over the King is chequered with gold.

This is one of several such rolls known to have survived that record the openings of Henry VIII's parliaments. They are the latest in a long tradition of heraldic rolls in England, and this example is from the prolific workshop of Sir Thomas Wriothesley. Two later copies of it survive in the British Library (MS Add. 22306), and in the Bodleian Library (MS Ashmole 13), the latter made for the seventeenth-century antiquary Elias Ashmole. It is by no means clear how far these rolls can be taken to be accurate records of attendance: not everyone present at the opening of Parliament returned to take part in subsequent business. Their purpose seems to have been primarily as a record of precedence, for future reference.

PROVENANCE: Given to Trinity College by John Allen, B.D., Fellow (d.1778), in 1772: according to the eighteenth-century antiquary William Cole, Allen acquired it in Cheshire.

LITERATURE: James 1900–1904, III, 248; London, British Library, MS Add.5831 (notes by William Cole); Wagner and Sainty 1967; Wagner 1967; Anglo 1968.   DMcK

137

Statutes of the Order of the Garter

In English
England, 1520s

Parchment, 25 fols., 230 × 175 mm, text 150 × 110 mm, 23 long lines, ruled in red ink

SCRIPT: Gothic bookhand (cursive)

BINDING: blind-stamped calf over boards, 16th c.

Gonville and Caius College, MS 514/736

T HE ORDER OF THE GARTER was instituted at Windsor Castle by Edward III in 1348 as a secular Order of Chivalry, a knightly equivalent to the medieval religious orders. Such guild-like Orders became fashionable and widespread in Europe in the fourteenth century, and were usually formed from secular noblemen who never entered the religious life. Other models may have been tourneying societies; the seats of the members of the Order of the Garter in St George's Chapel at Windsor faced one another like two opposed tournament teams. The formal character of these Orders or guilds was reflected in their limited membership, possession of statutes, the holding of regular meetings like a religious chapter, and the conferral of an identifying mark which in other contexts might be called a 'device'. Such marks formed one part of the late-medieval obsession with rank, formality, ritual and precedence, as well as more generalized celebrations of war and military culture. Obligations to the monarch were also carefully set out in such statutes.

These Orders flourished throughout the later Middle Ages because they lent lustre to the person of the monarch. The Caius copy of the statutes dates to around 1522, since they were revised in this form in that year by the exceptionally image-conscious Henry VIII. *The Statuts amd Ordynances of the moste noble Ordre of Saynte George named the Gartyer* open on fols. IV–2 with a fine coat of arms consisting of a crest with a griffin quarterly or and azure on a cap of maintenance encircled by a garter supported by two beasts each with three horns, gorged with crowns. This is a very fine presentation copy made for a member of the Order.

PROVENANCE: given to the College by Robert Wright (probably Robert Wright, Baron of the Exchequer, d.1689).

LITERATURE: James 1907–1908, II, 585.

PB

138

Statutes and Armorial of the Order of the Golden Fleece

In French
Southern Netherlands, probably Valenciennes, 1563
SCRIBE and ARTIST: Jacques le Boucq
(act. *c.*1560–*c.*1565)

Parchment, 153 fols., 300 × 200mm, varying size of text block, number of lines and ruling

SCRIPT: Gothic bookhand (hybrida)

BINDING: gold-stamped calf over pasteboards, defaced arms, fleece and flint-and-steel stamps, traces of two clasps on fore-edge, gilt and gauffered edges, late 16th c.

Fitzwilliam Museum, MS 187

In 1429 the Duke of Bedford invited Philip the Good, Duke of Burgundy (1419–1467), to join the English Order of the Garter *(see no. 137)*. Philip declined. The following year, while celebrating his marriage to Isabella of Portugal in Bruges, he founded his own Order of the

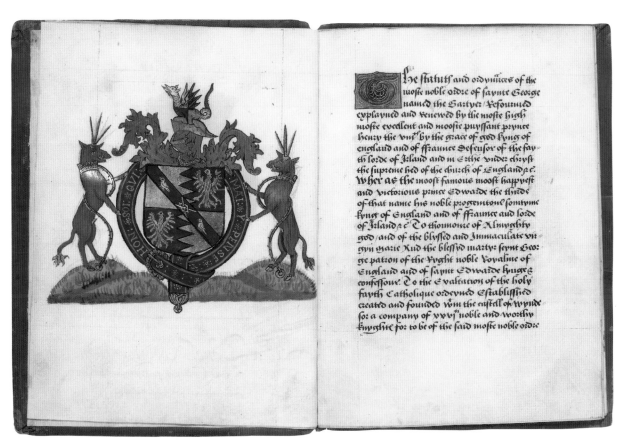

Owner's arms. Gonville and Caius College, MS 514/736, fols. IV–2

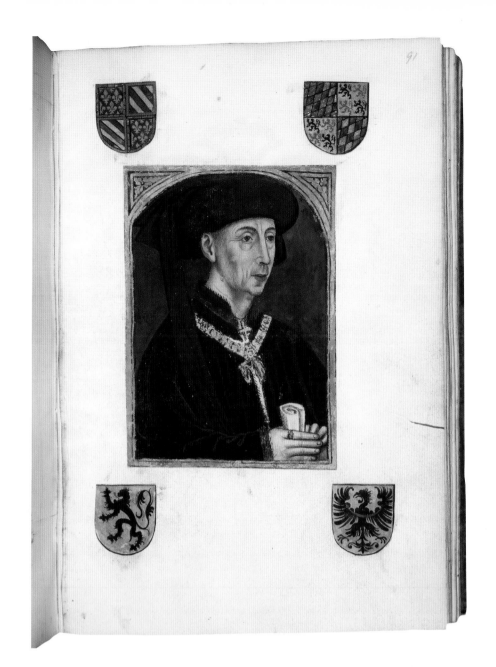

Philip the Good.
Fitzwilliam Museum,
MS 187, fol. 91

Golden Fleece. It united the aristocratic elite of the vast Burgundian territories in loyalty to their sovereign and became a powerful body of government that held its regular meetings, or chapters, in major cities of the Duke's domain.

This manuscript traces the history of the Order from its foundation in 1430 until 1559 when Philip II of Spain assumed the right to appoint new members without summoning chapters. Its first half contains the foundation documents of the Order in their revised version of 1446. They include the Statutes describing the members' rights and duties, the Ordinances stipulating the obligations and privileges of the four officers, namely the Chancellor, the Treasurer, the Griffier, and the King of Arms, and the Ceremonial for feasts and chapters. The second half of the manuscript contains the Order's succinct history in a register of its meetings and newly elected members between 1430 and 1559, and the

Armorial, a catalogue of the knights' heraldic shields. The major text divisions are embellished with illusionistic strewn-pattern borders and the first meeting to be presided over by a new ruler – starting with Philip the Good and finishing with Philip II of Spain – is framed in a Renaissance cartouche and introduced by a full-page design with the sovereign's arms. The consistent script and illumination establish that the manuscript was completed within a single campaign. The date 1563 appears on the title page and on decorated borders throughout the volume. The scribe recorded his name, Jacques le Boucq, and the place where he completed his work, Valenciennes, within the painted cartouche on fol. 93, which suggests that he was responsible for the illumination as well. The full-page armorial plates are surrounded with texts by an expert calligrapher and share their pigments and ornamental vocabulary with the strewn-pattern borders and the Renaissance cartouches. Nicholas Pickwoad has suggested (in conversation) that the binding may well be the original one and once contained the arms of the owner no doubt, a member of the Order.

The portrait of Philip the Good displayed here was painted on a separate piece of parchment by a different artist. It shows the Duke in full three-quarters view, clad in his fur-trimmed coat and black hat, or chaperon, the latest Burgundian fashion, wearing a cross and the collar of the Order of the Golden Fleece, holding a scroll, and gazing past the onlooker in a withdrawn, contemplative mode. It is a copy of a now lost portrait, the official 'likeness' of the Duke. Together with similar contemporary depictions, it established the fashion for half-length commemorative portraits promoting the image of pious nobility (Campbell 1979; Campbell 1990). The lost prototype probably created before the mid-1440s and traditionally ascribed to Rogier van der Weyden, but more recently associated with Jan Van Eyck, inspired numerous copies on panel, of which the most accomplished are now in Bruges, Groeningemuseum, and in Dijon, Musée des Beaux-Arts (Campbell 1985, no. 76; de Vos 1999, 372–73). Parchment copies would have functioned as independent portraits too, but they also featured in de luxe manuscripts of the Statutes of the Order of the Golden Fleece. Although the depictions of rulers introducing the account of the first chapter over which they presided were normally full-length images, a manuscript made around 1520 most probably for Charles V contains half-length portraits of the type seen here (Vienna, Österreichische Nationalbibliothek, MS 2606). In emulation of such celebrated copies of the Statutes, the patron of the Fitzwilliam manuscript may have ordered a replica of Philip's portrait for his own copy or he may have already owned the image and added it to the book. While the date of the portrait itself is hard to establish, the addition seems contemporary with the execution of the volume, since the portrait is surrounded by the arms of Burgundy and Flanders, the lion of Flanders, and the eagle of the Holy Roman Empire, all painted on pieces of parchment by the manuscript's main scribe-artist.

Two fifteenth-century illuminations were added to the manuscript at a later date. The first, glued to the lifted front pastedown, is a border fragment showing the flint-and-steel badge of the Order of the Golden Fleece, the initials 'C' and 'M' linked with a love knot, and the motto of Charles the Bold and Margaret of York *Je lay enprins, bien en aviegne* ('I have started it, may good come of it'). The second, pasted on fol. 129, is a miniature showing a chapter of the Order presided over by Charles the Bold and identified beneath in a seventeenth-century inscription as the 1473 meeting in Valenciennes. The miniature came from a copy of Guillaume Fillastre's

three-volume *Histoire de la Toison d'Or*. During the 1468 Bruges Chapter Guillaume Fillastre, former councillor of Philip the Good, Bishop of Tournai since 1460, and Chancellor of the Order since 1461, delivered a sermon on the six fleeces known from ancient and biblical sources, and linked them with the six virtues to be pursued by the knights of the Order (Cockshaw 1984; Brussels 1996, 119–27). At Charles the Bold's request, he began to develop this idea into a six-volume work. His death in 1473 allowed him to complete only three volumes, which he presented to Charles at the 1473 Chapter in Valenciennes. The Cambridge miniature documents this occasion.

Among the copies of Fillastre's *History* to which the Fitzwilliam fragments might have belonged originally, the most relevant is the set made for Charles the Bold between 1473 and 1477. Its second and third volumes are now in Vienna (Haus-, Hof- und Staatsarchiv, MS 2) and Copenhagen (Kongelige Bibliotek, MS 465–2), but the first volume survives in only two fragments (Dijon, Bibliothèque municipale, MS 2948 and Épinal, Musée de l'Imagerie, MS 345; Cockshaw 1984; Brussels 1996, 134–36). The Cambridge miniature does not match the fine illumination in the Vienna and Copenhagen manuscripts, and must have belonged to a different set of Fillastre's *History*. However, the exquisitely painted border fragment is identical with those in the Vienna and Copenhagen manuscripts and must have graced the opening miniature of the first volume, now in Dijon, which lacks all four borders.

Pierre Cockshaw recorded that the first volume of Charles the Bold's set had been destroyed before 1810. The provenance of the Fitzwilliam manuscript establishes that this may have happened as early as 1650. The inscription beneath the border fragment documents the ownership of Julius Chifflet. As Chancellor of the Order of the Golden Fleece from 1648 and author of its history printed by Moretus in 1652, he had unlimited access to the Order's Archives and to the ducal library, one of which would have housed Charles the Bold's set of Fillastre's *History*. So did his father, Jean-Jacques Chifflet, who was sent on a research trip to the Low Countries by Philip IV in 1626, published his history of the Order in 1632, and left many of his books to Julius. Either father or son may have helped themselves to mementos from the Order's glorious past, if they did not carry the whole volume away.

PROVENANCE: probably Jean-Jacques Chifflet (1588–1660); Julius Chifflet (*c.*1610–1676); acquired by Viscount Fitzwilliam in 1814; his bequest, 1816.

EXHIBITED: Cambridge 1993, no. 47.

LITERATURE: James 1895a, 395–96.

SP

289

139

Doge's Commission

In Latin and Italian
Venice, 1524
ARTIST: Benedetto Bordone (*c.*1450/1455–1539)
and workshop

Parchment, 49 fols., 240 × 165 mm, text 175 × 108 mm,
26 long lines, ruled in pale black ink

SCRIPT: Humanistic cursive

BINDING: gold-tooled red leather over boards, 18th c.;
re-backed, Cambridge University Library, 1980

Cambridge University Library, MS Dd.10.23

ISSUED BY THE DOGES OF VENICE and known as *Dogali* (the Venetian form for the standard Italian *Ducali*), Commissions were essentially contracts of employment for high-ranking officials. This commission was given in September 1524 to Vincenzo Zantani, who was appointed Commander of the Galleys by Doge Andrea Gritti (1523–1539). The Doge's notary Petrus Grasolarius signed the document on fol. 38v. Vincenzo Zantani's initials and arms are suspended from the text's frame in a typically illusionistic Renaissance fashion. This person-alized vocabulary is added to a feature common to most *Dogali*, the Lion of St Mark, patron of Venice. The city of Venice is suggested in the background of the top cartouche. The saints flanking the *incipit* page are Louis of Anjou (1274–1297), the Franciscan bishop of Toulouse canonized in 1317, and Vincent Ferrer (1350–1419), the Dominican friar canonized in 1455. They signal Vincenzo Zantani's private devotion in a document, which is otherwise concerned with his public service and secular power.

Commissions doubled as status symbols. To reinforce their importance as icons of the individual's power and the family's prestige, the recipients often had them illus-trated by leading contemporary artists. The design of this page framed in liquid gold, the atmospheric land-scapes of the cartouches, the fine border of blue and gold foliage are from the workshop of Benedetto Bor-done *(see no. 172)*. One of the most prolific and versatile Venetian artists of the late fifteenth and early sixteenth centuries, he was heavily involved in the illumination of *Dogali* and *Guiramenti*, or oaths of office (Mariani Canova 1968–1969a; Mariani Canova 1968–1969b; Armstrong 1996; Armstrong 1998). Since their dates and original ownership are often explicit, these documents present an invaluable source for the study of individual artists as well as the development of general trends and fashions in Renaissance manuscript illumination.

PROVENANCE: Vincenzo Zantani (1524, name, arms and initials on fol. 2, name on fol. 38v); John Moore, Bishop of Ely (1707–1714); presented to the Library by George I in 1715.

LITERATURE: University Library 1856–1867, I, 419; Robinson 1988, no. 12, pl. 363.

SP

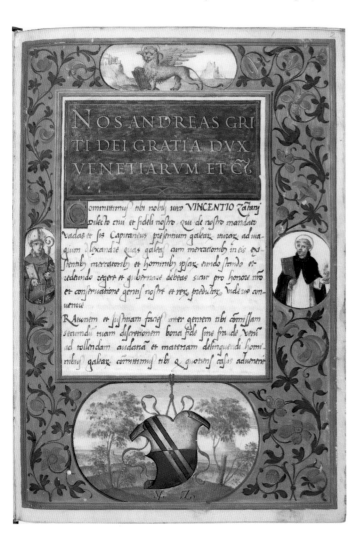

Incipit page with St Mark's lion, the owner's arms, Saints Louis of Toulouse and Vincent Ferrer. Cambridge University Library, MS Dd.10.23, fol. 2

OPPOSITE: St Mark, St Peter, and St Sebastian. Fitzwilliam Museum, Marlay cutting It. 43

140

Leaf from a Doge's Commission

In Latin
Venice, 1535
ARTIST: Master 'T°. Ve' (act. c.1520–c.1575)

Parchment, 230 × 158 mm
SCRIPT: Humanistic cursive

Fitzwilliam Museum, Marlay cutting It. 43

THIS IS ONE of seventeen leaves at the Fitzwilliam Museum, which belonged to Venetian Commissions spanning the entire sixteenth century. It once opened a *Dogale* similar in function to the one described in *no. 139*, but illuminated on a more ambitious scale. It was issued by Doge Andrea Gritti (1523–1539) for Pietro Dechataipetra, or de Tagliapietra, who was made podestà

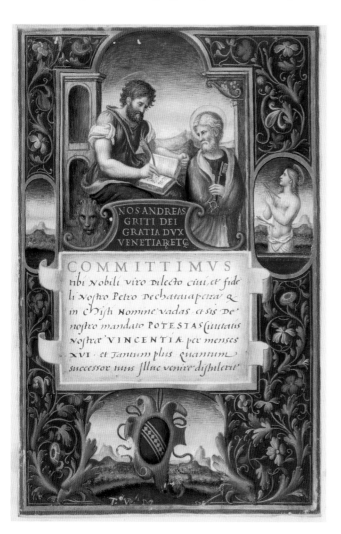

of Vicenza in 1535. His arms are prominently set against the landscape in the lower border. While St Mark and his symbol, the Lion, stand for the city of Venice, the owner ensured the protection of his patron saint, Peter, and of St Sebastian to whom he must have been particularly devoted.

The inscription 'T°. Ve. Dep. 1578' scratched at the foot of the image is a later addition. It purports to be the signature of Titian, but is probably no more than a sign of wishful thinking on behalf of a later owner or bait for a potential buyer. It was after this inscription that Giulia Maria Zuccolo Padrono named the artist of the Fitzwilliam leaf, attributing to him a large number of *Dogali* and *Guiramenti* (Padrono 1971). He was the head of a prolific workshop in Venice from the 1520 until the 1570s, specializing in the illumination of documents. Though a direct link with Titian cannot be substantiated, the style of the Master 'T°. Ve' is a witness to the triumph of Mannerism in contemporary Venetian illumination.

PROVENANCE: Pietro de Tagliapietra; Libri no. 563 pencilled on the verso; Charles Brinsley Marlay (1831–1912); his bequest, 1912.

EXHIBITED: London 1975, no. 15.

LITERATURE: Padrono 1971; Wormald and Giles 1982, 123–24; Philadelphia 2001, no. 77.

SP

141

Patent of nobility

In Spanish
Spain, Valladolid, 1576

Parchment, 48 fols. (contemporary ink foliation on fols. 2–21; modern foliation includes pastedowns as fols.1 and 50), 304 × 215 mm, 201 × 121 mm, 36 long lines, ruled in red ink
SCRIPT: Gothic bookhand (textualis)

BINDING: contemporary blind-stamped brown leather over boards made of printed leaves pasted together; traces of four ties; the forty-eight leaves form a single gathering sewn at three points through the central fold with a twisted cord of red, yellow and white silk threads; they were once attached to the seal described on fol. 48v and now lost

Cambridge University Library, MS Add. 4130

PATENTS OF NOBILITY are among the most frequently illuminated Spanish documents of the sixteenth century. Their numbers swelled during the reign of Philip II (1556–1598), who was anxious to exclude the most powerful nobles from the highest offices of government, chose low-born, hard-working, and ambitious professionals as his secretaries, and surrounded himself with loyal courtiers from the ranks of the lesser nobility, giving them honorary titles, but rarely landed income (Álvarez 1998; Williams 2001). Since they are dated and firmly associated with local families, who were normally responsible for their decoration, patents of nobility offer a rich and still under-explored source for the study of Spanish illumination of the period.

This *Carta Executoria* conferred noble status to Juan Perez de Medinilla. It was granted in Valladolid on 28 March 1576 and signed by members of the royal council on fol. 48v. The half-page historiated initial on fol. 4v shows Philip II, his feeble legs barely touching the floor, but his finger pointing to his name on the right and to the lengthy list of his titles and territorial claims, which occupies the entire text space and still ends incomplete with '*et cetera*'. This is the visual and verbal statement of a monarch at the height of his power; the second half of the sixteenth century is often named 'the age of Philip II'. The miniature below shows St Francis with two suppliants, Bartolomeo de Medinilla and Fray Alonso Velazquez, presumably the ancestors of Juan Perez de

Medinilla and his wife, Juana Velazquez, who appear at the top of the facing page. They are shown praying to the Virgin and accompanied by family members, all grouped around the proudly displayed Medinilla arms.

The different scale and style of the figures and strewn-flower borders reveals that the facing pages were not illuminated by the same artist. Indeed, the family members and their arms are painted on the first leaf of a bifolio, which was added to the rest of the manuscript made up of a single gathering. Originally, the leaf with Philip II (fol. 4), which is a conjoint of the penultimate text leaf (fol. 47), faced the first text page (fol. 7). It was numbered '2' by the scribe and begins with gold ink script against a blue panel. Identical gold lettering on blue, green or red panels, matching the name of Philip II on fol. 4v, opens the text sections down to fol. 15v. After that, the artist abandoned the project, for lack of time or money, and the scribe inserted the sub-titles. The illumination on fol. 4v and the text decoration until fol. 15v were executed simultaneously with the text in Valladolid. The leaf with the family members was added towards the end of the sixteenth century. Whether intended to reassert the family's status or to serve as commemorative images, the

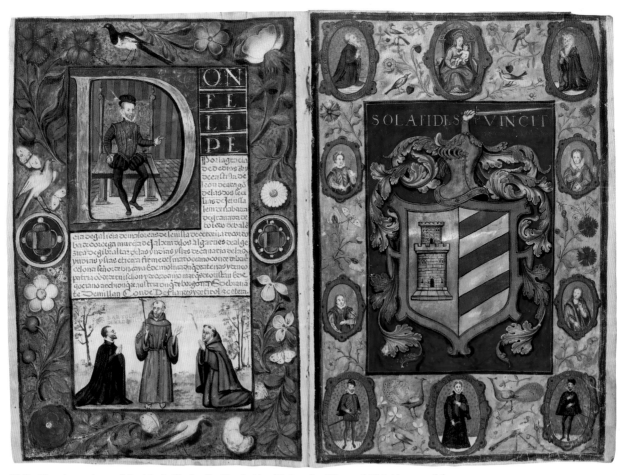

Philip II and members of the Medinilla family. Cambridge University Library, MS Add. 4130, fols. 4v–5

small medallions provide close parallels to contemporary portrait miniatures and demonstrate the origins of this genre in manuscript illumination.

PROVENANCE: Juan Perez de Medinilla (1576); purchased from Bernard Quaritch (General catalogue 1882, no. 11104) by Samuel Sandars and bequeathed to the Library in 1894.

LITERATURE: unpublished.

SP

142

La anatomia de España

In Spanish
Spain, 1598

Paper (cf. Briquet 1477, 2296, 12928), 151 fols. (contemporary pagination 3–148), 228 × 166 mm, 173 × 103 mm, 22 long lines, ruled in plummet and framed in red ink

SCRIPT: Humanistic cursive

BINDING: contemporary red velvet over wooden boards, traces of two pairs of red velvet fastening devices, gilt edges; brown leather spine, 19th c.

Cambridge University Library, MS Gg.6.19

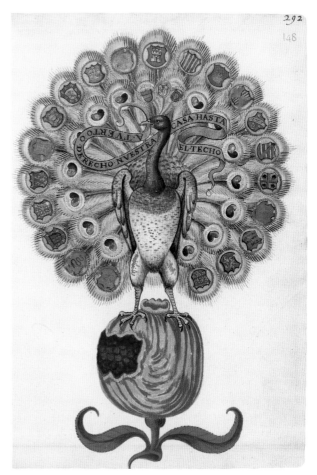

Philip II as a Peacock. Cambridge University Library, MS Gg.6.19, fol. 148

THIS BRIEF HISTORY of the House of Castile and its relationship with the kingdoms of the Iberian Peninsula and other European dynasties is accompanied by numerous genealogical tables. The most peculiar of them shows the dynastic trees of Castile, Aragon, England, France, and the Holy Roman Empire extending their branches from the mid-twelfth through the mid-sixteenth century and crossing swords or exchanging friendly handshakes across the double page opening (fols. 36v–37, *fig. 34*). The historical narrative begins in the early eleventh century and ends with a passionate invective against the Habsburg kings of Spain. The title page (fol. 2) is framed by the columns of the Castilian kingdom which support the arms of old Spain and stand on pedestals inscribed: *Miedo, Sospecha, Usurpacion, Hipocresia, Perfidia, Tirania, Homocidia,* and *Bastardia* (fear, suspicion, usurpation, hypocrisy, treachery, tyranny, murder, and bastardy). The attack on Philip II (r. 1556–1598) is vitriolic. His vices, listed in the closing paragraph (fol. 147), are personified by the peacock shown here (fol. 148). His tail expanded and emblazoned with the arms of territories claimed by Philip II, the peacock perches on top of a pomegranate, the badge of Granada which Philip's celebrated ancestors, the 'Catholic Monarchs' Ferdinand of Aragon and Isabella of Castile, had added to their joint arms in 1492 after their

conquest of the Moorish Kingdom of Granada, the last stronghold of Islam in the Iberian peninsula. The scroll reads: *A tuerto o derecho nuestra casa hasta el techo* ('By hook or by crook this is our house up to the roof'). The final decades of Philip II's rule were marked by plague, famine, economic and military disasters, and imperial aggression (Álvarez 1998; Williams 2001). His authority was eroded by the endless war in the Low Countries which drained Castilian resources, the defeat of the Armada in 1588, the usurpation of the Portuguese crown, and the ignominious campaign against Aragon in the early 1590s.

The text reveals that its anonymous author was stimulated by a French history of Spain, probably Mayerne Turquet's *Histoire générale d'Espagne* (1587), and that he was a religious connected with the Sorbonne and well informed about the current situation of the Jesuit Order. He would have been familiar with the ideas of his contemporary, Juan de Mariana (1535–1624), a Jesuit historiographer, biblical scholar and political theorist (Soons 1982). Mariana, who had spent five years at the Jesuit College in Paris and had witnessed the Night of St Bartholomew, first printed his Latin *History of Spain* in Toledo in 1592 and had the Castilian translation ready for the press in 1598. The following year, he was to publish his princely manual, *On the king and his educa-*

tion, which condemned 'the profligacy of our princes' and justified tyrannicide. However, *On the king and his education* was commissioned for Philip III and did not contain direct attacks on his father, while the *History of Spain*, for which Mariana sought Philip II's patronage, ended with Ferdinand the Catholic. By contrast, *La anatomia de España* focuses on most recent history. Its title page is dated 1598, although the text makes no mention of the king's death or of his long illness. Critical tracts against Philip II began to circulate shortly after his death on 13 September 1598 (Kamen 1997, 317–19). Whether in tune with or in anticipation of them, this volume demonstrates one of the uses of manuscripts that endured long after the advent of printing. With images as eloquent as the text, it was a powerful vehicle for the exchange of ideas within a limited, perhaps exclusive and secretive circle of like-minded intellectuals.

PROVENANCE: John Moore, Bishop of Ely (1707–1714); presented to the Library by George I in 1715.

LITERATURE: University Library 1856–1867, III, 222–23.

SP

143

Portolan Chart of the Mediterranean

Italy, Messina, 1584
ARTIST: Joan Martines (act. *c.* 1556–1591)

Parchment, irregularly shaped skin, approximately 580 × 937 mm
SCRIPT: various capital and minuscule inscriptions

Trinity College, MS R.4.50

THE COLLECTIONS of manuscripts in Cambridge, surprisingly, include only two Mediterranean portolan charts, or maps with a set of sailing directions known in Italian as *portolani*. The present example, the earlier of the two, features the whole Mediterranean and was drawn in Messina by Joan Martines in 1584; the second, of the Aegean Sea, was made by Estienne Bremond in Marseilles in the mid-seventeenth century (Cambridge University Library, MS Plans 697).

About one hundred and eighty of the surviving sea charts and atlases date from the fourteenth and fifteenth centuries, the earliest surviving portolan being the *Carte Pisane* (known by its French name) from the last quarter of the thirteenth century. The sixteenth and seventeenth centuries saw an enormous increase in manuscript charts of the Mediterranean; more than 675 maps and atlases provide the projection of the coastline, already well-established by tradition.

All that is known of Joan Martines comes from inscriptions found on his maps between 1556 (not 1550, as is sometimes claimed) and 1591. Altogether thirty works, either atlases or sea charts, are signed by him, with another fifteen attributable to him – and more if we look at the attributions in sale catalogues. Martines worked in Messina, where he signed his first dated work: *Joan Martines en Messina Añy 1556*. He was still there in 1587, to judge from an atlas done in that year. In 1590 and 1591 he is attested in Naples, as cosmographer of the King of Spain, signing one of his atlases *Joan martines De messina cosmographo Del Rey nro. segnor En Napoles Añy 1591*. He was evidently from Messina, although he may have had Majorcan or Catalan ancestors. The place names of his maps, with Spanish and Catalan as well as Italian elements, testify to the varied influences on Mediterranean cartography in the later sixteenth century.

Five charts, dated between 1564 and 1590 and signed by Martines, centre on the Mediterranean; three also include a large section of the coastline of Northern Europe, and one is of the Black Sea. The five charts of the Mediterranean are: map 62.1 × 97cm, signed 'Joan Martines en Messina Añy 1564', London, British Library, Add. MS 17540; map 58 × 96 cm, signed 'Joan martines en Messina Añy 1565', Madrid, Librería Gabriel Molina (on loan to Museo Naval, Madrid); map 53 × 75cm, signed 'Joan Martines en Messina anno 1571', Piacenza, Marchese Casati (in 1882); map 58 × 93.7cm, signed 'Joan Martines En messina Añy 1584', Cambridge, Trinity College, MS R.4.50; map 47.2 × 99.6cm, signed 'Joan martines DE Messyna cosmographo del Rey nro segnor En napoles Añy 1590', Bordighera, Istituto di Studi Liguri. On the west of the Trinity College map, at the level of the neck of the animal that provided the vellum, are represented the Virgin and the Child flanked by St James and St Anthony. The coastline of the Mediterranean and the Black Sea is shown in a continuous line, from Saffi (*zaniffi*) in Morocco to Cape Finisterre (*c. de finisterra*) in Galicia. The map is illustrated with vignettes, harbours and towns all around the Mediterranean. On the European side are Barcelona (*barcelona*), Marseilles (*Marzella*), Genoa (*yenoua*), Venice (*venessia*), Dubrovnik (*Ragussa* as it was called) and Thessaloniki (*Salonich*); while on the African coast are vignettes for Arzila (*Alzerra*), a city taken by the Portuguese in 1471, Algiers (*alger*), Bone (*bona*), Tripoli (*tripol d berberia*) and Cairo. Jerusalem, with its distinctive cross, is of course shown inland. Another town, on a hill on the northeast of the Red Sea, represents Mount Sinai.

The decorative character of the map is stressed by

scales of distances, but also by seven wind roses, each with thirty-two lines in black, red and green. The coastline is often drawn in a rather mannered way, with a series of creeks and inlets, and with capes and peninsulas between them; in the cases of Illyria and the Aegean Sea, it looks like the pieces of a jigsaw puzzle. Martines's maps were clearly luxurious items made for rich patrons, such as Philip II of Spain.

PROVENANCE: unknown.

LITERATURE: James 1900–1904, II, 164; Rey Pastor and Garcia Camarero 1960, 110 (1584); Ibáñez Cerdá 1973, no. 22; Astengo 1996, 31, no. UKCI; Astengo 2000, 175, no. UKCI.   JMM

Portolan Chart of the Mediterranean.
Trinity College, MS R.4.50

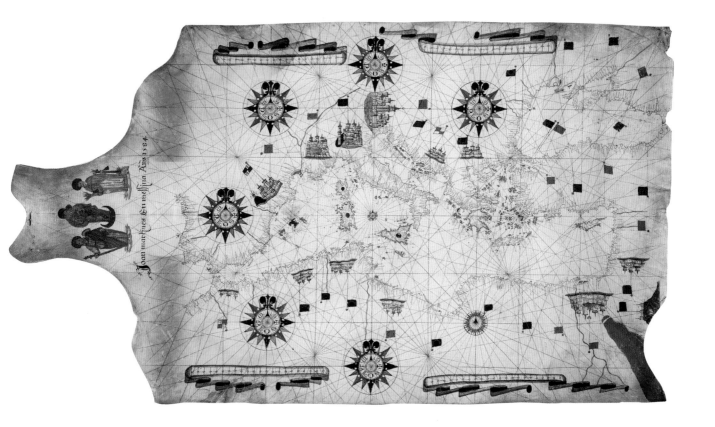

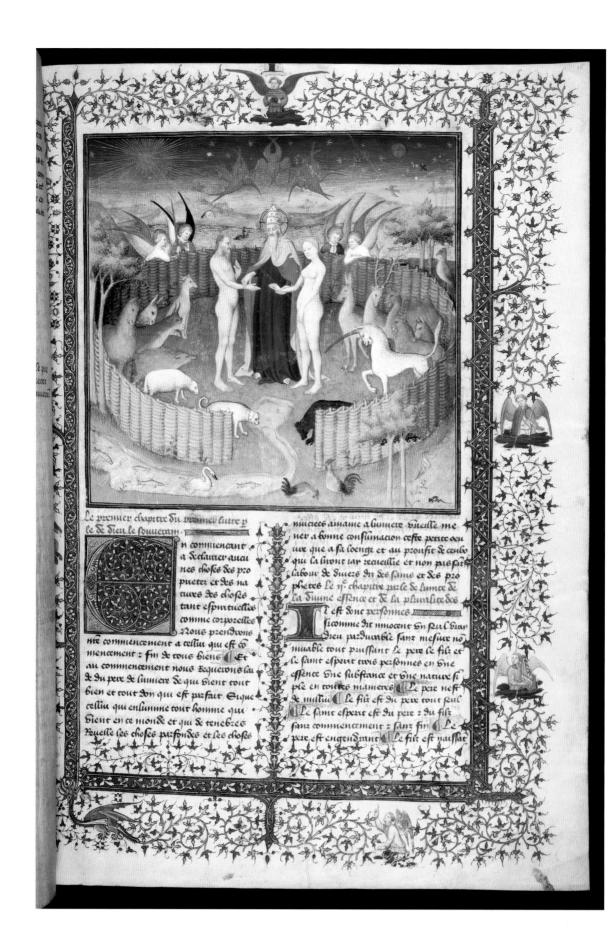

Le premier chapitre du premier liure p le de dieu le souuerain.

N commencant a declairer aucunes choses des propietez et des natures des choses tant espirituelles comme corporelles Nous prendrons nre commencement a celui qui est commencement z fin de tous biens Et au commencement nous requerons la de du pere de lumiere de qui uient tout bien et tout don qui est parfait Et que cestui qui enlumine tout homme qui uient en ce monde et qui de tenebres Nuelle les choses parfondes et les choses

nucieces a maine a lumiere Nuelle me ner a bonne consumacion ceste petite oeu ure que a sa loenge et au proufit de ceulx qui la sront par recueillie et non pas sauz labour de diuers dis des saime et des pro phetes Le ij chapitre parle de lumne essence et de la pluralite des est donc personnes

Si comme dit innocent un seul diable dieu pardurable sanz mesure no muable tout puissant Le pere le filz et le saint esperit trois personnes en une essence une substance et une nature si ple en toutes manieres Le pere nest de nului Le filz est du pere tout seul Le saint esperit est du pere z du filz sanz commencement z sanz fin Le pere est engendrant Le filz est naissant

THE MEDIEVAL ENCYCLOPEDIA: SCIENCE AND PRACTICE

Peter Jones

THE BOOK OF GENESIS told of the creation of the universe and of mankind, and of how mankind first lived in harmony with the rest of creation, and then wilfully disturbed it *(fig. 35)*. The Fall meant that mankind no longer had access to untroubled knowledge of the created world. For the Christian Middle Ages this was a story about order, knowledge and human limitations. Science – as an enterprise to recover knowledge about nature and providence – was an attempt, inevitably doomed to imperfect success by the Fall, to mirror that original harmony and order of creation in the human mind.

The idea of completeness, to which our modern encyclopedias aspire, was also of great importance to medieval authors and compilers. Whether it was applied to *omnis res scibilis* (the entire realm that could in theory be known), or to the field of a particular science, the attempt should be made to be exhaustive, to include all the possible objects of inquiry. In practice it was recognized that no individual or team of collaborators could hope to achieve that ideal. Indeed the practical needs of the reader were often anticipated, in terms of providing summaries and manuals that would be of use to those readers in digesting the work of more compendious authorities. But there are some manuscripts put together by individuals in which we can recognize a personal aspiration towards that ideal of completeness. The *Liber cosmographiae* (book of writings on the cosmos) of John de Foxton is one such work, known only through the unique copy shown *(no. 156)* here. Foxton, an obscure Yorkshire cleric living around the turn of the fifteenth century, probably put his compilation together to please a patron. This explains the costly illuminations of personifications of the planets, a zodiac and a bloodletting man. The whole work was designed as a compendium of popular science, and was put together from a variety of different sources. Yet Foxton also personalized the text and the pictures in such a way as to leave much for his patron and later readers to puzzle over, hiding meanings in ciphers and deliberately allusive pictures.

Foxton's illuminated figures are at one extreme of illustrations of medieval science. Diagrams, sometimes drawn sketchily by the scribe of a manuscript, but at other times much elaborated, are at the opposite extreme. Diagrams often served mnemonic purposes and in line with medieval theories of memory made use of visual designs that were thought to be peculiarly effective in stimulating recall. Placing the concept to be memorized on top of the picture of a familiar object or person was a favourite device. The cherub's wings in a work on the wings of angels *(fig. 36, no. 145)* were shown as constructed of feathers inscribed with the different angelic virtues – more easily remembered in this visual form than as a simple list written into the column of the book. One of the most powerful devices, and still in use today as an aid to memory, was the drawing of architectural structures on which to situate elaborate tables of information. Arcades of graceful rounded arches were used to articulate the canon tables showing the correspondences of different passages in the Gospels *(nos. 8, 10)*. Less usual is the array of pointed arches rising

Fig. 35. The Marriage of Adam and Eve. Fitzwilliam Museum, MS 251, fol. 16

up from the bottom of the page like the tracery of a Gothic window, and which house a diagram of the structure of the medieval church, from the papacy at the top to the parish level at the bottom *(no. 146)*. Harking back to the Temple at Jerusalem as the ancient architectural metaphor for the body of true believers that made up the Church, the metaphor for *'ecclesia'* is brought up to date when embodied in the form of mounting rows of Gothic arches.

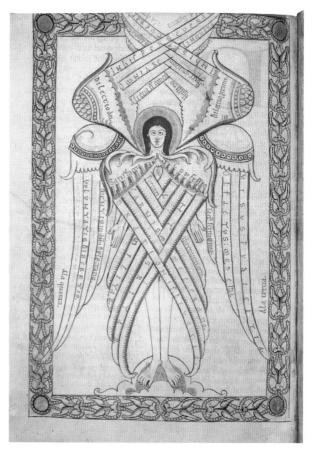

Fig. 36. Cherub. Corpus Christi College, MS 66, fol. 100

The sciences of the *quadrivium*, arithmetic, music, geometry and astronomy, addressed the numerical relationships and harmonies to be found in creation. Boethius, the sixth-century Christian philosopher, provided the early Middle Ages with its definition of the *quadrivium* and the most authoritative summations in two of its branches, those of arithmetic and music. From a pragmatic point of view there was much to be gained in assisting the teaching and memorizing of the abstract relationships that characterized these sciences by expressing them on the page in diagrammatic form. The concepts involved could be expressed by diagrams making use of simple geometrical figures, squares, circles, triangles, etc, or combining them in more elaborate figures to express more complex relationships. An early twelfth-century manuscript of Boethius *(no. 144)* uses coloured diagrams of this sort to illustrate both *De arithmetica* and *De institutione musica*. It also contained two figural drawings, one that shows Boethius in person presenting his book to his father-in-law Symmachus, and the other in which he is portrayed with Pythagoras, Plato, and Nichomacus of Gerasa, his most important philosophical sources. So Boethius is seen in dialogue with the ancients *and* as a channel for communicating their science in book form to the Christian world.

The medieval manuscript book lent itself to a kind of modular construction by which separate parts in the form of booklets containing one text or several could be built up by owners who brought the parts together within the boards or wrappers of a single book. Compilation could take on the character of a physical process of assembly, bringing together texts that had been written as separate units. This was a kind of do-it-yourself encyclopedism, inviting the combination of diverse parts into a whole that would approach incrementally to the ideal of a complete science of creation. One of the more eccentric of the manuscripts produced this way is the Anglo-Norman 'library' *(no. 151)*. As extraordinary as its cube shape is the fact that one scribe working in the English West Midlands around 1330 seems to have written all the texts brought together within its covers. The unknown person who commissioned the writing of the series of fifty-five texts that make up the book seems at first sight to be omnivorous in his taste in subject matter. There are devotional texts, literary, political and historical texts, as well as works on cosmology and physiognomy that conform better to our ideas of what an encyclopedia of the natural world should contain. There is however a thread to be discerned that links the disparate genres and texts we encounter in this manuscript, that is preoccupation with the prediction of future events. Many of the texts are concerned with prophecy, revelation, or prognostication, and suggest a single mind at work in the assembling of the 'library.' Only two texts though are illustrated. The illuminations in the Apocalypse of St John and in *L'Image du Monde* of Gossouin of Metz are conventional in their programme and suggest that illustration was not central to the planning of the book, but an incidental result of including two texts with a tradition of visual accompaniment.

The medieval maps of the world known as *Mappae mundi* have sometimes been described as visual encyclopedias. They are certainly different in intention and execution from modern projections in world maps like that of Mercator, which concentrate on physical geography and are drawn rigorously to scale. The way in which textual information from the Bible, classical and legendary sources find expression in visual form onto these maps, including Paradise, animals, and human monuments like the pyramids, encourages the idea that they were compiled in much the same way as an encyclopedic text. By contrast, texts like the *Imago mundi* of Honorius of Autun seem to provide a visual equivalence in their descriptions of the constituent parts of the world to the *Mappae mundi*. The Hereford world map is the most famous example of the *Mappae mundi* in England, but the earliest English version in the manuscript displayed here *(no. 145)* belongs to the text of the *Imago mundi* and is necessarily considerably smaller than the Hereford version, though still busy with detail. It is not simply a visual equivalent to an encyclopedic text or an assembly of literary sources. The map has its own visual logic in relating its various components to points of the compass and it is selective in choosing what to display.

The thirteenth century is usually thought of as the classic age of medieval encyclopedism. Several authors belonging to the mendicant Orders, Dominicans and Franciscans especially, constructed vast encyclopedic works which quickly superseded earlier texts in popularity. Perhaps the most famous of all was Bartholomaeus Anglicus, a Franciscan master at Paris whose *De proprietatibus rerum* ('On the properties of things') was compiled around 1245. It was intended to provide a gloss on things and places mentioned in the Bible for student friars and others. It became a textbook in Paris in 1284, a source for preachers, and was translated into English in 1398 by John Trevisa. There were nineteen books in all, written out in double columns. The early manuscript versions were not illustrated. In fact, encyclopedias on the scale of *De proprietatibus rerum* and the *Speculum historiale* or the even larger threefold *Speculum maius* of Vincent of Beauvais, did not require illustration for their original purposes of providing help to student preachers. Most surviving copies therefore are without illustration. Illuminated copies of these works were commissioned by royal or noble patrons who considered the work a prestigious ornament to their libraries. In the case of Bartholomaeus it was the French translation, *Des proprietez des Choses*, by Jean Corbechon that was the most likely to be illuminated, usually with prefatory pictures for each book. The copy displayed here was made for Amadeus VIII, Count of Savoy in 1414, and as one would expect of a book destined for the grandson of the great Duc de Berry, it is magnificently illuminated *(fig. 35, no. 152)*. The subject-matter of its illustrations bears witness to the Count's personal interest in medicine and alchemy.

299

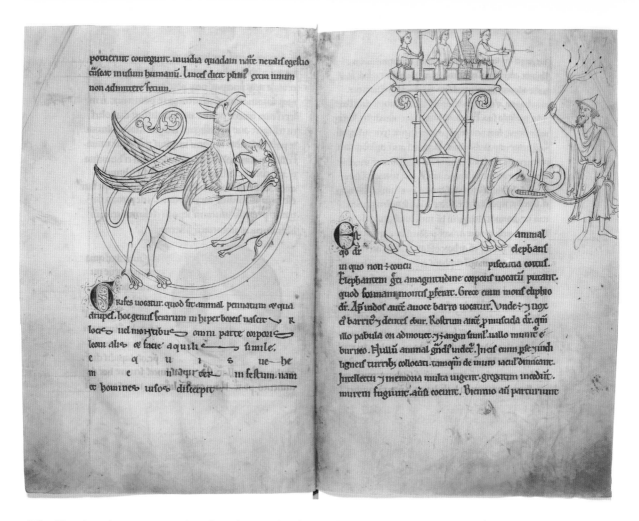

The Bestiary is a text associated with Cambridge before all other places. Not only are some of the finest manuscripts of the Bestiary to be found in its libraries, but Montague Rhodes James, the great cataloguer of manuscripts, Provost of King's College, and Director of the Fitzwilliam Museum, opened up the study of the Bestiary. His introduction to the Roxburghe Club facsimile of the University Library Bestiary *(no. 147)* published in 1928 was the first comprehensive account of Latin Bestiaries and their classification into textual groups or families. The first Bestiary catalogued by James was the Sidney Sussex College copy *(no. 148)*, one of the few Bestiary manuscripts to have been written and illuminated in France rather than England. English monastic houses seem to have shown an interest in Bestiary texts that goes back to at least the early twelfth century, and the fashion for Bestiary production seems to have lasted until the mid-fourteenth century. Today we look at Bestiary manuscripts mainly to marvel at the illuminations of real and mythical beasts, enjoying the strange deviations from realism that seem to have overcome the artists, even when the texts themselves are reasonably faithful descriptions of the appearance of animals. But of course the point of both text and illustration was not to create works of natural history in the modern sense, but to use animals as appropriate stimuli to reflection on Christian beliefs, conduct and prophecies. The animals in Bestiary illustrations are supposed to provide cues for this meditative process among the monks, not to register zoological detail. That is why in so many cases the animals are shown with faces or attitudes expressive of human emotion, for each beast has its own distinctive moral or prophetic attributes. Mythical beasts are just as significant as ones that can be observed in daily life, for both kinds are equally subject to the moralizing imagination that uses them as vehicles for religious instruction *(fig. 37)*.

Fig. 37. A griffin and an elephant. Cambridge University Library, MS Ii.4.26, fols. 6v–7

There is considerable room for variation in both the text and illustrations to medieval Bestiaries. The common origin of the various texts of the Bestiary was the Greek *Physiologus*, translated into Latin perhaps as early as the fifth century. There is no surviving manuscript earlier than the eighth century, and there is another gap between the tenth- and twelfth-century Bestiaries. As a result of these gaps and divergences in transmission, certain animals might be included in one example and left out of another. The Sidney Sussex College manuscript *(no. 148)* opens with the *Aviarium* of Hugh of Fouilloy, an extended meditation on birds with twenty-five illustrations, which imitates the Bestiary's structure and Christian allegorization. But the abridged Bestiary proper that follows the *Aviarium* has a variant text with fewer illustrations than normal, and two illustrations clearly abandoned because they duplicated the *Aviarium*. Nor was the Bestiary and its imitators the only source of figures of animals in medieval manuscripts. There was an alternative tradition of text and illustration on animals available in medical works, particularly the *Medicina ex quadrupedis* ('Medicine from quadrupeds') of Sextus Placitus *(no. 150)*. An illustrated Anglo-Saxon example of this work, which discusses the medicinal uses of animal parts, is found in the mid-eleventh-century British Library Cotton MS Vitellius C.iii. The illustrations, though less likely to include mythological beasts, were also uncontrolled by the requirement of faithfulness to nature, since the medical text had no descriptions of animals like lions and elephants, but only recipes for their use.

We might imagine that, since plants played such a central role in the therapeutic repertoire of healers of all kinds in the Middle Ages, they would be illustrated frequently as an aid to identifying and finding herbs in the wild. In fact, illustrated Herbals are surprisingly few and far between, and pictorial values tended to prevail over practical ones in the examples that have survived. We may doubt whether the monastic herb garden and the relatively few Herbals that can be identified with monastic library collections were often interdependent. The dominant illustrated Herbal tradition up to the fourteenth century was the *Herbarius* corpus associated with Apuleius Platonicus. The *Herbarius* corpus was a combination of texts on the medicinal use of herbs, animals and minerals that included a good deal of magical lore and prayers of a distinctly pagan cast. The illustrations that survive balance pictures of plants with scenes of action, mythical figures and medical treatment, as well as the scorpions and snakes against which the herbs might be prescribed. Manuscripts like the Trinity College Herbal *(no. 150)*, which is a rough and ready product by comparison with most others of the *Herbarius* corpus, are still a long way from being plant identification manuals. Surprisingly fourteenth- and fifteenth-century Herbals were even less likely to be illustrated than the earlier ones. The most frequently found texts, Macer's verse Herbal and the *Circa instans* text (so-called from its opening words), were far more often copied without illustrations, despite their evident practical use in medicine. On the other hand, luxury Herbals like the great book created for Francesco Carrara II, Lord of Padua (London, British Library, Egerton MS 2020), or the *Tacuinum sanitatis* ('Handbook of health') manuscripts were galleries of sumptuous plant portraits and fashion plates rather than the handbooks of practising physicians.

For an unique English example of a surgical manual that was illustrated with marginal pictures of plants we have to turn to the works of the fourteenth-century surgeon John of Arderne. Cambridge has the one manuscript of a Middle English

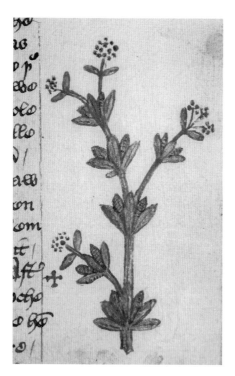

translation of his writings that has a full programme of illustration, including numerous well-observed plants prescribed for medical use in the text *(fig. 38)*. It could not be included in the exhibition due to its extremely fragile condition. John of Arderne's willingness to explore the usefulness of drawings on surgical operations, instruments and *materia medica* marks him out from his more illustrious Continental counterparts who were university educated rather than craft trained, and whose texts are far more scholastic in content and format. But surgical illustration in Europe did in fact have a pedigree that went back to the thirteenth century, when the work of the first independent surgical author of the West, Roger Frugardi of Parma, was provided with a set of marginal illustrations in an Anglo-Norman manuscript of his *Chirurgia (no. 153)*. Tinted drawings accompany most of the chapters of Roger's work, and take their inspiration from individual sentences in the text. The surgeon is shown as an authoritative and commanding figure, while his patients display their ailments or submit themselves to the knife, with little dignity or sympathy from the artist. The illustrations to this manuscript certainly do more to boost the prestige of the surgeon than to instruct the viewer in the performance of surgical operations. In that respect John of Arderne's illustrative programme is much more sensitive to the practical needs of the trainee surgeon than this earlier example.

Texts written by physicians were less likely to be illustrated in the Middle Ages than the works of surgeons. University medicine was logocentric, being largely a matter of commentating on texts and disputation, though it was always recognized that the practical end of medicine was to keep the body healthy, or restore it to health. One of the rare examples of the *Articella*, the group of texts used in the teaching of university medicine, attracting an illustrator is seen in Cambridge, King's College MS 21 *(fig. 39)*. The physician is seen in his archetypal pose, examining the patient's urine sample. Even in the matter of anatomy, where we might imagine that visual knowledge would have played a vital role, little interest was shown in using illustrations or models to convey that knowledge. A cycle of illustrations that originated in the Alexandrian medical school of late Antiquity, which we now call the five (or more properly nine) figure series, survived into the Middle Ages, though university physicians seem to have paid remarkably little attention to it. The thirteenth-century copy of this series found in the Gonville and Caius College manuscript *(no. 154)* belonged to the Premonstratensian Order at Hagnaby in Lincolnshire rather than to a physician. The figures are quite stylized in form, not at all based on observational data, but reflecting the body systems and organs as they were supposed to function within the system of physiology taught by Galen and later classical authorities. They are more like aides-memoires for the student than maps of the human body for the practitioner.

Fig. 38. Saxifrage. Emmanuel College, MS 69, fol. 72, detail

The only areas where illustration played a significant role in medical practice in the later Middle Ages were the occult sciences of astrology and alchemy. These impacted on the discipline of medicine between the thirteenth and fifteenth centuries, and in both cases they led to the development of visual aids to the practice of those ancillary sciences. In astrology the pictures are best described as instruments of prognosis, for they were used to determine the outcome of illnesses and the likely success of treatment. Some of them were no more than diagrams from which the practitioner could derive results once he had the necessary information about the patient and his diagnosis. The simplest form of all was the Zodiac Man, on whose body was marked the Signs of the Zodiac, so that the doctor would know when to let blood from the body according to the relationship between the moon and the Zodiac Signs. Others required tables of data about the movements of planets and their relations at different times of the year, and the instrument was a means of simplifying calculations. The most complex of all required moving parts and gave rise to parchment volvelles, or rotating wheels attached to the page. They allowed the doctor to read the results by moving the fingers on the dials. The example in the Gonville and Caius College miscellany *(no. 155)* is only one of a number of astrological and prognostic devices in the manuscript. Less practically oriented were the elaborate figures of constellations that accompanied the text of the *Astronomica* of the late Roman writer Hyginus *(no. 158)*. This kind of illustration was associated more with princely patrons than practitioners, allowing for stylish colour drawings of the mythological figures supposed to be discerned in the patterns of stars visible from earth. These are products of enthusiasm for humanistic learning, and a delight in the elaborate and ornamental.

Alchemy also gave scope to those who delighted in the exotic, particularly in the symbolic illustrations to the parchment rolls containing the works of the English fifteenth-century alchemist George Ripley (see, for example, Fitzwilliam Museum, MS 276★ and Yale, Beinecke Library, Mellon MS 41). The mysterious illustrations were a perfect equivalent to the deliberately opaque text. But there were also alchemical illustrations that were practical guides to the apparatus and processes necessary for turning the basic ingredients into quintessences that could be used in medicine or in the refinement of base metals into precious ones. The Corpus Christi College manuscript *(no. 157)* is an example of the English interest in the literature about the quintessence, thought to have been written by John of Rupescissa and Ramon Lull, and which was transmitted in the late fourteenth and early fifteenth centuries from Catalonia to England.

Fig. 39. Physician examining urine sample. King's College, MS 21, p.149

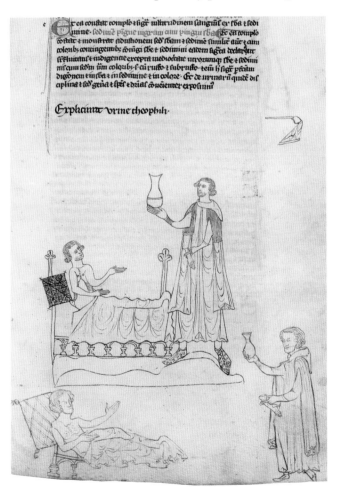

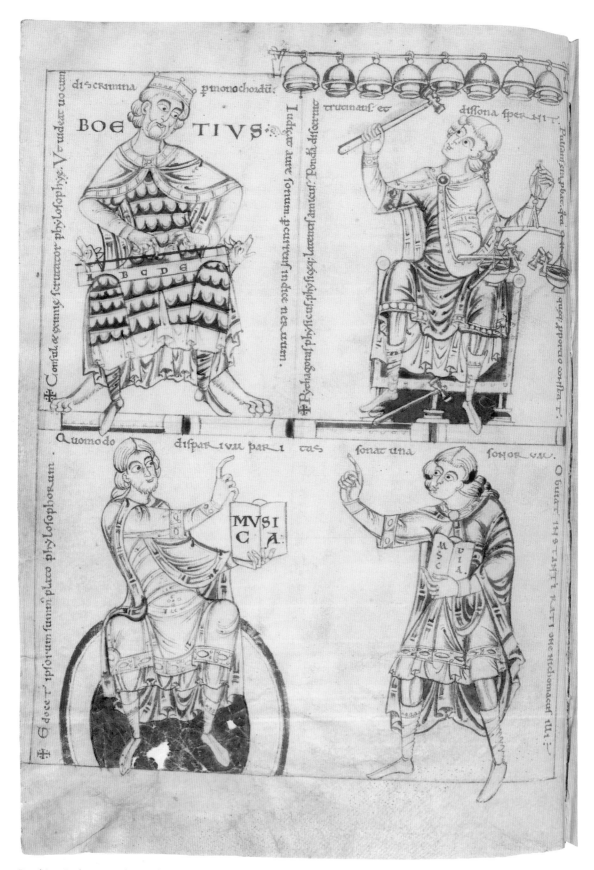

Boethius, Pythagoras, Plato and Nichomacus. Cambridge University Library, MS Ii.3.12, fol. 61v

144

Boethius, *De arithmetica, De musica*

In Latin
England, Canterbury, Christ Church, first third
of the twelfth century

Parchment, ii (paper) + 137 + ii (paper) fols., 292 × 205 mm,
text 221 × 129 mm, 32 lines, ruled in plummet

SCRIPT: late Caroline minuscule

BINDING: calf over boards, 17th c.; repaired 1959

Cambridge University Library, MS Ii.3.12

THIS VOLUME brings together the standard textbooks on two of the subjects of the *quadrivium*: Boethius's treatises on arithmetic and music. In each, the text is accompanied with numerous diagrams, carefully drawn in brown, red and green. The manuscript is best known for two pictorial frontispieces: an uncoloured pen drawing of Boethius presenting the *De arithmetica* to his father-in-law, Symmachus (fol. 1) and a magnificent tinted full-page framed miniature of Boethius and three ancient philosophers, Pythagoras, Plato and Nichomacus, whose theories acted as the principal sources for Boethius's own music theory (fol. 61v). The pairing of *De musica* with *De arithmetica* rather than with other more recent works of music theory and practice (as in a contemporary Christ Church manuscript, Cambridge, Trinity College, MS R.15.22, with which Ii.3.12 is textually very closely related), presents the text within the context of the theoretical study of music. Christopher Page has suggested that a diagram illustrating pitch notation on fol. 125v (also present in R.15.22) may reflect something of the practice of music, could represent a keyboard and organ pipes, and thus be the earliest known English representation of a keyboard. This suggestion is, however, treated with some caution by Peter Williams in his major study of the early medieval organ.

It is unclear whether the manuscript was originally conceived as a single unit. The text of *De musica* begins on a new quire, and the ruling pattern is slightly different. The hand of the main scribe of both texts is very similar, if not the same (a rather awkward example of the characteristic post-Conquest Christ Church variety of Caroline minuscule), but the hands of the other scribes and rubricators are different. If the texts were originally produced as two independent units, then the miniature that now acts as a frontispiece to *De musica* must have been added, since it is located on the final verso of the last quire of *De arithmetica*. If so, it might account for the disparity between the evidence for dating provided, on the one hand, by the rubrication of *De musica* (the work of a rubricator identified by Gullick in a number of late-eleventh and early twelfth-century Christ Church books) and the historiated initial on fol. 62v, also typical of early twelfth-century Christ Church books; and on the other hand, by the much more developed Romanesque style of the miniature, which had led the manuscript to be dated to the second quarter of the century.

PROVENANCE: Christ Church (15th c., ex-libris inscriptions, fols. 2, 62, 130); Richard Holdsworth, Master of Emmanuel College (d.1649); his bequest, 1649; received by the University Library in 1664.

EXHIBITED: London 1984b, no. 30

LITERATURE: University Library 1856–1867, III, 418–419; Dodwell 1954, 23, 35, 37, 39, 64, 66, 74, 121; Kauffmann 1975, no. 41; Page 1979; Heslop 1984, 204; Manion, Vines and de Hamel 1989, 123–24; Williams 1993, 183; Gibson and Smith 1995, 42; Gameson 1999, no. 32; Gullick and Pfaff 2001, 291.

TW

145

Honorius Augustodunensis, *Imago Mundi*, and other texts

In Latin
England, probably Durham, *c.*1190

Parchment, i (modern paper) + 57 + i (modern paper) fols. paginated and foliated, 298 × 217 mm, text 225–242 × 154–166 mm, 2 columns, 33–43 lines, ruled in plummet

SCRIPT: Gothic bookhand (textualis)

BINDING: tan calf, by J.P. Gray, Cambridge, 1954

Corpus Christi College, MS 66, part I

THE MANUSCRIPT is a Romanesque collection of what would now be called 'social sciences', a compilation of geography, history and cosmology. It appears to have formed one volume with the University Library manuscript *(no. 146)* before Matthew Parker separated them. It opens with the *Imago Mundi* of Honorius Augustodunensis (*c.*1070–*c.*1140), an account of the geography of the world, the measurement of time and the history of mankind from the fall of the rebel angels to the betrothal of the future Emperor Henry V to Matilda, daughter of Henry I of England in 1110. This section is prefixed by a detailed and lightly coloured map of the world, tended by four gesticulating angels. The second principal text is an ingenious chronicle

305

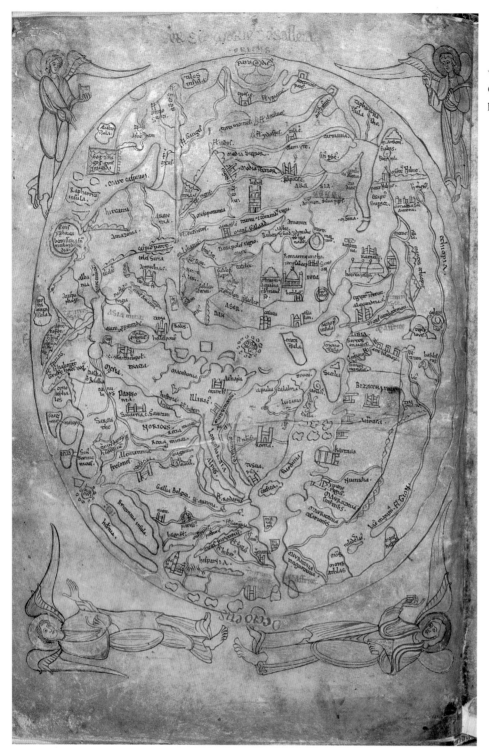

providing an unbroken line of descent from Adam to Henry II, King of England 1154–89. Full-page illustrations here are a Wheel of Fortune, reassuringly showing that even great kings can tumble backwards again into obscurity, and a fearsome Woden, the Norse god, with his seven sons. Shorter texts at the end include a work on the wings of angels ascribed here to Clement of Lanthony, with an illustration assigning different virtues to each feather of a cherub's wings. One component is dated 1188 (p.98).

The world map is by far the oldest of its kind in England, and it has attracted enormous interest and a vast bibliography since its first publication by Richard Gough in 1780. It shows the world with Paradise (the far east) at the top, Africa to the right, and Europe in the foreground. It includes tiny drawings of hills and rivers and ancient monuments, such as the pyramids ('the granaries of Joseph') and the Tower of Babel. It is the earliest in a small family of illustrated world maps, which culminates about a century later in the celebrated

Mappa Mundi at Hereford Cathedral. It is complicated by the fact that the prologue here ascribes the *Imago Mundi* to an otherwise unknown Henry, Canon of Mainz. The probable explanation is that the name is simply a miscopying or an acceptable variant of 'Honorius', but the map, which is not in fact integral with the text, is often cited under the misnomer of the *Mappa Mundi* of Henry of Mainz. It is not found with any other manuscript of the *Imago Mundi*.

By the early thirteenth century the manuscript belonged to the Cistercian Abbey at Sawley, near Clitheroe in the far west of Yorkshire. It is such an improbably grand book for a small and struggling Cistercian foundation that it is most likely to have been made elsewhere. As first proposed by Mynors (1939), the genealogy and its pictures are derived, probably directly, from a manuscript in Durham Cathedral Library, MS B. II. 35. The selection of texts here is characteristic of the anthologizing work of the early twelfth-century historian there, Symeon of Durham. The fine illumination of the manuscript is closely related to that of a group of luxury manuscripts, including a giant Bible, commissioned probably in Durham itself by Hugh de Puiset, Bishop of Durham. On his death Bishop Puiset presented the monks of Durham with his collection of seventy-six manuscripts. They included one listed at the time as '*Mappa Mundi*' which, to judge from the context, may have been a title given to a volume rather than a single sheet. It was possibly the book displayed here, sent off soon after the bishop's death to the Abbey at Sawley, perhaps because the genealogies, at least, were duplicated in Durham. If not, it was almost certainly copied and illuminated at Durham, doubtless, in part, at least, from the manuscript called '*Mappa Mundi*' then in the Bishop's possession.

PROVENANCE: perhaps Hugh de Puiset, Bishop of Durham (1153–1195); Sawley Abbey, Yorkshire; Matthew Parker (1504–1575); his bequest, 1575.

EXHIBITED: Munich, 1995, no. D.92

LITERATURE: Gough 1780, 6, pl. III; James 1912b, I, 137–45; Mynors 1939, 41; Destombes 1964, 48, no. 25.3; Kauffmann 1975, no.102; Dumville 1977–1980; London 1984b, 130; Dalché 1988, 183; Lecoq 1990; Bell 1992, 74; von den Brinken 1992, 69–70; Chekin 1993, 501–504; Meehan 1994, 442–47; Flint 1995, 99–100, 108–110, 166; Lewis 1995, 283; Harvey 1996, 27, 39; Harvey 1997; Rollason 1998, 5–6; Meehan 1998, 136–37; Norton 1998, 62–104, pls.9–16, 19; Story 1998, 209–10; von den Brinken 1998, 40, pl. VII, Lawrence-Mathers 2003, 119, 256–7.

C DE H

146

Gildas, *De excidio Britanniae*; Gilbert of Limerick, *De statu ecclesie*; Gerald of Wales, *Descriptio Hybernie and Descriptio Cambrie*, and other texts

In Latin
England, probably Durham, *c.*1190 and Bury St Edmunds, third quarter of the thirteenth century

Parchment, ii + 270 + xiii fols., 295 × 200 mm, text 208–240 × 138–162 mm, 36–43 lines, ruled in plummet, individual foliation of each work, continuous pagination
SCRIPT: Gothic bookhand (textualis)
BINDING: red morocco, D. Cockerell 1967

Cambridge University Library, MS Ff.1.27

L IKE ITS SISTER MANUSCRIPT *(no. 145)*, this compilation of miscellaneous historical, ecclesiastical and encyclopedic works enjoyed a complex history almost certainly beginning at Durham in the late 1180s or early 1190s. The authors are distinguished: Gildas and Nennius, the historians of Britain; Bede, who was amongst the first to define the English people and the early history of its religion; the Irish reforming bishop Gilbert of Limerick; and the peppery and brilliant twelfth-century cleric Gerald of Wales, whose writings on Wales and Ireland were celebrated. It also includes the *Historia Dunelmensis* of Symeon of Durham (pp.121–186) and twenty-one lines of Old English verse on the city of Durham and its relics, *c.*1104–*c.*1109, the last extant poem in regular Old English metre. These texts were of especial interest to Durham Cathedral Priory and perhaps to Hugh de Puiset *(see no. 145)*. The parts containing the works of Gerald of Wales were added to the book only when it passed to the University; these had been written and illuminated in the middle of the thirteenth century at Bury. The relationship of the various components of the book to the manuscript in Corpus Christi College has been elucidated (Norton, 1998).

By far the most important illumination in the manuscript is that on p.238, a fully-coloured *Imago ecclesie* or Image of the Church illustrating Gilbert of Limerick's *De statu ecclesie* (pp.237–42). Gilbert, Bishop of Limerick, was the first papal legate in Ireland. His text *De statu ecclesiae* was very likely written as a programme of reform for the Irish synod of 1111. Its focus is a diagram of the general order of the Church. This is a fine example of the use of architecture to structure ideas and memory. The text sets out to explain the hierarchy of the Church

307

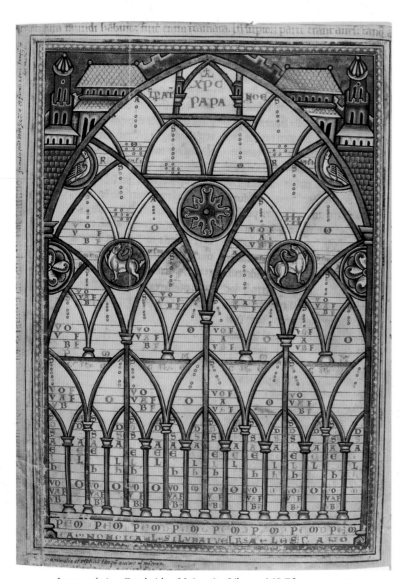

Imago ecclesiae. Cambridge University Library, MS Ff.1.27, p. 238

If the current arguments about the relationship between the two parts of this manuscript are valid, this diagram was executed *c.*1190 at Durham, and is in effect the earliest undeniably 'Gothic' illumination in English, and possibly European, art. The designer saw pointed arches as being congruent with the pyramids that form the basic module of the text. Though sometimes likened to a Gothic window, the distribution of the arches is strikingly similar to, but may even pre-date, the 'syncopated' layered wall arcading found towards 1200 in the aisles of St Hugh's choir and the eastern transepts at Lincoln Cathedral.

The illuminations in the section from Bury are related to the Norwich-area Carrow Psalter (Baltimore, Walters Art Museum, MS 34; Morgan 1982–1988, no. 118 for the group). The marginalia illustrating Giraldus on Ireland may be compared with the earlier but related imagery in London, British Library, Royal MS 13.B.viii and Dublin, National Library of Ireland, MS 700 (Morgan 1982–1988, no. 59 and cf. no. 116).

PROVENANCE: perhaps Hugh de Puiset (d.1195), bishop of Durham; Sawley Abbey, Yorkshire; Matthew Parker (1504–1575), given to the University Library in 1574.

LITERATURE: University Library 1856–1867, II, 318–29; James 1912b, I, 138, 145; Ker 1964, 16, 177, 335, Suppl. 5; Dumville 1974; Kauffmann 1975, no. 102; Meehan 1994; Norton 1998.

PB

by working up from the smallest units to the largest by means of what Gilbert calls a series of pyramids. Starting at the lower left, the basic pyramidal units are the parish, whose officers number seven from the priest down, and the monastery or nunnery, headed by an abbot or abbess. These units are divided into seven ranks, but also into three other categories familiar by the twelfth century: those who pray (*oratores*), plough (*aratores*) and fight (*bellatores*). These categories include the laity, male and female, labelled V and F. The next major unit governing the parishes and the monasteries is the diocese, which is embraced by the archdiocese, and finally the primatial church ruled by a primate. This Church is in turn headed by the Pope, whose type is Noah, and over whom presides Christ. Each stage of the ecclesiastical hierarchy finds a corresponding rank in the secular hierarchy, from the Emperor downwards. Gilbert's text finds its most accurate counterpart in terms of layout and lettering in a fairly simple diagram in another Durham manuscript of the period (Durham Cathedral, MS B. II. 35, fol. 36v; *see also no. 145).*

147

Bestiary

In Latin
England, perhaps Lincolnshire, *c.*1200

Parchment, iv (i paper, ii–iv modern vellum) + 74 + iii (modern vellum) fols., 282 × 190 mm, text 202 × 127 mm, 24 long lines, ruled in plummet

SCRIPT: Gothic bookhand (textualis)

BINDING: quarter tawed skin over oak boards, by D. Cockerell, 1928

Cambridge University Library, MS Ii.4.26

THIS IS THE EARLIEST of three Bestiaries in the exhibition. These are famous manuscripts because of their wonderful illustrations of animals and their quaint accounts of exotic and fabulous creatures then believed

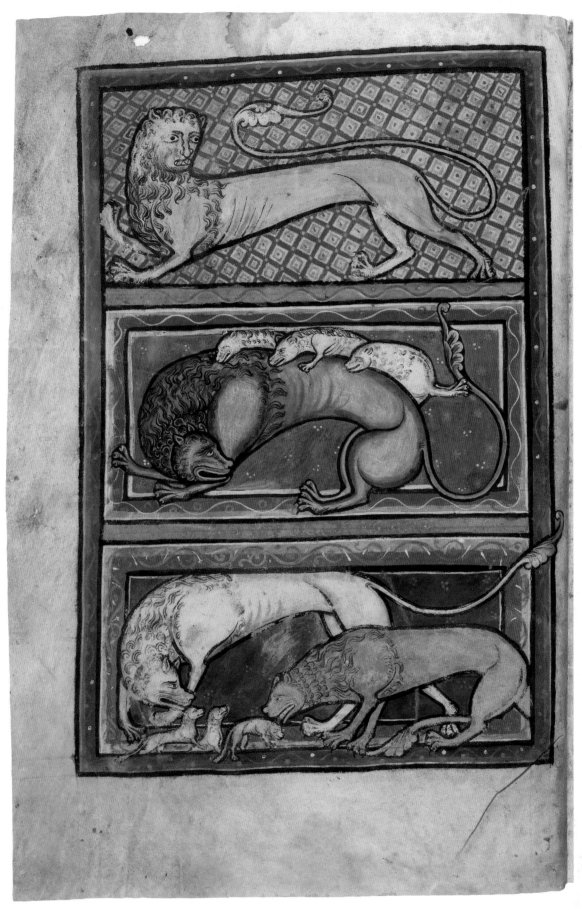

Lions. Cambridge University Library, MS Ii.4.26, fol.1v

to inhabit remote parts of the world. Bestiaries are a characteristically English phenomenon. Of about sixty-five recorded manuscripts, around fifty were made in medieval England. The modern English obsession with animals, both in the home and in the wild, goes back in Bestiary manuscripts to the first half of the twelfth century. However, the Bestiary is not simply a record of natural history. It is a strictly religious book, used mostly in monasteries. It belongs to a time when there was no concept of natural evolution. God evidently made the world and all living creatures for a purpose. In the way that every sentence of the Bible was believed to conceal multiple layers of meaning – literal, prophetical and moral – so too God's other revelation, the natural world, was believed to be divinely encoded with different levels of meaning to be discovered by patient reflection. Each animal in a Bestiary is described literally, often (in the case of familiar beasts) remarkably accurately. Then the text usually offers one or more suggestions as to why God had made that creature behave as it does: as prophecies or reminders of biblical events, for instance, or as examples of behaviour to be imitated or avoided by the Christian monk. This is why Bestiaries include improbable creatures of legend, such as unicorns and yales. The compilers probably had doubts as to the animals' authenticity, but would have preferred to err by inclusiveness rather than risk careless rejection of what might be part of God's specific revelation. Biblical editors have always felt the same about the Apocrypha.

Cambridge University Library MS Ii.4.26 is one of the best-known Bestiaries by the chance that it was selected by M.R. James for his Roxburghe Club facsimile of 1928, with an introduction giving the first comprehensive account of Latin Bestiaries and their classification into textual groups or 'families'. The facsimile was, for many years, the most easily available edition of the Latin text. It was translated in 1954 by T.H. White, who had already populated his Arthurian romance, *The Sword in the Stone*, 1938, with mythical creatures taken from the Cambridge Bestiary. In fact, the manuscript is neither the earliest nor the best Bestiary from the point of view of natural history, as noted by Yapp. It is, however, quite beautiful. It opens with two full-page coloured miniatures with multiple scenes from the lives of lions. It continues with ninety-seven illustrations, four of them with colour added and the remaining ninety-three from fol. 6v onwards mostly simply drawn in ink. Occasionally there are splashes of colour, but it is probable that the artist intended them to be plain drawings. The unerring confidence of the draughtsman is impressive and in a few quick strokes even birds and animals are given personality and life. The expressions of the creatures graphically convey their ferocity, fear, meekness and wonder. The pictures are often in rectangular or circular frames, some of which interact playfully with the page layout, disappearing behind the ruling or entwined through the coloured initials.

Below the end of the text on fol.73 there is an early sixteenth-century inscription, apparently 'Jacobus Thomas heysson – Thys ys ye Abbaye of Rev[…]', with the end of the crucial word cropped away in the outer margin. Even part of the 'v' is now lost. The only English abbey beginning with these letters was the Cistercian house of Revesby, in Lincolnshire, founded in 1142, which may be where the manuscript was on the eve of the Reformation. Appropriately, its only remains are a medieval deer park. The text of the Cambridge Bestiary is related to a group of other copies including New York, Pierpont Morgan Library, M. 81, which belonged to a canon of Lincoln in 1187. Nigel Morgan has noted that the artist of the present manuscript was almost certainly responsible for Baltimore, Walters Art Museum, MS W. 793, a chronicle of *c*.1200 with a single drawing showing the Battle of Lincoln in 1141, and the well-known Guthlac Roll in the British Library (Harley Roll Y.6), which is presumably from, and was probably made at, Crowland Abbey in southern Lincolnshire, where Guthlac's relics were translated in 1196. Revesby is about thirty miles north of Crowland and twenty east of Lincoln. An origin in Lincolnshire certainly seems possible.

PROVENANCE: perhaps Revesby Abbey; Osbert Fowler, registrar of King's College; his gift to the University Library, 1655.

EXHIBITED: London 1987–1988, no. 252.

LITERATURE: University Library 1856–1867, III, 463–64; James 1928; White 1954; McCulloch 1960, 35, 36; Ker 1964, 158; Morgan 1982–1988, no. 21; Yapp 1985, 1–3; Muratova 1990, 82; Hassig 1995, 3, 4, 23, 24, 36 etc.; Baxter 1998, 21, 130, 137, 140, 147, 150, 175, 177–79; Wheatcroft 1999, 144, fig.2; Brown 2002, 39.

C DE H

148

Hugh of Fouilloy, *Aviarium* and Bestiary

In Latin
France, Paris, *c*.1230–*c*.1250

Parchment, i (paper) + 43 + 14 (an unrelated eleventh-century manuscript from Durham) + i (paper) fols., 297 × 212 mm, text 211 × 148 mm, 2 columns, 32 lines, ruled in plummet

SCRIPT: Gothic bookhand (textualis)

BINDING: reversed calf over pasteboards, 17th c.

Sidney Sussex College, MS 100

THIS WAS THE FIRST BESTIARY encountered by M.R. James in his cataloguing of the manuscripts of the Cambridge colleges and it initiated a pursuit of animals which occupied him for decades. The manuscript is unusual for various reasons, including the fact that it was made in France. It is one of four copies, all Continental, which open with the *Aviarium* of Hugh of Fouilly (*c.*1100–*c.*1173), Prior of St Laurent-au-Bois at Heilly, near Amiens. This part comprises fols. 1–26v. It is a text on birds with even more extensive interpretations of their religious significance than in a traditional Bestiary. The *Aviarium* often circulated on its own and over 40 copies are recorded. In four manuscripts, however, including this, the text was supplemented by an abridged Bestiary supplying standard accounts of animals too. The others are Paris, Bibliothèque nationale de France, MS lat. 2495; Chalons-sur-Saône, Bibliothèque municipale, MS 14, from La Ferté Abbey; and Valenciennes, Bibliothèque municipale, MS 101, from the Abbey of St-Amand. All are from the thirteenth century.

The Sidney Sussex manuscript has twenty-five illustrations of birds and eighteen of animals and natural phenomena. The scribe left spaces in the Bestiary portion for two further illustrations, those for the pelican (fol. 35v) and the calladrius bird (fol. 38). They were never supplied because both occur, or did occur (the manuscript is now

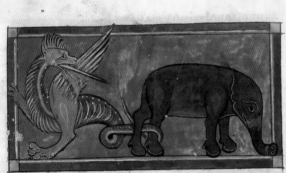

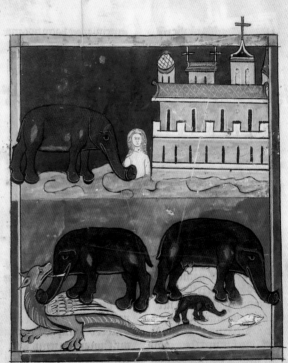

Elephants. Sidney Sussex College, MS 100, fols. 33v–34

incomplete), in the *Aviarium* portion at the beginning and the artist realized he would be duplicating pictures. The pelican was on the leaf once before fol. 9 and the calladrius on the leaf once after fol. 20. To judge from this oversight alone, one might suppose that the scribe was unfamiliar with the double text and that perhaps this was the first time he had copied the two components together.

The miniatures have been attributed to a Parisian workshop known as the Bari Atelier from a Missal in this style now in the Church of San Nicola in Bari in southern Italy (Clark 1989). Certainly the style has extremely close parallels with miniatures executed in Paris in the mid-century but it may be that it should be attributed to somewhere like Reims, outside but within the orbit of Paris

The manuscript was certainly in England by the fifteenth century, when names of birds and also other scribbles in Middle English were added by several childish hands, one of whom signs herself 'keterina' (fol. 35v). The manuscript has been roughly treated and it is defective and damaged. It was clearly out of a binding for some time, for the outer pages are rubbed and stained, including marks apparently left by a tankard or mug. It was given to the College by Thomas Jennings, a clergyman in Essex. Later it was bound up with a portion of a smaller eleventh-century liturgical book from Durham Cathedral Priory, which had probably reached Sidney Sussex from a different source.

PROVENANCE: given to the College by Thomas Jennings (*c.*1554–1607).

EXHIBITED: London 1908, no. 82.

LITERATURE: Bernard 1697, 106, no. 762; James 1895d, 115–22; James 1928, 11; Pfaff 1980, 179 and 299; McCulloch 1960, 32, pl.VIII.3; Clark 1982, 73; Yapp 1985, 5; Clark 1989, 41, 42; Rogers 1996, 79; Baxter 1998, 87, 148; Stones forthcoming.

C DE H

149

The Peterborough Bestiary

In Latin
England, *c.*1300–*c.*1310

Parchment, bound with other texts, iv (paper) + ii (medieval parchment) + 180 (Psalter of Hugh of Stukely) + 8 (chronicles of Peterborough) + 22 (Bestiary) + iv (paper) fols., 346 × 230 mm, text 260 × 163 mm, 2 columns, 42 lines, ruled in plummet

SCRIPT: Gothic bookhand (textualis)

BINDING: blind-tooled blue morocco, British Museum bindery, 1956

Corpus Christi College, MS 53

THIS IS ONE of the last great Bestiaries, produced as a luxurious volume for bibliophilic delight or pious contemplation at a time when the accounts of the more bizarre animals in the text were already outdated. It is of exceptional size and is illuminated with a large opening historiated initial followed by one hundred and four framed pictures of animals, birds and fish. It is known as the Peterborough Bestiary because it is bound with an even more opulently illuminated Psalter which belonged to Hugh of Stukely, who was Prior of Peterborough Abbey probably in the 1320s. It is likely but not absolutely provable that the Bestiary was already part of the composite volume before its acquisition by Matthew Parker, if only because Parker had no especial interest in Psalters or Bestiaries but would have cared immensely for the two short chronicles from Peterbrough sandwiched between them. There was a strong tradition of Bestiaries at Peterborough, beginning with a *Liber bestiarium*, given by St Æthelwold on the Abbey's refoundation in the late tenth century, and including three books on animals recorded in the fourteenth-century Peterborough library catalogue.

Lucy Sandler has suggested that the artist of the Peterborough Bestiary also worked on three other manuscripts. They are: Oxford, Jesus College, MS D.40, a Psalter probably from the diocese of London; Paris, Bibliothèque Mazarine, MS 34, a Bible probably made for Anthony Bek, Bishop of Durham (1284–1311), and later owned by Henry V, who gave it to Sheen Priory; and New York, Pierpont Morgan Library, G. 50, the De Lisle Hours, probably made for Margaret de Beauchamp (d.1339), wife of Robert de Lisle. The close association of Bek with the royal court suggests London or Westminster as a possible origin.

Unusually for a Bestiary, the book is arranged rather like a Breviary, with a formal liturgical script in two columns, and with highly finished miniatures in rectan-

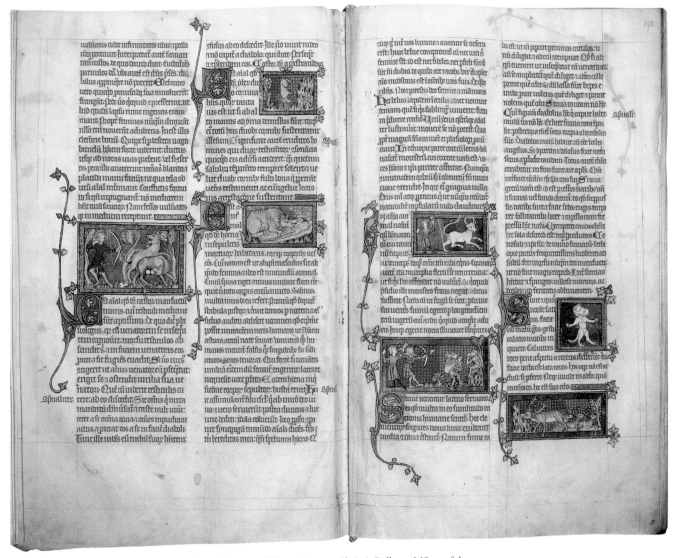

Beavers, Ibex, Hyena, 'Bonnacon', Monkeys, Satyr, and Deer. Corpus Christi College, MS 53, fols. 191v–192

gles up to column-width in size. There are small versal initials, as in a Psalter. It looks like a book for private piety rather than for general monastic edification. Very many chapters have separate paragraphs marked *spiritualiter*, to introduce the moral or theological lessons to be learned from the animals' habits. Frequently the chapters are introduced by head-and-shoulder portraits of people looking into the text. Most are men, sometimes bearded, sometimes in hats. One is a bishop, on fol. 202v, in a chapter comparing a dove with a great preacher. A king appears only once, on fol. 201v. It prefaces the account of the partridge, which is accused of mating with other males and of forgetting its true nature in the frenzy of unnatural passion. If this is a court manuscript, then the king gazing into this chapter may allude to

Edward II, whose intimacy with Piers Gaveston in *c*.1307–1312 was causing very great scandal. It would be entirely consistent with a stylistic dating for the book.

PROVENANCE: probably Peterborough Abbey, perhaps from the library of the priors; Matthew Parker (1504–1575); his bequest, 1575.

LITERATURE: James 1912b, 105–11; James 1921; James 1928, 20, no. 33; McCulloch 1960, 37, pls. II.2, III.5, V.2b, VI.1a; Yapp 1985, 13; Sandler 1986, no. 23; Robinson 1988, no. 127, pl. 133a–b; Hassig 1995, 9, 178, 179, 264; Baxter 1998, 147, 150, 154–5, 174, 176–7; Derolez 2003, pl. 27; Kauffmann 2003, 207; Sandler and de Hamel 2003.

C DE H

150

Apuleius Platonicus, *Herbarius*

In Latin
Germany, fourteenth century

Paper, i (fragment of a tenth-century Bible containing Gen. 43:1) + 273 fols. (unknown number of leaves missing at end of codex, medieval foliations indicate other leaves lost after fols. 46, 74, 78, 86, 88, 93, 97), 210 × 140 mm, text not bounded by ruling

SCRIPT: Gothic bookhand (hybrida)

BINDING: Red niger morocco, by Douglas Cockerell, 1966

Trinity College, MS O.2.48

WITH OVER eight hundred images, this is the most extensively illustrated Herbal in the Herbarius corpus. Named after Apuleius Platonicus, this corpus survives in more than sixty known copies and includes several other texts on medicinal simples usually found together. Many of the illustrations can be traced back to Late Antique prototypes. They depict plants, animals, and minerals that could be used in medicine, as well as thirty-eight figural scenes whose origins are more controversial, sometimes claimed for the fifth or sixth century, sometimes for as late as the thirteenth century. Different hands are involved in the illustrations, and some of them are 'very rough' in the words of M.R. James. The manuscript does not follow the usual order of the texts in the Herbarius corpus, but is made up as follows:

1. *Precationes* (prayers to be recited while gathering herbs or preparing medications)
2. Antonius Musa, *De herba vetonica* (betony)
3. Apuleius Platonicus, *Herbarius*
4. Pseudo-Dioscorides, *Liber medicinae ex herbis feminis* ('female' herbs used in medicine)
5. *Passio vulnerum* (short text on wound healing)
6. Unidentified herbal based on a Latin version of Dioscorides, *De materia medica*
7. *De taxone liber* (on the use of the badger)
8. Sextus Placitus, *Liber medicinae ex animalibus et avibus* (medical use of animals and birds)

The illustrations are concentrated in the herbal sections and include figural scenes not found elsewhere in the Herbarius corpus manuscripts. The most dramatic accompany narrative passages like those on the herb martagon or herb of Salomon. The chapter on *Herba salamonis* in

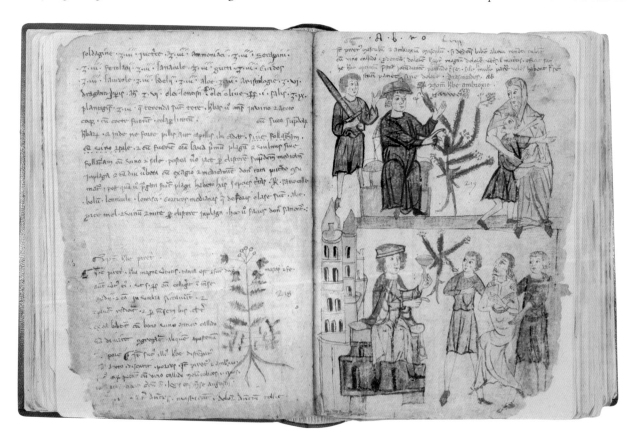

Herba piretri and *Herba ambroxie*. Trinity College, MS O.2.48, fols. 62v–63

the *Liber medicinae ex herbis feminis* (4) is accompanied by an image of the son and daughter of a noble woman who were troubled by demons until the use of a herbal amulet recommended by the blessed Augustine freed them (fol. 56). This image is not found in other illustrated versions of this text. Yet, the majority of the figure illustrations resemble those found in related manuscripts of the Herbarius corpus and show consultations of doctor and patient. Authoritative figures like Galen or Hippocrates, robed impressively in decorated gowns and wearing caps, stand at their patients' bedside or sit on chairs while their patients stand before them. Patients and attendants are smaller in size. Plant illustrations are crudely drawn and somewhat spindly in appearance, but pick out enough characteristics to distinguish one plant from another of a similar kind. Dogs, snakes, and scorpions are depicted at points in the text where plants are described as remedies for their bites or stings. The Sextus Placitus text is illustrated with animals and birds in a style found in thirteenth-century Bestiaries.

The manuscript texts are written around the illustrations on the page, and the book as a whole does not give the impression of being carefully designed or executed. There are corrections and additions in later hands in the book by cursive hands, particularly in respect of the names of plants. These suggest that it was read and used by German speakers. Despite its figural illustrations this seems to have been a manuscript that was designed for practical use, and continued to be used by those interested in *materia medica*.

PROVENANCE: given to Trinity College by Roger Gale in 1738.

LITERATURE: James 1900–1904, vol. III, 162–3; Howald and Sigerist 1927; Grape-Albers 1976; Maggiulli and Giolito 1996; Jones 1999; Collins 2000; Totelin 2003.

PJ

151

Gossuin of Metz, *L'Image du Monde*

In Anglo-Norman
England, West Midlands, *c.*1330

Parchment, ii + 633 fols., 217 × 145 mm, text 157–163 × 110 mm, 2 columns (except 261v–264v, 265v–279v, 328v–345v, and 407–439v, 1 column), 36–40 lines ruled in crayon

SCRIPT: Gothic bookhand (textualis)

BINDING: light brown leather over boards, by S. Cockerell, 1972

Cambridge University Library, MS Gg.1.1

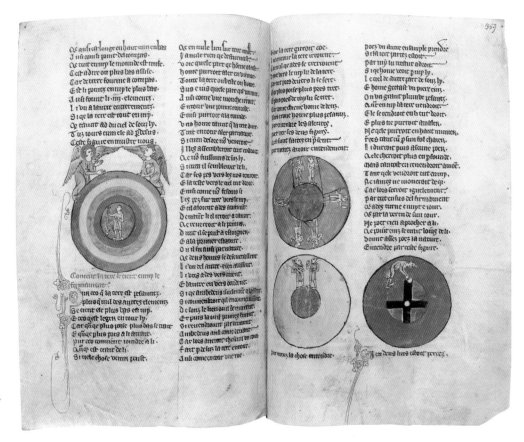

Cosmological diagrams. Cambridge University Library, MS Gg.1.1, fols. 358v–359

THIS BOOK has been referred to as a library in itself. The small format of the pages combines with the great number of leaves to give the manuscript an extraordinary shape, almost a cube. There are 55 texts, if not more, depending on how they are counted, mostly in Anglo-Norman but with a sprinkling of Latin texts and one in Middle English. No other single manuscript contains so many separate Anglo-Norman texts. They combine devotional with political and didactic subjects, exhibiting a recurring interest in prognostication and prophecy. Remarkably, they appear to be the work of a single scribe. The illustrations too show the work of a single hand, in the diagrams accompanying the text *L'Image du Monde* as well as in the series of miniatures illustrating the Apocalypse.

The diagrams are closely linked to the versified cosmology text, which calls at points in the poem for *'ceste figure'*. The artist confines the diagram to the place in the column where the text reference appears. In each picture the cosmos is signified by all that is contained within the pen drawn circle and the earth by a green sphere at the centre of the cosmos. On the verso page the figure with a spade personifies the heaviest element, earth, the other three elements lying outside the solid earth concentrically. Angels tend the pure celestial air of the heavens in the circle beyond the elemental world. On the facing recto the three diagrams represent extremely simple thought experiments. The first two show the imagined journey from one side of the world to the other by two individuals going in opposite directions; the conclusion is that they will meet on the other side, and if the circuit was continued would meet again where they first started. The final diagram shows a heavy weight dropped through an imagined hole in the earth's surface and its final lodging place at the centre. The human figures in these diagrams are rendered as little more than ciphers, cartoon figures in a highly schematized cosmos.

The other main series of illuminations in the book contains illustrations to the Apocalypse of St John. The combination of secular and religious images within the same book is not unusual at this time, and the same artist was responsible for both. In this case the interest of the commissioner of this great 'library' of texts in the natural world and in the future might have comprehended both the structure of the cosmos and the 'final things' in the history of the world. The singular illustration of the faculties of the human mind is designed to show its topography, a diagram of the microcosm to set alongside those of the macrocosm. The artist drew on well-established traditions of illustration in Anglo-Norman texts for the principal series of images, though it is unusual to find these traditions represented in such a large and varied miscellany of texts.

PROVENANCE: 'bought of Mr Washington' (inscription on fol. IV referring to John Washington, a mid-seventeenth century London bookseller); John Moore, bishop of Ely (1707–1714); presented to the Library by George I in 1715.

LITERATURE: University Library 1856–1867, III, 1–8; Meyer 1886, 283–340; Prior 1913; Flint, 1983, 7–153; Dean 1999, 18, 43, 66, 85, 198, 202, 217.

PJ

152

Jean Corbechon, *Des Proprietez des Choses*

In French
France, Paris, *c.*1415
ARTIST: Boucicaut Master (act. *c.*1400–*c.*1415)

Parchment, 363 fols., 405 × 285 mm, text 298 × 190 mm, 2 columns, 49 lines ruled in hard point
SCRIPT: Gothic bookhand (hybrida)
BINDING: gold-tooled calf over pasteboards, 18th c.

Fitzwilliam Museum, MS 251

THIS COPY of the illustrated encyclopedia of Bartholomaeus Anglicus is one of the few such great secular books for which we can trace payment and identify for whom it was written and illuminated. The opening miniature shows the work being presented to the French King Charles VI by its translator into French, the Augustinian hermit Jean Corbechon. By the side of the royal throne stands the great patron Jean, Duc de Berry. The book was paid for in Paris in 1414 by the Duke's grandson, Amadeus VIII, then Count of Savoy, and it is his patronage that accounts for the Madonna lilies that are such a prominent part in five of the paintings and one of the borders. The translation into French of the popular encyclopedia was made in 1372, and it is this event that is commemorated in the opening miniature, with Amadeus's grandfather so prominently depicted leaning on the throne (the translation was actually presented to Charles V, though the King shown is Charles VI). The dozen earliest copies of the translation seem to share a programme of illustration of a broadly standardized kind and the manuscript ordered by Amadeus belongs to this tradition of large and magnificently illuminated books. However there are specific features of the Fitzwilliam manuscript that seem to be closely related to the interests of its patron, Amadeus VIII.

In the miniature that introduces the medical book of *Des Proprietez des Choses* we find the physician not

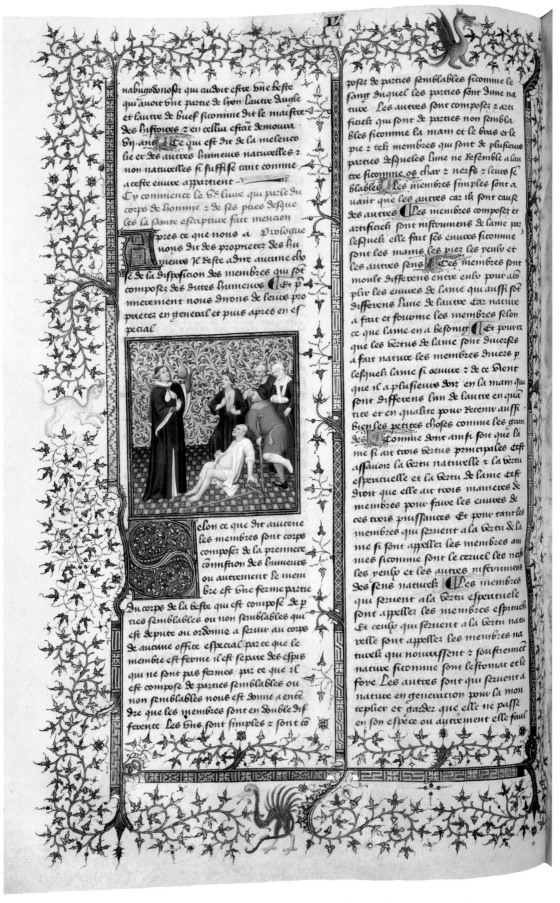

Physician with his Patients. Fitzwilliam Museum, MS 251, fol. 54v

lecturing as usual, but with the sick. The physician is shown in a blue academic robe with red hood and sleeves, and holds up a urine glass, his badge of office as well as a diagnostic tool. Before him stands a tableau of patients illustrating different maladies. One standing patient bares his chest with a wound; another in white sits on the ground, a crutch to one side, and shows his swollen stomach; a third in red on a crutch has a bandaged leg; a fourth with beard exhibits a wounded hand, and finally there is a lady in blue with a bandaged arm in sling. Collectively they show the range of complaints with which a physician must deal, as described in the text. The triangular composition recalls the Funeral of St Jerome in the *Belles Heures* of the Duc de Berry, also a depiction of physical suffering. The effect is dramatic and evokes the viewer's sympathy for the sick and respect for the physician. Medicine was one of Amadeus's life-long interests, and he employed many physicians and alchemists. He commissioned works on the philosopher's stone and potable gold, both means to the relief of suffering. Another miniature in the book, that on elements and humours, also shows medicinal jars.

The nineteen paintings of Fitzwilliam MS 251 introducing different books of the encyclopedia were products of the workshop of the Boucicaut Master, to which a number of the finest Parisian works of the period can be attributed. The patronage of the manuscript and its lavish presentation demonstrate a nobleman's taste for conspicuous display as opposed to the use of Bartholomaeus Anglicus' encyclopedia as a school-book or resource for sermon making. Most Latin copies were made for academic or homiletic purposes, but copies of the French translation seem to have been intended for the private reading and delectation of men like Amadeus VIII of Savoy.

PROVENANCE: Amadeus VIII of Savoy (1383–1451); presented to the Museum by Brigadier Archibald Stirling of Keir in 1897.

EXHIBITED: Cambridge 1966, no. 70; Paris 2000, 95 and no. 93; Paris 2004a, no. 27.

LITERATURE: Meiss 1968, 58–9,79–80, 115, fig. 452–7; Byrne 1977, 90–8; Byrne 1978, 149–64; Wormald and Giles 1982, 172–5; Byrne 1984, 118–35; Bagliani 1990, 197; Meyer 1996, 368–75.

PJ

153

Roger of Parma, *Chirurgia*

In Anglo-Norman
England, *c.*1230– *c.*1240

Parchment, ii (paper) + 331 (including fol. 95bis) + ii (paper) fols., 198 × 155 mm, text 142 × 113 mm, 21 lines, ruled in hard point
SCRIPT: Gothic bookhand (textualis)
BINDING: gold-tooled dark calf, 17th c., rebacked 20th c.

Trinity College, MS O.1.20

THE *CHIRURGIA* of Roger of Parma, compiled around 1180, is the first Western surgical work to attract figural illustrations. It is also the first independent medieval work on surgery. It seems that the figures at the bottom of the page in this manuscript were not planned at the time of writing, but added subsequently – no other similar illustrations have been found elsewhere. The illustrations are closely related to the Anglo-Norman translation of Roger's text, sometimes taking their inspiration from individual sentences or phrases. In the displayed opening the central figure seems to offer coins from a purse – in fact these are the *magdaliones* (round medicaments sold by spicers) called for to help heal the wound made by the surgical incision. The razor and forceps shown are likely to be accurate renderings of surgical instruments of the time. There are forty-nine separate illustrations (excluding the initial by a different artist at the beginning, and another sketch of the doctor at the end), related to separate chapters of the text. Many are plain drawings in brown ink, but some are tinted in yellow, brown and green. The style of the drawings has proved difficult to relate convincingly to other work, though it bears some resemblance to the Cambridge University Library Bestiary *(no. 147)*. The style mixes static figures of the surgeon, whose authority is conveyed by a seated pose and formal clothing, with dynamic poses for the patient and helpers. The various diseases are differentiated by exaggerated features or dramatic gestures on the part of the patient.

Trinity MS O.1.20 is one of the earliest and most important collections of medical texts to survive in Anglo-Norman. It contains a series of practical texts, including general works on therapeutics (principally the *Practica brevis* of Platearius), women's ailments and beauty, and advice to doctors. Following the illustrated Anglo-Norman *Chirurgia* comes a Latin text of the same work (incomplete, fols. 300–24), and an incomplete treatise on confession (fols. 325–30v) with spaces for initials never completed. The book really consists of four separate parts, the work of different scribes. There is an *ad*

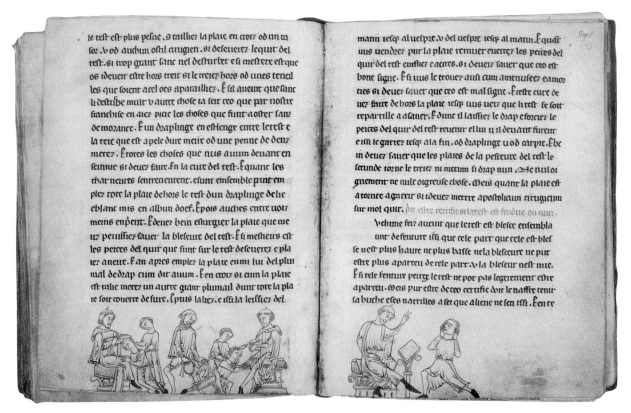

Depressed Fracture of the Cranium. Trinity College, MS O.1.20, fols. 242v–243

hoc quality to the compilation of the book, with treatises left unfinished, evidence of excerpting from longer texts, free translations, and additions of recipes and charms.

The surgical illustrations to the Roger text should not be judged as indispensable guides to manual operations. They enhanced the visual interest and beauty of the manuscript but would have had very limited instructional value for the viewer. The artist repeats motifs like rows of apothecary jars and round trays of medicinal simples rather than telling the story of distinct operations. He or she is much concerned with symmetry of design on the page and with decorative patterning, often at the expense of technical clarity. In these respects the artist's response to the text is best compared with interpretations of other narrative texts, romances, histories and biblical stories, rather than with the informational diagrams of modern practical manuals.

PROVENANCE: Thomas Gale (d.1702); presented to Trinity College by Roger Gale in 1738.

EXHIBITED: London 1908, no. 78; London 1987–1988, no. 312.

LITERATURE: James 1900–1904, III, 23–8; Meyer 1903, 75–95; Sudhoff 1914, 33–42; Ross 1940, 15–272; Hunt 1982; Morgan 1982–1988, no. 78; Hunt 1990, 142–44; Hunt 1994; Green, 1997, 92; Hunt 1997, 68–115.

PJ

154

Anatomy

In Latin, Middle English, and Flemish
England, thirteenth century and *c.*1440
SCRIBE: John Welles (act. *c.*1440)

Parchment, 6 fols. (13th c., 200 × 160 mm) + 104 fols. (parchment and paper, *c.*1440, 210 × 150 mm) fols.

SCRIPT: Gothic bookhand (hybrida)

BINDING: limp leather, wallet with flap, 15th c; repaired by S. Cockerell, 1987

Gonville and Caius College, MS 190/223

THIS MANUSCRIPT is a composite assembled in the fifteenth century, probably with its usefulness for medical practice in mind. Except for the opening gathering of anatomical drawings and captions, the manuscript is made up of three booklets of fifteenth century medical material. These were all (but for the last leaves) written by Brother John Welles, canon of the Premonstratensian Abbey of Hagnaby, to which he probably gave it himself. He wrote the excerpted *Experimenta* or *Liber receptarum ad fistulas* of the English fourteenth-century surgeon,

319

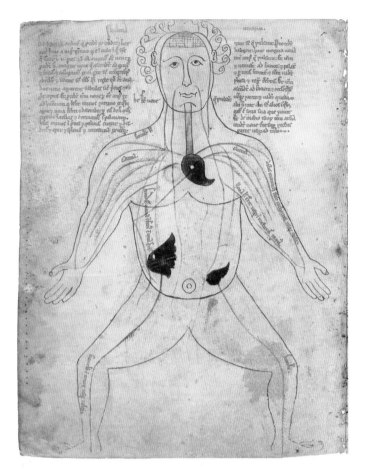

John of Arderne, and illustrated them with many of the marginal drawings of instruments, plants, diseases, etc., that usually accompany Arderne's complete treatise on *fistula-in-ano* (operation on the rectum) and *Liber medicinalium*. This work was completed, he tells us, in 1440. The other later texts are also practical medical works, including a gloss on the *Viaticum* of Constantinus Africanus, and a number of recipes and charms have been added later in Middle English, Latin and Flemish.

The anatomical drawings at the beginning of the manuscript were presumably thought of as suitable companions to the practical works when the manuscript was put together, perhaps by Welles himself. They are witnesses to a very ancient series of figures whose origins have been traced to the medical schools of Alexandria at the beginning of the Christian era. Each of the nine figures is given a title, such as *istoria arteriarum*, and represent various systems and organs of the body. Veins and arteries are followed by bones, nerves, muscles, genitalia, the abdominal organs, the matrix and female genitalia, and the brain and eyes. Collectively the systems and organs were meant to provide a visual guide to the workings of the human body, rather than a descriptive anatomy based on dissection of an actual body. There is therefore a considerable amount of schematization in the representing of the systems and organs, with simplified geometrical shapes and mirror symmetry accentuated at the expense of more pictorial qualities. Their use in teaching at the Alexandrian schools probably meant that this simplification and schematization was present in the diagrams in this nine-figure series from the beginning of its long history.

The descriptive text is written around or over the drawings of the systems and organs. Not much information beyond labelling of the parts is provided, except for a succinct account on the leaves containing the nerve and muscle men. Fuller versions of the text can be found in other manuscripts of this series. How useful the Premonstratensian canons of Hagnaby found this guide to anatomy of two centuries earlier is hard to say – the sorts of anatomical text that normally accompanied surgical writings did not usually come accompanied by visual aids, and were far more discursive in character.

PROVENANCE: Hagnaby Abbey, Linconshire, 15th c.; given to the College by William Moore in 1659.

LITERATURE: Sudhoff 1907, 51–59, pls. 13, 14; James 1907–1914, I, 218–19; Herrlinger 1970, 10–4; O'Neill 1977, 538–49; Robinson 1988, no. 240, pl. 233; O'Neill 1993, 91–105; Rand-Schmidt 2001, 47–50.

PJ

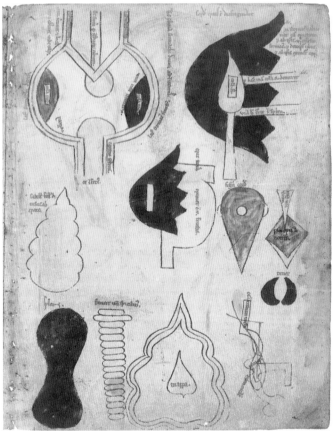

Vein man. Gonville and Caius College, MS 190/223, fol. 2v

Internal organs. Gonville and Caius College, MS 190/223, fol. 5

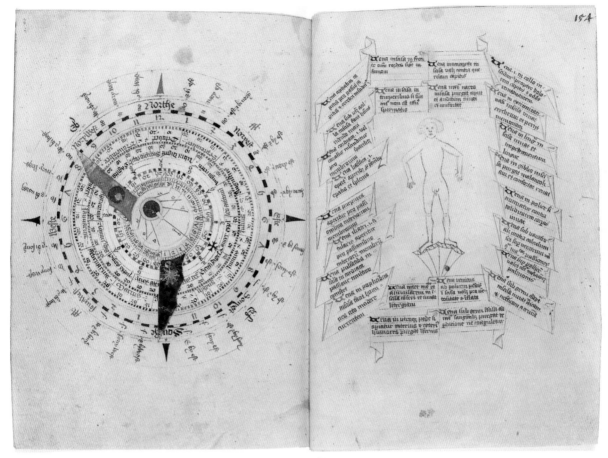

Vein man and the volvelle. Gonville and Caius College, MS 336/725, fols. 153v–154

155

Medicine and Astrology

In Middle English and Latin
England, c.1480– c.1500

Parchment, 168 fols. (fol. 49 occurs twice; leaf between fols. 52 and 53 not numbered; no fol. 77; fols. 86 and 92 occur twice; leaf after fol. 97 numbered fol. 97a; leaf after fol. 124 not numbered), 244 × 172 mm, text 166 × 98 mm, 33 long lines, ruled in crayon

SCRIPT: Gothic bookhand (hybrida)

BINDING: tanned calf, 18th c.

Gonville and Caius College, MS 336/725

IN FIFTEENTH-CENTURY ENGLAND, growing lay interest in medicine, astrology and alchemy led to flourishing production of manuscripts containing texts in Latin and Middle English, and to a lesser extent Anglo-Norman. There is evidence that this scientific production became increasingly standardized, and books may have been prepared not for individual customers but in anticipation of a potential market. A group of such manuscripts probably produced in London has been identified, marked by shared textual content, and by format, script, and decoration. The second part of MS 336/725 (fols. 104–157) is related to this group, and along with its twin, Tokyo, Collection of Toshi Takamiya, MS 33, belongs to a second generation of books that seemingly copy features of the original 'Sloane group'. The texts in the manuscript (the first part of which is dated rather earlier, probably in the 1460s) include part of the Surgery of Guy de Chauliac in Middle English translation, a compendium on uroscopy, the plague tract of John of Burgundy in Latin, and a variety of short medical, astrological and alchemical texts. But this manuscript is distinguished throughout for the number and elaboration of its prognostic diagrams and parchment instruments for medicine and astrology.

These include the golden table of Pythagoras, used to foretell the outcomes of illnesses and other events, sets of urine glasses to help diagnosis (although the colours were not supplied in one set), a zodiacal man with signs for different parts of the body, a vein man showing where to let blood for particular complaints, and an astrological volvelle. Shown here are the vein man and the volvelle. The vein man stands in the distinctive frog pose descended from images of Late Antiquity; missing are the indication lines that should link the veins to the illnesses for which they should be opened. The captions state, for example, that the vein in the big toe should be bled for windiness of the stomach.

The volvelle was used for predicting the best time to provide medical treatment. On the outside we see the points of the compass in English, then the hours, days, and months. Inside these are the days within astrological houses and states of digestion. Finally we come to the days of the moon on the innermost ring. The movable dial has the signs for the planets and an aperture through which to see the size of the moon. There are two pointing indexes for the sun and the moon respectively. By setting these correctly the medical practitioner could estimate the relationship between solar and lunar days and the ruling astrological signs. If these were propitious on a particular day he or she could be confident of a successful outcome in giving a medicine or letting blood. We should remember that ownership of manuscripts with these impressive instruments and diagrams had as much to do with the prestige of the practitioner as the convenience for diagnosis and prognosis.

PROVENANCE: given to the College by William Moore, 1659.

LITERATURE: James 1907–1914, I, 378–80; Wallner 1971; Harley 1982; Voigts 1990, 54n. 10; Voigts 1994; Rand-Schmidt 2001, 60–72.

PJ

156

John de Foxton, *Liber cosmographiae*

In Latin
England, 1385–1408
SCRIBE: John de Foxton (c.1369–c.1440)

Parchment: vi + 81 + iii fols., 255 × 175 mm, text 190 × 225 mm, 2 columns, 38–41 lines, ruled in hard point

SCRIPT: Gothic bookhand (textualis)

BINDING: dark calf with gilt armorial centrepiece, 17th c.; rebacked by J.P. Gray, 20th c.

Trinity College, MS R.15.21

JOHN DE FOXTON's *Liber cosmographiae* is an illustrated compendium of popular science in one hundred and four chapters, probably written by the author and compiler. Most of the book was made up by excerpts accumulated over a considerable time, and in this sense it represents a lifetime's work. Foxton was a Yorkshire cleric who may have been associated with the extraordinary scientific library of the Augustinian Priory in York. Almost all of his source texts for the *Liber cosmographiae* were to be found there. The first twenty-eight chapters, roughly those dealing with the elements, meteorology and health, particularly diet and obstetrics, are taken verbatim (but without acknowledgement) from the *De naturis rerum* of the Flemish Dominican Thomas of Cantimpré, an encyclopedia written around 1240. Other works used by Foxton

belong to the encyclopedic tradition. Being an unbeneficed chaplain for most of the period of compilation of his book, Foxton would not have intended such an elaborate compilation for his own use, but for that of a noble patron. In return he may have expected, and received, promotion to a benefice. Nevertheless, it was John de Foxton himself who seems to have given his book to an obscure convent in Knaresborough after its completion.

The illustrations to the work range from astronomical tables drawn up by Foxton himself to elaborate figures drawn to show the temperaments and the planets (the Signs of the Zodiac were planned but never executed). There are similarities between the planetary figures in the *Liber cosmographiae* and the miniatures painted by John Siferwas in the first two-thirds of the Sherborne Missal (London, British Library, Add. MS 74236); perhaps Fox-

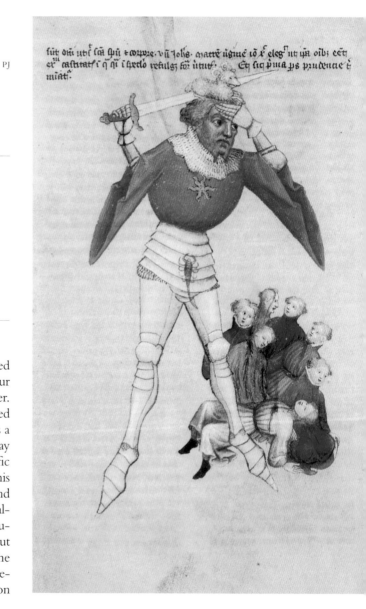

ton's book was sent to Siferwas's workshop for illumination, although it was far from York. There is a curious lack of finish about the manuscript in other respects, as if the appropriate decorative scheme to go with the illuminations had never been attempted.

The main idea of Foxton's compilation is that the planets influence the four elements and humours, and hence all life. The first four pictures are of the temperaments, sanguine, somnolent, melancholy and choleric. These are keyed to the chapters on physiognomy. The remaining eight are by a superior artist, and include a zodiac and blood-letting man (keyed to phlebotomy tables). The most unusual are the series of planetary portraits illustrating mythographic chapters that are loosely based on John Ridwall's *Fulgentius metaforalis*. Mars (shown here) wears the armour called camail, above his head the sign of Aries the ram and on his belly Scorpio. He carries a sword and the gesture to his head is one of anger. At his feet are his children, stricken by war. Each of the personified planets combines different attributes, Zodiacal Signs, and mythological references, some of them hard to decipher even with the aid of the text. Thus Luna, the moon, is shown as a man, although the text tells us that the ancients show Luna with the face of a woman. The same desire to embellish the mysteries of the text may also have lain behind Foxton's employment of ciphers to conceal the meaning of chapters on prognostication within the text of the *Liber cosmographiae*. He certainly did not intend to make it easy for his patron or later readers.

PROVENANCE: given by Foxton to the Trinitarian convent of Knaresborough, Yorkshire (colophon, fol. 77); bequeathed to Trinity College by Archbishop Whitgift (d.1604).

EXHIBITED: London 1908, no. 155; London 1930, no.561; Vienna 1962, no. 150; Brussels 1973, no.77; Lisbon 2000, no. 20.

LITERATURE: James 1900–1904, II, 358–61; Saxl and Meier 1953, III, I, xxxiii–iv, 428–30, III, II, pls. 90, 92, figs. 233–6; Friedman 1982, 219–35; Friedman 1983, 391–418; Friedman 1988; Robinson 1988, no.356; Vandendriessche 1995, 529–37; Scott 1996, no. 31

PJ

Mars. Trinity College, MS R.15.21, fol. 44v

157

John of Rupescissa, *Liber de consideratione quintae essentiae*, etc.

In Latin and Catalan
Southern France, possibly Roussillon area,
early fifteenth century

Parchment (outer and middle leaves of gatherings, to fol.119) and paper, ii + 132 + i fols., 218 × 144 mm, text 150 × 95 mm, 30 lines, ruled in hard point and plummet

SCRIPT: Gothic bookhand (textualis and hybrida)

BINDING: vellum over pasteboards, calfskin back, 17th c.

Corpus Christi College, MS 395

THIS BOOK testifies to the fascination with pseudo-Lullian alchemy amongst English doctors of the fifteenth century. A number of copies of the works of John of Rupescissa, an author known as pseudo-Ramon Lull, and various anonymous fourteenth-century writers on the medical uses of the quintessence were imported to England from southern France or Catalonia at this time. Pseudo-Lullian alchemy is characterized by techniques for creating and using quintessential remedies based on the multiple distillation of wine and other substances, for which huge medical benefits are claimed. Equally characteristic is the use of instructional diagrams and tables of relationship between substances to explain alchemical propositions. These visual features gave alchemy a distinctive 'look', particularly when accompanied by pictures of alchemical apparatus. But the full-page illustrations of lunaria grass found in this manuscript, accompanied here by explanatory captions in Catalan, are very unusual.

Lunaria grass is unique in putting forth its fifteen leaves in accordance with the waxing and the waning of the moon. The pages exhibited demonstrate this process stage by stage, and the rather refined young man holds a caption that explains the relationship to astrology (also indicated by the planetary symbols above the plant). Lunaria was thought to have exceptional powers as a medicine on the fifteenth day of the moon. A Latin text explaining this curious plant and its benefits for thirteen different ailments was added to the original manuscript by an English fifteenth-century hand, presumably that of one of its first English owners. This text comes immediately before the illustrations, to which the scribe refers. In the margin the same scribe has added that the leaves of lunaria not only cure quartan fever, but all desperate illnesses, God willing. Distilling of the quintessence of the lunaria would amplify its powers still

323

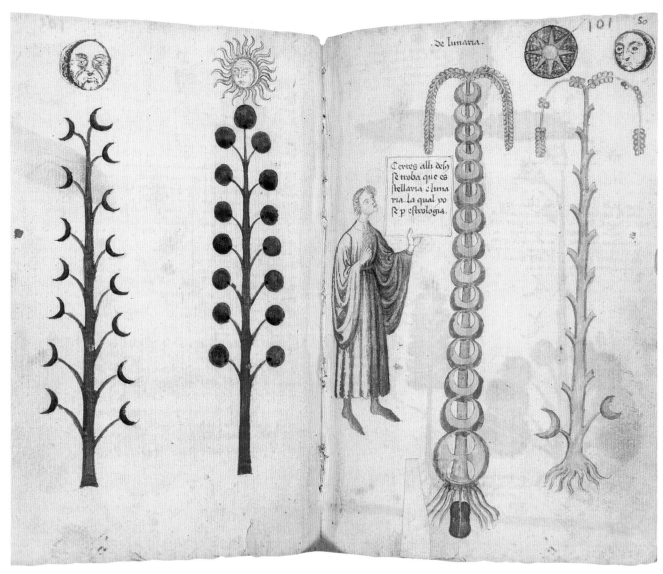

Lunaria Grass. Corpus Christi College, MS 395, fol. 49v–50

further. Overleaf are portraits of different varieties of lunaria by the same artist, showing roots and flowers as well as leaves. The illustrations are painted as coloured washes with ink outlines. The style of plant portraiture is rather formalized and stiff despite the concern in the captions for distinguishing the varieties of lunaria. The diagrams found elsewhere in the manuscript are executed in coloured inks with capitals touched in yellow.

A number of Latin texts on alchemy and necromancy by the same English hand that wrote the lunaria text have been added to the original manuscript, either in gaps in the original, or on paper leaves added to the end. Later still a well-known English alchemist, Robert Green of Welby (c.1467–1540), has substituted his own name for that of the original scribe of these additions. The manu-

script has thus become an important witness to the development of the English style of medicinal alchemy from its pseudo-Lullian origins on the Continent. So influential did this school of thought become that several English physicians applied for a licence to practise quintessential alchemy in an attempt to rescue King Henry VI from his fits of madness in the 1450s.

PROVENANCE: Robert Green of Welbe (c.1506); Matthew Parker (1504–1575); his bequest, 1575.

LITERATURE: James 1912b, II, 255–58; Watson 1985, 312–13; Bohigas 1985, 42; Pereira 1989, 22–37; Pereira 1990, 41–54; Wilkins 1993, 108.

PJ

158

Hyginus, *Astronomica*

In Latin
Italy, Mantua, *c.*1475

Paper, 63 + ii fols., 2 raised pastedowns, 217 × 145 mm, text area variable, 26 lines to a full page, no visible ruling

SCRIPT: Humanistic cursive

BINDING: white pigskin over oak boards, by Robert Proctor, 1992; preserved remains of contemporary binding, alum tawed skin stained pink over paper boards

Fitzwilliam Museum, MS 260

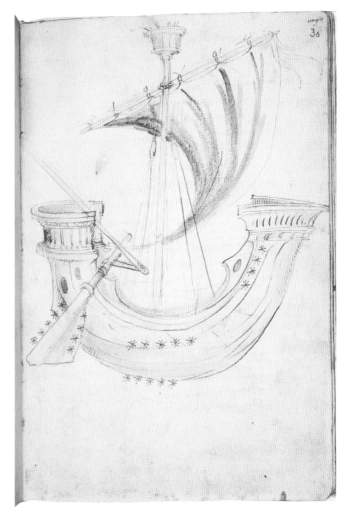

The mythical ship Argo. Fitzwilliam Museum, MS 260, fol. 30

THE *ASTRONOMICA* OR *POETICON ASTRONOMICON* of Hyginus was written at the end of the first or the beginning of the second century AD. It is divided into an introduction and four parts. In Books II and III Hyginus names forty-two constellations, discussing the mythological stories associated with each, and its place in the sky at night. These two books became very popular with Humanists and bibliophiles of the late fifteenth century, partly because they seemed to offer access to the classical tradition of astronomical learning, without reference to Islamic or medieval intermediaries, partly because they offered scope for illustrations that interpret mythological themes while offering exact observation of the heavens.

This manuscript is closely associated with the court of the Gonzaga in Mantua, whose enthusiasm for astrology was marked (another contemporary copy of Hyginus belonging to the Gonzaga was formerly Dyson Perrins MS 92). The two books of Hyginus are here in reverse order. Book III is illustrated with 33 outline drawings of the constellations, in sepia tinted with colours, marked with red stars, while Book II is unillustrated. The names of each constellation have been written by the scribe in a tiny hand in the top right corner, as an indication to the artist of the figure required. This copy is written on paper rather than vellum, and perhaps reflects a personal commission rather than a presentation copy. The drawings and script are less elaborately finished than in other contemporary copies, and the decoration is minimal; by comparison the copy of Hyginus belonging to Lodovico Gonzaga was decorated with a profusion of Renaissance vases, cornucopias, plinths, dolphins, columns and sphinxes, and contains Lodovico's coat of arms.

At some time in its history five pages and images have gone missing after fols. 1, 7, 20, 24, and 25. The text of the book omits the Greek quotations in the original, or transliterates the Greek into Latin, often wrongly. The text and illustration of the page exhibited deals with the constellation 'Argo'. The illustrator depicts a contempo-

rary vessel with blue sails to represent the mythical Greek ship. The position of individual stars within the constellation is marked on the drawing by the red stars, and the form of the 'Argo' is no obstacle to fixing the stars in the sky as they would have appeared in the time of Hyginus. Other pages show the Signs of the Zodiac, which form the band of sky that seems, from the earth, to contain the paths of the seven planets. Zodiacal astrology was at the peak of its intellectual authority and influence in the late fifteenth and early sixteenth centuries, and many noble and wealthy patrons sought to own books that combined elegant drawings with information about the stars.

PROVENANCE: Leonora Gonzaga (1493–1543), ownership inscription, fols. 1, i; Giuseppe Scotti and Mauricio Aymi, ownership inscriptions, fol. i; purchased for the Museum from Jacques Rosenthal of Munich (Catalogue 27, no. 2) in 1901.

LITERATURE: Saxl and Meier 1953, III, I, liii, 328, 439; Wormald and Giles 1982, 192–94.

PJ

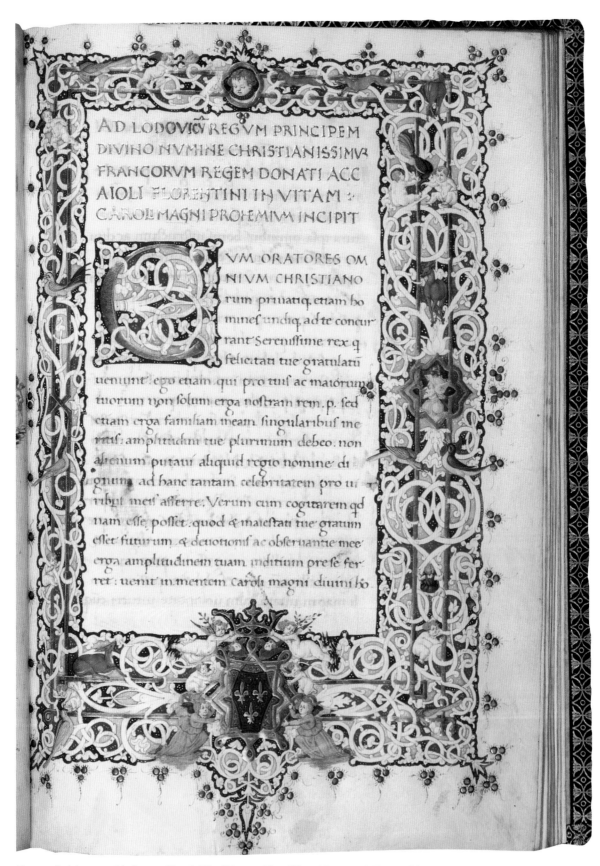

AD LODOVICŨ REGVM PRINCIPEM
DIVINO NVMINE CHRISTIANISSIMŪ
FRANCORVM REGEM DONATI ACC
AIOLI FLORENTINI IN VITAM :
CAROLI MAGNI PROHEMIVM INCIPIT

VM ORATORES OM
NIVM CHRISTIANO
rum priuatiq. etiam ho
mines undiq. ad te concur
rant Serenissime rex q
felicitati tue gratulati
ueniunt. ego etiam qui pro tuis ac maiorum
tuorum non solum erga nostram rem. p. sed
etiam erga familiam meam. singularibus me
ritis, amplitudini tue plurimum debeo. non
alienum putaui aliquid regio nomine di
gnum. ad hanc tantam celebritatem pro u
ribus meis afferre. Verum cum cogitarem qd
nam esse posset. quod & maiestati tue gratum
esset futurum. & deuotionis ac obseruantie mee
erga amplitudinem tuam. inditium pre se fer
ret. uenit in mentem Caroli magni diuini ho

Fig. 40. *Incipit* page with Arms of Louis XI of France. Fitzwilliam Museum, MS 180, fol. 2

7

THE HUMANISTIC MANUSCRIPT

Jonathan Alexander

I N ITALY in the early fifteenth century a revolution took place, first in Florence, and very soon after in the rest of the peninsula, in the script and decoration of the manuscript book. The new script, now known as 'humanistic script', was referred to by contemporaries as *littera antica*. The innovators in Florence were Coluccio Salutati, Niccolò Nicoli and Poggio Bracciolini. Visitors can contrast the various forms of Gothic script, which had developed between 1150 and 1400, in other sections of the exhibition. They will find the Gothic letter forms less familiar, since the alphabet we use today is basically that reintroduced by the Humanists. The Gothic scripts are cramped and angular, letter forms often run together, and some letters, 'r' and long 's' for example, are unfamiliar. The Gothic scribes also used many abbreviations.

The twelfth-century manuscripts which the early Humanists took as models are written, on the other hand, in a clear round minuscule (or lower case – a printer's term) alphabet. The letters of this alphabet, though they may have looked 'antique' to contemporaries, were certainly not known in ancient Rome. They had been invented in the Frankish Empire at the end of the eighth century. This new minuscule alphabet became the standard form for writing texts required in the monastic communities and the cathedral schools and its use was encouraged by the Emperor Charlemagne (d.814) and his successors as part of the cultural revival of the ninth century. As such it spread all over Europe.

The majuscule (capital or upper case) alphabets used for headings and initials in the minuscule scripts did on the other hand include letter forms found on Roman inscriptions of the early Empire, especially the seriffed alphabet, as used on the column of Trajan for example. The capitals in humanistic manuscripts tend to return to these more monumental early Roman capitals *(no. 165)*. Other forms of capitals, the uncial letters for example, developed later in the Roman period, and there were further experiments in majuscule letters in the Gothic period. Capital letters, as we all know from the many forms we are required to fill in to-day, tend to be more legible, but are slower to write, because they necessitate more lifts of the pen. The few antique de luxe codices to survive are entirely written in various capital alphabets. The Carolingian minuscule, therefore, introduced speed but without sacrificing legibility.[1]

The historicising use of the 'new/old' humanistic script in Italy was in some ways comparable to its Carolingian predecessor as part of a cultural revival. The early Humanists aimed to reform Latin spelling and usage, to improve the texts of known classical authors by consulting earlier and better exemplars, and to rediscover lost works by Roman writers. In general they sought to revive the philological study of ancient literature, which soon came to include Greek literature as well. Their aim was to make this study a central part of the educational curriculum. In their search for ancient texts in monastic and cathedral libraries, not only in Italy but in other parts of Europe as well, Poggio and his contemporaries would have come across both Carolingian and Romanesque manuscripts, but manuscripts made in Italy in the Romanesque period were obviously much more accessible. These were

written in a weighty, rounded and legible version of Carolingian minuscule and many survived still in Tuscany and Central Italy. In any case, even if the minuscule script is a more complicated matter as to its origins, it was not from Carolingian manuscripts but from such Italian Romanesque manuscripts that the style of decoration of the initials in the earliest manuscripts written in humanistic script was closely copied. The new initials were at first very simply decorated with small capitals accompanied by a stylized plant scroll, generally not painted but reserved on the cream-coloured membrane. This plant ornament has come to be referred to as 'white-vine' or in Italian *'bianchi girari'*. The interstices of the scroll were filled with a mosaic of simple, cheap colours, red, yellow, green and blue.

Such sober initials in the earliest examples may have been felt suitable in not distracting attention from the text. More importantly, like the script they distanced the texts from liturgical and religious texts. The latter continued to be written in the various forms of the Gothic alphabet which developed from the early thirteenth century onwards. Their illumination with gold and more varied pigments and with a whole variety of styles of decoration, also included illustrations, as the Humanist texts for the most part did not. However, as time went on the two styles began to intermingle. Already in the second decade of the fifteenth century in Florence the white-vine was invaded by motifs from the richer vocabulary of the religious manuscripts, birds, animals, real and imaginary, butterflies and more naturalistic vegetation and flowers *(fig. 40; no 161)*. They also commonly contained author portraits, and often little scenes were included in the borders of the frontispieces. The latter continued to be the main form of illumination with narrative miniatures still relatively uncommon. Another ubiquitous feature became the small naked boys, now known as 'putti', but described in some contemporary texts as *'spiritelli'*.[2] They were probably consciously borrowed by the illuminators from antique sarcophagi or from the contemporary sculpture of artists like Donatello.[3] Often they flank an owner's coat-of-arms in the centre of the lower margin of the page *(nos. 161, 162, 163)*. Sometimes they are winged, sometimes not, though whether that changed their meaning is unclear. The artists in the earliest manuscripts may have been also the scribes. As the work became more complex they were evidently professional craftsmen, many of whom are documented in payment accounts, tax returns and property transactions and wills.[4] The white-vine initials started to acquire border extensions and these might fill one, two or, for an important frontispiece, all four sides as a continuous framing border. A typical example is the Eusebius illuminated for Pope Pius II by Gioachino de Gigantibus, who, born in Southern Germany, was evidently trained in Florence *(no. 163)*. Unusually he worked as both scribe and artist. No great claims for him as the latter can be made, as a comparison with a de luxe example of Florentine illumination of the highest quality, a manuscript produced by the famous *cartolaio* Vespasiano da Bisticci for presentation to Louis XI of France, makes clear *(no. 161)*.[5]

From Florence the white-vine style spread south to Rome and Naples. It was also adopted with variations by the other main regional schools, in the Veneto, in such important centres as Ferrara and Bologna and, though with less enthusiasm, in Milan. It was also used after printing was introduced to Italy in spaces left blank by the printers for the initials to be inserted by hand. This occurs in the earliest books printed at Subiaco outside Rome in 1465, in Venice, where the first book was printed in 1469, and elsewhere all over Italy. However by about 1500 white-

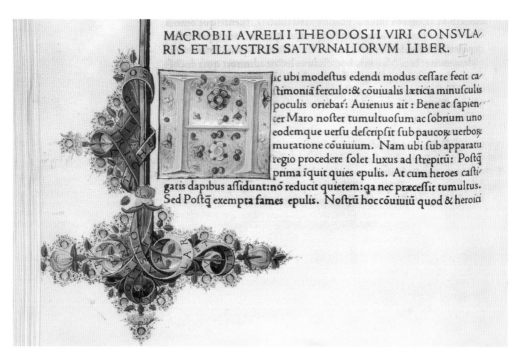

MACROBII AVRELII THEODOSII VIRI CONSVLA/
RIS ET ILLVSTRIS SATVRNALIORVM LIBER.

ιc ubi modeſtus edendi modus ceſſare fecit ca/
timoniā ferculo:& cōuiualis læticia minuſculis
poculis oriebat: Auienιus ait : Bene ac ſapien/
ter Maro noſter tumultuoſum ac ſobrium uno
eodemque uerſu deſcripſit ſub paucoȝ uerboȝ
mutatione cōuiuium. Nam ubi ſub apparatu
ɾegio procedere ſolet luxus ad ſtrepιtū: Poſtɋ
prima ſquit quies epulis. At cum heroes caſti/
gatis dapibus aſſidunt:nō reducit quietem:qa nec præceſſit tumultus.
Sed Poſtɋ exempta fames epulis. Noſtrū hoccōuiuiū quod & heroιci

Fig. 41. Faceted
initial. Cambridge,
Trinity College,
Inc. VI.18.52,
book II, detail

vine had gone out of fashion almost everywhere. In Florence it had begun to be replaced in luxury humanistic codices already in the 1460s.

In Padua and the Veneto other important experiments with decoration using antique motifs took place from the mid-century. They result in the use of 'faceted initials' (*littera prismatica*), in manuscripts from the 1450s onward (*no. 166*).[6] These were archaeologically exact capitals with serifs and were painted to simulate the third dimension (*fig. 41, see also nos. 165, 166*). Illuminators in the North-east also experimented with other ways of making the letter form three-dimensional, for example by incorporating columns, globular forms, or sculpted figures (*fig. 42, see also no. 174*). A second original development in the 1450s is the architectural frontispiece. The title or often the initial page of text was framed by pillars or columns which uphold a pediment (*nos. 172, 174*). These frontispieces are reminiscent of antique triumphal arches, of which a number had survived in Italy, the most famous being the Arch of Constantine in Rome. The architectural frontispiece quickly became fashionable throughout the rest of Italy. It was brought to Rome in the 1470s by illuminators trained in Padua or Venice, and later spread to Naples and to Lombardy. The fashion spread beyond the confines of humanistic texts and even some Books of Hours, especially in Naples, used such frames (*fig. 44, no. 100*). Due to the importance of the printing industry in Venice, it was also used in woodcut frontispieces there and came to be adopted in printed books all over Europe.[7]

Paduan and Venetian illuminators also enriched their frontispieces and initials in Humanist manuscripts with a wide variety of antique motifs, cornucopiae, vases, precious stones, jewels, coins and cameos, as well as classical mythological figures such as satyrs and centaurs (*nos. 167, 174, see also fig. 43, fig. 44, and nos. 100, 101, and 102*). An emphasis in all the arts of the Quattrocento on three dimensional illusionism and on *trompe-l'oeil* painting was put to use by the illuminators both to enrich their pages and for special effects in which they played off the two-dimensional space of the flat page against a three-dimensional illusion, either showing objects as if projecting above or out of the page, or playing with a deeper space illusionistically shown

as if extending behind it. Thus they painted frontispieces in which the text seems to be written on a placard attached by ropes to a building, or looks as if it has been written on some piece of parchment so ancient that it is torn and full of holes *(nos. 172, 174)*. They did the same with their initials, painting them as if they were three-dimensional objects which putti or satyrs could actually carry about or climb on to or through.

Printing was bound to replace the manuscript book eventually, but why and how this happened is too complex a question to discuss here.[8] Two things should be emphasized, however. First, in the initial stages there were many overlaps with the earlier hand-produced book, not only in decoration inserted by hand as already mentioned, but in *mise-en-page* and general design. It becomes clear how similar to manuscripts the three books in this section look, all printed on vellum and richly illuminated by hand *(nos. 172, 173, 174)*. Venice became the main centre of the new technology in Italy with the largest number of new editions and the longest print runs. For a time in the 1470s and 1480s the success of the Venetian printers opened up increased opportunities for the artists, even as the scribes were put out of business. Once print-

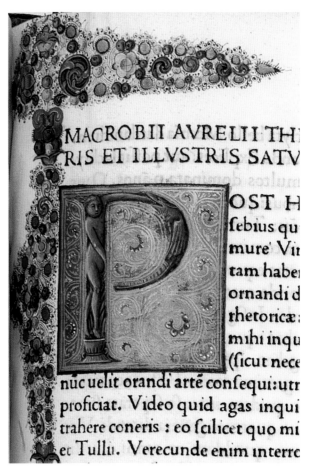

Fig. 42. Figural initial. Cambridge, Trinity College, VI.18.52, book V, detail

ers had found a way to illustrate their books with woodcuts, the artists too were threatened, though a few, including the so-called 'Pico Master' *(no. 173)* survived by providing designs for woodcut illustrations and frontispieces. A second point to be emphasized is that certain commissions, and some whole classes of books, for example the state documents of the Republic of Venice, continued to be executed in whole or in part by hand. An example of an important commission, and perhaps also a text which might not have had a sufficiently large market for a print-run, is the Aristoxenos, a Greek text copied in Rome for presentation to Francis I of France, *c.*1540 *(no. 171)*.

From an early period Humanism impacted on the rest of Europe. Poggio himself was in England from 1419–1423 as secretary to Cardinal Beaufort. Duke Humphrey of Gloucester (d.1447), brother of King Henry V, was in touch with the Humanist Pier Candido Decembrio in Milan and gave manuscripts to the library of Oxford University, now the Bodleian Library. He had intended to bequeath the remainder of his library to Oxford, but his nephew, Henry VI, appropriated them for his new foundation in Cambridge, King's College. Very few of his books have survived, but his example was soon followed by other fifteenth-century English Humanists, mainly churchmen. These patrons went to Italy either to study or on church and diplomatic business. They took the opportunity while there to buy humanistic manuscripts and some of the most important collectors bequeathed them to their college libraries, most notably William Gray (d.1478), Bishop of Ely, to Balliol College, Oxford, and Robert Flemmyng (d.1483), Dean of Lincoln Cathedral, to Lincoln College, Oxford.[9] Later acquisitions built on these riches.

Fig. 43. Jewelled
decoration.
Cambridge, Trinity
College, VI.18.52,
book III, detail

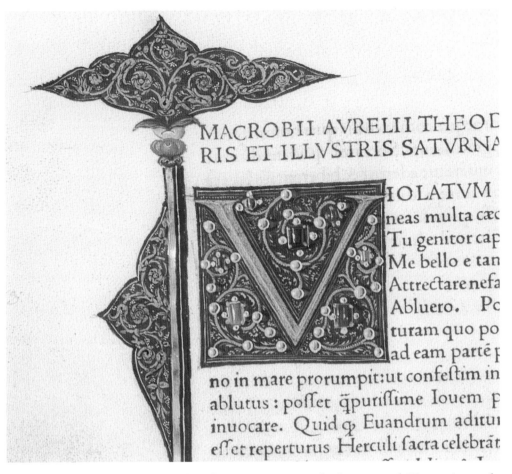

Cambridge University was less fortunate in its early donors and Humanist studies were only to become highly important there from the end of the fifteenth
century onwards (*see Collectors and Collecting in Cambridge, pp.17–21* and Introduction
to Section 8). Nevertheless, later acquisitions have enriched the holdings of the
Cambridge University Library, the Fitzwilliam Museum, and the Colleges with
outstanding examples of classical learning, such as Erasmus's Greek-Latin autograph *(no. 170)*. Manuscripts written by two of the greatest scribes of the period,
Piero Strozzi of Florence *(no. 161)* and Bartolomeo Sanvito of Padua *(no. 166)* are
included in the exhibition. Another important scribe to sign his work is Antonio
Toffio who worked in Rome for Pope Paul II *(no. 165)*. Some of the great
Renaissance patrons on either side of the Alps are represented in this and other
sections of the exhibition: Popes Pius II *(no. 163)* and Leo X *(no. 64)*, Cardinals
Giovanni d'Aragona *(no. 164)* and Albrecht of Brandenburg *(no. 97)*, Archbishop
Alessandro Carafa of Naples *(no. 48)* and Abbot Robert de Clercq *(no. 57)*, Bernardo
Bembo *(no. 166)*, the Medici *(no. 101)*, the Strozzi *(no. 100)*, Louis XI of France
(no. 161), and Francis I of France *(no. 171)*. Though many of the artists remain anony-
mous those whose names are known through signed or documented works include
Domenico di Niccolò Pollini *(no. 159)*, Francesco d'Antonio del Cherico of
Florence *(no. 161)*, Gioachino de Gigantibus *(no. 163)*, Niccolò Polani *(no. 165)*,
Benedetto Bordone of Venice *(no. 172)*, Cristoforo Majorana *(no. 100)*, Gherardo di
Giovanni del Fora *(no. 101)*, and Attavante degli Attavanti *(nos. 64, 104)*.

Among the anonymous artists is the prolific 'Master of Ippolita Sforza', working

331

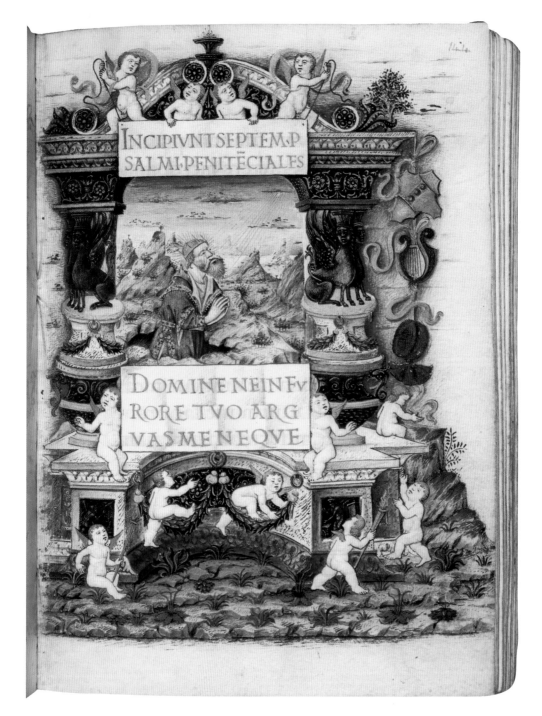

Fig. 42.
Architectural
frontispiece with
King David.
Fitzwilliam
Museum, MS 153,
fol. 144

in Milan from the 1430s to the 1460s *(no. 160)*. The text he was set to illuminate in 1443, Suetonius' Lives of the Roman Emperors, is eminently humanistic, but his style continues to be a version of the courtly International Gothic Style. Artists in other parts of Italy react against this style's emphasis on elegance of line in the drapery forms, its idealized refinement of the human figure, and its particular range of harmonious colour. By the 1430s this was a style of the past. Nevertheless artists such as, Belbello da Pavia, the Master of the Bologna Breviary, and the 'Master of the Vitae Imperatorum' continued to practise it, ignoring the changes in other parts of Italy. They used it indiscriminately for classical and Christian religious texts, though they mainly worked on the latter. Their illumination lacks almost totally the antiquarian vocabulary developed by Florentine or Paduan artists and this continues to be true of much Lombard illumination even into the 1470s. The 'Ippolita Master' is particularly close to the 'Vitae Master' and both illuminators use a particular type of abstracted foliage initial in non-Christian texts, but it seems quite independent of the white-vine used in the rest of Italy and whatever its origins it is not a historicising copying of the initials of Romanesque manuscripts illuminated in Lombardy.

The work of these Lombard illuminators serves to draw attention to the fact that there were many different styles of illumination in Italy at this time. The illuminators were not necessarily consistent in their use of particular styles of decoration for particular types of text, religious or secular. They were also in close contact with the styles practised in the monumental arts in their own geographic areas. For illuminators in the North Mantegna was the crucial influence. Paduan antiquarianism was an essential ingredient of his style and as several important illuminators were trained, as was Mantegna, in the workshop of Squarcione in Padua, their stylistic kinship is hardly surprising. In Tuscany illuminators were similarly closely aware of what contemporary painters and sculptors were doing. Finally it must also not be forgotten that illuminators, like other artists, frequently travelled in search of work, thus further spreading stylistic innovations.

Though the representation in this section of types of humanistic decoration in Italian manuscripts is far from complete, it may be supplemented with examples from other sections. From the exhibition taken as a whole the visitor will get a good sense of just how high the standards of book production were in Italy in the fifteenth century. The books are distinguished by their generous size, their fine parchment, wide margins (when they have not been later cut down), clear, regular script, often reaching very high standards of penmanship, and lastly by sophisticated illumination which is remarkably varied in style, and is also technically accomplished in its use of gold and varied pigments. The original bindings, when preserved, complete the sense of a professionally organized and highly sophisticated craft practised to the highest standards of quality. When the books are displayed open, the way script and decoration balance and complement one another is a constant aesthetic pleasure to the eye.

REFERENCES

1   This is, obviously, an oversimplified account of a complex history. For an introduction with further bibliography see Brown 1990. For the handwriting of the early Humanists see de la Mare 1973; for the earliest humanistic script in Florence, see de la Mare 1977; and for Florentine scribes more generally de la Mare 1985. For a summary on the development of scripts, *(see The Making of a Medieval Manuscript, pp.23–36)*.

2   Dempsey 2001.

3   They occur commonly in fourteenth-century Neapolitan manuscripts of the so-called Orimina group, and in the work of some Bolognese artists, Zebo da Firenze for example.

4   The sheer amount of documentation in the Florentine archives is impressive. See D'Ancona 1962b.

5   For Florentine illumination see Garzelli 1985. The older general accounts in Salmi 1954 and Alexander 1977 should be supplemented by the following important exhibition catalogues: Paris 1984a, London and New York 1994–1995, Vatican City 1995, and Florence 1997 for illumination throughout the peninsula; for regional schools, see Milan 1958, Ferrara 1998, Padua 1999, Naples and Valencia 1998.

6   Alexander 1988.

7   Smith 2000.

8   Armstrong's discussion in London and New York 1994–1995 is an up-to-date account of the illumination of printed books in Italy with recent bibliography. The literature on printers and printing in Italy is, of course, vast. See also Armstrong 2003a.

9   For Humanism in England see Oxford 1970.

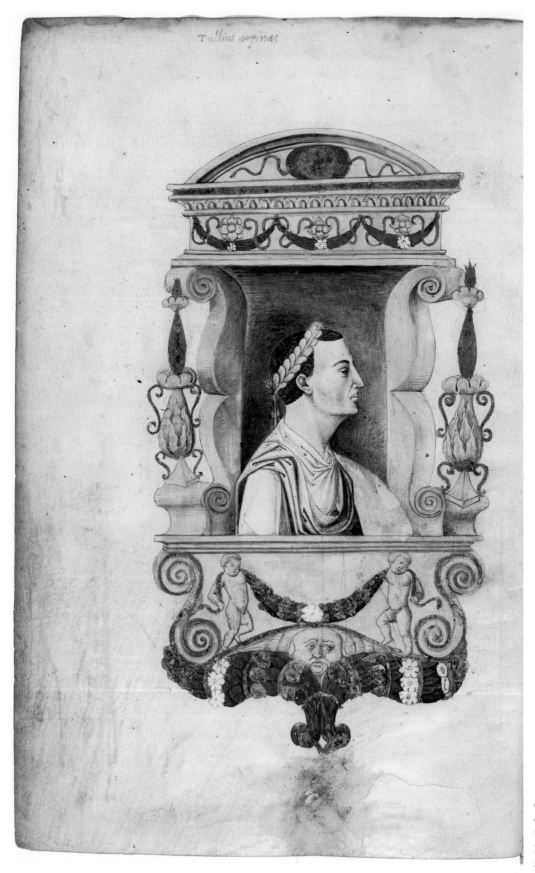

Cicero.
Cambridge
University
Library, MS Add.
8442, fol. 2v

159

Marcus Tullius Cicero, *De officiis*

In Latin
Italy, Florence, *c.*1430
ARTIST: Giovanni di Antonio Varnucci (1416–1457)
SCRIBE: Domenico di Niccolò Pollini (1395–1473)

Parchment, ii (20th c.) + 63 + ii (20th c.) fols., 281 × 183 mm, text 194 × 108 mm, 32 long lines, ruled in hard point
SCRIPT: Humanistic minuscule
BINDING: alum tawed pigskin over wooden boards by Rivière and Son, 20th c.

Cambridge University Library, MS Add. 8442

CICERO, more than any other Roman author, became the model for the humanistic revival of classical Latin grammar, rhetoric, philosophy, and ethics. In Florence, he enjoyed an even greater popularity, as some of his writings, notably *De officiis*, lent support to Coluccio Salutati's republican ideology. As well as producing de luxe manuscripts for wealthy patrons, many Renaissance scribes made fair copies for their own use. One of them was the Florentine scribe Domenico di Niccolò Pollini (1395–1473) to whom Sydney Cockerell and Albinia de la Mare attributed this Cicero. That he made good use of the volume is revealed by the three layers of annotations. First, he copied the brief marginal subject headings, or *notabilia*, simultaneously with the main text, in the same black ink. Corrections and variant readings penned in pale ink indicate that he collated his copy with another one. While reading, he added longer, more discursive comments with a smaller, finely cut quill. These are closely related to another manuscript, containing Cicero's *Tusculanae disputaiones* and *De finibus*, signed by Niccolò Pollini, and dated 1431 (New Haven, Yale University, Beinecke Library, Marston MS 184; Shailor 1992, III, 342–44, pl. 16). Almost identical in size, it echoes the page layout and scribal techniques of the Cambridge Cicero, down to the unusually long horizontal catchwords positioned right in the centre of the lower margin. The two manuscripts may have been intended as a set.

The text decoration in the Yale and Cambridge volumes, white vine scrolls on thin, earthy green, peach, and blue background, is also identical. Barbara Shailor has suggested that it was added at a later stage in the Yale manuscript and Albinia de la Mare attributed it to the young Giovanni Varnucci. The Cambridge Cicero lends strong support to this attribution. Its pale colour scheme matches that of the Yale volume. It may have been added

after Pollini had used the manuscript for some time and probably for presentation to the person whose arms have been fully erased from the medallion beneath Cicero's portrait. Yet, it seems unlikely that the text and the illustration are separated by more than a decade. The somewhat clumsy application of the gold leaf is hardly the work of an accomplished illuminator. Furthermore, the robust portrait of Cicero, with its densely hatched modelling and pronounced sculptural qualities, anticipates the forceful busts Giovanni Varnucci painted in the 1440s and 1450s (Garzelli 1985, 27–29). Like his brother, Bartolomeo Varnucci (1410–1479), Giovanni was strongly influenced by contemporary Florentine sculpture, notably by Donatello's low reliefs. Framed in a marble niche beneath an architectural canopy, Cicero's image appears as if in relief.

The importance of the frontispiece lies less in its technical execution and the conventions of contemporary portraiture than in the novelty of its concept. It depicts an ancient bust of the type that would have been familiar to Varnucci's contemporaries. The passion among antiquarians for classical sculpture, coins, and cameos inspired the vocabulary of the *all'antica* style developed by the visual arts from the 1450s onwards. The Cambridge Cicero is one of its earliest manifestations. Well into the 1470s, Cicero's works were illustrated with the conventional author portrait (Lazzi 2000). Even when the settings included allusions to Antiquity, such as classical arches, niches, pedestals, or sculptures, Cicero himself was shown in the attire and with the attributes of a fifteenth-century academic, as the symbolic personification of Renaissance rhetoric and philosophy. Idealized as the Cambridge portrait may seem, it nevertheless represents the classical Cicero in the same antiquarian spirit in which the manuscript reconstructs his text.

PROVENANCE: ownership inscriptions 'Christophorus Fabertinus Gallus' (15th c., fol. 2), 'In Casa del ?Retiereng' (15th c., fol. 62); gift from Fran. Daniel to Aloisius Cassano Serra (18th c., fol. 1v); Arnold Mettler; purchased at his sale, Sotheby's, London, 26–27 April 1937, lot 267, by Robinson for £52; Sir Geoffrey Keynes (1887–1982); purchased by the Library in 1982.

LITERATURE: Cockerell 1951, 13; Keynes 1964, 3, MS 10, pl. II; de la Mare 1985, 493.

SP

160

Suetonius, *Vitae duodecim Caesarum*

In Latin
Italy, Milan, 1443
ARTISTS: Master of Ippolita Sforza (act. *c*.1430–*c*.1470)
and assistant
SCRIBE: Milano Borro (act. *c*.1430–*c*.1450)

Parchment, ii (paper, 19th c.) + 191 + ii (paper, 19th c.) fols.
210 × 148 mm, text 125 × 75 mm, 29 long lines ruled in faint
brown ink

SCRIPT: Humanistic minuscule

BINDING: gold-tooled dark blue morocco over wooden boards,
by Zaehnsdorf, 19th c.

Fitzwilliam Museum, MS McClean 162

THE INTEREST in Roman history at the Visconti court is well attested by this manuscript, signed and dated in 1443 by the Milanese scribe Milano Borro. As the work of Suetonius (69–140), Hadrian's secretary who boasted first-hand knowledge of the imperial court, the *Lives of the Caesars* would have had a special appeal to the manuscript's original owner, Gian Matteo Bottigella of Pavia. Appointed superintendent of ecclesiastical benefices in the duchy of Milan in 1443 when this manuscript was made, he became secretary of Filippo Maria Visconti in 1444 and secret councillor of Gian Galeazzo Sforza in 1477. His arms, motto *Sic necesse est* ('As necessary'), device (the compasses), and initials dominate the border of the *incipit* page (fol. 1). The compasses and motto also shape the opening initial A. The Christ monogram with a ducal coronet in the upper border and the knotted cloth above Bottigella's crest are the devices of Filippo Maria Visconti often used in manuscripts made for his courtiers.

The miniature displayed here shows Emperor Vespasian in full armour. The sword evokes his military triumphs, while the model of Rome refers to his ambitious building campaigns and renovation of the city, praised by Suetonius (fol. 169v). Originally, each Life was introduced by a foliage initial and a facing miniature of the relevant Emperor. Of the twelve portraits only three survive: Otto (fol. 153), Vespasian (fol. 164v), and Domitian (fol. 178v). The rest can be reconstructed from another copy of Suetonius also made for a Visconti courtier (Princeton University Library, Kane MS 44). His initials I and O are surrounded by the same Visconti devices as in the Cambridge Suetonius. They appear, as Suzanne Reynolds pointed out (in correspondence), in a contemporary Livy (Holkham Hall, MS 345) and await identification. The Princeton Suetonius was copied by Milano Borro in 1433 and preserves all twelve portraits painted by the Master of the Vitae Imperatorum, the leading artist at the Visconti court *c*.1430–*c*.1450 *(see no. 55)*. He was named after another copy of Suetonius (Paris, Bibliothèque nationale de France, MS ital. 131), a vernacular translation of the Latin text he illuminated for Filippo Maria Visconti

Incipit page with arms and devices of Gian Matteo Bottigella. Fitzwilliam Museum, MS McClean 162, fol. 1

in 1431. The large group of manuscripts first attributed to the Master of the Vitae Imperatorum (Toesca 1912, 528–32) continues to be reshaped to include numerous illuminators working in his idiom and often collaborating on copies of the same text made for the Dukes' courtiers (Stones 1969; Toesca 1969; Mariani Canova 1978; Cappugi 1985; Stefani 1985; Melograni 1990; Melograni 1993; Manfredi and Melograni 1996; Heid-Guillaume and Ritz 1998, 30–43). The Cambridge Suetonius, invariably attributed until now to the Master of the Vitae Imperatorum, is best understood in this context.

While inspired by the Princeton miniatures, the Cambridge portraits are by an assistant of the Master of the Vitae Imperatorum. His heavy and static figures, executed in thin washes, contrast with the diminutive forms and vivid painterly technique of the opening page in the Cambridge Suetonius. Its layout is based on a design the Master of the Vitae Imperatorum used in the Princeton Suetonius and in the Holkham Hall Livy, maintaining a balance of scale between text and decoration. The artist of the Cambridge Suetonius overwhelmed the text with exuberant borders. The closest parallels are three other manuscripts made for Gian Matteo Bottigella (Budapest, National Museum, MS 161; Paris, Bibliothèque nationale de France, MS nouv. acq. lat. 504; Philadelphia, Free Library, Lewis MS 54; the last two were copied by Milano Borro). The floral ornament, its layout, and the crest with the female hybrid holding the compasses and motto are identical in all four manuscripts. The triangular crowns of the trees growing on the marginal islands, the rounded faces with full cheeks and pouting lips, the segmented treatment of the putti's grey flesh, and the delicately modelled, fluttering robes draw on the vocabulary of the Master of the Vitae Imperatorum. Yet, they are the salient features of his most accomplished follower, the Master of Ippolita Sforza. Named after the manuscripts Ippolita brought to Naples in 1465 when she married Alfonso, Duke of Calabria, this artist occupied the same prestigious position in the Sforza court during the third quarter of the fifteenth century that his Master enjoyed under the Visconti (Toscano 1996–1997; Naples and Valencia 1998, 483–89). The Cambridge Suetonius predates the earliest manuscripts attributed to the Master of Ippolita Sforza as an independent artist, a Virgil of 1450 and a Macrobius of c.1455, which reveals the development of the Suetonius marginalia (Valencia, Biblioteca Universitaria, MS 768–766; El Escorial, Monasterio de San Lorenzo de El Escorial, Biblioteca, MS q.I.1; Toscano 1996–1997; Naples and Valencia 1998, no. 49 and 4). The Cambridge manuscript shows him as the main artist and preserves his earliest known use of an initial formed of the owner's motto and

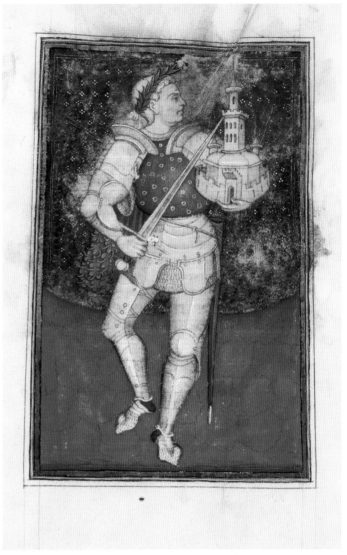

Emperor Vespasian. Fitzwilliam Museum, MS McClean 162, fol. 164v, detail

devices, another feature he inherited from his Master and developed to its full potential.

PROVENANCE: Gian Matteo Bottigella (doc. 1443–1479); Leo Olschki; purchased from him by Frank McClean in 1892 and bequeathed to the Museum in 1904.

EXHIBITED: Cambridge 1966, no. 86.

LITERATURE: James 1912a, 312–13; Toesca 1930, 111; Morison 1952, 2; Pellegrin 1955, 233; Stones 1969, 11; D'Ancona 1970, 14, 18, 130; Stefani 1985, 876; Robinson 1988, no. 229, pl. 241 Melograni 1990, 306.

SP

337

161

Donato Acciaiuoli, *Vita Caroli Magni*

In Latin
Italy, Florence, 1461
ARTISTS: Francesco di Antonio del Chierico
(act. *c*.1452 – d.1484) and assistant
SCRIBE: Messer Piero di Benedetto Strozzi
(1416–*c*.1492)

Parchment, vi + 26 + viii fols. 245 × 165 mm, text
155 × 80 mm, 26 long lines ruled in hard point
SCRIPT: Humanistic minuscule
BINDING: dark blue morocco, gilt and lined with pink silk, 19th c.

Fitzwilliam Museum, MS 180

ON 2 JANUARY 1462 the Florentine ambassadors presented the recently crowned Louis XI of France (1461–1483) with a de luxe copy of the *Life of Charlemagne*, a gift of considerable intellectual, artistic, symbolic,

and monetary value. Befitting its royal destination, the manuscript is a monument of the intellectual and aesthetic principles of the Italian Renaissance. Based on twelfth-century Tuscan decoration, the white vine-scroll, which surrounds the text and the royal arms of France on the *incipit* page, became the hallmark of early humanistic illumination. The frontispiece heralds another major humanistic contribution to book design, the ancestor of the modern title page. It also looks back to the dedication roundels in de luxe Carolingian manuscripts. Their imperial associations would have seemed particularly appropriate in a royal presentation copy and this is emphasized by the French arms surmounted by the crown and suspended by putti above the roundel.

The author, Donato Acciaiuoli (1428–1478), belonged to the prominent family of Florentine bankers, civil and ecclesiastical officials that served the Medici for generations. A renowned mathematician, philosopher, and Aristotelian scholar, he represented Florence at the two centres crucial for European politics at the time, the Papal Curia and the French court. He was the Medici's ambassador to Louis XI in 1461. This copy of Acciaiuoli's text was produced by Vespasiano da Bisticci (*c*.1422–1498),

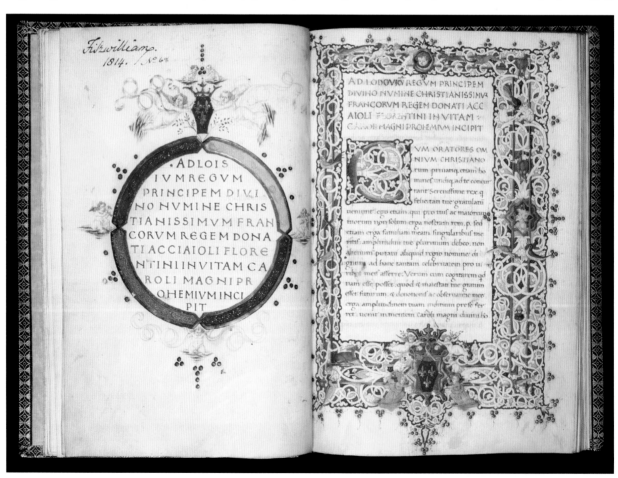

Dedication to Louis XI and *incipit* page. Fitzwilliam Museum, MS 180, fols. 1V–2

the 'prince of booksellers' who enjoyed the friendship of leading Humanists, like Donato Acciaiuoli, and the clientele of discerning collectors, including the Medici. Vespasiano described the presentation of this manuscript to Louis XI in his account of Donato's life.

Vespasiano entrusted the writing to his close friend and frequent collaborator, Messer Piero di Benedetto Strozzi, whom he called 'the most beautiful scribe of this age and the most accurate' (da Bisticci 1976, II, 426). He commissioned the decoration from Francesco di Antonio del Chierico, the favourite illuminator of the Medici. The dedication frontispiece and the decoration to the prologue are by Francesco di Antonio himself. They show him at a transitional stage in his career when the firm drawing and heavy modelling of his early work was developing into the light, dynamic, briskly sketched figures, and the mild, elusive, almost ethereal palette of his documented, post-1463 manuscripts. The opening page to the main text was illuminated by an artist who remains anonymous, but whose crisp outlines, saturated colours, firm modelling, facial features, and ornamental details follow Antonio del Chierico's early work faithfully enough to suggest a Master-apprentice relationship. This artist collaborated with del Chierico on several important commissions, most notably in two other manuscripts produced by Vespasiano da Bisticci and copied by Piero di Benedetto Strozzi: the Medici Pliny (Florence, Biblioteca Medicea Laurenziana, MS Plut. 82, 3) and Alfonso of Aragon's Livy (Florence, Biblioteca Nazionale, Banco rari 34–36). He also worked on his own, for example, in a copy of Ptolemy's *Cosmography* (Moscow, Russian State Library, MS f.68 no. 215) and in a Cicero copied by Piero Strozzi (Vienna, Österreichische Nationalbibliothek, MS 11).

The close connections of author, bookseller, scribe, and illuminators with the Medici account for the manuscript's outstanding quality and demonstrate the importance of de luxe manuscripts as subtle political tools. Few diplomatic gifts could have evoked the Humanist ideal of the learned monarch more successfully or offered the French king a more flattering statement than the Life of his glorious predecessor, written in a script and introduced by a frontispiece that recreated the finest manuscripts of the Carolingian Renaissance.

PROVENANCE: Louis XI of France (1461–1483); Auguste Chardin (no. 450 in his catalogue of 1811); acquired by Viscount Fitzwilliam in 1814; his bequest, 1816.

EXHIBITED: Cambridge 1966, no. 96.

LITERATURE: Milanesi 1865, 7, 25; Searle 1876, 11–13; James 1895a, 386; de la Mare 1965, 64; Alexander and de la Mare 1969, 40; da Bisticci 1970–1976, II, 33; Garzelli 1985, 140, fig. 403; de la Mare 1985, 530; de la Mare 1994, 91, pl. 34.

SP

162

Lactantius, *Opera*

In Latin
Italy, Rome, 1460
SCRIBE: Johannes Gobellini de Lins (doc.1457–1464)

Parchment, i (paper lined with leather, 19th c.) + 336 + i (paper lined with leather, 19th c.) fols., 337 × 223 mm, text 212 × 102 mm, 29 long lines ruled in hard point

SCRIPT: Humanistic minuscule

BINDING: blind- and gold-tooled leather over wooden boards, 19th c.

Fitzwilliam Museum, MS McClean 115

ON SATURDAY, 7 JUNE 1460 the scribe completed this manuscript and signed it 'Johannes G. de Lyns'. In another manuscript dated 1459 (Paris, Bibliothèque Sainte-Geneviève, MS CCL in-fol. 12) he gave his full name, Johannes Gobellini de Lins, and described himself as a '*librarius*' in the household of Niccolò Forteguerri of Pistoia (1419–1473), Bishop of Teano and treasurer of Pius II (1458–1464) *(see no. 163)*. It was for Niccolò that he copied the Cambridge Lactantius. Documented as papal scribe between 1461 and 1464, Johannes Gobellini de Lins worked mainly for members of the Roman Curia (Ruysschaert 1968). Niccolò Forteguerri had befriended the future pope and distinguished Humanist Enea Silvio Piccolomini during his student years in Siena. When Piccolomini became Cardinal in 1456, he invited Niccolò to join him in Rome. As Bishop of Teano, Forteguerri carried out diplomatic missions for the new Pope at the courts of Naples and Urbino, and co-ordinated Pius II's military campaign against the Ottoman Turks. The red hat over Forteguerri's arms on fol. 2 in the Cambridge manuscript confirms that he received it in 1460 when Pius II made him Cardinal. The arms on fol. 4v have been overpainted.

While the manuscript reveals a lot about the patron and the scribe, it remains silent on the identity of the artist. M.R. James remarked on the German flavour of the illumination and this is hardly surprising. Pius II, who had been Frederick III's imperial poet and diplomat between 1442 and 1455, attracted an international team of scholars, scribes, and artists to Rome *(see no. 163)*. Johannes Gobellini de Lins, who came from the area around Bonn, may have recommended a compatriot for the project. Whatever his origin and training, the illuminator blended artistic traditions from both sides of the Alps. Lactantius has the facial features of a Northerner and the *studiolo* of an Italian scholar. The putti, ubiquitous in humanistic manuscripts, are in the company of Bosch-

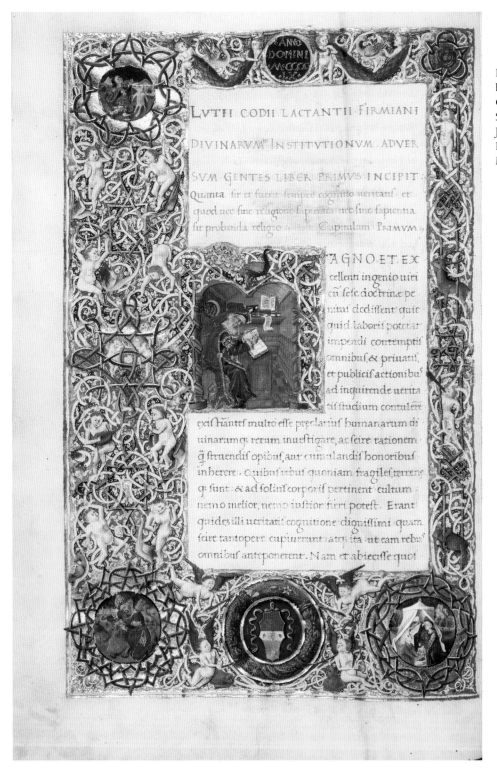

Lactantius in his study, border medallions with Gideon with the Fleece, Samson with the Lion, and Judith with Holofernes. Fitzwilliam Musuem, MS McClean 115, fol. 4v

inspired hybrids and grotesques. The Italian white-vine scroll borders are enlivened by medallions, in which Gideon kneels beside the fleece, Samson defeats the lion, and Judith has just beheaded Holofernes. They reflect a passion for biblical typology and pictorial narrative best paralleled in the block book editions of the *Biblia Pauperum* and the *Speculum Humanae Salvationis*, which inspired the border scenes in some devotional manuscripts north of the Alps in the following decade *(see no. 92)*. Yet, their relationship with Lactantius' text remains as elusive as the artist himself.

PROVENANCE: Niccolò Forteguerri (1419–1473); Ulrico Hoepli; purchased from him by Frank McClean and bequeathed to the Museum in 1904.

EXHIBITED: Cambridge 1966. no. 94.

LITERATURE: James 1912a, 251–53, pls. LXXIII, LXXIV; Ruysschaert 1968, 255–56; Robinson 1988, no. 223, pl. 281.

SP

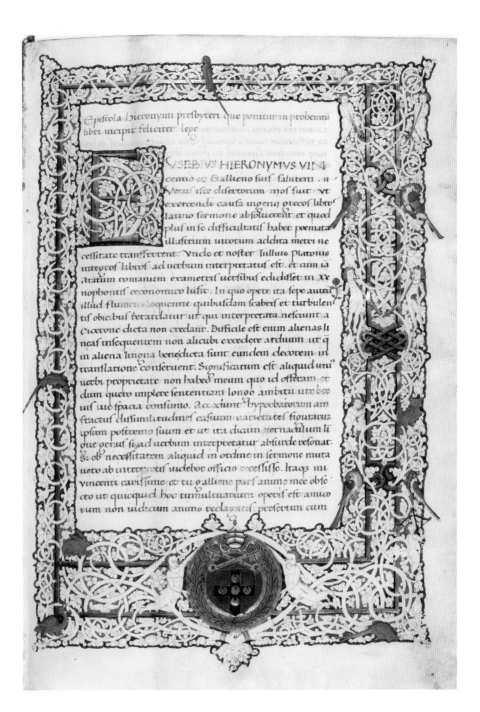

163

Eusebius of Caesarea, *Chronica*

In Latin, translated by St Jerome
Italy, Rome, 1460–1464
ARTIST: Gioacchino di Giovanni de Gigantibus
(doc.1460–1481)

Parchment, i + 150 + i fols. 333 × 230 mm, text 173 × 127 mm,
28–32 lines ruled in hard point

SCRIPT: Humanistic minuscule

BINDING: marbled paper over pasteboards, 19th c.

Cambridge University Library, MS Mm.3.1

COMPOSED BY EUSEBIUS, Bishop of Caesarea
(d. *c.*340), in the early fourth century, this comparative chronology of biblical history and contemporary
events in Egypt, Rome and other parts of the ancient
world was translated by the end of the century from
Greek into Latin by St Jerome. Like other patristic texts,
the *Chronicle* was particularly popular with Renaissance
ecclesiastical patrons. Pietro Donato, the bibliophile
Bishop of Padua (1428–1448), brought a Carolingian
copy to Padua in the 1430s (Oxford, Merton College,
MS 315; London and New York 1992, no. 7). Its text
and layout were copied, in various recensions, for humanistic prelates, including Donato's successor in Padua,
Fantino Dandolo (1450–1459), and Cardinal Bessarion
(1439–1472). The arms in the lower border of the

Cambridge manuscript reveal that this copy was made for Pope Pius II (r.1458–1464).

Although Humanists had served the Roman Curia since the time of Poggio Bracciolini, Enea Silvio Piccolomini was the first true Humanist on St Peter's throne (Naville 1984). Educated in Siena and Florence, he pressed his intellectual achievements and worldly passions into the service of leading ecclesiastical and secular patrons. As secretary to Cardinal Albergati and the antipope Felix V in the 1430s, and as imperial poet and diplomat of Frederick III between 1442 and 1455, Piccolomini was exposed to the unstable political climate in Europe and the Ottoman invasion in the East, both problems that would dominate his pontificate. When Constantinople fell to Mehmet II in 1453, Enea Silvio famously wrote from Frederick III's court in Graz: '…of the two lights of Christendom, one has been extinguished'. This passion for the union of Roman and Greek cultural heritage, both ancient and Christian, is evident in his interest in this text composed and translated by two distinguished Fathers of the early Greek and Latin Churches.

The time spent at Frederick III's court may also account for the international team of scribes and artists that Enea Silvio Piccolomini attracted to Rome during his pontificate. One of them was the Bavarian calligrapher and illuminator Gioacchino de Gigantibus from Reesen near Rotenburg (Ruysschaert 1968, 267–80; Naples 1997, 24, 32; Naples and Valencia 1998, 437–40). First documented in 1460 in Siena, Piccolomini's home town, for the next decade Gioacchino de Gigantibus worked both there and in Rome, in the bottega of Jacopo da Fabriano (act.1452–1477), another illuminator appreciated by Pius II and represented in Cambridge collections (Fitzwilliam Museum, MS 172). Between 1471 and 1480 Gioacchino de Gigantibus, as royal 'scriptor' and 'miniador', produced his most ambitious manuscripts for the Aragonese court at Naples, before returning to papal service in 1481.

The illumination of the Cambridge Eusebius is among Gioacchino's finest early works. The putti, with their large foreheads, wig-style hair, coral beads, and long trumpets are his hallmark. The burnished gold initial and frame, entwined in white vine scroll, set against blue, green and pink background, and inhabited by birds, hares, and putti, were the staples of early humanistic decoration. Gioacchino remained faithful to them throughout his career, although the Veneto-Paduan *all'antica* style was reaching Rome by the early 1470s and Naples by the early 1480s. If he chose to ignore these in his later works, in the early 1460s he had not yet seen the Mantegnesque illumination and polychrome textual ornaments of the Eusebius copies made in Padua in the 1450s. A Paduan copy reached Rome

with Bartolomeo Sanvito around 1464–1465 (London and New York 1992, no. 7; de la Mare 1999, 500; *see no. 165 and 166*). By then Gioacchino had completed the Cambridge volume and its patron, Pius II, was dead.

PROVENANCE: Pope Pius II (r. 1458–1464); John Moore, bishop of Ely (1707–1714); presented to the Library by George I in 1715.

LITERATURE: University Library 1856–1867, IV, 173; London and New York 1992, 125.

SP

164

Bonaventure, *Super IV Sententiarum*

In Latin
Italy, Florence and Naples, 1484
ARTIST: Matteo Felice (act. *c.*1455 – *c.*1495)

Parchment, 345 fols. (contemporary red ink foliation i–vi, 1–338, vii), 338 × 245 mm, 228 × 147 mm, 2 cols., 48 lines ruled in pale black ink

SCRIPT: Gothic bookhand (textualis)

BINDING: gold-tooled brown leather over pasteboards; two pairs of holes left from lost fastenings on fore-edge, 17th c.

Cambridge University Library, MS Gg.3.22

THIS VOLUME displays the salient features that marked scholastic works throughout the Renaissance period. It contains Bonaventure's commentary on Peter Lombard's *Sentences* – both key texts of scholastic theology – written in a formal Gothic script and set out in two columns. It was copied in Florence in 1484, as the colophon on fol. 338v informs us, by a scribe who specialized in scholastic texts. He produced many of them for Federico da Montefeltro, including another copy of Bonaventure on Lombard's *Sentences* (Vatican City, Biblioteca Apostolica Vaticana, MS Urb. lat. 144; de la Mare 1985, App. I, no. 99). The Cambridge copy was made for Giovanni of Aragon (1456–1485), the fourth child of King Ferrante I of Naples. Giovanni's early death at the age of twenty-nine did not prevent him from enjoying a remarkable career and amassing an impressive library. His ecclesiastical appointments began in 1461, when he was only nine, and culminated in 1477 when he received the Cardinal's hat from Sixtus IV. This manuscript was presented to him when he was at the height of his power. In August 1484 he returned from a diplomatic mission to Hungary, where his sister Beatrice ruled as Matthias Corvinus' queen, and Innocent VIII, who had just succeeded Sixtus IV, appointed him papal

Bonaventure writing in his study, border with Cardinal Giovanni of Aragon's arms. Cambridge University Library, MS Gg.3.22, fol. 1

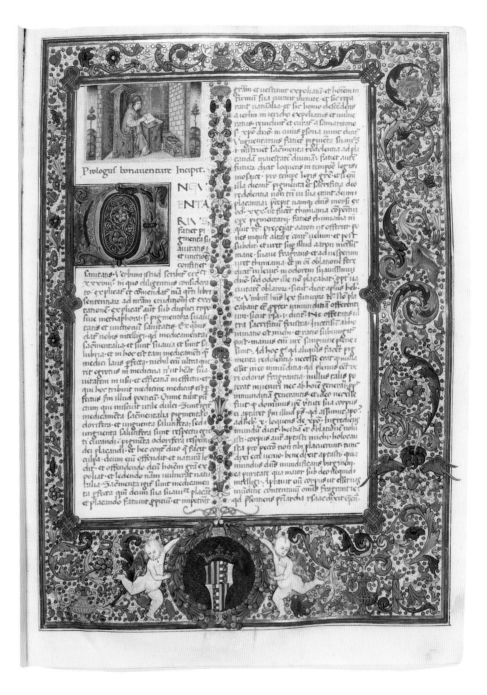

legate to Bologna, before entrusting him, later that year, with the diocese of Esztergom (Gran).

Cardinal Giovanni must have commissioned a set of Bonaventure's work, since the copy of his commentary on the second book of Lombard's *Sentences* is now Cambridge University Library, MS Gg.3.23 (de la Mare 1984, 293; Haffner 1997, no. 37, 323–25). It shares the main features of MS Gg.3.22: two columns of text written in Gothic script on 47 lines, identical ruling frame, size of text block, red running headings and foliation by the original scribe. Yet, it was copied by a different Florentine scribe and was probably illuminated in

Florence. The colour scheme and floral types of its border are typical of Florentine illumination. They have no parallels in contemporary Neapolitan manuscripts, which contain either the old-fashioned white vine scrolls, or the innovative Veneto-Paduan *all'antica* frontispieces, or the Ferrarese-Neapolitan floral borders seen in the Bonaventure volume displayed here. Giovanni had a strong preference for Florentine scribes. Foremost among them was Antonio Sinibaldi (1443 – d. before 1528), who was in Naples between 1477 and 1480 at Giovanni's invitation, and continued to copy manuscripts for the Cardinal from Florence, notably a Quintilian now at the

Fitzwilliam Museum (MS McClean 160; de la Mare 1984, 260–61, 277; *fig. 11*). Yet, his de luxe manuscripts were illuminated either by Gaspare da Padova in Rome (Naples and Valencia 1998, 453–64) or by the leading Neapolitan artists, Cristoforo Majorana *(see nos. 100, 103)* and Matteo Felice *(see no. 99)*. The illumination of MS Gg.3.22 was attributed to the latter (de la Mare 1984, 293).

The combination of floral borders with gold and navy bars, and the prominent knotwork in the centre and corners are ubiquitous in Matteo Felice's manuscripts *(see no. 99)* The putti's facial types in the Cambridge volume characterize Felice's late period, when the subtle modelling in his works of the 1460s and 1470s gave way to the firm, somewhat dry outlines found in a set of Plato's works he illuminated for King Ferrante in 1491–1493 and in incunables decorated for Aragonese patrons (British Library, Harley MSS 3481–3482; Toscano 1995; Naples and Valencia 1998, 289–98). The depiction of Plato in his study in Harley MS 3482, fol. 4, is related to the Cambridge miniature of Bonaventure. The composition derives from one of Felice's earliest and most inventive works, a Seneca illuminated for Alfonso the Magnanimous around 1455 (Paris, Bibliothèque nationale de France, MS lat. 17842, fol. 1; Toscano 1995, figs. 2, 3).

Giovanni may have commissioned the Cambridge set as early as 1482 when Bonaventure was canonized by Sixtus IV. Bonaventure's halo in the Cambridge miniature signals his saintly status and the Cardinal's hat is a flattering reference to Giovanni's patronage. Originally, Giovanni's own red hat was depicted above the Aragonese arms in the lower border, but was later painted over with the royal crown as in the other manuscripts, which passed upon his death to the Royal Library. The Cambridge volumes were among the 138 manuscripts Cardinal Georges I d'Amboise (d.1516) bought from King Federico III of Naples between 1502 and 1504. They are no. 30 (MS Gg.3.23) and no. 32 (MS Gg.3.22) in his inventory of 1508 (Delisle 1868–1881, I, 235; Mazzatinti 1897, CXXII)

PROVENANCE: Cardinal Giovanni of Aragon (1456–1485); Royal Library of Naples; Cardinal Georges d'Amboise (d.1516); John Moore, Bishop of Ely (1707–1714); presented to the Library by George I in 1715.

LITERATURE: University Library 1856–1867, III, 68; de la Mare 1984, 293; de la Mare 1985, 466–7, 550, App. I, no. 99 and Addenda, 599; Robinson 1988, no. 39, pl. 327; Haffner 1997, no. 36, 20–23, fig. 42.

SP

165

Macrobius, *Convivia Saturnalia*

In Latin
Italy, Rome, 1466
ARTIST: Niccolò Polani (doc.1459–1471)
SCRIBE: Antonio Tophio (act. *c.*1460–*c.*1470)

Parchment, 180 fols, 319 × 224 mm, text 197–203 × 90–113 mm, 29 long lines, ruled in hard point
SCRIPT: Humanistic minuscule
BINDING: red morocco over wooden boards, blind-tooled frame and central panel of interlaced ropework; sewn on six double tawed skin sewing supports, endbands at head and tail, four brass catchplates and traces of four velvet straps; fastening from front to back, gilt and gauffered edges, late 15th c.

Cambridge University Library, MS Add. 4095

THIS MANUSCRIPT preserves the most important work of the fifth-century Neoplatonic philosopher Macrobius (fl. 430). As an evaluation of Virgil's poetry and religious beliefs, it was of particular interest to Renaissance scholars. The Cambridge volume formed a magnificent set, together with a copy of *In Somnium Scipionis*, Macrobius' commentary on Cicero's *Dream of Scipio*, now in the Vatican (MS Ottob. lat. 1137; Barker-Benfield 1975; Barker-Benfield 1983, 223). The colophon on fol. 180v records that the Cambridge volume was completed in Rome in April 1466 by Antonio Tophio, one of the most prominent scribes in the household of Pope Paul II (Fairbank 1965; Ruysschaert 1968; Fairbank 1970; Fairbank 1971; Ruysschaert 1986). It shows Tophio emulating the style of the celebrated Bartolomeo Sanvito *(see no. 166)* with whom he collaborated in the Vatican volume. The relationship between these two masters of the humanistic pen has provoked continuous discussions. Our understanding was greatly advanced by the work of the late Albinia de la Mare who pointed out that Tophio developed his style through a systematic imitation of Sanvito's hand; that before establishing himself in Rome in 1469, Sanvito visited in 1464/5; and that he collaborated with Tophio on the Macrobius set, drawing the image and completing the text on fol. 33 of the Vatican volume (de la Mare 1984; de la Mare 1999, 499).

The Cambridge volume shows Tophio mastering Sanvito's minuscule almost beyond recognition and adopting the colourful epigraphic capitals for which Sanvito was famous. The illustration of the *incipit* page is unusually rich and highly individual. The opulent floral ornament, with its distinctive colour scheme of crimson, purple, gold, and silver, engulfs the faceted initial and the borders filled with classical motifs, cameos, birds, animals, and landscape medallions. Similar alternating lines of gold, purple, red, and green epigraphic capitals, faceted initials, and floral backgrounds mark the remaining text divisions (fols. 3, 4, 11, 57v, 69, 92, 99, 128v, 147v); fol. 92 includes two medallions with views of the bridge and Castle of Sant' Angelo. Jonathan Alexander recognized the artist's hand in two contemporary manuscripts, Tophio's copy of Aulus Gellius (London, British Library, Burney MS 175) and a Caesar copied by Sanvito (Milan, Biblioteca Ambrosiana, MS A. 243 inf.; Alexander 1970b, 30, 38). The arms in both have been overpainted. The original shield in the Am-

brosiana Caesar, just barely visible and still unidentified, may have been identical with that in the Cambridge Macrobius, before it was painted over with the present arms thought to be those of the Contarini family of Venice. The artist responsible for all three manuscripts was Niccolò Polani, a priest in the households of Pius II and Paul II (Ruysschaert 1968; Ruysschaert 1973; Piacentini 1983, 376–77, 385; de la Mare 1999, 499). His only known signed manuscript is a copy of Augustine's *The City of God* (Paris, Bibliothèque Sainte-Geneviève, MS CCL in-fol. 12), copied in 1459 for Niccolò Forteguerri by Johannes Gobelini de Lins *(see no. 162)*.

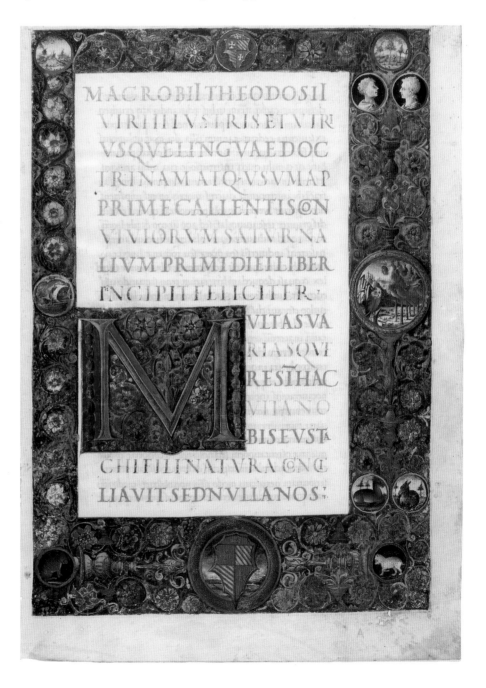

Incipit page. Cambridge University Library, MS Add. 4095, fol. 1

Documented as miniaturist in the papal accounts between 1459 and 1471, Polani was among the earliest proponents of the classicising style in Rome.

PROVENANCE: Comte de Toustain, Château de Vaux-sur-Auve; his sale, Sotheby's, London, 9 July 1884, lot 148; no. 26739 probably in a Quaritch catalogue; '830009' (perhaps in a Quaritch catalogue) and '2,241' inscribed inside lower cover; purchased from Quaritch by Samuel Sandars (1837–1894) in 1884 for £50; his bequest, 1894.

EXHIBITED: London 1891, 23, no. E.1, pl. XXI; London 1893–1894, no.115–17; Cambridge 1989–1990, no.93.

LITERATURE: Wardrop 1963, pl. 4; Fairbank 1965, pls. 3, 4; Fairbank 1970, 160, 162; Alexander 1970b, 24, 30, 38; Fairbank 1971, 8; Robinson 1988, no.96, pl. 294; Sheppard 1997, back cover; de la Mare 1999, 499.

SP

166

Horace, *Opera*

In Latin
Italy, Rome, 1485–1492
SCRIBE AND ARTIST: Bartolomeo Sanvito (1435–1511)

Parchment, iv (fol. i 20th c.) + 167 (fols. 1–165 foliated by Bembo) + iii (fol. iii 20th c.), 165 × 100 mm, text 113 × 60 mm, 25 long lines, ruled in hard point

SCRIPT: Humanistic cursive

BINDING: alum tawed skin over boards, by Roger Powell, 20th c.

King's College, MS 34

THIS ELEGANT VOLUME was copied by the distinguished Renaissance scribe, Bartolomeo Sanvito, whose cursive script inspired the type designed for the Aldine Press and known to this day as Italic. Albinia de la Mare grouped under his name 117 complete manuscripts, a further six to which he contributed, and over sixty volumes written by others, but containing his celebrated polychrome epigraphic capitals seen here (de la Mare 1999; de la Mare 2002). This manuscript was made for the Venetian intellectual and diplomat, Bernardo Bembo (1433–1519), one of Sanvito's closest friends (they had met in Padua in the 1450s) and earliest patrons.

The King's College Horace comes late in the series of manuscripts Sanvito copied for his friend between the 1450s and the 1490s. Sanvito had moved to Rome around 1463, and Bembo's visits there in 1485 or 1487 are compatible with the style of script and illumination. A date before November 1492 is established by Bernardo's annotation on

fol. 159, recording the names of the Venetian *oratores* who left for Rome on 9 November 1492 to congratulate the newly-elected Alexander VI. This topical note, Bembo's contents list (fol. ii), index of *incipits* (fol. 166), and literary-philosophical marginalia are characteristic of his attempts to blend the pursuits of a Renaissance intellectual with the *vita activa* of a statesman. On the end flyleaf, Bembo copied Horace's description of a quiet life spent away from worldly passions, among books and learned men, from the main text on fol. 110, and summed it up as 'the true meaning of life'.

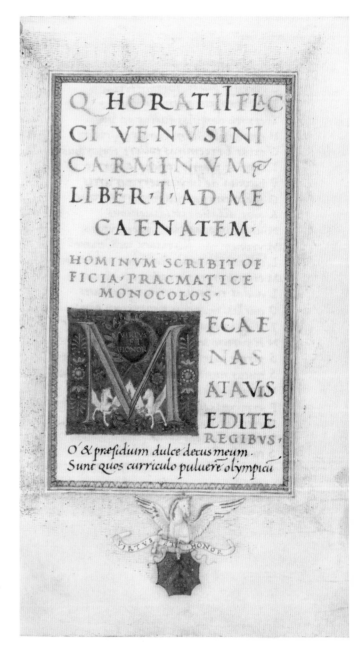

Incipit page with Bernardo Bembo's arms, motto, and device. King's College MS 34, fol. 1

In addition to the King's College Horace, at least twelve other manuscripts have been associated with both Sanvito and Bembo (Giannetto 1985; de la Mare 1999; de la Mare 2002). Two of them are closely related to the King's College volume: a Horace in Cambridge, England (University Library, MS Dd.15.13) and a Sallust in Cambridge, Mass. (Harvard University, Houghton Library, MS Richardson 17). Probably made for Bembo's travels some time before 1477, the tiny book at the University Library (104 × 77 mm) was the second of Sanvito's five copies of Horace (de la Mare 2002). It reflects his use of three distinct textual sources: a Florentine manuscript of Horace made c.1470 and corrected by him (London, British Library, Harley MS 3510), printed editions of the 1470s, and the first copy of Horace he made in Padua c.1460 for Marcantonio Morosini (Austin, University of Texas, MS HRHRC 35) from the celebrated tenth-century manuscript that had belonged to Petrarch (Florence, Biblioteca Medicea Laurenziana, MS Plut. 34, 1). Bembo's marginal annotations and corrections in the University Library copy suggest further editorial work and may explain why he received a second, improved Horace some ten years later. The King's College volume preserves features from the two earlier copies, but shares many more with the two later ones made by Sanvito c.1483–1485 for Ludovico Agnelli, apostolic protonotary and former secretary of Cardinal Gonzaga (Budapest, National Széchény Library, MS 419), and for Gioacchino Torriano of Venice c.1490 (New York, Public Library, Spencer MS 48). Both received elaborate frontispieces and may reflect Sanvito's hope for new patrons after the death of Cardinal Gonzaga in 1483.

Turning to the Harvard Sallust, it is so close in size, format, and page layout to the King's College Horace that the two manuscripts must have been conceived as companion volumes. They exemplify the slim, tall format introduced by Sanvito in copies of classical texts and later adopted by Aldus Manutius for his 'pocket-size' editions of ancient authors. Their opening pages display Bembo's arms, motto *Virtus et Honor* ('virtue and honour'), and emblem, the winged Pegasus, as well as Sanvito's epigraphic capitals and cursive hand. Most importantly, they are among the few manuscripts (out of the large body of material ascribed to Sanvito the illuminator in Ruysschaert 1986 and Erdreich 1993) that indisputably show him working as both scribe and artist (Erdreich's most recent work on Sanvito as an illuminator will be presented in a volume of Albinia de la Mare's research on Sanvito currently edited by Laura Nuvoloni). The King's College Horace opens with a leaf stained purple, a feature of ancient imperial manuscripts revived by the early antiquarians. It faces the *incipit* page, which shows Sanvito's characteristic colour scheme of gold, blue, red, green, and purple in the initial, background, and epigraphic capitals. The same pigments were used for the floral decoration, classicising border, and purple 'shredded' background of the faceted *P* initial at the opening of Horace's *Epistles* (fol. 91v). They are echoed in the ornamental vocabulary and colour scheme of the Harvard Sallust. With his Roman patron dead and his thoughts turning towards his native Padua, Sanvito committed both pen and brush to the books of Bernardo Bembo, a life-long friend who was also one of the most influential men in the Veneto.

PROVENANCE: Bernardo Bembo (1433–1519); Pietro Bembo (1470–1547); Henry Wotton (1568–1639) who purchased it in Venice from Bembo's descendants in the 1610s and gave it to Samuel Collins on 14 Dec. 1630; John Pearson, Bishop of Chester, who presented it to the College in 1672.

LITERATURE: James 1895b, 53–54; James 1895c, viii; Wardrop 1963, 29, 33, 50; Clough 1966/1971, 3, 12 n.22; Clough 1980, 43, figs. 2, 3; Clough 1984, 308, pls. 3, 4; Giannetto 1985, 299–301; de la Mare 1999, 503; de la Mare 2002.

SP

167

Herodian, *Historiae de imperio*

In Latin, translated by Angelo Poliziano
Italy, Rome, c.1490

Parchment, i + 162 + i fols., 238 × 124 mm, text 158 × 67 mm, 22 long lines ruled in crayon

SCRIPT: Humanistic cursive

BINDING: contemporary, sewn on four double tawed skin supports; olive-brown morocco over wooden boards, gold-tooled interlaced frame and centre piece; four leather straps with brass catches and shell-shaped lip catchplates, closing front to back; gilt and gauffered edges; clasps renewed and spine replaced; red label with the year 1490

Cambridge University Library, MS Add. 4114

THIS MANUSCRIPT demonstrates the blend of Florentine Humanist scholarship and Veneto-Paduan classicism in Rome during the 1490s. It contains the first Latin translation of the History of the Roman Empire written by the Greek historian, Herodian of Syria (170–240). The translation was prepared by Angelo Poliziano (1454–1494), the leading Florentine poet, philosopher and classical scholar (Branca 1983). He enjoyed the patronage of Lorenzo de' Medici and became the tutor of Lorenzo's son, Giovanni, the future Leo X *(see no. 64)*. In 1484 he was sent as Lorenzo's envoy to congratulate the Venetian Giovanni Battista Cibò on his election as Innocent VIII (1484–1492). As the dedication in this manuscript records, the Pope commissioned the translation of Herodian and Poliziano presented it to him in 1487. Innocent VIII welcomed the presentation copy (Rome, Biblioteca Nazionale, MS V.E. 1005) as 'a great ornament of our library'. During his research and diplomatic visits to the Papal Curia and the Veneto, Poliziano was at the heart of intellectual and diplomatic exchange between Florence, Venice and Rome.

The Cambridge Herodian reflects this exchange. It was made for a member of the Brescian family of Gambara, whose arms are displayed in the lower border of fol. 4. Gianfrancesco Gambara (d.1511), who was involved in Venetian military campaigns throughout his life, provided his children with sound humanistic education. His eldest son, Uberto Gambara (1489–1549), was made apostolic protonotary by Leo X and rose to Cardinal.

The format of the Cambridge Herodian is modelled on Bartolomeo Sanvito's slim, tall copies of classical texts *(see no. 166)*. The binding is among the earliest Roman gold-tooled examples modelled on the Paduan Mamluk style of the 1460s and probably brought to Rome by Sanvito in 1469. The manuscript preserves the refined Italic hand popular with the Roman followers of Bartolomeo Sanvito, particularly with pupils of Pomponio Leto and members of the household of Cardinal Francesco Gonzaga.

Among the marginal subject headings, or *notabilia*, penned by the original scribe and drawing the reader's attention to major events, personalities, ancient monuments, and moral-philosophical values, there are three notes on the corrupt Greek original (fols. 68, 84v, 111v). Begging the reader to treat the passages with caution and not to blame the translator, they derive from the exemplar Poliziano dictated to his disciples (Florence, Biblioteca Medicea Laurenziana, MS Rinuccini 20). The same annotations are found in other copies of Poliziano's translation, notably in a manuscript made in 1487 for a member of the Cibò family (London, British Library, Add. MS 23773, fols. 61v, 100, 142). It was copied by Alessandro Verazano and illuminated by Attavante in the typically Florentine style of the 1480s *(see no. 64 and 104)*.

The Cambridge Herodian was illuminated in the markedly different Veneto-Paduan style. Liquid gold faceted initials, whose three-dimensional effects are enhanced by illusionistic frames and entwined foliage, introduce the dedicatory preface and eight books (fols. 1, 4, 29v, 55, 79v, 100, 113v, 128, 148). The titles of the preface and the first book are inscribed in gold capitals on blue tablets and embellished with *all'antica* borders displaying vases, satyrs' masks, and strings of coral beads on 'shredded' gold or violet backgrounds. Their graceful, almost fragile elegance resembles the work of Francesco Marmitta of Parma, one of the most sophisticated and elusive artists of the decades around 1500 (Toesca 1948; Quazza 1985; Quazza 1990; Bacchi et al. 1995). A painter, illuminator, and goldsmith, Marmitta was particularly attuned to the 'jewelled' style of the Master of the London Pliny and Girolamo da Cremona *(see no. 174)*. He brought it to perfection, during his Roman sojourn, in the Missal of Cardinal Domenico

Incipit page with *all'antica* borders and arms of Gambara. Cambridge University Library, MS Add. 4114, fol. 4

della Rovere (1442–1501), one of the most distinguished art patrons in the Papal Curia (Turin, Museo Civico d'Arte Antica, Inv. gen. 497, inv. part. 6; Romano 1990; Bacchi et al. 1995, 115–44, no. 14). The Missal, illuminated in Rome *c.*1490–1492, offers numerous comparisons, and suggests a contemporary date for the Cambridge Herodian.

PROVENANCE: member of the Gambara family of Brescia (arms, fol. 4); Enrico Gambera, created Count Palatine and invested with Mirabello in 1499 (ownership inscription dated 22 Oct. 1511 inside lower cover); purchased by Petrus Axen. Husum-Slesuicensis in Venice (inscription dated May 1667 inside lower cover); Baron Achille Seilière; purchased at his sale (Paris, 7 May, 1890, lot 1230) by Ellis & Elvey (no. 273 in their catalogue); Samuel Sandars (1837–1894); his bequest, 1894.

EXHIBITED: London 1891, 23.

LITERATURE: Maïer 1965, 59–60; Hobson 1989, 78–79, fig. 65.

SP

168

Texts on Alexander the Great and Cicero, *Tusculanae disputationes*

In Latin
Flanders, Bruges, 1471–1478

Parchment, 158 fols. (foliated 1–21 in modern pencil, 1–84 and 1–52 in fifteenth-century red ink), 325 × 235 mm, text 215 × 155 mm, 38 long lines ruled in crayon

SCRIPT: Gothic bookhand (textualis)

BINDING: nineteenth-century leather over wooden boards; fifteenth-century strap with metal clasp, two pins and *fenestra* ('Quintus Curtius et questionum Tuscularum *(sic)* Tulii') on lower cover, four metal bosses, centre and corner pieces on each cover reused from the de luxe green Camelot covers recorded in the mid-sixteenth-century catalogue (Derolez 1979, 5–6, 41)

Peterhouse, MS 269

FEW MANUSCRIPTS reveal as much about their owners as this miscellany does about Raphael de Mercatellis (*c.*1437–1508). One of the many illegitimate children of Philip the Good of Burgundy (1419–1467), Mercatellis embarked on an early ecclesiastical career, becoming Abbot of the Benedictine Monastery of St Bavo in Ghent in 1478 and Bishop of Rhosus in Cilicia in 1487. His lucrative benefices, diplomatic missions as Philip's envoy to France and the Netherlands, and numerous privileges as councillor of Archduke Maximilian allowed him to indulge his luxurious tastes. Among his greatest

extravagances was the assembling of the first great humanistic library in Flanders (Derolez 1979). Some sixty manuscripts survive, out of nearly one hundred, and this volume belongs to the formative period of Mercatellis' library, which he had started in 1463 the year of his appointment as Abbot of St Peter in Oudenburg. Mercatellis spent most of his term in his native Bruges, where this volume was made. Its composite structure, content and script are representative of the Abbot's humanistic tastes.

The manuscript is written in a formal Gothic hand which nevertheless shows a conscious effort to imitate the humanistic minuscule, increasingly popular in copies of classical texts. Derolez and Arnould demonstrated that a number of manuscripts were copied in this style for Mercatellis and other collectors by Bruges scribes in the 1470s. Three of them collaborated on the Cambridge miscellany. The first part (fols. 1–20) contains texts on Alexander the Great's adventures in the East, popular throughout the Middle Ages and the Renaissance, that is the Latin summary of Pseudo-Callisthenes' Greek Alexander Romance, the letter Alexander allegedly wrote to his former tutor Aristotle, and his apocryphal correspondence with Dindimus, King of the Brahmans. They were copied by a scribe who was also responsible for the first two books of the next section in the miscellany, Quintus Curtius Rufus' equally popular novel *Historia Alexandri Magni*. The rest of the novel was copied by a second scribe and a third one completed the volume with Cicero's *Tusculanae disputationes*. The texts by Curtius and Cicero, independently foliated in contemporary red ink, were copied from printed editions. This is typical of the library of Mercatellis: like the other great fifteenth-century Flemish bibliophile, Louis de Bruges, Lord of Gruuthuse (d.1492), his passion for manuscripts was as strong as his dislike for printed books. Yet, his concern about the accuracy of the text is documented by his use of printed editions, and by his numerous corrections and annotations. The inscription added at the end of the volume in 1495 states that Mercatellis purchased (*'comparavit'*) and corrected (*'correxit'*) the volume. Derolez highlighted the problem this poses for many of Mercatellis' manuscripts, which were almost certainly acquired before the date recorded in these inscriptions. One possible solution is to translate *'comparavit'* with 'compared', as Mercatellis continued to collate and correct his texts long after he had acquired them. Since Curtius' 'History of Alexander' (except for the first two books) was copied from the 1471 Venetian edition of Vindelinus de Spira and Mercatellis' arms as Abbot of St Bavo on fol. 1 of the Alexander texts and fol. 40 of the Cicero section were clearly added to the main decoration after 1478 by a different hand, the production of the manuscript can be dated between these years. Mercatellis' enigmatic monogram

hiſtoriarū alexandri magni liber prim⁹   fo. p̃

Quinti curci ruffi hiſtoriarū Alexandri magni regis macedonū liber primus feliciter incipit

LEXANDER VESANVS IVVENIS QVI NICHIL NISI grande concepit aūo et cui pro virtute felix temeritas fortune ceſſit in gloriā: etatis ſue xx. agens annū. adorſus eſt expugnare regnū pſarum: etate quidē tantis rebus imatura: ſed abunde ſufficienti Erat eū uir in adoleſcente ſupra potenciā humanā animi magnitudine predit⁹ Hui⁹ autē magnitudinis future multa preceſſiſſe legitur prodigia Nā ea nocte qua mater eius olimpias eū concepit: viſa eſt p quiete cū ingenti ſerpente voluptari Quippe profecto maius humana mortalitate opus vtero tulit. die qua nat⁹ eſt due aquile ſupra culmen dom⁹ regis philippi patris eius a mane vſq̄ ad veſperū cōſederunt: omen duplicis imperii europ̃ ſci. et aſie preferentes Eade quoq̄ die pater eius duarū victoriarū nuncium accepit. qd̄ omen vniuerſarū teriarū victoriam portendebat Puer acerrim⁹ litterarū ſtudns erudit⁹ fuit Fracta puericia p quinquennū apud athenas ſub ariſtotele phōrum omnū inclito creuit: cui philipp⁹ iamdudū ſcripſerat ſe non tam gaudere qd̄ ei filius nat⁹ erat ꝗ quod temporib⁹ eius natus erat Die quadā dum cauſa luſitationis exiret vrbe. vidit quedam cynicū ſub ueſtibulo porte qui cum ab eo petit ereu reſpondit non decere alexandrū Ite cynico petente aureū. non decet inquit alexander cynicū Ita quadā verborū faſcencia negans vtruq̄ ſuridens abiit Paulo vero poſt cum tranſiret per eādem portā cū ſodalibus ſuis reſtitit ante dolū diogenis Cumq̄ illi plurimas offerret expenſas noluit diogenes recipe Alexandro vero inſtante: vt magnū inquit diogenes michi munus exhibeas: ſole te abſente rogo venire pmittas. preſencia tua michi nocet: abſentia nūꝗ nocuit Duodecimū agens annum cum tot et tantas victorias patris audiret: inter ſocios fertur ſleuiſſe dicens. nichil ſibi vincendū patris virtute relictū Philippo vero ipſū quadam die increpante ꝗ eos quorū amiciā munerib⁹ cōparauerat ſibi fideles eſtimaret: reſpondit. A caritate inquit iſtud michi pater prouenit Deniq̄ decedente philippo ſucceſſit in regno macedonū: vicis et virtutib⁹ patre maior Vterq̄ ſiquidē bellicoſ⁹ et auid⁹ fuit regnandi ſed neuter cū amicis regnare voluit Pater amari filius nolebat timeri. nulla apud patré vincendi ratio turpis apud filiū nulla videbatur difficilis. filius apte: pater artib⁹ bella tractabat. hic deceptis ille palam fuſis hoſtibus gaudebat. pater conſilio prudencior: filius animo magnificencior Vterq̄ liberalib⁹ artib⁹ inſtruct⁹: ſi filius apud ariſtotelé. philippus oratione: alexander reb⁹ preſtancior. hic bland⁹ pariter et inſidioſus alloquio. et qui plura pmittet ꝗ daret. ille reb⁹ ꝗ verbis munificencior. alexander fide philippus verbis et oratione preminebat Pater diuiciarū queſtu ꝗ cuſtodia ſollercior: filius i alto

Portenta diuiſa

infanti Ariſtoteles ph̃s

Diogenes ph̃s

LYS was added, probably at the same time as the arms, on fol. 57 of Curtius' text.

Unlike the content and the script, the decoration of the manuscript, with one notable exception, reveals no attempt to emulate the new developments of Italian or Northern Renaissance illumination. While the Alexander texts at the beginning have only penwork initials, most of Curtius's text and all of Cicero's received conventional Gothic foliage initials and acanthus borders. The only exception among his surviving manuscripts is the opening page of Curtius' text illustrated here. It received the owner's monogram, an elaborate initial, and a border with flowers and insects depicted as if scattered over the surface of the page. This illusionistic style first appeared in Flemish manuscripts in the mid-1470s and was established as the most fashionable trend in Bruges by the end of the decade. While this border was certainly added after the illumination in the rest of the volume, since its text was missing in the printed edition and was supplied from a different source by a different scribe, we must not necessarily assume a very long interval between the two campaigns of illumination. Strewn-flower borders co-existed with conventional ones in manuscripts of the 1470s and 1480s. If Mercatellis, who remained committed to the traditional style throughout his life, showed interest in the new trend on one single occasion, this is likely to have happened at the very beginning of his career as a young collector when the illusionistic borders first came into fashion. Since the Alexander texts preceding Curtius in the present volume are neither illuminated nor supplied with running headers and contemporary foliation, nor recorded in the *fenestra* from the original binding, we can be fairly certain that Mercatellis' manuscript once opened with this elaborate and trendy illumination.

PROVENANCE: Raphael de Mercatellis (c.1437–1508); given to the College by Algernon Peyton in 1666.

EXHIBITED: Cambridge 1993, no. 73.

LITERATURE: James 1899, 341–43; Ross 1965, 129; Van Acker 1977, 162 n.8, 193 n.72, 198 n.124; Derolez 1979, 3, 21–22, 24, 28, 30, 41–44; Derolez 1982, 146; Robinson 1988, 110; Arnould 1991, I, 50–59.

SP

Strewn-flower border and Raphael de Mercatellis' monogram. Peterhouse, MS 269, fol. 22

169

William Caxton, *Moralised Ovid*

In English
England, *c.*1483
ARTIST: Caxton Master (act. *c.*1470–*c.*1490)

Paper, iii + 272 + ii fols., 312 × 215 mm, text 200 × 140 mm, 2 columns, 30 lines, ruled in red ink, 2 watermarks: a gothic letter 'y' and a cross, and a covered tankard

SCRIPT: Gothic bookhand (cursive)

BINDING: full brown morocco over pasteboards, British Museum, 1969

Magdalene College, Old Library MS F.4.34 (Books I–IX; Books X–XV are Magdalene College, Pepys MS 2124)

THIS TRANSLATION of Ovid, from a French prose version rather than from the standard French *Ovide moralisée*, was made by Caxton himself. The colophon states that it was translated by William Caxton at Westminster on 22 April 1480 in the twentieth year of the reign of King Edward IV. The colophon would appear to have been taken over from the exemplar by this copyist. The book is probably from Caxton's printing shop at Westminster, though there is no indication that the text was ever used as a copy for printing. Dr Paul Needham suggested (in conversation) a dating around 1483, based on the evidence of the watermarks in the Median paper.

The text is decorated with embellished ascenders on the top lines and flourishes on the initials and single coloured Lombard letters in a manner typical of the Low Countries or north-west Germany in the later fifteenth century. There are also two-to-four-line blue and red penwork initials. A nineteen-line space for a miniature was left at the beginning of each of the fifteen books, but only four were completed. If the book was designed as a presentation copy, it was left unfinished.

Kathleen Scott attributed three of the miniatures to the Caxton Master: the one of Ovid himself, the Fall of Phaeton and the story of Cadmus. The story of Pyramus and Thisbe exhibited here and made famous by its inclusion in Shakespeare's play *A Midsummer Night's Dream*, does not appear to be by him. The natural tones of the colours used and the drawing style are very different from those of the Caxton Master. The illustration is a narrative sequence of the incidents in the story, all represented as if they were different groups within one picture. Pyramus and Thisbe in their city and the famous wall can be seen, as well as the two lovers outside the city and Pyramus plunging his sword into his breast watched by the lion. Thisbe is wearing a dress of a type fashionable in the 1460s and 1470s.

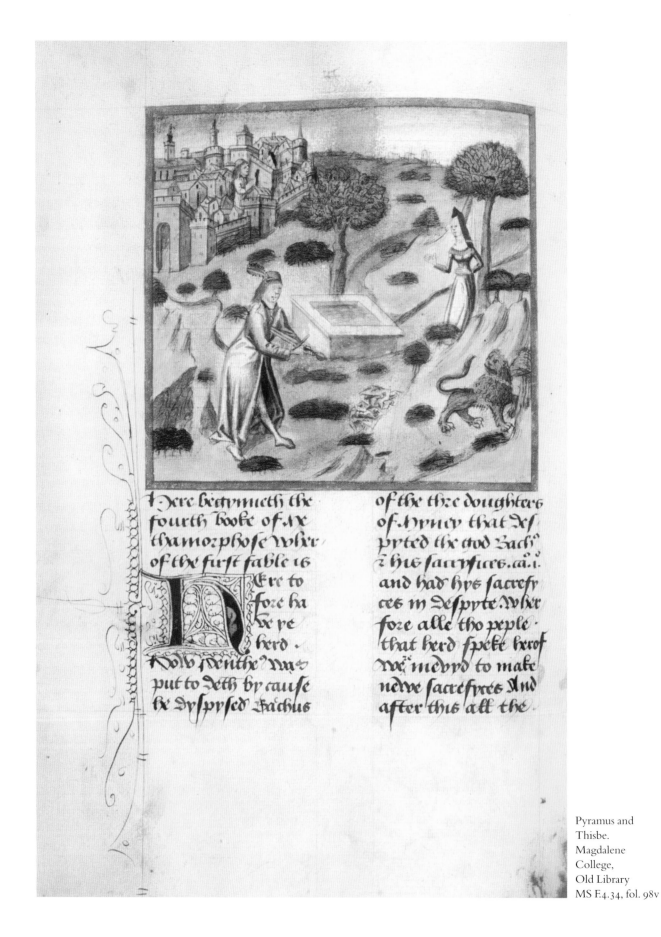

Pyramus and
Thisbe.
Magdalene
College,
Old Library
MS F.4.34, fol. 98v

PROVENANCE: Old Library, MS F.4.34 belonged to Sir Thomas Phillipps (d.1872), was sold at Sotheby's, 27 June 1966, lot 318.; and was acquired by Magdalene College in 1970. Pepys MS 2124 belonged to Rychard Wastfield, the Audely family, and Lord Lumley (1534–1609); it was purchased by Samuel Pepys in 1688 and bequeathed to the College in 1703.

LITERATURE: *Metamorphoses* 1968; Carter 1971; Blake 1973, 88–89; Scott 1976; Ker 1977, 233; Beadle and McKitterick 1992, 51–54.

RMCK

170

Libanius and others, *Declamationes*

In Latin and Greek
Northern Netherlands, Louvain, 1503
SCRIBE: Erasmus of Rotterdam (1469–1536)

Paper (fols. 3–4, parchment), quarto, vi + 63 + ii fols., 205 × 135 mm, text 140 × 85 mm, 15 long lines, ruled in hard point

SCRIPT: Humanistic cursive

BINDING: brown calf over pasteboards, 18th c., rebacked

Trinity College, MS R.9.26

THIS MANUSCRIPT consists of three declamations, the first by Libanius (AD 314–c.393) and the other two anonymous. It was written out by Erasmus at Louvain in 1503 and has been decorated in the Southern Netherlands, probably in Brabant, presumably by a professional illuminator. Libanius, a teacher of rhetoric and a prolific writer, whose pupils probably included John Chrystostom, spent most of his career at Constantinople, Nicomedia and Antioch. Of his surviving orations, many are addressed to or concern the Emperor Julian, whose funeral oration he composed in AD 365. Besides these, he has left no fewer than 1600 letters in addition to a large corpus of other rhetorical exercises. The imaginary oration which Erasmus places first in his trio takes an Homeric theme, and is placed in the mouth of Menelaus, who as King of Sparta, brother of Agamemnon and husband of Helen seeks restitution from the Trojans. Erasmus set out his own translations of the three orations first, and followed them with the original Greek texts: the manuscript on which he based his work seems to have been of little authority. He dedicated the work to Nicolas Ruistre, or Ruterius (c.1442–1509), Bishop of Arras and Chancellor of the University of Louvain. Ruterius was a bibliophile, and other of his manuscripts survive in Brussels and Louvain. The rats on the edge of Ruterius's arms allude to his posi-

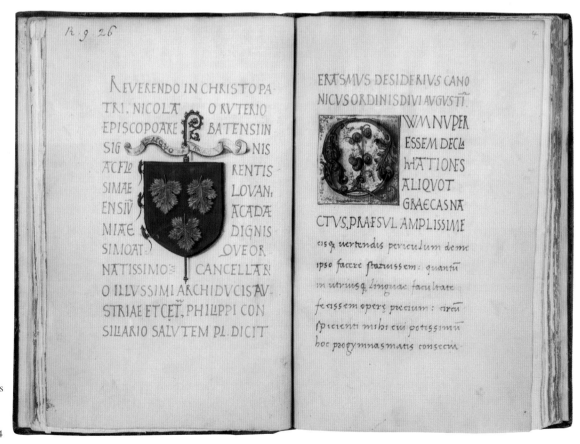

Dedication and arms of Nicolas Ruterius. Trinity College, MS R.9.26, fols. 3v–4

tion as Bishop of Arras. Erasmus clearly prepared this book in the hope that he would continue to prove to be a patron to him as he had been to others. As he explained in his dedicatory letter, he had chosen to follow Cicero's precept in his translation, weighing the meaning rather than counting the words. The volume is dated 17 November 1503, and Ruterius's duties at the Burgundian court had already led that autumn to the commissioning from Erasmus of a panegyric to welcome Philip the Handsome back from Spain. Ruterius rewarded Erasmus with ten gold pieces (approximately 30 shillings sterling at the time) for his present of the Libanius. The work was not printed until 1519, by Dirk Martens at Louvain.

PROVENANCE: Nicolas Ruterius; Abraham Ortelius (1527–98); his nephew, Jacobus Colius Ortelianus, or Jacob Cool (1563–1628); presented to Trinity College by Hugh Peter (BA Trinity College, 1618, chaplain to the parliamentary army, executed 1660), in 1657.

EXHIBITED: Brussels 1969, no. 16.

LITERATURE: James 1900–1904, II, 268–69; Garrod 1949; Bernardinello 1979, no. 61; Mynors and Thomson 1975, 71–79; Bietenholz and Deutscher 1985–1987, III, 177–78; Robinson 1988, no. 352, pl. 350.

DMCK

171

Aristoxenus, *On the Elements of Harmony*, etc.

In Greek
Italy, Rome *c.*1540
SCRIBE AND ARTIST (fols. 1–18): Giovanni Onorio de Maglie (act. *c.*1524 – 1563)

Paper, 181 fols, 287 × 215 mm, text 197–225 × 115–125 mm, 30–40 long lines, ruled in hard point, rubrics, running headers
SCRIPT: Greek minuscule
BINDING: marbled paper over pasteboards, gilt and gauffered edges, nineteenth century.

Cambridge University Library, MS Kk.5.26

THIS MISCELLANY of texts covers subjects as diverse, and yet inter-related, as music and the nature of horses. It opens with the three books on harmonics, which are almost all that survives from the enormous output of the fourth-century Aristotelian philosopher Aristoxenus. The *incipit* page makes a clear statement about its royal patronage. The headpiece includes the device (salamander) and motto (*'Erit Christianorum lumen*

in igne at auro praestantior', 'The light of Christians will surpass even gold on fire) of Francis I (1514–1547). The putti support the arms of France above the dedication panel. Francis I, an exemplary monarch of the High Renaissance, and a discriminating bibliophile and patron of the arts, assembled a collection of Greek manuscripts at Fontainebleau rivalling that of the Vatican.

This volume was copied by three scribes, responsible for fols. 1–18, 20–62, and 64–181 respectively. Henri Omont identified the first one, who copied Aristoxenus' treatise on music, as Giovanni Onorio de Maglie in Otranto whose career spanned the rule of five pontiffs, from the Farnese Pope Paul III to the Medici Pope Pius IV. Documented between 1535 and 1563 as 'instaurator' at the Vatican Library, Onorio was entrusted with reversing the consequences of the sack of Rome in 1527. He was working in Rome by 1524 and probably took his post as early as 1515, succeeding Demetrios Damilas, the first Greek copyist officially employed at the Vatican Library (Canart 1977–1979, 282; Staikos 1998, I, 138). The subtitle, running headers, and pagination, as uniform as those in contemporary printed texts, betray Onorio's involvement in the design of Greek types, notably for Cardinal Ridolfi's edition of Eustathius' commentary on Homer.

Onorio was paid for the copying, restoration, binding and, most intriguingly, illumination of manuscripts. These payments may often reflect his role as a project manager. In addition to the Cambridge volume, other manuscripts produced by Onorio preserve the work of distinct scribes and artists, some of whom emulated his hand. Among the imitators is the scribe of another Cambridge manuscript (Corpus Christi College, MS 248, fols. 107v–236v) who was tentatively identified as Onorio (Young 1953, 32; de Meyier 1964, 261; Agati 2001, 69, 255, 257).

While the decoration of Onorio's finest commissions varies in style and quality, it conforms to the design seen here – a headpiece, the salient feature of *incipit* pages in Greek manuscripts; the author's name and title in Onorio's characteristic, *diminuendo* capitals, closely related to his type faces; an ornamental initial; and the owner's arms flanked by putti above a dedication panel. A copy of Dio Cassius' *Life and Rule of Octavian* (Cambridge, Mass., Harvard University, Houghton Library, MS Typ. 144), which Onorio produced for his major patron, Cardinal Alessandro Farnese, shows a similar layout, probably by the same hand. This and the Cambridge Aristoxenus may preserve Onorio's own art work. The treatment of the title initials and the liquid gold frames is identical. The floral ornament in the headpiece matches the decoration at the beginning of the next two books of Aristoxenus' treatise, undoubtedly penned by Onorio.

Onorio's de luxe manuscripts were produced for

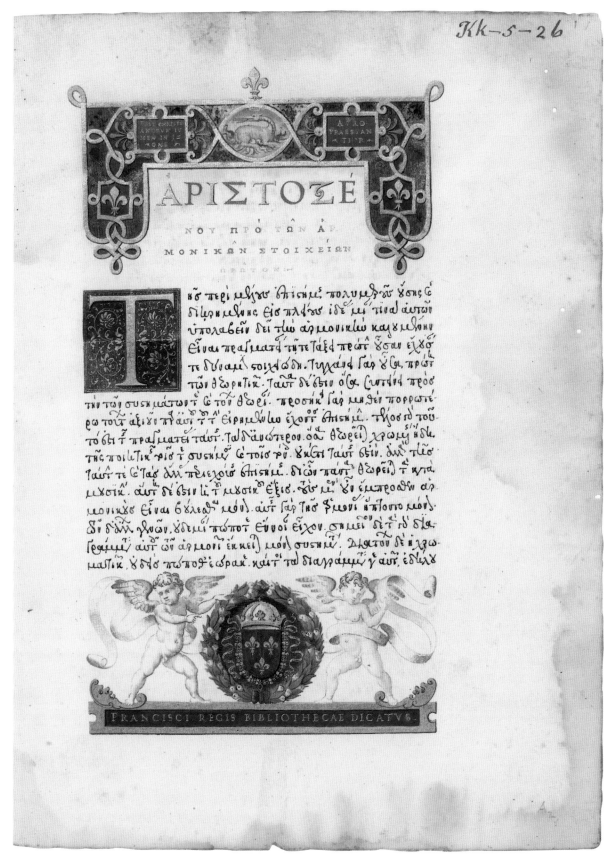

Incipit page with arms of Francis I. Cambridge University Library, MS Kk.5.26, fol. 1

wealthy ecclesiastical patrons who gravitated around the Vatican. Francis I's main agents were his ambassadors to Italy, all bishops well net-worked at the Curia. Henri Omont suggested that the Cambridge manuscript was among the first fifty Greek volumes acquired by Francis I as early as 1529 through Jeronimo Fondulo of Cremona, Cardinal Salviati's secretary and future tutor of Henry II. Yet, the date of Fondulo's purchase has been corrected to 1539 and the list Omont associated with it refers to a copy not of Aristoxenus, but of Aristides (Paris, Bibliothèque nationale de France, MS gr. 2456; Reeve 1981, 145 n.20; Reeve 1986, IX, XV). The script, increasingly vertical and abbreviated, and the watermark, crossed arrows surmounted by a star (fol. 19; cf. Briquet 6289), are characteristic of the most productive phase of Onorio's career, from the late 1530s through the 1540s (Agati 2001, 88–89, 110–31). The last, unfinished treatise on the nature of horses, copied on different paper by another scribe, had its title inserted by Angelos Vergikios, who left Venice for Paris in 1538 to become the leading Greek scribe at Fontainebleau under Guillaume Budé. Even if the volume was not produced as a unit, it was at Fontainebleau, in its current content, by the late 1540s; it features in the alphabetical and subject catalogues of the Greek manuscripts completed by Vergikios in 1550.

PROVENANCE: Francis I; John Moore, Bishop of Ely (1707–1714); presented to the Library by George I in 1715.

LITERATURE: University Library 1856–1867, III, 694–97; Omont 1889, 17, 305; Gamillscheg and Harlfinger 1981, no. 174; Reeve 1981, 145 n. 20; Agati 2001, 69, 255, 257.

SP

172

Dio Chrysostomus, *De regno*

In Italian, translated by Francesco Piccolomini
Italy, Venice, 1471
PRINTER: Christoph Valdarfer
ARTIST: Benedetto Bordone (1450/1455–1530)

Parchment, 73 fols. (unfoliated), 205 × 140 mm, royal octavo, handwritten signatures

Roman type (110R)

BINDING: old red morocco over cushioned wooden boards, sewn on four double sewing supports, ropework central panel and frame, two leather straps with metal hook clasps and lip catchplates, closing front to back, green and cream endbands, 16th c.

Cambridge University Library, SSS 15.5

THIS SPLENDID PAGE encapsulates one of the most important transitional stages in the history of the book. The art of illumination experienced its last flowering on the pages of printed books, starting in early incunables and lasting well into the sixteenth century. In 1469 the German Johannes de Spira brought the new technology to Venice and obtained a monopoly for printing there. His death in 1470 invited competition. Christoph Valdarfer was among the first to establish the business which by 1500 would transform Venice into the most important centre of printing in Europe. Yet, in those early days printing was a risky enterprise, requiring substantial investment. To appeal to wealthy bibliophiles, the early printers produced elaborate editions on vellum, modelled on de luxe illuminated manuscripts. The growing number of books and the wealthy clientele attracted some of the most inventive artists to Venice.

This volume, one of the first printed by Christoph Valdarfer, exemplifies the popularity of classical texts among the early printers and their aristocratic patrons. At the request of Nicholas V (r.1447–1455), Dio Chrysostomus' Greek treatise on government was translated into Latin by Francesco Piccolomini (1439–1503), the future Pius III. Piccolomini's address at the beginning of the text praises the Pope's choice of this work as 'the most appropriate and necessary for the rule of a good prince'. In January 1469, Francesco Piccolomini, who had been papal legate to Germany, dedicated his Italian translation to Maximilian I (r.1493–1519), praising the Emperor's *moderantia* and the greatness of the House of Austria. The original owner of the Cambridge volume remains unknown, but the elaborate frontispiece painted on vellum implies a wealthy patron whose involvement in contemporary politics may have been encoded, as Jonathan Alexander suggested, in the animals and mythical creatures depicted on the left.

The frontispiece has been attributed to Benedetto Bordone, one of the most versatile artists of the Veneto. During his long career in Padua and Venice, documented between 1480 and 1530, his style changed significantly and his skills were applied to the design of woodcuts, as well as to the illumination of manuscripts and printed books (Billanovich 1968; Mariani Canova 1968–1969b; Mariani Canova 1969, 68–74, 122–30, 156; Massing 1990; London and New York 1994–1995, 45–46, no.97, 104, 118; Armstrong 1996; Armstrong 1998; Padua 1999, no.146, 147, 151, 152, 171–75; Armstrong 2001; Armstrong 2003). His only signed works are two of the four legal incunables illuminated for Peter Ugelheimer (Gotha, Landesbibliothek, Mon. Typ. 1477, 20 (13), Justinian's *Digestum novum* dated 1477, and Mon. Typ. 1479, 20 (4), Gregory's *Decretales* dated 1479; London and New York 1994–1995, no.97; Modena 1999, no.147) and the Evangeliary for Santa

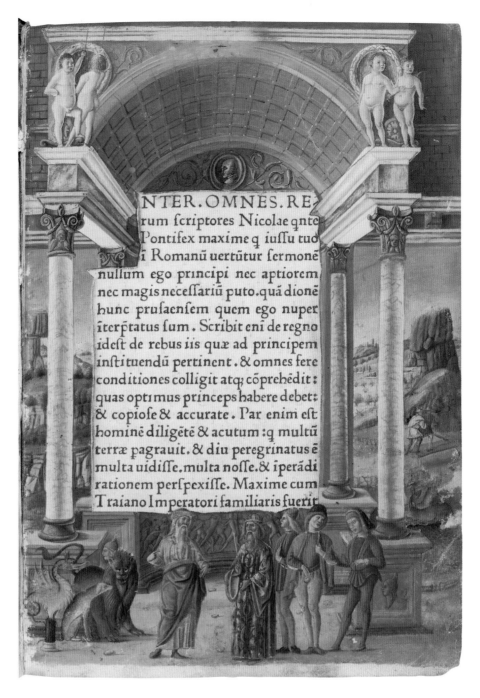

Architectural frontispiece.
Cambridge University
Library, SSS 15.5, fol. 1

Giustina in Padua of 1523–1525 (Dublin, Chester Beatty Library, MS W.107; London and New York 1994–1995, no.118). They exemplify the beginning and the end of his career. The Cambridge Chrysostomus is particularly close to the Gotha Justinian and may well be Bordone's earliest surviving work, datable between 1471 and the mid-1470s. It shows the early development of the architectural frontispiece which evolved in the Gotha volume into sophisticated cityscapes and freestanding monuments enriched with the jewelled ornament Girolamo da Cremona brought to Venice by 1475. The Chrysostomus frontispiece is conceived in four planes. The distant landscape is partially blocked by the text. Suspended on a parchment scroll, the treatise on government is framed and introduced by the Roman arch, the powerful symbol of imperial rule. The strings that attach the text to the putti's ankles draw the viewer's eye to the frontal columns. Beneath and in front of them, Dio Chrysostomus converses with Trajan. The last line of text, just above the figures, records the philosopher's close relationship with the Roman Emperor and goes on to say, overleaf, that the two of them often travelled together. The image bridges and anticipates the text, creating one of the most meaningful examples of Renaissance illusionism to be found in an incunable.

PROVENANCE: London, Puttick and Simpson, 7–10 April 1892, lot 533; purchased by Samuel Sandars (1837–1894); his bequest, 1894.

LITERATURE: de Roover 1953; Oates 1954, no.1647; Alexander 1969, 16–17.

SP

357

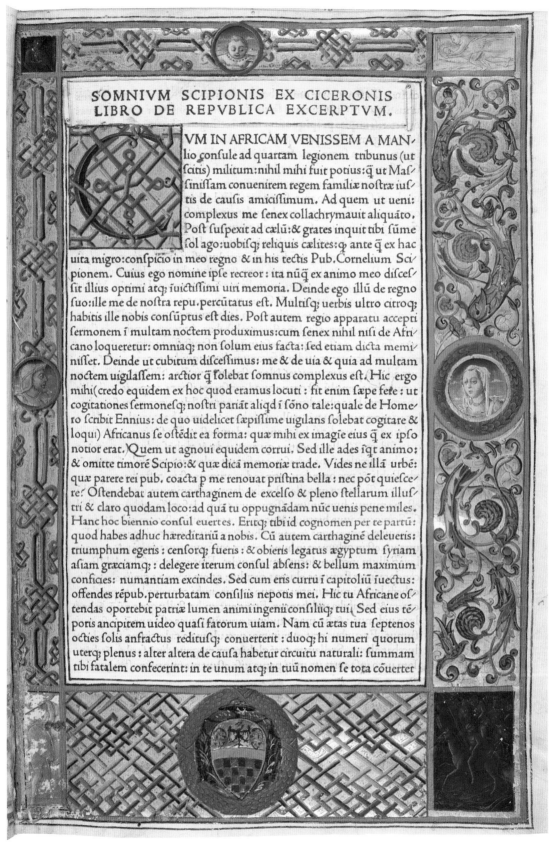

SOMNIVM SCIPIONIS EX CICERONIS LIBRO DE REPVBLICA EXCERPTVM.

VM IN AFRICAM VENISSEM A MAN-
lio consule ad quartam legionem tribunus (ut
scitis) militum:nihil mihi fuit potius:q̄ ut Mas-
sinissam conuenirem regem familiæ nostræ ius-
tis de causis amicissimum. Ad quem ut ueni:
complexus me senex collachrymauit aliquāto.
Post suspexit ad cælū:& grates inquit tibi sūme
sol ago:uobisq; reliquis cælites:cp ante q̄ ex hac
uita migro:conspicio in meo regno & in his tectis Pub.Cornelium Sci-
pionem. Cuius ego nomine ipse recreor : ita nūq ex animo meo disces-
sit illius optimi atq; iuictissimi uiri memoria. Deinde ego illū de regno
suo:ille me de nostra repu.percūtatus est. Multisq; uerbis ultro citroq;
habitis ille nobis consūptus est dies. Post autem regio apparatu accepti
sermonem ī multam noctem produximus:cum senex nihil nisi de Afri-
cano loqueretur: omniaq; non solum eius facta: sed etiam dicta memi-
nisset. Deinde ut cubitum discessimus: me & de uia & quia ad multam
noctem uigilassem: arctior q̄ solebat somnus complexus est. Hic ergo
mihi(credo equidem ex hoc quod eramus locuti : fit enim sæpe fere : ut
cogitationes sermonesq; nostri pariāt aliqd ī sōno tale:quale de Home-
ro scribit Ennius: de quo uidelicet sæpissime uigilans solebat cogitare &
loqui) Africanus se ostēdit ea forma: quæ mihi ex imagīe eius q̄ ex ipso
notior erat.)Quem ut agnoui equidem corrui. Sed ille ades īqt animo:
& omitte timoré Scipio:& quæ dicā memoriæ trade. Vides ne illā urbē:
quæ parere rei pub. coacta p me renouat pristina bella : nec pōt quiesce-
reˀ Ostendebat autem carthaginem de excelso & pleno stellarum illus-
tri & claro quodam loco:ad quā tu oppugnādam nūc uenis pene miles.
Hanc hoc biennio consul euertes. Eritq; tibi id cognomen per te partū:
quod habes adhuc hæreditariū a nobis. Cū autem carthaginé deleueris:
triumphum egeris : censorq; fueris : & obieris legatus ægyptum syriam
asiam græciamq; : delegere iterum consul absens: & bellum maximūm
conficies: numantiam excindes. Sed cum eris curru ī capitoliū iuectus:
offendes rēpub.perturbatam consiliis nepotis mei. Hic tu Africane os-
tendas oportebit patriæ lumen animi ingenū consiliiq; tui. Sed eius tē-
poris ancipitem uideo quasi fatorum uiam. Nam cū ætas tua septenos
octies solis anfractus reditusq; conuerterit : duoq; hi numeri quorum
uterq; plenus : alter altera de causa habetur circuitu naturali: summam
tibi fatalem confecerint: in te unum atq; in tuū nomen se tota cōuertet

Incipit page with arms of Pico della Mirandola. Trinity College, VI.18.52, fol. 1

173

Macrobius, *Expositio in somnium Scipionis, Convivia Saturnalia*

In Latin
Italy, Venice, 1472
PRINTER: Nicolas Jenson (*c.*1435–1480)
ARTIST: Master of the Pico Pliny (act. *c.*1469–*c.*1494)

Parchment, ii (i paper, 18th c.) + 164 + i (paper, 18th c.) fols., 315 × 220 mm, printed area 218 × 136 mm, median folio
Roman type
BINDING: red turkey leather gilt over pasteboards, 18th c., Pembroke Library

Trinity College, VI.18.52

T HIS SUMPTUOUS BOOK contains the works of the fifth-century neo-Platonist Macrobius, particularly popular with Renaissance scholars for the commentary on Virgil and the synthesis of ancient views on the structure of the universe *(see no. 165)*. It was printed by Nicolas Jenson, the Frenchman sent to Germany by Charles VII to learn the new technology of printing, who transformed it into an art, and who was elevated to a Count Palatine by Sixtus IV. Designing the most elegant of Roman types, he involved leading artists and wealthy bibliophiles in the production of the most opulent incunables in fifteenth-century Venice (Lowry 1991, 82–87; London and New York 1994–1995, 35–47; Armstrong 2003; *see no. 174*). This copy was illuminated for Giovanni Pico della Mirandola (1463–1494), the celebrated Florentine neo-Platonist, who read and collected books with a voracious appetite. He wrote *On the Dignity of Man*, and was charged with heresy for his belief in the unity of pagan, Jewish, Christian, and Muslim thought (Craven 1981). Since his arms are surmounted by a black clerical hat, the illumination must have been completed after 1473 when Cardinal Francesco Gonzaga appointed him apostolic protonotary. Pico was barely ten and this must have been one of the first books in his future great library. If the annotations on the Roman calendar in the margins of the *Saturnalia* (fols. 67–68) are in his hand, they may reveal an early antiquarian and scientific interest or a life-long use of the book.

This Macrobius is the earliest of three volumes illuminated for Giovanni Pico della Mirandola by the Master of the Pico Pliny. Named after the latest volume, a Pliny manuscript copied for Giovanni in 1481 (Venice, Biblioteca Nazionale Marciana, MS Lat. VI, 245 [=2976]; the second one is Jenson's 1478 edition of Plutarch, Berlin, Kupferstichkabinett, MS 78 D.16), this prolific artist was responsible for some of the most innovative and diverse book illustration produced in Venice in the 1470s and 1480s (Armstrong 1990; London and New York 1993–1994, 41–42, fig. 28, no.102, no.103). His media and techniques ranged from sepia drawings and monochrome illuminations to fully-painted architectural frontispieces and woodcuts. Within two decades, he experienced a remarkable evolution, always remaining at the forefront of new developments.

The Cambridge Macrobius exemplifies the work of the Pico Master's early career in affirming his wide repertoire and restless search for diverse aesthetic expression. The *incipit* page combines a faceted initial, lush foliage border, colourful strap work, portrait medallions, and monochrome figural compositions with a shy, early attempt at illusionism in the scroll curling around the printed title. These features re-appear in the initials and one-sided borders at the beginning of each book of *Cicero's Dream* (fols. 3v, 29) and the *Saturnalia* (fols. 48, 80v, 88v, 102v, 107, 123v, 145), but continue to develop and diversify (figs. 41, 42, 43). The geometrical strap work (fols. 1, 123v) gives way to a more sinuous interlace (fols. 29). The lush foliage border (fol. 1) sprouts zoomorphic hybrids and grotesques (fols. 48, 102v, 145). The blue faceted initials (fols. 1, 3v, 29, 48, 123v) turn pink (fol. 80v) or gold (fol. 88v), and acquire monochrome blue and pink putti first as a backdrop (fol. 102v) and then as their own structural elements (fols. 107, 145). A most unexpected 'jewelled' initial and border (fol. 88v) makes a guest appearance, one of the earliest in Venetian illumination *(see no. 174)*. As if to harmonize the symphony of shapes and colours, characteristically Ferrarese floral sprays grace every third text division (fols. 3v, 80v, 107). It is tempting to interpret this catalogue of styles current in Padua, Mantua, and Ferrara during the 1460s as suggestive of the Pico Master's early training. Yet, they are more likely to reflect the climate of Venice as a crossroads of traditions within the *Terra firma* and beyond. The illumination of the Cambridge Macrobius is a show piece of the artist's rich vocabulary, experimental spirit, and virtuoso techniques.

LITERATURE: Armstrong 1990, 37; Armstrong 1991, fig. 6.4; London and New York 1994–1995, 206.

SP

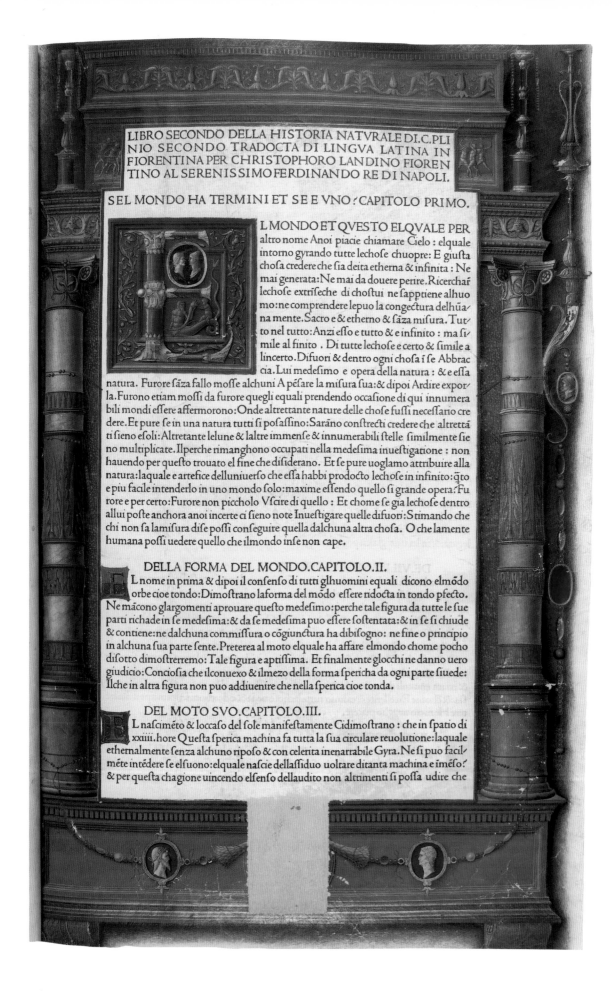

LIBRO SECONDO DELLA HISTORIA NATVRALE DI.C.PLI
NIO SECONDO TRADOCTA DI LINGVA LATINA IN
FIORENTINA PER CHRISTOPHORO LANDINO FIOREN
TINO AL SERENISSIMO FERDINANDO RE DI NAPOLI.

SEL MONDO HA TERMINI ET SE E VNO: CAPITOLO PRIMO.

L MONDO ET QVESTO ELQVALE PER
altro nome Anoi piacie chiamare Cielo: elquale
intorno gyrando tutte lechose chuopre: E giusta
chosa credere che sia deita etherna & infinita: Ne
mai generata: Ne mai da douere perire. Ricerchar
lechose extriseche di chostui ne sapptiene alhuo
mo: ne comprendere lepuo la congectura delhûa
na mente. Sacro e & etherno & sâza misura. Tut
to nel tutto: Anzi esso e tutto & e infinito : ma si
mile al finito . Di tutte lechose e certo & simile a
lincerto. Difuori & dentro ogni chosa i se Abbrac
cia. Lui medesimo e opera della natura : & e essa
natura. Furore sâza fallo mosse alchuni A pésare la misura sua: & dipoi Ardire expor
la. Furono etiam mossi da furore quegli equali prendendo occasione di qui innumera
bili mondi essere affermorono: Onde altrettante nature delle chose fussi necessario cre
dere. Et pure se una natura tutti si posassino: Sarâno constrecti credere che altrettâ
ti sieno esoli: Altretante lelune & laltre immense & innumerabili stelle similmente sie
no multiplicate. Ilperche rimanghono occupati nella medesima inuestigatione : non
hauendo per questo trouato el fine che disiderano . Et se pure uoglamo attribuire alla
natura: laquale e artefice delluniuerso che essa habbi prodocto lechose in infinito: qto
e piu facile intenderlo in uno mondo solo: maxime essendo quello si grande opera. Fu
rore e per certo: Furore non piccholo Vscire di quello : Et chome se gia lechose dentro
allui poste anchora anoi incerte ci sieno note Inuestigare quelle difuori: Stimando che
chi non sa lamisura dise possi conseguire quella dalchuna altra chosa. O che lamente
humana possi uedere quello che ilmondo inse non cape.

DELLA FORMA DEL MONDO. CAPITOLO. II.

L nome in prima & dipoi il consenso di tutti glhuomini equali dicono elmôdo
orbe cioe tondo: Dimostrano laforma del môdo essere ridocta in tondo pfecto.
Ne mâcono glargomenti aprouare questo medesimo: perche tale figura da tutte le sue
parti richade in se medesima: & da se medesima puo essere sostentata: & in se si chiude
& contiene: ne dalchuna commissura o côgiunctura ha dibisogno: ne fine o principio
in alchuna sua parte sente. Preterea al moto elquale ha affare elmondo chome pocho
disotto dimostrerremo: Tale figura e aptissima. Et finalmente glocchi ne danno uero
giudicio: Conciosia che ilconuexo & ilmezo della forma spericha da ogni parte siuede:
Ilche in altra figura non puo addiuenire che nella sperica cioe tonda.

DEL MOTO SVO. CAPITOLO. III.

L nasciméto & loccaso del sole manifestamente Cidimostrano : che in spatio di
xxiiii. hore Questa sperica machina fa tutta la sua circulare reuolutione: laquale
ethernalmente senza alchuno riposo & con celerita inenarrabile Gyra. Ne si puo facil
méte intédere se elsuono: elquale nascie dellassiduo uoltare ditanta machina e iméso:
& per questa chagione uincendo elsenso dellaudito non altrimenti si possa udire che

174

Pliny the Elder, *Natural History*

In Italian, translated by Cristoforo Landino
Italy, Venice, 1476
PRINTER: Nicolas Jenson (*c*.1435–1480)
ARTIST: Master of the London Pliny (act. *c*.1470–1490)

Parchment, iii (paper) + 415 + iii (paper) fols., 386 × 250 mm, royal folio

Roman and Greek types (115R and 115Gk)

BINDING: gold-tooled Russia leather over pasteboards, 19th c.

Cambridge University Library, Inc. I.B.3.2 (1360)

PRIZED BY RENAISSANCE SCHOLARS as the most comprehensive anthology of ancient knowledge about the natural world, Pliny's *Natural History* was first printed by Nicolas Jenson in Latin in 1472. By the following year the Florentine Humanist Cristoforo Landino (1424–1492) had translated it into Italian and dedicated it to Ferdinand of Aragon, King of Naples (r.1458–1494). Jenson's 1476 edition of the Italian translation was one of the most ambitious and best documented printing campaigns in fifteenth-century Italy (London and New York 1994–1995, nos. 84, 85). Initiated and sponsored by the Florentine banking firm of Filippo and Lorenzo Strozzi, Landino's translation was to be printed in 1000 copies on paper, provided by the Venetian merchant family of the Agostini, and distributed through booksellers in Rome, Naples, Pisa, Siena, Bruges, and London, as well as Florence and Venice. Jenson was particularly attuned to demands at the top end of the market (Lowry 1991, 82–87; London and New York 1994–1995, 35–47; Armstrong 2003). In addition to the paper copies, he printed some twenty copies on parchment to be illuminated by leading artists for the project's sponsors, their associates, and distinguished bibliophiles. The present Cambridge copy is one of them and Lilian Armstrong suggested (in correspondence) that it might have been made for the Agostini. It is unfortunate that the erased arms prevent a firm identification.

In her pioneering work (1981) on illuminated Venetian incunables, Lilian Armstrong attributed the frontispiece to the Master of the London Pliny. Named after a copy of Jenson's 1472 edition of the *Natural History* (London, British Library, IC19662; Armstrong 1981, no.36, 30–49),

he was among the most inventive and productive painters of classical imagery in Venice during the 1470s. He probably moved south with Cardinal Giovanni of Aragon (1456–1485), as no works illuminated by him for Venetian patrons are known after 1480, while he worked on a number of manuscripts copied in Rome or Naples in the 1480s and 1490s (de la Mare 1984, 256–57; London and New York 1994–1995, no.46, 90).

The magnificent frontispiece of the Cambridge Pliny is datable to the late 1470s. By that time, the rich, jewelled style of Girolamo da Cremona, who came to Venice before 1475, was exerting strong influence on Venetian illuminators. Both aspects are fully developed in the Cambridge Pliny: the imposing wall monument, the smooth columns, the text attached to them with beaded strings, the exquisite candelabra, precious stones, and cameos. These features and the rich colour scheme are mirrored in a copy of Plutarch's *Parallel Lives* printed by Jenson in 1478 and illuminated by the Pliny Master for a member of the Agostini family (Dublin, Trinity College, Fag. GG. 2.I, 2; London and New York 1994–1995, no. 92). The treatment of the opening initials in the Cambridge Pliny and the Dublin Plutarch is identical. Made of purple crystal cylinders with joints of gold acanthus and hybrid profiles, and set against a green plaque with floral ornament in black and yellow, they represent the most developed stage of the so-called faceted initial. A paper copy of Jenson's 1476 Pliny at the Fitzwilliam Museum (McClean Inc. 115) illustrates this evolution through its initials, illuminated in the three main styles found in humanistic books: the white-vine scroll, the plane faceted initial, and its later, precious stone version. In addition to the cameo with bust portraits identified as *Divus Augustus* and *Diva Faustina*, the frontispiece preserves another important feature of the Pliny Master's repertoire, the Triton and putto carved in high relief. Similarly elaborate initials composed of blue, pink and green acanthus, and crystal cornucopiae on burnished gold ground open the remaining thirty-six books, making the Cambridge Pliny one of the most sumptuous Venetian incunables.

PROVENANCE: names of Jane Argall, Mary Argall, and Ann Chittham inscribed on flyleaves; John Moore, Bishop of Ely (1707–1714); presented to the Library by George I in 1715.

LITERATURE: Waagen 1854–1857, III, 452–53; Oates 1954, no.1640; Alexander 1969, 17–18; Armstrong 1981, no.41, ill.98–99; Armstrong 1986, 87, 91, ill.58.

SP

Architectural frontispiece. Cambridge University Library, Inc. I.B.3.2 (1360), fol. 22

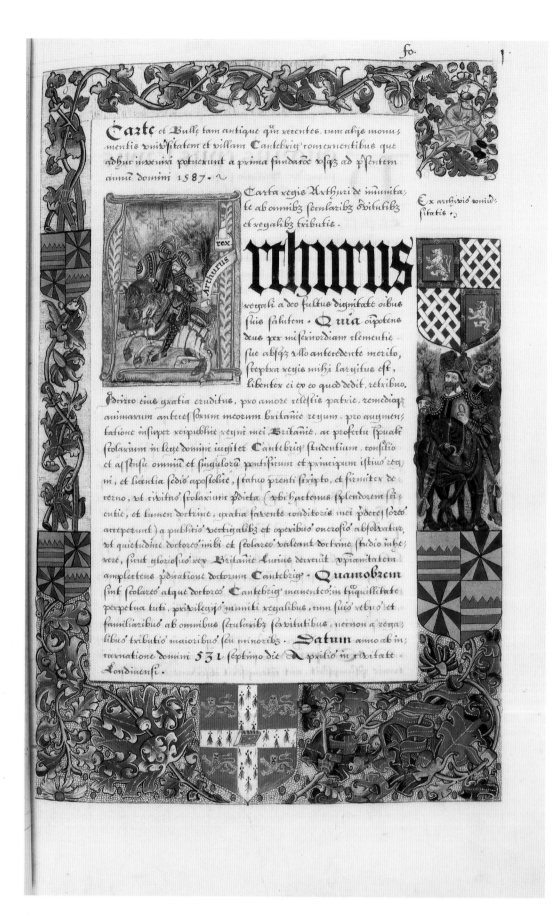

Carte et Bulle tam antique qn recentes, cum alijs monu;
mentis vniuersitatem et villam Cantebrig conceruentibus que
adhuc inuenia potuerunt a prima fundatoe vsqz ad presentem
annum domini 1587.

Carta regis Arthuri de immunita;
te ab omnibz secularibz oneribz
et regalibz tributis.

Ex archiuio vniu;
sitatis

rex.

Arthurus

rthurus

regali a deo fultus dignitate oibus
suis salutem. Quia oipotens
deus per misericordiam clementie
sue absqz vllo antecedente merito,
sceptra regis mihi largitus est,
libenter ei eo eo quod dedit, retribuo.

Idcirco eius gratia eruditus, pro amore celestis patrie, remediogz
animarum anteceessorum meorum britanie regum, pro augmen;
tatione insuper reipublice regni mei Britanie, ac profectu spuali
scolarium in lege domini iugiter Cantebrig studentium, consilio
et assensu omniu et singuloru pontificum et principum istius reg;
ni, et licentia sedis apostolice, statuo presenti scripto, et firmiter de
cerno, vt ciuitas scolarium pdicta (vbi hactenus splendorem sci;
entie, et lumen doctrine, gratia fauente conditoris mei pdecessores
acceperunt) a publicis vectigalibz et operibus onerosis absoluatur,
vt quietudine doctores inibi et scolares valeant doctrine studio inhe;
rere, sicut gloriosus rex Britanie Lucius decreuit ypianitatem
amplectens pdicatione doctorum Cantebrig. Quamobrem
sint scolares atque doctores Cantebrig manentes in tranquillitate
perpetua tuti, priuilegijs muniti regalibus, cum suis rebus et
familiaribus ab omnibus secularibz seruitutibus, necnon a rega;
libus tributis maioribus seu minoribz. Datum anno ab in;
carnatione domini 531 septimo die Aprilis in ciuitate
Londinensi.

Fig. 45.
King Arthur.
Cambridge
University
Archives,
Hare A, vol. 1,
fol. 1

MANUSCRIPTS AND DOCUMENTS FOR CAMBRIDGE UNIVERSITY

Nigel Morgan and Nicholas Rogers

Manuscripts for the Curriculum

The emergence of the universities in Europe in the late twelfth and early thirteenth centuries created a new demand for the class of books required by scholars and students.[1] It also had a lasting effect on the places where manuscript books were made. Up to the second half of the twelfth century the majority of books were made in monastic centres, but the demand for 'university books' made the cities where the universities were located into important centres of book production. Scribes and illuminators are well documented in Bologna, Oxford and Paris in the first half of the thirteenth century, and in Cambridge from the late thirteenth century onwards.[2] In the case of England, not only university texts, but also liturgical and devotional books were made in Oxford and Cambridge. The earliest of such books with illumination that might have been made in Cambridge or East Anglia c.1250 is a copy of the pastoral care treatise, the *Summa* of Richard of Wethringsette (fl. c.1200–c.1232), the first Chancellor of the University at some time between 1215 and 1232 *(no. 177)*.[3] Both centres remained active until c.1350, but in the last hundred and fifty years of the Middle Ages, London came to dominate as the major book producing centre in the country, while Oxford and Cambridge declined. By that time, it seems that the universities were already well stocked with copies of the texts required for study, and the majority of surviving manuscripts of this type were made before 1350.

In Cambridge collections, the three college libraries still possessing a large number of university books of c.1200–1350, are Gonville and Caius, Pembroke and Peterhouse.[4] Many of these manuscripts have medieval marks of ownership by these colleges. In addition, the University Library and the Fitzwilliam Museum have several university books of the thirteenth and fourteenth centuries, but they were not acquired until the eighteenth century at the earliest, and are not necessarily books from the libraries of English universities. The function of such books for scholarly study inevitably resulted in relatively few being illuminated, but some are decorated with historiated and ornamental initials. Well-established canon and civil lawyers, members of the higher clergy, and even scholars and students from richer families may have purchased the more expensive, illuminated copies. Some of these books were pledged to secure loans from the loan chests of the universities and have inscriptions in them recording the deposit.[5]

The majority of illuminated university texts are law books, and some of them also belonged to monastic libraries (e.g. Trinity College, MS B.16.46). Some university books were produced at Oxford or Cambridge, whereas others were imported from Bologna, Paris and Toulouse.[6] The copies made in Italy sometimes arrived with only sparse or incomplete decoration and were illuminated by English artists on arrival (e.g. two copies of Justinian's *Codex* in Gonville and Caius College,

MS 10/10 and MS 11/11, and a copy of Gregory IX's *Decretals* in the Fitzwilliam Museum, MS McClean 136).[7] A richly decorated copy of around 1335–1350 of a Compendium on the *Liber sextus* with miniatures and full borders was made entirely in England (St. John's College, MS A.4).

The texts of these books cover most of the required reading for the curriculum of the various subjects. Those that contain more specialized scholarly texts hardly ever have any decoration. The universities of Oxford and Cambridge had faculties of the arts, law, medicine and theology, with that of medicine being by far the smallest in student numbers. The arts in a medieval university comprised some subjects which in modern times would be considered as science, and also parts of the philosophy course were studied by theology and medical students. The teaching of the faculty of arts was spread over the *Trivium*, which consisted of Grammar, Rhetoric and Logic, the *Quadrivium*, which consisted of Arithmetic, Music, Geometry and Astronomy, and, finally, Philosophy, which was divided into Natural Philosophy, Moral Philosophy and Metaphysics. Law comprised both Canon Law, that is law related to the Church, and civil law. Colleges or Halls in both universities varied considerably in the numbers of students and scholars they had in the various faculties.[8] Some had arts, law or theology students and scholars predominating, but for medicine no college had more than a few members.

The faculty of the arts required the greatest number of texts as defined for the curriculum.[9] The faculty of law required fewer, but in particular the most up-to-date commentaries on law, which were mostly by scholars at the great centre of legal study, the University of Bologna. Medicine also had a limited number of essential texts. Only few basic texts were required for theology students, but the large number of commentaries on the Bible by the Church Fathers, Augustine, Gregory, Jerome and Ambrose, as well as by medieval authors such as Peter Lombard (*c.*1100–1160) and Thomas Aquinas (1224–1274), were essential for study and were needed in a theology library.[10]

Study in many areas of the faculty of arts was dominated by the works of Aristotle, with commentaries by scholars of Late Antiquity such as Porphyry (234 – *c.*305) and Boethius (*c.*475/80–524), by Arab scholars such as Avicenna (980–1037) and Averroes (1126– 1198), and by contemporary thirteenth- or fourteenth-century scholars, mainly those working at Paris and Oxford.[11] Illuminated examples of collections of text for the logic course are copies of Porphyry, Boethius and Aristotle *(no. 176* and Gonville and Caius College, MS 494/263), and for the natural philosophy course copies of Aristotle *(no. 175* and Fitzwilliam Museum, MS McClean 155).

Canon Law required the collections of law texts called Decretals, with commentaries by leading Bolognese Canon lawyers, such as Gratian (fl. *c.*1150), Accursius (1185–1263), Hostiensis (Henricus de Segusio, *c.*1200–1271), Guido de Baysio, 'The Archdeacon' (*c.*1250–1313), and Giovanni d'Andrea (*c.*1270–1348)).[12] Many illuminated copies of these texts are in Cambridge libraries. The earliest is the *Decretum* of Gratian (e.g. Corpus Christi College, MS 10 and Fitzwilliam Museum, MS 183). Revised sets of Decretals were compiled under Popes Innocent IV (e.g. Gonville and Caius College, MS 605/513 and Peterhouse, MS 80), Gregory IX (e.g. Fitzwilliam Museum, MS McClean 136 and Gonville and Caius College, MS 252/496) and Boniface VIII, the *Liber sextus*. Commentaries on these were made by Bolognese scholars, such as Guido de Baysio whose commentary on Gratian's *Decretum* is known as the Rosarium (Gonville and Caius College, MS 255/474),

Geoffrey of Trani on Gregory IX's Decretals (Gonville and Caius College, MSS 163/84 and 172/93, and Pembroke College, MS 167), Hostiensis on Gregory IX's Decretals (Gonville and Caius College, MS 30/19, Pembroke College, MS 183, and Trinity College, MS B.16.46), and Giovanni d'Andrea on the *Liber Sextus* (Gonville and Caius College, MS 256/661).

Civil law required the Digest of Justinian, often in editions with commentaries,[13] e.g. *Digestum vetus* with gloss of Accursius (Gonville and Caius College, MS 8/8), *Digestum vetus* books XXXIX–L (Gonville and Caius College, MS 14/130), *Digestum novum* with gloss of Accursius (Gonville and Caius College, MS10/10). Also required were Justinian's *Codex novus* (e.g. Books I–IX, Gonville and Caius College, MS 22/138, Gonville and Caius College, MS 589/499, Books I–IX with gloss of Accursius, Gonville and Caius College, MS 11/11) and his *Institutiones* (Gonville and Caius College, MS 248/493). The majority of these law books were made in Bologna and Toulouse and exported to Paris, Oxford, Cambridge and other northern European universities.

Medicine required the Canon of Avicenna, the *Aphorisms* of Hippocrates, Galen's *Liber Tegni* with the *Isagoge*, or Introduction, to it by Johannitius, Philaretus on the pulse, Theophilus on urines, and some additional texts.[14] An example of an *Ars medicinae* compilation of many of these medical university texts is St. John's College, MS D. 24.

Theology required first and foremost the Bible.[15] The need from the early thirteenth century of both students and teachers to possess copies results in a change from the large-scale monastic Bibles *(no. 19, no. 21)* to copies of smaller size *(no. 30)*, some others being even smaller and fully portable. Above all in Paris, but also in Oxford and Cambridge, such books were produced in the thirteenth century.[16] Biblical concordances were produced by thirteenth-century university scholars such as the Dominican Hugh of Saint-Cher (e.g. the handsomely decorated Pembroke College, MS 8). After the Bible, a standard text book was the Sentences of Peter Lombard (*c.*1100–1160), of which the earliest copies date to the second half of the twelfth century, before the period of university book production began following the emergence of the University of Paris in the 1170s and 1180s. An illuminated English copy of the Sentences of *c.*1300, perhaps from Oxford, is Gonville and Caius College, MS 290/682, and another copy, with the commentary of John Duns Scotus is Gonville and Caius College, MS 49/26. Also needed were commentaries on the books of the Bible by the Church Fathers, medieval authors and contemporary university men such as Thomas Aquinas (e.g. his commentaries on the four Gospels, Trinity College, MSS B.4.18 and B.4.19).[17]

To these books, directly linked to the required reading for the curriculum, can be added encyclopedic works, above all *Speculum historiale* by the Dominican Vincent of Beauvais, and *De proprietatibus rerum* by the Franciscan Bartholomaeus Anglicus, as well as the standard work of penitential literature, *De casibus poenitentiae*, also by a Dominican, Raymund de Peñafort *(no. 177)*.[18] A splendid illuminated three-volume text of the *Speculum* of Vincent of Beauvais which belonged to St. Augustine's, Canterbury, is divided between Corpus Christi College, MSS 13, 14 and St. John's College, MS B.21. An illuminated copy of Bartholomaeus Anglicus is Gonville and Caius College, MS 280/673, and a Raymond de Peñafort with historiated initials, survives in Corpus Christi College, MS 474.

The arrangement of the texts of these university books was specially designed to allow for both the commentary and additional users' notes to be placed around the main text. For law books the main text is of two columns framed on all four sides by the commentary, and allowing a wide border for additional notes of comment to be made by the owners.[19] For the Aristotle manuscripts, the main text is in a larger size script than the gloss, as in twelfth-century glossed texts with an ample surrounding margin for notes.

Book production in the university cities was strictly controlled in regard to the accuracy of the text exemplars given to the scribes. A system was devised to speed up production in which a text was divided into sections (*pecia*) which could be distributed to a number of scribes.[20] The export of books from one centre to another was strictly controlled to ensure that correct texts were always disseminated.[21] These university texts were but part of the history of book production in the university cities. The scribes and illuminators established in such places worked for a wide circle of patrons, for members of the clergy and the religious Orders, and for lay people. Although the need for production of books for the universities resulted in scribes and artists basing themselves in the university cities, their activity, even from the beginning, extended to provide a diversity of texts for a much wider readership.

Illuminated Documents

Charters, letters patent and similar official documents are essentially public documents, intended for exhibition. Their existence underpinned the legal status and privileges of Cambridge University and its constituent colleges. This authority was recognized during the Peasants' Revolt in 1381 when rioters in Cambridge cast many of the early University muniments onto a bonfire on Market Hill. Fortunately some survived, such as early examples of charters embellished by illuminated initials, a practice which developed in England in the second half of the thirteenth century. Since it seems to have been usual in the fourteenth and fifteenth centuries for the recipient to arrange for the illumination of the document,[22] the early Cambridge charters are valuable pointers to the practice of illumination in Cambridge. The documentary evidence for book production in Cambridge has yet to be evaluated properly, but there is a good body of circumstantial evidence for Cambridge illuminators to be placed alongside the few names as yet retrieved from archives.

Cambridge University Archives Luard 7★, an *inspeximus* of 1291 *(no. 178)* has been compared to a Breviary of Ely Cathedral Priory (Cambridge University Library, MS Ii.4.20).[23] This stylistic link reinforces an attribution to Cambridge rather than London. Similarly, Luard 33a★ *(no. 179)* has been shown to be by the same artist as a Psalter with an Ely diocesan calendar in Brescia, and has links with the Psalter of Simon de Montacute *(no. 77)* and the Zouche Hours (Oxford, Bodleian Library, MS lat. liturg. e. 41), both intended for use in the diocese of Ely.[24] The location of the artist of the Trinity Hall foundation charter of 1353 (Trinity Hall, Muniments 77) is less clear-cut. Norwich, the seat of Bishop Bateman, might be considered as a possibility, but it is most likely that the artist was one of those who migrated from Oxford to Cambridge in the 1340s.[25]

Statutes, which were restricted in circulation to the bodies that they regulated, were usually devoid of decoration. Pembroke College, Archives Box A.12, a late-fourteenth-century copy of that college's statutes, with its neat bicoloured pen initials, is typical of this genre [26]. The inclusion of full-page miniatures in the Old Proctor's Book *(no. 180)* would appear to be prompted by its use in ceremonies, most notably the *Magna Congregatio* at which the townsmen swore to uphold the privileges of the University. The miniatures are a visual equivalent of the cosmopolitan nature of the late medieval University, drawing on several Continental influences. The members of the University were well placed to respond, if they so wished, to intellectual and artistic developments that were transmitted by means both of imported books and visiting scholars. Even if the Caesar Master's decoration of the Pembroke letter of 1448 to Henry VI *(no. 182)* does not necessarily prove his presence in Cambridge, his employment does reveal that Cambridge was open to Italian Humanism.[27]

Iconographically, these early charters and statutes are of interest for their representations of academics. The 1291 charter *(no. 178)* displays an awareness of academic hierarchy. Two *magistri* are shown kneeling, while behind them stand two doctors, in differently coloured robes, perhaps representing different faculties. In Luard 15★, of 1309, the King is shown giving the charter to a coifed figure. This could be a lawyer, or, by analogy with the thirteenth-century seal of the University, a proctor, a suitable person for a document concerned with the punishment of delinquent scholars. Luard 33a★ *(no. 179)*, which provided protection for the Chancellor against false imprisonment, includes the figure of a sergeant with his mace, whose power is curtailed by the letters patent being given. It is noteworthy that academics do not appear in the King's College Charter *(no. 181)*, which illustrates a dialogue between the King in parliament and the patrons of the college. The dedication of the college is also the subject of the Trinity Hall Charter *(no. 183)*, which has a *Gnadenstuhl* Trinity in the initial. The seated, crowned Virgin and Child in the Old Proctor's Book may also be seen as patronal in nature, possibly even reflecting a devotional image in the University Church of Great St Mary's.

The impact of printing on Cambridge, even prior to the advent of John Siberch as the first University Printer in 1520, is reflected in the woodcut-like images of the four Evangelists and the Crucifixion (the latter unfortunately badly defaced) in Cambridge University Archives, Collect. Admin. 2, dating from *c*.1490. Printing transformed the provision of textbooks and, to a lesser extent, liturgical books, but limners were still employed for special commissions. A London-based illuminator was responsible for the rich display of heraldic and foliage decoration on the opening page of the letters patent of 1505 by which Henry VII granted leave to his mother to refound God's House as Christ's College. The artist was identified by Janet Backhouse as one of the group of Dutch illuminators covered by the collective title of Masters of the Dark Eyes, who carried out other work for Lady Margaret Beaufort.[28] London illuminators linked with the Court or the Chancery were responsible for the Elizabethan charters of Trinity Hall, Emmanuel and Sidney Sussex. Also probably based in London, but practising in a distinctive style related to contemporary German work, was the main artist of the two-volume collection of University documents made by Robert Hare *(no. 184)*. The iconographic programme testifies to the variety of motives that impelled him to make such a compilation. The scenes of University ceremonies have a practical aspect similar to heralds' representations of ceremonies, whereas the image of King Arthur and the heraldic displays *(fig. 43)* are more conventionally antiquarian. The desire of an

Elizabethan Catholic to protect the record of the past is proclaimed in the daring dedicatory images of the Four Doctors of the Church.

Illumination of documents continued in Cambridge into the seventeenth century. One of the last practitioners was John Scott (d.1638). He is best known for his description of the University and Colleges of Cambridge, emblazoned with coats of arms, of which at least thirteen versions survive, made at various dates between 1615 and 1627.[29] The Sidney Sussex copy (MS 66), given to Samuel Ward in 1619, prompted a gift of £3. 10s. More typical of the type of work carried out by the last generation of Cambridge limners is the penwork depiction of Queen Elizabeth in the *Registrum Magnum* of Sidney Sussex College, for which John Scott junior was paid 2s. 6d. in 1638. This is a rustic reinterpretation of the pen initial to the 1594 licence to found the college. The impulse to dignify important documents by means of figure decoration was a constant from the thirteenth to the seventeenth century, despite cultural and religious changes.

REFERENCES

1   On the rise of the universities see Rashdall 1987.

2   For Bologna see Stelling-Michaud 1963, Devoti 1994, and Gibbs 2002. For Paris see Rouse and Rouse 1988, Rouse and Rouse 2000, and Paris 1974. For Oxford and Cambridge see Parkes in Catto and Evans 1992, Pollard 1955, Pollard 1964, Michael 1988, Michael 1993. Illuminated copies from Oxford are catalogued in Morgan 1982–1988, cat. nos. 145, 146 (a), (b), 156 (a), (b), (c) and further discussed in Camille 1985 and Camille 1995.

3   See Goering 1995 for the *Summa* and its author.

4   Unfortunately, many of the illuminated copies in Pembroke and Peterhouse have been mutilated by cutting out their historiated and decorated initials. The surviving medieval library catalogues of the Cambridge colleges are fully described with identification of extant manuscripts in Clarke and Lovatt 2002.

5   On the loan chests see Pollard 1939–1940, Lovatt 1993 (for Cambridge) and Catto 1984, 267–68, 276–77 (for Oxford).

6   A c.1300 Parisian illuminated copy of Gratian's Decretum is Fitzwilliam Musem, MS 262, and a c.1300 copy of Gregory IX's Decretals from Toulouse is Fitzwilliam Museum, MS McClean 136.

7   Alexander 1980.

8   Cobban 1982 gives comparative figures of theology and law students in various colleges of Oxford and Cambridge. Fletcher 1994 gives an overview of the strengths of the various faculties at Oxford and Cambridge.

9   Weisheipl 1964 gives a complete listing of the books required at Oxford in the early fourteenth century. See also Catto 1984 and Catto and Evans 1992 for Oxford, and Leader 1988, 108–69 for Cambridge.

10 For Bible study in the Middle Ages see Smalley 1983 and de Hamel 2001A, 92–113.

11 Callus 1943 discusses at length the rise of Aristotelian studies in thirteenth-century Oxford. For the Aristotle texts in general see Lohr 1982 and Dod 1982.

12 The text and illumination of these books is fully discussed, using many examples from Cambridge libraries, in Pink 1959 and Cambridge 2001 where most of the illuminated examples mentioned in this essay are discussed in detail. For medieval Canon Law and lawyers see Brundage 1995 and Owen 1990. For Oxford see Boyle 1964, Boyle in Catto 1984, 531–64, Barton in Catto and Evans 1992, 281–314; for Cambridge see Leader 1988, 192–201 and Brundage 1993. For the commentaries on the various texts, including civil law, see Dolazalek 2002.

13 For civil law at Oxford see Barton in Catto 1984, Catto and Evans 1992 and for Cambridge Leader 1988, 192–201.

14 On texts required for the faculty of medicine see Kibre 1978. For medicine at Cambridge and Oxford see Leader 1988, 202–10 and Getz in Catto and Evans 1992, 373–406.

15 For the theology faculties at Oxford and Cambridge see Little 1930, Little and Pelster 1934, Catto in Catto 1984, 471–518, Courtenay and Catto in Catto and Evans 1992, 1–34, 175–280, and Leader 1988, 170–91.

16 For illuminated copies probably made in Oxford and Cambridge see Morgan 1982–1988, cat. nos. 66, 69, 70, 75. Excellent discussions of small Bibles of the thirteenth century are in Light 1994 and de Hamel 2001, 114–39.

17 For biblical commentaries see de Hamel 2001, 92–113.

18 For manuscripts of texts by Dominican university men in Cambridge libraries see Cambridge 1988.

19 On this arrangement of text see Parkes 1976 and Cambridge 2001, 54–68.

20 On the *pecia* system in Bologna, Paris and Oxford see Destrez 1935, Talbot 1958, Pollard 1978, Bataillon 1988, Rouse and Rouse 1988, Rouse and Rouse 1994 and Soetermeer 2002.

21 See Stelling-Michaud 1963 and Bataillon 1988.

22 Danbury 1989, 160.

23 Morgan 1982–1988, II, 38 n. 40.

24 Dennison 1986b.

25 Dennison 1993, 27–31, pl. 16.

26 Grimstone 1997, fig. 5.

27 Oxford 1970, no. 90.

28 Carley and Backhouse 1997.

29 Baker 1993.

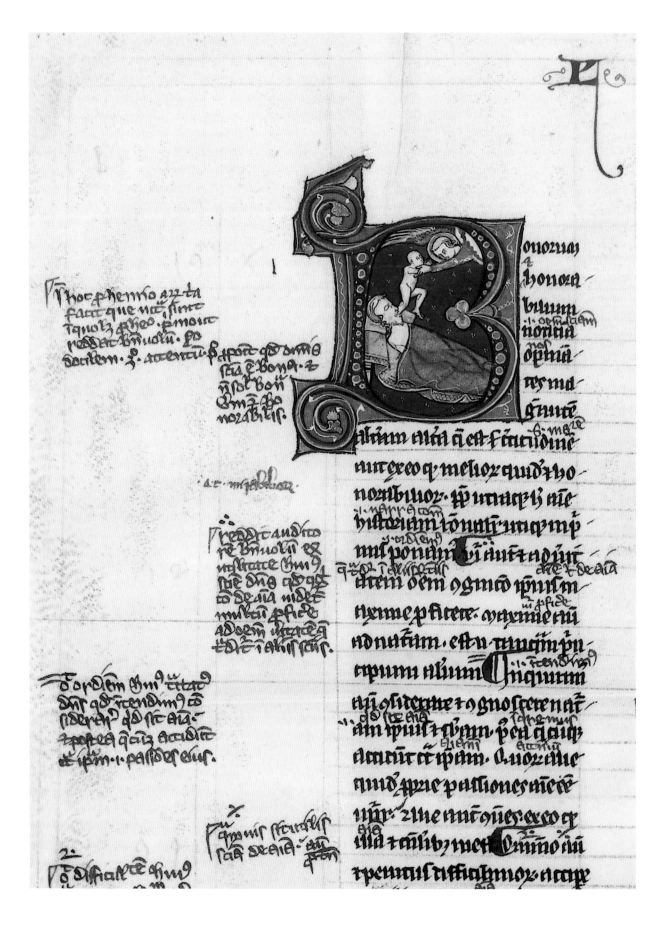

175

Aristotle, *Phisica, De Celo et Mundo, Metheora, De Anima, De Memoria et Reminiscentia, Metaphysica*

In Latin
England, probably Oxford, *c*.1260

Parchment, i (paper) + 269 + i (paper) fols., 296 × 215 mm, text 145 × 84 mm, 2 columns, 31 lines, ruled in crayon
SCRIPT: Gothic bookhand (textualis)
BINDING: marbled paper boards and brown leather spine, by D. Cockerell, 1968

Cambridge University Library, MS Ee.2.31

THIS IS A BOOK essential for the philosophy course in a thirteenth-century university, whose key texts were the works of Aristotle (Weisheipl 1964, Dod 1982, Catto 1984, Leader 1988, Catto and Evans 1992). It comprises most of the texts required for two parts of the philosophy course, natural philosophy and metaphysics. The first five texts contained in this volume are for the study of natural philosophy and are referred to as the *libri naturales*. His *Phisica* was the fundamental book on natural science, the *De Celo et Mundo* discussed the motion of the universe and the physical theory of the spheres, the *Metheora* was concerned with the elements and the chemical composition of bodies, the *De Anima* with the soul as the active force in living things, and *De Memoria et Reminiscentia* is a work on psychology. Finally, Aristotle's *Metaphysica* was the basic text for the course on Metaphysics. The manuscript does not contain the texts required for the third part of the philosophy course, that on moral philosophy, which consisted of Aristotle's *Nicomachean Ethics, Economics* and *Politics*. The page layout is designed to facilitate study. Aristotle's text occupies a relatively small area in the centre of the page, generously allowing for the addition of a commentary (in this case that of Averroes) on passages of Aristotle indicated by paraphs and such notes as the reader wished to add (Lohr 1967, Lohr 1982). Also, the lines of Aristotle's text are sufficiently spaced to accommodate interlinear notes.

Together with the next manuscript, which contains texts for the logic course *(no. 176)*, this is one of the rela-tively few university books to have extensive illumina-tion. Historiated or ornamental initials with short border extensions are placed at the head of each of the six texts and at the beginning of their constituent chapters. The pages are designed and ruled to accommodate annota-tions by future readers. The problem for the artist was to devise appropriate images for the opening initials of these philosophical texts, and it is often difficult to inter-pret what the chosen images might mean. The *Phisica* opens with a seated tonsured figure teaching a group of students sitting on the ground (fol. 1). For its Book II a standing woman rests her hands on the bar of the open-ing initial E (fol. 7v). The *De Celo et Mundo* has a bust of Christ holding an orb and blessing, with green waves of the sea and brown land below (fol. 67). This compo-sition is clearly based on the initial frequently found for Psalm 68 in Psalters whose opening verse 'Save me O God, for the waters are come in even to my soul' is illus-trated by a bust of Christ above a man standing in the water. The *Metheora* opens with a man turning a wind-mill (fol. 130), famous as perhaps the earliest example of a windmill in English art. The choice of subject relates to the text's discussion of the elements, including the winds. The *De Anima* initial has a dying man in bed with his soul being taken up by an angel (fol. 164v), and is obviously related to the soul in life and after death discussed in the text. Finally, the *Metaphysica* has Christ seated holding an orb (fol. 195). The remaining texts and their constituent books have ornamental initials.

The figure style and ornamental decoration compares with a workshop of artists probably based in Oxford *(see no. 176)*. It specialized in university text books: at least ten such manuscripts can be attributed to the same artists. The most extensively decorated of these univer-sity books is similar in content to the Cambridge volume (London, British Library, Harley MS 3487). A late pro-duct by the same workshop is the famous Oscott Psalter (London, British Library, Add. MS 50000), which has similar motifs for its small figure initials.

PROVENANCE: John Moore, Bishop of Ely (1707–1714); presented to the Library by George I in 1715.

LITERATURE: University Library 1856–1867, II, 47–48; Lacombe 1939, 360, no.260; Parkes 1976, 124, 126; Camille 1985b, 33, figs. 4, 13; Morgan 1982–1988, II: 125, 127, 131.

NJM

The human soul. Cambridge University Library, MS Ee.2.31, fol. 164v, detail

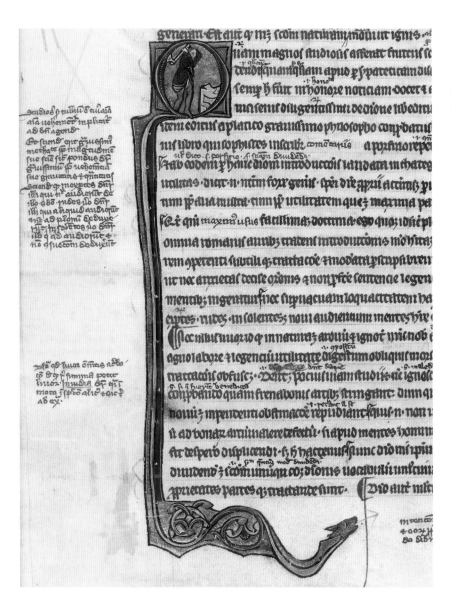

176

Porphyry, *Isagoge*; Aristotle, *Praedicamenta, Perihermenias*; Gilbert of Poitiers (attrib.), *Liber sex principiorum*; Boethius, *Topica, Liber de divisione*; Aristotle, *De Sophisticis Elenchis, Topica, Analytica Priora et Posteriora*

In Latin
England, probably Oxford, *c.*1260

Parchment, iii (paper) + 236 + ii (paper) fols., 341 × 230 mm, text 164 × 94 mm, 28 long lines, ruled in brown ink and plummet

SCRIPT: Gothic bookhand (textualis)

BINDING: dark green leather over wooden boards, 19th c.

Pembroke College, MS 193

IN THIRTEENTH-CENTURY UNIVERSITIES the arts course required the study of logic for which there were set texts (Weisheipl 1964, Dod 1982, Catto 1984, Leader 1988, Catto and Evans 1992). This university book contains the texts required for the logic course. The first four texts comprised the so-called *logica vetus*, which was studied over three terms. The final four works of Aristotle were called the *logica novus* with one term devoted to each of the texts. The works of Aristotle were the core of the syllabus but three commentaries by other writers were included (Lohr 1967, Stump 1978, Lohr 1982). Porphyry (234–*c.*305), a Greek scholar, wrote an introduction (*isagoge*) to Aristotle's *Categories* (Minio-Paluello 1966, XVII, LVI, 5–31). His Greek text was translated into Latin by Boethius. The *Liber sex principiorum* is of uncertain authorship, but has been attributed to Gilbert of Poitiers (*c.*1080–1154) a leading scholar of the School of Chartres (Minio-Paluello 1966, 35–59). The work is also concerned with Aristotle's *Categories*. The final works in the curriculum by an author other than Aristotle are by the Roman philosopher Boethius (*c*.480–524). He wrote a commentary on Cicero's *Topica* and a treatise on *Topics*, *De topicis differentiis*, concerned with the discovery of arguments. This is of course of particular relevance to logic, which is concerned with judging and evaluating arguments. Boethius's *Liber de divisione* is another work concerned with logic.

These compilations of university texts usually lack illumination, but several have historiated and ornamental initials with partial border extensions at the beginning of each text. Perhaps these were purchased by richer students or by their teachers. Unfortunately many of the historiated or ornamental initials have been cut out of this book. Only two of the historiated initials survive. Boethius's *Liber de divisione* begins with an initial of a man chopping a piece of wood (fol. 39). This subject might be derived from the title of the work. Aristotle's *Analytica Posteriora* begins with an initial showing a man and woman in bed (fol. 215), a subject difficult to explain from the accompanying text. The short partial borders and initials have in some cases birds or animals perched on them.

The figure style and ornament place this volume among manuscripts produced by a workshop of artists probably based in Oxford *c*.1250–*c*.1270: a Psalter (Preston, Harris Museum), two Bibles (Oxford, All Souls College, MS 2 and New York, Pierpont Morgan Library, G. 42), a Bestiary (Cambridge, Trinity College, MS R.14.9) and at least ten university text books *(see no. 175)*. The feature of the birds or animals perched on border extensions or initials can be paralleled in a copy of Aristotle's *Libri naturales* made by this workshop (London, British Library, Harley MS 3487). A discovery by the late Michael Camille, who devoted much study to these university books, demonstrated that already from *c*.1230 such books were being made in Oxford. He discovered a *c*.1230 copy of Aristotle's works on logic, with a textual content similar to that of Pembroke 193, partly decorated by the Oxford illuminator William de Brailes, who is documented as working in that city between 1238 and 1252 (Vatican City, Biblioteca Apostolica Vaticana, MS Borghesiana 58). It begins with Porphyry's *Isagoge* illustrated by an initial, not by de Brailes, showing a seated tonsured figure instructing a group of students seated before him, the same iconography as occurs at the beginning of the compilation of Aristotle's *Libri naturales (no. 175)*. De Brailes uses the same subject for the opening initial of the *Analytica Priora*, and also for the *Analytica Posteriora*, but with the hand of God intervening from above in the latter initial.

PROVENANCE: three ownership inscriptions of the fourteenth and fifteenth centuries (fol. 236v) reveal that by the second half of the fourteenth century this book belonged to Pembroke College, founded as the Hall of Valence Mary in 1347. Unfortunately, it cannot be identified in the *c*.1490 list of benefactors and their gifts of books.

LITERATURE: James 1905a, 180–81; Lacombe 1939, 342, no. 221; Camille 1985a, 32; Morgan 1982–1988, II, 125; Camille 1995, 294 n. 10.   NJM

177

Raymond of Peñafort, *Summa de casibus*, etc.

In Latin
England, *c*.1250

Parchment, 173 fols., 272 × 202 mm, text 166–72 × 103–9 mm with 47–48 lines, 164–168 × 101–103 mm with 42 lines and 169–197 × 124 mm with 47–54 lines, ruled in pencil or crayon

SCRIPT: Gothic bookhand (textualis)

BINDING: quarter niger by J.P. Gray, 1963; early pattern of lozenges and flowers on fore-edges

Cambridge University Library, Add. MS. 3471

THIS MANUSCRIPT contains the *Summa de casibus penitentie* of St Raymond of Peñafort with his *Summa de matrimonio* appearing as the fourth book; the *Summa* of Richard of Leicester or Wethringsette; and the *Templum domini* of Robert Grosseteste. The two last works appear together in five other manuscripts. All three texts were relevant to the pastoral work of parish priests and confessors and to the *cura animarum* (care of souls). Master Richard of Leicester was Rector of Wetheringsett in Suffolk and, by *c*.1222, Chancellor of Cambridge University. He is the first recorded Chancellor and was still in office *c*.1232. His *Summa 'Qui bene presunt presbiteri'* is a pastoral manual for confessors, written after the Fourth Lateran Council of 1215 and probably before 1222. A popular and influential work, it survives, at the latest count, in sixty-two manuscripts. In the words of its current editor, together with Thomas of Chobham's *Summa confessorum* it 'established a new type of didactic religious literature that would flourish for centuries on English soil' (Goering 1995, 142, 153 and n.42).

The most recent of the works contained in Add. MS. 3471 is Raymond's *Summa de matrimonio*, written *c*.1234–35. It is likely that the manuscript was written not long after this, for the accomplished hand suggests a date in the mid-thirteenth century. There are numerous glosses in at least three thirteenth/fourteenth-century hands. The table of contents to Raymond's *Summa* contains rubrics encircled in blue and brown with penwork flourishing.

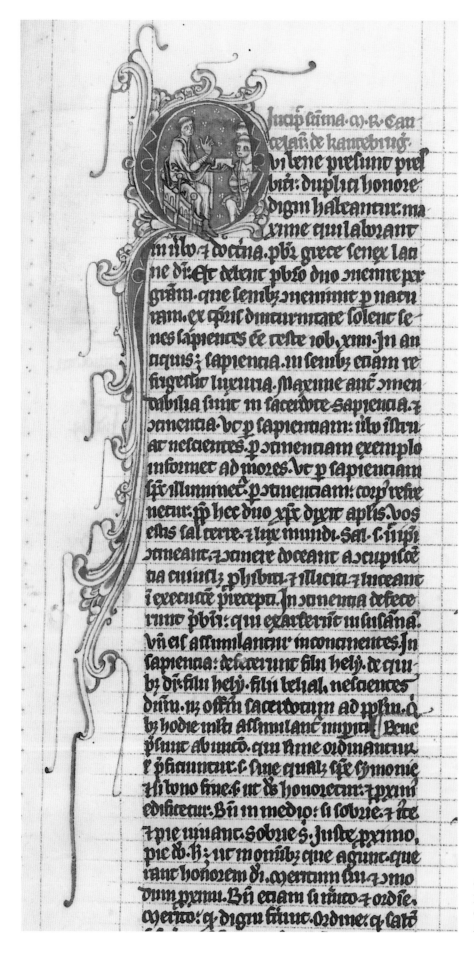

374

Each of the *Summae* opens with an illuminated initial, apparently by the same artist (fols. 11, 125). The first of these depicts two Dominicans against a burnished gold ground; one (representing the author, Raymond of Peñafort) is handing a book to another. The second initial depicts the author, Richard of Wethringsette, seated and lecturing (Emden 1963, 679) or presiding at an inception ceremony (Hackett 1970, 147). This initial may be the earliest representation of Cambridge academic dress, but it is doubtful if it is accurate in detail (Hackett 1970, 147). On the first page of Grosseteste's work (fol. 170) is an elaborate penwork initial. At the foot of the page there is an elegant drawing of the *Templum domini*, its roof supported on seven columns. The style of illumination is comparable to that of Psalters made for Peterborough Abbey and an East Anglian Bible (No. 68; London, Society of Antiquaries, MS 59; Oxford, Bodleian Library, MS Auct. D.4.8; Morgan, 1982–1988, nos. 45, 47, 75), and it is likely that the manuscript was produced in East Anglia.

PROVENANCE: 'M. Lee', 'Thomas Huckell Lee' (ownership inscriptions, 19th c.); Thomas Phillipps (MSS. 7402 and 22339); purchased by the Library at his sale, Sotheby's, London, 6 June 1898, lot 622.

LITERATURE: Smalley and Lacombe 1931, 141; Kuttner 1937, 443–45; Glorieux 1938, I, no. 118a; Emden 1963, frontispiece and 367, 679; Hackett 1970, 47–49, 147–48; Kaeppeli 1970–1993, III, 285–86; Bloomfield, Guyot, Howard and Kabealo 1979, nos. 4583, 5982; Morgan 1982–1988, II, 38 n.40; Goering and Mantello 1985; Goering 1992, 86–95; Goering 1995, 143–59; Sharpe 1997, 519; unpublished descriptions by Jayne Ringrose and Paul Binski. PNRZ

178

Letter patent of Edward I confirming privileges of Cambridge University

In Latin
England, London and Cambridge, issued 6 Feb. 1292

Parchment, 470 × 410 mm, portion of Great Seal of Edward I attached

SCRIPT: Secretary

Cambridge University Archives, MS Luard 7★

ROYAL CHARTERS granted to institutions such as Cambridge University have the signal advantage of being dated *(see no. 133)*; so, aside from their intrinsic

interest, they can offer landmarks in the history of illumination. Luard 7★ gives us some indication of what sort of illumination was conducted in Cambridge itself towards 1300. With the possible exception of item *177* in the exhibition it is the earliest Cambridge illumination. The preparation, writing and sealing of a royal charter such as this was the business of the Royal Chancery in London. But the addition of the illumination, in this case an initial letter, could be left to the grantee to supply later on (but probably not much later). In Luard 7★ a pink-red and blue initial E for *Edwardus dei gratia Rex* (etc.) depicts King Edward I, in blue, presenting the charter directly to a doctor of Canon Law in *cappa clausa*, a doctor of civil law in *cappa manicata*, and two kneeling doctors of theology in *cappe clause*. The evidence for thinking that this initial was executed in Cambridge and not London is provided by a small Breviary and Missal made *c.*1290–1300 for Ely Cathedral Priory, now Cambridge University Library, MS Ii.4. 20. This has initials in the same style, and since it is intrinsically probable that the monks of Ely were having their liturgical books illuminated in their own region rather than London, Cambridge is pointed to as the origin of both works. Similar

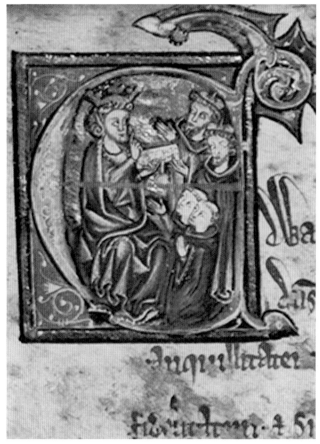

King Edward I presenting the Charter to Cambridge Doctors. Cambridge University Archives, MS Luard 7★, detail

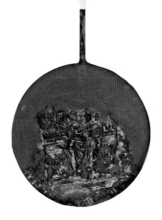

King Edward I presenting the Charter
to Cambridge Doctors.
Cambridge University Archives,
MS Luard 7★

connections between Ely and Cambridge are implied by the next item *(no. 179)*. The direct but neat and crisp idiom is generally in keeping with styles of illumination practised in south-eastern England towards 1300.

PROVENANCE: in the archives of the University since it was issued.

EXHIBITED: London 1987–1988, no.319.

LITERATURE: Morgan 1982, 38 n.40; Owen 1988, 4; Danbury 1989, 168; Fox 1998, fig. 231.

PB

179

Royal writ under Great Seal conferring jurisdictions on the Chancellor

In Latin
England, London and Cambridge, issued 19 Sept. 1343

Parchment, 420 × 290 mm

SCRIPT: Secretary

Cambridge University Archives, MS Luard 33a★

Luard 33a★, issued under the Great Seal of England, confirms the Cambridge-Ely connection apparent in the earlier charter Luard 7★ *(no. 178)*. Though damaged and much conserved, it is immediately apparent that this work is artistically a good deal more elaborate, in keeping with the showy ornateness of English illumination in the generation before the Black Death. To the right hand side it shows King Edward III with an orb and a cross holding a scroll, together with a soldier in a basinet holding a mace. The King is addressing the Chancellor of Cambridge, kneeling to the left hand side in blue, also with an inscribed scroll and with a sergeant behind him in a brown tunic, holding a mace. Above, a weird winged creature in blue with hooves holds up two shields (England quartered with France, and gules, a fess dancetty with three escalopes (?) argent), which are supported from above by an angel emerging from clouds. Bar and vinescroll ornament frames the left border. The Chancellor is Thomas de Northwood (confirmed 1340; Tanner 1917, 16; Emden 1963, 427–28). The style of the work is quite close to one hand (e.g. fol. 7) of the Vienna Bohun Psalter (Vienna, Österreichische Nationalbibliothek, MS 1826★), and to the circle of the Psalter of Simon de Montacute, Bishop of Ely *(no. 78*; Sandler 1986, nos. 133, 112). Accordingly it offers some general pointers to the dates of those related works and to the continued existence of illuminators working in Cambridge for the University and other organizations (Dennison 1986b).

PROVENANCE: in the archives of the University since issued.

LITERATURE: Dennison 1986b, 56, figs. 21–2; Owen 1988, 7; Danbury 1989, 168.

PB

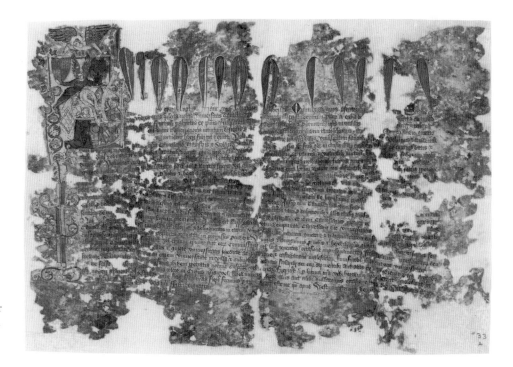

King Edward III addressing the Chancellor of Cambridge University. Cambridge University Archives, MS Luard 33★

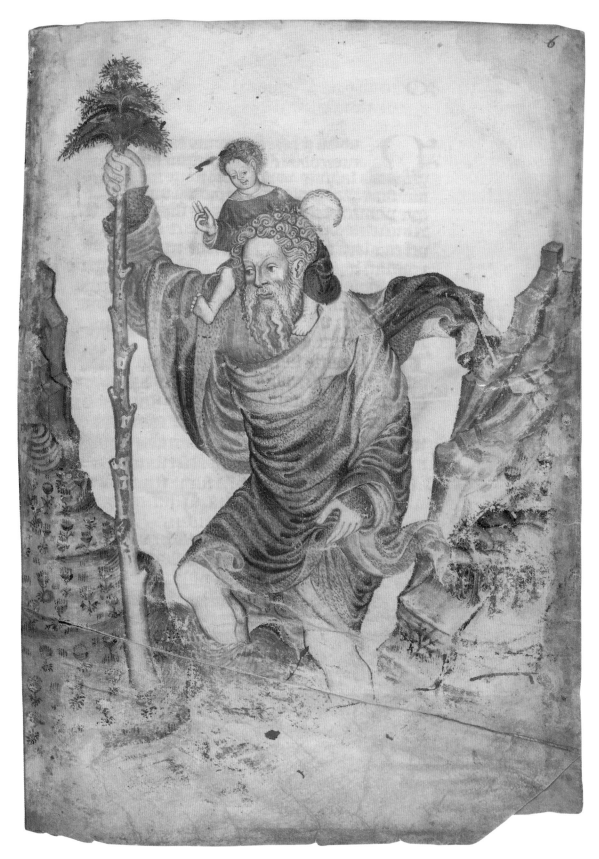

St Christopher carrying the Christ Child. Cambridge University Archives, Collect. Admin. 3, fol. 6

180

The Old Proctor's Book

In Latin
England, Cambridge, c.1390

Parchment, 48 fols., 284 × 190 mm, text 205 × 118 mm,
32 lines, ruled in brown ink

SCRIPT: Gothic bookhand (cursive; textualis, fols. 6v–7v)

BINDING: lower cover, blind-stamped calf with latten mounts,
clasps and staple for carrying chain, end of 15th c.; upper cover,
calf over pasteboard, early 19th c.; spine, vellum, 19th c., late

Cambridge University Archives, Collect. Admin. 3

THE OLD PROCTOR'S BOOK consists of the greater part of a collection of University statutes and related documents prepared for the use of the proctors, the Chancellor's executive officers. A date after c.1385–1389 is indicated by the inclusion of the obit of Master William Gotham in the Calendar, and the absence of a statute relating to the commemoration of the Chancellor Michael de Causton suggests a date before 1396. Other portions of the original book are now to be found in Collect. Admin. 1, fols. 60–80, and Collect. Admin. 2, fols. 107–10. Its creation may have been a result of the reorganization of records after the partial destruction of the University's muniments during the Peasants' Revolt of 1381. It includes two full-page tinted drawings: St Christopher carrying the Christ Child, who holds an eye-like orb, on fol. 6, and the Virgin and Child enthroned under a canopy with niches inhabited by members of the University and laity, including a figure accompanied by the heraldic device of a bull's head, on fol. 8. These images are intended to underline the solemnity of oaths sworn by civic officials. In the Junior Proctor's Book of c.1490 (Collect. Admin. 2) there is a badly defaced full-page Crucifixion, together with small miniatures of the Evangelists accompanying the Gospel extracts on which the oaths were sworn. A thirteenth-century example of sacred images in the context of oaths is London, Public Record Office E. 36/266, the Black Book of the Exchequer (Morgan 1982–1988, no. 83). St Christopher may be included on account of his popularity as an atropaic figure, but it is significant that in the Beaufort Hours (London, British Library, Royal MS 2. A.xviii, fol. 12) he is invoked against lies and false witness.

Evidence has been put forward for manuscript illumination in Cambridge in the first half of the fourteenth century (Dennison 1986b; Michael 1988), but this is a unique example of Cambridge figural illumination at the end of the century. The drawings illustrate the diversity of influences upon English art in the late fourteenth century. The stippling of the pigments and even the very colours used are suggestive of Lombard influence. The figure of St Christopher has parallels in the Paris *Tacuinum Sanitatis* (Paris, Bibliothèque nationale de France, MS nouv. acq. lat. 1673). Certain other features point more towards the German Imperial lands. The rocks between which St Christopher wades resemble those in Bohemian wall paintings at Karlstein. St Christopher's distinctive facial type, with strong nasal bridge and eyebrows, can be found in works of art produced in the lands of the Teutonic Order. The inhabited architectural setting for the Virgin and Child can be paralleled in Bohemian art, but the artist may have been inspired by the use of the motif in English or Flemish seals and brasses. This heterogeneity is reminiscent of the *mélange* of styles in the Pepysian Sketchbook (Cambridge, Magdalene College, Pepys MS 1916). It is now recognized that Bohemian art, though significant, was just one element in an eclectic range of influences upon metropolitan art in the late fourteenth century (Binski 1997). The University of Cambridge, with its international academic contacts, was as likely a place as the court of Richard II for a manifestation of International Gothic.

PROVENANCE: in the archives of the University since issue.

LITERATURE: Peek and Hall 1962, 27, pl.1; Hackett 1970, 260–85; Rogers 1986; Cobban 1988, pl. K; Robinson 1988, no. A2.

NR

181

Charter upon Act of Parliament for the Foundation of King's College, Cambridge

In Latin
England, London, 1446
ARTIST: William Abell (doc.1450–d.1474)
SCRIBE: John Broke (doc.1443–1450)

Parchment, 5 membranes, 710 × 982 mm, text 620 mm wide,
ruled in plummet

SCRIPT: Secretary

Seal: The Golden Seal of Henry VI (identical with the Second
Great Seal of Henry IV) (Wyon 1887, Nos. 79A, 80A), green
wax, blue, gold and white thread

King's College Archives KC/18

THE LAVISHNESS of the decoration of this charter, no less that the extent of the concessions, exemptions and privileges which it confers, indicates the importance of the foundation of King's College to Henry VI. The layout of the charter points to a close collaboration between the scribes and the illuminator. The calligraphic penwork heading, with interlaced letter forms and elaborate cadels, was written first by an unidentified scribe. Then the text of the charter was written by John Broke, clerk of the chancery. Finally an elaborate iconographic programme was provided by the illuminator, William Abell. The king, wearing a closed crown and an ermine-lined mantle, is depicted within the calligraphic H of 'Henricus', kneeling at a prie-dieu, holding the charter and gesturing to a scroll inscribed *Fiat ad laudem gloriam et cultum tuum'*, ('Be it done to thy praise, glory and worship'). Behind him are the Lords Spiritual and Temporal,

headed by the Lord Chancellor, Archbishop Stafford, and Cardinals Beaufort and Kemp. Below, heading a group of sixteen Members of Parliament, is the Speaker of the House of Commons, holding a scroll inscribed in Law French *'Prient les comunes'*, ('The Commons request'). This is echoed by the Lords' *'Et nous le prioms auxi'*, ('And we also request it'). The process of parliamentary petitioning is reflected by a heavenly hierarchy. Henry's prayer is directed to the patrons of the College. St Nicholas intercedes with the Blessed Virgin, who is shown being borne up to Heaven to be crowned by the Trinity. Morgan has noted that Mary, with her mantle held open by the angels, appears as a Madonna of Mercy mediating the grace of the Trinity to the assembled Parliament. Further indicators of heavenly protection

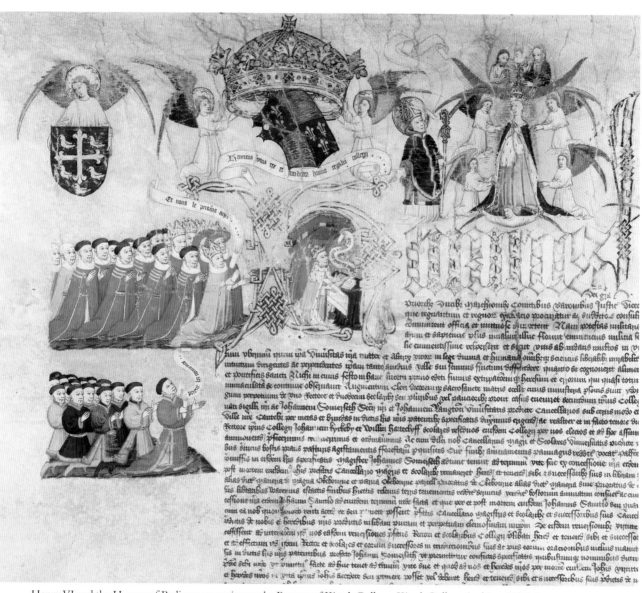

Henry VI and the Houses of Parliament praying to the Patrons of King's College. King's College Archives KC/18

are the angels bearing the crown above the royal arms and the demi-angels holding the arms of Saints Edward the Confessor and Edmund. With the exception of a few narrative images in chronicles, this is the earliest representation of the Houses of Parliament. The familiarity with the parliamentary process, which is revealed by such details as the distinctions of rank in the peers' robes, led Powell and Wallis to speculate that the artist was involved in the preparation of illustrated records of parliamentary procedure similar to those made by Tudor heralds *(see no. 136)*. The motif of ranks of petitioning figures is to be found in an earlier document decorated by William Abell or his workshop, the 1444 Letters Patent to the Leathersellers' Company (London 2003–2004, *no. 131*).

The King's Charter was identified as the work of the London illuminator William Abell by Erna Auerbach, who noted its stylistic similarity to Eton College ECR EA.3, of 5 March 1446, for which Abell was paid 26s. 8d. (Auerbach 1954, 20). Abell was the supervisor of the will of Thomas Fyssh, limner (d.1450), from whom he inherited the apprentices Robert FitzJohn and William Butler. Abell lived in the parish of St Nicholas Shambles, of which he was churchwarden in 1452–1453 and 1470–1471. From 1469 until his death in 1474 Abell rented shops in Paternoster Row, the centre of the London book trade (Christianson 1990, 59–60). In 1454 he was enrolled in the Parish Clerks' Fraternity of St Nicholas, which was patronized by several people involved in book production (James 2004, 36). Abell's precise, rather hard style was particularly well suited to heraldic decoration. His hand can be recognized in the grants of arms to the Haberdashers, of 1446, and the Tallow Chandlers, of 1456. Characteristic of his work are the bony head types, often with heavy upper eyelids, of the Lords and Commons, and angular drapery folds, exemplified by St Nicholas. Alexander noted a stylistic similarity to the work of the artist of Trinity College, Cambridge MS B.11.7, the so-called Cornwall Master. It has been suggested that the Cornwall Master may be Thomas Fyssh (Rogers 1994, 183).

PROVENANCE: at King's College since it was issued.

EXHIBITED: Brussels 1973, no.82; London 2003–2004, no.20.

LITERATURE: Heywood and Wright 1850, 299–359 ; Cooper 1860–1866, I, 178–81; Saltmarsh 1933, 87, fig. 5; Auerbach 1954, 20–21; Powell and Wallis 1968, 477–78, pl.XIV; Alexander 1972, 166, 167, pl.2; Alexander 1983, 152, pl.13; Cobban 1988, pl.M; Danbury 1989, 160; Morgan 1994, 238; Scott 1996, II, 264, 265, 267.   NR

182

Letter addressed to King Henry VI

In Latin
England, probably Cambridge, May 1448
ARTIST: The Caesar Master (act. *c.*1440–*c.*1460)

Parchment, 1 membrane, 240 × 385mm, text 110 × 310mm, 19 long lines, ruled in plummet

SCRIPT: Secretary

Seal: Common seal of Pembroke College, red wax

Pembroke College Archives, College Box A 19

UNDER JOHN LANGTON, Master from 1428 to 1447, Pembroke College received several benefactions from Henry VI of Cambridgeshire property derived from alien priories that had been sequestered during the wars with France. Langton, who was also chaplain to the King and Treasurer of Calais, was consecrated Bishop of St David's in King's College Chapel on 7 May 1447, but died on 22 May. Associated with Langton in royal service was John Somerset, Fellow of Pembroke from 1416, Physician to the King, and executor of Humphrey, Duke of Gloucester. Langton and Somerset were both involved in the early stages of the foundation of King's College. The appointment of a new Master, Hugh Damlet, was an appropriate point at which to render formal thanks to the King, thereby reminding him of Pembroke's continuing needs.

In the letter, dated 20 May 1448, the College thanks the King, who has brought it from the depths of poverty to a sufficiency unimagined hitherto. In return, the indebted scholars offer mites, like the widow in the Gospel. Four times every year, on the feasts of Saints Fabian and Sebastian, Chad, Medard and Gildard, and Kenelm, the Mass *Salus populi*, with music, would be celebrated by the Fellows for the King and his two kingdoms, and in Rogationtide would be held the Office of the Dead with a Requiem Mass, during the King's life, for the souls of Henry V and Catherine his consort. After the King's decease, the Office of the Dead would be celebrated annually, in perpetuity, for the souls of the King, Margaret his consort, his parents and all his ancestors. These provisions would be incorporated in the statutes of the College, and all fellows elected henceforth would have to take an oath to observe this statute along with the others in the book of statutes. In function this document is similar to a monastic letter of confraternity, bestowing spiritual benefits upon a benefactor. It is probable that a pair of documents was executed, one of which was given to the King.

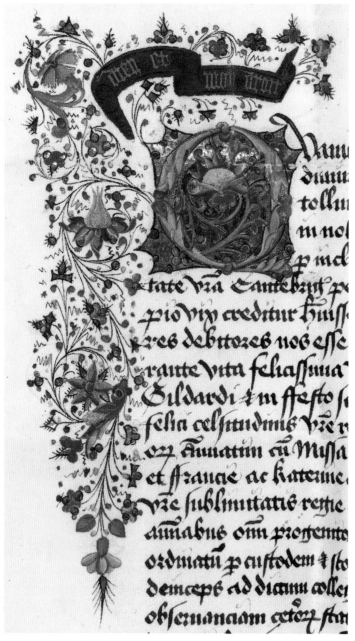

Initial Q and Scroll with Royal Motto. Pembroke College Archives, College Box A 19

The document bears the College's common seal, now fragmentary, showing Christ displaying his wounds, seated on the roof of a building probably intended to represent the College Chapel, which is supported by the outstretched hands of the Foundress, Marie de St Pol, and her husband, Aymer de Valence, Earl of Pembroke (Ringrose 1993, 95). This seal, together with that of the University, was attached to the book of the College Statutes referred to in the letter (Pembroke College Archives, College Box A12), and the sealing of this

document seems to indicate that it has the status of a College statute. Another version of this letter, written in the same distinctive Secretary hand, with an elaborate penwork crowned Q and the royal motto above, is preserved in Pembroke College Archives (Soham D7).

Above the initial Q in the letter shown here is a scroll bearing the motto 'Dieu et mon droit', 'God and my right'. Henry VI is the first King of England whose use of this motto – which is still the royal motto – is confirmed by clear contemporary evidence. It is incorporated in the penwork of the Letters Patent of 12 February 1441 founding King's College (Danbury 1989, 174). The decorative repertoire is quite distinct from standard English illumination of the 1440s. The initial Q, with its 'wheat-ear' structure and acanthus flower, is Italianate in appearance, and the neat flowers and geometric foliage of the border can be paralleled in Flemish manuscripts of the 1440s. The letter is the second earliest dated example of the work of a Continental illuminator working in England named the Caesar Master (Scott 1980, 41–44). It is still not clear whether he was an Italian who had added Netherlandish elements to his repertoire or a Netherlander who had received training in Italy. His earliest known work is Florence, Biblioteca Riccardiana, MS 952, written by Milo de Carraria in London in 1447. He also illuminated additions made for Richard, Duke of York to a Book of Hours produced in Flanders (Ushaw, St Cuthbert College, MS 43). A copy of Johannes de Bado Aureo, De Arte Heraldica, made for Sir Hugh Fenne of Herringby, Norfolk (Oxford, Bodleian Library, MS Laud. misc. 733), contains figural illumination by him that is clearly Italian in character. It would appear that the Caesar Master was itinerant, obtaining commissions chiefly from Humanist scholars. This document is of significance in that it almost certainly adds Cambridge to the places in which the Caesar Master operated.

PROVENANCE: Pembroke College Archives.

EXHIBITED: Cambridge 1998.

LITERATURE: Cobban 1988, pl. N; Scott 1996, II, 278; Grimstone 1997, 28, fig. 19.

JR/NR

183

Charter upon Act of Parliament of Elizabeth I

In Latin
England, London, probably Westminster, 1559

Parchment: 1 membrane, 479 × 672 mm, text 272 × 462 mm, 44 lines, ruled in red ink

SCRIPT: Secretary

SEAL: First Great Seal of Elizabeth I, engraved by Dericke Anthony (Wyon 1887, Nos. 111, 112), brown wax, silver thread

Trinity Hall Muniments 79

THIS CHARTER, issued at Westminster on 13 May 1559, serves as a confirmation of the Charters of Trinity Hall. The issuing of such confirmatory charters is often an indicator of political turmoil. In the reign of Edward VI, Trinity Hall had nearly been amalgamated with Clare to form a new college for the study of civil law. To obviate a repetition of such a move at the beginning of Elizabeth's reign, at a time when royal commissioners were visiting the University and depriving Catholic masters and fellows, Henry Harvey, the conservative conformist who was Master of Trinity Hall from 1558 to 1585, took the precaution of obtaining parliamentary approval of Bishop Bateman's foundation of 1350.

Illuminated royal charters usually have an enthroned image of the sovereign in the initial, a reprise of the subject-matter of the obverse of the Great Seal. The

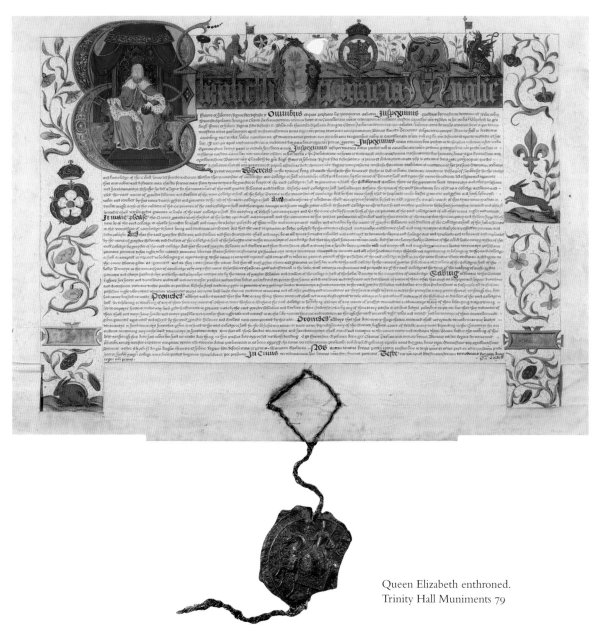

Queen Elizabeth enthroned.
Trinity Hall Muniments 79

383

earliest known instance of this is London, Society of Antiquaries, MS 607, Letters Patent granted by Edward I in 1280 to Glastonbury Abbey (Danbury 1989, 168–69).

The image of Queen Elizabeth presented here is of a standard type used on legal documents until *c.*1580 (Auerbach 1954, 121). Unfortunately, the Queen's face is rubbed, making a stylistic assessment difficult. A similar depiction in the 1559 indenture by which the Poor Knights of Windsor were founded (London, Public Record Office, E. 36/277) has been attributed by Strong to Livina Teerlinc (Strong 1987, 55), but there is no reason for invoking her name in this instance. The banner-bearing heraldic animals, crowned Tudor rose and fleur-de-lis are standard features of Tudor charters. They can be found, for example, in the 1557 Letters Patent of Philip and Mary (Clerkenwell, St John's Gate) by which the Knights Hospitaller were restored in England (Riley-Smith 1999, 87). This document has rather loose floral decoration with flattened flower-heads, similar to that on the Trinity Hall Charter.

The Trinity Hall Charter is the earliest of three Elizabethan documents in Cambridge with portraits of the Queen. Of a far higher quality than the Trinity Hall example is the miniature on the Letters Patent of 11 January 1584, granting licence to Sir Walter Mildmay to found Emmanuel College, which has been attributed to Nicholas Hilliard (Bendall, Brooke and Collinson 1999, pl. 1). At Sidney Sussex College the initial E of the licence of 25 July 1594, enabling the Earl of Kent and Sir John Harington to found the college, contains a delicate pen drawing of Elizabeth (Sidney Sussex 1996, 47–49, pl.).

PROVENANCE: in Trinity Hall since issue.

LITERATURE: Madden 1902, 101–2; Pink 1929, 17; Crawley 1976, 56–57.

NR

184

Robert Hare, *Registrum novum monumentorum universitatis Cantebrigie*

In Latin, French and English
England, probably London, 1587–1589

VOLUME I: Parchment, xxx + 368 + 7 fols., 365 × 227 mm, text 215 × 125 mm, 36 lines, ruled in brown ink

VOLUME II: Parchment, xiv + 435 fols., 361 × 223 mm, text 227 × 127 mm, 36 lines, ruled in brown ink

SCRIPT: Secretary

BINDING: Contemporary or near contemporary, calf over wooden boards, each volume with bosses (not all extant), fastenings and inscriptions under horns

Cambridge University Archives, Hare A, i–ii

MEDIEVAL RELIGIOUS HOUSES and other ecclesiastical establishments preserved deeds, charters and other writings by which they bolstered and defended their possessions and rights. They copied these documents into cartularies and registers, which served as a form of security in the event of loss or damage to the originals. The University of Cambridge was no exception to this practice. The earliest register to survive (Cambridge University Archives, Collect. admin. 7) was a private compilation by Thomas Markaunt, fellow of Corpus Christi College, and senior proctor in 1417–1418. It contains university statutes and royal, papal and other documents. It came into the university's possession only in 1594, through the gift of Robert Hare. Hare had become a fellow commoner of Gonville Hall in 1545, but he left Cambridge without taking a degree and entered the Inner Temple. He was Clerk of the Pells from 1560 to *c.*1571. Thereafter he devoted himself to antiquarian pursuits. He is principally associated not with Markaunt's register but with a massive collection of university charters and privileges in two volumes, which he compiled at the suggestion of the Vice-Chancellor, John Copcot. The first of these volumes is displayed. They were completed in 1589 and presented to the University in 1590, when the Public Orator addressed a letter of thanks to Hare. Hare presented or bequeathed two further (but less opulent) versions of his collection to the University, one for the use of the Registrary (Hare B, i–iii) and one for the Vice-Chancellor (Hare C, i–iv).

The source of the texts is always specified: they derive mainly from the public records, but some are from university archives. Little is known about the circumstances of the production of Hare A. It is likely that

Robert Hare employed scribes and illuminators in London. Their work is of a high order. The preface (Vol. I, fol. vi) contains representations of the Four Doctors of the Church with the symbols of the Evangelists and is followed by two pages of heraldic shields. The arrangement is chronological, divided by the reigns of the English kings. Each reign begins with decorated borders of foliage and heraldic arms, meticulously executed. The first reign is that of King Arthur, whose entirely fictitious charter of 7 April 531 is transcribed *'ex archivis universitatis'*. Arthur is depicted in armour and on horseback in both the illuminated initial 'A' and the right border *(see fig. 45)*. Below the latter are Hare's arms, which feature again and again in the volumes. The next reign is King John's, with sparser decoration (fol. 13); but the tendency is for borders and initials to become more sumptuous with each reign. A fitting climax is the opening of the section for the reigning monarch, Elizabeth I (Vol. II, fol. 377). In Volume I are two illuminations different in style from the rest of the illustrative matter. One depicts the mayor of Cambridge taking an oath before the Chancellor of the University to maintain peace between the town and the University. It accompanies the text of letters patent of Edward III requiring the mayor and other representatives of the town to take this oath annually. The second accompanies Richard II's grant to the university of the supervision of weights and measures in the town. It shows University officials surveying them and destroying false ones (fol. 276v; Peek and Hall 1962, pl.13). These illustrations underline the function of Hare's collection, which was to reinforce not only the national and international standing of the university but also the manifold aspects of its jurisdiction over the town of Cambridge.

The massive volumes of Hare's *Registrum* show that even in the late sixteenth century the tradition of medieval manuscript production, and more especially decoration and illumination, was still alive.

PROVENANCE: Presented to the University of Cambridge by Robert Hare, 1590.

LITERATURE: Cooper 1842–1908, III, 45–46; Venn 1897–1901, I, 34; Clark 1904, 575–76; Peek and Hall 1962; Owen 1988, 33; Hiatt 2004, pl. 3.

PNRZ

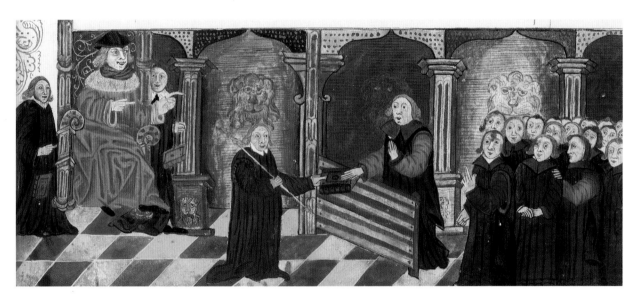

The mayor of Cambridge taking an oath before the Chancellor of the University. Cambridge University Archives, Hare A, I, fol. 152, detail

GLOSSARY

Apocalypse
The Revelation of St John the Divine, the last book of the Bible

Arma Christi
A symbolic image of the Instruments of the Passion of Christ found in the later Middle Ages

Bestiary
A book of animals, birds and reptiles in which their habits are described and moralized. Many of the creatures are fantastic and mythological (*see* p.298)

Bifolium
Two pages made up of a single sheet of vellum. Bifolia were inserted inside each other to make up a quire

Bindings *see* pp.27–29

Book of Hours
A prayer book based on liturgical service books, used mainly for private devotions

Calendar
Listing of the feast days and saints' days of the year, frequently illustrated with Labours of the Months and Signs of the Zodiac

Canon Tables
A concordance table of references to passages occurring in two or more of the four Gospels compiled by Eusebius of Caesarea in the fourth century and usually arranged in columns under arches

Canonical Hours
The eight monastic church services prescribed for the twenty-four hour day as the Divine Office: Matins, Lauds, Prime, Terce, Sext, Nones, Vespers, Compline

Common of Saints
Offices used in common for saints not commemorated in the Missal or Breviary by an individual service

Decretals
Collections of law texts, most famously, that of Gratian.

Evangelist Symbols
The four Evangelists frequently represented symbolically by four winged creatures derived from Ezekiel's vision: St Matthew – the Angel; St Mark – the Lion; St Luke– the Ox; St John – the Eagle

Explicit
Closing words of a text (Latin 'it ends')

Fore-edge
The painting of the cut outer edges of a bound manuscript with decorative patterns, often heraldic

Gloss
Notes in the margin or between the lines of a book containing comments, interpretations or explanations of the passages of a text

Grisaille
Monochrome painting in neutral greys or beiges only

Historiated Initial
An initial letter enclosing a narrative or symbolic scene

Incipit
Opening words of text (Latin 'it begins')

Littera prismatica
Faceted initials

Liturgical Books
Antiphonal, Benedictional, Breviary, Epistle Lectionary, Gospels, Gospel Lectionary, Gradual, Manual, Missal: Temporal and Sanctoral, Ordinal, Pontifical (*see* pp.119–123).

Majuscule
An upper-case letter, whether uncials, rustic or square capitals

Minuscule
A lower-case letter. **Caroline Minuscule** is of the Caroligian and Anglo-Saxon periods

Pecia system
Text divided into sections and distributed to a number of scribes, which are later returned and collated

Pietà
An image of the Virgin with the dead body of Christ across her lap

Pigments *see* pp. 27–28

Plummet
A 'pencil', piece of lead used to rule lines

Postilla
Digest of patristic and medieval teaching

Quadrivium
The division of the curriculum into the Liberal Arts of arithmetic, music, geometry and astronomy

Rustic capitals
A Roman alphabet whose distinctive form is a capital A without a cross-bar; it is generally characterized by a narrowness of letter, the contrast of thick and thin strokes and large serifs

Sarum Use
The 13th-century liturgical texts and practices of Salisbury by the Province of Canterbury, but not the Province of York and the Diocese of Hereford, which kept their own Use. The **Use of Rome** is also common in Continental medieval manuscripts

Scripts *see* pp. 29–31

Tawed skin
Taw makes hide into leather without the use of tannin esp. by soaking in a solution of alum and salt

Tetramorph
The union of the four symbols of the Evangelists – the angel, lion, ox and eagle – into one figure

Tree of Jesse
A diagram in the form of a branching tree, with figural components, showing the descent of Christ from David and his father Jesse, usually recumbent at the foot

Trivium
The Liberal Arts of Grammar, Rhetoric and Logic in the curriculum

Typology
Presenting episodes of the Life of Christ with incidents of the Old Testament held symbolically to have been foreshadowed

Uncial
A Roman alphabet with distinctive capital letters of equal height and generally rounded forms. **Half-uncial** script has ascenders and descenders (*see* p.29)

Vulgate
The Latin text of the Bible as translated by St Jerome

BIBLIOGRAPHY

Books and Articles

AGATI 2001: M.L. Agati, *Giovanni Onorio da Maglie: copista Greco (1535–1563)*, Bolletino dei classici, Suppl. 20, Rome, 2001

ALDIS WRIGHT 1873–1878: W. Aldis Wright, *Generydes,* Early English Text Society OS 55, 70, London 1873–1878

ALEXANDER 1969: J.J.G. Alexander, 'Notes on Some Veneto-Paduan Illuminated Books of the Renaissance', *Arte Veneta* 23 (1969), 9–20; repr. in Alexander 2002, 106–141

ALEXANDER 1970A: J.J.G. Alexander, *The Master of Mary of Burgundy: A Book of Hours for Engelbert of Nassau*, London, 1970

ALEXANDER 1970B: J.J.G. Alexander, 'A Manuscript of Petrarch's Rime and Trionfi', *Victoria and Albert Museum Yearbook* 2 (1970), 27–40; repr. in Alexander 2002, 142–68

ALEXANDER 1971: J.J.G. Alexander, 'A lost leaf from a Bodleian Book of Hours', *Bodleian Library Record 8* (1971), 248–51

ALEXANDER 1972: J.J.G. Alexander, 'William Abell "lymnour" and 15th Century English Illumination', in *Kunsthistorische Forschungen Otto Pächt zu seinem 70. Geburtstag*, ed. A. Rosenauer and G. Weber, Salzburg, 1972, 166–72

ALEXANDER 1977: J.J.G. Alexander, *Italian Renaissance Illuminations*, New York and London, 1977

ALEXANDER 1978: J.J.G. Alexander, *Insular manuscripts: 6th to the 9th century*, A Survey of Manuscripts Illuminated in the British Isles 1, London, 1978

ALEXANDER 1980: J.J.G. Alexander, 'An English Illuminator's Work in some Fourteenth-Century Italian Law books at Durham', in *Medieval Art and Architecture at Durham Cathedral*, British Archaeological Association Conference Transactions 3 (1980), 149–53; repr. in Alexander 2002, 55–65

ALEXANDER 1983: J.J.G. Alexander, 'Painting and Manuscript Illumination for Royal Patrons in the Later Middle Ages', in *English Court Culture in the Later Middle Ages*, ed. V.J. Scattergood and J.W. Sherborne, London, 1983, 141–91

ALEXANDER 1985: J.J.G. Alexander, 'Italian Illuminated Manuscripts of the Fourteenth to the Sixteenth Centuries in British Collections', in Sesti 1985, I, 99–126; repr. in Alexander 2002, 22–54

ALEXANDER 1988: J.J.G. Alexander, 'Initials in Renaissance Illuminated Manuscripts: The Problem of the So-called *littera mantiniana*', in *Renaissance- und Humanistenhandschriften*, ed. J. Autenrieth and U. Eigler, Munich, 1988, 145–55; repr. in Alexander 2002, 169–98

ALEXANDER 1992: J.J.G. Alexander, *Medieval Illuminators and Their Methods of Work*, New Haven and London, 1992

ALEXANDER 2002: J.J.G. Alexander, *Studies in Italian Manuscript Illumination*, London, 2002

ALEXANDER AND DE LA MARE 1969: J.J.G. Alexander and A.C. de la Mare, *The Italian Manuscripts in the Library of Major J.R. Abbey*, London, 1969

ÁLVAREZ 1998: M.F. Álvarez, *Felipe II y su tiempo*, Madrid, 1998

ANDRIEU 1938–1942: M. Andrieu, *Le Pontifical romain au Moyen Âge*, Studi e Testi 86–88, 99, Vatican City, 1938–1942

ANGLO 1968: S. Anglo, *The Great Tournament Roll of Westminster*, 2 vols., Oxford, 1968

ARMSTRONG 1981: L. Armstrong, *Renaissance Miniature Painters & Classical Imagery: The Master of the Putti and his Venetian Workshop*, London, 1981

ARMSTRONG 1986: L. Armstrong, 'The Agostini Plutarch: An Illuminated Venetian Incunable', in *Treasures of the Library, Trinity College Dublin*, ed. P. Fox, Dublin, 1986, 86–96

ARMSTRONG 1990: L. Armstrong, 'Il Maestro di Pico: un miniatore veneziano del tardo Quattrocento', *Saggi e Memorie di Storia dell' Arte* 17 (1990), 7–39

ARMSTRONG 1991: L. Armstrong, 'The Impact of Printing on Miniaturists in Venice after 1469', in *Printing the Written Word: The Social History of Books, circa 1450–1520*, ed. S. Hindman, Ithaca, 1991, 174–202

ARMSTRONG 1994–1995: L. Armstrong, 'The Hand-Illumination of Printed Books', in London and New York 1994–1995, 35–47

ARMSTRONG 1996: L. Armstrong, 'Benedetto Bordon, miniator, and Cartography in Early Sixteenth-Century Venice', *Imago Mundi* 48 (1996), 65–92

ARMSTRONG 1998: L. Armstrong, 'Benedetto Bordon, Aldus Manutius, and LucAntonio Giunta: Old Links and New', in *Aldus Manutius and Renaissance Culture*, ed. D. Zeidberg, Florence, 1998, 161–83

ARMSTRONG 2001: L. Armstrong, 'Woodcuts for Liturgical Books Published by LucAntonio Giunta in Venice, 1499–1501', *Word and Image* 17 (2001), 65–93

ARMSTRONG 2003: L. Armstrong, 'The Hand Illumination of Venetian Bibles in the Incunable Period', in *Incunabula and Their Readers: Printing, Selling, and Using Books in the Fifteenth Century*, ed. K. Jensen, London, 2003, 83–113

ARMSTRONG 2003A: L. Armstrong, *Studies of Renaissance Miniaturists in Venice*, 2 vols., London, 2003

ARNOULD 1991: A. Arnould, *The Art Historical Context of the Library of Raphael de Mercatellis*, Ph.D. thesis, 2 vols., Ghent, 1991

ASHBURNHAM 1853–1861: *Catalogue of the Manuscripts at Ashburnham Place*, 3 vols., privately published, 1853–1861

ASTENGO 1996: C. Astengo, *Elenco preliminare di carte ed atlanti nautici manoscritti eseguiti nell'area mediterranea nel periodo 1500–1700 e conservati presso enti pubblici*, Genova, 1996

ASTENGO 2000: C. Astengo, *La cartografia nautica mediterranea dei secoli XVI e XVII*, Genova, 2000

AUERBACH 1954: E. Auerbach, *Tudor Artists*, London, 1954

AVRIL 1972: F. Avril, 'Un chef-d'oeuvre de l'enluminure sous le règne de Jean le Bon: la Bible Moralisée manuscrit français 167 de la Bibliothèque nationale', *Monuments et Mémoires de l'Académie des Inscriptions et Belles Lettres, Fondation Eugène Piot* 58 (1972), 91–125

AVRIL 1982: F. Avril, 'Les manuscrits enluminés de Guillaume de Machaut, Essai de chronologie', *Guillaume de Machaut, Colloque-table ronde, organisé par l'université de Reims*, Actes et colloques 23, Paris, 1982, 118–133

AYTO AND BARRATT 1984: J. Ayto and A. Barratt, ed., *Aelred of Rievaulx's De Institutione Inclusorum, Two English Versions.* Early English Text Society OS 287, Oxford, 1984

AVRIL, DUNLOP AND YAPP 1989: F. Avril, L. Dunlop and B. Yapp, *Les Petites Heures du Duc de Berry. Kommentar zu Ms. lat. 18014 der Bibliothèque nationale, Paris*, Lucerne, 1989

AVRIL AND STIRNEMANN 1987: F. Avril and P.D. Stirnemann, *Manuscrits enluminés d'origine insulaire VIIe–XXe siècle*, Paris, 1987

BACCHI ET AL. 1995: A. Bacchi, B. and R. Bentivoglio-Ravasio, A. de Marchi, S. Pettenati, *Francesco Marmitta*, Torino, 1995

BACKHOUSE 1967–1968: J. Backhouse, 'A Victorian Connoisseur and His Manuscripts: the Tale of Mr Jarman and Mr Wing', *The British Museum Quarterly* 32 (1967–1968), 76–92

BACKHOUSE 1985: J. Backhouse, *Books of Hours*, London, 1985

BACKHOUSE 1993: J. Backhouse, *The Isabella Breviary*, London, 1993

BAGLIANI 1990: *Les manuscrits enluminés des comtes et ducs de Savoie*, ed. A.P. Bagliani, Turin, 1990

BAILEY 1971: T.W. Bailey, *The Processions of Sarum and the Western Church*, Toronto, 1971

BAKER 1993: J.H. Baker, 'John Scott and the College Arms (1615)', *St Catharine's College Society* (1993), 42–43

BALTEAU ET AL. 1929–: Balteau, J., A. Rastoul, and M. Prévost, ed. *Dictionnaire de biographie française*, vols. 1–, Paris, 1929–

BANGE 1923: E.F. Bange, *Eine Bayerische Malerschule des XI. und XII. Jahrhunderts*, Munich, 1923

BANNISTER 1910–1911: H.M. Bannister, 'Irish Psalters', *Journal of Theological Studies* 12 (1910–1911), 278–82

BARKER-BENFIELD 1975: B.C. Barker-Benfield, 'The Manuscripts of Macrobius' commentary on the Somnium Scipionis', D.Phil. thesis, Oxford, 1975

BARKER-BENFIELD 1983: 'Macrobius', in Reynolds 1983, 222–32

BAROFFIO 1999: G. Baroffio, *Iter Liturgicum Italicum*, Padua, 1999

BARRATT 1995: A. Barratt, ed., *The Seven Psalms, A Commentary on the Penitential Psalms translated from the French into English by Dame Eleanor Hull*, Early English Text Society OS 307, Oxford, 1995

BARTHÉLÉMY 1854: C. Barthélémy, *Rational ou manuel des divins offices*, 5 vols., Paris, 1854

BATAILLON 1988: L.J. Bataillon, 'Les textes théologiques et philosophiques diffusés à Paris par *exemplar* et *pecia*', in *La production du livre universitaire au moyen âge. Exemplar et Pecia*, ed. L.J. Bataillon, B.G. Guyot, and R.H. Rouse, Paris, 1988, 155–63

BATELY 1991: J. Bately , 'The nature of Old English prose', in *The Cambridge Companion to Old English Literature*, ed. M. Godden and M. Lapidge, Cambridge, 1991, 71–87

BAXTER 1998: R. Baxter, *Bestiaries and their Uses in the Middle Ages*, Stroud, 1998

BEADLE 2005: R. Beadle, 'Sir John Fastolf's French Books', in *Medieval Texts in Manuscript Context*, ed. G. Caie and D. Renevey, Lisse, 2005 (in press)

BEADLE AND MCKITTERICK 1992: R. Beadle and R. McKitterick, *Catalogue of the Pepys Library at Magdalene College Cambridge, V: Manuscripts, part I, Medieval*, Cambridge, 1992

BEL 1998: *Ridono le Carte: Medieval and Renaissance Illumination*, BEL Catalogue 2, ed. M. Bollati, R. Gibbs, S. Hindman, S. Marcon, Milan, 1998

BELL 1992: D.N. Bell, *An Index of Authors and Works in Cistercian Libraries in Great Britain*, Cistercian Studies Series 130, Kalamazoo, 1992

BELTING 1990: H. Belting, *The Image and its Public in the Middle Ages. Form and Function of Early Paintings of the Passion*, New Rochelle, 1990

BENDALL, BROOKE AND COLLINSON 1999: S. Bendall, C. Brooke and P. Collinson, *A History of Emmanuel College, Cambridge*, Woodbridge, 1999

BENNETT 1973: A. Bennett, 'The Place of Garrett 28 in thirteenth-century English illumination', Ph.D. dissertation, Princeton, 1973

BENNETT 2002: Adelaide Bennett, 'Commemoration of Saints in Suffrages: From Public Liturgy to Private Devotion,' in *Objects, Images, and the Word: Art in the Service of the Liturgy*, ed. Colum Hourihane, Princeton, 2003, 54–78

BENT 1983: M. Bent, 'The Machaut Manuscripts Vg, B and E', *Musica Disciplina* 37 (1983), 53–82

BERENSON 1930: B. Berenson, 'Italian Illustrators of the Speculum Humanae Salvationis', in B. Berenson, *Studies in Medieval Painting*, New Haven, 1930, 102–37

BERGAMINI 1986: G. Bergamini, 'Un breviario francescano del XIV secolo nel Museo di Cividale del Friuli', *Le Venezie francescane* n.s. 3 (1986), 29–42

BERKOVITS 1964: I. Berkovits, *Illuminated Manuscripts from the Library of Matthias Corvinus*, Budapest, 1964

BERLINER 1955: R. Berliner, 'Arma Christi', *Münchener Jahrbuch für bildende Kunst* 6 (1955), 33–152

BERNARD 1697: E. Bernard, *Catalogi Librorum Manuscriptorum Angliae, Pars Altera*, 1697

BERNARDINELLO 1979: Silvio Bernardinello, *Autografi greci e greco-latini in occidente*, Padua, 1979

BETHERUM 1952: D. Betherum, *The homilies of Wulfstan*, Oxford, 1952

BETKA 2002: U. Betka, *Marian Images and Laudesi Devotion in Late Medieval Italy ca.*

1260–1350, Ph.D. thesis, University of Melbourne, 2001, published UMI, Michigan, 2002

BIEMANS 1984: J.A.A.M. Biemans, *Middelnederlandse bijbelhandschriften*, Verzameling van Middelnederlandse bijbelteksten, Catalogus, Leiden, 1984

BIETENHOLZ AND DEUTSCHER 1985–1987: *Contemporaries of Erasmus*, ed. Peter G. Bietenholz and Thomas B. Deutscher, 3 vols., Toronto, 1985–1987

BILLANOVICH 1968: M. Billanovich, 'Benedetto Bordone and Giulio Cesare Scaligero', *Italia medioevale e umanistica* 11 (1968), 187–256

BINSKI 1991: P. Binski, 'Abbot Berkyng's Tapestries and Matthew Paris's Life of St Edward the Confessor', *Archaeologia* 109 (1991), 89–95

BINSKI 1995: P. Binski, *Westminster Abbey and the Plantagenets: Kingship and the Representation of Power 1200–1400*, New Haven and London, 1995

BINSKI 1996: P. Binski, *Medieval Death: Ritual and Representation*, London, 1996

BINSKI 1997: P. Binski, 'The *Liber Regalis*: Its Date and European Context', in *The Regal Image of Richard II and the Wilton Diptych*, ed. D. Gordon, L. Monnas, and C. Elam, London 1997, 233–46

BISCHOFF 1965: B. Bischoff, 'Die Hofbibliothek Karls des Grossen', in *Karl der Grosse: Lebenswerk und Nachleben*, ed. Helmut Beumann et al., 5 vols., Düsseldorf, 1965–1968, II, 42–62; revised version in B. Bischoff, *Mittelalterliche Studien: ausgewählte Aufsätze zur Schriftkunde und Literaturgeschichte*, 3 vols., Stuttgart, 1966–1981, III, 149–170; English translation by M. Gorman in B. Bischoff, *Manuscripts and Libraries in the Age of Charlemagne*, Cambridge, 1994, 56–75.

BISCHOFF 1990: B. Bischoff, *Latin Palaeography: Antiquity and the Middle Ages*, transl. D. Ó Cróinín and D. Ganz, Cambridge, 1990

BISHOP 1918: E. Bishop, 'On the origin of the Prymer', in E. Bishop, *Liturgica historica*, Oxford, 1918, 211–37

BISHOP 1953: T.A.M. Bishop, 'Notes on Cambridge Manuscripts I', *Transactions of the Cambridge Bibliographical Society* 1 (1953), 432–41

BISHOP 1954–1958: T.A.M. Bishop, 'Notes on Cambridge Manuscripts II', *Transactions of the Cambridge Bibliographical Society* 2 (1954–1958), 185–99

BISHOP 1967: T.A.M. Bishop, 'The Copenhagen Gospel Book', *Nordisk Tidskrift for Bok- och Bibliotekvasen* 54 (1967), 33–41

BISHOP 1971: T.A.M. Bishop, *English Caroline Minuscule*, Oxford, 1971

BLAKE 1962: *Liber Eliensis*, ed. E. O. Blake, Camden Society 3rd ser., London, 1962

BLAKE 1973: N.F. Blake, *Caxton's own prose*, London, 1973

BLOOMER 1992: W. Bloomer, *Valerius Maximus and the Rhetoric of the New Nobility*, London, 1992

BLOOMFIELD, GUYOT, HOWARD AND KABEALO 1979: M.W. Bloomfield, B.–G. Guyot, D.R. Howard and T.B. Kabealo, *Incipits of Latin Works on the Virtues and Vices, 1100–1500 A.D.*, Cambridge, Mass., 1979

BLOOMFIELD-SMITH 2004: D. Bloomfield-Smith, *The Walrus Said: A Long Silence is Broken*, Lewes, 2004

BOFFEY 1995: J. Boffey, 'Annotations in Some Manuscripts of *Troilus and Criseyde*', *English Manuscript Studies, 1100–1700* 5 (1995), 1–17

BOHIGAS 1985: P. Bohigas, *Sobre Manuscrits i Biblioteques*, Montserrat, 1985

BONNIWELL 1944: W. Bonniwell, *A History of the Dominican Liturgy*, New York, 1944

BOSKOVITS 1975: M. Boskovits, *Pittura fiorentina alla vigilia del Rinascimento, 1370–1400*, Florence, 1975

BOSKOVITS 1984: M. Boskovits, *The Fourteenth Century. A Critical and Historical Corpus of Florentine Painting*, sec. 3, vol. 9, Florence, 1984

BOUSMANNE 1997: B. Bousmanne, 'Item a Guillaume Wyelant aussi enlumineur', in *Willem Vrelant, un aspect de l'enluminure dans les Pays-Bas méridionaux sous le mécénat des ducs de Bourgogne Philippe le Bon et Charles le Téméraire*, Turnhout, 1997

BOUSMANNE AND VAN HOOREBEECK 2000: *La Librairie des ducs de Bourgogne. Manuscrits conserves à la Bibliothèque royale de Belgique*, I, ed. B. Bousmanne and C. Van Hoorebeeck, Turnhout, 2000

BOUTEMY 1954–1955: A. Boutemy, 'Le type de l'evangéliste et la lettre ornée dans les evangiles rémois du IXe siècle', *Bulletin de la Société Nationale des Antiquaires de France* (1954–1955), 25–28

BOYLE 1964: L. Boyle, 'The Curriculum of the Faculty of Canon Law at Oxford in the First Half of the Fourteenth Century', in *Oxford Studies presented to Daniel Callus*, ed. R.W. Southern, Oxford, 1964, 135–62

BOYLE 1984: L. E. Boyle, 'Canon Law before 1380', in Catto 1984, 531–64

BRÄM 1997: A. Bräm, *Das Andachtsbuch der Marie de Gavre*, Wiesbaden 1997

BRANCA 1983: V. Branca, *Poliziano e l'umanesimo della parola*, Turin, 1983

BRANNER 1977: R. Branner, *Manuscript Painting in Paris During the Reign of Saint Louis: A Study of Styles*, Berkeley and Los Angeles, 1977

BRIEGER 1967: P.H. Brieger, *The Trinity College Apocalypse*, London, 1967

BRIEGER 1968: P.H. Brieger, *English Art 1215–1307*, 2nd edn, Oxford, 1968

BRINKMANN 1987–1988: B. Brinkmann, 'Neues vom Meister der Lübecker Bibel', *Jahrbuch der Berliner Museen* 29–30 (1987–1988), 123–61

BRINKMANN 1992: B. Brinkmann, 'Fitzwilliam 1058–1975 and the 'Capriccio' in Flemish Book Illustration', in *Fifteenth-Century Flemish Manuscripts in Cambridge Collections, Transactions of the Cambridge Bibliographical Society* 10.2 (1992), 203–214

BRINKMANN 1997: B. Brinkmann, *Die flämische Buchmalerei am Ende des Burgunderreichs: Der Meister des Dresdener Gebetbuchs und die Miniaturisten seiner Zeit*, 2 vols., Turnhout, 1997

BRISCOE 1998: *Valerius Maximus, Factorum ac dictorum memorabilium Libri IX*, ed. J. Briscoe, Leipzig 1998

BROOKE 1996: C.N.L. Brooke, *A History of Gonville and Caius College*, Woodbridge, 1996

BROWN 1990: M.P. Brown, *A Guide to Western Historical Scripts from Antiquity to 1600*, London and Toronto, 1990

BROWN 1996: M.P. Brown, *The Book of Cerne: Prayer, Patronage and Power in Ninth-century England*, London and Toronto, 1996

BROWN 1998: M.P. Brown, 'Sir Robert Cotton, Collector and Connoisseur', in *Illuminating the Book: Makers and Interpreters. Essays in Honour of Janet Backhouse*, ed. M.P. Brown and S. McKendrick, London, 1998, 281–98

BROWN 2002: M.P. Brown, 'Marvels of the West', *English Manuscript Studies, 1100–1700* 10 (2002), 34–59

BROWNRIGG 1978: L.L. Brownrigg, 'Manuscripts containing English Decoration 871–1066, Catalogued and Illustrated: a review', *Anglo-Saxon England* 7 (1978), 239–66

BRÜCKMANN 1973: J. Brückmann, 'Latin Manuscript Pontificals and Benedictionals in England and Wales', *Traditio* 29 (1973), 391–458

BRUINSMA 1992: E. Bruinsma, 'The *Lettre Bourguignonne* in Cambridge University Library Nn.3.2 and other Flemish Manuscripts: A Method of Identification', in *Fifteenth-Century Flemish Manuscripts in Cambridge Collections, Transactions of the Cambridge Bibliographical Society* 10.2 (1992), 156–164

BRUNDAGE 1993: J.A. Brundage, 'The Cambridge Faculty of Canon Law and the Ecclesiastical Courts of Ely', in *Medieval Cambridge: Essays on the Pre-Reformation University*, ed. P.N.R. Zutshi, Woodbridge, 1993, 21–45

BRUNDAGE 1995: J.A. Brundage, *Medieval Canon Law*, London, 1995

BUBENICEK 1980: V. Bubenicek, 'Le mortifiement de Vaine Plaisance (1455) de René d'Anjou, littérature et spiritualité', in *La littérature angevine médiévale*. Actes du colloque du samedi 22 mars 1980, Angers, 1980, 177–98

BUCHHOLZ 1888: G. Buchholz, *Ekkehard von Aura. Untersuchungen zur deutschen Reichsgeschichte unter Heinrich IV und Heinrich V*, Leipzig, 1888

BUCK 1997: S. Buck, *Holbein am Hofe Heinrichs VIII.*, Berlin, 1997

BUCKLOW 2000: S. Bucklow, 'Paradigms and Pigment Recipes: Natural Ultramarine', *Kunsttechnologie* 14.1 (2000), 5–14

BUDNY 1997: M. Budny, *Insular, Anglo-Saxon, and Early Anglo-Norman Manuscript Art at Corpus Christi College, Cambridge: an illustrated catalogue*, 2 vols., Kalamazoo, MI, 1997

BÜHLER 1949: C.F. Bühler, 'Sir John Fastolf's manuscripts of the *Epître d'Othéa* and Stephen Scrope's translation of this text', *Scriptorium* 3 (1949), 123–28

BÜHLER 1970: *The Epistle of Othea, translated from the French text of Christine de Pisan by Stephen Scrope*, ed. C.F. Bühler, London, 1970

BUSBY 2000: K. Busby, *Codex and Context: Reading Old French Verse Narrative in Manuscript*, Amsterdam, 2000

BÜTTNER 1983: F.O. Büttner, *Imitatio pietatis.*

Motive der christlichen Ikonographie als Modelle zur Verähnlichung, Berlin, 1983

BÜTTNER 2005: *The Illuminated Psalter: Studies in the Content, Purpose and Placement of its Images*, ed. F.O. Büttner, Turnhout, 2005

BYRNE 1977: D. Byrne, 'Two Hitherto Unidentified Copies of the 'Livre des propriétés des choses' from the Royal Library of the Louvre and the Library of Jean de Berry', *Scriptorium* 31 (1977), 90–98

BYRNE 1978: D. Byrne, 'The Boucicaut Master and the Iconographical Tradition of the "Livre des propriétés des choses"', *Gazette des Beaux-Arts* sér.6, 92 (1978), 149–64

BYRNE 1984: D. Byrne, 'Manuscript Ruling and Pictorial Design in the Work of the Limbourgs, the Bedford Master, and the Boucicaut Master', *The Art Bulletin* 66 (1984), 118–35

BYVANCK 1923A: A.W. Byvanck, 'Noord-Nederlandsche miniaturen, V. Een schilderschool te Delft,' *Oudheidkundig Jaarboek* 3 (1923), 188–201

BYVANCK 1923B: A.W. Byvanck, 'Utrechtsche miniaturen', *Het Gildeboek* 6 (1923), 1–11, 63–80, 106–17, 179–95

BYVANCK 1930: A.W. Byvanck, 'De Meester van Zweder van Culemborg en de Utrechtsche miniaturen', *Oudheidkundig Jaarboek* Ser. 3, 10 (1930), 127–39

BYVANCK 1937: A.W. Byvanck, *La miniature dans les Pays-Bas septentrionaux*, trans. A. Haye, Paris, 1937

BYVANCK 1943: A.W. Byvanck, *De middeleeuwsche boekillustratie in de Noordelijke Nederlanden*, Antwerp-Utrecht, 1943

BYVANCK AND HOOGEWERFF 1922–1926: A.W. Byvanck and G.J. Hoogewerff, *La miniature hollandaise dans les manuscrits des 14e, 15e et 16e siècles*, 3 vols., The Hague, 1922–1926

CABROL 1904: F. Cabrol, 'Le book of Cerne. Les liturgies celtiques et gallicanes et la liturgie romaine', *Revue des Questions Historiques* 76 (1904), 210–22

CADEI 1984: A. Cadei, *Giovannino de Grassi e Belbello da Pavia. Studi di miniatura Lombarda*, Rome, 1984

CAHN 1982: W. Cahn, *Romanesque Bible Illustration*, Ithaca, New York, 1982

CALKINS 1991: R. G. Calkins, 'The Question of the Origins of the Master of Catherine of Cleves', in van der Horst and Klamt 1991, 327–34

CALLUS 1943: D.A. Callus, 'Introduction of Aristotelian Learning to Oxford', *Proceedings of the British Academy* 29 (1943), 229–81

CALLUS 1948: D.A. Callus, 'The "Tabula super Originalia Patrum" of Robert Kilwardby O.P.', in *Studia mediaevalia in honorem admodum reverendi patris Raymundi Josephi Martin*, ed. B. Van Helmond, Bruges, 1948, 243–70

CAMES 1966: G. Cames, 'Recherches sur les origines du Crucifix à trois clous', *Cahiers Archéologiques* 16 (1966), 185–202

CAMILLE 1985A: M. Camille, 'Seeing and Reading: some visual implications of medieval literacy and illiteracy', *Art History* 8 (1985), 26–47

CAMILLE 1985B: M. Camille, 'Illustrations in Harley MS 3487 and the Perception of Aristotle's *Libri naturales* in Thirteenth-Century England', in *England in the Thirteenth Century*, Proceedings of the 1984 Harlaxton Symposium, ed. W.M. Ormrod, Harlaxton, 1985, 31–44

CAMILLE 1985C: M. Camille, 'The Illustrated Manuscripts of Guillaume de Deguileville's "Pélerinages" 1330–1426,' PhD thesis, University of Cambridge, 1985

CAMILLE 1995: M. Camille, 'An Oxford University textbook illuminated by William de Brailes', *Burlington Magazine* 137 (1995), 292–99

CAMPBELL 1979: L. Campbell, *Van der Weyden*, London, 1979

CAMPBELL 1985: L. Campbell, *The early Flemish pictures in the collection of Her Majesty the Queen*, Cambridge, 1985

CAMPBELL 1990: L. Campbell, *Renaissance Portraits : European Portrait-painting in the 14th, 15th and 16th centuries*, New Haven and London, 1990

CANART 1977–1979: P. Canart, 'Démétrius Damilas, *alias* le "librarius Florentinus"', *Rivista di studi bizantini e neoellenici* 14–16 (1977–1979), 281–347

CAPPUGI 1985: E. Cappugi, 'Contributo alla conoscenza dell' 'Inferno' Parigi-Imola e del suo miniatore detto Il Maestro del Vitae Imperatorum', in Sesti 1985, I, 285–96

CARLEY 2000: J.P. Carley, *The Libraries of Henry VIII*, Corpus of British Medieval Library Catalogues 7, London, 2000

CARLEY AND BACKHOUSE 1997: J.P. Carley and J. Backhouse, 'Remembrances of Lady Margaret Beaufort in the Archives: her Foundation Document and her Signatures', *Christ's College Magazine* 222 (1997), 14–17

CARLINO 1996–1997: L. Carlino, 'L'inedita "Cronaca Universale" in Rotulo da Cremona: alcune questioni di iconografia', *Rivista di storia della miniatura* 1–2 (1996–1997), 55–60

CARLVANT 1982: K. Carlvant, 'Collaboration in a Fourteenth-Century Psalter: The Franciscan Iconographer and the Two Flemish Illuminators of MS 3384, 8° in the Copenhagen Royal Library', *Sacris Erudiri* 25 (1982), 135–166

CARTER 1971: J. Carter, 'The Caxton Ovid', *The Book Collector* (Spring 1971), 7–18 .

CATTO 1984: *The History of the University of Oxford, I: The Early Oxford Schools*, ed. J.I. Catto, Oxford, 1984

CATTO AND EVANS 1992: *The History of the University of Oxford, II: Late Medieval Oxford*, ed. J.I. Catto and R. Evans, Oxford, 1992

CAVANAUGH 1988: S.H. Cavanaugh, 'Royal Books: King John to Richard II', *The Library*, 6th ser., 10.4 (1988), 304–16

CHADD 2002: *The Ordinal of the Abbey of the Holy Trinity Fécamp, Parts II, III & IV*, ed. D. Chadd, Henry Bradshaw Society 112, London, 2002

CHADWICK 2001: H. Chadwick, *The Church in Ancient Society, from Galilee to Gregory the Great*, Oxford, 2001

CHALLIS 1998: Kate Challis, 'Marginalized Jewels: The Depiction of Jewellery in the Borders of Flemish Devotional Manuscripts', in *The Art of the Book – Its Place in Medieval Worship*, ed. M. M. Manion and B. J. Muir, Exeter, 1998, 253–89.

CHARDIN 1811: Auguste Chardin, *Catalogue de livres précieux, manuscrits et imprimés sur peau-vélin, du cabinet de M.***, Paris, 1811

CHAVANNES-MAZEL 1992: C.A. Chavannes-Mazel, 'The Twelve Ladies of Rhetoric in Cambridge [CUL MS Nn.3.2]', in *Fifteenth-Century Flemish Manuscripts in Cambridge Collections, Transactions of the Cambridge Bibliographical Society* 10.2 (1992), 139–155

CHEKIN 1993: L.S. Chekin, 'Mappae Mundi and Scandinavia', *Scandinavian Studies* 65 (1993), 487–520

CHIHAIA 1988: P. Chihaia, *Immortalité et décomposition dans l'art du Moyen Âge*, Madrid, 1988

CHRISTIANSON 1990: C.P. Christianson, *A Directory of London Stationers and Book Artisans 1300–1500*, New York, 1990

CIARDI DUPRÉ DAL POGGETTO 1984: M.G. Ciardi Dupré dal Poggetto, 'La libreria di coro dell'Osservanza e la miniatura senese del quattrocento', in *L'Osservanza di Siena: la basilica e i suoi codici miniati*, testi di Cecilia Alessi, Siena, 1984, 111–154

CLARK 1904: John Willis Clark, *Endowments of the University of Cambridge*, Cambridge, 1904

CLARK 1982: W.B. Clark, 'The Illustrated Medieval Aviary and the Lay-Brotherhood', *Gesta* 21 (1982), 63–74

CLARK 1989: W.B. Clark, 'The Aviary-Bestiary at the Houghton Library, Harvard', in *Beasts and Birds of the Middle Ages, The Bestiary and its Legacy*, ed. W.B. Clark and M.T. McMunn, Philadelphia, 1989, 26–52

CLARK 1995: R.J.H. Clark, 'Raman Microscopy, Application to the Identification of Pigments on Medieval Manuscripts', *Chemical Society Reviews* 24 (1995), 187–96

CLARKE 2001: M. Clarke, *The Art of All Colours: Medieval Recipe Books for Painters and Illuminators*, London, 2001

CLARKE AND LOVATT 2002: P.D. Clarke, R. Lovatt, *The University and College Libraries of Cambridge*, Corpus of British Medieval Library Catalogues 10, London, 2002

CLAY 1931: C. Clay, 'An Illuminated Charter of Free Warren, dated 1291', *Antiquaries Journal* 11 (1931), 129–32

CLOUGH 1966/1971: C.H. Clough, 'Pietro Bembo's Library Represented in the British Museum', *British Museum Quarterly* 30 (1966), 3–17; rev. ed. *Pietro Bembo's Library as Represented in the British Museum*, London, 1971

CLOUGH 1980: C.H. Clough, 'Die Bibliothek von Bernardo und Pietro Bembo', *Librarium* 23 (1980), 41–56

CLOUGH 1984: C.H. Clough, 'The Library of Bernardo and of Pietro Bembo', *The Book Collector* 33 (1984), 305–31

COBBAN 1982: A.B. Cobban, 'Theology and Law in the Medieval Colleges of Oxford and Cambridge', *Bulletin of the John Rylands Library* 65 (1982), 57–77

COBBAN 1988: A.B. Cobban, *The Medieval English Universities: Oxford and Cambridge to c.1500*, Berkeley, 1988

COCKERELL 1905: S.C. Cockerell, *A Psalter*

and Hours executed before 1270 for a lady… probably Isabelle of France, London, 1905

COCKERELL 1906: S.C. Cockerell, 'The Parisian Miniaturist Honoré', *Burlington Magazine* 10 (1906), 186–91

COCKERELL 1907: S.C. Cockerell, *The Gorleston Psalter*, London, 1907

COCKERELL 1930: S.C. Cockerell, *The Work of W. de Brailes*, Roxburghe Club, 1930

COCKERELL 1951: S.C. Cockerell, 'Signed Manuscripts in my Collection', *Book Handbook* 2.1 (1951), 13–18

COCKSHAW 1984: P. Cockshaw, 'De la réalisation d'un livre à sa destruction: l'exemplaire de l'histoire de la Toison d'Or de Charles le Téméraire', in *Liber Amicorum Herman Liebaers*, ed. F. Vanwijngaerden, J.-M. Duvosquel, J. Mélard, and L. Viaine-Awouters, Brussels, 1984, 201–212

COLISH 1991: M.C. Colish, 'From *Sacra pagina* to *theologia*: Peter Lombard as an Exegete of Romans', *Medieval Perspectives* 6 (1991), 1–19

COLLINS 1960: A.J. Collins, *Manuale ad usum percelebris ecclesiae Sarisburiensis*, Henry Bradshaw Society, 91, 1960

COLLINS 2000: M. Collins, *Medieval herbals: the illustrative traditions*, London, 2000

COMBLEN-SONKES AND LORENTZ 1995: M. Comblen-Sonkes and P. Lorentz, *Musée du Louvre, Paris II. Corpus de la peinture des anciens pays-bas méridionaux et de la principalité de Liège au quinzième siècle* 17, Brussels, 1995

CONNOLLY 1998: M. Connolly, *John Shirley: Book Production and the Noble Household in Fifteenth-Century England*, Aldershot and Brooklines, 1998

CONTI 1981: A. Conti, *La miniatura Bolognese: Scuole e botteghe 1270–1340*, Bologna, 1981

COOPER 1842–1908: C.H. Cooper, *Annals of Cambridge*, 5 vols., Cambridge, 1842–1908

COOPER 1860–1866: C.H. Cooper, *Memorials of Cambridge*, new edn, 3 vols., Cambridge, 1860–1866

CORBIN 1947: S. Corbin, 'Les Offices de la Sainte Face', *Bulletin des Études Portugaises* 11 (1947), 1–65

CORRIE 1987: R. Corrie, 'The Seitenstetten Missal and the Persistence of Italo-Byzantine Influence at Salzburg', *Dumbarton Oaks Papers* 41 (1987), 111–23

COWLING 2002: George Chastelain, Jean Robertet, Jean de Montferrant, *Les Douze Dames de Rhétorique*, ed. David Cowling, Geneva, 2002

CRAVEN 1981: W.G. Craven, *Giovanni Pico della Mirandola, Symbol of His Age: Modern Interpretations of a Renaissance Scholar*, Geneva, 1981

CRAWLEY 1976: C. Crawley, *Trinity Hall: The History of a Cambridge College, 1350–1975*, Cambridge, 1976

CRONIN 1922: *Rogeri Dymmok Liber contra XII Errores et Hereses Lollardorum*, ed. H.S. Cronin, Wyclif Society, London, 1922

CSAPODI AND CSAPODI-GÁRDONYI 1969: C. Csapodi and K. Csapodi-Gárdonyi, *Bibliotheca Corviniana*, Shannon, 1969

CUNNINGHAM 1966: A. Cunningham, *Aurelii Prudentii Clementis Carmina*, CCSL 126, Turnhout, 1966

DA BISTICCI 1970–1976: V. da Bisticci, *Le Vite*, ed. A. Greco, 2 vols., Florence, 1970–1976

DALCHÉ 1988: P. Gautier Dalché, *La 'Descriptio mappae mundi' de Hughes de Saint-Victor*, Paris, 1988

DANBURY 1989: E. Danbury, 'The Decoration and Illumination of Royal Charters in England, 1250–1509: An Introduction', in *England and her Neighbours, 1066–1453: Essays in Honour of Pierre Chaplais*, ed. M. Jones and M. Vale, London, 1989, 157–79

D'ANCONA 1914: P. D'Ancona, *La miniatura Fiorentina*, 2 vols., Florence, 1914

D'ANCONA 1957 (published 1959): M.L. D'Ancona, 'Don Silvestro dei Gherarducci e il Maestro delle Canzoni', *Rivista d'arte* 32 (1957, published 1959), 3–37

D'ANCONA 1962A: M.L. D'Ancona, 'Jacopo del Giallo e alcune miniature del Corer', *Bolletino dei Musei Civici Veneziani* 7.2 (1962), 1–23

D'ANCONA 1962B: M. L. D'Ancona, *Miniatura e miniatori a Firenze dal XIV al XVI secolo. Documenti per la storia della miniatura*, Florence, 1962

D'ANCONA 1966–1967: M.L. D'Ancona, 'Un libro d'ore di Francesco Marmitta da Parma e Martino da Modena al Museo Correr', *Bollettino dei Musei Civici Veneziani* 11.2 (1966), 18–35 and 12.4 (1967), 9–28

D'ANCONA 1970: M.L. D'Ancona, *The Wildenstein Collection of Illuminations. The Lombard School*, Florence, 1970

D'ANCONA 1978: M.L. D'Ancona, 'I corali di S. Maria degli Angeli ora nella Biblioteca Laurenziana e le miniature da essi asportate', in *Miscellanea di studi in memoria di Anna Saitta Revignas*, Florence, 1978, 213–35

D'ANCONA 1994: M.L. D'Ancona, *The Illuminators and Illuminations of the Choir Books from Santa Maria degli Angeli and Santa Maria Nuova and Their Documents*, Florence, 1994

DAVRIL AND THIBODEAU 1995–2000: A. Davril and T.M. Thibodeau, *Guillelmi Duranti Rationale Divinorum Officiorum*, 3 vols., *Corpus Christianorum* 140, 140A, 140B, Turnhout, 1995–2000

DEAN 1999: R. J. Dean, *Anglo-Norman Literature: a Guide to Texts and Manuscripts*, Anglo-Norman Text Society, O.P. no. 3, London, 1999

DEARDEN 1966: J.S. Dearden, 'John Ruskin, the Collector: with a Catalogue of the Illuminated and Other Manuscripts formerly in his Collection', *The Library*, 3rd ser., 21 (1966), 124–54

DEARMER 1922: P. Dearmer, *Fifty Pictures of Gothic Altars*, London, 1922

DE BRUIN 1980: C.C. de Bruin, *Tleven ons heren Ihesu Cristi. Het Pseudo-Bonaventura-Ludolfiaanse Leven van Jesus*, Verzameling van Middelnederlandse bijbelteksten, Miscellanea 2, Leiden, 1980

DE HAMEL 1980: C.F.R. de Hamel, 'Manuscripts of Herbert of Bosham', *Manuscripts at Oxford, an Exhibition in Memory of R.W. Hunt*, ed. A.C. de la Mare and B.C. Barker-Benfield, Oxford, 1980, 38–41

DE HAMEL 1984: C.F.R. de Hamel, *Glossed Books of the Bible and the Origins of the Paris Booktrade*, Woodbridge and Dover, 1984

DE HAMEL 1986: C.F.R. de Hamel, *A History of Illuminated Manuscripts*, Oxford, 1986

DE HAMEL 1992A: C.F.R. de Hamel, 'A Contemporary Miniature of Thomas Becket', *Intellectual Life in the Middle Ages: Essays Presented to Margaret Gibson*, ed. L. Smith and B. Ward, London and Rio Grande, 1992, 179–184

DE HAMEL 1992B: C.F.R. de Hamel, *Scribes and Illuminators*, London, 1992

DE HAMEL 2001A: C.F.R. de Hamel, *The Book: A History of the Bible*, London, 2001

DE HAMEL 2001B: C.F.R. de Hamel, *The British Library Guide to Manuscript Illumination*, London, 2001

DE KESEL 1992: L. de Kesel, 'Cambridge University Library MS Add. 4100: A Book of Hours illuminated by the Master of the Prayer Books of circa 1500?', in *Fifteenth-Century Flemish Manuscripts in Cambridge Collections, Transactions of the Cambridge Bibliographical Society* 10.2 (1992), 182–202

DE LA MARE 1965: A.C. de la Mare, 'Messer Piero Strozzi, a Florentine Priest and Scribe', *Calligraphy and Palaeography: Essays Presented to Alfred Fairbank on his Seventieth Birthday*, ed. A.S. Osley, London, 1965, 55–68

DE LA MARE 1972–1976: A.C. de la Mare, 'A Fragment of Augustine in the Hand of Theodoricus Werken', *Transactions of the Cambridge Bibliographical Society* 6 (1972–1976), 285–90

DE LA MARE 1973: A.C. de la Mare, *The Handwriting of the Italian Humanists*, vol. I, fasc. 1, Oxford, 1973

DE LA MARE 1977: A.C. de la Mare, 'Humanist Script: the First Ten Years', in *Das Verhältnis der Humanisten zum Buch*, ed. F. Kraft and D. Wuttke, Boppard, 1977, 89–110

DE LA MARE 1984: A.C. de la Mare, 'The Florentine Scribes of Cardinal Giovanni of Aragon', in *Il libro e il testo*. Atti del Convegno Internazionale, Urbino, 20–23 Settembre 1982, ed. C.Questa and R. Raffaelli, Urbino, 1984, 243–93

DE LA MARE 1985: A.C. de la Mare, 'New Research on Humanistic Scribes in Florence', in Garzelli 1985, I, 393–600

DE LA MARE 1994: A.C. de la Mare, 'A Palaeographer's Odyssey', in *Sight and Insight. Essays on Art and Culture in Honour of E.H. Gombrich at 85*, ed. J. Onians, London, 1994, 89–107

DE LA MARE 1999: A.C. de la Mare, 'Bartolomeo Sanvito da Padova, copista e miniatore', in Padua 1999, 495–505

DE LA MARE 2002: A.C. de la Mare, 'Marginalia and Glosses in the Manuscripts of Bartolomeo Sanvito of Padua', in *Talking to the Text: Marginalia from Papyri to Print*. Proceedings of a Conference held at Erice 26 September–3 October 1998 as the 12th Course of International School for the Study of Written Records, ed. V. Fera, G. Ferraù, S. Rizzo, Messina, 2002, 459–555

DE LA MARE AND HELLINGA 1977–1980: A.C. de la Mare and L. Hellinga, 'The First Book Printed in Oxford: the Expositio symboli of Rufinus', *Transactions of the Cambridge Bibliographical Society* 7 (1977–1980), 184–244

DELAISSÉ 1968: L.M.J. Delaissé, *A Century of*

Dutch Manuscript Illumination*, Berkeley and Los Angeles, 1968

DELISLE 1868–1881: L. Delisle, *Le cabinet des manuscrits de la Bibliothèque Impériale*, 3 vols., Paris, 1868–1881

DELISLE 1907: L. Delisle, *Recherches sur la librairie de Charles V*, Paris, 1907

DELISLE AND MEYER 1901: L. Delisle and P. Meyer, *L'Apocalypse en Français au XIIIe siècle*, Paris, 1901

DE MARINIS 1947–1952: T. de Marinis, *La biblioteca napoletana dei re d'Aragona*, 4 vols., Milan, 1947–1952; *Supplemento*, 2 vols., Verona, 1969

DE MEYIER 1964: K.A. de Meyier, 'Scribes grecs de la Renaissance', *Scriptorium* 18 (1964), 258–266

DEMPSEY 2001: C. Dempsey, *Inventing the Renaissance Putto*, Chapel Hill, North Carolina, 2001

DENNISON 1986A: L. Dennison, 'An Illuminator of the Queen Mary Psalter Group: the Ancient 6 Master', *Antiquaries Journal* 66 (1986), 287–314

DENNISON 1986B: L. Dennison, '"The Fitzwarin Psalter and its Allies": a Reappraisal', in *England in the Fourteenth Century: Proceedings of the 1985 Harlaxton Symposium*, ed. W.M. Ormrod, Woodbridge, 1986, 42–66

DENNISON 1986C: L. Dennison, 'The Artistic Context of Fourteenth Century Flemish Brasses', *Transactions of the Monumental Brass Society* 14 (1986), 1–38

DENNISON 1990A: L. Dennison, ' "Liber Horn", Liber Custumarum and Other Manuscripts of the Queen Mary Psalter Workshops', in *Medieval Art, Architecture and Archaeology in London*, ed. L. Grant, British Archaeological Association Conference Transactions 10 (1990), 118–34

DENNISON 1990B: L. Dennison, 'Oxford, Exeter College MS 47: The Importance of stylistic and Codicological Analysis in its Dating and Localization', in *Medieval Book Production, Assessing the Evidence*, ed. L.L. Brownrigg, Los Altos Hills, 1990, 41–60

DENNISON 1993: L. Dennison, 'Some Unlocated Leaves from an English Fourteenth-Century Book of Hours now in Paris', in *England in the Fourteenth Century: Proceedings of the 1991 Harlaxton Symposium*, ed. N. Rogers, Stamford, 1993, 15–33

DEROLEZ 1979: A. Derolez, *The Library of Raphael de Mercatellis*, Ghent, 1979

DEROLEZ 1982: A. Derolez, 'The copying of printed books for humanistic bibliophiles in the fifteenth century', in *From Script to Book*, ed. H. Bekker-Nielsen, Odense, 1986, 140–60

DEROLEZ 2003: A. Derolez, *The Palaeography of Gothic Manuscript Books from the Twelfth to the Early Sixteenth Century*, Cambridge, 2003

DE ROOVER 1953: F.E. de Roover, 'Per la storia dell'arte della stampa in Italia: come furono stampati a Venezia tre dei libri primi in volgare', *La Bibliofilia* 55 (1953), 107–117

DESPRES 1998: D.L. Despres, 'Immaculate Flesh and the Social Body: Mary and the Jews', *Jewish History* 12.1 (1998), 47–69

DESTOMBES 1964: M. Destombes, *Mappemondes, A.D. 1200–1500*, Amsterdam, 1964

DESTREZ 1935: J. Destrez, *La Pecia dans les manuscrits universitaires du XIIIe et XIVe siècles*, Paris, 1935

DEUTSCHE 1986: G. N. Deutsche, *Iconographie de l'illustration de Flavius Josèphe au temps de Jean Fouquet*, Leiden, 1986

DE VOS 1999: D. de Vos, *Rogier van der Weyden: the Complete Works*, Antwerp, 1999

DEVOTI 1994: L. Devoti, 'Aspetti della produzione del libro a Bologna: il prezzo di copia del manoscritto giuridico tra XIII e XIV secolo', *Scrittura e civiltà* 18 (1994), 77–142

DE VREESE 1931: W. de Vreese, *De eerste Bliscap van Maria*, The Hague, 1931

DEWICK 1895: E.S. Dewick, 'On a Ms Pontifical of a Bishop of Metz of the Fourteenth Century', *Archaeologia* 54 (1895), 411–24

DEWICK 1902: E.S. Dewick, *The Metz Pontifical*, Roxburghe Club, 1902

DE WINTER 1980: P.M. de Winter, 'Une réalisation exceptionelle d'enlumineurs français et anglais vers 1300: le bréviaire de Renaud de Bar, evêque de Metz', *Actes du 103e congrès national des Sociétés savantes, Nancy-Metz (1978), Archéologie (1980), 27–61

DE WINTER 1982: P. de Winter, 'The Grandes Heures of Philip the Bold, Duke of Burgundy: The Copyist Jean L'Avenant and his Patrons at the French Court', *Speculum* 57 (1982), 786–842

DE WINTER 1985: P. de Winter, *La bibliothèque de Philippe le Hardi duc de Bourgogne (1364–1404)*, Paris, 1985

DE WIT 1926: C. de Wit, 'Noord-Nederlandsche miniaturen', *Het Gildeboek* 9 (1926), 122–25

DE WIT 1927: C. de Wit, *Die Utrechtschen Miniaturen des 15. Jahrhunderts*, Ph.D. Dissertation, Ludwig-Maximilians-Universität zu München, 1927, Berlin, 1937

DE WIT 1929A: C. de Wit, 'Het atelier der Utrechtsche miniaturen en een kapittel uit de geschiedenis van het Karthuizerklooster Nieuw-Licht', *Oudheidkundig Jaarboek*, Ser. 3, 8 (1929), 264–71

DE WIT 1929B: C. de Wit, 'Uit geschiedenis der Utrechtsche miniaturen', *Oudheidkundig Jaarboek* Ser. 3, 8 (1929), 272–77

DICKINSON 1861–1883: F. H. Dickinson, *Missale ad usum insignis et praeclarae ecclesiae Sarum*, Burntisland, 1861–1883, repr. 1970

DI MAURO 1992: A. Di Mauro, 'Un contributo alla mnemotecnica medievale: il "Compendium Historiae in Genealogia Christi" in una redazione pisana del XIII secolo', in *Atti del III Congresso di Storia della Miniatura Italiana, Cortona, 20–23 Ottobre 1982*, Florence, 1992, 453–67

DIMINUTO DEVOCIONARIO 1995: *Diminuto devocionario del Museo arqueológico nacional*, 2 vols., ed. A. Dominguez Rodriguez and F Javier Docampo Capilla, Madrid, 1995

DIRINGER 1967: D. Diringer, *The Illuminated Book*, London, 1967

DOD 1982: B.G. Dod, 'Aristoteles Latinus', in *The Cambridge History of Later Medieval Philosophy*, ed. N. Kretzmann, A. Kenny and J. Pinborg, Cambridge, 1982, 45–79

DODWELL 1954: C.R. Dodwell, *The*

Canterbury School of Illumination, 1066–1200, Cambridge, 1954

DODWELL AND TURNER 1965: C.R. Dodwell and D.H. Turner, *Reichenau Reconsidered*, Warburg Institute Surveys 2, London, 1965

DOGAER 1987: G. Dogaer, *Flemish Miniature Painting in the 15th and 16th Centuries*, Amsterdam, 1987

DOLEZALEK 1985: G.R. Dolezalek, *Repertorium manuscriptorum veterum Codices Iustiniani*, 2 vols., Frankfurt, 1985

DOLEZALEK 2002: G.R. Dolezalek, '*Libri magistrorum* and the Transmission of Glosses in Legal Textbooks (12th and Early 13th Century)', in *Juristische Buchproduktion im Mittelalter*, ed. V. Colli, Frankfurt, 2002, 315–49

DOYLE 1983: A.I. Doyle, 'English Books In and Out of Court from Edward III to Henry VI', in *English Court Culture in the Later Middle Ages*, ed. V.J. Scattergood and J.W. Sherborne, London, 1983, 163–81

DOYLE 1990: A.I. Doyle, 'Book Production by the Monastic Orders in England (*c.*1375–1530): Assessing the Evidence', *Medieval Book Production, Assessing the Evidence, Proceedings of the Second Conference of The Seminar in the History of the Book to 1500, Oxford, July 1988*, ed. L.L. Brownrigg, Los Altos Hills, 1990, 1–19

DOYLE 1997: A.I. Doyle, 'Stephen Dodesham of Witham and Sheen', in *Of the Making of Books, Medieval Manuscripts, their Scribes and Readers, Essays presented to M.B. Parkes*, ed. P.R. Robinson and R. Zim, Aldershott, 1997, 94–115

DUMVILLE 1972: D.N. Dumville, 'Liturgical drama and panegyric responsory from the 8th century. A reexamination of the origin and contents of the 9th-century section of the Book of Cerne', *Journal of Theological Studies* n.s. 23 (1972), 374–406

DUMVILLE 1974: D.M. Dumville, 'The Corpus Christi 'Nennius'', *Bulletin of the Board of Celtic Studies* 25 (1974), 369–80

DUMVILLE 1977–1980: D.N. Dumville, 'The Sixteenth-Century History of Two Cambridge Books from Sawley', *Transactions of the Cambridge Bibliographical Society* 7 (1977–1980), 427–44

DUMVILLE 1987: D.N. Dumville, 'English square minuscule script: the background and earliest phases', *Anglo-Saxon England* 16 (1987), 147–79

DUMVILLE 1991–1995: D.N. Dumville, 'On the Dating of Some Late Anglo-Saxon Liturgical Manuscripts', *Transactions of the Cambridge Bibliographical Society* 10 (1991–1995), 40–57

DUMVILLE 1992 : D.N. Dumville, *Liturgy and the Ecclesiastical History of Late Anglo-Saxon England*, Woodbridge, 1992

DUMVILLE 1994: D.N. Dumville, 'English Square Minuscule Script: the mid-century phases', *Anglo-Saxon England* 23 (1994), 133–64

DURAND 1503: Guillaume Durand, *Le racional des divins offices*, ed. A. Verard, Paris, 1503

DURRIEU 1912A: P. Durrieu, *Les heures a l'usage d'Angers de la collection Martin Le Roy*, Paris, 1912

DURRIEU 1912B: P. Durrieu, 'Le maître des

"Grandes Heures de Rohan" et les Lescuier d'Angers', *Revue de l'art ancien et moderne* 32 (1912), 81–98, 161–83

EARP 1989: L. Earp, 'Machaut's Role in the Reproduction of his Works', *Journal of the American Musicological Association* 42 (1989), 478–79

EARP 1995: L. Earp, *Guillaume de Machaut, A Guide to Research*, New York and London, 1995

EDWARDS 1991: A.S.G. Edwards, 'Beinecke MS 661 and Early Fifteenth-Century English Manuscript Production', *Yale University Library Gazette*, LXVI, Supplement, 1991, 181–89

EGBERT 1940: D.D. Egbert, *The Tickhill Psalter and Related Manuscripts*, New York and Princeton 1940

ELLIS & ELVEY 1890: Ellis & Elvey, *Catalogue of Ancient & Modern Books and Manuscripts*, 70, London, 1890

EMDEN 1957–1959: A.B. Emden, *A Biographical Register of the University of Oxford to A.D. 1500*, 3 vols., Oxford, 1957–1959

EMDEN 1963: A.B. Emden, *A Biographical Register of the University of Cambridge to 1500*, Cambridge, 1963

EMDEN 1974: A.B. Emden, *A Biographical Register of the University of Oxford A.D. 1501–1540*, Oxford, 1974

EMMERSON 1999: R.K. Emmerson, 'Reading Gower in a Manuscript Culture: Latin and English in Illustrated Manuscripts of the *Confessio Amantis*', *Studies in the Age of Chaucer* 21 (1999), 143–86

EMMERSON 2004: R. K. Emmerson, 'Picturing Visionary Narratives: The Marginal Images in the Hours of Isabella Stuart,' unpublished lecture delivered at the Columbia University Medieval Forum, New York, 16 October 2004

EMMERSON AND LEWIS 1985: R.K. Emmerson and S. Lewis, 'Census and Bibliography of Medieval Manuscripts containing Apocalypse Illustrations, ca. 800–1500, II', *Traditio* 41 (1985), 367–409

EMMERSON AND LEWIS 1986: R. K. Emmerson and S. Lewis, 'Census and Bibliography of Medieval Manuscripts Containing Apocalypse Illustrations, ca. 800–1500, III', *Traditio* 42 (1986), 443–72

ENLUMINURES 2001: *Illuminations: Middle Ages, Renaissance*, ed. S Hindman with M. Bolati, G. Fruler, P. Palladino, Les Enluminures Catalogue 10, Paris, 2001

ENRIGHT-CLARK SHOUKRI 1974: *Liber Apologeticus de Omni Statu Humanae Naturae*, ed. D. Enright-Clark Shoukri, London and New York, 1974

ERDREICH 1993: E.C. Erdreich, '"Qui hos cultus…pinxerit": Illumination Associated with Bartolomeo Sanvito (*c.*1435–*c.*1512)', Ph. D. dissertation, Johns Hopkins University, Baltimore, 1993

ERNST 1991: U. Ernst, *Carmen figuratum. Geschichte des Figurengedichts von den Antiken Ursprüngen bis zum Ausgang des Mittelalters*, Pictura et poesis 1, Cologne, 1991

EUBEL 1914: C. Eubel, *Hierarchia Catholica Medii Aevi*, 8 vols., Regensburg, 1913–1978

EVANS 1980: M. Evans, 'The geometry of the mind', *Architectural Association Quarterly* 12.4 (1980), 32–55

EVANS 1987: M. Evans, 'New Light on the "Sforziada" Frontispieces of Giovan Pietro Birago', *British Library Journal* 13 (1987), 232–47

EVANS 1992: M. Evans, *The Sforza Hours*, London, 1992

EVANS AND BRINKMANN 1995: M. Evans and B. Brinkmann, with a contribution by H. Herkommer, *The Sforza Hours, Add. MS 34294 of the British Library, London*, Lucerne, 1995

FAIRBANK 1965: A. Fairbank, 'Antonio Tophio', *Journal of the Society for Italic Handwriting* 45 (1965), 8–14

FAIRBANK 1970: A. Fairbank, 'Antonio Tophio and Bartolomeo Sanvito', in *Essays in Honour of Victor Scholderer*, ed. D.E. Rhodes, Mainz, 1970, 159–64

FAIRBANK 1971: A. Fairbank, 'Sanvito and Tophio', *Journal of the Society for Italic Handwriting* 68 (1971), 7–9

FASSLER AND BALTZER 2000: *The Divine Office in the Latin Middle Ages*, ed. M.E. Fassler and R.A. Baltzer, Oxford, 2000

FEDERICI, DI MAJO AND PALMA 1996: C. Federici, A. di Majo and M. Palma, 'The Determination of Animal Species Used in Medieval Parchment Making: Non-Destructive Identification Techniques', *Bibliologia* 14 (1996), 146–53

FERRARI 1999: M. Ferrari, *Il "Liber sanctae crucis" di Rabano Mauro. Testo – immagine – contesto*, Lateinische Sprache und Literatur des Mittelalters 30, Bern, 1999

FINKE 1963: U. Finke, 'Utrecht – Zentrum nordniederländischer Buchmalerei', *Oud Holland* 78 (1963), 27–66

FLEMING 1969: J. V. Fleming, *The Roman de la Rose: A Study in Allegory and Iconography*, Princeton, 1969

FLETCHER 1994: J. M. Fletcher, 'Some unusual aspects of the English medieval universities and the relation of this to certain materials used in the Faculty of Arts', in *Manuels, programmes de cours et techniques d'enseignement dans les universités médiévales*, ed. J. Hamesse, Louvain-la-Neuve, 1994, 371–83

FLINT 1983: *Honorius Augustodunensis Imago Mundi*, ed. V.I.J.Flint, *Archives d'histoire doctrinale et littéraire du Moyen Age* 57 (1983), 7–153

FLINT 1995: V.I.J. Flint, 'Honorius Augustodunensis of Regensberg', *Authors of the Middle Ages, Historical and Religious Writers of the Latin West*, II, 5–6, ed. P.J. Geary, Aldershot, 1995, 95–103

FLODOARD 1886: Flodoard of Reims, *Historia Remensis ecclesiae*, ed. G. Waitz, *Historia Remensis ecclesiae*, MGH Scriptores XIII, Hannover, 1886, and M. Stratmann, MGH Scriptores nova series, Hannover, 1998

FOSSIER 1980–1981: F. Fossier, 'Chroniques universelles en forme de rouleau à la fin du Moyen-Âge', *Bulletin de la Société des Antiquaires de France* (1980–1981), 163–83

FOSTER 1976–1977: B. Foster, *The Anglo-Norman Alexander (Le Roman de toute chevalerie*) by Thomas of Kent, Anglo-Norman Text Society 29–33 (1976–1977)

FOX 1998: P. Fox, ed., *Cambridge University Library. The Great Collections*, Cambridge, 1998

FRERE 1894–1932: W.H. Frere, *Bibliotheca Musico-Liturgica: a descriptive handlist of the musical and Latin-liturgical manuscripts of the middle ages preserved in the libraries of Great Britain and Ireland*, 2 vols., London, 1894–1932; repr. Hildesheim, 1967

FRERE 1899: W. H. Frere, *Exposition de la messe from La Legende dorée of Jean de Vignay, with Illuminations Reproduced from Fitzwilliam Museum MS. 22*, Alcuin Club Collection 2, London, 1899

FRERE 1901–1908: W.H. Frere, *Pontifical Services illustrated from Miniatures of the XVth and XVIth Centuries*, 4 vols., Alcuin Club Collections 3, 4, 8, 12, London and New York, 1901–1908

FRERE 1935: W.H. Frere, *Studies in early Roman liturgy, III: The Roman Epistle-Lectionary*, Alcuin Club Collections 32, Oxford, 1935

FRERE AND BROWN 1904–1915: W.H. Frere and L.E.G. Brown, *The Hereford Breviary*, 3 vols., Henry Bradshaw Society, 26, 40, 46, 1904–1915

FREULER 1997: G. Freuler, *Tendencies of the Gothic in Florence: Don Silvestro dei Gherarducci. A Critical and Historical Corpus of Florentine Painting*, sec. 4, vol. 7, pt. 2, Florence, 1997

FRIEDMAN 1982: J.B. Friedman, 'The cipher alphabet of John de Foxton's Liber cosmographiae', *Scriptorium* 36 (1982), 219–35

FRIEDMAN 1983: J.B. Friedman, 'John Siferwas and the mythological illustrations in the Liber cosmographiae of John de Foxton', *Speculum* 58 (1983), 391–418

FRIEDMAN 1988: *John de Foxton's Liber Cosmographiae (1408): an Edition and Codicological Study*, ed. J. B. Friedman, Leiden, 1988

FRIESEN 1993: M. Friesen, *Der Rosenroman für François I*, Graz, 1993

FRY 1905: R.E. Fry, 'On Two Miniatures by the de Limbourg,' *Burlington Magazine* 7 (1905), 435–45

FUGLESANG 1980: S.H. Fuglesang, *Some Aspects of the Ringerike Style: a phase of Scandinavian art*, Medieval Scandinavia Supplements 1, Odense, 1980

GAMBER 1963: K. Gamber, *Codices liturgici latini antiquiores*, Freiburg, 1963

GAMESON 1994: *The Early Medieval Bible: Its Production, Decoration and Use*, ed. R. Gameson, Cambridge, 1994

GAMESON 1995: R. Gameson, 'English Manuscript Art in the Late Eleventh Century: Canterbury and its Context', *Canterbury and the Norman Conquest: Churches, Saints and Scholars, 1066–1109*, ed. R. Eales and R. Sharpe, London, 1995, 95–144

GAMESON 1996: R. Gameson, 'Book Production and Decoration at Worcester in the Tenth and Eleventh Centuries', *St Oswald of Worcester: life and influences*, ed. N. Brooks and C. Cubitt, Leicester, 1996, 194–243

GAMESON 1999: R. Gameson, *The Manuscripts of Early Norman England (c.1066–1130)*, Oxford, 1999

GAMILLSCHEG AND HARLFINGER 1981: E. Gamillscheg and D. Harlfinger, *Repertorium der griechischen Kopisten 800–1600. vol. I: Handschriften aus Bibliotheken Grossbritanniens*, Vienna, 1981

GANZ 1994: D. Ganz, 'Mass Production of Early Medieval Manuscripts: The Carolingian Bibles from Tours', in Gameson 1994, 53–62

GARROD 1949: H.W.Garrod, 'Erasmus and his English patrons', *The Library*, 5th ser., 4 (1949), 1–13

GARRISON 1953: E.B. Garrison, 'A Lucchese Passionary related to the Sarzana crucifix', *Art Bulletin* 35 (1953), 109–19

GARZELLI 1985: A. Garzelli, *Miniatura fiorentina del rinascimento 1440–1525: Un primo censimento*, 2 vols., Florence, 1985

GATCH 1977: M. McC. Gatch, *Preaching and theology in Anglo-Saxon England: Aelfric and Wulfstan*, Toronto and Buffalo, 1977

GATCH 1991: M.McC. Gatch, 'Perceptions of eternity', in *The Cambridge Companion to Old English Literature*, ed. M. Godden and M. Lapidge, Cambridge, 1991, 190–205

GEE 2002: L.L. Gee, *Women, Art and Patronage from Henry III to Edward III 1216–1377*, Woodbridge, 2002

GHISALBERTI 1960–: Ghisalberti, A. M. *Dizionario biografico degli Italianani*, vols. 1–, Rome, 1960–

GIANNETTO 1985: N. Giannetto, *Bernardo Bembo, umanista e politico Veneziano*, Florence, 1985

GIBBS 2002: R. Gibbs, 'The Development of the Illustration of Legal Manuscripts by Bolognese Illuminators between 1241 and 1298', in *Juristische Buchproduktion im Mittelalter*, ed. V. Colli, Frankfurt, 2002, 173–218

GIBSON 1989: M. T. Gibson, 'The Twelfth-Century Glossed Bible', *Papers presented to the Tenth International Conference on Patristic Studies held in Oxford in 1987*, ed. E. A. Livingstone, Studia Patristica 23, Leuven, 1989, 232–44

GIBSON 1994: M. Gibson, 'Carolingian Glossed Psalters', in Gameson 1994, 78–100

GIBSON, HESLOP AND PFAFF 1992: M. Gibson, T.A. Heslop and R.W. Pfaff, *The Eadwine Psalter: text, image and monastic culture in twelfth-century Canterbury*, London, 1992

GIBSON AND SMITH 1995: *Codices Boethiani: a conspectus of manuscripts of the works of Boethius, I: Great Britain and the Republic of Ireland*, ed. M.T. Gibson and L. Smith, Warburg Institute Surveys and Texts 25, London, 1995

GILSON 1922: J.P. Gilson, 'Friar Alexander and his Historical Interpretation of the Apocalypse', *Collectanea Franciscana* 2, ed. C.L. Kingsford, Manchester, 1922, 20–36

GLORIEUX 1938: P. Glorieux, *Répertoire des maîtres en théologie de Paris au XIIIe siècle*, 2 vols, Paris, 1938

GLUNZ 1933: H.H. Glunz, *The Vulgate in England from Alcuin to Roger Bacon*, Cambridge, 1933

GNEUSS 2001: H. Gneuss, *Handlist of Anglo-Saxon Manuscripts: a List of Manuscripts and Manuscript Fragments Written or Owned in England up to 1100*, Tempe, AZ, 2001

GOERING 1992: J. Goering, *William de Montibus (c.1140–1213): The schools and the literature of pastoral care*, Toronto, 1992

GOERING 1995: J. Goering, 'The summa "Qui bene presunt" and its author', in *Literature and Religion in the later Middle Ages: Philological studies in honor of Siegfried Wenzel*, ed. R.G. Newhauser and J.A. Alford, Binghamton, 1995, 142–59

GOERING AND MANTELLO 1985: J. Goering and F.A.C. Mantello (eds), *Robert Grosseteste: Templum dei*, Toronto, 1985

GOODALL 1997: J.A. Goodall, 'Heraldry in the Decoration of English Medieval Manuscripts', *Antiquaries Journal* 77 (1997), 179–220

GORISSEN 1973: F. Gorissen, *Das Stundenbuch der Katharina von Kleve*, Berlin, 1973

GOUGAUD 1935: L. Gougaud, 'Études sur les Ordines Commendatio Animae', *Ephemerides Liturgicae* 49, 1935, 3–27

GOUGH 1780: R. Gough, *British Topography, or, An Historical Account of what has been done for Illustrating the Topographical Antiquities of Great Britain and Ireland*, London, 1780

GRANSDEN 1974–1982: Gransden, *Historical Writing in Britain, c.550 to the sixteenth century*, 2 vols., London, 1974–1982

GRAPE-ALBERS 1976: H. Grape-Albers, *Spätantike Bilder aus der Welt des Arztes. Medizinische Bilderhandschriften der Spätantike und ihre mittelalterliche Überlieferung*, Wiesbaden, 1976

GREEN 1994: D.H. Green, *Medieval Reading and Listening. The Primary Reception of German Literature 800–1300*, Cambridge, 1994

GREEN 1997: M. Green, 'A Handlist of Latin and Vernacular Manuscripts of the so-called Trotula texts', *Scriptorium* 51 (1997), 80–104

GRÉMONT 1971: D. B. Grémont, 'Lectiones ad prandium à l'abbaye de Fécamp aux xiiie siècle', *Cahiers Léopold Delisle* 20. 3–4 (1971), 3–41

GRETSCH 1999: M. Gretsch, *The Intellectual Foundations of the Benedictine Reform*, Cambridge, 1999

GRIFFITHS 1983: J. Griffiths, '"Confessio Amantis": the Poem and its Structure', in *Gower's Confessio Amantis. Responses and Reassessments*, ed. A.J. Minnis, Woodbridge, 1983, 163–78

GRIMSTONE 1997: *Pembroke College, Cambridge: A Celebration*, ed. A.V. Grimstone, Cambridge, 1997

GROTEFEND 1891–1898: H. Grotefend, *Zeitrechnung des deutschen Mittelalters und der Neuzeit*, Hannover 1891–1898, repr. 1997

GUARDA 1986: D. Nebbiai-Dalla Guarda, 'Les listes médiévales de lectures monastiques', *Revue Bénédictines* 96 (1986), 271–326

GULLICK 1996–1999: M. Gullick, 'The Origin and Date of Cambridge, Corpus Christi College MS 163', *Transactions of the Cambridge Bibliographical Society* 11 (1996–1999), 89–91

GULLICK 1998: M. Gullick, 'Professional Scribes in Eleventh- and Twelfth-Century England', *English Manuscript Studies 1100–1700*, 7 (1998), 1–24

GULLICK AND PFAFF 2001: M. Gullick and R.W. Pfaff, ' The Dublin Pontifical (TCD 98 [B.3.6]): St Anselm's ?', *Scriptorium* 55 (2001), 284–94

GY 1984: P-M. Gy, 'La Bible dans la liturgie du Moyen Âge', in *Le Moyen Âge et la Bible*, ed. P. Riché and G. Lobrichon, Paris, 1984, 537–52

HACKETT 1970: M.B. Hackett, *The Original Statutes of Cambridge University: The Text and Its History*, Cambridge, 1970

HAFFNER 1997: T. Haffner, *Die Bibliothek des Kardinals Giovanni d'Aragona (1456–1485)*, Wiesbaden, 1997

HAMBURGER 1988: J. Hamburger, 'The Casanatense Missal and Painting in Guelders in the Early Fifteenth Century', *Wallraf-Richartz-Jahrbuch* 48–49 (1988), 7–44

HAMBURGER 1991: J. Hamburger, 'The Casanatense and the Carmelite Missals: Continental Sources for English Manuscript Illumination of the Early 15th Century', in van der Horst and Klamt 1991, 161–73

HAMER 1993: R. Hamer, 'From Vignay's *Légende dorée* to the Earliest Printed Editions', in *Legenda aurea – la Légende dorée (XIIIᵉ – XVᵉ s.)*, Actes du Congrès international de Perpignan, séances "Nouvelles recherches sur la *Legenda aurea*", *Le moyen français* 32 (1993), 71–81

HÄNSEL-HACKER 1952: I. Hänsel-Hacker, 'Die Miniaturmalerei einer Paduaner Schule im Ducento', *Jahrbuch der Österreichischen Byzantinischen Gesellschaft* 2 (1952), 105–48

HÄNSEL-HACKER 1954: I. Hänsel-Hacker 'Die Fresken der Kirche St Nikolaus bei Matrei in Östtirol, das Werk einer Paduaner malerschule des 13. Jhs.', *Jahrbuch der Österreichischen Byzantinischen Gesellschaft* 3 (1954), 109–22

HARDMAN 1997: P. Hardman, 'Interpreting the Incomplete Scheme of Illustration in Cambridge, Corpus Christi College MS 61', *English Manuscript Studies* 6 (1997), 52–69

HARDWICK 1858: *Thomas of Elmham, Historia Monasterii S. Augustini Cantuariensis*, ed. C. Hardwick, Rolls Series 8, London, 1858

HARLEY 1982: M.P. Harley, 'The Middle English contents of a fifteenth-century medical handbook', *Mediaevalia* 8 (1982), 171–88

HARPER 1991: J. Harper, *The Forms and Orders of Western Liturgy from the Tenth to the Eighteenth Century*, Oxford, 1991; repr. 1993, 1994, 1995

HARRIS 1983: K. Harris, 'The Origins and Make-up of Cambridge University Library MS Ff.1.6', *Transactions of the Cambridge Bibliographical Society* 8 (1983), 299–325

HARRIS 2000: K. Harris, 'The Patronage and Dating of Longleat House MS 24: A Prestige Copy of the Pupilla Oculi Illuminated by the Master of the Troilus Frontispiece', in *Prestige, Authority and Power in Late Medieval Manuscripts and Texts*, ed. F. Riddy, York, 2000, 35–54

HARTHAN 1977: J. Harthan, *Books of Hours and Their Owners*, London, 1977

HARVEY 1996: P.D.A. Harvey, *Mappa Mundi, The Hereford World Map*, London, 1996

HARVEY 1997: P.D.A. Harvey, 'The Sawley Map and Other World Maps in Twelfth-Century England', *Imago Mundi* 49 (1997), 33–42

HASELOFF 1938: G. Haseloff, *Die Psalterillustration im 13 Jahrhundert. Studien zur Buchmalerei in England, Frankreich un den Niederländen*, Kiel, 1938

HASSIG 1995: D. Hassig, *Medieval Bestiaries, Text, Image, Ideology*, Cambridge, 1995

HAWORTH 1980: K.R. Haworth, *Deified virtues, demonic vices and descriptive allegory in Prudentius' Psychomachia*, Amsterdam, 1980

HEID-GUILLAUME AND RITZ 1998: C. Heid-Guillaume and A. Ritz, *Manuscrits médiévaux de Chambéry: textes et enluminures*, Paris, 1998

HEIMANN 1932: A. Heimann, 'Der Meister der "Grandes Heures de Rohan" und seine Werkstatt,' *Städel-Jahrbuch* 7–8 (1932), 1–61

HELMBOLD 2002: A.J. Helmbold, 'Speaking Volumes: Chaucer and the Legacy of the *Troilus* Frontispiece', PhD thesis, University of Alberta, 2002

HENDERSON 1967: Henderson, G., 'Studies in English Manuscript Illumination II', *Journal of the Warburg and Courtauld Institutes* 30 (1967), 71–137

HENDERSON 1968: G. Henderson, 'Studies in English manuscript illumination III', *Journal of the Warburg and Courtauld Institutes*, 31 (1968), 108–113

HENDERSON 1982: G. Henderson, *Losses and lacunae in insular art: the third G.N. Garmonsway Memorial Lecture delivered on 9 May 1975 in the University of York*, York, 1982, repr. in Henderson 1985, I, 1–45

HENDERSON 1983: G. Henderson, 'The Seal of Brechin Cathedral', in *From the Stone Age to the 'Forty-Five': Studies presented to R.B.K. Stevenson*, ed. Anne O'Connor and D.V. Clarke, Edinburgh, 1983, 399–415

HENDERSON 1985: G. Henderson, *Studies in English Bible Illustration*, 2 vols., London, 1985

HENDERSON 1987: G. Henderson, *From Durrow to Kells: the Insular Gospel Books, 650–800*, London 1987

HENDERSON 1991: G. Henderson, 'The meaning of leaf 5 of Fitzwilliam MS 330', *Burlington Magazine* 133 (1991), 682–86

HENDERSON 1993–1994: G. Henderson, '"The foxes have holes", once again', *Wiener Jahrbuch für Kunstgeschichte* 46/47 (1993–1994), 245–54

HENDERSON 1999: G. Henderson, *Vision and Image in Early Christian England*, Cambridge, 1999

HENDERSON 1994: J. Henderson, *Piety and Charity in Late Medieval Florence*, Oxford, 1994

HENDERSON 1874: W.G. Henderson, *Missale ad usum insignis ecclesiae Eboracensis*, Surtees Society, 59–60, 1874

HENDERSON 1969: W.G. Henderson, *Missale ad usum percelebris ecclesiae Herefordiensis*, Leeds, 1874; repr. 1969

HENRY 1960: F. Henry, 'Remarks on the decoration of three Irish Psalters', *Proceedings of the Royal Irish Academy* 61C, no. 2 (1960), 23–40

HERMANS 2004: J.M.M. Hermans, *Zwolse boeken voor een markt zonder grenzen 1477–1523*, Bibliotheca Bibliographica Neerlandica, Series Major 1, `t Goy-Houten, 2004

HERRLINGER 1970: R. Herrlinger, *History of Medical Illustration*, New York, 1970

HESBERT 1963–1979: R.-J. Hesbert, *Corpus Antiphonalium Officii*, 6 vols., Rome, 1963–1979

HESLOP 1984: T.A. Heslop, ' "Dunstanus Archiepiscopus" and Painting in Kent around 1120', *Burlington Magazine* 125 (1984), 195–204

HESLOP 1990: T.A. Heslop, 'The Production of *De Luxe* Manuscripts and the Patronage of King Cnut and Queen Emma', *Anglo-Saxon England* 19 (1990), 151–95

HEYWOOD AND WRIGHT 1850: *The Ancient Laws of the Fifteenth Century, for King's College, Cambridge, and for the public school of Eton College*, ed. J. Heywood and T. Wright, London, 1850

HIATT 2004: Alfred Hiatt, *The making of medieval forgeries*, London, 2004

HILPERT 1985: Hans-Eberhard Hilpert, 'Geistliche Bildung und Laienbildung: Zur Überlieferung der Schulschrift *Compendium historiae in Genealogia Christi* (*Compendium veteris testamenti*) des Petrus von Poitiers (†1205) in England', *Journal of Medieval History* 11 (1985), 315–31

HINDMAN 1977A: S. Hindman, 'The Case of Simon Marmion: attributions and documents', *Zeitschrift für Kunstgeschichte* 40 (1977), 185–204

HINDMAN 1977B: S. Hindman, *Text and Image in Fifteenth-Century Illustrated Dutch Bibles*, Verzameling van Middelnederlandse bijbelteksten, Miscellanea 1, Leiden, 1977

HINDMAN 1986: S. L. Hindman, *Christine de Pizan's "Epistre Othéa". Painting and Politics at the Court of Charles V*, Pontifical Institute of Medieval Studies, Studies and Texts 77, Toronto, 1986

HINDMAN 1989: S. Hindman, *Four Miniatures by Simon Bening*, London, 1989

HINDMAN ET AL. 1997: *The Robert Lehman Collection. Vol. IV Illuminations*, ed. S. Hindman, M.L. D'Ancona, P. Palladino, M.F. Saffiotti, New York, 1997

HOBSON 1989 : A. Hobson, *Humanists and Bookbinders: the Origins and Diffusion of the Humanistic Bookbinding 1459–1559 with a Census of Historiated Plaquette and Medallion Bindings of the Renaissance*, Cambridge, 1989

HOFFMANN 1925: E.W. Hoffmann, 'Der künstlerische Schmuck der Corvin-Codices', *Belvedere*, 8 (1925), 130–55

HOFFMANN 1969: E.W. Hoffmann, 'Simon Marmion reconsidered', *Scriptorium* 23 (1969), 243–71

HOFFMANN 1973: E.W. Hoffmann, 'Simon Marmion or "The Master of the Altarpiece of St. Bertin": a problem in attribution', *Scriptorium* 27 (1973), 263–90

HOFFMANN 1986: H. Hoffmann, *Buchkunst und Königtum im ottonischen und frühsalischen Reich*, Schriften der Monumenta Germaniae Historica 30, I, Stuttgart, 1986

HOHLER 1972: C. Hohler, 'The Red Book of Darley', in *Nordiskt Kollokvium II i latinsk liturgiforskning*, Institutionem för klassika språk vid Stockholms Universitet, Stockholm, 1972, 39–47

HOLTER 1938: K. Holter, 'Eine Wiener Handschrift aus der Werkstatt des Meisters des Zweder von Culenborg', *Oudheidkundig Jaarboek*, Ser. 4, 7 (1938), 55–59

HOOGEWERFF 1936: G.J. Hoogewerff, *De Noord-Nederlandsche schilderkunst*, I, The Hague, 1936

HOOGEWERFF 1937: G.J. Hoogewerff, *De Noord-Nederlandsche schilderkunst*, II, The Hague, 1937

HOOGEWERFF 1961: G.J. Hoogewerff, 'Gelderse miniatuurschilders in de eerste helft van de XVde eeuw', *Oud Holland*, 76 (1961), 3–49

HOWALD AND SIGERIST 1927: *Antonii Musae de herba vettonica liber. Pseudo Apulei Herbarius. Anonymi de Taxone liber. Sexti Placiti liber medicinae ex animalibus*, ed. E. Howald and H.E. Sigerist, *Corpus Medicorum Latinorum* 4, Leipzig, 1927

HUBERT 1928: J. Hubert, 'Quelques vues de la cité au XVe siècle dans un bréviaire parisien', *Mémoires de la Société Nationale des Antiquaires de France*, 77 (1928), 25–42

HUGGLER 1934: M. Huggler, 'Der Bilderkreis in den Handschriften der Alexander-Apokalypse', *Antonianum* 9 (1934), 85–150

HUGHES 1970: K.Hughes, 'Some aspects of Irish influence on early English private prayer', *Studia Celtica* 5 (1970), 48–61

HUGHES 1982: A. Hughes, *Medieval Manuscripts for Mass and Office*, Toronto, 1982

HUGHES 1984: M.J. Hughes, 'Margaret of York, Duchess of Burgundy: Diplomat, Patroness, Bibliophile and Benefactress', *The Private Library* 3rd. ser, 7 (1984), 2–17, 53–78

HUGLO 1988: M. Huglo, *Les Livres du Chant Liturgique*, Turnhout, 1988

HULL 1994: C.S. Hull, 'The Douai Psalter and Related East Anglian Manuscripts', unpublished Ph.D thesis, Yale University, 1994

HULL 2001: C.S. Hull, 'Abbot John, Vicar Thomas and M.R. James: The Early History of the Douai Psalter', in *The Legacy of M.R. James*, ed. L Dennison, Donington, 2001, 118–27

HUNT 1982: T. Hunt, *The Medieval Surgery*, Woodbridge, 1982

HUNT 1990: T. Hunt, *Popular Medicine in Thirteenth-century England: Introduction and Texts*, Cambridge, 1990

HUNT 1994: T. Hunt, *Anglo-Norman Medicine I: Roger Frugard's Chirurgia and the Practica Brevis of Platearius*, Woodbridge, 1994

HUNT 1997: T. Hunt, *Anglo-Norman Medicine II: the Shorter Treatises*, Woodbridge, 1997

HUNTER BLAIR AND MYNORS 1959: P. Hunter Blair and R.A.B. Mynors, *The Moore Bede: Cambridge University Library Ms Kk.5.16*, Copenhagen, 1959

HUTCHINSON 1974: G.E. Hutchinson, 'Attitudes toward Nature in Medieval England: The Alphonso and Bird Psalters', *Isis* 65 (1974), 5–37

IBÁÑEZ CERDÁ 1973: J. Ibáñez Cerdá (introd.), *Atlas de Joan Martines 1587*, Madrid, 1973

INNES AND MCKITTERICK 1994: M. Innes and R. McKitterick, 'The writing of history', in R. McKitterick, *Carolingian Culture: Emulation and Innovation*, Cambridge, 1994, 193–220

JACKSON 1969: R. Jackson, 'The *Traité du Sacre* of Jean Golein', *Proceedings of the American Philosophical Society* 113 (1969), 305–24

JAMES 1600: T. James, *Ecloga Oxonio-Cantabrigienses*, London, 1600

JAMES 1895A: M.R. James, *A Descriptive catalogue of the Manuscripts in the Fitzwilliam Museum*, Cambridge, 1895

JAMES 1895B: M.R. James, *A Descriptive Catalogue of the Manuscripts other than Oriental in the Library of King's College, Cambridge*, Cambridge, 1895

JAMES 1895C: M.R. James, *A Descriptive Catalogue of the Manuscripts in the Library of Eton College*, Cambridge, 1895

JAMES 1895D: M.R. James, *A Descriptive Catalogue of the Manuscripts in the Library of Sidney Sussex College, Cambridge*, Cambridge, 1895

JAMES 1898: M.R. James, *A Descriptive Catalogue of Fifty Manuscripts from the Collection of Henry Yates Thompson*, Cambridge, 1898

JAMES 1899: M.R. James, *A Descriptive Catalogue of the Manuscripts in the Library of Peterhouse*, Cambridge, 1899

JAMES 1900–1904: M.R. James, *The Western Manuscripts in the Library of Trinity College, Cambridge*, 4 vols., Cambridge, 1900–1904

JAMES 1903: M.R. James, *The Ancient Libraries of Canterbury and Dover*, Cambridge, 1903

JAMES 1904: M.R. James, *The Western Manuscripts in the Library of Emmanuel College: A Descriptive Catalogue*, Cambridge, 1904

JAMES 1905A: M.R. James, *A Descriptive Catalogue of the Manuscripts in the Library of Pembroke College, Cambridge*, Cambridge, 1905

JAMES 1905B: M.R. James, *A Descriptive Catalogue of the Western Manuscripts in the Library of Clare College, Cambridge*, Cambridge, 1905

JAMES 1905C: M.R. James, *A Descriptive Catalogue of the Western Manuscripts in the Library of Christ's College, Cambridge*, Cambridge, 1905

JAMES 1907: M.R. James, *A Descriptive Catalogue of the Manuscripts in the Library of Trinity Hall*, Cambridge, 1907

JAMES 1907–1914: M.R. James, *A Descriptive Catalogue of the Manuscripts in the Library of Gonville and Caius College, Cambridge*, Cambridge, 1907–1914

JAMES 1909A: M.R. James, *A Descriptive Catalogue of the Manuscripts in the College Library of Magdalene College, Cambridge*, Cambridge, 1909

JAMES 1909B: M.R. James, *The Trinity Apocalypse*, Roxburghe Club, 1909

JAMES 1912A: M.R. James, *A Descriptive Catalogue of the McClean Collection of Manuscripts in the Fitzwilliam Museum*, Cambridge, 1912

JAMES 1912B: M.R. James, *A Descriptive Catalogue of the Manuscripts in the Library of Corpus Christi College Cambridge*, 2 vols., Cambridge, 1912

JAMES 1913: M.R. James, *A Descriptive catalogue of the Manuscripts in the Library of St John's College, Cambridge*, Cambridge, 1913

JAMES 1916: M.R. James, *The Chaundler MSS*, Roxburghe Club, London, 1916

JAMES 1920: M.R. James, *La Estoire de Seint Aedward le Rei*, Roxburghe Club, Oxford, 1920

JAMES 1921: M.R. James, *A Peterborough Psalter and Bestiary of the Fourteenth Century*, Oxford, Roxburghe Club, 1921

JAMES 1925: M.R. James, *A Descriptive Catalogue of the Manuscripts in the Library of St. Catharine's College, Cambridge*, Cambridge, 1925

JAMES 1928: M.R. James, *The Bestiary, being a Reproduction in Full of the Manuscript Ii.4.26 in the University Library, Cambridge, with Supplementary Plates from Other Manuscripts of English Origin, and a Preliminary Study of the Latin Bestiary as Current in England*, Oxford, Roxburghe Club, 1928

JAMES 1931: M. R. James, *The Apocalypse in Art*, The Schweich Lectures of the British Academy 1927, London, 1931

JAMES 1935: M.R. James, *The Canterbury Psalter*, London, 1935

JAMES 1936: M.R. James, *The Bohun Manuscripts*, Roxburghe Club, 1936

JAMES 1936–1937: M.R. James, 'An English Picture-Book of the Late Thirteenth Century', *The Walpole Society* 25 (1936–1937), 23–32, pls. IX–XVI

JAMES 2004: *The Bede Roll of the Fraternity of St Nicholas*, ed. N.W. James and V.A. James, London Record Society 39, London, 2004

JAMES ET AL. 1902: M.R. James, *A Descriptive Catalogue of the Second Series of Fifty Manuscripts in the Collection of Henry Yates Thompson*, Cambridge, 1902

JAMES AND BERENSON 1926: *Speculum Humanae Salvationis, being a Reproduction of an Italian Manuscript of the Fourteenth Century*, ed. M.R. James and B. Berenson, Oxford, 1926

JEFFERSON 1995: L. Jefferson, 'Two Fifteenth-Century Manuscripts of the Order of the Garter', *English Manuscript Studies 1100–1700* 5 (1995), 18–35

JENKINSON 1915: H. Jenkinson, 'Mary de S. Paulo, Foundress of Pembroke College, Cambridge', *Archaeologia* 66 (1915), 401–46

JENNI AND THOSS 1982: U. Jenni and D. Thoss, *Das Schwarze Gebetbuch*, Frankfurt am Main, 1982

JONES 1999: *Medicina Antiqua*, ed. P.M. Jones, London, 1999

JONES AND UNDERWOOD 1992: M.K. Jones and M. Underwood, *The King's Mother: Lady Margaret Beaufort Countess of Richmond and Derby*, Cambridge, 1992

JUNG 1982: M.-R. Jung, 'Les "Douze Dames de Rhétorique"', in *Du mot au texte. Actes du IIIème Colloque International sur le Moyen francais, Düsseldorf, 17–19 septembre 1980*, ed. P. Wunderli, Tübingen, 1982), 229–40

JUSTICE 1993: S. Justice, 'The Illustrated Anglo-Norman Metrical Apocalypse in England', Ph.D. dissertation, Princeton University, 1993

KAEPPELI 1970–1993: T. Kaeppeli, *Scriptores Ordinis Praedicatorum Medii Aevi*, 4 vols, Rome, 1970–1993

KAMEN 1997: H. Kamen, *Philip of Spain*, New Haven and London, 1997

KAUFFMANN 1975: C.M. Kauffmann, *Romanesque Manuscripts, 1066–1190*, Survey of Manuscripts Illuminated in the British Isles 3, London and Boston, 1975

KAUFFMANN 1996: C.M. Kauffmann,

'Elkanah's Gift: Texts and Meaning in the Bury Bible Miniature', *Journal of the Warburg and Courtauld Institutes* 59 (1996), 279–85

KAUFFMANN 2003: C.M. Kauffmann, *Biblical Imagery in Medieval England, 700–1550*, London and Turnhout, 2003

KEITEL 1982: E. Keitel, 'La tradition manuscrite de Guillaume Machaut', *Guillaume de Machaut, Colloque-table ronde, organisé par l'université de Reims*, Actes et colloques 23, Paris, 1982, 75–94

KENDRICK 1999: L. Kendrick, *Animating the Letter: The Figurative Embodiment of Writing from Late Antiquity to the Renaissance*, Columbus, Ohio, 1999

KER 1957: N.R. Ker, *Catalogue of Manuscripts containing Anglo-Saxon*, Oxford, 1957

KER 1964: N.R. Ker, *Medieval Libraries of Great Britain: A List of Surviving Books*, London, 1964

KER 1977: N.R. Ker, *Medieval Manuscripts in British Libraries, II, Abbotsford-Keele*, Oxford, 1977

KER 1981: N.R. Ker, 'The books of Philosophy distributed at Merton College in 1372 and 1375', in *Medieval Studies for J.A.W. Bennett*, ed. P.L. Heyworth, Oxford, 1981, 347–94

KER AND PIPER 1992: N.R. Ker and A.J. Piper, *Medieval Manuscripts in British Libraries, IV, Paisley – York*, 1992

KEYNES 1964: G. Keynes, *Bibliotheca Bibliographici*, London, 1964

KEYNES 1985: S. Keynes, 'King Athelstan's Books', *Learning and Literature in Anglo-Saxon England: studies presented to Peter Clemoes on the occasion of his sixty-fifth birthday*, ed. M. Lapidge and H. Gneuss, Cambridge, 1985, 143–201

KEYNES 1992: S. Keynes, *Anglo-Saxon Manuscripts and Other Items of Related Interest in the Library of Trinity College, Cambridge*, Old English Newsletter Subsidia, 18, Binghamton, NY, 1992

KEYNES 2005: S. Keynes, 'Wulfsige, Monk of Glastonbury, Abbot of Westminster, and Bishop of Sherborne (993–1002)', in *St Wulfsige and the Sherborne Abbey Millenium 998–1998*, ed. K. Barker, D. Hinton and A. Hunt, (in press)

KEYNES AND LAPIDGE 1983: S. Keynes and M. Lapidge, *Alfred the Great: Asser's Life of King Alfred and other contemporary sources*, Harmondsworth, 1983

KIBRE 1978: P. Kibre, 'Arts and Medicine in the Universities of the Later Middle Ages', in *The Universities in the Late Middle Ages*, ed. J. Ijsewijn and J. Paquet, Leuven, 1978, 213–27

KLAUSER 1935: T. Klauser, *Das römische Capitulare evangeliorum. Texte und Untersuchungen zu seiner ältesten Geschichte*, Liturgiegeschichtliche Quellen und Forschungen 28, Münster-in-Westfalen, 1935

KNOWLES 1954: B. Knowles, 'Jean de Vignay, un traducteur du XIVe siècle,' *Romania* 75 (1954), 353–83

KÖNIG 1989: E. König, *Boccaccio Decameron*, Stuttgart, 1989

KÖNIG 2001: E. König, *Das Guemadeuc-Stundenbuch: Der Maler des Antoine de Roche und Guido Mazzoni aus Modena*, Ramsen, 2001.

KOSMER 1973: E. Kosmer, 'A Study of the Style and Iconography of a Thirteenth-Century Somme le Roi (British Library Ms. Add. 54180)', Ph.D. Diss., Yale University, 1973

KÖSTER 1979: K. Köster, 'Kollectionen metallener Wallfahrts-Devotionalien und kleiner Andachtsbilder, eingenäht in spätmittelalterlicher Gebetbuch-Handschriften', in *Das Buch und sein Haus, 1. Erlesenes aus der Welt des Buches*, ed. R. Fuhlrott and B. Haller, Wiesbaden, 1979, 77–130

KÖSTER 1984: K. Köster, 'Gemalte Kollectionen von Pilgerzeichen und religiösen Medaillen in flämischen Gebet- und Stundenbüchern des 15. und frühen 16. Jahrhunderts. Neue Funde in Handschriften der Gent-Brügger Schule', *Liber Amicorum Herman Liebaers*, ed. F. Vanwijngaerden et al., Brussels, 1984, 485–535

KRÄMER 1989: S. Krämer, *Mittelalterliche Bibliothekskataloge Deutschlands und der Schweiz. Handschriftenerbe des deutschen Mittelalters, I, Aachen-Kochel*, Munich, 1989

KREN 1992: *Margaret of York, Simon Marmion and the Visions of Tondal*, ed. T. Kren, Malibu, 1992

KUPFER-TARASULO 1979: M. Kupfer-Tarasulo, 'A Rosary Psalter Illuminated by Simon Bening,' *Quaerendo* 9 (1979), 209–26

KUTTNER 1937: Stephan Kuttner, *Repertorium der Kanonistik (1140–1234)*, Vatican City, 1937

KUYPERS 1902: A.B. Kuypers, *The Prayer Book of Aeluald the Bishop*, Cambridge, 1902

KVĚT 1931: J. Květ, *Illuminované rukopisy Královny Rejčky. Příspěvek k dějinám české knižní malby ve století XIV.*, Prague, 1931

LACAZE 1991: C. Lacaze, 'A Little-Known Manuscript from the Workshop of Master Pancraz', in van der Horst and Klamt 1991, 255–63

LACOMBE 1939: G. Lacombe, *Aristoteles Latinus. Pars Prior*, Rome, 1939, 2nd ed., Bruges, 1957

LACOMBE 1955: G. Lacombe, L. Minio-Paluello, *Aristoteles Latinus. Pars Posterior*, Cambridge, 1955

LADNER 1973: P. Ladner, 'Das Missale von Sant'Antonio di Ranverso in Lausanne', *Zeitschrift für schweizerische Kirchengeschichte* 67 (1973), 121–39

LANGLOIS 1910: E. Langlois, *Les manuscrits du Roman de la Rose: description et classement*, Travaux et Mémoires de l'Université de Lille, n.s. I, *Droit, Lettres*, v. 7, Lille, 1910; repr. Geneva, 1974

LAPIDGE 1982: M. Lapidge, 'The study of Latin texts in late Anglo-Saxon England: the evidence of Latin glosses', in *Latin and the vernacular languages in early medieval Britain*, ed. N. Brooks, Leicester, 1982, 99–140

LAPIDGE 1991: M. Lapidge, ed., *Anglo-Saxon Litanies of the Saints*, Henry Bradshaw Society 106, London, 1991

LAPIDGE 1992: M. Lapidge, 'Abbot Germanus, Winchcombe, Ramsey and the Cambridge Psalter', in *Words, Texts and Manuscripts: studies in Anglo-Saxon Culture presented to Helmut Gneuss on the occasion of his sixty-fifth birthday*, ed. M. Korhammer, Woodbridge, 1992, 99–129

LATRIE 1877: Guillaume de Machaut, *La prise d'Alexandrie; ou, Chronique du roi Pierre 1er de Lusignan*, ed. L. de Mas Latrie, Geneva, 1877

LAWLEY 1880–1883: S.W. Lawley, *Breviarium ad usum insignis ecclesiae Eboracensis*, 2 vols., Surtees Society, 71, 75, 1880–1883

LAWRENCE-MATHERS 2003: A. Lawrence-Mathers, *Manuscripts in Northumbria in the Eleventh and Twelfth Centuries*, Woodbridge, 2003

LAW-TURNER 2004: F. Law-Turner, 'Campaign to save a masterpiece', *Art Quarterly* (winter 2004), 44–48

LAW-TURNER 2005: F. Law-Turner, *The Ormesby Psalter*, Oxford, 2005

LAZZI 2000: Giovanna Lazzi, 'Iconografia Ciceroniana nella tradizione del ritratto miniato', *Ciceroniana*, nuova ser. 11 (2000), 79–93

LEADER 1988: *A History of the University of Cambridge, I: The University to 1546*, ed. D.R. Leader, Cambridge, 1988

LECLERCQ 1956: J. Leclercq, 'Textes et manuscrits cisterciens dans diverses bibliothèques', *Analecta sacri ordinis cisterciensis* 12 (1956), 289–310

LECOQ 1990: D. Lecoq, 'La Mappemonde d'Henri de Mayence, ou l'image du monde au XIIe siècle', *Iconographie médiévale: Image, texte, contexte*, ed. G. Duchet-Suchaux, Paris, 1990, 155–207

LEFF 1968: G. Leff, *Paris and Oxford Universities in the Thirteenth Century*, New York, 1968

LEGARÉ 2003: A.-M. Legaré, 'Un manuscrit inédit de la *Légende dorée* enluminé par le Maître des Heures de Dresde et le Maître de Marguerite de Liedekerke. Recyclage ou camouflage?,' unpublished lecture delivered at the symposium *Illuminating the Renaissance: Burgundian Identities, Flemish Artists and European Markets*, Los Angeles, The J. Paul Getty Museum, September 5–6, 2003

LEGARÉ 2004: A.M. Legaré, *Le Pèlerinage de Vie humaine en prose de la Reine Charlotte de Savoie*, Ramsen, 2004

LEGG 1901: L.G.W. Legg, *English Coronation Records*, Westminster, 1901

LEGG 1916: J.W. Legg, *The Sarum Missal*, Oxford, 1916; repr. 1969

LEMAIRE 1983: C. Lemaire, 'Quatre fermoirs de reliure armoriés d'origine laïque provenant des Pays-Bas méridionaux datant du XVe siècle', *Le livre et l'estampe* 29.113–114 (1983), 7–16

LEMAIRE 1993: C. Lemaire, 'Les manuscrits de Jean II, comte d Oettingen ou la fin d'une légend', in *Miscellanea Martin Wittek: Album de codicologie et de paléographie offert à Martin Wittek*, ed. A. Ramman and E. Manning, Louvain and Paris, 1993, 243–51

LENZUNI 1992: *All'ombra del Lauro. Documenti librari della cultura in età Laurenziana*, ed. A. Lenzuni, Florence, 1992

LEPROUX 2001: G.-M. Leproux, *La peinture à Paris sous le règne de François I*, Paris, 2001

LEROQUAIS 1924: V. Leroquais, *Les Sacramentaires et les Missels manuscrits des bibliothèques publiques de France*, 3 vols., Paris, 1924

LEROQUAIS 1927–1943: V. Leroquais, *Les Livres d'heures manuscrits de la Bibliothèque*

Nationale, 3 vols. with a supplement, Paris, 1927–1943

LEROQUAIS 1934: V. Leroquais, *Les Bréviaires manuscrits des bibliothèques publiques de France*, 5 vols., Paris, 1934

LEROQUAIS 1937: V. Leroquais, *Les Pontificaux manuscrits des bibliothèques publiques de France*, 3 vols., Paris, 1937

LEROQUAIS 1940–1941: V. Leroquais, *Les Psautiers manuscrits latins des bibliothèques publiques de France*, 2 vols., Mâcon, 1940–1941

LEVISON 1946: W. Levison, *England and the Continent in the Eighth Century*, Oxford, 1946

LEWIS 1985: F. Lewis, 'The Veronica: Image, Legend and Viewer', in *England in the Thirteenth Century, Proceedings of the 1984 Harlaxton Symposium*, ed. W.M. Ormrod, Harlaxton, 1985, 102–106

LEWIS 1987: S. Lewis, *The Art of Matthew Paris in the Chronica Majora*, Berkeley, 1987

LEWIS 1990: F. Lewis, 'From Image to Illustration: the Place of Devotional Images in the Book of Hours', in *Iconographie médiévale. Image, texte, contexte*, ed. G. Duchet-Suchaux, Paris, 1990, 29–48

LEWIS 1995: S. Lewis, *Reading Images: Narrative Discourse and Reception in the Thirteenth-Century Illuminated Apocalypse*, Cambridge, 1995

LEWIS 1996: F. Lewis, 'The wound in Christ's side and the instruments of the Passion: gendered experience and response', in *Women and the Book: assessing the Visual Evidence*, ed. L.M. Smith, J.H.M. Taylor, London, 1996, 204–29

LEWIS 2001: S. Lewis, 'Parallel Tracks – Then and Now: the Cambridge Alexander Apocalypse', *New Offerings, Ancient Treasures: Studies in Medieval Art for George Henderson*, ed. P. Binski and W. Noel, Stroud, 2001, 367–88

LIEFTINCK 1969: G. Lieftinck, *Boekverluchters uit de omgeving van Marie van Bourgondië*, Brussels, 1969

LIGHT 1984: L. Light, 'Versions et révisions du texte biblique', *Le Moyen Age et la Bible*, ed. P. Riché and G. Lobrichon, Paris, 1984, 55–93

LIGHT 1994: L. Light, 'French Bibles c.1200–30: A New Look at the Origin of the Paris Bible', in Gameson 1994, 155–76

LIPPE 1899–1907: R. Lippe, *Missale Romanum Mediolani 1474*, 2. vols., Henry Bradshaw Society 17, 33, 1899–1907

LITTLE 1930: A. G. Little, 'The Friars and the Foundation of the Faculty of Theology in the University of Cambridge', *Mélanges Mandonnet* 2 (1930), 389–401

LITTLE 1937: A.G. Little, *Franciscan History and Legend in English Medieval Art*, Manchester, 1937

LITTLE AND PELSTER 1934: A.G. Little and F. Pelster, *Oxford Theology and Theologians c.1282–1302*, Oxford, 1934

LOHR 1967: C.H. Lohr, 'Medieval Latin Aristotle Commentaries, Authors A–F', *Traditio* 23 (1967), 314–413

LOHR 1982: C.H. Lohr, 'The Medieval Interpretation of Aristotle', in *The Cambridge History of Later Medieval Philosophy*, ed. N. Kretzmann, A. Kenny and J. Pinborg, Cambridge, 1982, 80–98

LONGO 1998: *La Porpora: realtà e immaginario di un colore simbolico*, Atti del Convegno di studio, Venezia, 24 e 25 ottobre 1996, ed. O. Longo, Venice, 1998

LOVATT 1993: R. Lovatt, 'Two Collegiate Loan Chests in Late Medieval Cambridge', in *Medieval Cambridge: Essays on the Pre-Reformation University*, ed. P.N.R. Zutshi, Woodbridge, 1993, 129–65

LOVETT 2000: P. Lovett, *The British Library Companion to Calligraphy, Illumination and Heraldry*, London, 2000

LOWDEN 2003: J. Lowden, 'Illuminated Books and the Liturgy: Some Observations', in *Objects, Images and the Word: Art in the Service of the Liturgy*, ed. C. Hourihane, Princeton, 2003, 17–53

LOWRY 1991: M. Lowry, *Nicholas Jenson and the Rise of Venetian Publishing in Renaissance Europe*, Oxford, 1991

LUARD 1858: H. R. Luard, *Lives of Edward the Confessor*, Rolls Ser. 3, London, 1858

LYNA 1926: F. Lyna, *Le mortifiement de vaine plaisance de René d'Anjou*, Brussels, 1926

LYNA 1928: F. Lyna, 'Onbekende miniaturen van den Girartmeester (Jehan de Dreux)', *Het Boek* 17 (1928), 179–85

MACAULAY 1900–1901: G.C. Macaulay, *The English Works of John Gower*, 2 vols., Early English Text Society, ES 81 and 82, London, 1900–1901

MCCANN 1952: *Rule of St Benedict*, transl. J. McCann, London, 1952

MCCULLOCH 1960: F. McCulloch, *Medieval Latin and French Bestiaries*, University of North Carolina, Studies in the Romance Languages and Literatures 33, Chapel Hill, 1960

MCGURK 1961: P. McGurk, *Latin Gospel Books form A.D. 400 –to A.D. 800*, Brussels and Amsterdam, 1961

MCGURK 1986: P. McGurk, 'Text', in *The York Gospels*, ed. N. Barker, London, 1986, 43–63

MCGURK 1994: P. McGurk, 'The Oldest Manuscripts of the Latin Bible', in Gameson 1994, 1–23

MCGURK AND ROSENTHAL 1995: P. McGurk and J. Rosenthal, 'The Anglo-Saxon Gospelbooks of Judith, Countess of Flanders: their text, make-up and function', *Anglo-Saxon England* 24 (1995), 251–308

MCILWAIN 1999: M. McIlwain, 'The Gorleston Psalter', unpublished Ph.D thesis, Institute of Fine Arts, New York, 1999

MACKINLAY 1942: A.P.MacKinlay, *Arator: the codices*, Cambridge, Mass., 1942

MACKINLAY 1951: Arator, *Historia apostolorum*, ed. A.P. MacKinlay, CSEL 72, Vienna, 1951

MCKITTERICK 1978: D.J. McKitterick, *The Library of Sir Thomas Knyvett of Ashwellthorpe, c.1539–1618*, Cambridge, 1978

MCKITTERICK 1986: D.J. McKitterick, *Cambridge University Library. A History. The eighteenth and nineteenth centuries*, Cambridge, 1986

MCKITTERICK 2004: R. McKitterick, *History and Memory in the Carolingian World*, Cambridge, 2004

MCKITTERICK ET AL. 2004: *The Trinity Apocalypse*, ed. D.J. McKitterick, N. Morgan,

I. Short and T. Webber, London and Toronto, 2004

MCLACHLAN 1975: E. P. McLachlan, 'The Pembroke College New Testament and a Group of Unusual English Evangelist-Symbols', *Gesta* 14 (1975), 3–18

MADDEN 1902: H.E. Madden, *Trinity Hall*, London, 1902

MADDOCKS 1986: H. Maddocks, 'Illumination in Jean de Vignay's *Légende dorée*,' in *Legenda aurea: sept siècles de diffusion*, Actes du colloque international sur la *Legenda aurea*: texte latin et branches vernaculaires à l'Université du Québec à Montréal 11–12 mai 1983, Montreal and Paris, 1986, 155–59

MADDOCKS 1991: H. Maddocks, 'Pictures for Aristocrats: The Manuscripts of the *Légende dorée*,' in *Medieval Texts and Images: Studies of Manuscripts from the Middle Ages*, ed. Margaret M. Manion and Bernard J. Muir, Chur and Sydney, 1991, 1–23

MAGGIULLI AND GIOLITO 1996: G. Maggiulli, M.F.B. Giolito, *L'altro Apuleio: Problemi aperti per una nuova edizione dell'Herbarius*, Naples, 1996

MAÏER 1965: I. Maïer, *Les Manuscrits d'Ange Politien*, Geneva, 1965

MANFREDI AND MELOGRANI 1996: A. Manfredi and A. Melograni, 'Due nuovi codici del "Magister Vitae Imperatorum"', *Aevum* 70 (1996), 295–311

MANION, VINES AND DE HAMEL 1989: M. Manion, V. Vines and C. de Hamel, *Medieval & Renaissance Manusacripts in New Zealand Collections*, London, 1989

MARCOLINI 1999: S. Marcolini, 'La descente d'Orphée aux enfers dans L'Epistre d'Othéa de Christine de Pizan: un veritable echec?', *Studi Urbinati* B 69 (1999), 239–64

MARIANI CANOVA 1968–1969A: G. Mariani Canova, 'La decorazione dei documenti ufficiali in Venezia dal 1460 al 1530', *Atti del Istituto Veneto di scienze, lettere ed arti* 126 (1968–1969), 319–34

MARIANI CANOVA 1968–1969B: G. Mariani Canova, 'Profilo di Benedetto Bordone, miniatore padovano', *Atti del Istituto Veneto di scienze, lettere ed arti* 126 (1968–1969), 99–121

MARIANI CANOVA 1969: G. Mariani Canova, *La miniatura veneta del rinascimento: 1450–1500*, Venice, 1969

MARIANI CANOVA 1978: G. Mariani Canova, *Miniature dell' Italia settentrionale nella Fondazione Giorgio Cini*, Venice, 1978

MARIANI CANOVA 1988: G. Mariani Canova, 'Da Bologna a Padova, dal manoscritto alla stampa: Contributi alla storia dell' illustrazione degli incunaboli giuridici', in *Rapporti tra le università di Padova e Bologna* (Contributi alla storia dell' Università di Padova 20), Padua, 1988, 25–69

MARKS AND MORGAN 1981: R. Marks and N. Morgan, *The Golden Age of English Manuscript Painting 1200–1500*, New York, 1981

MARROW 1968: J.H. Marrow, 'Dutch Manuscript Illumination before the Master of Catherine of Cleves: The Master of the Morgan Infancy Cycle', *Nederlands Kunsthistorisch Jaarboek*, 19 (1968), 51–113

MARROW 1984: J.H. Marrow, 'Simon Bening in 1521: A Group of Dated Miniatures, in

Liber Amicorum Herman Liebaers, ed.
F. Vanwijngaerden, J.-M. Duvosquel,
J. Mélard, and L. Viaine-Awouters,
Brussels, 1984, 537–59

MARROW 1991: J.H. Marrow, 'Dutch
Manuscript Painting in Context:
Encounters with the Art of France, the
Southern Netherlands and Germany', in
van der Horst and Klamt 1991, 53–88

MARROW 1998: J.H. Marrow, 'History,
Historiography, and Pictorial Invention in
the *Turin-Milan Hours*', in *In Detail: New
Studies of Northern Renaissance Art in Honor
of Walter S. Gibson*, ed. L.S. Dixon, Turnhout,
1998, 1–14

MARROW 2002: J.H. Marrow, 'The Pembroke
Psalter-Hours', in *'ALS ICH CAN'. Liber
Amicorum in Memory of Professor Dr. Maurits
Smeyers*, ed. B. Cardon, J. Van der Stock,
D. Vanwijnsberghe et al., 2 vols., Leuven,
2002, I, 861–902

MARROW 2003: J.H. Marrow, 'L'enluminure
dans les anciens Pays-Bas septentrionaux',
in: *L'art flamand et hollandaise. Le siècle des
primitifs 1380–1520*, ed. C. Heck, Paris,
2003, 297–329

MARSDEN 1994: R. Marsden, 'The Old
Testament in Late Anglo-Saxon England:
Preliminary Observations on the Textual
Evidence', in Gameson 1994, 101–124

MARTIN 1964: C. Martin, 'Walter Burley', in
Oxford Studies presented to Daniel Callus,
Oxford, 1964, 194–230

MARTIN AND VEZIN 1990: *Mis-en-page et mise
en texte du livre manuscrit*, ed. H.-J. Martin
and J. Vezin, Paris, 1990

MASLAKOV 1984: G. Maslakov, 'Valerius
Maximus and Roman historiography. A
study of the *exempla* tradition', in *Aufstieg
und Niedergang der römischen Welt* II, 32.1,
ed. W. Haase, 1984, 437–96

MASON 1990: E. Mason, *St Wulfstan of
Worcester c.1008–1095*, Oxford, 1990

MASSING 1990: J.-M. Massing, '*The Triumph of
Caesar* by Benedetto Bordone and Jacobus
Argentoratensis: Its Iconography and
Influence', *Print Quarterly* 7 (1990), 2–21

MAYR-HARTING 1991: H. Mayr-Harting, *The
coming of Christianity to Anglo-Saxon
England*, 3rd edition, London, 1991

MAZZATINTI 1897: G. Mazzatinti, *La biblioteca
dei re d'Aragona in Napoli*, Rocca S. Casciano,
1897

MEARNS 1913: J. Mearns, *Early Latin Hymnaries*,
Cambridge, 1913

MEEHAN 1994: B. Meehan, 'Durham Twelfth-
Century Manuscripts in Cistercian Houses',
in *Anglo-Norman England, 1093–1193*, ed.
D. Rollason, M. Harvey and M. Prestwich,
Woodbridge, 1994, 439–49

MEEHAN 1998: B. Meehan, 'Notes on the
Preliminary Texts and Continuations to
Symeon of Durham's *Libellus de Exordio*', in
*Symeon of Durham: Historian of Durham and
the North*, ed. D. Rollason, Stamford, 1998,
128–37

MEERSSEMAN 1960: G.G. Meersseman, *Der
Hymnos Akathistos im Abendland, II, Gruss-
Psalter, Gruss-Orationen, Gaude-Andachten
und Litaneien*, Freiburg, 1960

MEISS 1963: M. Meiss, 'French and Italian
Variations on an Early Fifteenth-Century

Theme: St. Jerome and His Study', *Gazette
des Beaux-Arts* 62 (1963), 147–70

MEISS 1967: M. Meiss, *French Painting in the
Time of Jean de Berry. The Late Fourteenth
Century and the Patronage of the Duke*,
2 vols., London 1967

MEISS 1968: M. Meiss, *French Painting in the
Time of Jean de Berry: The Boucicaut Master*,
London, 1968

MEISS 1974: M. Meiss, with the assistance of
S.O. Dunlap Smith and E.H. Beatson,
*French Painting in the Time of Jean de Berry:
The Limbourgs and Their Contemporaries*,
2 vols., New York, 1974

MEISS AND THOMAS 1973: M. Meiss and
M. Thomas, *The Rohan Master: A Book of
Hours*, New York, 1973

MELOGRANI 1990: A. Melograni, 'Appunti di
miniatura lombarda. Ricerche sul "Maestro
delle Vitae Imperatorum"', *Storia dell' arte*
70 (1990), 273–314

MELOGRANI 1992: A. Melograni, 'I corali
quattrocenteschi della Collegiata di S.
Lorenzo a Voghera', *Storia dell'Arte* 75
(1992), 117–64

MELOGRANI 1993: A. Melograni, 'Il Messale di
Guglielmo Lampugnani miniato dal
"Maestro delle Vitae Imperatorum"
(Holkham Hall, MS 34)', *Studi di Storia dell'
arte* 4 (1993), 9–25

MELOGRANI 1995: A. Melograni, 'Miniature
inedite del Quattrocento lombardo nelle
collezioni americane', *Storia dell'arte* 83
(1995), 5–27

MERKL 1999: Ulrich Merkl, *Buchmalerei in
Bayern in der ersten Hälfte des 16. Jahrhunderts*,
Regensburg, 1999

MERTON 1912: A. Merton, *Die Buchmalerei in
St Gallen*, Leipzig, 1912

METAMORPHOSES 1968: *The Metamorphoses of
Ovid: translated by William Caxton, 1480*,
New York, 1968

MEYER 1879: P. Meyer, 'Les manuscrits
français de Cambridge, I, Saint John's
College', *Romania* 8 (1879), 305–42

MEYER 1886: P. Meyer, 'Les manuscrits français
de Cambridge', *Romania* 15 (1886), 236–357

MEYER 1895: P. Meyer, 'La descent de Saint
Paul en enfer', *Romania* 24 (1895), 357–91

MEYER 1896: P. Meyer, 'Version Anglo-
Normande en vers de l'Apocalypse',
Romania 25 (1896), 174–257

MEYER 1903: P. Meyer, 'Les manuscrits français
de Cambridge', *Romania* 32 (1903), 75–95

MEYER 1996: H. Meyer, 'Die illustrierten
lateinischen Handschriften im rahmen der
Gesamt überlieferung der Enzyclopädie des
Bartholomäus Anglicus', *Frühmittelalterliche
Studien* 30 (1996), 368–75

MICHAEL 1981: M.A. Michael, 'The Harnhulle
Psalter-Hours: an Early Fourteenth-Century
English Illuminated Manuscript at Downside
Abbey', *Journal of the British Archaeological
Association* 134 (1981), 81–99

MICHAEL 1988: M.A. Michael, 'Oxford,
Cambridge and London: towards a theory
for 'grouping' gothic manuscripts',
Burlington Magazine 130 (1988), 107–115

MICHAEL 1993: M.A. Michael, 'English
Illuminators c.1190–1450: A Survey from
Documentary Sources', *English Manuscript
Studies* 4 (1993), 62–113

MILANESI 1865: G. Milanesi, 'Il viaggio degli
ambasciatori fiorentini al re di Francia nel
MCCCCLXI descritto da Giovanni di
Francesco di Neri Cecchi loro cancelliere',
Archivio Storico Italiano, ser. III, 1.1 (1865),
1–29

MILLAR 1926: E.G. Millar, *English Illuminated
Manuscripts, Xth to the XIIIth Century*, Paris,
1926

MILLAR 1927: E.G. Millar, *The Library of A.
Chester Beatty: a Descriptive Catalogue of the
Western Manuscripts*, Oxford, 1927

MILLAR 1953: E.G. Millar, *An Illuminated
Manuscript of La Somme le Roy attributed to
the Miniaturist Honoré*, Roxburghe Club,
Oxford, 1953

MILLAR 1959: E.G. Millar, *The Parisian
Miniaturist Honoré*, London, 1959.

MINIO-PALUELLO 1961: L. Minio-Paluello,
Aristoteles Latinus. Codices Supplementa Altera,
Bruges, 1961

MINIO-PALUELLO 1966: L. Minio-Paluello,
*Porphyrii Isagoge et Anonymi Fragmentum vulgo
vocatum 'Liber sex principiorum'*, Aristoteles
Latinus I, 6–7, Bruges and Paris, 1966

MISCHLEWSKI 1995: A. Mischlewski, *Un ordre
hospitalier au Moyen Âge. Les chanoines reguliers
de Saint-Antoine-en-Viennois*, Grenoble, 1995

MOMBELLO 1967: G. Mombello, *La tradizione
Manoscritta dell' "Epistre d'Othéa" di Christine
de Pizan. Prolegomeni all'edizione del testo*.
Memorie dell'Accademia delle Scienze di
Torino, Classi di scienze morali, storiche e
filologiche, ser. 4, 15, Torino, 1967

MOORE 1936: P.S. Moore, *The Works of Peter of
Poitiers*, Notre Dame, Ind., 1936

MORAND 1962: K. Morand, *Jean Pucelle*,
Oxford, 1962

MORGAN 1982–1988: N. Morgan, *Early
Gothic Manuscripts*, 2 vols., A Survey of
Manuscripts Illuminated in the British Isles
4, Oxford and London, 1982–1988

MORGAN 1992: N. Morgan, 'Old Testament
Illustration in Thirteenth-Century
England', in *The Bible in the Middle Ages: Its
Influence on Literature and Art*, ed. B.S. Levy,
Binghamton, 1992, 149–98

MORGAN 1993–1994: N. Morgan, 'Longinus
and the Wounded Heart', *Wiener Jahrbuch
für Kunstgeschichte* 46–47 (1993–1994),
507–18, 817–20

MORGAN 1994: N. Morgan, 'The Coronation
of the Virgin by the Trinity and Other
Texts and Images of the Glorification of
Mary in Fifteenth-Century England', in
*England in the Fifteenth Century: Proceedings
of the 1992 Harlaxton Symposium*, ed.
N. Rogers, Stamford, 1994, 223–41

MORGAN 1996: N. Morgan, 'Chronicles and
histories', in Turner 1996, vol. 7, 241–44

MORGAN 1999: N. Morgan, 'Texts and Images
of Marian Devotion in English Twelfth-
Century Monasticism and their Influence
on the Secular Church', in *Monasteries and
Society in Medieval Britain. Proceedings of the
1994 Harlaxton Symposium*, ed. B. Thompson,
Harlaxton Medieval Studies 6, Stamford,
1999, 117–36

MORGAN 2001: N. Morgan, 'The Introduction
of the Sarum Calendar into the Dioceses of
England in the Thirteenth Century', in
Thirteenth Century England, VIII, ed. M.

Prestwich, R. Britnell and R. Frame, Woodbridge, 2001, 179–206

MORGAN 2002: N. Morgan, 'Patrons and Devotional Images in English Art of the International Gothic *c.*1350–1450', in *Reading Texts and Images. Essays on Medieval and Renaissance Art and Patronage in honour of Margaret M. Manion*, ed. B.J. Muir, Exeter, 2002, 93–121

MORGAN 2003: N. Morgan, 'An SS Collar in the Devotional Context of the Shield of the Five Wounds', in *The Lancastrian Court. Proceedings of the 2001 Harlaxton Symposium*, ed. J. Stratford, Harlaxton Medieval Studies 13, Donington, 2003, 147–62

MORGAN 2004: N. Morgan, 'The Torments of the Damned in Hell in Texts and Images in England in the Thirteenth and Fourteenth Centuries', in *Prophecy, Apocalypse and the Day of Doom. Proceedings of the 2000 Harlaxton Symposium*, ed. N. Morgan, Harlaxton Medieval Studies 12, Donington, 2004, 250–60

MORGAN 2005: N. Morgan, 'Patrons and their Devotions in the Historiated Initials and Full-Page Miniatures of 13th-Century English Psalters', in Büttner 2005, 205–18

MORGAND 1893: *Répetorie méthodique de la librairie de Damascène Morgand*, Partie I, Paris, 1893

MORISON 1952: S. Morison, *Byzantine Elements in Humanistic Script*, Chicago, 1952

MORSE 1991: R. Morse, *Truth and Convention in the Middle Ages. Rhetoric, Representation and Reality*, Cambridge, 1991

MROCZKO 1966: T. Mroczko, 'Illustracje apokalipsy we wroclawskim komentarzu Aleksandra O.F.M.', *Rocznik historii sztuki* 6 (1966), 7–45

MUHLETHALER 1985: J.-C. Muhlethaler, 'Un manifeste poetique de 1463: les "Enseignes" des Douze Dames de Rhétorique', in *Les Grandes Rhétoriqueurs. Actes du Ve Colloque International sur le Moyen Français, Milan, 6–8 mai 1985*, ed. S. Cigada , Milan, 1985, I, 83–101

MÜLLER 1973: Hans-Georg Müller, *Hrabanus Maurus – de laudibus sanctae crucis. Studien zur Überlieferung und Geistesgeschichte mit dem Faksimile Textabdruck aus Codex Reg. lat. 124 der Vatikanischen Bibliothek*, Beihefte zum Mittelateinischen Jahrbuch 11, Ratingen, 1973

MUNBY 1972: A.N.L. Munby, *Connoisseurs and Medieval Miniatures 1750–1850*, Oxford, 1972

MURATOVA 1990: X. Muratova, 'Les manuscrits-frères: un aspect particulier de la production des Bestiaires enluminés en Angleterre à la fin du XIIᵉ siècle', in *Artistes, Artisans et Production Artistique au Moyen Age, Colloque internationale, 1983*, ed. X. Barral i Altet, Picard, 1990, 69–92

MYNORS 1939: R.A.B. Mynors, *Durham Cathedral Manuscripts to the End of the Twelfth Century*, Durham, 1939

MYNORS 1949–1953: R.A.B. Mynors, 'A Fifteenth-Century Scribe: T. Werken', *Transactions of the Cambridge Bibliographical Society* 1 (1949–1953), 97–104

MYNORS AND THOMSON 1975: Erasmus, *Correspondence*, Letters 142–297, transl. R.A.B. Mynors and D.F.S. Thomson, Toronto, 1975

NAPIER 1967: *Wulfstan: Sammlung der ihm zugeschriebenen Homilien* , ed. A.S. Napier, Dublin and Zürich, 1967; repr. 1993

NAUGHTON 1991: J. Naughton, 'A Minimally-intrusive Presence: Portraits in Illustrations for Prayers to the Virgin', in *Medieval Texts and Images: Studies of Manuscripts from the Middle Ages*, ed. Margaret M. Manion and Bernard J. Muir, Chur, Philadelphia and Sydney, 1991, 111–126

NAVILLE 1984: C.-É. Naville, *Enea Silvio Piccolomini: l'uomo, l'umanista, il pontefice (1405–1464)*, Bologna, 1984

NEISNER 1995: M. Niesner, *Das Speculum Humanae Salvationis der Stiftsbibliothek Kremsmünster*, Cologne, Weimar, Vienna and Böhlau, 1995

NOEL 1995: W. Noel, *The Harley Psalter*, Cambridge, 1995

NOEL 2004: W. Noel, *The Oxford Bible Pictures*, Luzern and Baltimore, 2004

NORDENFALK 1975: C. Nordenfalk et al., *Medieval and Renaissance miniatures from the National Gallery of Art*, Washington DC, 1975

NORTON 1998: C. Norton, 'History, Wisdom and Illumination', in *Symeon of Durham: Historian of Durham and the North*, ed. D. Rollason, Stamford, 1998, 61–105

NORTON-SMITH 1979: J. Norton-Smith, *Bodleian Library MS Fairfax 16*, London, 1979

NUTTALL 2004: P. Nuttall, *From Flanders to Florence: the Impact of Netherlandish Painting 1400–1500*, New Haven and London, 2004

OATES 1954: J.C.T. Oates, *A Catalogue of the Fifteenth-Century Printed Books in the University Library, Cambridge*, Cambridge, 1954

OATES 1986: J.C.T. Oates, *Cambridge University Library, a History. From the beginnings to the Copyright Act of Queen Anne*, Cambridge, 1986

OBBEMA 1997: P. Obbema, 'Tussen Zwolle en Kampen', *Nieuw Letterkundig Magazijn* 14–15 (1995), 28–29

OFFNER 1930: R. Offner, *The Fourteenth Century. A Critical and Historical Corpus of Florentine Painting*, sec. 3, vol. 2, pt. 1, New York, 1930

OFFNER AND BOSKOVITS 1987: R. Offner, *The Fourteenth Century. A Critical and Historical Corpus of Florentine Painting*, sec. 3, vol. 2, pt. 1, ed. M. Boskovits, Florence, 1987

OHLGREN 1992: T.H. Ohlgren, ed., *Anglo-Saxon Textual Illustration: photographs of sixteen mansucripts with descriptions and index*, Kalamazoo, MI, 1992

OMAN 1950: C. Oman, 'The Swinburne Pyx', *Burlington Magazine* 92 (1950), 337–41

O'MEARA 2001: C.F. O'Meara, *Monarchy and Consent: The Coronation Book of Charles V of France*, London and Turnhout, 2001

OMONT 1889: H. Omont, *Catalogue des manuscrits grecs de Fontainebleau sous François Ier et Henry II* , Paris, 1889

O'NEILL 1977: Y. V. O'Neill, 'The Fünfbilderserie – a bridge to the unknown', *Bulletin of the History of Medicine* 51 (1977), 538–49

O'NEILL 1993: Y.V. O'Neill, 'Diagrams of the medieval brain: a study in cerebral localization', in *Iconography at the Crossroads. Papers from the colloquium sponsored by the Index of Christian Art, Princeton University, 23–24 March 1990*, ed. B. Cassidy, Princeton, 1993, 91–105

ORR 1995: M.T. Orr, 'Illustration as Preface and Postscript in the Hours of the Virgin of Trinity College MS B.11.7', *Gesta* 34.2 (1995), 162–76

ORTH 1976: M.D. Orth, 'Progressive Tendencies in French Manuscript Illumination 1515–1530: Godefroy le Batave and the 1520s Hours Workshop,' PhD dissertation, Institute of Fine Arts, New York University, 1976

ORTH 1980: M.D. Orth, 'Geofroy Tory et l'enluminure. Deux livres d'Heures de la collection Doheny,' *Revue de l'Art* 50 (1980), 40–47

ORTH 1988: M.D. Orth, 'French Renaissance Manuscripts: The 1520s Hours Workshop and the Master of the Getty Epistles,' *The J. Paul Getty Museum Journal* 16 (1988), 33–60

ORTH 1989: M.D. Orth, 'Antwerp Mannerist Model Drawings in French Renaissance Books of Hours: A Case Study of the 1520s Hours Workshop,' *Journal of The Walters Art Gallery* 47 (1989), 77–90

ORTH 2005: M. Orth, *French Renaissance Manuscripts 1515–1570*, London and Turnhout, 2005 (forthcoming)

OTAKA AND FUKUI 1977: Y. Otaka and H. Fukui, *Apocalypse Anglo-Normande (Cambridge, Trinity College, MS R.16.2)*, Osaka, 1977

OTTOSEN 1993: K. Ottosen, *The Responsories and Versicles of the Latin Office of the Dead*, Aarhus, 1993

OWEN 1988: D.M. Owen, *Cambridge University Archives: A Classified List*, Cambridge, 1988

OWEN 1990: D.M. Owen, *The Medieval Canon Law: Teaching, Literature and Transmission*, Cambridge, 1990

PÄCHT 1948: O. Pächt, *The Master of Mary of Burgundy*, London, 1948

PÄCHT 1963: O. Pächt, 'Zur Entstehung des "Hieronymus im Gehäus"', *Pantheon* 21 (1963), 131–142

PÄCHT 1977: O. Pächt, 'René d'Anjou Studien II', *Jahrbuch der Kunsthistorischen Sammlungen in Wien* 73 (1977), 17–32

PÄCHT 1987: O. Pächt, 'Der Salvator Mundi des Turiner Stundenbuches', *Florilegium in honorem Carl Nordenfalk octogenarii contextum*, Nationalmuseums skriftserie, NS 9, Stockholm, 1987, 181–190

PÄCHT AND JENNI 1975: O. Pächt and U. Jenni, *Holländische Schule*, 2 vols., Die illuminierten Handschriften und Inkunabeln der Österreichischen Nationalbibliothek III, Vienna, 1975

PÄCHT, JENNI AND THOSS 1983: O. Pächt, U. Jenni and D. Thoss, *Flämische Schule I*, 2 vols., Die illuminierten Handschriften und Inkunabeln der Österreichischen Nationalbibliothek VI, Vienna, 1983

PÄCHT AND THOSS 1990: O. Pächt and D. Thoss, *Flämische Schule II*, 2 vols., Die illuminierten Handschriften und Inkunabeln der Österreichischen Nationalbibliothek VII, Vienna, 1990

PADOVANI 1978: S. Padovani, 'Su Belbello da Pavia e sul 'Miniatore di San Michele a Murano', *Paragone* 29 (1978), 25–34

PADRONO 1971: G.M.Z. Padrono, 'Il Maestro 'To. Ve.' e la sua bottega: Miniature Veneziane del XVIo secolo', *Arte Veneta* 25 (1971), 53–71

PAGE 1979: C. Page, 'The earliest English Keyboard: new evidence from Boethius', *Early Music* 7 (1979), 308–14

PALAZZO 1998: E. Palazzo, *A History of Liturgical Books from the Beginnings to the Thirteenth Century*, Collegeville, 1998

PALAZZO 1999: E. Palazzo, *L'évêque et son image. L'illustration du Pontifical au moyen âge*, Turnhout, 1999

PANAYOTOVA 2001: S.D. Panayotova, 'Peter of Poitiers's *Compendium in Genealogia Christi*: the Early English Copies', in *Belief and Culture in the Middle Ages: Studies Presented to Henry Mayr-Harting*, ed. R. Gameson and H. Leyser, Oxford, 2001, 327–41

PANAYOTOVA 2005A: S.D. Panayotova, 'Art and Politics in a Royal Prayerbook', *Bodleian Library Record* (April 2005), forthcoming

PANAYOTOVA 2005B: S.D. Panayotova, 'A Ruskinian project with a Cockerellian flavour', *The Book Collector* (2005), forthcoming

PANAYOTOVA 2006: S.D. Panayotova, 'The Way of the Psalms', in *The Medieval Bible as a Way of Life*, ed. G. Dinkova-Bruun and J.A. Harris, Routledge, 2006, forthcoming

PANOFSKY 1927: E. Panofsky, 'Imago Pietatis', in *Festschrift M.J. Friedländer*, Leipzig, 1927, 261–308

PANOFSKY 1953A: E. Panofsky, 'Guelders and Utrecht. A Footnote on a Recent Acquisition of the Nationalmuseum at Stockholm', *Konsthistorisk Tidskrift*, 22 (1953), 90–102.

PANOFSKY 1953B: E. Panofsky, *Early Netherlandish Painting: Its Origins and Character*, Cambridge, 1953

PAREDI 1961: A. Paredi, *La Biblioteca del Pizolpasso*, Milan, 1961

PARKER 1969: E. Parker, 'A Twelfth-Century Cycle of New Testament Drawings from Bury St Edmunds Abbey', *Proceedings of the Suffolk Institute of Archaeology* 31 (1969), 263–302

PARKER AND LITTLE 1994: E.C. Parker and C.T. Little, *The Cloisters Cross, Its Art and Meaning*, New York, 1994

PARKES 1976: M.B. Parkes, 'The Influence of the Concepts of *Ordinatio* and *Compilatio* on the Development of the Book', in *Medieval Learning and Literature. Essays presented to Richard William Hunt*, ed. J.J.G. Alexander and M.T. Gibson, Oxford, 1976, 120–41

PARKES 1979: M.B. Parkes, *English Cursive Book Hands, 1250–1500*, London, 1979

PARKES 1982: M.B. Parkes, *The Scriptorium of Wearmouth-Jarrow: the Jarrow Lecture 1982*, Jarrow, 1982; repr. in Parkes 1991, 93–120

PARKES 1988: M.B. Parkes, 'Book Provision and Libraries at the Medieval University of Oxford', *The University of Rochester Library Bulletin* 40 (1988), 28–43; repr. in Parkes 1991

PARKES 1991: M.B. Parkes, *Scribes, Scripts and Readers: Studies in the Communication, Presentation and Dissemination of Medieval Texts*, London, 1991

PARKES 1997: M.B. Parkes, 'Archaizing Hands in English Manuscripts', in *Books and Collectors 1200–1700: essays presented to Andrew Watson*, ed. J.P. Carley and C.G.C. Tite, London, 1997, 101–141

PARKES AND BEADLE 1980: M.B. Parkes and R. Beadle, *Geoffrey Chaucer. The Poetical Works. A facsimile of Cambridge University Library MS Gg.4.27*, 3 vols., Woodbridge, 1980

PARKES AND SALTER 1978: M.B. Parkes and E. Salter, *Troilus and Criseyde, Geoffrey Chaucer, A Facsimile of Corpus Christi College, Cambridge, MS 61*, Cambridge, 1978

PARRY 1977: M. Parry, '"Candor Illaesus": The "impresa" of Clement VII and Other Medici Devices in the Vatican Stanze', *Burlington Magazine* 119 (1977), 676–86

PARSONS 1975: *Tenth century studies*, ed. D. Parsons, London, 1975

PARTSCH 1981: S. Partsch, *Profane Buchmalerei der bürgerlichen Gesellschaft im spätmittelalterlichen Florenz: Der Specchio Umano des Getreidehändlers Domenico Lenzi*, Worms, 1981

PARUSSA 1999: G. Parussa, ed., *Christine de Pizan. Epistre Othea*, Textes Littéraires Français, Genève, 1999

PEARSALL 1961: D.A. Pearsall, 'Notes on the Manuscript of "Generydes"', *The Library*, 5th ser., 16 (1961), 205–10

PEARSALL 2004: D. Pearsall, 'The Manuscripts and Illustrations of Gower's Works', in *A Companion to Gower*, ed. S. Echard, Woodbridge, 2004, 73–97

PEEK AND HALL 1962: H.E. Peek and C.P. Hall, *The Archives of the University of Cambridge: An Historical Introduction*, Cambridge, 1962

PEILE 1910–1913: J. Peile, *Biographical Register of Christ's College 1505–1905 and of the Earlier Foundation, God's House 1448–1505*, 2 vols., Cambridge, 1910–1913

PELLEGRIN 1955: E. Pellegrin, 'Bibliothèques d'humanistes lombards de la cour des Visconti Sforza', *Bibliothèque d'Humanisme et Renaissance* 17 (1955), 218–245

PELLEGRIN 1955–1969: E. Pellegrin, *La bibliothèque des Visconti et des Sforza ducs de Milan au Xve siècle*, Paris, 1955; *Supplément*, Florence, 1969

PERDRIZET 1933: P. Perdrizet, *Le calendrier parisien à la fin du Moyen Âge*, Paris, 1933

PEREIRA 1989: M. Pereira, *The Alchemical Corpus Attributed to Raymond Lull*, Warburg Institute Surveys and Texts 18, London, 1989

PEREIRA 1990: M. Pereira, 'Lullian alchemy: aspects and problems of the Corpus of alchemical works attributed to Ramon Llull (XIV–XVII centuries)', *Catalan Review* 4 (1990), 41–54

PERRIN 1989: M Perrin, 'Le "De laudibus sanctae crucis" de Raban Maur et sa tradition manuscrite au IXe siècle', *Revue d'histoire des textes* 19 (1989), 191–240

PETERSON 1994: E.A. Peterson, 'The textual basis for visual errors in French Gothic Psalter illustration', in Gameson 1994, 177–204

PFAFF 1970: R.W. Pfaff, *New Liturgical Feasts in Later Medieval England*, Oxford, 1970

PFAFF 1980: R.W. Pfaff, *Montagu Rhodes James*, London, 1980

PFAFF 1995: R.W. Pfaff, ed., *The Liturgical Books of Anglo-Saxon England*, Old English Newsletter, Subsidia 23, Kalamazoo, MI, 1995

PIACENTINI 1983: P. Scarcia Piacentini, 'I codici', in P. Cherubini et al., 'Il costo del libro', in *Scrittura, biblioteche e stampa a Roma nel Quattrocento*, ed. M. Miglio et al., Littera Antiqua 3, Vatican City, 1983, 359–401

PICKERING 1980: F.P. Pickering, *The Calendar Pages of Medieval Service Books*, Reading, 1980

PICKWOAD 1994: N. Pickwoad, 'The conservation of Cambridge, Corpus Christi College MS 197B', in *Conservation and Preservation in Small Libraries*, ed. N. Hadgraft and K. Swift, Cambridge, 1994, 114–22

PINK 1929: H.L. Pink, *List of Trinity Hall Documents to 1600*, Cambridge, 1929

PINK 1959: H.L. Pink, 'Decretum Manuscripts in Cambridge University', *Studia Gratiana* 7 (1959), 235–50

PLUMMER 1964: J. Plummer, *Liturgical Manuscripts for the Mass and the Divine Office*, New York, 1964

POLLARD 1939–1940: G. Pollard, 'Mediaeval Loan Chests at Cambridge', *Bulletin of the Institute of Historical Research* 17 (1939–1940), 113–29

POLLARD 1955: G. Pollard, 'William de Brailes', *Bodleian Library Record* 5 (1955), 202–209

POLLARD 1964: G. Pollard, 'The University and the Book Trade in Medieval Oxford', *Miscellanea Medievalia* 3 (1964), 336–44

POLLARD 1978: G. Pollard, 'The *Pecia* system in the Medieval Universities', in *Medieval Scribes, Manuscripts and Libraries: essays presented to N.R. Ker*, ed. M.B. Parkes and A. G. Watson, London, 1978, 145–61

POPE 1967–1968: J. Pope, *Homilies of Aelfric: a supplementary collection*, 2 vols., Early English Text Society, OS 259 and 260, London, 1967–1968

PORCHER 1959: J. Porcher, *The Rohan Book of Hours*, London, 1959

PORQUET 1890: *Catalogue de Livres Rares et Précieux Manuscrits et Imprimés composant la Bibliothèque de Feu M. Le Baron Ach. S(eillière)*, Paris, Charles Porquet, 1890

POWELL 1998: S. Powell, 'Lady Margaret Beaufort and her Books', *The Library*, 6th ser., 20 (1998), 197–240

POWELL AND WALLIS 1968: J.E. Powell and K. Wallis, *The House of Lords in the Middle Ages: A History of the English House of Lords to 1540*, London, 1968

POWICKE 1931: M. Powicke, *The Medieval Books of Merton College*, Oxford, 1931

PRIEBSCH 1896: R. Priebsch, *Deutsche Handschriften in England*, I, Erlangen, 1896

PRIOR 1913: O. H. Prior, *L'Image du Monde de Maitre Gossouin: rédaction en prose*, Lausanne and Paris, 1913

PROCTER AND WORDSWORTH 1879–1886: F. Procter and C. Wordsworth, *Breviarium ad usum insignis ecclesiae Sarum*, 3 vols., Cambridge, 1879–1886; repr. 1970

QUAZZA 1985: A. Quazza, 'La Biblioteca del Cardinal Domenico della Rovere: I Codici Miniati di Torino', in Sesti 1985, II, 655–700

QUAZZA 1990: A.Quazza, 'La commitenza di Domenico della Rovere nella Roma di Sisto IV', in Romano 1990, 13–40

RABEL 1992: C. Rabel, 'L'illustration du *Rational des Divins Offices* de Guillaume Durand', in *Guillaume Durand, Évêque de Mende (v. 1230–1296), canoniste, liturgiste et homme politique*, ed. P.-M. Gy, Paris, 1992, 171–81

RAIMES 1908: F. Raimes, 'Robert de Reymes of Bolam, Shortflatt and Ayden Castle', *Archaeologia Aeliana*, 3 ser., 4 (1908), 313–8

RAIMES 1939: A.L. Raimes, 'The Family of Reymes in Wherstead in Suffolk', *Proceedings of the Suffolk Institute of Archaeology* 23 (1939), 89–115

RANDALL 1966: L.M.C. Randall, *Images in the Margins of Gothic Manuscripts*, Berkeley, 1966

RAND-SCHMIDT 2001: K.A. Rand-Schmidt, *The Index of Middle English Prose. Handlist 17: Manuscripts in the Library of Gonville and Caius College, Cambridge*, Woodbridge, 2001

RASHDALL 1987: H. Rashdall, *The Universities of Europe in the Middle Ages*, ed. F.M. Powicke and A.B. Emden, 3 vols., 2nd ed, Oxford, 1987

RASMUSSEN 1998: N.K. Rasmussen, *Les pontificaux du haut Moyen Age. Genèse du livre liturgique de l'évêque*, Louvain, 1998

RAWCLIFFE AND WILSON 2004: *Medieval Norwich*, ed. C. Rawcliffe and R. Wilson, London and New York, 2004

REANEY 1969: *Manuscripts of Polyphonic Music (c.1320–1400)*, ed. G. Reaney, Répertoire international des souces musicales, ser.B, iv:2, Munich, 1969

REEVE 1981: M.D. Reeve, 'Five dispensable manuscripts of Achille Tatius', *JHS* 101 (1981), 144–45

REEVE 1986: Longus, *Daphnis et Chloe*, ed. M.D. Reeve, Leipzig, 1986

REY PASTOR AND GARCIA CAMARERO 1960: J. Rey Pastor and E. Garcia Camarero, *La cartografia Mallorquina*, Madrid, 1960.

REYNOLDS 1983: *Texts and transmission: A survey of the Latin Classics*, ed. L.D. Reynolds, Oxford, 1983

REYNOLDS 2005: C. Reynolds, 'The Workshop of the Master of the Duke of Bedford: Definitions and Identities', in: *Patrons, Authors and Workshops: Books and Book Production in Paris around 1400*, ed. G. Croenen and P. Ainsworth, Leuven, 2005 (forthcoming)

RÉZEAU, 1986: P. Rézeau, *Répertoire d'incipit des prières francaises à la fin du moyen âge*, Geneva, 1986

RICKERT 1952: M. Rickert, *The Reconstructed Carmelite Missal*, London, 1952

RICKERT 1965: M. Rickert, *Painting in Britain: The Middle Ages*, 2nd edn, Harmondsworth, 1965

RILEY-SMITH 1999: J. Riley-Smith, *Hospitallers: The History of the Order of St John*, London, 1999

RING 1949: G. Ring, *A Century of French Painting 1400–1500*, London, 1949

RINGROSE 1993: J. Ringrose, 'The Medieval Statutes of Pembroke College', in *Medieval Cambridge: Essays on the Pre-Reformation University*, ed. P.N.R.Zutshi, Woodbridge, 1993, 93–127

ROBBINS 1939: R.H. Robbins, 'The Arma Christi Rolls', *Modern Language Review* 34 (1939), 415–21

ROBBINS 1952: R.H. Robbins, *Secular Lyrics of the XIVth and XVth Centuries*, Oxford, 1952

ROBIN 1985: F. Robin, *La cour d'Anjou-Provence. La vie artistique sous le règne de René*, Paris, 1985

ROBINSON 1988: P.R. Robinson, *Catalogue of Dated and Datable Manuscripts c.737–1600 in Cambridge Libraries*, 2 vols., Cambridge, 1988

ROBINSON 1997: P.R. Robinson, 'A Twelfth-Century *Scriptrix* from Nunnaminster', in *Of the Making of Books: medieval manuscripts, the scribes and readers, essays presented to M.B. Parkes*, ed. P.R. Robinson and R. Zim, Aldershot, 1997, 73–93

ROGERS 1982: N. Rogers, 'Books of Hours produced in the Low Countries for the English market in the fifteenth century', M. Litt. dissertation, University of Cambridge, 1982

ROGERS 1986: N.J. Rogers, 'The Old Proctor's Book: A Cambridge Manuscript of *c.1390*', in *England in the Fourteenth Century: Proceedings of the 1985 Harlaxton Symposium*, ed. W.M. Ormrod, Woodbridge, 1986, 213–23

ROGERS 1987: N.J. Rogers, 'Fitzwilliam Museum Ms 3–1979: A Bury St. Edmunds Book of Hours and the Origins of the Bury Style', in *England in the Fifteenth Century: Proceedings of the 1986 Harlaxton Symposium*, ed. D. Williams, Woodbridge, 1987, 229–43

ROGERS 1994: N. Rogers, 'The Artist of Trinity B.11.7 and his Patrons', in *England in the Fifteenth Century: Proceedings of the 1992 Harlaxton Symposium*, ed. N. Rogers, Stamford, 1994, 170–86

ROGERS 1995: N. Rogers, 'The Early History of Sidney Sussex College Library', in *Sidney Sussex College, Cambridge, Historical Essays in Commemoration of the Quatercentenary*, ed. D.E.D. Beales and H.B. Nisbet, Woodbridge, 1996, 75–88

ROGERS 2001: N. Rogers, 'Some Curiosa Hagiographica in Cambridge Manuscripts Reconsidered', in *The Legacy of M.R. James*, ed. L. Dennison, Donington, 2001, 194–210

ROLLASON 1998: D. Rollason, 'Symeon's Contribution to Historical Writing in Northern England', in *Symeon of Durham: Historian of Durham and the North*, ed. D. Rollason, Stamford, 1998, 1–13

ROMANO 1990: G. Romano, ed., *Domenico della Rovere e il Duomo Nuovo di Torino: Rinascimento a Roma e in Piemonte*, Torino, 1990

ROPER 1993: S. Roper, *Medieval English Benedictine Liturgy*, New York, 1993

ROSS 1940: D.J.A.Ross, 'Some thirteenth-century French versions of the Chirurgia of Roger of Salerno', Ph.D. thesis, London, 1940

ROSS 1956: D.J.A. Ross, 'A check-list of manuscripts of three Alexander texts: The Julius Valerius Epitome, the Epistola ad Aristotelem and the Collatio cum Dindimo', *Scriptorium* 10 (1956), 127–32

ROSS 1963: D.J.A. Ross, *Alexander historiatus. A Guide to Medieval Illustrated Alexander Literature*, London, 1963; revised ed. Frankfurt, 1988

ROSS 1969: D.J.A. Ross, 'A thirteenth century Anglo-Norman workshop illustrating secular literary manuscripts', in *Mélanges offerts à Rita Lejeune*, Gembloux, 1969, 689–94

ROUSE AND ROUSE 1988: R.H. Rouse and M.A. Rouse, 'The Book Trade in the University of Paris ca. 1250–ca. 1350', in *La production du livre universitaire au moyen âge. Exemplar et Pecia*, ed. L.J. Bataillon, B.G. Guyot, and R.H. Rouse, Paris, 1988, 41–114; reprinted in M.A. Rouse and R.H. Rouse, *Authentic Witnesses: Approaches to Medieval Texts and Manuscripts*, Notre Dame, 1991, 259–325

ROUSE AND ROUSE 1994: R.H. Rouse and M.A. Rouse, 'The Dissemination of Texts in Pecia at Bologna and Paris', in *Rationalisierung der Buchherstellung im Mittelalter und in der frühen Neuzeit*, ed. P. Rück, Marburg an der Lahn, 1994, 69–77

ROUSE AND ROUSE 2000: R.H. Rouse and M.A. Rouse, *Manuscripts and their Makers: Commercial Book Producers in Medieval Paris 1200–1500*, 2 vols., London/Turnhout, 2000

RUSHFORTH 2002: R. Rushforth, *An Atlas of Saints in Anglo-Saxon Calendars*, ASNC Guides, Texts, and Studies, Cambridge, 2002

RUSSELL 1980: F. Russell, 'A Gothic miniature from Murano', *Burlington Magazine* 122.923 (1980), 117–18

RUSSELL 1986: V. Russell, 'Evidence for a Stemma for the De Vignay MSS: St. Nicholas, St. George, St. Bartholomew, and All Saints', in *Legenda aurea: sept siècles de diffusion*, Actes du colloque international sur la *Legenda aurea*: texte latin et branches vernaculaires à l'Université du Québec à Montréal 11–12 mai 1983), Montreal and Paris, 1986, 131–54

RUYSSCHAERT 1968: J. Ruysschaert, 'Miniaturistes 'romains' sous Pie II', in *Enea Silvio Piccolomini Papa Pio II. Atti del Convegno per il quinto centenario della morte e altri scritti*, ed. D. Maffei, Siena, 1968, 245–82

RUYSSCHAERT 1969: J. Ruysschaert, 'Le miniaturiste "romain" de l'"opus" de Michele Carara', *Scriptorium* 23 (1969), 215–24

RUYSSCHAERT 1973: J. Ruysschaert, 'Le Liber juramentorum de la Chambre Apostolique sous Paul II', in *Miscellanea in memoria di G. Cencetti*, Turin, 1973, 285–291

RUYSSCHAERT 1986: J. Ruysschaert, 'Il copista Bartolomeo San Vito miniatore padovano a Roma dal 1469 al 1501', *Archivio della Società di storia patria* 109 (1986), 37–47

SAENGER 1985: P. Saenger, 'Books of Hours and the Reading Habits of the Later Middle Ages', *Scrittura e Civiltà* 9 (1985), 239–69

SALMI 1951: M. Salmi, 'Contributo a Belbello da Pavia', *Miscellanea Galbiati* 2 (1951), 231–38

SALMI 1954: M. Salmi, *Italian Miniatures*, New York, 1954

SALMON 1962: P. Salmon, *The Breviary through the Centuries*, Collegeville, 1962

SALTMARSH 1933: J. Saltmarsh, 'The Muniments of King's College', *Proceedings of the Cambridge Antiquarian Society* 33 (1933), 83–97

SANDLER 1974: L.F. Sandler, *The Peterborough Psalter in Brussels and other Fenland Manuscripts*, London, 1974

SANDLER 1985: L.F. Sandler, 'A note on the

illuminators of the Bohun Manuscripts', *Speculum* 60 (1985), 364–72

SANDLER 1986: L.F. Sandler, *Gothic Manuscripts 1285–1385*, A Survey of Manuscripts Illuminated in the British Isles 5, Oxford, 1986

SANDLER 2002: L.F. Sandler, 'Three Psalters for the Bohun Family', in *Reading Texts and Images. Essays on Medieval and Renaissance Art and Patronage in honour of Margaret M. Manion*, ed. B.J. Muir, Exeter, 2002, 123–51

SANDLER 2003: L.F. Sandler, 'Lancastrian Heraldry in the Bohun Manuscripts', *The Lancastrian Court*, Proceedings of the 2001 Harlaxton Symposium, ed. J. Stratford, Harlaxton Medieval Studies 13, Donington, 2003, 221–32

SANDLER 2004: L.F. Sandler, *The Lichtenthal Psalter and the Manuscript Patronage of the Bohun Family*, London, 2004

SANDLER AND DE HAMEL 2003: L.F. Sandler and C. de Hamel, *The Peterborough Bestiary, MS.53 (fols.189–210v), The Parker Library, College of Corpus Christi and the Blessed Virgin Mary, Cambridge*, Commentary on the Facsimile Edition, i, Luzern, 2003

SANDON 1984–: N. Sandon, *The Use of Salisbury*, Newton Abbot, 1984– (in progress)

SAUL 1997A: N.E. Saul, *Richard II*, New Haven, 1997

SAUL 1997B: N.E. Saul, 'Richard II's Ideas of Kingship', in *The Regal Image of Richard II and the Wilton Diptych*, ed. D. Gordon, L. Monnas and C. Elam, London, 1997, 27–32

SAUL 2001: N. Saul, *Death, Art, and Memory in Medieval England: The Cobham Family and their Monuments, 1300–1500*, Oxford, 2001

SAXL AND MEIER 1953: F. Saxl and H. Meier, *Catalogue of Astrological and Mythological Illuminated Manuscripts of the Latin Middle Ages*, 3 vols., London, 1953

SCATTERGOOD 1983: V.J. Scattergood, 'Literary Culture at the Court of Richard II', in *English Court Culture in the Later Middle Ages*, ed. V.J. Scattergood and J.W. Sherborne, London, 1983, 29–43

SCHELLER 1995: R.W. Scheller, *Exemplum, Model-Book Drawings and the Practice of Artistic Transmission in the Middle Ages (ca.900–ca.1470)*, Amsterdam, 1995

SCHILLER 1990–1991: G. Schiller, *Ikonographie der christlichen Kunst, 5, Die Apokalypse des Johannes*, 2 vols., Gütersloh, 1990–1991

SCHMALE AND SCHMALE-OTT 1972: *Frutolfs und Ekkehards Chroniken und die Anonyme Kaiserchronik*, ed. F.-F. Schmale and I. Schmale-Ott, Darmstadt, 1972

SCHMALE-OTT 1971: I. Schmale-Ott, 'Untersuchungen zu Ekkehard von Aura und zur Kaiserchronik', *Zeitschrift für bayerische Landesgeschichte* 34, 1971, 403–61

SCHMIDT 2001: G. Schmidt, 'Chaucer in Italy, Some Remarks on the 'Chaucer Frontispiece' in Ms 61, Corpus Christi College, Cambridge', *New Offerings, Ancient Treasures, Studies in Medieval Art for George Henderson*, ed. P. Binski and W. Noel, Stroud, 2001, 478–89

SCHMOLINSKY 1991: S. Schmolinsky, *Der Apokalypsenkommentar des Alexander Minorita*, Hannover, 1991

SCHRADER, ROBERTS AND MAKOWSKI 1992: *Arator's On the acts of the Apostles (De actibus apostolorum)*, ed. R.J. Schrader, J.L. Roberts and J.F. Makowski, Atlanta, Georgia, 1992

SCHULLIAN 1981: D.M. Schullian, 'A revised list of MSS of Valerius Maximus', in *Miscellanea Augusto Campana, Medioevo e Umanesimo* 44–45 (1981), 695–728

SCOTT 1911: C.R. Scott, *Collegium Divi Johannis Evangelistae 1511–1911*, Cambridge, 1911

SCOTT 1976: K.L. Scott, *The Caxton Master and his Patrons*, Cambridge Bibliographical Monographs 8, Cambridge, 1976

SCOTT 1980: K.L. Scott, *The Mirroure of the Worlde: MS Bodley 283 (England c.1470–1480)*, Roxburghe Club, Oxford, 1980

SCOTT 1996: K.L. Scott, *Later Gothic Manuscripts 1390–1490*, 2 vols., A Survey of Manuscripts Illuminated in the British Isles 6, London, 1996

SCOTT 2000: K.L. Scott, 'Limner Power: A Book Artist in England c.1420', in *Prestige, Authority and Power in Late Medieval Manuscripts and Texts*, ed. F. Riddy, York, 2000, 55–75

SCOTT 2002: K.L. Scott, *Dated & Datable English Manuscript Borders, c.1395–1499*, London, 2002

SEARLE 1876: W.G. Searle, *The Illuminated Manuscripts in the Library of the Fitzwilliam Museum, Cambridge*, Cambridge, 1876

SECOMSKA 1975: K. Secomska, 'The Miniature Cycle in the Sandomierz *Pantheon* and the Medieval Iconography of Alexander's Indian Campaign', *Journal of the Warburg and Courtauld Institutes* 38 (1975), 53–71

SECOMSKA 1977: K. Secomska, *Legenda Aleksandra Wielkiego w "Pantheonie" sandomierskim: miniatury w Kodeksie z 1335 roku*, Wroclaw, 1977

SESTI 1985: E. Sesti, ed., *La Miniatura italiana tra Gotico e Rinascimento*, Atti del II Congresso di Storia della Miniatura Italiana, Cortona, 24–26 Settembre 1982, 2 vols., Florence, 1985

SEYMOUR 1995: M.C. Seymour, *A Catalogue of Chaucer Manuscripts*, I, *Works before the Canterbury Tales*, Aldershot, 1995

SHACKLETON-BAILEY 2000: *Valerius Maximus, Memorable doings and sayings*, ed. and trans. D.R. Shackleton-Bailey, Cambridge, Mass., 2000

SHAILOR 1992: B. A. Shailor, *Catalogue of Medieval and Renaissance Manuscripts in the Beinecke Rare Book and Manuscript Library Yale University*, 3 vols., New York, 1984–1992

SHARPE 1996: R. Sharpe et al., *English Benedictine Libraries: the shorter catalogues*, Corpus of British Medieval Library Catalogues 4, London, 1996

SHARPE 1997: R. Sharpe, *A Handlist of the Latin Writers of Great Britain and Ireland before 1540*, Turnhout 1997

SHEINGORN 1995: P. Sheingorn, ' "And flights of angels sing thee to thy rest": The Soul's Conveyance to the Afterlife in the Middle Ages', in *Art into Life. Collected Papers from the Kresge Art Museum Medieval Symposia*, ed. C.G. Fisher and K.L. Scott, East Lansing, 1995, 155–92

SHEPPARD 1997: *A Guide to the Census of Western Medieval Bookbinding Structures to 1500 in British Libraries*, ed. J. Sheppard, 1997

SHERBORNE 1983: J.W. Sherborne, 'Aspects of English Court Culture in the Later Fourteenth Century', in *English Court Culture in the Later Middle Ages*, ed. V.J. Scattergood and J.W. Sherborne, London, 1983, 1–27

SIDNEY SUSSEX 1996: *Sidney Sussex College Annual*, 1996

SIMON 1978: P. Simon, *Die Fünfzehn Zeichen in der Handschrift Nr. 215 der Gräflich von Schönborn'sche Bibliothek zu Pommersfelden*, Ph.D. dissertation, Munich, Ludwig-Maximilians-Universität, 1975, published 1978

SINCLAIR 1982: K.V. Sinclair, *French Devotional Texts of the Middle Ages. A Bibliographic Manuscript Guide. First Supplement*, Westport, 1982

SKELTON AND HARVEY 1986: *Local Maps and Plans from Medieval England*, ed. R.A. Skelton and P.D.A. Harvey, Oxford 1986

SKIDMORE 1996: C.J. Skidmore, *Practical ethics for Roman gentlemen: the work of Valerius Maximus*, Exeter, 1996

SMALLEY 1937: B. Smalley, 'La Glossa Ordinaria', *Recherches de théologie ancienne et médiévale* 9 (1937), 365–400

SMALLEY 1973: B. Smalley, *The Becket Conflict and the Schools*, Oxford, 1973

SMALLEY 1983: B. Smalley, *The Study of the Bible in the Middle Ages*, 3rd edn, Oxford, 1983

SMALLEY AND LACOMBE 1931: B. Smalley and G. Lacombe, 'The Lombard's commentary on Isaias and other fragments', *The New Scholasticism*, 5 (1931), 123–62

SMEYERS 1999: M. Smeyers, *Flemish Miniatures from the 8th to the mid-16th Century*, trans. K.Bowen and D. Imhoff, Leuven, 1999

SMITH 1976: M. Smith, *Prudentius' Psychomachia. A re-examination*, Princeton, 1976

SMITH 2000: M. Smith, *The Title Page: Its Early Development 1460–1510*, London and Newcastle, Delaware, 2000

SMITH 2001: L. Smith, *Masters of the Sacred Page: Manuscripts of Theology in the Latin West to 1274*, Notre Dame, 2001

SMITH 2003: K.A. Smith, *Art, Identity and Devotion in Fourteenth-Century England*, London, 2003

SOETERMEER 2002: F. Soetermeer, 'Exemplar und Pecia. Zur Herstellung juristischer Bücher in Bologna im 13 und 14 Jahrhundert', in *Juristische Buchproduktion im Mittelalter*, ed. V. Colli, Frankfurt, 2002, 481–516

SOONS 1982: A. Soons, *Juan de Mariana*, Boston, 1982

SOTHEBY'S 2004: Sotheby's, The Library of the Earls of Macclesfield, pt 3, 22 June 2004

SOUKOUPOVÁ 1984: H. Soukoupová, 'Illuminované rukopisy z kláštera bl. Anežky v Praze Na Františku', *Časopis Národního Muzea v Praze* 153.2 (1984), 69–97

SPILLING 1978: H. Spilling, 'Angelsächsische Schrift in Fulda', in *Von der Klosterbibliothek zur Landesbibliothek. Beiträge zum zweihundertjährigen Bestehen oder Hessischen Landesbibliothek Fulda*, ed. A. Brall, Stuttgart, 1978, 47–98

SPILLING 1980: H. Spilling, 'Das Fuldaer Skriptorium zur Zeit Hrabanus Maurus', in *Hrabanus Maurus. Lehrer. Abt und Bischof*, ed.

R. Kottje and H. Zimmermann, Wiesbaden, 1980, 165–81

SPILLING 1992: H. Spilling, *Opus magnentii Hrabani Mauri in honorem sanctae crucis conditum. Hrabans Beziehung zu seinem Werk*, Fuldaer Hochschulschhriften 18, Frankfurt, 1992

SPILLING 1996: H. Spilling, 'Das frühe Phase karolingische Minuskel', in *Fulda in der Welt der Karolinger und Ottonen Kloster*, ed. G. Schrimpf, Frankfurt, 1996, 249–84

SPRIGGS 1964: G.M. Spriggs, 'Unnoticed Bodleian Manuscripts illuminated by Herman Scheerre and his School, I, Manuscripts of Works by John Gower', *Bodleian Library Record*, 7 (1964), 193–99

STADTHUBER 1950: J. Stadthuber, 'Das Laienstundengebet vom Leiden Christi in seinem mittelalterlichen Fortleben', *Zeitschrift für katholischen Theologie* 72 (1950), 282–325

STAIKOS 1998: K. Staikos, *Charta of Greek Printing*, 2 vols (Cologne, 1998)

STANGE 1929: A. Stange, 'Beiträge zur Sächsischen Buchmalerei des 13 Jahrhunderts', *Münchener Jahrbuch der bildenden Kunst*, 6 (1929), 302–44

STEFANI 1985: L. Stefani, 'Per una storia della miniatura lombarda da Giovannino de' Grassi alla scuola Cremonense della II metà del Quattrocento: appunti bibliografici', in Sesti 1985, II, 823–881

STELLING-MICHAUD 1963: S. Stelling-Michaud, 'Le transport international des manuscrits juridiques bolonais entre 1265 et 1320', in *Mélanges d'histoire économique et sociale en hommage au professeur Antony Babel*, ed. Anne-Marie Piuz and Jean-François Bergier, Geneva, 1963, I, 95–127

STERLING 1987–1999: C. Sterling, *La peinture médièvale à Paris 1300–1500*, 2 vols., Paris, 1987–1990

STETTINER 1895–1905: R. Stettiner, *Die illustrierten Prudentiushandschriften*, Berlin, 1895–1905

STONEMAN 1999: W.P. Stoneman, *Dover Priory*, Corpus of British Medieval Library Catalogues 5, London, 1999

STONES 1969: A. Stones 'An Italian Miniature in the Gambier-Parry Collection', *The Burlington Magazine* 111 (1969), 7–12 A.

STONES 1996: A. Stones, 'The Illustrations of BN, fr. 95 and Yale 229', in *Word and Image in Arthurian Literature*, ed. K. Busby, New York, 1996, 203–60

STONES FORTHCOMING: M.A. Stones, *Manuscripts Illuminated in France: Gothic Manuscripts, c.1260–1320*, London and Turnhout, forthcoming

STORY 1998: J.E. Story, 'Symeon as Annalist', in *Symeon of Durham: Historian of Durham and the North*, ed. D. Rollason, Stamford, 1998, 202–13

STRATFORD 1999: J. Stratford, 'The Early Royal Collections and the Royal Library to 1461', *The Cambridge History of the Book in Britain, Volume III. 1400–1557*, ed. L. Hellinga and J.B. Trapp, Cambridge, 1999, 255–66

STRONG 1987: R. C. Strong, *Gloriana: The Portraits of Queen Elizabeth I*, London, 1987

STRONGMAN 1977: S. Strongman, 'John Parker's manuscripts: an edition of the lists in Lambeth Palace MS 737', *Transactions of the Cambridge Bibliographical Society* 7 (1977), 1–27

STUMP 1978: E. Stump, *Boethius's De topicis differentiis*, Ithaca, 1978

SUCKALE 1977: R. Suckale, 'Arma Christi', *Städel Jahrbuch* 6 (1977), 177–208

SUDHOFF 1907: K. Sudhoff, 'Anatomische Zeichnungen (Schemata) aus dem 12. und 13. Jahrhundert und eine Skelettzeichnung des 14. Jahrhunderts', in *Studien zur Geschichte der Medizin, Heft I: Tradition und Naturbeobachtung in den Illustrationen medizinischer Handschriften und Frühdrucke vornehmlich des 15. Jahrhunderts*, Leipzig, 1907, 51–59

SUDHOFF 1914: K. Sudhoff, 'Beiträge zur Geschichte der Chirurgie im Mittelalter', *Studien zur Geschichte der Medizin* 10 (1914), 33–42

SWARZENSKI 1901: G. Swarzenski, *Die Regensburger Buchmalerei des X. und XI. Jahrhunderts, Denkmäler der süddeutschen Malerei des frühen Mittelalters* 1, Stuttgart, 1901; repr. 1969

TALAMO 1997: E.A. Talamo, *Codices cantorum. Miniature e disegni nei codici della Cappella Sistina*, Florence, 1997

TALBOT 1958: C.H. Talbot, 'The Universities and the Medieval Library', in *The English Library before 1700*, ed. F. Wormald and C.E. Wright, London, 1958, 66–84

TANNER 1917: J. R. Tanner, ed., *The Historical Register of the University of Cambridge*, Cambridge, 1917

TEMPLE 1976: E. Temple, *Anglo-Saxon Manuscripts 900–1066*, A Survey of Manuscripts Illuminated in the British Isles 2, London, 1976

TESTA 1986: J. A. Testa, *The Beatty Rosarium: A Manuscript with Miniatures by Simon Bening*, Studies and Fascsimiles of Netherlandish Illuminated Manuscripts 1, Doornspijk, 1986

TESTA 1994: J.A. Testa, 'An Unpublished Manuscript by Simon Bening,' *Burlington Magazine* 136 (1994), 416–26

TEVIOTDALE 1992: E.C. Teviotdale, 'Some Thoughts on the Place of Origin of the Cotton Troper', *Cantus Planus: papers read at the fourth meeting of the Cantus Planus study group of the International Musicological Society, Pécs, Hungary 3–8 September 1990*, ed. L. Dobszay, Budapest, 1992, 407–12

TEVIOTDALE 1995: E.C. Teviotdale, 'The "Hereford Troper" and Hereford', *Medieval Art, Architecture and Archaeology at Hereford*, ed. David Whitehead, British Archaeological Association Conference Transactions 15 (1995), 75–81

THOBY 1959: P. Thoby, *Le Crucifix des Origines au Concile de Trente*, La Roche-sur-Yon, 1959

THOMAS 1985: M. Thomas, *Psautier de Saint-Louis*, Codices selecti 37, Graz, 1985

THOMPSON 1907: H. Yates Thompson, *A Descriptive Catalogue of Twenty Illuminated Manuscripts Nos. LXXV to XCIV (replacing twenty discarded from the original number) in the Collection of Henry Yates Thompson*, Cambridge, 1907

THOMPSON 1907–1918: H.Y. Thompson, *Illustrations of 100 Manuscripts in the Library of H.Y. Thompson*, 7 vols., London, 1907–1918

THOMPSON 1912: H. Yates Thompson, *A Descriptive Catalogue of Fourteen Illuminated Manuscripts*, Cambridge, 1912

THOMPSON 1956: D.V. Thompson, *The Materials and Techniques of Medieval Painting*, New York, 1956

THOMPSON 1960: Cennino D'Andrea Cennini, *The Craftsman's Handbook: The Italian "Il Libro dell'Arte"*, trans. D.V. Thompson, New Haven, 1933; repr. New York, 1960

THOMSON 1949: H.J. Thomson, *Prudentius*, 2 vols., Cambridge, Mass., 1949

THOMSON 1982: R. Thomson, 'Identifiable books from the pre-Conquest library of Malmesbury Abbey', *Anglo-Saxon England* 10 (1982), 1–19

THOMSON 1985: R.M. Thomson, *Manuscripts from St Albans Abbey 1066–1235*, 2 vols., 2nd edn, Woodbridge, 1985

THOMSON 2001: R.M. Thomson, *The Bury Bible*, Woodbridge and Tokyo, 2001

TOESCA 1912: P. Toesca, *La pittura e la miniatura nella Lombardia dai piú antichi monumenti alla metà del Quattrocento*, Milan, 1912; repr. 1966

TOESCA 1930: P. Toesca, *Monumenti e studi per la storia dell miniatura Italiana. La collezione di Ulrico Hoepli*, Milan, 1930

TOESCA 1948: P. Toesca, 'Di un miniatore e pittore emiliano Francesco Marmitta', *L'Arte* 17 (1948), 33–39

TOESCA 1969: I. Toesca, 'In margine al "Maestro delle Vitae Imperatorum"', *Paragone* 20.237 (1969), 73–77

TOSCANO 1995: G. Toscano, 'Matteo Felice: un miniatore al servizio dei re d'Aragona di Napoli', *Bollettino d'Arte* 93–94 (1995), 87–118

TOSCANO 1996–1997: G. Toscano, 'In margine al Maestro delle Vitae Imperatorum e al Maestro di Ippolita Sforza. Codici Lombardi nelle collezioni aragonesi', *Rivista di storia della miniatura* 1–2 (1996–1997), 169–78

TOSWELL 1997: M.J. Toswell, 'St Martial and the Dating of Late Anglo-Saxon Manuscripts', *Scriptorium* 51 (1997), 3–14

TOTELIN 2003: L. Totelin, 'Herbs and People: Figural Illustrations to the Herbarius in MS Trinity O.2.48', M. Phil. dissertation, Cambridge, 2003

TOYNBEE 1946: M. R. Toynbee, 'The Portraiture of Isabella Stuart, Duchess of Brittany (c.1427–after 1494),' *Burlington Magazine* 88 (1946), 300–05

TREUHERZ 1972: J. Treuherz, 'The border decoration of Milanese manuscripts c.1350–1420', *Arte Lombarda* 36 (1972), 71–82

TRINITY APOKALYPSE 2004: *Die Trinity-Apokalypse – The Trinity Apocalypse*, Luzern, 2004

TURNER 1968–1969: D.H. Turner, 'The Development of Maître Honoré', *British Museum Quarterly* 33 (1968–1969), 53–65

TURNER 1996: *The Dictionary of Art*, ed. J.S. Turner, 34 vols., London, 1996

TUVE 1964: R. Tuve, 'Notes on the Virtues and Vices', *Journal of the Warburg and Courtauld Institutes* 27 (1964), 42–72

ULLMANN 1960: B.L. Ullmann, *The Origins and Development of Humanistic Script*, Rome, 1960

UNIVERSITY LIBRARY 1856–1867: *A Catalogue of the Manuscripts Preserved in the Library of the*

University of Cambridge, ed. C. Hardwick, J.E.B. Mayor and H.R. Luard, 6 vols., Cambridge 1856–1867

URBÁNKOVÁ 1957: E. Urbánková, *Rukopisy a vzácné tisky Prazské Universitní knihovny*, Prague, 1957

VAN ACKER 1977: K.G. Van Acker, 'De librije van Raphaël de Mercatellis, abt van Sint-Baas en bisschop van Rhosus', *Archives et Bibliothèques de Belgique* 48 (1977), 143–98

VAN BUREN 1996: A.H. van Buren, 'The Genesis of the Eyckian Book of Prayers and Masses,' *Heures de Turin-Milan: Inv. No. 47, Museo Civico d'Arte Antica, Torino*, 2 vols., commentary volume, ed. A. H. van Buren, J. H. Marrow and S. Pettenati, Lucerne, Faksimile Verlag Luzern, 1996

VAN BUREN 1999: A.H. van Buren, 'Die Rezeption der Rolin-Madonna durch die Zeitgenossen Jan van Eycks – Eine Rekonstruktion auf der Grundlage von Texten und Bildkopien', *Porträt – Landschaft – Interieur. Jan van Eycks Rolin Madonna im ästhetischen Kontext*, ed. Christiane Kruse and Felix Thürlemann, *Literatur und Anthropologie* 4, Tübingen, 1999, 147–64

VAN BUREN 2002: A.H. van Buren, 'Dreux Jehan and the *Grandes Heures* of Philip the Bold', in *'ALS ICH CAN'. Liber Amicorum in Memory of Professor Dr. Maurits Smeyers*, ed. B. Cardon, J. Van der Stock, D. Vanwijnsberghe et al., 2 vols., Leuven, 2002, II, 1377–1414

VANDENDRIESSCHE 1995: G. Vandendriessche, 'The representation of the four temperaments and their medical correlates in de Foxton's Liber Cosmographiae (1408)', in *Flanders in a European Perspective. Proceedings of the International Colloquium, Leuven, 7–10 September 1993*, ed. M.Smeyers and B. Cardon, Louvain, 1995, 529–37

VAN DER HOEK 1991: K. van der Hoek, 'The North Holland Illuminator Spierinck: Some Attributions Reconsidered', in van der Horst and Klamt 1991, 275–86

VAN DER HORST AND KLAMT 1991: K. van der Horst and J.-C. Klamt, ed., *Masters and Miniatures, Proceedings of the Congress on Medieval Manuscript Illumination in the Northern Netherlands (Utrecht, 10–13 December 1989)*, Doornspijk, 1991

VAN DIJK 1963: S.J.P. van Dijk, *Sources of the Modern Roman Liturgy. The Ordinals of Haymo of Faversham and Related Documents 1243–1307*, 2 vols., Leiden, 1963

VAN DIJK AND WALKER 1960: S.J.P. van Dijk and J.H. Walker, *The Origins of the Modern Roman Liturgy*, London, 1960

VAN LEEUWEN 1975: C.G. van Leeuwen, *Denkbeelden van een vliesridder. De Instruction d'un jeune Prince van Guillebert van Lannoy*, Amsterdam, 1975

VAUGHAN 1958: R. Vaughan, *Matthew Paris*, Cambridge, 1958

VENN 1897–1901: John Venn, *Biographical History of Gonville and Caius College*, 3 vols, Cambridge, 1897–1901

VERDON 1978: T. Verdon, *The Art of Guido Mazzoni* New York, 1978

VEZIN 1973: J. Vezin, 'La répartition du travail dans les "scriptoria" carolingiens', *Journal des Savants* (1973), 212–27

VEZIN 1980: J. Vezin, 'Le point d'interrogation, un élément de datation et de localisation des manuscrits: l'exemple de Saint-Denis aux IXe siècle', *Scriptorium* 34 (1980), 181–96

VITZTHUM 1907: Graf G. Vitzthum, *Die Pariser Miniaturmalerei von der Zeit des hl. Ludwig bis zu Philipp von Valois und ihr Verhältnis zur Malerei in Nordwesteuropa*, Leipzig, 1907

VOGEL 1986: C. Vogel, *Medieval liturgy. An introduction to the sources*, Washington D.C., 1986

VOIGTS 1990: L.E. Voigts, 'The 'Sloane group': related scientific and medical manuscripts from the fifteenth century in the Sloane collection', *British Library Journal* 16 (1990), 50–53

VOIGTS 1994: L.E.Voigts, 'The Golden Table of Pythagoras', in *Popular and Practical Science of Medieval England*, ed. L. Matheson, East Lansing MI, 1994, 123–39

VON DEN BRINCKEN 1957: A.-D. von den Brincken, *Studien zur lateinischen Weltchronistik bis in das Zeitalter Ottos von Freising*, Düsseldorf, 1957

VON DEN BRINKEN 1992: A.-D. von den Brincken, *Fines Terrae: Die Enden der Erden und der vierte Kontinent auf mittelalterlichen Weltkarten*, Hannover, 1992

VON DEN BRINCKEN 1998: A.-D. von den Brincken, 'Mappe del Medio Evo: mappe del cielo e della Terra', *Ciecli e terre nei secoli XI–XII, Orizzonti, percezioni, rapporti*, Atti della tredicesima Settimana internazionale di studio Mendola, 22–26 agosto 1995, Milan, 1998, 31–50

VON EUW AND PLOTZEK 1979–85: A. von Euw and J. Plotzek, *Die Handschriften der Sammlung Ludwig*, 4 vols., Cologne, 1979–85

VŠETEČKOVÁ 1995: Z. Všetečková, 'Some Remarks on the Osek Lectionary (NK Praha Osek 76)', *Umění* 43 (1995), 219–223

WAAGEN 1854–1857: G.F. Waagen, *Treasures of Art in Great Britain*, 4 vols., London, 1854–1857

WAAGEN 1857: G.F. Waagen, *Galleries and Cabinets of Art in Great Britain, being an Account of More than Forty Collections of Paintings, Drawings, Sculptures, MSS, &c &c. Visited in 1854 and 1856, and now for the First Time Described*, London, 1857

WACHTEL 1955: A. Wachtel, *Alexander minorita Expositio in Apocalypsim*, Weimar, 1955

WAGNER 1967: A. Wagner, *Heralds of England; a history of the Office and College of Arms*, London, 1967, pl. xiv

WAGNER AND SAINTY 1967: A. Wagner and J.C.Sainty, 'The origin of the introduction of peers in the House of Lords', *Archaeologia* 101 (1967), 119–50

WALLACE 1983: K. Y. Wallace, *La Estoire de Seint Aedward le Rei*, Anglo-Norman Text Society, 41, London, 1983

WALLACE-HADRILL 1983: J.-.M. Wallace-Hadrill, *The Frankish Church*, Oxford, 1983

WALLER 1981: K. M. Waller, 'The Library, Scriptorium and Community of Rochester Cathedral Priory, *c.*1080–1150', Unpublished Ph.D. dissertation, University of Liverpool, 1981

WALLNER 1971: B. Wallner, *A Middle English Version of the Introduction to Guy de Chauliac's*

'Chirurgia Magna' Edited from the Manuscripts, Acta Universitatis Lundensis Sectio I, Theologica Juridica Humaniora 12, Lund, 1971

WALPOLE AND MASON 1922: A.S. Walpole and A.J. Mason, *Early Latin Hymns*, Cambridge, 1922

WARDLE 1998: *Valerius Maximus, Memorable deeds and sayings Book 1*, trans. with commentary by D. Wardle, Oxford, 1998

WARDROP 1963: J. Wardrop, *The Script of Humanism*, Oxford, 1963

WATSON 1985: A.G. Watson, 'Robert Green of Welby, alchemist and Count Palatine *c.*1467–*c.*1540', *Notes and Queries*, New Ser. 302, no. 3 (1985), 312–13

WATSON 2000: A.G. Watson, 'Robert Hare's Books', in *The English Medieval Book: Studies in Memory of Jeremy Griffiths*, ed. A.S.G. Edwards, V. Gillespie and R. Hanna, London, 2000, 209–32

WATSON 2003: R. Watson, *Illuminated Manuscripts and Their Makers*, London, 2003

WEBBER 1997: T. Webber, 'Latin Devotional Texts and the Books of the Augustinian Canons of Thurgarton Priory and Leicester Abbey in the Late Middle Ages', *Books and Collectors 1200–1700: essays presented to Andrew Watson*, ed. J.P. Carley and C.G.C. Tite, London, 1997, 27–42.

WEISHEIPL 1964: J.A. Weisheipl, 'Curriculum of the Faculty of Arts at Oxford in the early fourteenth Century', *Mediaeval Studies* 26 (1964), 143–85

WHEATCROFT 1999: J.H. Wheatcroft, 'Classical Ideology in the Medieval Bestiary', in *Mark of the Beast: The Medieval Bestiary in Art, Life, and Literature*, ed. D. Hassig, New York, 1999, 141–59

WHITE 1954: T.H. White, *The Book of Beasts, Being a Translation from a Latin Bestiary of the Twelfth Century*, New York, 1954

WIECK 1988: R.S. Wieck, *The Book of Hours in Medieval Art and Life*, London, 1988

WIECK 1997: R.S. Wieck, *Painted Prayers. The Book of Hours in Medieval and Renaissance Art*, New York, 1997

WIECK 1999A: R.S. Wieck, with a contribution by K.M. Hearne, *The Prayer Book of Anne de Bretagne*, Luzern, 1999.

WIECK 1999B: R.S. Wieck, 'The Death Desired: Books of Hours and the Medieval Funeral', in *Death and Dying in the Middle Ages*, ed. E.E. DuBruck and B.I. Gusick, New York, 1999, 431–76

WIECK 2001: R.S. Wieck, 'The Book of Hours', in *The Liturgy of the Medieval Church*, ed. T.J. Heffernan, E.A. Matter, Kalamazoo, 2001, 473–513

WIECK 2002: R.S. Wieck, 'Special Children's Books of Hours in the Walters Art Museum', in *'ALS ICH CAN' Liber Amicorum in Memory of Professor Dr. Maurits Smeyers*, ed. B. Cardon, Jan Van der Stock, D. Vanwijnsberghe et al., 2 vols., Leuven, 2002, II, 1629–39.

WIELAND 1985: G. Wieland, 'The glossed manuscript: classbook or library book?', *Anglo-Saxon England* 14 (1985), 153–73

WIERDA 1995: L.S. Wierda, *De Sarijs-handschriften. Studie naar een groep laat-middeleeuwse handschriften uit de IJsselstreek* (voorheen toegeschreven aan de Agnietenberg bij Zwolle), Zwolle, 1995

WILKINS 1993: N. Wilkins, Catalogue des manuscrits français de la Bibliothèque Parker (Parker Library), Corpus Christi College, Cambridge, 1993

WILLIAMS 1993: P. Williams, The Organ in Western Culture, 750–1250, Cambridge, 1993

WILLIAMS 2001: P. Williams, Philip II, Basingstoke and New York, 2001

WILMART 1932: A. Wilmart, Auteurs spirituels et textes dévots du moyen âge latin, Paris, 1932; repr. 1971

WILMART 1935: A. Wilmart, 'Le grand poème Bonaventurien sur les sept paroles du Christ en Croix', Revue Bénédictine 47 (1935), 235–78

WILSON 1992: B. Wilson, Music and Merchants: The Laudesi Companies of Republican Florence, Oxford, 1992

WILSON AND WILSON 1984: A. Wilson and J.L. Wilson, A Medieval Mirror, Speculum Humane Salvationis, 1324–1500, Berkeley, Los Angeles and London, 1984

WOLF 1982: H. Wolf, Die Meister des Breviarium Grimani, Berlin, 1982

WOOD 2001: Ian Wood, The Missionary life. Saints and the Evangelisation of Europe 400–1050, London, 2001

WOODRUFF 1930: H. Woodruff, The illustrated manuscripts of Prudentius, Cambridge, 1930

WORDSWORTH 1901–1902: C. Wordsworth, Ordinale Sarum sive Directorium Sacerdotum, 2 vols., Henry Bradshaw Society, 20, 22, 1901–1902

WORDSWORTH 1904: C. Wordsworth, The Ancient Kalendar of the University of Oxford, Oxford, 1904

WORDSWORTH 1920: C. Wordsworth, Horae Eboracenses: The Prymer or Hours of the Blessed Virgin Mary according to the Use of the Illustrious Church of York, Surtees Society 132, 1920

WORDSWORTH AND LITTLEHALES 1904: C. Wordsworth and H. Littlehales, The Old Service Books of the English Church, London, 1904

WORMALD 1939: F. Wormald, English Benedictine Kalendars after AD1100, I, Henry Bradshaw Society, 77, 1939

WORMALD 1946: F. Wormald, English Benedictine Kalendars after AD1100, II, Henry Bradshaw Society, 81, 1946

WORMALD 1954: F. Wormald, The Miniatures in the Gospels of St Augustine, Cambridge, 1954

WORMALD 1972: F. Wormald, 'A Manuscript Processional', Kunsthistorische Forschungen Otto Pächt zu seinem 70 Geburtstag, ed. A. Rosenauer, Salzburg, 1972, 129–34

WORMALD 1988: F. Wormald, 'The Fitzwarin Psalter and its Allies', in Francis Wormald, Collected Writings, II. Studies in English and Continental Art of the Later Middle Ages. Oxford, 1988, 88–102

WORMALD AND GILES 1982: F. Wormald and P.M. Giles, A Descriptive Catalogue of the Additional Manuscripts in the Fitzwilliam Museum, Cambridge, 1982

WRIGHT 2001: D. Wright, The Roman Vergil

and the Origins of Medieval Book Design, Toronto, 2001

WÜSTEFELD 1992: W.C.M. Wüstefeld, 'Delftse handschriftenproduktie en de boeken van de familie Van Assendelft', Delfia Batavorum Jaarboek (1992), 9–42

WÜSTEFELD 2003: W.C.M. Wüstefeld, 'A remarkable prayer roll attributed to the Master of Sir John Fastolf (Rouen c.1440, Museum Catharijneconvent Utrecht, MS ABM h4a)', Quarendo 33 (2003), 233–46

WYON 1887: A.B. Wyon and A. Wyon, The Great Seals of England, London, 1887

YAPP 1985: B. Yapp, 'A New Look at English Bestiaries', Medium Aevum 51 (1985), 1–19

YORKE 1988: A. Yorke, Bishop Aethelwold: His Career and Influence, Woodbridge, 1988

YOUNG 1953: C.C. Douglas Young, 'A codicological inventory of Theognis Manuscripts', Scriptorium 7 (1953), 3–36

ZIINO 1978: A. Ziino, 'Laudi e miniature fiorentine del primo Trecento', Studi musicali 7 (1978), 39–83

ZIINO AND ZAMEI 1999: A. Ziino and F. Zamei, 'Nuovi frammenti di un disperso laudario fiorentino', in Col dolce suon che da te piove: Studi su Francesco Landini e la musica del suo tempo, in memoria di Nino Pirrotta, ed. A. Delfino and M.T. Rosa-Barezzani, Florence, 1999, 485–505

ZSUPPÀN 1970: Jean Robertet, Œvres, ed. M. Zsuppàn, Genève, 1970

Exhibition Catalogues

BORDEAUX 1954: Flandres, Espagne, Portugal du XVe au XVIIe siècle, ed. M.-M. Gilberte, Musée des Beaux Arts, Bordeaux, 1954

BRAUNSCHWEIG 1995: Heinrich der Löwe und seine Zeit, ed. J. Luckhardt and F. Niehoff with G. Biegel, Herzog Anton Ulrich-Museum, Braunschweig, Munich, 1995

BRUGES 1981: Vlaamse Kunst op perkament. Handschriften en miniaturen te Brugge van de 12de tot de 16de eeuw, Gruuthusemuseum, Bruges, 1981

BRUSSELS 1959: La miniature flamande, ed. L.M.J. Delaissé, Bibliothèque royale de Belgique, Brussels, 1959

BRUSSELS 1969: Erasmus en België, Bibliothèque royale de Belgique, Brussels, 1969

BRUSSELS 1973: English Illuminated Manuscripts 700–1500, ed. J.J.G.Alexander and C.M.Kauffmann, Bibliothèque royale de Belgique, Brussels, 1973

BRUSSELS 1996: L'Ordre de la toison d'or de Philippe le Bon à Philippe le Beau (1430–1505): Idéal ou reflet d'une société?, ed. P. Cockshaw and C. Van den Bergen-Pantens, Brussels, Bibliothèque royale de Belgique, Turnhout, 1996

CAMBRIDGE 1966: Illuminated Manuscripts in the Fitzwilliam Museum, ed. F. Wormald and P.M. Giles, Fitzwilliam Museum, Cambridge, 1966

CAMBRIDGE 1975: Matthew Parker's legacy: books and plate, ed. R.I. Page and G.H.S. Bushnell, Corpus Christi College, Cambridge, 1975

CAMBRIDGE 1976: William Caxton, ed. J. Cook and B. Jenkins, University Library, Cambridge, 1976

CAMBRIDGE 1982: Cambridge Music Manuscripts, 900–1700, ed. I. Fenlon, Fitzwilliam Museum, Cambridge, 1982

CAMBRIDGE 1985: Anglo-Saxon manuscripts and other items of related interest in the library of Trinity College, Cambridge: an exhibition organized in connection with the conference of the International Society of Anglo-Saxonists, Cambridge, 19–23 August 1985, notes compiled by S. Keynes, Trinity College, Cambridge, 1985

CAMBRIDGE 1988: The Dominicans in Cambridge 1238–1538, ed. P.N.R. Zutshi, R. Ombres, and N. Morgan, University Library, Cambridge, 1988

CAMBRIDGE 1988–1989: The Dutch Connection, ed. P. Woudhuysen, Fitzwilliam Museum, Cambridge, 1988

CAMBRIDGE 1989–1990: Splendours of Italian Illumination, unpublished list assembled by J.J.G. Alexander, Fitzwilliam Museum, Cambridge, 1989–1990

CAMBRIDGE 1993: Splendours of Flanders, ed. A. Arnould and J.-M. Massing, Fitzwilliam Museum, Cambridge, 1993

CAMBRIDGE 1998: Celebrating Pembroke, Fitzwilliam Museum, Cambridge, 1998, no catalogue

CAMBRIDGE 2001: Illuminating the Law: Legal Manuscripts in Cambridge Collections, ed.

S. L'Engle, R. Gibbs, and P. Clarke, Fitzwilliam Museum, Cambridge, London and Turnhout, 2001

CAMBRIDGE, MASS. 1989: Italian Humanists in Ten Manuscripts from the Houghton Library, ed. J. Hankins, Houghton Library, Cambridge, Mass., 1989

CLEVELAND, SAN FRANCISCO AND NEW YORK 2003: Treasures of a Lost Art: Italian Manuscript Painting of the Middle Ages and Renaissance, ed. P. Palladino, Cleveland Museum of Art, Cleveland, Fine Arts Museum, San Francisco, and Metropolitan Museum of Art, New York, New Haven and London, 2003

COLOGNE 1982: Die Messe Gregors des Grossen, ed. U. Westfehling, Schnütgen Museum, Cologne, 1982

COLOGNE 1992: Biblioteca Apostolica Vaticana: Liturgie und Andacht im Mittelalter, ed. J. M. Plotzek and U. Surmann, Erzbischöfliches Diözesanmuseum, Cologne, 1992

DIJON AND CLEVELAND 2004–2005: L'art à la cour de Bourgogne: Le mécénat de Philippe le Hardi et de Jean sans Peur (1364–1419), Dijon, Musées des Beaux-Arts, and Cleveland, The Cleveland Museum of Art, Paris, 2004

EVANSTON 2001: Manuscript Illumination in the Modern Age, ed. Sandra Hindman, Mary and Leigh Block Museum of Art, Evanston, 2001

FERRARA 1998: *La Miniatura a Ferrara dal tempo di Cosmè Tura all'eredità di Ercole Roberti*, ed., F. Toniolo, Palazzo Schifanoia, Ferrara, 1998

FLORENCE 1997: *Umanesimo e Padri della Chiesa. Manoscritti e incunaboli di testi patristici da Francesco Petrarca al primo Cinquecento*, ed. S. Gentile, Biblioteca medicea laurenziana, Florence, 1997

LISBON 2000: *The image of time: European manuscript books*, Calouste Gulbenkian Museum, Lisbon, 2000

LONDON 1874: *Illuminated Manuscripts*, Burlington Fine Arts Club, London, 1874

LONDON 1886: *Catalogue of a Series of Illuminations from Manuscripts principally of the Italian and French Schools*, Burlington Fine Arts Club, London, 1886

LONDON 1891: *Exhibition of Bookbindings*, Burlington Fine Arts Club, London, 1891

LONDON 1893–1894: *Exhibition of Early Italian Art from 1300–1550*, New Gallery, London, 1893–1894

LONDON 1908: *Exhibition of Illuminated Manuscripts*, ed. S.C. Cockerell, Burlington Fine Arts Club, London, 1908

LONDON 1923: *Exhibition of British Primitive Painting*, Royal Academy of Arts, London, 1923

LONDON 1930: *Exhibition of English Medieval Art*, Victoria and Albert Museum, London, 1930

LONDON 1934: *Exhibition of British Art*, Royal Academy, London, 1934

LONDON 1939: *British Medieval Art*, Burlington Fine Arts Club, London, 1939

LONDON 1953–1954: *Flemish Art 1300–1700*, ed. O. Pächt, Royal Academy of Arts, London, 1953

LONDON 1959: *Treasures of Cambridge*, Goldsmith's Hall, London, 1959

LONDON 1975: *Andrea Palladio, 1508–1580*, ed. H. Burns with L. Fairbairn and B. Boucher, Arts Council of Great Britain, London, 1975

LONDON 1983: *Early Italian Paintings and Works of Art, 1300–1480*, Mattheisen Fine Arts, London, 1983

LONDON 1984A: *The Golden Age of Anglo-Saxon Art 966–1066*, ed. J. Backhouse, D.H. Turner and L. Webster, British Museum, London, 1984

LONDON 1984B: *English Romanesque Art 1066–1200*, ed. G. Zarnecki, J. Holt and T. Holland, Hayward Gallery, London, 1984

LONDON 1985: *Hidden Friends: an Exhibition of Illuminated Manuscripts from the Comites Latentes Collections*, ed. C. de Hamel, Sotheby's, London, 1985

LONDON 1987–1988: *Age of Chivalry: Art in Plantagenet England 1200–1400*, ed. J.J.G. Alexander and P. Binski, Royal Academy of Arts, London, 1987

LONDON 1991: *The Making of England: Anglo-Saxon Art and Culture AD 600–999*, ed. Janet Backhouse and L. Webster, British Museum, London, 1991

LONDON 1993: *Making and Meaning: The Wilton Diptych*, ed. D. Gordon, National Gallery, London, 1993

LONDON 1997: *The Transformation of the Roman World AD 400–900*, ed. L. Webster and M. Brown, British Museum, London, 1997

LONDON 1999–2000: *The Apocalypse*, ed. F. Carey, British Museum, London, 1999

LONDON 2003: *Painted Labyrinth: the World of the Lindisfarne Gospels*, ed. M.P. Brown, British Library, London, 2003

LONDON 2003–2004: *Gothic Art for England 1400–1547*, ed. R. Marks and P. Williamson, Victoria and Albert Museum, London, 2003

LONDON AND NEW YORK 1992: *Andrea Mantegna*, ed. J. Martineau, Royal Academy of Arts, London and Metropolitan Museum, New York, Milan, 1992

LONDON AND NEW YORK 1994–1995: *The Painted Page: Italian Renaissance Book Illumination 1450–1550*, ed. J.J.G. Alexander, Royal Academy of Arts, London and Pierpont Morgan Library, New York, Munich, 1994

LOS ANGELES AND LONDON 2003–2004: *Illuminating the Renaissance: The Triumph of Flemish Manuscript Painting in Europe*, ed. T. Kren and S. McKendrick, J. Paul Getty Museum, Los Angeles and Royal Academy of Arts, London, Los Angeles, 2003

MANCHESTER 1959: *Romanesque art*, Art Gallery, Manchester, 1959

METZ 1989: *Metz enluminée*, Bibliothèque-Médiathèque, Metz, 1989

MILAN 1958: *Arte Lombarda dai Visconti agli Sforza*, Palazzo Reale, Milan, 1958

MILAN 1988: *Arte in Lombardia tra Gotico e Rinascimento*, ed. M. Boskovits et al., Palazzo Reale, Milan 1988

NANCY 1984: *Écriture et enluminure en Lorraine au Moyen Âge*, Musée historique lorrain, Nancy, 1984

NAPLES 1997: *Libri a corte: Testi e imagini nella Napoli aragonese*, ed. A.P.D. Murano, Biblioteca nazionale, Naples, 1997

NAPLES AND VALENCIA 1998: *La Biblioteca reale di Napoli al tempo della dinastia aragonese*, ed. G. Toscano, Castel Nuovo, Naples and Biblioteca General I Històrica de la Universitat, Valencia, 1998

NEW YORK 1982: *The Last Flowering: French Painting in Manuscripts, 1420–1530 from American Collections*, ed. J. Plummer and G. Clark, Pierpont Morgan Library, New York, 1982

NEW YORK 1988–1989: *Painting in Renaissance Siena 1420–1500*, ed. K. Christiansen, L.B. Kanter, and C.B. Strehlke, Metropolitan Museum of Art, New York, 1988

NEW YORK 1992–1993: *The Bernard Breslauer Collection of Manuscript Illuminations*, ed. W.M. Voelkle, R.S. Wieck, and M.F.P Saffiotti, Pierpont Morgan Library, New York, 1992

NEW YORK 1994: *Painting and Illumination in Early Renaissance Florence 1300–1450*, ed. L.B. Kanter et al., Metropolitan Museum of Art, New York, 1994

NORWICH 1973: *Medieval Art in East Anglia 1300–1520*, ed. P. Lasko and N.J. Morgan, Norwich Castle Museum, Norwich, 1973

OTTAWA 1972: *Art and the Courts: France and England from 1259 to 1328*, ed. P. Brieger and P. Verdier, National Gallery of Canada, Ottawa, 1972

OXFORD 1970: *Duke Humphrey and English Humanism in the Fifteenth Century*, ed. R.W Hunt and A.C. de la Mare, Bodleian Library, Oxford, 1970

PADUA 1999: *La miniatura a Padova dal medioevo al settecento*, ed. G. Baldissin Molli, G. Canova Mariani, F. Toniolo, Palazzo della ragione, Modena, 1999

PARIS 1968A: *La librairie de Charles V*, ed. F. Avril, Bibliothèque nationale de France, Paris, 1968

PARIS 1968B: *L'Europe gothique XIIe–XIVe siècles*, Musée du Louvre, Paris, 1968

PARIS 1974: *La vie universitaire parisienne au XIIIe siècle*, Chapelle de la Sorbonne, Paris, 1974

PARIS 1981: *Les Fastes du Gothique. Le siècle de Charles V*, ed. F. Baron et al, Galeries nationales du Grand-Palais, Paris, 1981

PARIS 1984A: *Dix siècles d'enluminure italienne (VIe – XVIe siècles)*, ed. F. Avril, Y. Zaluska and M.-T. Gousset, Bibliothèque nationale de France, Paris, 1984

PARIS 1984B: *Altdorfer et le realisme fantastique dans l'art allemand*, Centre Culturel du Marais, Paris, 1984

PARIS 1993: *Les manuscripts à peinture en France 1440–1520*, ed. F. Avril and N. Reynaud, Bibliothèque nationale de France, Paris, 1993

PARIS 1998: *L'Art au temps des rois maudits, Philippe le Bel et ses fils 1285–1328*, Galeries nationales du Grand Palais, Paris, 1998

PARIS 2000: *Visions du futur: une histoire des peurs et des espoirs de l'humanité*, Galeries nationales du Grand Palais, Paris, 2000

PARIS 2004A: *Moyen Âge entre ordre et désordre*, Musée de la musique, Paris, 2004

PARIS 2004B: *Paris 1400: Les arts sous Charles VI*, Musée du Louvre, Paris, 2004

PHILADELPHIA 2001: *Leaves of Gold: Manuscript Illumination from Philadelphia Collections*, ed. J.R. Tanis, Philadelphia Museum of Art, Philadelphia, 2001

SAINT PETERSBURG AND FLORENCE 1996: *Flemish Illuminated Manuscripts 1475–1550*, ed. M. Smeyers and J. Van der Stock, State Hermitage Museum, Saint Petersburg and Museo Bardini, Florence, Ghent and New York, 1996

UTRECHT 1996: *The Utrecht Psalter in medieval art: picturing the Psalms of David*, ed. K. van der Horst, W. Noel and H. Wüstefeld, Museum Catharijneconvent, Utrecht, Tuurdijk, 1996

UTRECHT AND NEW YORK 1989–1990: *The Golden Age of Dutch Manuscript Painting*, intro. J.H. Marrow, ed. H.L.M. Defoer, A.S. Korteweg and W.C.M. Wüstefeld, Museum Catharijneconvent, Utrecht and Pierpont Morgan Library, New York, Stuttgart and New York, 1989–1990

VATICAN CITY 1995: *Liturgia in Figura: Codici liturgici rinascimentali della Biblioteca Vaticana*, ed. G. Morelli and S. Maddalo, Vatican Library, Vatican City, 1995

VENICE 1995: *I libri di San Marco*, ed. S Marcon, Biblioteca Nazionale Marciana, Venice, 1995

VIENNA 1962: *Europäische Kunst um 1400*, Kunsthistorisches Museum, Vienna, 1962

INDEX I:

MANUSCRIPTS AND PRINTED BOOKS CITED IN THE CATALOGUE

References to manuscripts and printed books cited here are given to their relevant catalogue number, in bold figures where the manuscript is exhibited and in normal figures where citations occur. Where manuscripts and printed books are cited in the introductory essays to the Catalogue and the different sections, references are given to page and figure numbers.

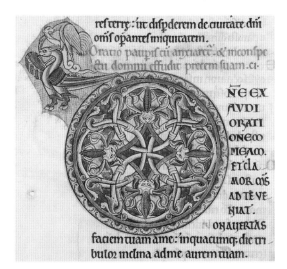

Corpus Christi College MS 4, fol. 33v, detail

INDEX II:

SCRIBES, ARTISTS, PRINTERS, COMMISSIONERS AND ORIGINAL OWNERS OF MANUSCRIPTS AND PRINTED BOOKS DISPLAYED IN THE EXHIBITION

The numbers refer to catalogue entries